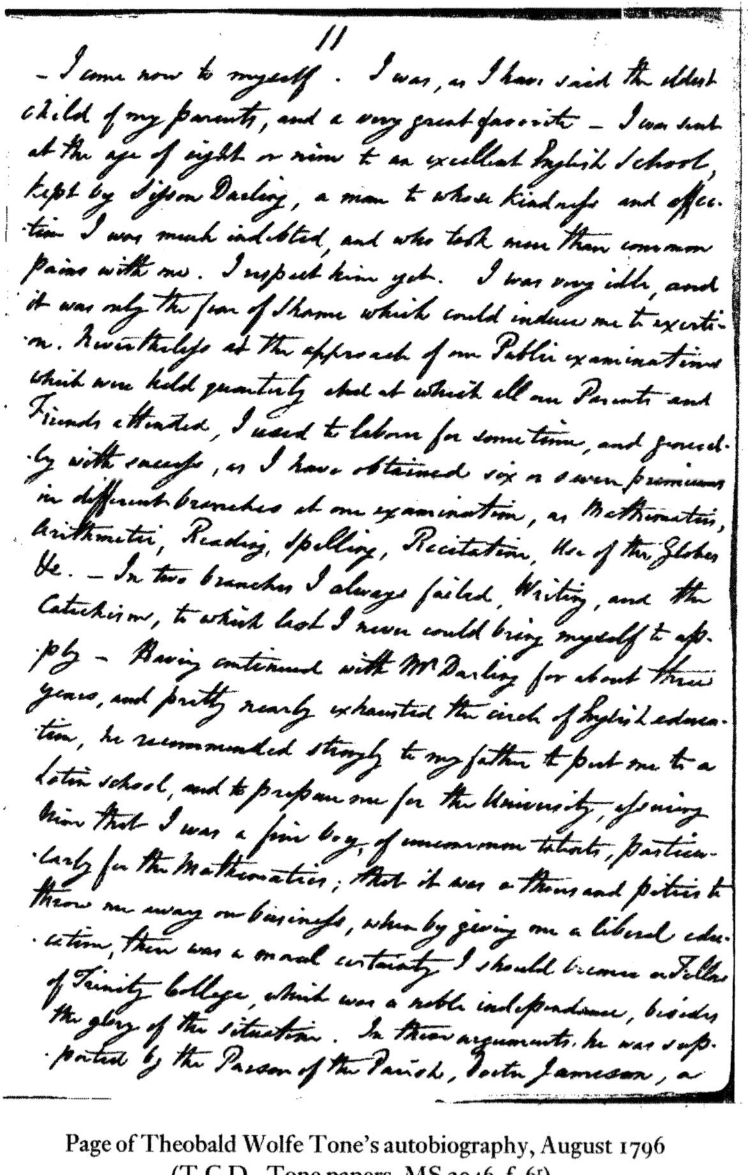

11

— I come now to myself. I was, as I have said the eldest
child of my Parents, and a very great favorite — I was sent
at the age of eight or nine to an excellent English School,
kept by Sisson Darling, a man to whose kindness and affec-
tion I was much indebted, and who took more than common
pains with me. I respect him yet. I was very idle, and
it was only the fear of Shame which could induce me to exerti-
on. Nevertheless at the approach of our Public examinations
which were held quarterly and at which all our Parents and
Friends attended, I used to labour for some time, and generall-
y with success, as I have obtained six or seven premiums
in different branches at one examination, as Mathematics,
Arithmetic, Reading, Spelling, Recitation, Use of the Globes
&c. — In two branches I always failed, Writing, and the
Catechism, to which last I never could bring myself to ap-
ply — Having continued with Mr Darling for about three
years, and pretty nearly exhausted the circle of English educa-
tion, he recommended strongly to my father to put me to a
Latin school, and to prepare me for the University, assuring
him that I was a fine boy, of uncommon talents, particu-
larly for the Mathematics; that it was a thousand pities to
throw me away on business, when by giving me a liberal edu-
cation, there was a moral certainty I should become a Fellow
of Trinity College, which was a noble independance, besides
the glory of the situation. In these arguments he was sup-
ported by the Parson of the Parish, Doctor Jameson, a

Page of Theobald Wolfe Tone's autobiography, August 1796
(T.C.D., Tone papers, MS 2046, f. 6r).
Reproduced by courtesy of the Board of Trinity College, Dublin

# THE WRITINGS OF
# Theobald Wolfe Tone
## 1763–98

THE WRITINGS OF THEOBALD WOLFE TONE, 1763–98

| | |
|---|---|
| Volume I | Tone's career in Ireland to June 1795 |
| Volume II | America, France and Bantry Bay (August 1795 to December 1796) |
| Volume III | France, the Rhine, Lough Swilly and death of Tone (January 1797 to November 1798) |

THE WRITINGS OF

# Theobald Wolfe Tone 1763–98

VOLUME II

America, France and Bantry Bay,
August 1795 to December 1796

Edited by

T. W. MOODY, R. B. McDOWELL
and
C. J. WOODS

CLARENDON PRESS · OXFORD

*This book has been printed digitally and produced in a standard specification in order to ensure its continuing availability*

OXFORD
UNIVERSITY PRESS

Great Clarendon Street, Oxford OX2 6DP

Oxford University Press is a department of the University of Oxford.
It furthers the University's objective of excellence in research, scholarship,
and education by publishing worldwide in

Oxford New York

Auckland Cape Town Dar es Salaam Hong Kong Karachi
Kuala Lumpur Madrid Melbourne Mexico City Nairobi
New Delhi Shanghai Taipei Toronto
With offices in
Argentina Austria Brazil Chile Czech Republic France Greece
Guatemala Hungary Italy Japan South Korea Poland Portugal
Singapore Switzerland Thailand Turkey Ukraine Vietnam

Oxford is a registered trade mark of Oxford University Press
in the UK and in certain other countries

Published in the United States
by Oxford University Press Inc., New York



First published in paperback 2009



ISBN 978-0-19-820879-2 (Hbk)
ISBN 978-0-19-956407-1 (Pbk)

Cover illustration: portrait of Theolbald Wolfe Tone in what is said to be a Volunteer uniform. Once the property of his friend Peter Burrowes, the portrait is now in the National Gallery of Ireland, by whose courtesy it is reproduced. The artist is unknown.

Printed and bound in Great Britain by
CPI Antony Rowe,
Chippenham, Wiltshire

# EDITORS' PREFACE

THIS edition of the writings of Theobald Wolfe Tone (1763–98), lawyer, United Irishman, agent of the Catholic Committee and later an officer in the French revolutionary army, the first of three volumes of which appeared on 30 October 1998, is intended to be complete and largely to supersede the two-volume *Life of Theobald Wolfe Tone ... written by himself and ... edited by his son, William* (Washington, 1826). It consists mainly of Tone's correspondence, diaries, autobiography, pamphlets, public addresses and miscellaneous memoranda (both personal and public); it is based on the original MSS if extant or on the most reliable printed version. The larger portion of the Tone papers (including the diaries and autobiography) is in Trinity College, Dublin; the remaining portion (mainly letters to his wife) was for many years in the possession of his great-great granddaughter, Katherine Dickason of Short Hills, New Jersey, who died on 20 September 1995, and is now held by Mrs Dickason's granddaughter, Mrs Kit Prendergast. This volume ('America, France and Bantry Bay, August 1795 to December 1796') is to be followed shortly by volume III ('France, the Rhine, Lough Swilly and death of Tone, January 1797 to November 1798'), which will include corrigenda, addenda, a bibliography of Theobald Wolfe Tone and an index to all three volumes.

*Editorial practice*

The editors' intention has been to publish all of Tone's writings together with letters to him and some contemporary documents relating to his career. All matter in each document (e.g. date, address, etc., of letters) has been printed if extant. The arrangement is strictly chronological. Letters and other documents whose dates fall within those of a diary sequence have been inserted in their appropriate places within the sequence. Therefore the autobiography (which appears in this volume) is to be found among documents for August and September 1796 (when it was written). The original spelling has been retained. Punctuation and (to a larger degree than in volume I) use of capitals have been silently standardised. Dates have been supplied in some cases, as explained in headnotes. The eighteenth-century practice of underlining or italicising names of persons and places, direct speech and literary quotations has been followed only for literary quotations, which are italicised, as are French and Latin words in documents largely in English. In the case of French official documents the republican calendar (in which the year begins at the autumn equinox and is divided into ten months, each with a name taken from the season) has been silently converted to the Gregorian in the headings and notes. The dating of Tone's diaries (but not of other documents) has been standardised in the form '12 Oct. 1796'. Numerous footnotes are supplied to elucidate the text of the documents. We have followed the conventions laid down in T. W. Moody, 'Rules for contributors to *Irish Historical Studies' in I.H.S.*, suppl. I (Jan. 1968), except that references to the first and third volumes are in the form 'see above, vol. I, p. 533'.

*Acknowledgements*

We are grateful to the board of Trinity College, Dublin, for permission to publish documents in the Tone and Sirr collections of MSS and to refer to the College muniments; to the family of the late Mrs Katherine Dickason of Short Hills, New Jersey, for permission to publish documents in the Tone family papers; to the director of the National Archives (Ireland) for permission to publish various documents in the Rebellion papers; to the trustees of the Public Record Office, London, for permission to quote from documents in the Home Office papers; to the director of the Public Record Office of Northern Ireland for permission to quote from documents in the Drennan and Abercorn papers; to the trustees of the British Library for permission to quote from a document in the Pelham papers and a document formerly in the India Office Library; to the director of the Archives Nationales, Rue des Francs-Bourgeois, Paris, for permission to publish or quote from documents in the records of the Directoire Exécutif; to the director of the Archives des Affaires Étrangères, Quai d'Orsay, Paris, for permission to publish documents in three series (Correspondance Politique, Angleterre, Mémoires et documents, Angleterre, and dossiers personnels); and to the director of the Service Historique de l'Armée de Terre, Château de Vincennes, Val-de-Marne, for permission to cite information in the Archives de la Guerre dossiers personnels series.

The number of people who over the years have helped in one way or another is so large that we cannot attempt to thank them all by name without inadvertently omitting some and so causing pain. We can only acknowledge that our debt of gratitude to them is immense and hope that the final result of their assistance gives satisfaction.

The project of editing Tone's writings was begun in 1963. One of the editors, T. W. Moody, died on 11 February 1984.

R. B. McDowell
C. J. Woods

22 August 2001

# CONTENTS



## THE DOCUMENTS

# ABBREVIATIONS

| | |
|---|---|
| *Allgemeine deutsche Biographie* | *Allgemeine deutsche Biographie* (56 vols, Leipzig, 1875–1912) |
| *Alumni Dubl.* | G. D. Burtchaell and T. U. Sadleir, *Alumni Dublinenses: a register of students [etc.] ... of Trinity College* (2nd ed., Dublin, 1935) |
| Archives de la Guerre | Archives historiques de la Guerre, Château de Vincennes |
| Archives des Affaires Étrangères | Archives du Département des Affaires Étrangères, quai d'Orsay, Paris |
| Archives Nationales | Archives Nationales, rue des Francs-Bourgeois, Paris |
| *Biographie nouvelle des contemporains* | *Biographie nouvelle des contemporains* (20 vols, Paris, 1820–5) |
| *Biographie universelle ancienne et moderne* | *Biographie universelle ancienne et moderne* (85 vols, Paris, 1811–62) |
| *Commons' jn. Ire.* | *Journals of the house of commons of the kingdom of Ireland* (19 vols, Dublin, 1796–1800) |
| *D.A.B.* | *Dictionary of American biography* (20 vols, New York & London, 1928–37) |
| *D.E.P.* | *Dublin Evening Post* |
| *D.N.B.* | *Dictionary of national biography* (66 vols, London, 1908–9) |
| Debidour, *Recueil des actes du Directoire Exécutif* | Antonin Debidour (ed.), *Recueil des actes du Directoire Exécutif* (4 vols, Paris, 1910–17) |
| Desbrière, *Projets et tentatives* | Édouard Desbrière, *Projets et tentatives de débarquement aux îles Britanniques, 1793–1805* (4 vols in 5, Paris, 1900–02) |
| *Dict. biog. franç.* | *Dictionnaire de biographie française* (Paris, 1933– ) |
| *Dict. parl. franç.* | Adolphe Robert and Gaston Cougny, *Dictionnaire de parlementaires français* (5 vols, Paris, 1889–91) |
| *Drennan letters* | *The Drennan letters ..., 1776–1819*, ed. D. A. Chart (Belfast, 1931) |
| Elliott, *Tone* | Marianne Elliott, *Wolfe Tone, prophet of Irish independence* (New Haven, 1989) |
| Fétis, *Biog. des musiciens* | F. J. Fétis, *Biographie universelle des musiciens* (2nd ed., 10 vols, Paris, 1860–84) |
| G.E.C., *Peerage* | G. E. C[okayne], *The complete peerage of England, Scotland, Ireland, Great Britain and the United* |

| | |
|---|---|
| | *Kingdom* (8 vols, Exeter, 1887–98; 2nd ed. by Vicary Gibbs et al., 13 vols, London, 1910–40) |
| *Gent. Mag.* | *Gentleman's Magazine* |
| *H.J.* | *Hibernian Journal* |
| *I.H.S.* | *Irish Historical Studies* |
| Lajarte, *Bibliothèque musicale* | Théodore Lajarte, *Bibliothèque musicale du théâtre de l'opéra* (2 vols, Paris, 1878) |
| *Life* | *Life of Theobald Wolfe Tone . . . written by himself and . . . edited by his son, William* (2 vols, Washington, 1826) |
| Lyonnet, *Dict. des comédiens* | Henry Lyonnet, *Dictionnaire des comédiens français* (2 vols: i, Paris, 1908; ii, Geneva, n.d.) |
| MacDermot, *Tone* | Frank MacDermot, *Theobald Wolfe Tone: a biographical study* (London, 1939) |
| Madden, *United Irishmen* | R. R. Madden, *The United Irishmen: their lives and times* (1st ed., 3 series in 7 vols, Dublin, 1842–6; 2nd ed. in 4 vols, London, 1857–60) |
| *N.S.* | *Northern Star* |
| Nat. Arch. (Ire.) | National Archives (Ireland), Dublin |
| *Nouvelle biographie générale* | *Nouvelle biographie générale* (46 vols, Paris, 1855–66) |
| *Parl. reg. Ire.* | *The parliamentary register; or . . . debates of the house of commons of Ireland* (17 vols, Dublin, 1782–1801) |
| P.R.O. | Public Record Office, London |
| P.R.O.N.I. | Public Record Office of Northern Ireland |
| Rowan, *Autobiography* | *Autobiography of Archibald Hamilton Rowan*, ed. W. H. Drummond (Dublin, 1840) |
| Six, *Dict. des généraux & amiraux* | Georges Six, *Dictionnaire biographique des généraux et amiraux français de la Révolution et de l'Empire, 1792–1814* (2 vols, Paris, 1934) |
| T.C.D. | Trinity College, Dublin |
| Tone (Dickason) papers | Tone family papers in the possession of the late Mrs Katherine Dickason, Short Hills, New Jersey, U.S.A. |

Most sources used for headnotes and footnotes are included in the 'Bibliography of Theobald Wolfe Tone' (below, vol. III).

# AMERICA, FRANCE AND BANTRY BAY, AUGUST 1795 TO DECEMBER 1796

Theobald Wolfe Tone arrived in the United States of America on 1 August 1795. Having to maintain a wife and family, he busied himself in finding a farm in which to invest his small capital. But it cannot be said that he was very enthusiastic about his prospects as a farmer and politics soon beckoned. During the winter of 1794–5 the European strategic situation had considerably changed. France was definitely on the offensive and it seemed she was at last in a position to give Ireland the assistance offered to nations struggling to be free by the Convention in November 1792. Before leaving Ireland Tone had expressed to a few of his close political associates his intention, once he arrived in America, of exploring the possibility of making back across the Atlantic for France and trying to obtain French assistance. He approached the French minister to the United States, Pierre Auguste Adet, who at first was diplomatically cool. But in November, having received letters from Ireland informing him that a revolutionary situation was fast developing there, Tone again approached Adet. By then the minister, who had had time to make inquiries, was much more friendly. On 1 January 1796 Tone sailed for Le Havre.

By the time Tone arrived in France the heroic age of the revolution was passed. It may be said to have ended with the fall of Robespierre in July 1794. By 1796 the mass of Frenchmen were craving for stability, social, political and economic, and there were signs that strong elements of continuity with pre-revolutionary France persisted. But party passions, personal ambitions and class conflict, the strain of a great war and steady inflation were keeping the community in a state of ferment. Since the summer of 1789 many venerable and venerated institutions had been swept away or reorganised, traditional standards challenged, privileges abolished and careers in politics, administration and the fighting services thrown open to youth and talent. It was an epoch for gifted and enterprising spirits. Paris was the hub of the new France. Its 600,000 inhabitants were close packed and its impressive public buildings and spacious parks were surrounded by networks of narrow streets of high houses. Parisians were intensely interested in politics and prices. There was much poverty and discontent and a considerable display of conspicuous consumption as the new ruling world of France began to enjoy itself after the short but terrifying era when political puritans were saving the country.

A few months before Tone arrived the constitution of Year III, designed to safeguard a status quo that satisfied the moderate and mellowed revolutionaries who were in power after the Thermidorian *coup d'état*, had come into operation. It established a bicameral legislature, the representative house, the Council of

Five Hundred (*Conseil des Cinq Cens*), being elected on a property franchise. Executive power was vested in five directors, elected by the legislature, under whom there were six ministers. The new regime was threatened from both the left and the right. Soon after Tone reached Paris the Directory firmly suppressed a conspiracy or agitation led by Babeuf, an advanced social reformer vehemently hostile to all vested interests. About a year later pressure from the right began to mount, a powerful conservative opposition emerging in the legislature, having among its leaders Charles Pichegru, who had acquired a great, if overrated, reputation as a soldier. Two of the directors, Lazare Carnot and François Barthelémy, sympathised with the opposition but their three colleagues led by Paul Barras decided to use the army to defeat the conservatives. On 4 September 1797 (18 Fructidor Year V) military detachments surrounded the Tuilleries where the Council of Five Hundred was sitting and a number of members were arrested and deported to Cayenne.

Tone comments on these events, but his attitude to French politics was governed by his concentration on his main objective—securing French aid for an Irish revolution. This meant that he wanted France to have a strong administration able to wage war vigorously, and he certainly did not want to get himself and his cause involved in French domestic politics. In any event, for some time after he arrived in France he was feeling his way in a strange environment. Nevertheless, his comments on conditions and happenings in France and in French-occupied Europe are often penetrating. Even when he misses the mark he reveals the impression revolutionary France made on an alert observer. Moreover, it is clear that what he saw and heard on his travels was playing a considerable part in shaping his political opinions. There are many indications in his diaries—he called them his journals—that the policy of the first government of an independent Ireland might have been significantly influenced by Tone's reactions to conditions in France (where he spent most of the period 1796–8) and in Holland (which he visited in 1797).

Tone began work in Paris with obvious handicaps. His funds were limited; he was not at first fluent in French; and he lacked official status—even by revolutionary standards. When Lord Edward Fitzgerald and Arthur O'Connor arrived on the Continent in the summer of 1796 and Edward Lewines arrived there in the spring of 1797 they were the designated envoys of the executive committee of the United Irishmen. But Tone left Ireland before the militant Irish radicals had built up a strong organisation; he could claim to be a well-known political publicist whose wide contacts and experience entitled him to be treated with respect as an interpreter of Irish revolutionary opinion; he could also claim—and there is support for this in some of the documents printed below—to have the approval, confidence and backing of leading members of the Dublin and Belfast societies of United Irishmen and even of representatives of the Catholic Committee and the Defenders.

He had of course advantages. His diaries show that he united diplomatic gifts of a high order with charm, ardour and undauntable optimism. Moreover, he had arrived at an opportune moment. In the early stages of the war, during 1792 and 1793, it seemed as if France was bound to be defeated by the great European coalition arrayed against her. But revolutionary fervour and drive had ruthlessly mobilised men and material on a scale hitherto unknown. By a combination of mass and mobility the allied armies were checked and finally hurled over the French frontiers. The Austrian Netherlands and Holland were overrun, and in 1795 Prussia, Spain and Holland all withdrew from the war—Holland becoming an ally or satellite of France. So when in the autumn of 1795 Carnot, 'the organiser of victory', was elected a member of the Directory and assumed control of the French war effort, France possessed the initiative. For 1796 Carnot planned a great three-pronged attack against Austria, the armies commanded by Moreau, Jourdan and Bonaparte being directed against the territories under Austrian control. During the summer Jourdan and Moreau advanced rapidly but they were opposed by the Archduke Charles, a master of the art of war, and in the autumn were driven back pell-mell to the Rhine. But in Italy Bonaparte, by a series of swift, unexpected moves broke the Sardinians, drove the Austrians out of Lombardy and frightened the small states of central and southern Italy into submission.

Carnot also devoted considerable attention to that seemingly intractable strategic problem—how to inflict a crippling blow on Great Britain, France's successful and apparently impregnable foe. To men bred in the traditions of land warfare the essence of the problem lay in the exasperating existence of the English Channel. Assuming Great Britain's naval predominance—and that had to be assumed in 1796—it was difficult to see how a large army could be flung across the Channel, landed in southern England and supplied and reinforced. Admittedly in 1793 the Committee of Public Safety, with a fine disregard of reality, issued an imperative directive to the ministry of the marine to prepare plans for landing 100,000 men on the English coast, and Lazare Hoche, a young officer high in the committee's favour, called in ringing terms for attack on England. 'Point de manoeuvres', he added, 'point d'art; du fer, du feu et du patriotisme'.[1]

With a major frontal attack for the moment ruled out, the Directory in 1796 contemplated starting a *chouannerie* in the British Isles; and since the Vendée and Brittany had demonstrated how important it was for forces waging a guerrilla war to have the sympathy and support of the local population, Ireland was obviously a theatre worth considering.[2] On 19 June the Directory issued instructions to Hoche, commander of the *Armée des côtes de l'Océan*, for an attack on Ireland. 'To detach Ireland from England', these laid down, 'is to reduce the latter to be nothing more than a second-class power'. Three expeditions were to be sent to

[1] Édouard Desbrière, *Projets et tentatives aux îles Britanniques* (4 vols, Paris, 1900–02), i, 30, 32.

[2] For an account of Hoche's Irish expedition based on a wide range of French sources, see Desbrière, *Projets et tentatives*, i, 57–232. E. H. S. Jones in his *An invasion that failed: the French expedition to Ireland, 1796* (Oxford, 1950) uses both British and French material. See also various articles in John A. Murphy (ed.), *The French are in the bay: the expedition to Bantry Bay, 1796* (Cork and Dublin, 1997), esp. Hugh Gough, 'Anatomy of a failure' (pp 9–24).

Ireland. The first, numbering about 5,000 men, was to be conveyed from Brest to Ireland by a squadron that was being dispatched to India. The second expedition, of about 6,000 men, was also to sail from Brest. The men for these forces were to be drawn from the *Armée des côtes de l'Océan*. A third force, of about 5,000 men, composed mainly of foreign deserters under French officers, was to sail from Holland and call at Ostend.[1] All three expeditions were to start about the beginning of September and make for Galway Bay. The quality of the troops suggests that the Directory intended the expedition, in co-operation with the Irish insurgents, to stage a *chouannerie* on a large scale. On receiving these instructions, Hoche obtained permission to visit Paris. He seems to have been fired by the possibilities of an Irish expedition but nevertheless believed the plan required to be modified. Presumably partly as a result of his comments the project outlined in the instructions was reshaped. About the middle of July, Hoche was named as the commander-in-chief of a force of 15,000 men which was to be sent to Ireland and it was settled that once he was established there reinforcements would follow. It was left open for some time at what point the landing should be made. The strength of the United Irishmen's organisation in the north was an argument in favour of landing there; but the longer the sea voyage, the greater the danger from the British navy, and so it was settled in the end that the landing should be on the south-west coast, at Galway Bay, the Shannon estuary or Bantry Bay. In November the ministry of the marine decided in favour of Bantry Bay as having an excellent anchorage.

To what extent Tone was responsible for the Directory's decision to launch a large-scale expedition under a first-class general against Ireland, it is impossible to say. He was not alone in drawing the attention of the French government to Ireland, but his two memorials, drawn up in February 1796, provided the most convincing exposition of the arguments in favour of a major thrust at Ireland.

During his visit to Paris in July 1796 Hoche met Tone and the two men took an immediate liking to one another. If Tone was only 33, Hoche was not quite 28. His career to some extent epitomised the revolution. In 1789 he had been a corporal in the French guards. Four years later he was a staff officer distinguished for his resolution and revolutionary ardour. By the end of the year he was a general of a division and in command of the army of the Moselle; after very hard fighting he relieved Landau at the beginning of 1794. A self-confident, domineering, flamboyant leader of men, he aroused the suspicions of the Committee of Public Safety and early in 1794 was imprisoned in the Conciergerie. Released after the fall of Robespierre, he was sent to fight the rebels in the west of France. He defeated the royalist landing at Quiberon, and showed not only ability in conducting a wearying and disheartening campaign but also political acumen. He realised the importance of religion to the Breton peasant and he insisted that catholicism should be tolerated. Large and strongly built, highly strung and

[1] Desbrière, *Projets et tentatives*, i, 107–9. The quoted matter is as translated by the editors.

restless, Hoche was a fascinating blend of a rough and untutored soldier and a man of natural charm and intellect.

A week after his first meeting with Hoche, Tone was commissioned *chef de brigade* in the French army. The French authorities probably regarded this appointment as a simple method of subsidising an Irish exile and providing Hoche, to whose staff he was immediately attached, with a political adviser. For Tone, however, the commission admitted him to a profession which for years he had wished to join; and he set to work to turn himself into a competent professional soldier.

A joint naval and military operation is bound to present difficulties of its own. With the best of good will one arm of the forces may fail to comprehend the problems of the other. In 1796 the French army was confident it could snatch victory from the most adverse of circumstances. But it had very little experience of amphibious warfare. The French navy was in a thoroughly unhappy condition. A force that demanded a considerable degree of technical knowledge, during the early years of the revolution it had lost a high proportion of its officers. The naval dockyards had been disorganised by strikes and riots and had difficulty in obtaining stores—wood for spars, linen for sails and cordage. The Baltic trade had stopped and Brest had for its hinterland a region where communications were frequently cut by royalist rebels.[1]

Hoche and his staff were infuriated by the delays that arose in fitting out the expedition—and their irritation and discernible contempt for the navy communicated itself to Tone's diary. Frustrated and bored, Tone had already, before leaving Paris *en route* for Brest on 17 September, turned to writing his memoirs. By the time he left Rennes he had completed some 35,000 words of autobiography and begun another pamphlet, *An address to the people of Ireland on the present important crisis*, which was completed at Brest by 22 November and printed there for distribution in Ireland. At last, on 15 December 1796, the expedition sailed. By then it was a time of the year when bad weather could be expected, but this, though a handicap, was not wholly a disadvantage.

By remarkably good fortune, on 19 December, thirty-four ships, including the *Immortalité*, carrying Admiral Bouvet, second in command of the fleet, and General Grouchy, Hoche's second in command, found themselves together some 200 km to the south of Mizen Head. However, among their missing consorts was the *Fraternité*, carrying Hoche and Admiral Morard de Galles. It had sailed well off course, too far to the south-west, and when after struggling against adverse winds it arrived off the Irish coast on 30 December, the rest of the fleet was making back for France. Earlier, on 20 December, Bouvet directed the ships under his command to make for Bantry Bay, which had been chosen as the landing place. An unfavourable wind and faulty navigation placed the fleet on the 21st slightly to the west of the entrance to the bay. Then, when after tiresome tacking the ships were entering the bay, the weather worsened. The wind rose, the sea

[1] P. J. Levot, *Histoire de la ville et du port de Brest sous le Directoire et le Consulat* (Brest, 1875), pp 144–53.

mounted; it became obviously difficult to use small craft for landing operations and the ships themselves were tossing in a rough sea in a high wind near a rugged coast—a situation abhorrent to a seaman. While Bouvet must have been haunted by the prospect of seeing the sails of British warships rounding the entrance to the bay, Grouchy and the senior officers he could consult (including Tone) were, after some discussion, in favour of landing the force at their disposal (about 6,400 men) and striking boldly into Munster. The weather moderated for a short spell and there was a possibility that a landing would have been feasible, but Grouchy, though professionally highly competent and personally courageous, had not the fire and drive required to arouse enthusiasm for a forlorn hope. Nor of course were he and his fellow officers technically qualified to assess the difficulties involved in manoeuvring ships off the Cork coast in stormy winter weather. Bouvet certainly recognised these difficulties. First, he emphasised that it was impossible to land troops until the weather improved. Then during the early evening of 25 December, having lost an anchor, he made out of Bantry Bay into the open sea. The other ships during the next twenty-four hours followed his example and started to straggle back to France. In the event, of the 45 ships that sailed, 34 (including the *Indomptable* with Tone on board) returned to French ports, 11 being lost. It was not an episode that the French army and navy could contemplate with satisfaction. The conception had been bold and success had been remarkably near, which made it all the more exasperating that the expedition had been rendered futile by a combination of accident and human error.

Nor could the British navy derive much satisfaction from a survey of the fortunes of Hoche's expedition. Admittedly, Rear Admiral Pellew's frigates stationed off Brest and Vice Admiral Kingsmill's small squadron based on Cork had done their utmost to harry the enemy and inflict some loss on the French fleet. But one of the most remarkable features of the episode was the failure of the Channel fleet, which was responsible for the blockade of Brest, to take effectual action. The fleet was divided, an advance squadron under Rear Admiral Colpoys being stationed off Brest, rather too far out to sea, and a reserve under Admiral Bridport at Plymouth, some 400 km from Brest. When Colpoys learned that the French fleet had got out of Brest, being afraid to take up its pursuit in the wrong direction, he first stayed on his station and then, distressed by bad weather and anxious to get news, he fell back to Falmouth. As for Bridport, though he seems to have shown a lack of urgency, he was certainly held up by adverse winds, so that he was not finally clear of port until 3 January 1797. The judgement of one naval historian on British naval strategy and the French expedition to Bantry Bay is well justified: 'an inadequate force at the decisive spot, inadequately maintained and dependent upon a reserve as large as itself but unready and improperly stationed—such were the glaring faults'.[1]

[1] A. T. Mahon, *The influence of sea power on the French revolution and empire, 1793–1812* (London, 1893), i, 366.

# To Thomas Russell, 7 August 1795

T.C.D., Sirr papers, MS 868/2, ff 2r–2v; printed in Bulmer Hobson (ed.), *The letters of Wolfe Tone* (Dublin, [1920]), pp 34–7.

The passages shown in italics below were printed, with insignificant verbal changes, in the *Northern Star* (Belfast), 15 Oct. 1795, under the statement: 'the following is extracted from a letter received from a reputable gentleman who went out passenger in the *Cincinnatus* to his friend in this town'.

Philadelphia, Augt 7, 1795

My dear Tom,

As the post for Europe closes this evening, *I have barely time to inform you that we are all arrived safe and well after a passage of 7 weeks in which the only adventure which occurred worth relating was that we were boarded*[1] *about the middle of the 6th week by three British frigates*[2] *who pressed, with circumstances of great insolence and barbarity, 50 of our people therein including all the hands save one, so that if we fortunately had not had moderate weather, it would have been next to a miracle if we had ever got in.* You will judge how this circumstance went down with me, especially when I tell you that I was very near having the honor myself to serve the King when I least dreamt of it, and I dare say if the scoundrels had known my name I should certainly have been detained. So much for this just and necessary war. *My stay here has been so short (two days) that you will judge I can have no news of any kind for you.* I have not even called on Smith to present my bills for acceptance[3] but shall tomorrow. The country is beautiful but it is like a beautiful scene in a theatre—the effect at a proper distance is admirable but it will not bear a minute inspection, the features are large, the weeds rank, the grasses coarse, but distance blends all that and renders the whole a singular, certainly, and, in my mind, a beautiful landscape. I am obliged to speak of the face of the country, for as yet I know so little of the people that it would not be candid to speak what I am inclined to think of them. However, to my friend I whisper that I believe them not to be amiable; they seem selfish and interested, and they do fleece us, Émigrés, at a most unmerciful rate. All this however is a secret between us. *What I am competent to say with certainty is that the public mind is in a prodigious ferment here regarding the treaty with England, which is universally condemned*, with the exception of the Chamber of Commerce of New York, which you who know that state

[1] The *Northern Star* reported the boarding of the *Cincinnatus* by three British frigates on 25 July at a point 38° 40' N. by 73° W. ('a few hours' sail from the American coast') and the impressment of forty-six passengers and all but one of the sailors on board. It added that the American government should not ignore the incident. (*N.S.*, 1 Oct. 1795).

[2] According to a passage in Tone's autobiography, written over a year later and emended by his son, the ships were the *Thetis*, Capt. Cochrane, the *Hussar*, Capt. Rose, and the *Esperance*, Capt. Wood, but this information may not be altogether accurate (see below, p. 335).

[3] See above, vol. I, p. 532.

and the spirit of commerce will not wonder at.[1] Two thirds of the Senate are necessary to sanction a treaty and the numbers on the division were 20 to 10, exactly the number required.[2] *What the President will do is not known but I suppose he will sanction the Treaty, in which case he will outlive his hard and well-earned popularity, a circumstance which I for one shall most heartily regret; at the same time God forbid any sense of past services should overbear truth and justice. He will live too long for the mischiefs attendant, on which I refer you to Juvenal's 10th Satyr*, or rather to Johnson's translation thereof.[3] I have now done with American politics.

The time is so very short that I cannot write to my friends in Belfast. We therefore beg you will go to Simms, Wm & Rob[er]t,[4] to Neilson, to McDonnell,[5] to Sinclaire[6] and to every one to whom we are obliged, which is indeed every one we know, in Belfast and assure that we do entertain and ever shall the warmest sense of their kindness and the sincerest affection for them personally. If the shortness of the time would at all admit it we would write to everybody, but the cruel post office closes *this evening*; in a week or ten days we shall know more of our own prospects and situation and then we will write in detail; till then, my dear Tom, God almighty bless you. The girls add a P.S. *Shew this letter to every one.*

Yours most truly
T. W. Tone

I have just sealed a letter to my father[7] and very wisely forgot to tell him how to direct to me, so do you write and tell him to direct to the care of Messrs Rabb,[8] Philadelphia, and they will forward it.

## Matilda Tone to Thomas Russell, 7 August 1795

T.C.D., Sirr papers, MS 868/2, ff 3r–3v; added to the preceding letter; printed in Bulmer Hobson (ed.), *The letters of Wolfe Tone* (Dublin, [1920]), p. 37.

My dearest Tom,

I cannot let this letter go without telling you that I am well & happy, by which you may guess that all those on whom my life & soul depend are so also. I shall not attempt to mention what I felt at parting [from] you, for no language can express it. Write to y[ou]r sister[9] for me & remember me to all my dear friends

[1] The treaty between Great Britain and the United States (usually known as the Jay treaty) signed in Nov. 1794. It provided that British troops should be withdrawn from the territories assigned by the peace of 1783 to the United States and that the debts due to British merchants and compensation for injuries to American merchants should be settled by commissioners. It also included clauses regulating commercial relations between the two countries. (Clive Parry (ed.), *The consolidated treaty series* (Dobbs Ferry, N.Y., 1969– ), li, 243–72).

[2] On 24 June the Senate agreed to the ratification of the treaty by 20 votes to 10 (*Journal of the executive proceedings of the Senate*, i, 186).

[3] Juvenal's tenth satire, imitated by Samuel Johnson (1709–84) in the *The vanity of human wishes* (1749).

[4] William and Robert Simms. [5] Dr James MacDonnell. [6] William Sinclair.

[7] Peter Tone (see below, p. 37, n. 3). [8] See below, p. 14. [9] Margaret Russell.

at Belfast; tell them I consider my seeing them as the happiest circumstance of our life. I will write to them the first opportunity. Adieu, my dearest Tom, give my love to John[1] when you write, & believe me ever your affectionate friend

Matilda Tone

Mary sends her love, specially to Will Simms, but the paper is full, she has not room to write it. *Write to us instantly*.

her
Mary × Tone
mark

The thermometer here is at 92![2]—fine roasting weather. You may judge of the heat by the effect it has on my writing.[3]

Mr Tho^s^ Russell
Belfast
Ireland
p[er] Schooner *Nancy*.

## To Pierre Auguste Adet, 10 August 1795

Tone (Dickason) papers.

Pierre Auguste Adet (1763–1834), physician and chemist; entered French government service at the time of the revolution; French minister to the United States of America, June 1795–Nov. 1796 (*Dict. biog. franç.*).

The copy from which this is taken is in a French hand and contains linguistic errors.

Philadelphia, Aug^t^ 10, 1795

Citizen Minister,

I have the honor to leave for your perusal the trial of the late William Jackson, published in Ireland,[4] and I beg leave to point out particularly to your notice page 63, wherein there is the statement of England admirably drawn up, and also page 64, wherein there is a statement of Ireland written by me,[5] the substance of which I had the honor this morning to quote to you in conversation and on the authenticity of which you may rely.

In addition to the facts contained in that paper (which the shortness of the time prevents me from transcribing), I beg leave to mention to you that I presume England is the enemy the most formidable to France of the whole confederacy against her, as well by her money as by her navy. It is a circumstance not

[1] One of Russell's brothers. [2] i.e. 92 degrees Fahrenheit, or about 33 degrees Celsius.
[3] From 'Mary sends her love' is in Tone's hand. The letter is postmarked 6 Oct. 1795.
[4] William Sampson, *The trial of the Rev. William Jackson . . . for high treason . . .* (Dublin, 1795).
[5] Above, vol. I, pp 505–6.

known, I fear, in France that two thirds of that navy are manned by Irishmen;[1] neither is it known that since the commencement of the present war Ireland has furnished to England no less than 180,000 men for the fleet and army; that England draws all the provisions for her fleet, and much of them for her troops in the West Indies and elsewhere, from Ireland in a war; that if Ireland were merely to withhold her support from England, that nation could scarcely by possibility carry on a war; but if on the other hand she were to join and co-operate with France, it must operate the certain destruction of England, and by consequence to the establishment of the liberty of mankind. The idea of any invasion of England will be folly. The nation there would oppose it as one man. In Ireland it is directly the reverse: every man except the aristocracy and their immediate dependants would support it. I speak within bounds when I say that seven eight[h]s of the Irish people would join an invading army provided they were satisfied as to the principle of which the invasion was made.

For that purpose it would be necessary for the general or the deputy with the French army, immediately on the landing being affected [*sic*], to publish a proclamation declaring that they came not as enemies but as allies, to enable the people to redress their grievances, to assert their rights, to subvert the ancient tyranny of their oppressors and to establish the independance of Ireland on the ruins of the English usurpation; it should promise the most perfect freedom to the exercise of all religion, at the same time suggesting the necessity of abolishing all unjust distinctions and oppressive establishments; it should assure protection in persons and properties to all who should demean themselves as good citizens and friends to the liberty of their country, at the same time denouncing the severest penalties on all those who should adhere to the cause of the enemy; it should call upon the people to choose provisional deputies to frame a form of government, and it should pledge the faith of the French Republic to guarantee that form, subject only to this condition, that it should be totaly separated from and independant of England. If such a proclamation were published, I have no doubt but it would ensure the support of seven eight[h]s of the people.

The army now in Ireland, I dare say, is not less than 30,000 men of which 17,500 are militia, all Irishmen and very fine troops. The remaining 12,500 are made of the ruins of the British army from Flanders, new levied and several regimens of Scotch fencibles.[2] These last are in a most wretched state as to appearance and discipline—I am confident that by proper measures the whole, at least of the militia, could be gained over, such as rewarding them highly at first;

[1] From 1793 to Nov. 1796 the total number of Irishmen enlisted for the naval and marine forces was 16,515 and it has been estimated that Irishmen made up about one-twelfth of the navy (G. E. Manwaring and Bonamy Dobree, *The floating republic* (London, 1935), p. 101). If the muster books of the ships of the line at Trafalgar provide a true sample about 25 per cent of the lower deck at the beginning of the nineteenth century was Irish (R. B. McDowell, *Ireland in the age of imperialism and revolution* (Oxford, 1979), pp 493–4).

[2] The Irish house of commons had resolved on 10 Feb. 1795 to maintain 23,478 regulars for home defence together with a militia force of 22,699 (*Commons' jn. Ire.*, xvi, 48). Fencibles were regulars enlisted for home defence.

promoting the most intelligent to the rang of subalterns in the Irish army, addressing proper proclamations to them on the enormity of fighting against their own country and relations to which Irishmen are very much attached. All those measures however would be done most effectually by the Irish provisional government.

Similar and perhaps most effacious [*sic*] and important measures, might [be] adopted with regard to the navy, two thirds of which are Irish Catholics. If an Irish provisional Government were once established they might publish a proclamation calling on all Irishmen in the English navy to return home, and declaring that all British ships whether of war or otherwise brought in by them should be their absolute property, and further that such of them as chose to enter in the Irish navy should have a liberty of chusing their own officers as high as the captains together with increase pay and a fair division of prize money. All this should be as strongly as possible contrasted with their present situation and hopes and even if it did not succeed in bringing many of them over, it would [have] raised such a spirit of suspicion and distrust and such a foundation for mutiny and desertion in the British navy as must very materially embarrass her operations by sea. I believe no British admiral would like to meet a French fleet with two thirds of his ship's crews Irish and such a proclamation hanging on his head.

A great variety of measures of a similar nature suggest themselves to me, but I wish to avoid running too much into detail and therefore pass them over.

England and France are now committed in a contest that cannot end but in the subversion of the government of the one country or the other. England is only assailable with effect thro' Ireland. I submit to you, Citizen Minister, the difference which it should make to the French republique to have Ireland her ally instead of her enemy.

It remains now to consider of the measure by which this can be established. France have got Holland with her hands;[1] she has got rid of the king of Prussia.[2] By the taking of Luxembourg and, I hope by this time, of Mayence,[3] the Emperor[4] is desirable[5] from giving her much trouble if he be not indeed reduced to beg peace in her own terms; Spain is at her feet.[6] England alone remains with a rancorous animosity to the Republic and a determination to carry on the war as it should seem alone, which let it never be forgotten, she is enabled to do solely

[1] *Recte* 'France has got Holland within her hands'? The stadtholder of the United Provinces (Holland) having fled to England in Jan. 1795, the Patriot party gradually seized power and on 16 May set up the Batavian Republic in close alliance with France.

[2] Frederick William II (1744–97), king of Prussia, 1786–97, ceded the left bank of the Rhine to France by the treaty of Basle, 5 Apr. 1795.

[3] Luxemburg, the last remaining stronghold in the Austrian Netherlands, was captured by France on 25 June 1795. Mayence, at the confluence of the Rhine and Main, was besieged by the French from Jan. 1795 until local republicans took control in Oct. and was not incorporated into the French republic until Nov. 1797.

[4] Francis II (1768–1835), holy Roman emperor, 1792–1806, afterwards emperor of Austria.

[5] The sense seems to require 'prevented'.

[6] Spain, at war with France since Mar. 1793, came to terms on 27 July 1795, ceding her part of Santo Domingo.

or at least principally by the military resources which she draws from Ireland. What then should be the object of France? England and she cannot exist together. Let her then bend all her attention and strain her mighty resources to level that proud nation with dust. She has the command of the Dutch fleet; let her make peace with Spain on the condition of having the use of the Spanish fleet, even tho' she buys it by the surrender of all her conquests. Let her by these means get the command of the channel but for one week and the business is done. Let 20,000 men land in Ireland with a proper quantity of arms and ammunition, the more of both the better and with a general whose name is known at their head and the power of England in Ireland and on the ocean is gone for ever. This great event, which at once ascertains [*sic*] the security of the Republic and destruction of the only enemy she has to fear, may be accomplished with a loss of men, money and honor less than it will require to take the single town of Mayence.

Now is the critical period the people of Ireland are prepared, they want nothing but the means to begin a rallying point to ressort to until they can organise themselves and draw out their own resources. They are for the first time in three six [*sic*] hundred years united among themselves and all sects and parties save the aristocracy and the rich join in the utmost hatred and abhorrence of England and an affectionate regard for the French Republic, to which alone they look for relief from the tyranny of their oppressor. If the present period be suffered to elapse, it never will return; England knows her danger in Ireland, the French does not, and if a peace be once made, she will use such measures in Ireland as will render it impossible for her ever hereafter to emancipate herself, in which she will be supported by aristocracy and the rich in Ireland, who could rather sacrifice their own liberties and the independence of their country than endanger one shilling of their property in the event of a war.

It is not even necessary for the success of the measure that France should retain the command of the channel; it is sufficient if the landing can be made once with the forces I have mentioned. Ireland will be then enabled to proceed on her own resources; but it would be absolutely necessary at first to send a large supply of arms and ammunition with some money to pay the troops until arrangements could be made. It would also be expedient that a considerable part of the French troops should be artillonistre [*sic*], in which Ireland is deficient. Less than 20,000 could not do and more would be unnecessary as Ireland could furnish 500,000 soldiers.

Upon the whole I presume that the detaching so powerful a member of the British Empire as Ireland is from England and uniting her in friendship with the French Republic is a me[a]sure to France of the highest consequence that the bare neutrality of Ireland would be an object which the Republic should be glad to purchase at almost any price if she were apprised of the immense importance of that country to England in a military point of view; that she have now an opportunity for ever to detach Ireland from England and united it to herself by the strongest ties of gratitude and of interest that from the geographical situation of Ireland and her natural produces [*sic*] and advantages she would be a most invaluable ally to France in case of any future war with England, who would be then placed completely between two fires; that the immense supplies of provisions soldiers and seamen which are now drawn from Ireland by England and employed against France, and without [which] England could scarcely if at all carry on the war, would in that event be transported to France and employed against England; that a separation from England and an alliance with France is the most earnest wish of the great majority of Irish people; that it would be for the glory of the République to emancipate a country that has now for seven hundred melancholy years groaned under the yoke of British tyranny; that she will thereby give a deadly blow to the power of his most mortal enemy; that it will [be] a fair revenge of the tumult and insurrection raised by England in the bowels of France, in La Vendée, Lyon et Toulon; that the attempt, whether it succeeds or fails as to Ireland, must be nearly equally destructive to England, to whom victories only there would destroy her best resources and that the outfit of the expedition would be almost the all expense to France, which Ireland, if she succeeded, would most gladly repay with interest and finally that there and there only is the period at which all this may be accomplished, which if suffered to elapse will never return—all this strikes so strongly on my mind, that I cannot believe that if the French government were properly apprise[d] of the true state of Ireland, they would not immediately and at any expense attempt the invasion.

I have to apologise, Citizen Minister, for the length of this, [as] well as for its incorrectness, but the time is so short that I cannot make [it] more perfect, and I find the intense heat of this climate so different from that I have been use[d] to [as to] affect my head extremely. Such as it is I submit it to you and I shall [be] but to[o] happy if the hints I have thrown out can in any the least degree redound[1] to the glory of the Republic and the emancipation of my own dear country.

Health and fraternity

Scribed T. Wolfe Tone
True copy:
E. Anissoy[2]

## Memorandum by Tone on the state of Ireland, 13 August 1795

Archives Nationales, Archives du Directoire Exécutif, AF III, carton 64, dossier 264. There is another copy in Archives des Affaires Étrangères, Corresp. Politique Angleterre, cote 589, ff 129–30v. The minor differences between the two copies have not been noted.

[1] Meaning here 'accrue'.

[2] Not identified. Presumably he made this copy of Tone's original and handed it to Tone. It does not read like a 'true copy'.

This is presumed to be a translation of the 'Mémoire' later referred to by Adet (see below, p. 24) and the 'Memorial' referred to by Tone himself in his Autobiography (see below, p. 337).

There is a full translation (or retranslation) of the copy in Archives des Affaires Étrangères in J. J. St Mark, 'Wolfe Tone's diplomacy in America, August–December 1795' in *Éire-Ireland*, vii (1972), no. 4, pp 7–9.

du 13 Août 1795

D'après la situation de l'Irlande, présentée au Comité de Salut Public l'année dernière,[1] on a du croire que la paix en Irlande ne serait que l'assoupissement honteux d'un peuple qui supporte patiemment les outrages d'une nation plus puissante. On a dû croire que les Irlandais étaient prêts à fraterniser avec les forces de la République dont ils croyaient que l'intérêt était de leur envoyer du secours qu'ils ont attendu avec impatience.

Les causes qui depuis tant de siècles les ont rendus malheureux sous le joug de l'Angleterre ont été aggravées depuis plusieurs mois par presque tous les maux que la force et l'intrigue jointes à la corruption et à la violence peuvent produire. Parmi plusieurs autres outrages, des taxes exhorbitantes ont été levées pour soutenir une cause qu'ils haïssent. On a créé des lois ec[c]lésiastiques, injustes et oppressives. On a manifesté le désir de dépouiller les Irlandais de leur existence politique et de mettre le comble à leur esclavage en les unissant à l'Angleterre.[2] Leur indépendance nationale à présent n'est qu'un nom et une raillerie, et est sujette à tous les inconvéniens de l'utilité provinciale. Ils ne l'ont souffert que parce qu'ils ne pouvaient l'empêcher, car la réunion avec l'Angleterre a été longtems comparée au supplice inventé par Mézence[3] qui attachait un cadavre à un corps vivant. Cette réunion projetée a rempli tous les coeurs d'indignation et chacun brûle d'en venir aux mains avec ses oppresseurs. Que dans ce moment, 20,000 Français descendent en Irlande avec des armes et des munitions, et ils formeront le noyau d'une armée qui détruira la tyrannie anglaise et rendra la liberté au monde entier.

L'Angleterre ne peut éxister sans l'Irlande, son pouvoir déstructeur serait anéanti sans elle. Toutes les fois qu'il lui a plu de s'engager dans une guerre, les pauvres Irlandais ont été forcés par la destruction de leurs manufactures &c. de mourir de faim, ou de s'engager dans les armées ou dans la Marine, dont ils composaient ordinairement les deux tiers.

Une révolution en Irlande ôteraient à la Grande Bretagne la source de la force; et ils ne prendraient pas les armes contre leurs parents et leurs amis. Dans le dernier mouvement qui a eu lieu,[4] la milice (qui est la force principale) s'est comportée de manière à montrer qu'elle n'en agirait pas de la sorte.

L'Irlande a trop longtems été le magasin de l'Angleterre. Au lieu de l'employer au soutien de ses citoyens et à l'augmentation de la population, son

[1] Perhaps an allusion to the memorandum on the situation in Ireland which Tone drafted on 14 or 15 Apr. 1794 (above, vol. I, pp 504–8).

[2] The proposed union of Ireland with Great Britain.

[3] Mezentius, mythical king of the Tyrrhenians, noted for his cruelty.

[4] Not identified.

sol fertile n'a servi qu'au pâturage des bestiaux, et l'Angleterre en a tiré exclusivement ses provisions pour ses armées navales et ses colonies; dépourvue des provisions de l'Irlande, l'Angleterre ne pourrait plus subsister.

S'il se faisait une révolution en Irlande, l'Écosse essayerait aussi de s'émanciper; elle avait dernièrement, et peut-être à présent, des agens en Irlande pour concerter de communs efforts.[1]

La crainte d'une révolution en Irlande a engagé l'Angleterre à tourner de ce côté une partie de ses forces; elle y a envoyé dix-huit régimens anglais avec les débris de son armée du Continent; ceci joint à la milice irlandaise monte environ à 30,000 hommes; ils ont formé quatre camps, d'environ 5,000 hommes chaque, et en ont mis un dans chaque province; le sud de l'Irlande est l'endroit le plus convenable pour une invasion; dans le nord, où les volontaires étaient en plus grand nombre, la majeure partie du peuple est armé et discipliné, et n'auraient besoin que d'un peu de secours; là ils sont pénétrés d'amour pour la liberté et d'admiration pour la révolution française.

Les circonstances suivantes prouvent la bonne volonté du Peuple pour la France:

Malgré les efforts des gens éclairés pour retenir les insurrections locales qui ne pouvaient que diminuer la force du peuple et augmenter celle de leurs oppresseurs, las enfin de souffrir, il s'est soulevé dans plusieurs endroits, et tous ceux qui étaient en état de porter les armes ont juré 'que si les Français faisaient une descente, il les les seconderaient de tous leur pouvoir et rompraient entièrement avec George 3'.

Si une descente en Irlande avait lieu, il paraîtrait utile que ceux qui seraient envoyés par la République déclarent que leur but serait l'affranchissement, et non la conquête, de l'Irlande; et qu'ils leur garantissent l'indépendance, les droits de conscience et la liberté des religions et des opinions.

Une maison de commerce à Belfast,[2] qui [a] des fonds considérables disponibles, désirerait savoir s'[il] y aurait moyen d'envoyer des bâtimens chargés de provisions en France. Elle désirerait aussi savoir s'il lui serait permis d'armer dans les ports français des corsaires contre les Anglais.

Une autre compagnie,[3] qui a fait le commerce du coton de la manière la plus

[1] One authority on relations between Scottish and Irish radicals in the 1790s states that 'the facts behind Tone's claim are unclear' but suggests that one such agent may have been James Tytler, the polymath Scottish radical who fled Scotland for Belfast in Jan. 1794 and moved in radical circles there under the name of Donaldson (Elaine W. McFarland, *Ireland and Scotland in the age of reason* (Edinburgh, 1994), pp 136–8). When in Ireland, Tytler (1747?–1805) was an associate of Tone's friend Russell; he moved to America in July 1795 (*D.N.B.*; *Journals and memoirs of Thomas Russell, 1791–4*, ed. C. J. Woods (Dublin, 1991), pp 151, 173–4, 176). In a letter written from Salem, Massachusetts, very probably to Russell, on 7 Sept. 1795 Tytler refers warmly to Tone, Rowan, Reynolds and Tandy, whom he knows to be in Philadelphia, which he expects to visit (T.C.D., Sirr papers, MS 868/2, ff 182–3).

[2] Not identified.

[3] Very probably O'Brien and Comerford's which in 1787 had a callico and cotton factory at Balbriggan, Co. Dublin, a textile printing works at Palmerstown and a warehouse in Merchants Quay, Dublin, 'for the purpose of carrying on the business of manufacturing and printing on a plan correct, extensive and novel in the kingdom'. The partners were Denis Thomas O'Brien and John Comerford, both members of the

étendue en Irlande, voudrait savoir si elle éprouverait quelqu'encouragement en allant s'établir en France.

La réponse de ces demandes faites au Ministre de la République française pourrait être communiquée à leurs correspondans à Philadelphie, qu'ils ont chargés de la lui présenter.

Pour traduction conforme

## Memorandum by Tone on his brother Mathew, August 1795

Archives Nationales, Archives du Directoire Exécutif, AF III, carton 64, dossier 264. There is another copy in Archives des Affaires Étrangères, Corresp. Politique Angleterre, cote 589, ff 128r–128v.

This document, which is not in Tone's hand, is obviously a translation from the English. For its dating, see Autobiography (below, p. 337). The numerous but minor differences between the two versions have not been noted.

Under the impression that his brother Mathew is a prisoner at Guise, Tone seeks his release, explaining that Mathew Tone left Ireland in Aug. 1794 with the intention of joining the French army. In fact Mathew Tone was released in May 1795 and was to arrive in America in Dec. 1795 (see below, p. 265).

Au Citoyen Adet, Ministre Plénipotentiaire de la République Française près les É[tats] U[nis] d'Amérique.

Mémoire de Theobald Wolf Jone [*sic*] dernièrement arrivé de Belfast dans le royaume d'Irlande

Citoyen Ministre,

J'ai l'honneur de vous représenter que mon frère Mathieu Jone [*sic*], pénétré d'admiration pour la République Française et de haine pour la tyrannie anglaise, a quitté l'Irlande sous un nom supposé de William Brown au mois d'août 1794 avec l'intention de se joindre à l'armée française et de sacrifier sa vie pour la cause de la liberté et de l'égalité.

En conséquence de ce projet, il partit pour Hambourg, et delà pour Dunkerque, où, à son arrivée s'étant déclaré irlandais, il fut arrêté et mis en prison vers la fin de l'année 1794.

Il écrit aussitôt à Archibald Hamilton Rowan, alors à Paris, qui présentait son mémoire au Comité de Salut Public, mais on ne fit aucune démarche en sa faveur.

Il a été depuis transféré parmi les prisonniers de guerre à Guise,[1] où il a eu une maladie très dangéreuse; il y a perdu ses habits et dépuisé l'argent qui lui restait. Il a fait encore plusieurs démarches pour obtenir sa liberté, mais elles ont été vaines.

Catholic Committee. In 1795 the firm provided Tone with bills of exchange to enable him to transfer money from Ireland to America. (*D.E.P.*, 18 Dec. 1787; see above, vol. I, pp 320, n. 1, 429, n. 3, and 532).

[1] A garrison town in the Aisne, 180 km north-east of Paris.

Mr Rowan, à son départ de Paris, l'a recommandé au Citoyen Madgit[1] pour lui faire avoir un passe-porte sous le nom de William Brown; mais il me semble que cela a été sans succès; ainsi j'ignore absolument le sort de mon frère, et ne sait pas s'il est mort ou vivant.

Permettez-moi donc de vous représenter que mon frère n'avait d'autre motif en allant en France que son zèle et son amour pour la cause de la Liberté et de la République; que j'ai moi-même souffert pour cette cause; que j'ai été banni de mon pays pour mon attachement à la France (comme vous le savez); de plus, que moi et mon frère, nous sommes encore prêts a sacrifier notre vie pour une belle cause. Permettez-moi donc de réclamer de votre justice et de la magnanimité de votre République que mon frère, comme sous le nom de William Brown, soit mis en liberté et renvoyé en Amérique par la prochaine occasion. Le tout vous est soumis respectueusement.

## To Thomas Russell, 1 September 1795

Nat. Arch. (Ire.), Rebellion papers, 620/16/3/3.

Philadelphia, Sept. 1st, 1795

Dear Tom,

I wrote to you immediately on my arrival here on the 6th of last month, as I recollect, which letter[2] I sent haphazard by the post office and therefore it may probably never reach you, at least unless the Irish post office has exceeding improved its morality since I left Europe; but now having the opportunity of a private hand, I hope what I am about to write may come safe. Of myself and family I have little to add. About a week ago we removed to Westchester, 25 miles from this place, where we shall live much cheaper than we can do here, and yesterday I returned here on business which may detain me a week. We are all well and I hope may continue so notwithstanding the heat of the weather, which is most dreadfully oppressive.

Having now been a month in this country and made many inquiries, I am a little more competent to speak my opinion than when I wrote last. The result of my observation is a most unqualified dislike of the people. They, I mean those of Philadelphia, seem a selfish, churlish, unsocial race, totally absorbed in making money, a mongrel breed, half English, half Dutch, with the worst qualities of both countries. The spirit of commerce hath eaten up all other feeling, and the

[1] Nicholas Madgett (b. 1738) had by 1798 spent forty years in France. He was employed by the Committee of Public Safety and then worked in the translation section in the ministry of foreign affairs. His rank was that of 'sous-chef' of a bureau (there were ten bureaux in the ministry and sixteen sous-chefs). Madgett was believed by a British government source to be one of the instruments of the Directory 'in everything that relates to Ireland'. In 1797 he retired. (Nat. Arch. (Ire.), Rebellion papers, 620/1/216, Suspects book; Archives Nationales, AF III, 52–3, dossier 2B; Frédéric Masson, *Le Département des Affaires Étrangères pendant la révolution* (Paris, 1877)).

[2] Above, pp 1–3. It is dated, in fact, 7 Aug. 1795.

pride of mercantile wealth is, I promise you, little beneath the lofty pretensions of your aristocracy. We are splitting here fast into two great parties, the rich and the poor. I mean poor relatively, for as to absolute poverty, there seems to me to be no such thing in America. The Treaty with England[1] is the question on which they are now at issue; but in fact it is but a text.[2] The real state is Aristocracy against Democracy, and I know you will rejoice to hear that against all the weight of property and Government influence Democracy is daily gaining ground. The more I consider the question the more I am convinced of the wicked folly of intrusting power long in the hands of one man, no matter how virtuous and how able. Power long exercised would corrupt an angel. I do believe from my very soul that Washington is a very honest man, and a sincere American according to his own theory. But he is a high-flying aristocrat and in the present contest between the parties he has developed so much of his character and principles as to produce a visible change in the sentiments of numbers. He has already within this few days [*sic*] sustained some sharp attacks in the papers, and it is no longer a damnable heresy to doubt the infallibility of the President. When people once desert principles and attach themselves to men, adieu to all public virtue! The Government here is in some respects most admirably constructed yet it is wonderful how uniformly alike the spirit of aristocracy will work everywhere. In order to procure an address to the President in favor of the Treaty from the merchants & traders of Philadelphia,[3] the directors of the banks went round and insinuated pretty plainly that those who refused should remember their discounts. Is not that a manœuvre that would do honor to the old countries? By this and similar means an address was procured here and another from the merchants of New York, to both which, as concurring with his own sentiments, the President returned very cordial answers,[4] but to all those numerous ones from all parts of the Union reprobating the Treaty, he returned one and the same answer, and one sufficiently lofty and dignified, the spirit of which was, in effect that they should leave politics to those who had made them their study and not put their judgement, grounded on partial views, in competition with his, who had combined the general interests of the whole state.[5] See now what it is to continue a wise and good man, for I believe Washington to be both, in such a station as President for seven years! What do people want with presidents?

Whenever he shall die, I do believe the aristocracy of America will receive their mortal blow. It was, you may remember, our opinion in Europe and all I have yet seen here tends to confirm my expectation. They are anchored in his great and just reputation, and even that is now beginning to fail them. Whenever they lose him, their sole support is gone.

[1] See above, p. 2, n. 1. [2] *Recte* 'pretext'?

[3] *The writings of George Washington*, ed. J. C. Fitzpatrick (39 vols, Washington, 1931–44), xxxiv, 278–9, 280.

[4] Ibid., pp 252–3, 294–5, 297, 301, 303.

[5] In his reply Washington pointed out that the treaty had been ratified by the Senate and that he hoped 'experience will show that the public interest required the course which has been pursued' (ibid., p. 301).

I can hardly think with patience of the abominable selfishness of spirit which has regulated the public conduct of America during this war between France and England, yet for this the people are not to blame, it is their government, or more properly speaking their aristocracy, for the House of Representatives are sincere Republicans; and this, if I wanted anything to confirm me in my political creed, would completely furnish it. In America, a representative government, a measure of no less consequence than one including peace or war, the highest possible concern of a nation, has been carried by the two upper Estates, manifestly against the sense of the great majority of the People. See now what Aristocracy is however modified! I suppose as much has been done as could well be done to neutralise it in the Constitution of America, but in vain, it still retains its noxious activity. What is it to me whether it is an aristocracy of merchants or of peers, elective or hereditary? It is still an aristocracy, incompatible with the existence of genuine liberty. Here now is the interest of America, save that of my lords the merchants, sacrificed, her character engaged, her friend,[1] to whom she owes her existence, deserted in the hour of extreme necessity, to gratify her ancient tyrant,[2] who persecuted her to the very verge of her own destruction, and why? to bring in more dollars to the chests of the mercantile peerage of America. I see more clearly than ever, or, more properly, the theory is now supported by the fact, that liberty must destroy aristocracy under every possible modification or surrender her existence. She can keep no terms, admit no composition with her, she must, to borrow Grattan's expression when he was surprised by his passion into a fit of honesty, 'extinguish Aristocracy or Aristocracy will extinguish her'.[3] You have in Ireland the blessing of privileged order, and an hereditary peerage, not to mention the best of sovereigns, whom I mention with honor. We have here a president, elected for four years, a senate for two, with a property qualification;[4] surely if any modification could extract the poison from Royalty and Aristocracy, this would have done it. Yet see how it is—here are twenty-one men controlling the almost universal sense of five millions and the single instance of misgovernment and national degradation which must ever follow national ingratitude that I have yet seen here has been the work of the aristocratic part of the Administration of America. Do not however imagine from what I write to you that I am so foolish as to write or speak thus here. I keep, and shall, a profound silence. I bless God I am no American. I have but one country to where[5] [ ] and wherever fortune may drive me I shall never consi[der] myself for an instant released from my natural allegiance to her.

[1] France. [2] England.

[3] In reply to an address from the Dublin catholics voted at the end of February 1795 Grattan, having declared that he trembled at the return of their 'old task-masters' who had been removed from power by Fitzwilliam, added 'they will extinguish Ireland—or Ireland must remove them' (*D.E.P.*, 17 Mar. 1795).

[4] United States senators were chosen by the state legislatures. To be eligible it was necessary to be resident in the state, to have been a citizen for nine years and to have attained the age of thirty (Constitution of 1787, sect. III).

[5] In the MS about 6.5 cm of the next line are cut out. About five words are lost.

I have written to you now a volume of American politics. Let me beg of you in return to send me by the first safe conveyance, the Post Office being always excepted and forbidden, a full state of everything in Ireland since my departure together with all manner of papers, pamphlets &c., relating to Irish affairs; let me also know how my old masters the Catholics got[1] on or whether they got on at all. You know me better than any man knows me, and suit your letter accordingly.

Hamilton Rowan is here and well—his adventures since he left Ireland are curious enough.[2] We are very much together.[3] Reynolds[4] is also here, but I believe he writes to his friends, as well as Rabb,[5] whom I have found very friendly. For my own affairs, I went to Smith[6] on whom I had my bills, which he accepted, and as I thought he might from his residence know the country I consulted him as to my going back;[7] but he dissuaded me from it, especially from the days during the present bloody war which is carried on there, those counties which I had in contemplation being exposed to the ravages of the Indians and the event being very uncertain.[8] As I have no great talents for the tomahawk, I have therefore given up the idea of going into the woods, and I think now, if my means will admit it, of settling, I believe, in Rhode Island, which promises a more salubrious climate and, all things considered, cheaper land than Pen[n]sylvania. I think land here has found its level; that is to say, what is well circumstanced is sold at a very high rate, and what is sold for little money is ill circumstanced. I am for a thousand reasons of temper, habit and above all fortune, or rather the want of fortune, not

[1] Or 'get'? Here and five words on the MS is unclear.

[2] Hamilton Rowan, having escaped from Newgate in May 1794, on arrival in France was arrested at Roscoff as a British spy. On his release he travelled to Paris and had an interview with Robespierre shortly before Thermidor. After a year, 'much discontented with the distracted state of Paris, where they were too busy with their own intestine divisions to think of assisting Ireland', he secured through Madgett a passport enabling him to embark for the United States of America under the assumed name of James Thomson. (Rowan, *Autobiography*, esp. pp 240–1, 259, 261).

[3] Sarah Anne Hamilton Rowan wrote to her husband from Ireland on 19 Sept. 1795: 'the arch-deceiver T[one] has quit the country, and it is to be feared he may go where you are. I think it my duty to say that, if this should be the case, you ought to avoid all connection with him, and it is as well to say at once what is the fact—*his friend cannot be mine*; his wicked principles and artful manners have destroyed us' (ibid., p. 286). On 27 Oct., apparently after hearing from her husband, she wrote to him: 'Reynolds and Tone are not exactly the people you ought to make your constant companions, though there is no reason for absolutely shunning even Tone; however, you ought to be aware of him, and I hope he will not again fall in your way.' (ibid., pp 287–8).

[4] James Reynolds (see above, vol. I, p. 499, n. 5, and Addenda, below, vol. III). Implicated in the Jackson affair, he fled to America in May 1794, and joined the radical, Anglophobe circle of John Beckley (Michael Durey, *Transatlantic radicals and the early American republic* (Lawrence, Kansas, 1997), passim).

[5] At the beginning of May 1795, William Rabb inserted an advertisement in the *Northern Star* stating that he was leaving Belfast to set up a commission business in Philadelphia; he was recommended by several of Tone's Belfast friends including Robert and William Simms (*N.S.*, 4 May 1795).

[6] William Smith, junior, to whose firm Tone's bill of exchange was to be presented (see above, vol. I, p. 532). Described as a 'merchant', he had premises at 13 South Front St., Philadelphia (Edmund Hogan, *The prospect of Philadelphia* (Philadelphia, 1795), p. 113).

[7] i.e. to the back country, the undeveloped parts to the west.

[8] Tone seems to be referring to the Ohio country, where Iroquois were resisting the occupation of their lands by colonists.

adapted, I find, at least to Pen[n]sylvania. No man is fit to go back but either one with a great capital who can force things, or a very small capital who can labour hard himself and family. Now you know I believe I stand in neither one predicament nor the other. Do not think, however, that I am dispirited by this. I have not escaped so many dangers, and subdued so many difficulties, to get swamped at last here. One way or other I shall make it out, and in the worst event I shall console myself with the reflection that I am suffering in consequence of an endeavour to serve my country to the very best of my ability, my judgement and my conscience; a reflection from which I have a thousand times derived unspeakable consolation and support.

Believe me, dear Tom, the greatest of the numberless heavy losses I sustained in leaving Ireland, and especially in leaving Belfast, my adopted mother, was the loss of your society, and I speak for us all. There does not a day elapse that we do not speak of you, nor a ridiculous or absurd idea or circumstance arise that we do not regret that you are not with us to share and enjoy it with us. You know how exactly our humours concurred, and that particular style of conversation which we had framed for ourselves and which was to us so exquisitely pleasant; those strained quotations, absurd phrases and extravagant sallies, which people in the unreserve of affectionate intercourse indulge themselves in—all these we yet enjoy, but woefully curtailed by your absence—if anything brighter than ordinary occurs the first idea is 'Ah, poor Tom! I wish he was here with us now!'[1]

It is a selfish wish. Never come here unless you are driven. Stick to your country, to the last plank, as I would have done had I been able—much as I regret your absence, I cannot in conscience wish you were with us. You & I have known Ireland. I think in the course of this winter, during much of which I must be idle, of diverting the spleen by writing Memoirs of the Catholic Comm[itt]ee,[2] on the plan I mentioned to you, and sending them to Ireland. I have, I think, materials enough, and tho' men are very soon forgot when out of sight perhaps I may survive for six months so as that a work with my name may call the public attention a little. I shall be very moderate, and, I suppose I need not say to you, strictly and rigorously adhesive to truth. I think it may make, with a copious appendix, a large 8vo volume, which, printed in the very best manner, may sell (suppose by subscription) for half a guinea. If it is printed by subscription I must call on my friends in Belfast to exert themselves, and I should hope my old Catholic noble and approved good masters would not neglect me. I hope I may, if I succeed, get some character and some money, both of which will be very acceptable to me, for I am entirely too poor for America. I shall write to Chambers[3] on the subject,

[1] Tone seems to be recalling the scene in Shakespeare's *King Lear*, act III, in which Lear, Kent and Edgar are sheltering in a hovel from the storm. The words he quotes after 'poor Tom!' have not been found but they echo words spoken by Edgar in Nahum Tate's adaptation of the play (Dublin, 1758).

[2] Possibly 'Account of the proceedings of the Catholic Convention from 3 December 1792 to 9 April 1793', the document dated by the editors to *post* 16 August 1793 and printed above (vol. I, pp 464–85).

[3] John Chambers, the Dublin printer who did some work for Tone in 1791 (see above, vol. I, pp 132–3).

whom I think of giving it to, to print, as I know him to be an honest man and a good citizen. Pray remember in your answer to notice this part of my letter, and consult about it.

The heat is so oppressive here as very sensibly to affect my head and writing a long letter is a work of some difficulty. You will easily perceive the effect of the scirocco on this. I must therefore desire you will shew it to every one of my friends in Belfast and beg of them to consider it as addressed to each of them and let them answer it accordingly and give me a full account of everything relative to Ireland. Go particularly to Rob[er]t Simms and Sam Neilson, to W[illia]m Simms and McCrackens. You know I do not deal in professions, but the kindness I have ever received in Belfast, and most especially during my last stay there, when I so much needed it, I shall remember while I have life with sentiments of the warmest gratitude. Call in my name on McDonnell[1] and Sinclair, Tennent and McIlveen.[2] Call in short on all my friends and thank them in my name for their kindness to me. You will not say more for me than I feel.

I have said scarcely anything of Ireland thus far. Removed as I am, I know not how you may be proceeding, but I trust in the goodness of God you are doing well. I doubt not at all but the truth will finally prevail, but I am not like King Hezekiel,[3] for I wish that this great thing *should* happen in my day. At all events I have the consolation to think that in my humble station I have *to this hour* left *no one measure untried* which was likely to forward what I consider the cause of truth, justice and liberty.

Tell Tom Macabe I did not forget his last words to me in the boat. I hope my friend in Lisburne[4] is a good lad and sticks close to his business; diligence and steadiness will do wonders and I most heartily wish him success.

Tell Mrs Simms[5] we talk a thousand times of our excursion to Ram's Island.[6] I am sure we here shall not be so happy until we shall go there again, if ever that happens. I cannot look on this as my country, nor believe but some prosperous event may yet recall us. If it should ever so happen! Remember us affectionately to my great friend Mrs Neilson[7]—and to the Lion.[8] Writing this to you and recalling so many of those I most regard to my recollection is making me almost too melancholy to proceed. I will therefore stop here, wishing you and them health

[1] Dr James MacDonnell.

[2] Probably Gilbert McIlveen the younger, a proprietor of the *Northern Star* (see above, vol. I, p. 135).

[3] Tone probably means the prophet Ezekiel who foretold a new Jerusalem after the downfall of Israel. Cf. Ezekiel and 2 Chronicles, 29–32.

[4] Possibly Charles Hamilton Teeling (1778–1850), a son of Luke Teeling of Lisburn, Co. Antrim. He was imprisoned, 1796–7, and after 1802 settled at Dundalk, Co. Louth, as a linen-bleacher. (*D.N.B.*).

[5] Probably Mary Simms (1759?–1832), wife of Robert Simms (A. C. W. Merrick, *Old Belfast families* (Belfast, 1991), pp 255–6).

[6] On 11 June 1795, shortly before leaving Ireland, the Tones, together with the Simmses, Neilson and Russell, made an excursion to Ram's Island in Lough Neagh (see Autobiography, below, p. 333).

[7] Anne Neilson, wife of Samuel Neilson.

[8] Perhaps William Sampson (see below, p. 361, n. 1), joint author with Thomas Russell of *Review of the Lion of old England* (Belfast, 1794), a political satire (*Journals and memoirs of Thomas Russell, 1791–5*, ed. C. J. Woods (Dublin, 1991), pp 124, 146).

happiness and liberty. You have a country worth struggling for, whose value I never knew until I had lost it. May you be more fortunate than I have been. You never will be more so than I wish you

Yours most truly,
T. W. Tone

Any commands in the way of books, papers and letters, address for me, to the care of Mr Thos Stephens,[1] Bookseller, South Second St., Philadelphia. I have written to Dick McCormick to forward all my Dublin letters, &c., to Sam Neilson, so you will beg of him to take care of and transmit them, *by private hands*. Once more adieu, God bless you! Do not let my friends forget me.

Mr Thos Russell
Belfast
Ireland

## From John Keogh, 3 September 1795

*Life*, i, 291–3.

This document is said by William Tone to be 'from one of the chief Catholic leaders in Dublin, Sept. 3, 1795'. The author is identified in Matilda Tone Wilson to the editor of the *Truth Teller* (New York), 19 Oct. 1842, reprinted in *Nation* (Dublin), 17 Dec. 1842.

The letter given below, and the three that follow, reached Tone at about the end of Nov. 1795 (see Diary for 24 Feb. 1796, below, p. 77, and Autobiography, below, p. 339). William Tone states in a footnote (*Life*, i, 289): 'these last enigmatical letters, but of which the solution is easy, are those which determined my father's departure for France'.

[Sir],

I am told there is a vessel bound for Philadelphia to sail this day and determined to seize the opportunity to assure you that you live in the memory of those here whom I believe you considered worthy of your friendship. Is it to the hurry inseparable from the preparations for a long voyage that I am to impute your not answering a letter (not a short one) which I directed to you at Mr Neilson's?[2] Possibly it met the fate of many letters of late, to and from me, which were not thought to be worth delivering. However this may have been, let me know how is your health, and that of Mrs Tone and of your sister and children; whether you intend, like Cincinnatus[3] and your greater Washington, to follow the plough and, like them, to quit it when your country calls. Is young America engaged

[1] Thomas Stephens of 60 South Second St. advertised himself in his *Stephens's Philadelphia directory for 1796* as a 'wholesale and retail bookseller, stationer and importer'.

[2] Very probably at Samuel Neilson's in Belfast.

[3] Lucius Quinctius Cincinnatus (b. *c.* 519 B.C.), though twice dictator of Rome, worked on his farm.

entirely in clearing her woods? I trust that she knows how to appreciate genius when it flies to her shores for protection. But you will prefer knowing how your friends here proceed. To these inquiries. Since your departure a variety of applications were made by our great men to induce the people to have aggregate meetings to address the throne for Catholic emancipation; but these attempts are fruitless.[1] The people suspect the patriotism of their former leaders and they must by *actions* restore themselves to confidence, or leave the people to themselves. They will not go for half measures; their views are extended since your departure. Our unfortunate and misguided peasantry have become more outrageous; neither the gaol nor the gibbet deter them; they even meet death with firmness. The utmost exertions are used to suppress this spirit in the capital, where it is said that four thousand are already sworn;[2] many are thrown into Newgate.[3] I saw our friend P[eter] Burrowes about an hour since; he was just returned from Naas, where he was employed by the Crown in prosecuting Defenders. Two of them are condemned to death; one, whose name is O'Connor, after being found guilty made a speech in defence of the people.[4] Counsellor Burrowes considers these infatuated people as having enlisted men for the French in expectation of an invasion. It was proved that O'Connor swore many to be true to the French. This now appears to be the oath taken by all the Defenders. Our Bishop, Dr Troy, has excommunicated them, and they are not to be admitted to the sacraments at the hour of their death;[5] but this has also proved ineffectual. Religion and loyalty have lost their influence with those men, who rely upon their numbers, which are very great indeed.

A book has been published here on the best mode for the defence of Ireland.[6] The writer appears to be a scientific military man;[7] the work is full of French idioms. He points out the West as the most likely place for the enemy to

[1] At the beginning of Sept. 1795, the whig leaders suggested to some radicals, including Keogh, that a Dublin aggregate meeting should be held (R. B. McDowell, *Irish public opinion, 1750–1800* (London, 1944), pp 234–5).

[2] As Defenders.

[3] These arrests are reported in *Faulkner's Dublin Journal*, 27, 29 Aug., 1 Sept. 1795.

[4] Laurence O'Connor (d. 1795), a schoolmaster of Agher, Co. Meath, was charged with high treason, and found guilty on 31 Aug. 1795. He made a speech from the dock explaining the meaning of the terms 'love', 'liberty' and 'loyalty' in a paper which had been produced in evidence against him. Peter Burrowes was junior counsel for the crown. (*D.E.P.*, 5 Sept. 1795).

[5] A letter from the catholic archbishop of Dublin, John Thomas Troy, which was to be read from the altar in all the chapels of his diocese, excommunicated any person who had taken the Defenders' oath and not abjured it (ibid., 11 Aug. 1795).

[6] *On the defence of Ireland including observations on some other subjects connected therewith* (Dublin: P. Byrne, 1795). It was first advertised in *Dublin Evening Post*, 15 Aug. 1795. A second edition was published in Belfast in the following year. The lord lieutenant thought *On the defence of Ireland* 'sensible but of a dangerous tendency inasmuch as it exposed our weaknesses with great clearness; at the same time, however, it proposed a remedy' (Lord Camden to duke of Portland, 9 Jan. 1797, P.R.O., HO 100/69).

[7] The author was said to be Lieut-col. Maurice Bagenal St Leger Keatinge (*c.*1761–1835) of Narraghmore, Co. Kildare. He entered the army as a cornet, 1778; major, 1782; commanded 107th foot, 1794–5; M.P. for Co. Kildare, 1790–1802; a liberal, he was said to have been arrested, 1798; wrote several other works; died in Paris (*D.N.B.*; *Drennan letters* (1931), p. 276; R. G. Thorne (ed.), *The history of parliament: the house of commons, 1790–1820*, iv (London, 1986); Liam Chambers, *Rebellion in Kildare* (Dublin, 1998), passim).

land, stating that the S.W. winds would detain our fleets in the Channel, and permit a fleet from Brest to arrive here. He gives his opinion of the mode on which the enemy will proceed after landing, their route or march, dress for the armed peasantry, &c. and although he advises the method to oppose an invading enemy, yet this work appears extraordinary for a friend of Government at this time when the country is agitated beyond all former example, and might be dangerous in the hands of the enemy. This author recommends union, otherwise he asserts all resistance vain, in case of an invasion. I just now hear that this work is suppressed by Government. I think they are right. You have no doubt heard of our invasion of France and of the check we received at Quiberon.[1] But, at this moment, a large fleet is on the way thither[2] with Count D'Artois[3] on board.[4] 'Tis said when joined to Charette[5] they will amount to 75,000 men. We expect, on arrival of the packets, to hear of this landing. Louis XVIII[6] offers to pardon all his subjects if they will throw themselves at the foot of his throne; but he forgot to say where they will find it, which, I suppose, must postpone this proof of their attachment to him. But away with politics. Let us leave them to the great: for humble men, friendship is a fitter subject. Remember then, dear Tone, the many hours we spent in the garden in your favourite walk.[7] That these conversations impress your mind as they do mine, I can never doubt. How often have we anticipated your return to your friends—to your country? Those ideas can never be relinquished. I am sanguine in my expectations to see you and your family live in the country you love, suitable to your genius and your patriotism. I am growing old; you know 'tis the vice of age to become too much attached to interest; do not wonder then, if I should wish ardently that you may arrange your affairs so as to return to us, and if not soon, it may be too late for me, perhaps even for yourself. Cornelius[8] desires me to assure you of his affectionate regard; whenever you

[1] At the close of June 1795 a force of *émigrés* was landed on the Quiberon peninsula in Brittany. It was soon hemmed in by the republican forces commanded by Lazare Hoche. Though some of the royalists managed to re-embark, about 6,000 were compelled to surrender; of these 600 were summarily executed (J. W. Fortescue, *A history of the British army* (14 vols, London, 1899–1930), iv, 415–16).

[2] In August 1795 a small British force under the command of General John Doyle was landed on the Isle d'Yeu off the coast of the Vendée. Having accomplished nothing it was withdrawn in December. (Ibid., iv, 18–22).

[3] Charles Philippe, comte d'Artois, later Charles X (1757–1836); he was fifth son of the dauphin son of Louis XV (*Dict. biog. franç.*).

[4] Note by William Tone: 'the most curious details of this expedition are given in the memoirs of Count Vauban, an emigrant officer. But I suppose this work is not now to be procured.' Jacques Anne Joseph le Prestre, comte de Vauban (1754–1816), was an émigré officer who took part in the seizure of Quiberon. His *Mémoires historiques pour servir à l'histoire de la guerre de la Vendée* were published in two editions (Paris, 1806 and 1815).

[5] François Athanase Charette de la Coutrie (1763–96), leader of royalist insurgents in the Vendée; surrendered to government forces and was pardoned, Feb. 1795, but fought with émigré invaders at Quiberon, June 1795; captured and executed, 29 Mar. 1796, on orders of General Lazare Hoche (*Dict. biog. franç.*).

[6] Louis Stanislas Xavier, comte de Provence (1755–1824), fourth son of the dauphin son of Louis XV; emigrated, 1791. On the death of Louis XVI in 1793, he took the title of regent and after the death of his nephew in 1795 assumed the title of Louis XVIII.

[7] Probably at Mount Jerome.

[8] One of Keogh's sons, a student at Trinity College, Dublin (*Alumni Dubl.*).

return he expects to hear from you and will instantly pay you his respects *in person*. Our Government are making serious exertions to put down the Defenders. You, I am sure, join with me in earnest wishes that these unfortunate men may restrain from all violence, which must terminate in the destruction of many without any possible benefit to themselves or to the country. For, if they are aggrieved in rents, or otherwise, they cannot obtain redress by such means, which unite every man of property against them. Besides, it will naturally terminate in many associating in gangs as robbers and murderers. Your old companions of the Sub-committee are as you left them. I saw Mr MacCormick[1] this day for some time. His wishes for your return fully coincide with mine and he thinks that it will not be your fault and that you will omit nothing consistent with principles for so fair and honourable an object. And I own that I have such an opinion, let me say experience, of you, that I think you cannot fail to succeed in any attempt in the line of your profession. I know not, as yet, to whom I shall commit this letter, but will now go and inquire. Once more, Tone, remember and execute your garden conversation.

## From Robert Simms, 18 September 1795

*Life*, i, 283–4.

Dear Tone,

The newspapers will inform you of the French affairs and you will, I doubt not, have felt the same hopes and fears that we did respecting *peace*. We are now, however, in tolerable good spirits and the news of this day tends to invigorate us, which is the certain intelligence of the French having crossed the Rhine at Düsseldorf and taken the citadel of that place by assault.[2] With respect to our own affairs, they are not so well as I could wish, but still they are far from being in a bad way. The principal thing I dread is that the imprudence of some warm friends to their country may prematurely throw us into action. We are, however, generally in this quarter striving to repress the ardour of our fellow-labourers. The Defenders in County Meath, Dublin and Kildare have been throughout the summer very turbulent and excited general alarms amongst the great, but, as numbers of those unfortunate beings have suffered lately, they will probably for a time be quiet. But it is evident from the general sentiment of the lower classes of the people that it will be impossible Ireland can long remain in her present situation. They all look to the French and consider them as fighting *their* battles. The organization which you were made acquainted with amongst the Catholics in this neighbourhood continues to increase and has spread as far as Meath and

[1] Richard McCormick.

[2] The army of the Sambre-et-Meuse crossed the Rhine at Düsseldorf on 6 Sept. 1795 (*D.E.P.*, 17 Sept. 1795).

will probably go much farther, which will certainly produce powerful means if properly applied, but it will require great exertions to keep this organization from producing feuds among the different sects; for the Presbyterians in general, knowing nothing of their views and plans, look on them with great jealousy. These exertions shall not be wanting and let us hope the best.

R.S.

Belfast, 18th Sept. [1795]

## From Thomas Russell(?), 21 September 1795

*Life*, i, 289–90.

This letter is identified by William Tone as being 'from one of the leaders of the United Irish in Belfast, September 21st, 1795'. The author was very probably Thomas Russell. See C. J. Woods, 'The authorship of a letter received by Tone in America in 1795' in *Eighteenth-century Ireland*, v (1990), pp 192–4.

Reynolds[1] has at length broke his long silence and wrote to Neilson. He and . . . . . . .[2] were with your friend Smith,[3] who professed great willingness on the part of his employers to assist us, provided they are able. After informing N[eilson] of this, R[eynolds] recommends instant action whenever our crops are secured, and brings forward all the heroes of antiquity to support his arguments. But are we not gaining ground and our opponents rapidly losing? Why then make our country the seat of such speculations at present, when we are certain of having a more favourable opportunity some time hence? No doubt it would be a useful diversion to the Smiths.[4] And I consider R[eynolds]'s arguments only as a detail of what passed at the interview and not his own reasoning. For my part, I am firmly persuaded that it would be neither our interest nor that of the world to make the business very hazardous, or event doubtful. The bloodless manner in which the Smiths' hammer[5] was first introduced fascinated all parties; but it was only the firm friends to them were able to withstand the repeated shocks which a different conduct afterwards produced. Believe me, Tone, I am for no unnecessary procrastination. I think the hour is rapidly approaching and our business at present is preparation. Not the fixing a time, or saying, 'when the crops are in, or the corn secured', or any other definite time; but when we are prepared, let us embrace the first favourable moment that offers. A favourable speculation just now opens to our view: twenty-five thousand men of the best are going to the

[1] James Reynolds (see above, p. 14).

[2] Probably Archibald Hamilton Rowan, who after arriving in Philadelphia from France presented a memorandum to the French ambassador, Adet (Archives des Affaires Étrangères, Corresp. Politique Angleterre, cote 589; L. D. Woodward, 'Les projets de descente en Irlande et les réfugiés irlandais et anglais en France sous la Convention' in *Annales Historiques de la Révolution Française*, viii (1931), pp 23–4). The dotted space is given here as in *Life*.

[3] Probably Adet. [4] Probably the French. [5] Probably the French revolution.

West Indies. Their absence will, no doubt, make provisions plentier here and a demand for shoes and boots in the West Indies. I had almost forgot to mention that R[eynolds] speaks of an address to us from the Smiths, and that we may expect it immediately. A wilder scheme was never thought of; it would be the certain means of overrunning us with bulls,[1] which would prevent every idea of exertion. Despotism in the extreme, misery of every kind, and the banishment or death of all our best friends, would be the result. But, however, as you will have seen Smith a few months after R[eynolds], I am sure every idea of the kind will be dropt until some other arguments are ready to accompany it. I shall now drop the hammer &c. Neilson has been called away this morning by express to settle some serious disputes in County Armagh between the Peep-of-day-boys and Defenders.[2] C[harles] Teeling is there before him. I hope their efforts will be successful: that county has always been a plague to us.[3]

## From William Simms, 21 September 1795

*Life*, i, 290–91.

William Tone identifies this letter simply as being 'from another'. The author can be positively identified in the Autobiography (below, p. 339). The letter appears, from internal evidence, to have been written on the same day as the preceding one.

[Dear Tone],

I have been expecting very anxiously for some time past to hear from you. Government on this side the water are a good deal alarmed at the spreading of Defenderism amongst the militia. R.[4] is just returned from Dublin, where it is currently reported and generally believed that five or six thousand of the militia have taken the Defenders' oath. It is certain that a great many have. A fife major of the Fermanagh regiment has been sent to Newgate for having administered it to a number of privates in said regiment.[5] The societies of

[1] British troops.

[2] These disturbances, which culminated on 21 Sept. 1795 in a 'battle' at the Diamond, near Loughgall, Co. Armagh, led to the expulsion of some hundreds of catholics from the county and the formation by protestants of Orange lodges (Hereward Senior, *Orangeism in Ireland and Britain, 1795–1836* (London, 1966), pp 13–21, 29–31).

[3] In fact Neilson never reached the scene of the disturbances. Before he could do so, he was met on the road by Teeling, who convinced him of the impossibility that 'the maddened minds of either party could be rendered amenable to any rational control'. Teeling recalled much later: 'turning from the distracted County of Armagh, we entered into Down and there passed the night in the little village of Hallsmill on the banks of the Bann water. On the following morning we returned to our respective homes.' (C. H. Teeling, *Observations on the 'History and consequences of the battle of the Diamond'* (Belfast, 1838), p. 59).

[4] Possibly Thomas Russell.

[5] Camden in a letter to Pelham, 30 Aug. 1795, having referred to the arrest of a number of Defenders in Dublin, stated, 'we have sent for the fife major of the Fermanagh militia and one of the privates of the 7th dragoons who were the original persons who swore the information' (B.L., Pelham papers, Add. MS 33101, ff 248–249v).

United Irish are spreading fast throughout a large portion of Ulster. As you will no doubt have to lay out a good deal of money before you are *settled* as you could *wish*, if you have occasion, draw on me at sixty days sight for one or two hundred pounds: your bill shall be duly honoured and you may repay me at your convenience. I beg you will not be backward in doing this in case you find it at all necessary. Neilson received a letter last night from C[harles] Teeling,[1] from Portadown, where he is gone this day. There has been dreadful work there about the Defenders.

## Pierre Auguste Adet to the Committee of Public Safety, 1 October 1795

Archives des Affaires Étrangères, Corresp. Politique Angleterre, cote 589, ff 23r–23v; printed in L. D. Woodward, 'Les projets de descente en Irlande et les réfugiés irlandais et anglais en France sous la Convention' in *Annales Historiques de la Révolution Française*, viii (1931), p. 23.

There is an English translation in J. J. St Mark, 'Wolfe Tone's diplomacy in America, August–December 1795' in *Éire-Ireland*, vii (1972), no. 4, p. 7.

Adet states that Tone, 'an Irish patriot who has served the cause of the oppressed catholics', arrived in Philadelphia six weeks ago, came to see him straightaway and, at his request, has drafted a memorandum on the present state of Ireland.

*Légation de Philadelphie: Politique No. 20*

Philadelphie, le 9 vendémiaire l'an 4me de
La République Française une et indivisible

Le Ministre Plénipotentiaire de la République Française près les États-Unis
Aux Représentans du Peuple & Membres du Comité de Salut Public

Monsieur de Wolfe,[2] patriote irlandais, qui a servi la cause des catholiques opprimés, est arrivé à Philadelphie depuis six semaines. Fuyant la persécution qui menace, dans son pays, les amis de la liberté, il est venu chercher un asile sur le continent Américain.

Un objet plus important encore a déterminé son voyage: il est chargé par ses concitoyens de donner au Ministre de la République près les États Unis des renseignemens sur l'Irlande, sur les dispositions de ses habitans. Fidèle à l'engagement qu'il avoit pris avec eux, Monsieur de Wolfe est venu me trouver sitôt qu'il a été arrivé à Philadelphie. Après m'avoir justifié par des pièces matérielles de ses sentiments patriotiques, il m'a parlé de la situation actuelle de l'Irlande, du désir que les habitans avoient de briser leurs fers et d'être indépendants de l'Angleterre; puis il développa les avantages qui en résulteroient pour [la] République.

[1] See above, p. 22, nn 2, 3. [2] Theobald Wolfe Tone.

À ma demande, Monsieur de Wolff a rédigé un mémoire[1] sur cet objet. Je vous l'envoye avec [cette] lettre. Vous prononcerez dans Votre Sagesse, Citoye[ns] Représentants, sur le parti qu'il conviendra de prendre, d'après les données et les circonstances.

Salut et fraternité
signé P. A. Adet

## Extract from a despatch from Pierre Auguste Adet to the Committee of Public Safety, 1 October 1795

Archives des Affaires Étrangères, Corresp. Politique Angleterre, cote 589, f. 24.
Adet informs the committee of Tone's arrival and submits his memoranda.

Extrait d'une dépêche du Ministre de la Rép[ubliqu]e F[rançai]se près les États-Unis au Comité de Salut Public

Philadelphie, le 9 Vendémiaire an 4[e]

Le ministre de la République annonce au Comité l'arrivée de M. Wolsf [*sic*], Patriote irlandais, qui étoit chargé de lui faire des ouvertures de la part de ses compatriotes, amis de la liberté comme lui, et de lui manifester le désir de secouer le joug des Anglois avec le secours de la France.

Le ministre joint à la dépêche un mémoire[2] qu'il a fait rédiger par ces [*sic*] Irlandais, où l'on peint l'état actuel de l'Irlande, la haine tous les jours plus vive pour les Anglois, le vif ressentiment de l'oppression sous laquelle ils font gémir cette contrée, les mouvemens de révolte excités de toutes parts, le désir ardent de briser leurs fers, le succès très vraisemblable d'une descente des Français qui auroient sur le champ de nombreux auxiliaires.

À la même dépêche est joint aussi un mémoire[3] particulier de M. De Wolsf [*sic*] qui demande que son frère Mathieu Wolff Jone [*sic*],[4] qui n'étoit venu en France que pour y servir sous les drapeaux de la liberté et qui a été mis en prison, soit élargi et envoyé en Amérique par la plus prochaine occasion, avec un passe-port sous le nom de Williams Brown [*sic*] parce que les Anglais connaissent et haïssent trop son vrai nom.[5]

[1] Probably the memorandum of 13 Aug. 1795 (above, pp 7–10).
[2] As n. 1. [3] Above, pp 10–11. [4] *Recte* Mathew Tone.
[5] In February 1796 the French minister of war wrote to the minister of foreign affairs informing him that at the latter's request he had ordered the release of Mathew Tone, arrested at Dunkirk in April 1794 and held at Guise (Archives des Affaires Étrangères, Corresp. Politique Angleterre, cote 589, f. 133). But according to Tone's autobiography he had been released in May 1795 and arrived in America in the following December (see below, p. 265).

## To Arthur O'Connor, 20 October 1795

*Life*, i, 284–9.

William Tone identifies this document as 'Letter from my father to Arthur O'Connor, Esq., M.P., from America' and explains 'this letter, in the pressure of subsequent business, was never sent, but as it contains a clear and beautiful vindication of my father's conduct, I insert it here'.

Arthur O'Connor (1763–1852), M.P. for Philipstown, 1790–95. On 4 May 1795 he made a vehement speech in favour of catholic emancipation strongly criticising the existing order in Ireland. In 1796 he joined the United Irishmen. (*D.N.B.*; *Parl. reg. Ire.*, xv, 286–302).

Philadelphia, Oct. 20, 1795

Sir,

Within these few days, I met by chance with an Irish newspaper of some months standing in which was inserted an account of a debate in the Common Council at Cork on the subject of granting the freedom of that city to Mr Edward Byrne, wherein you took that part which your spirit and your principles demanded.[1] As my name was introduced in the argument by your adversaries to the discredit of the Catholic cause, and as you, in justifying that cause, were, I am satisfied, inadvertently led into an assertion that I had been dismissed by the Catholics in consequence of my connection, or supposed connection, with the late Mr Jackson and my wish to introduce a foreign enemy into Ireland, I feel it a duty to myself to acquaint you that I never was directly or indirectly dismissed by the Catholics; that my resignation was my own voluntary act wherein I did not even consult or advise with those of that body with whom I was most in habits of confidence, and that consequently whoever was your informant on that matter asserted what was not the fact.

I might rest here, but I have that respect for Mr O'Connor, that admiration for his uncommon talents and still more uncommon integrity, that I cannot resist the desire I feel to avail myself of the opportunity which chance has afforded me of detailing somewhat the grounds of my conduct; in the execution, or attempted execution, of which I found myself constrained to quit a country to whose emancipation I may now say I was ready to devote my life. I do this with the more eagerness because, judging from the speech which has immortalized you, I am satisfied we are agreed as to the grievances of Ireland, however we may differ as to the mode of redressing them.

My theory of Irish politics is comprised in these words: I trace all her miseries,

[1] The debate in the Cork court of D'Oyer Hundred held on 3 June on an order nominating Edward Byrne of Dublin to be a freeman of Cork is reported at considerable length in the *Dublin Evening Post* of 16 June 1795. In the course of the debate Arthur O'Connor stated that 'the Catholic Committee, far from conniving at what had come out in evidence on Mr Jackson's trial, had instantly dismissed Mr Tone from the secretaryship'.

so strongly described by you, to the blasting influence of England. How is that influence maintained? By perpetuating the spirit of internal dissension grounded on religious distinctions. How then is it to be obviated? By a cordial union of all the people. So far, I think, no honest Irishman can differ from me. On these principles I have acted and I will say, allowing for humble talents and limited situation, acted with success. I had the singular good fortune to be one of the very few men through whose means the Catholics of Dublin and the Dissenters of Belfast first came to understand each other; and to that union I know that what has been gained by the Catholics is owing. I know the members of your Parliament (I rejoice you are no longer contaminated by the association), even those who were the earliest and most decided friends to the Catholic cause; and I know how little *genuine principle* weighed with any one of them. I have had an opportunity to observe their shuffling and their speculating, their pushing and their parrying; and, what is more, the Catholics understand them as well as I do. They set out to raise themselves on the shoulders of the Catholics; they have assisted, in a certain degree, to raise them, but they have failed in making them their instruments. They are speculating stockjobbers on the rights of the people; but I prophecy they will have no cause to rejoice in the winding up of their accounts.

I presume up to the arrival of the unfortunate man[1] whose fortitude in a voluntary death must command the respect of the most virulent persecutor I am guiltless, though two years before that period, I had the honour to be made the subject of a furious philippic in the House of Lords by a man who had the meanness to possess himself of a copy of a private letter of mine and the baseness to falsify and misquote it.[2] The charge made against me, when stripped of the necessary legal and constitutional epithets, is that I wished to introduce a French force into Ireland, to subvert the present Government and establish a republic in its place. To this charge I shall give, as to the fact, no answer. But as to the principle, supposing it to be the case of an indifferent person, I think something at least may be said. Introducing a foreign enemy is a sounding phrase and very alarming to many; but I doubt whether the end may not justify even that measure in certain cases of the last extremity. As I have the honour to address a gentleman of respectable situation in a country yet subject to the laws of his Britannic Majesty, I shall beg leave to ask him what he thinks of the Whig noblemen and others who brought a foreign army and a foreign prince into England in 1688. If James II[3] had not been a fool and a coward, but had behaved like a man who was to contend for a crown, and if the Prince of Orange had been defeated, like Monmouth,[4] as war is very uncertain, I should be very glad to know what figure in history Lord Somers,[5]

[1] The Revd William Jackson. [2] See above, vol. I, pp 447–51.

[3] James II (1633–1701), king of England, 1685–8; he fled and was replaced by William of Orange as William III (*D.N.B.*).

[4] James Scott, also known as Fitzroy and Crofts (1649–85), illegitimate son of Charles II, who created him duke of Monmouth, 1663; he landed in the west of England on 11 June 1685 in an attempt to overthrow James II which ended in disaster (*D.N.B.*).

[5] John Somers (1651–1716), holding that James II had abdicated, negotiated with William of Orange in Nov. 1688; lord chancellor of England, 1697–1700; created Baron Somers, 1697 (*D.N.B.*).

Lord Halifax,[1] Bishop Burnet[2] and all the venerable fathers of the Whig interest would have made? Lord Somers rose to the woolsack; had he been placed in the Dock, as might have happened, what epithets would his Majesty's Attorney General have applied to him? Or, to come nearer to our own day, what is to be said for his Majesty's (present) loyal subjects of Corsica?[3] They felt, we must suppose, the yoke of France intolerable; they applied, we are told, for the protection of England; and in consequence they introduced a foreign force into their country to assist them in vindicating that liberty which they felt their own means inadequate to obtain. Here is the principle established in the strongest manner on the highest authority and in a case where I defy the ingenuity of man to find a difference except in the event:

> Multi eadem faciunt, diverso, crimina fato;
> Ille crucem pretium sceleris tulit, hic diadema.[4]

I do, for my part, think it possible to doubt the truth of what seems to be an axiom, that we are bound in all circumstances to stand or fall with England; and I think the time is rapidly approaching wherein it will be no more safe to broach that doctrine than it is now to hold the contrary. But the present state of Ireland is such that any man wishing to argue for her just rights is constrained to keep the strength of his case as much out of sight as possible and to scout and skirmish about the outposts instead of storming the enemy in the citadel; unless indeed he has a mind to discuss the point coolly in the King's Bench with the law officers of the crown, an experiment which I apprehend, from recent experience of the event of such investigations, few men will be now inclined to make.

But, to return to the original object of my letter. So far from being dismissed by the Catholics in consequence of Mr Jackson's trial, I can assure you that applications were made to them from a quarter that must naturally have had great weight with them, subsequent to his conviction and previous to introducing their bill, to induce them to disgrace me; which applications I must, though it is in my own case, say they did with great unanimity and justice refuse. The answer given was that I was in their service until the dissolution of their committee in April 1793, when they ceased to act as a body; that I was again called to their service at Christmas, 1794, on Lord Fitzwilliam's arrival;[5] that I had always acted

[1] George Savile (1633–95), created Viscount Halifax, 1668, and marquis, 1679, urged William of Orange as early as 1679 to come to England and was one of those who met him on his arrival in Dec. 1688 (*D.N.B.*).

[2] Gilbert Burnet (1643–1715) landed with William of Orange at Torbay on 5 Nov. 1688; he was bishop of Salisbury, 1689–1715 (*D.N.B.*).

[3] In 1793, Pasquale Paoli (1725–1807), the Corsican patriot, led a revolt against French rule in Corsica. He appealed to Great Britain for military assistance and in June 1794 the Corsican assembly offered the sovereignty of the island to George III. In Oct. 1796 Corsica was retaken by France. (*D.N.B.*).

[4] 'Many people commit the same crimes with different results; one carries off a cross as a reward for his crime, another a diadem' (Juvenal, *Satires*, xiii, 105).

[5] William Wentworth-Fitzwilliam (1748–1833), 2nd Earl Fitzwilliam, though a friend of Fox, joined Portland in taking office under Pitt, July 1794, and was appointed lord lieutenant of Ireland, 13 Dec. 1794 (*D.N.B.*). In fact he arrived in Ireland on 4 Jan. 1795. Tone must have been recalled by the Catholic Committee in anticipation of his arrival.

faithfully towards them; and that, as to any part of my conduct which happened during a period wherein we had no political connection, they did not feel it just, or necessary, by any act of theirs either to sanction or condemn it; and in this reply they steadily persevered. It is a circumstance which, its being in a degree a personal concern of my own, prevents my dwelling upon. Circumstanced as I then was, so convenient a scape-goat, and utterly incapacitated from defending myself, nothing but a sentiment of the most refined honour and strictest justice could have induced that body to protect me, as I must call it, by their refusal to comply with a requisition which, if my self-love does not influence my judgment, was base and dishonourable. What makes it more curious is that the party making the requisition had, a very few years before, thought me worth soliciting; and the cause of our breaking off was my refusal to withdraw myself from Catholic politics in which I was peremptory. Yet the very personage[1] who I am satisfied instigated the application for my disgrace, and who is now a noisy advocate for the Catholics, after first seeking me out and then breaking off all connection on the ground I have mentioned, insinuated to the Catholics that I must have purchased immunity from the Government by betraying their secrets, seeing I was not prosecuted. Luckily for me, they knew both our characters; and, though he was likely to be a great man, and I was ruined, they scorned to desert me in extremity. I know not whether my gratitude and admiration of their conduct exceeds my contempt for the man who took so safe and, as he thought, certain a mode of destroying one whose only offence, as to him, was rejecting his patronage when it was to be purchased at the surrender of principle.

I am sure you will make allowance for the feelings of a man in my situation. With regard to the opinions of most of the gentry of Ireland, I hold them in the most perfect contempt, but with regard to you it is a very different case. I entertain a sincere admiration of your talents and your principles, and I am sure you will credit me in this assertion when you reflect that you and I shall in all human probability never meet, nor do I see any possible contingency wherein you can be of the smallest service to me. It is because I look on you as a good Irishman that I give you this trouble. I was, in a part of my letter, going at large into the state of our common country, and I think I could justify myself on general principles; but considering the present state of things in Ireland, I thought it but right to stop. You are almost a stranger to me and a political correspondence, or even the appearance of one, might not be pleasant to you. I therefore stopt short and limited myself to the fact as to my dismission. As to my statement of it, any of the leading Catholics will satisfy you, if it be an object worth your inquiry; and I hope the contemplation of the honourable conduct of the Catholics to me will make you amends for such parts as are merely personal to myself. I am fully as anxious for their honour as for my own. To them I was ever, to the best of my ability, a faithful servant; and, as to the country at large, if I have been guilty of any offence

[1] George Ponsonby, a leader of the Irish whigs (see above, vol. I, p. 154, and Autobiography, below, pp 283–4).

of which, I bless God, my own conscience gives me the fullest acquittal, I am here making amends by a painful exile. I make no apology for this letter. You must know the value of a good man's approbation and therefore can sufficiently estimate my motive in addressing you.

I remain, Sir, with great respect
Your most obedient servant
Theobald Wolfe Tone

## To Thomas Russell, 25 October 1795

T.C.D., Sirr papers, MS 868/2, ff 13[r]–15[v]; printed in Bulmer Hobson (ed.), *The letters of Wolfe Tone* (Dublin, [1920]), pp 39–50. The MS seems to have been in better condition when read by Hobson.

Princeton, New Jersey, Oct[r] 25, 1795

D[ea]r Tom,

I begin to accom[m]odate myself to my situation, to forget that we are three thousand miles asunder, and sit down to write to you, as if I were still at Chateau Boue.[1] Short reckonings make long friends; and as I desire we may be so I bring my epistolary account up to this date by telling you that I have written to you on the 10th of Aug[us]t, the 20th of Sep[tembe]r and the 8th instant,[2] and I purpose writing about once a month, trusting to the mercy of the seas and the more inexorable post office for my letters reaching you. I have had one letter from you,[3] which I answered the day I got it; I also wrote to my friend Simms at the same time. Your letter was very nearly three months in coming, being dated the 11th of July. I desire you may write once a month, by the post, and as many bye letters as you can find safe hands to carry, and I shall do the like in return.[4]

I am here at an inn, and have been so, alone, these three days, waiting to sign and seal the deeds relating to my farm. It is a beautiful spot and, I believe, very healthy. The buildings are mean, and I purpose therefore erecting for myself a mansion in the course of the ensuing year, and in the meantime I shall do tolerably. The soil is light and sandy, and never has been properly cultivated, but I hope to shew the Jersey men a pattern. They are miserable farmers by all I can see. I have ninety (English) acres[5] cleared, and I intend to bring fifty of them into English cultivation, which is as much as I shall be able to manage properly, and far more profitable than thrice the extent, scratched over as it is here. I remember

[1] The cottage at Bodenstown, Co. Kildare, which had been Tone's home until his departure for America.

[2] The first of these letters, dated in fact 7 Aug. 1795, is given above (pp 1–2). The other two have not been found. Tone does not mention his letter to Russell of 1 Sept. 1795 (above, pp 11–17).

[3] Not found but evidently received on 8 Oct. 1795.

[4] Tone's name appears in a list of persons, published in the *Philadelphia Gazette*, 1 and 5 Sept. 1795, letters to whom were awaiting collection at the post office in Philadelphia.

[5] About 36 hectares.

once hearing a Down squire, Pottinger, say a smart rent was the best improver,[1] and truly I begin to think so. But I meditate greater things. When I am once fixed, to wit by next spring, I shall try by writing in the papers to form a farmers' club in this county with a small annual subscription to be laid out in purchasing an agricultural library, importing seeds &c. from Europe, for experiments, introducing articles from other states of the Union, and trying them here, perhaps giving small honorary premiums. I likewise, if I succeed so far, will try, at least, to introduce fai[rs] and markets on the Irish system, of which there is no trace here, to my great surprise; for in a country thinly peopled as this is, comparatively with Europe, such institutions as these periodical meetings when men can supply their mutual wants seem to me more peculiarly necessary. I have mentioned this to two or three people, and they all agree it would be a good thing, but nobody will stir in it. If, however, I get my club established next summer, and that we go on for one year, I hope to accomplish my scheme of the fairs & markets by which I shall have discharged my debt of gratitude to the United States for the asylum they have afforded me. I dare say you are amused with the idea of my being the father of a farming club after assisting in framing societies of so very different a nature; but I see no better way of being useful here. Independent of the practical excellence of the American Government, which leaves little ground for discontent, I have determined not to interfere in any degree, directly or indirectly, with their politics. I carry this so far that I shall never assume the rights of citizenship here, let my stay in the country be long or short, were it even to last for my life, *quod Deus avertat*! I am an inflexible Irishman and I will never by any act of mine devest myself of that name. Secluded, however, as I am from my own dear country, and of course unable to serve her as I wish, I will amuse myself and lighten if I can the weight of separation, by doing, or at least attempting, the little good that may be in my power.

I often think of an argument which you and I have held, in which I now feel experimentally that I was right and you were wrong, which indeed candor obliges me to allow has always been the case when we differed. You held that all countries were alike to a well-regulated mind. I do not wish you so ill as to desire you to be convinced of the contrary by such an experiment as I am now making, but if it ever should be your lot, I believe you will feel the irresistible affection with which a man is drawn to his native soil and how flat and uninteresting the politics and the parties of other countries appear. I would always except France; but even there the principle I speak of prevails, for she is contending for the liberty of every man's country.

Out of Ireland, I never shall be happy, but I have no doubt but I shall be perfectly easy; yet, well as I love her, I hope you do not think I would return to her in her present state. I would exist in no country, *permissu superiorum*. If Ireland is ever free, tho' I am fourscore, I will return, but not otherwise.

[1] Cf. Diary for 23 Oct. 1791 (above, vol. I, p. 146).

I see by the papers that the Defenders are becoming more formidable. I have the greatest compassion for them, for I know the extremity of their misery, and I do most sincerely deplore the rashness which drives them to sacrifice their unfortunate lives on the bayonets of the military. If they have leaders, as the papers say, surely every effort should be made by them to prevent such mad and unprofitable destruction. I see likewise that even in my own county, Kildare, ever so remarkable for peace and good order, the spirit of insurrection has intruded. Some persons have been arraigned for high treason, in swearing to join the French and W[illia]m Johnson was assigned as one of their counsel.[1] Pray let me know in your answer the result of this trial, for I look on the culprits as fellow sufferers. If the Government will hang every Irishman holding the same sentiment, I think his Majesty's Attorney General will have full employment. I see likewise a serious insurrection in Dublin among the soldiery, but I do not think it formidable, or at least very formidable, for it seems to involve no political principle, but to turn on points purely military.[2] At the same time a bad government must tremble at everything. If once the Army fluctuates, they are gone.

Now that I mention Irish affairs, let me have the papers as often as you have an opportunity. I did not get the *N[orthern] Stars* you sent last, for they were intercepted by Rabb and Reynolds, which vexed me; however I got sight of the one by chance in which mention was made of my departure,[3] for which I feel most sincerely obliged. It was a bold exertion of friendship towards a man in my situation. I should be curious to know whether the *Dublin Journal* took any notice of the paragraph.[4] Let me likewise have magazines, and any fugitive pieces worth sending—but all this I believe I mentioned in my last.

To return to my own affairs—I shall be for some time in pecuniary difficulties. I have latterly been so much involved in more serious ones that I disregard these. I shall extricate myself, partly, like an Irish gentleman, by selling my woods, and partly I must trust to that good providence that has so miraculously on more than one occasion, as you know, interfered to preserve me. One thing is in my favor—I never was in better health or spirits. My regret for the loss of my country is so mixed with opposite passions, with indignation and with hope, as little to affect me. I do not know, but circumstanced as I am it rather serves me by keeping my mind from stagnating. I have therefore resolved to keep a steady eye on Europe, but in the meantime to embark in my farming system, as if I were to continue here for ever. My great want is a friend, and the extent of that want, I leave to your feelings. Of my wife I need not speak to you who know her so well and love her so much; yet much as I delight in her, I feel a most painful chasm in the loss of

[1] On 13 Aug. 1795, at Athy assizes, William Johnson (see above, vol. I, p. 90, n. 2) was assigned as one of the counsel for Laurence O'Connor and five others charged with high treason. But when their trial came on at Naas on 31 Aug., he was not present and other counsel were assigned. (*Faulkner's Dublin Journal*, 15 Aug. 1795; *D.E.P.*, 5 Sept. 1795).

[2] On 23 and 24 Aug. the 104th and 111th foot stationed in Dublin mutinied on learning they were to provide drafts for the West Indies (*Faulkner's Dublin Journal*, 25 Aug. 1795).

[3] *N.S.*, 18 June 1795 (reprinted above, vol. I, p. 539).

[4] Tone's departure for America was not reported in *Faulkner's Dublin Journal*.

your society and almost wish, at times, that something were to happen which would drive you after me. If that were to be the case, emigration would to me lose *almost* all its pains, and you would have infinite advantages in my being before you, which I severely feel the want of. When I consider the perilous circumstances in which Ireland is placed at this moment, I am almost satisfied that one party or the other will speedily be forced to emigrate, and it is a great instance of the goodness of providence that there is such a country as this open to receive them. I refer you to my last, for my thoughts on emigration, as applied to your case, and I beg you will consider them very seriously.

In my first letters I wrote in terms of strong dislike which I very sincerely feel of many points in the American character. I believe however I guarded it by observing I was but just arrived, and that I spoke of the people of Philadelphia. They are a most disgusting race, eaten up with all the vice of commerce, and that vilest of all pride, the pride of the purse. In the country parts of Pen[n]sylvania the farmers are extremely ignorant and boorish, particularly the Germans and their descendants, who abound. There is something too in the Quaker manners extremely unfavorable to anything like polished society, but of all the people I have met here the Irish are incontestably the most offensive. If you meet a confirmed blackguard, you may be sure he is Irish. You will of course observe I speak of the lower orders. They are as boorish and ignorant as the Germans, as uncivil and uncouth as the Quakers, and as they have ten times more animal spirits than both, they are much more actively troublesome. After all, I do not wonder at, nor am I angry with them. They are corrupted by their own execrable Government at home; and when they land here and find themselves treated like human creatures, fed and clothed and paid for their labour, no longer flying from the sight of any fellow who is able to purchase a velvet collar to his coat, I do not wonder if the heads of the unfortunate devils are turned with such an unexpected change in their fortune and if their new gotten liberty breaks out, as it too commonly does, into petulance and insolence. For all this however it is perhaps scarcely fair to blame them but the fact is certain. In Jersey the manners of the people are extremely different. They seem lively and disengaged in comparison and that, among others, was one reason which determined me to settle in this state.

But if the manners of the Pen[n]sylvanians be unpleasant, their government is the best under heaven, and their country thrives accordingly. You can have no idea from anything you have ever seen or read or fancied of the affluence and ease in which they universally live, and as to the want of civility they do not feel it. What do you think of their government having paid off the whole of the debt incurred in the acquisition of their independence, and having at the moment a million and a half of dollars in advance in the National Bank for which they draw six per cent? Governor Mifflin[1] (the General) told me that in a very short time the State would be able to pay all their expenses by the interest of the money which

[1] Thomas Mifflin (1744–1800), merchant; revolutionary soldier, 1775–8; governor of Pennsylvania, 1790–99; anti-English and pro-French in sympathies (*D.A.B.*).

they were daily lodging in the Bank without drawing a dollar from the people. What do you say to a state not mortgaging its revenues to an irretrievable amount, but growing rich and living like a wealthy individual on their money in the funds? Then go and look at Ireland borrowing two million in one year, and for what? I have not temper to go on. These are the things that make men Republicans. These are the things for which the lives of thousands and of tens of thousands are on[1] a cheap purchase, and this will be yet, with God's assistance, the system of Ireland and of Europe. Governor Mifflin has promised me a statement of the affairs of Pen[n]sylvania, which if I obtain it I will transmit to you. If they be as he asserts and I doubt not they see it will be a curious document, and one sufficient, I should suppose, to imprint on the mind of every good subject an adequate horror of the miseries of republican governments and a rational attachment to the blessings of Monarchy. How sincerely an Englishman must despise such a pimping economy in the expenditure of the public money! ☞ *Take notice*, Pen[n]sylvania, in her constitution approaches the nearest to the doctrine of universal suffrage and perfect equality.

I have done for the present with politics. To come to business. Have you, as I desired in my last, by just and unjust means got together any money for me? If you have, I beg you will buy, in Belfast if you can, but if not in Dublin, 20 lb. of Lucerne seed, 30 lb. of sainfoin, 5 lb. of common furze seed and two or three quarts of the haw stones which grow on the white or haw thorn. Take care that the seeds be fresh, and do you get them packed up carefully in the sheet lead which comes round the tea. Rob[er]t Getty,[2] I dare say, will supply you, and have the whole inclosed in a small deal box pitched in all the seams and water tight—that McCracken will do for you. If you have money to allow it I also wish you would send me, in the same package, the Transactions of the Bath Society,[3] and the Linnæus[4] which McDonnell[5] gave me and I forgot to bring away from his house. I also wish exceedingly for Miller's *Gardener's Dictionary*, 2 vols, 4°;[6] but for this I fear you have not cash, nor perhaps have you any [*sic*]. I do not know whether they keep the furze seed for sale, but if not, it will be a pretty innocent amusement for you to go in person and gather it off the bushes for me and if I can do anything here in return command me. Let me see how you will execute all this like a man of business & direct the box to Thos Inglis[7] firm's correspondent.

This is a plaguy long letter, and tolerably miscellaneous, but what can a man do at an inn without books or company? When I get into my farm, you shall have letters of a less gigantic stature. I will now conclude. My wife, sister & children

[1] MS damaged. [2] See above, vol. I, p. 142, n. 3.

[3] *Letters and papers on agriculture, planting, &c. selected from the correspondence of the Bath and West of England Society for the encouragement of agriculture* . . ., of which several volumes had appeared by 1795.

[4] One of the 180-odd works published by Carolus Linnaeus (1707–78), the Swedish botanist.

[5] Dr James MacDonnell.

[6] *The gardener's dictionary* (2 vols, London, 1724; 8th ed., 1768), by Philip Miller (1691–1771) (*D.N.B.*).

[7] This reading is uncertain. Thomas Inglis has not been identified.

are all well. Matty[1] will write to you the moment we are settled. I enclose for your perusal, *and yours only*, a piece of secret history; burn it when you have read it.[2] Remember me most affectionately to all my friends in Belfast. Take special care of yourself, Dear Tom, and believe me to be ever most truly yours

William Penn[3]

Mr Tho[s] Russell
Belfast
Ireland[4]

## Pierre Auguste Adet to the Committee of Public Safety, 14 December 1795

Archives des Affaires Étrangères, Corresp. Politique Angleterre, cote 589, ff 94[r]–94[v].

Apparently this is a deciphered version of the letter of introduction Tone presented to the minister for foreign affairs after his arrival in Paris in February 1796. See below, pp 53–4, 56, 340–41.

There is an English translation in J. J. St Mark, 'Wolfe Tone's diplomacy in America, August–December 1795' in *Éire-Ireland*, vii (1972), no. 4, pp 9–10.

Légation de Philadelphie,
le 23 frimaire l'an 4[e] de la République française
une et indivisible

Le Ministre Plénipotentiaire de la Répub[liqu]e française près des États-Unis d'Amérique
Aux Citoyens composant le Comité de Salut Public de la Convention Nationale
Citoyens Représentans,

Cette lettre vous sera présentée par Mr Wolf Jones [*sic*]. Je vous ai déjà parlé de ce citoyen dans mon No. 20.[5] Je vous ai dit qu'à son départ de l'Irlande, il avait été chargé par ses concitoyens de présenter au Ministre de la République près les États-Unis une Mémoire en faveur des malheureux Irlandais, de lui faire une peinture fidèle de leur position, et de l'engager à la faire parvenir au Gouvernement françois. Wolf Jones [*sic*] s'est acquitté de sa Commission et m'a prouvé son attachement à la liberté. Il m'a d'ailleurs justifié de son caractère par ses preuves materielles.

Les renseignemens qu'il vient de recevoir de son pays, ainsi que tous les autres réfugiés d'Irlande, sont tels que pour séparer à jamais l'Irlande de l'Angleterre, il parait suffisant d'aider une insurrection déjà bien organisée. En réfléchissant sur

[1] Matilda Tone. [2] This document has not been found.
[3] Pseudonym. The letter is in Tone's hand.
[4] Postmarked 7 Dec. 1795. [5] Above, pp 23–4.

les suites d'un événement aussi impor[tant] j'ai pensé que je devais vous adresser Mr Wo[lf] Jones. Il vous fera un rapport exact sur l'Irlande, et vous indiquera tous les moyens qui pourront concourir à l'exécution d'un [projet?] dont le résultat serait l'émancipation d'un peuple opprimé et l'abaissement de la nouve[lle] Carthage.

Signé P. A. Adet

## John Beckley to James Monroe, 14 December 1795

New York Public Library, Monroe papers; printed in J. J. St Mark, 'Wolfe Tone's diplomacy in America, August–December 1795' in *Éire-Ireland*, vii (1972), no. 4, pp 10–11.

See Diary for 15 Feb. 1796 (below, pp 52, 53).

The words above the code numbers in the third paragraph are in a different hand and very probably were written in by Monroe after he had received the letter from the hands of Tone in Paris on 15 Feb. 1796.

John Beckley (1757–1807) was first clerk of the United States house of representatives, 1780–96 (*American national biography* (Oxford, 1999)).

James Monroe (1758–1831) was United States minister to France, June 1794–Nov. 1796; governor of Virginia, 1799–1802, 1811; secretary of state, 1811–16; president of the United States of America, 1816–24 (*D.A.B.*).

Philadelphia, 14th December 1795

My dear Sir,

I take occasion to introduce to you my friend Mr James Smith,[1] who has been about two years in our Western Country in pursuit of lands, and now visits Europe in search of a good market. He will come to Paris first, and then proceed to the Low Countries and elsewhere as circumstances may direct. Any notice or countenance you can consistantly afford him will be an obligation to me.

Congress commenced its session on Monday last, and my re-election as Cl[er]k of the H[ouse of] Rep[resentative]s was the first essay of party, and in the absence of 23 of my friends a vote was taken, of 30 against me and 48 in my favor. Mr Tazewell,[2] who lives with me during the session, writes you very fully by an opportunity that offers thro' M[onsi]e[ur] Adet, and I refer y[o]u to him for information generally, as also for Randolph's[3] vindication &c., &c.

[1] i.e. Tone, as explained in the encoded part of this letter.

[2] Henry Tazewell (1753–99), president of the American senate, 1795–9; an opponent of the Jay treaty (*D.A.B.*).

[3] Edmund Randolph (1753–1813), American secretary of state, 1794–5; resigned after the publication by the British minister to the United States of intercepted correspondence between the French minister at Philadelphia and the French government which could be read as implying that Randolph was acting dishonourably (*D.A.B.*).

The bear er here of is an agent from
812 1189 1649 1525 1352 1341 157 206 252
Ireland in whom you may confide. His object is
1615 149 1576 1243 1038 427. 1108 296 1341
to obtain of France aid in favor of his dis-
770 108 1352 841 550 149 396 1352 1108 697
tressed country what that aid should be & the
1359 1339 1380 698 550 1480 1569 673 812
man ner of giv ing it he will mention. The
443 988 1352 822 1465 410 182 1268 342. 812
French m[iniste]r I am tol d will aid the buying by
780 1515 145 1046 1105 707 1268 550 812 376 1461
a sacri fice[?] to his nation. You will act in this
101 1050 76 770 1108 275. 1243 1268 531 149 1160
man as you deem best. His name is
433 764 1243 483 1100. 1108 707 1341
T h e o b a l d W o l f e
865 1366 8 527 456 101 1598 707 1261 527 1598 738 8
T o n e. He is the fri end of Ham il ton
865 527 640 8. 182 1341 812 948 790 1352 775 983 1064
Row an and a per son in [whom] his coun trymen ful ly
547 157 673 101 211 149 1576 1108 1339 1150 1512 1593
confide.
427.

Decypher this by our friend Madison's cypher.

Yours truly & sincerely,
John Beckley

# Inscription by Tone in his Diary, 17 December 1795

T.C.D., Tone papers, MS 2047, f. 1$^{v}$.

'On the 16th of December', wrote Tone in his Autobiography, 'I arrived in New York and took my passage on board the ship *Jersey*' (below, p. 340). He may well have acquired at this time the series of notebooks in which his diary for the three remaining years of his life is recorded, for 'Note Book No. 1' is inscribed on the inner front cover as follows:

James Smith New York Dec$^{r}$ 17, 1795–

There is, however, no Diary narrative for this or any other day before 2 Feb. 1796. In his Autobiography Tone fills in the gap: 'I remained in New York for ten days . . . On the first of January, 1796, I sailed from Sandy Hook . . . bound for Havre de Grâce. Our voyage lasted exactly a month' (below, p. 340).

'James Smith' was the *alias* by which Tone was to be known henceforth, the purpose of which was to conceal his true identity from the British government. See preceding document.

## Margaret Tone to Thomas Russell, probably 26 January 1796

T.C.D., Sirr papers, MS 868/2, f. 18v.

This is one of seven family letters of 1796 concerning Arthur Tone in the Sirr papers. The others are printed in Frank MacDermot, *Theobald Wolfe Tone: a biographical study* (London, 1939), pp 25–9. It is from one of these, Arthur Tone to Russell, Jan. 1796 (MS 868/2, f. 18r), that Margaret Tone's letter is dated.

Margaret Tone née Lambert or Lamport (d. 1818) was Theobald Wolfe Tone's mother; she was living in Dublin in 1796, apparently at 25 South Earl St. or 20 Ross Lane (MacDermot, *Tone*, pp 4–5, 27, 28).

Mr Russell,

Arthur's sudden return[1] has thrown us into the greatest consternation. He went away intirely against our inclination and has returned naked without bringing us the [*word not deciphered*] of A [*word not deciphered*] to let us know what is the reason of it. He says his brother[2] has written his sentiments to you on the business. I beg if he has that you will not treat this letter as you have done my three former ones, but be so kind as to let us know what is the matter or what line of life chalked out for him, as he seems to dislike the sea of all things. His father[3] is so exasperated both at his going away and his return in the manner he has done that I believe it will be scarce possible to prevail on him to do anything for him, nor indeed is there much in his power, as we have but a small income of fifty pounds p[er] year to support us and that not longer than God spares his health to attend his employment and [*word not deciphered*] you have [*word not deciphered*] what you would to the contrary this every farthing upon Earth we have to depend upon however. If Arthur had not been taken from the business he chose for

[1] Arthur Tone (b. 1782–*fl.* 1811), Tone's youngest brother, accompanied him to America in the summer of 1795. He sailed for Ireland in Dec. 1795 with messages from Tone to the radical leaders but with instructions to say nothing to Peter and Margaret Tone about Tone's plans to go to France. It appears that later in 1796 he was a pupil at the Belfast Academy. He returned to America and subsequently arrived in Hamburg in June 1798; he participated in the Lough Swilly expedition, served in the Dutch navy and returned again to America in 1802. He served as a seaman in the American navy, 1809–11, after which nothing more is known of him. (William Grimshaw, *Incidents recalled* (Philadelphia, 1848), p. 17; MacDermot, *Tone*, pp 28–9; J. J. St Mark, 'The disappearance of Arthur Tone' in *Éire-Ireland*, xx, no. 3 (fall 1985), pp 56–70).

[2] Theobald Wolfe Tone.

[3] Peter Tone (d. 1805), coachmaker, farmer and, by 1795, an inspector of globes employed by the Dublin paving, lighting and cleansing commissioners and with an address at 27 Bride St. (*Gentleman's and Citizen's Almanack . . . for . . . 1795* (Dublin, 1795), p. 114; Elliott, *Tone*, passim).

himself we would have assisted him without calling on his brother. If there is any letters in Belfast for us I beg you may send them up.

I am, S[i]r, yours
M. Tone

## Report by Charles Delacroix to the Executive Directory, 27 January 1796

Archives des Affaires Étrangères, Corresp. Politique Angleterre, cote 589, ff 120–21.

An earlier version, 'présenté le [ ] Nivôse l'an 4$^{e}$' (i.e. 22 Dec. 1795 × 20 Jan. 1796), is in ibid., ff 117–18. Variants between the two versions are noted.

Charles Delacroix de Contaut (1741–1805) was French minister of foreign affairs, Nov. 1795–July 1797 (*Dict. biog. franç.*).

In the left-hand margin appears a summary: 'Amérique. L'affaire d'Irlande. Secret. Les réfugiés Irlandois à Philadelphie demandent que la France les seconde pour affranchir leur patrie du joug de l'Angleterre. Ouvertures faites à cet égard par un agent secret au M[inis]tre français près les États-Unis. Mesures proposées au Directoire.' (America. The Irish affair. Secret. The Irish refugees at Philadelphia ask for French support to free their country from the English yoke. This matter raised by a secret agent with the French minister to the United States. Measures proposed to the Directory.)

7 Pluv[iôse] an 4

### Rapport au Directoire Exécutif par le Ministre des Relations extérieures

Le mécontentement des Irlandais est à son comble. Depuis longtems ce peuple, opprimé par le despotisme anglais, avili par la privation de ses droits politiques et civils, n'attend que l'occasion favorable pour reconquérir son indépendance. Ses voeux appellent aujourd'hui la protection des Français pour accomplir ce généreux dessein.[1]

Par sa lettre du 9 Vendémiaire dernier,[2] le Ministre français près les États unis annonce l'arrivée à Philadelphie d'un patriote Irlandois nommé M. de Wolff[3] qui étoit chargé de lui faire des ouvertures de la part de ses compatriotes, amis de la liberté comme lui, et de lui manifester leur désir de secouer le joug anglais avec le secours de la France.

[1] The earlier version continues: 'L'instant approche peut-être où la République Française, en se déclarant pour l'Irlande et en y faisant une descente, pourra la délivrer de la domination anglaise, comme elle en affranchît l'Amérique. On enleverait à l'Angleterre la pépinière de ses flottes et de ses armées; on tarirait la source la plus féconde de ses richesses industrielles. Ce grand événement est préparé par les Irlandais eux mêmes; mais il doit être conduit avec sagesse; il éxige un concours de moyens tellement combinés que le succès ne puisse être douteux. Cet objet [est] de nature à fixer l'attention du Directoire Exécutif.'

[2] Above, pp 23–4. [3] i.e. Theobald Wolfe Tone.

Ces ouvertures on été faites au Ministre français dans les termes les plus propres à les faire accueillir favorablement. M. de Wolff, en exprimant l'impatience qu'éprouvent les Irlandois d'être indépendans de l'Angleterre, n'a pas oublié de déveloper les avantages qui en résulteroient pour la République française.

Le Ministre Adet a joint à sa dépêche un mémoire[1] qu'il a fait rédiger par cet agent secret, où l'on peint l'état actuel de l'Irlande, la haine des habitans de cette isle pour les Anglais, les mouvemens insurrectionnels excités de toutes parts, et le succès qu'obtiendroit une descente des Français; il paroit que nous y aurions sur le champ de nombreux auxiliaires.

Le Citoyen Adet a pris soin de s'assurer du caractère de cet Irlandois et de la réalité de sa mission.[2] Il dit positivement dans sa dépêche que M. de Wolff, qui a servi la cause des Catholiques, qui sont en Irlande le parti patriote, lui a justifié, par des pièces matérielles, de ses sentimens. Un autre fait vient à l'appui de cette assertion, c'est que M. de Wolff a un frère[3] qui, en 1793,[4] est passé en France pour demander du service dans nos armées contre les Anglais. Le Citoyen Adet pense que toutes ces considérations doivent lui attirer quelque confiance.[5]

J'avoue toutes fois que le catholicisme annoncé comme le point de ralliement des mécontens d'Irlande n'est pas fait pour rassurer beaucoup un gouvernement républicain. Pouvons-nous espérer d'avoir pour amis sincères au dehors les mêmes hommes qui nous déchirent au dedans? Ce rapprochement peut difficilement être sincère et la haine que les suppôts de Rome cherchent à inspirer à leurs sectaires contre les déffenseurs de l'égalité ne peut céder qu'a une haine plus forte encore, et au désir de s'assurer les moyens d'assouvir une juste vengeance. Eh bien! tout annonce que ce sentiment profond existe dans l'âme de l'Irlandais ulcéré, que son courage est plié depuis des siècles sous un joug de fer, mais qu'il n'est point rompû, qu'il peut se relever plus ferme que jamais, si le génie de la République fait luire à ses yeux l'aurore de l'espérance, que le sang de l'infortuné Jackson envoyé par le Comité de Salut public pour sonner en Irlande le tocsin de la résistance à l'oppression est devenu la semence d'une nuée de déffenseurs de la liberté prêts, s'il le faut, à devenir ses martyrs. Plusieurs se sont réunis à Philadelphie: ils pressent le Citoyen Adet de leur ménager l'appui du Directoire. À les en croire, leurs mesures sont prises, leurs moyens sont puissants; ils n'attendent pour éclatter que l'assurance d'un secours direct, ou tout au moins, d'une puissante diversion.[6]

Mais si ce projet auquel le Citoyen Adet a pris confiance, et dont l'éxécution contribueroit si puissamment à l'affoiblissement, à l'humiliation de l'orgueilleuse Albion, peut mériter l'attention du Directoire; ce n'est pas au delà de l'océan Atlantique qu'il peut être suivi. Ce n'est point à Philadelphie, c'est à

[1] Probably his Memorandum on the state of Ireland, 13 Aug. 1795 (above, pp 7–10).

[2] In the earlier version this para. begins: 'On pourrait soupçonner que M. de Wolff n'est autre chose qu'un agent secret des Ministres Britanniques, et sa démarche un nouveau piège qu'ils nous tendent. Mais notre Ministre à Philadelphie a pris soin . . .'.

[3] Mathew Tone. [4] *Recte* 1794 (see above, p. 10).

[5] In the earlier version this sentence reads: 'Toutes ces considérations réunies semblent devoir écarter les défiances qui pourraient naître sur cet Irlandais'.

[6] The earlier version lacks this paragraph.

Paris qu'il faut préparer l'exécution de [ce] plan à une distance aussi grande, le tenir nécessaire pour correspondre feroit nécessairement manquer le moment d'agir. Si le Directoire l'approuve, j'écrirai à notre Ministre Plénipotentiaire dans les États Unis d'engager M. de Wolff et ses amis à venir en France, où ils sont assurés d'obtenir bon accueil, afin d'y concerter les mesures à prendre pour préparer l'insurrection des Irlandais et en assurer le succès.[1]

Présenté le 7 Pluviôse l'an 4[e] de la République Française.

approuvé Le Tourneur[2]

## Diary, 2–15 February 1796

T.C.D., Tone papers, MS 2047, ff 2[v]–24[r]; *Life*, ii, 1–13.

These entries in Tone's diary are probably the first he made since leaving Ireland and are the earliest extant since that for 8 Feb. 1793.

No. 1
From February the 2nd to the 15th inclusive
1796
Paris[3]

### 2 Feb. 1796

I landed at Havre de Grâce[4] yesterday after a rough winter passage from New York of 31 days. The town ugly and dirty, with several good houses in alleys where it was impossible to see them. Lodged at the Hotel de Paix, fomerly the Hotel of the Intendant but reduced to its present state by the Revolution. '*My landlord is civil, but dear as the Devil.*'[5] Slept in a superb crimson damask bed; great luxury after being a month without having my cloaths off.

[1] In the earlier version this para. reads: 'Il serait prématuré de proposer les mesures d'éxécution pour un projet aussi important; mais je pense qu'il conviendrait mieux d'organiser le plan de cette entreprise à Paris qu'à Philadelphie. Je propose seulement au Directoire de me charger d'écrire à notre Ministre Plénipotentiaire dans les États Unis d'engager M. de Wolff à venir en France où il est assuré d'obtenir bon accueil afin d'y concerter la descente en Irlande, en s'assurant, par des intelligences directes, d'un parti puissant.'

[2] Charles Louis François Honoré Letourneur (1751–1817), member of the Legislative Assembly and the Convention; member of the Directory, 1795–7 (*Dict. parl. franç.*).

[3] In the MS the preceding headings are in a less logical order. It is evident that they were added after Tone's arrival in Paris. In *Life* they are omitted. See 'Inscription by Tone in his Diary, 17 December 1795' (above, pp 36–7).

[4] Le Havre in Normandy, just over 200 km north-west of Paris.

[5] Swift, 'Epigram on a window at an inn at Chester' (1726?).

## 3 Feb. 1796

Rose early. Difficult to get breakfast; got it at last in Daucourt's room.[1] Excellent coffee & very coarse brown bread, but as it happens I like brown bread. Walked out to see the lions;[2] none to see. Mass celebrating in the church & many people, especially women. Went into divers coffee houses; plenty of coffee but no papers. *No bread* in two of the coffee houses, but pastry![3] Singular enough. Dinner. And here, as matter of curiosity, follows our bill of fare which proves clearly that France is in a starving situation: an excellent soup; a dish of fish, fresh from the harbour; a fore quarter of delicate small mutton, like the Welsh; a superb turkey and a pair of ducks roasted; pastry, cheese and fruit after dinner, with wine *ad libitum* but still the *pain bis*.[4] Provoked with the Frenchmen grumbling at the bread; made a saying '*Vive le pain bis et la liberté!*'. I forgot the vegetables, which were excellent. Very glad to see such unequivocal proofs of famine. Went to the Comédie in the evening, a neat theatre and a very tolerable company. Twenty performers in the orchestre. House full. Several officers, very fine-looking fellows. The audience just as gay as if there were no such thing as war or brown bread in the world. Supper just like our dinner, with wine &c., &c.

Finance. The louis worth 5,000 livres or above 200 times its value in assignats; the six-franc piece in proportion.[5] My bill *per diem* for such entertainment as is above mentioned is *six francs* (viz. 5 shillings) and my crimson damask bed 20 sols, or ten pence; coffee in the morning 12 sols, or sixpence, so that I am starving in the manner I have described for the enormous sum of £00 " 6 " 4 a day.[6] Sad, sad! Paid for my seat at the theatre in the box next to that of the Municipalité! 80 livres in assignats or about 4*d.* sterling. Be it remembered I lodge at the principal hotel in Havre, and I doubt not but I might retrench perhaps one half by changing my situation, but hang saving————

## 4 Feb. 1796

A swindler in the Hotel; wishes to take me in; wants to travel with me to Paris; says he is an American and calls me Captain; is sure he has seen me somewhere; tell him perhaps it was in Spain; a close man but warm. It won't do! He tries his

[1] Preceding three words omitted from *Life*. Possibly it was the D'Aucourt who in Mar. 1788 was serving as an officer in the grenadiers (Archives de la Guerre, dossier) and who may have served in the West Indies (see below, p. 256).

[2] i.e. sights.

[3] Cf. 'I recollected the last shift of a great princess to whom it was told the peasants had no bread. Why then, said she, let them eat pastry.' (*The confessions of J. J. Rousseau*, trans. from the French (2 vols, Dublin, 1783), ii, 158)).

[4] Brown or wholemeal bread.

[5] The *louis* was a gold coin, normally worth 24 *livres*. The *livre*, also known as a *franc*, was divided into 20 *sols* or *sous*. The *assignats* were paper currency issued in 1789, and subsequently, on the security of property belonging to the nation. The *assignats* depreciated enormously and by Oct. 1795 the *assignat* with a nominal value of 100 *francs* was worth only 15 *sous* in coin.

[6] Tone found the cost of living in France low because he had brought with him from America £100 worth of gold *louis*, the purchasing power of which was greatly in excess of the much depreciated *assignats* (see below, p. 340).

wily arts on an old Frenchman and to my great surprise tricks him of about a guinea. The Frenchman finds it out and is in a rage; going to beat the *avanturier*,[1] who is forced to refund. This is the[2] first adventure. My friend was no American, which I very soon found out, for '*there is no halting before cripples*', as poor Richard says.[3]

## 5 Feb. 1796

A new arrangement with my landlord. I now pay 5*s*. a day for everything including my crimson damask bed. Walk out. Every third man a soldier, or with something of the military costume about him. In the evening the Comédie. *Blaise & Babet*, and the *Rigueurs du cloître*, a revolutionary piece;[4] applauses and honorable mention. I can account for the favorable reception of the latter piece; but the former is as great a favorite, tho' the fable is as simple as is possible. Two lovers fall out about a nosegay & a ribband and after squabbling thro' two acts are reconciled at last and marry &c. The sentiments and the music are pretty and pastoral; but what puzzles me is to reconcile the impression which the piece, such as I have described it, seemed to make on the audience with the sanguinary and ferocious part of the French character,[5] which is, to be sure, heteroclite beyond all calculation.

## 6 Feb. 1796

It is very singular, but I have had several occasions already to observe that there is more difficulty in passing silver than paper. I have seen money refused where assignats[6] have been taken currently. This is a phenomenon I cannot understand, especially when the depreciation is considered. The republican silver is received with great suspicion. People have got it into their heads that it is adulterated, but even so, surely it is worth, intrinsically, more than a bit of paper. So it is however that assignats are more current. The Comédie again. The Marsoilles Hymn[7] sung every night, and the verse '*Tremblez, Tyrans!*' always received with applause. The behaviour of the young men extremely decorous and proper, very unlike the riotous and drunken exhibitions I have been witness to in other countries. The women ugly, and some most grotesque headdresses.[8] Supper as usual excellent. The servants at the hotel remarkably civil, attentive and humble; infinitely more so than in the United States, which I mention because I have been so

[1] Meaning 'adventurer' or 'unscrupulous person'. [2] *Life*, ii, 2, has 'our' instead of 'the'.

[3] 'Poor Richard' was a pseudonym of Benjamin Franklin.

[4] *Blaise et Babet* was written by Jacques Marie Boutet Monvel. The second piece has not been further identified.

[5] Instead of 'sanguinary and ferocious part of the French character', *Life*, ii, 3, has 'sanguinary and ferocious character attributed to the French'. The remainder of the sentence is omitted.

[6] See above, p. 41, nn 5, 6.

[7] 'La Marseillaise', so called because it was sung by National Guard volunteers from Marseilles in 1792, became officially the national anthem on 14 July 1795.

[8] There is a sketch of woman with an elaborate headdress (f. 6r).

often tormented with blockheads arguing against liberty and equality as subversive of all subordination. I have *nowhere* met with more respectful attendance than here, nor better entertainment, and all for 5*s*. a day.

## 7 Feb. 1796, Sunday

I was curious to observe how this day would be kept in France. I believe nobody worked; the shops were half open, half shut, as I have seen them on holidays in other countries; everybody walking the streets. A vessel from Boston was wrecked last night within twenty yards of the Bason and an unfortunate Frenchwoman lost with two little children; she had fled to America early in the revolution and was now returning to her husband on the restoration of tranquility. God almighty help him! She might have been saved, alone, but she preferred to perish with her infants. It is too horrible to think of. Oh my babies, my babies, if your little bodies were sunk in the ocean what should I do?—but you are safe, thank God! Well, no more of that. Comédie again, house quite full, being Sunday. Madame Roussellois[1] principal singer; just such another in person, age, manner and voice as the late Mrs Kennedy,[2] but a much better actress.

## 8 Feb. 1796

An arrangement for Paris, at last. An American[3] has a hired coach, a very good one, and we, viz. D'aucourt and I, are to pay a louis apiece for our seats, and bear two thirds of the travelling expences, post horses &c. This is very comfortable, cheaper and much better than any public carriage. We are to set off early on Wednesday. I have now waited eight days on my companion, who, by the bye, does not improve on acquaintance; he is as proud as Lucifer and as mean as avarice can make him; I foresee we shall not live long together at Paris, but at first he will be absolutely necessary to me. Damn it and rot it, and sin it for me, that I cannot speak French! '*Rues they call them here*'.[4] '*Oh, that I had given that time to the tongues that I have spent in fencing and bear baiting*.'[5] Well, ''*Tis but in vain &c*.'[6] With God's blessing my little boys shall speak French. *Comédie* in the evening as usual &c., &c.—

8th. A pair of Casimir breeches—23# in cash.[7]

[1] Not identified.

[2] Probably Mrs Kennedy (d. 1793), an Irish actress and singer, well known in London (*D.N.B.*).

[3] This was apparently the Captain Sisson whom Tone refers to later (see Diary for 13 Feb., below, p. 49).

[4] Samuel Foote, *The Englishman in Paris* (1753), I, i.

[5] *Twelfth night*, I, iii.

[6] This refrain, quoted repeatedly by Tone, is to be found in *The buck's bottle companion* (London, 1775), and in Frederick Pilon, *The siege of Gibraltar: a musical farce* (1780), I, i.

[7] This line, which appears separately as a note on f. 8, is omitted from *Life*.

## 9 Feb. 1796

My lover,[1] the swindler, has been too cunning for us; he has engaged the fourth place in the coach, so we shall have the pleasure of his company on to Paris. He certainly has some design on our pockets, but I believe he will find himself defeated. Wrote to my family and to J.R. of Philadelphia[2] and gave the letters to Capt[n] Barons[3] who has promised to send them p[er] the *President*. Tired of Havre, which is dreadfully *monotone*;[4] and D'Aucourt's peevishness, proceeding partly from ill health, makes him not the pleasantest company in the world. Got our passports, engaged post horses, &c., &c. I do not bear the separation from my family well, yet I certainly do not wish them at present in France. If I can make out Mr W[illia]m Browne[5] I shall be better off. Poor P.P.[6] I shall never meet with such another agreeable companion in a post chaise.[7] Well, hang sorrow! But I am dreadfully lowspirited. '*Croker is a rhime for Joker! poor Dick*.'[8] *Comédie* as usual. Sad trash this evening—a boy of fifteen in love and married; introduced to his spouse by his nurse, confined to his room by his papa, and let out in order to be married; much fitter to peg a top or play marbles than to go a suitoring; yet the audience did not seem to feel any incongruity, tho' to heighten the absurdity his lover was Madame Roussellois, a fat woman of forty. It was excessively ridiculous to see her and the *amoureux de quinze ans* together, and to hear her singing '*Lindor a seu me plaire*';[9] she was easily pleased. The dresses at the theatre at Havre are handsomer and better appointed than I have seen anywhere except at London, which is wonderful considering it is but a small seaport town and the more so when one reflects on the price of admission. I suspect the Government must assist them, or I am sure they could not live on their receipts; if the fact be so, it is an additional *trait* in the resemblance of character between the French and Athenians, which is most striking. '*Panem et circenses*.'[10]

## 10 Feb. 1796

Up at 5 o'clock. A choice carriage lined with blue velvet; five horses; a French postilion a most grotesque figure; a cocked hat, a jacket, two great wisps of straw tied on his thighs and a pair of jack boots[11] as big as two American churns '*Their horses, their chevauxes they call them, ben't quite so nimble as our'n*.'[12] Set off

[1] Meaning here, ironically, 'wellwisher'. Tone seems to be referring to the 'swindler' mentioned in his Diary for 4 Feb. (above, p. 41).

[2] *Life*, ii, 4, has 'to Dr Reynolds of Philadelphia'.

[3] George Barons, captain of the ship on which Tone arrived from America (see below, p. 340).

[4] Translated in *Life*, ii, 4, as 'monotonous'.

[5] i.e. Mathew Tone (see above, p. 10). *Life*, ii, 4, has 'my brother Mathew'.

[6] Thomas Russell.

[7] Cf. 'an agreeable companion in a post-chaise' (George Colman, *Tit for tat* (1788), act III).

[8] 'Poor dear Dick. He us'd to say that Croaker rhim'd to joker.' (Goldsmith, *The good-natur'd man* (1768), act I).

[9] i.e. 'Lindor knew how to please me'.

[10] 'Bread and circuses' (Juvenal, *Satires*, x, 81). This quotation is omitted from *Life*.

[11] Diagram on f. 10[v], preceded by 'See, here it is!'

[12] Samuel Foote, *A trip to Calais* (1778), I.

for Paris. Huzza! The country flat and amazingly populous; the houses of the peasantry scattered as thick as they can lie; about a mean between an English cottage and an Irish cabbin or hovel, but if the house be inferior, there is an appearance in the spot of ground about far beyond what I have seen in England; every cottage stands in the middle of a parallelogram of perhaps an acre or two which is planted with trees and I suppose includes their *potagerie*, &c. The quantity of wood thus scattered over the face of the country is immense and has a beautiful effect; *every foot of ground* seems to me under cultivation, so there will be no starving, please God, this year. France, D'aucourt says, in a good year grows one third more than she consumes. No inclosures, but all the country open; excepting that circumstance not unlike Yorkshire, which I look upon as the finest part of England;[1] an orchard to every cottage besides rows of apple-trees without intermission by the road side; ☞![2] Why might it not be so in other countries whose climate differs but very little from that of Normandie? *Think of this!* The country still flat as a bowling green, but as interesting as much wood and the most perfect cultivation can make it. Again and again delighted with the prospect of the abundant harvest which a few months will produce. No streams, no meadows, but all tilled;[3] roads excellent. Arrive at Rouen two hours after nightfall; a beautiful approach to the town, thro' a noble avenue of trees, I believe, '*for it was so dark, Hal, thou couldst not see thy hand*'.[4] Lodge at the Hotel d'Égalité. '*Kind and tender usage*.'[5]

## 11 Feb. 1796

Set off at 10 o'clock. A hill immediately over Rouen of immense height and so steep that the road is cut in traverses. When at the top, a most magnificent prospect to look back over Normandie, with Rouen at your feet, and the Seine winding beautifully thro' the landscape. The face of the country pretty much as yesterday excepting that the cottages are not so detached but rather collected in small hamlets; a mean appearance and far inferior in all respects; the little plantations around the cottages set them off and hid all defects, but here they are grouped together and completely exposed; yet still they are far beyond the cottages I have been used to see. Very few towns, and those of a *sombre* appearance; the manufacturing towns of England beyond all comparison superior. The beauty of France is in the country. Pass two or three chateaus which are *very thinly* scattered; all shut up and deserted, their masters having been either guillotined, or being now on the right (viz. *the wrong*) bank of the Rhine. In general they are in a bad taste; no improvements round them, as in England, but built close on the road, and generally a dirty little hamlet annexed, the wretched

[1] Tone spent two years in England, Jan. 1787–Dec. 1788, and paid brief visits, Dec. 1792–Jan. 1793 and Mar.–Apr. 1795.

[2] No diagram but one was probably intended.

[3] Tone was passing through the Pays de Caux, a chalk plateau.

[4] *1 Henry IV*, II, iv.

[5] Preceding four words omitted from *Life*. Cf. 'his kind, tender usage of her, for whom he thought nothing too' (Charles Gildon, *A new rehearsal* (1714), act III), and 'his kind, his tender usage' (Charles Shadwell, *Rotherick O'Connor* (1720), act IV).

habitations of the slaves of the feudal system. Well, '*all those things are past and gone, just as if they had never been*'.[1] I can see the genius of the French *noblesse* was not adapted to the country. In England I suppose the seats of the gentry in the same kind of country would be as one hundred to one. Pass a beautiful valley with a stream[2] (the first I have seen) winding thro' it, and mount a second hill, almost as high as that above Rouen. Table land, cultivated as before, that is to say, *without a foot of ground wasted*. To my utter astonishment, a large flock of sheep! What, sheep in France! I suppose they must have swum over from England! Another flock! another! They '*sear mine eyeballs*'.[3] I could wish John Bull were here for one half hour, just to look at the fields of wheat that I am passing. It is impossible to conceive higher cultivation. I have seen nothing of a corn country like it in England. The roads this day but middling. Sleep at Magny.[4]

## 12 Feb. 1796

A most blistering bill for our supper, &c.* In great indignation and the more so because I could not scold in French. Passion is eloquent, but all my figures of speech were lost on the landlord. If this extortion resulted from any scarcity I would submit in silence, but it is downright villainy. Well ''*tis but in vain*', literally. Set off in a very ill humour, but soon reconciled to my losses by the smiling appearance of the country, still flat and richly cultivated. Breakfast at Pontoise. The serenity of my temper, which I had just recovered, ruffled completely by a second bill.† '*Landlords have flinty hearts, no tears can move them.*'[5] This comes of

* See, here it is![6] For a cold fowl, six eggs & 2 bottles of poor wine 32#[7] " 0, equal to £1 " 6 " 8.

Damn them!—

† See here it is!

| | |
|---|---|
| Wine . . . . . . . . | 2# |
| Ragout (execrable) . . | 5 |
| Leg of a cold turkey . . | 5 |
| Fire . . . . . . . . . | 1 |
| Coffee . . . . . . . | 3 |
| Eggs (six) . . . . . . | 2 |
| | 18# equal to 0 "15 " 0 |

Hell! Hell! Hell!.

I find I am an economist in travelling; it is an old theory of mine that every man, even the most extravagant, is an economist in something.[8]

[1] Source of quotation not identified. [2] At Fleury-sur-Andelle. [3] *Macbeth*, iv, i.
[4] Magny-en-Vexin, 60 km north-west of Paris.
[5] 'Parents have flinty hearts . . .' (Arthur Murphy, *The apprentice* (1756), II, iii).
[6] This note is omitted from *Life*. [7] i.e. 32 francs. [8] This note is omitted from *Life*.

riding in fine carriages, with blue velvet linings! We are downright *Milors Anglois*, and they certainly make us pay for our titles. Several vineyards, the first I have met with; an uninterrupted succession of corn, vines and orchards, as far as the eye can reach, rich and *riant* beyond description. I see now clearly that John Bull will be able to starve France. St Denis. The building for washing the royal linen, turned into an arsenal, and a palace into a barrack for the *Gendarmerie*. A church with the inscription '*Le peuple française* [*sic*] *reconnaît l'être suprême et l'immortalité de l'âme*'.[1] *Gros caillou*.[2] Several windmills turning, as if they were grinding corn, but to be sure they have none to grind; an artful fetch to deceive the worthy Mr Bull, and to make him believe there is still some bread in France—. In sight of *Paris at last*! Huzza! Huzza! I have now travelled one hundred and fifty miles in France, and I do not think I have seen one hundred and fifty acres uncultivated; the very orchards are under grain. All the mills I have seen were at work, and all the *chateaus* shut up without exception.

*Paris*. Stop at the Hotel des Étrangers, Rue Vivienne,[3] a magnificent house, but I foresee as dear as the Devil. My apartment in the third story, very handsomely furnished, &c., for 50#[4] p[er] month and so in proportion for a shorter time much cheaper than the Adelphi and other hotels in London; but I will not stay here, for all that; I must get into private lodgings. At 6 o'clock, dinner with D'aucourt at the *Restaurateur's*[5] in the Maison d'Égalité,[6] formerly the Palais Royal, which is within fifty yards of our Hotel. The bill of fare, printed, as large as a playbill, with the price of everything marked. I am ashamed to say so much on the subject of eating, but I have been so often bored with the famine in France that it is, in some degree, necessary to dwell upon it. Our dinner was a soup, roast fowl, fried carp, salad of two kinds, a bottle of Burgundy, coffee after dinner, and a glass of liqueur, with excellent bread (I forgot we had colliflowers in sauce) and our bill, for the whole, wine and all, was 1,500#,[7] in assignats,[8] which at the present rate (the louis being 6,500) is exactly £0 " 4. " 7½ ster[lin]g.[9] I wish to God our bill of fare was posted on the Royal Exchange for John Bull's edification. I do not think he would

[1] 'The French people acknowledge the supreme being and the immortality of the soul'. A similar legend was seen in Nov. 1796 by another traveller in France on the churches of several villages between Boulogne and Montreuil (A Lady, *A sketch of modern France in a series of letters . . . written in . . . 1796 and 1797* (London, 1798), pp 51–2).

[2] Perhaps a megalith. In *Life*, ii, 7, it is written 'Groscaillou'.

[3] The Hôtel des Étrangers, adjacent to the Palais Royal, was one of the best hotels in Paris (*A practical guide during a journey from London to Paris* (London, 1802)).

[4] Spelt out 'fifty francs' in *Life*, ii, 7.

[5] Probably the restaurant of Antoine Beauvilliers (see below, pp 98, 103).

[6] 'La Maison–Égalité est la cloaque non pas seulement de Paris, mais encore de toute la République. Les fripons de toute espèce fourmillent, les femmes prostituées y sortent d'une impudence qu'on ne peut peindre.' (F. V. A. Aulard, *Paris pendant la réaction thermidorienne et sous le Directoire* (5 vols, Paris, 1898–1902), iii, 55).

[7] Spelt out '1,500 livres' in *Life*, ii, 8.

[8] See the end of this entry for an appendix by Tone in which a translation of his bill is given. It is omitted from *Life*.

[9] In *Life*, ii, 8, this figure is given as '4*s.* 7$\frac{1}{10}$ *d.*'. There follows part of a note by Tone beginning 'What would I have given . . . ' and reproduced below (p. 48).

dine much better for the money even at the London Tavern,[1] especially if he drank such Burgundy as we did. The salon[2] in which we dined was most magnificent with looking glasses of immense size and illuminated with patent lamps. The company of a fashionable appearance, full as much so as ever I have seen at the Bedford coffee house;[3] in short everything wore a complete appearance of opulence and luxury. Walked round the Palais Royal, but too dark to see anything. Observed[4] a shop kept by J. B. Louvet.[5] Coffee houses all full as they can hold, but did not go into any of them. D'aucourt grumbling at the appearance of things not being half so brilliant as formerly. Believe he is fibbing a little. *Filles de joie sans nombre*.[6] A short explanation with D'aucourt perfectly amicable, which I hope will set us more at our ease than we have been. Bed.

Translation of our bill at the Restaurateur's in the Palais Royal.[7] Feby 12, 1796.

| | | | |
|---|---|---|---|
| Two loaves (excellent) | —— | Livres | 70 |
| Soup | —— | | 70 |
| Burgundy | —— | | 200 |
| Fowl | —— | | 270 |
| Salad | —— | | 200 |
| Colliflowers | —— | | 110 |
| Carp fried | —— | | 150 |
| Apricots, in Brandy | —— | | 100 |
| Coffee | —— | | 160 |
| Liqueurs | —— | | 160 |
| | | Livres | 1,490 |

What would I have given to have had P.P. with me! Indeed we would have discussed another bottle of the Burgundy, or, by our Lady, some two or three. '*The rogue has given me medicines to make me love him; yes, I have drank medicines.*'[8] How he would enjoy France, not excepting even her wines![9]

[1] The London Tavern, 123 Bishopsgate, was famous for its dinners, wines and turtle (H. B. Wheatley, *London past and present* (London, 1891), ii, 434–5).

[2] *Life*, ii, 8, has 'saloon'.

[3] Bedford coffee house under the piazza, Covent Garden (Bryant Lillywhite, *London coffee houses* (London, 1963), pp 114–15).

[4] *Life*, ii, 8, has 'Ascend'.

[5] Jean-Baptiste Louvet de Couvray, alias Louvet du Loiret (1760–97), novelist, bookseller and member of the Convention and of the Council of Five Hundred. He opposed the Jacobins and after Thermidor opened a bookshop in the 'galeries de bois' of the Palais Royal. (*Nouvelle biographie générale*; *Dict. parl. franç.*).

[6] This line, in which Tone alludes to 'countless women of pleasure', and the next are omitted from *Life*. An Englishwoman who visited this part of Paris a few months later recorded: 'the Palais Royal, now Égalité, . . . instead of being, as formerly, a rendez-vous for the beau-monde is degenerated into a receptacle for jobbers, speculators, gamblers, rogues and females of a certain disposition' (A Lady, *A sketch of modern France* (London, 1798), p. 169).

[7] From 'Translation of our bill' to 'Livres 1,490' omitted from *Life*.

[8] *1 Henry IV*, II, ii.

[9] This sentence omitted from *Life*. There is a facsimile reproduction of the bill in Elliott, *Tone*, plate 30.

## 13 Feb. 1796

Capt[ai]n Sisson, with whom we travelled up, called to breakfast. Settled our account of expences. From Havre to Paris is 160 miles, or thereabouts.[1] We lay two nights on the road, we were charged once or twice extravangtly [*sic*], we were driven with 4, 5 and two stages with 6 horses, and yet our expence for the whole was but 60 crowns, or £15, ster[lin]g, which was £5 apiece. In England to travel the same distance with four horses would have cost us, at the very lowest, double the money. So much for the relative expence of the two countries, which I am fond of comparing, and I think I know England pretty well. Council of war with D'aucourt; agreed to keep close for a day or two until we get French clothes made and then to pay my first visit to Monroe,[2] and deliver my letters; in the meantime to make enquiries &c. The *Directoire Exécutif* have presented Gen[era]l Jourdan[3] with six horses, magnificently caparisoned, a sword and a case of pistols. What a present for a republican general! I observe they have given nothing to Pichegru.[4] It looks odd that he should be passed over. Do they intend to fix the public attention on Jourdan? *Mind this*—I should be sorry if Pichegru were thrown into the shade. In the evening at the Grande Opéra, Théâtre des Arts.[5] *Iphigénie*.[6] The theatre magnificent, and, I should judge, about 100 performers in the orchestre. The dresses most beautiful, and a scrupulous attention to the *costume* in all the decorations, which I have never seen in London. The performers were completely Grecian statues animated, and I never saw so manifestly the superiority of the taste of the Ancients in dress, especially the women. Iphigénie (la citoyenne Chéron)[7] was dressed entirely in white, without the least ornament, and nothing can be imagined more truly elegant and picturesque. The acting admirable, but the singing very inferior to that at the Haymarket. The French cannot sing like the Italians. Agammemnon excellent, Clytemnœstra still better, Achilles abominable and more applauded than either of them. Sung in the old French style, which is most detestable; shaking and warbling on every note; vile, vile, vile! The others sung in a style sufficiently correct. The ballet, *L'offrande à la liberté*, most superb. In the centre of the stage was the Statue of Liberty with an altar blazing before her. She was surrounded by the characters in the Opera in their

[1] By the route taken by Tone it is 215 km or about 135 English miles.

[2] James Monroe, United States ambassador to France (see above, p. 35).

[3] Jean Baptiste Jourdan (1762–1833), commander of the army of Sambre-et-Meuse since its formation in 1794; marshal of France, 1804 (*Dict. biog. franç.*).

[4] Charles Pichegru (1761–1804) rose from the ranks; general of division, 1793; commander of the armée du Nord which conquered Holland, 1794–5; president of Conseil des Cinq-Cens, 1797; deported after 18 Fructidor an V; marshal, 1804 (Six, *Dict. des généraux & amiraux*).

[5] In 1792 a large theatre named the Théâtre National was built in the Rue de la Loi (Rue de Richelieu). In 1794 it was taken over for opera and ballet by the company which had been known as the Royal Academy of Music and renamed the Théâtre des Arts. (Max Aghion, *Le Théâtre à Paris au XVIII^e siècle* (Paris, 1926), pp 375–8).

[6] *Iphigénie en Aulide*, a tragic-opera in three parts by Durollet with music by Gluck (Lajarte, *Bibliothèque musicale du théatre de l'opéra*, i, 375–7).

[7] Anne Cameroy (b. 1767), wife of Augustin Athanase Chéron (1760–1829); she retired from the theatre, 1800 (*Dict. biog. franç.*).

beautiful Grecian habits. The civic air, '*Veillons au salut de l'empire*', was sung by a powerful base and received with transport by the audience. Whenever the word '*esclavage*' was uttered, it operated like an electric shock. The Marseilles Hymn was next sung and produced still greater enthusiasm; at the words '*Aux armes, Citoyens!*', all the performers drew their swords, and the females turned to them, as encouraging them. Before the last verse there was a short pause, the time of the music was changed to a very slow movement, and supported only by the flutes and oboes, a beautiful procession entered, first little children, like cherubs, with baskets of flowers; these were followed by boys a little more advanced with white javelins (the Hasta pura of the Ancients) in their hands; then came two beautiful female figures moving like the graces themselves, with torches blazing; these were followed by four Negroes, characteristically dressed and carrying two tripods between them which they placed respectfully on each side of the altar; next came as many Americans in the picturesque dress of Mexico, and these were followed by an immense number[1] of other performers, variously habited, who ranged themselves on both sides of the stage; the little children then approached the altar with their baskets of flowers, which they laid before the goddess, the rest in their turns succeeded, and hung the altar and the base of the statue with garlands and wreaths of roses; the two females with the torches approached the tripods, and, just touching them with the fire, they kindled into a blaze; the whole then knelt down, and all this was executed in cadence to the music and with a grace beyond description; the first part of the last verse, '*Amour sacré de la patrie*', was sung slowly and solemnly, and the words '*Liberté, Liberté chérie*' with an emphasis which affected me most powerfully. All this was at once pathetic and sublime beyond what I had ever seen, or could almost imagine, but it was succeeded by an incident which crowned the whole and rendered it indeed a spectacle worthy of a free republic. At the words '*Aux armes, Citoyens!*', the music changed again into a martial style, the performers sprang on their feet, and in an instant the stage was filled with National Guards, who rushed in with their bayonets fixed, their sabres drawn, and the Tricolor flag flying. It would be impossible to describe the effect of this. I never knew what enthusiasm was before, and what heightened it beyond all conception was that the men I saw before me were not hirelings acting a part; they were what they seemed, French citizens flying to arms to rescue their country from slavery; they were the men who had precipitated Cobourg[2] into the Sambre and driven Clairfait[3] over the Rhine, and were now on the eve of again hurrying to the frontiers to encounter fresh dangers and to gain fresh glory. *This* was what made the spectacle interesting beyond all description. I would willingly sail again from New York to enjoy again what I felt at that moment. *Set the ballets of the Haymarket*

[1] *Life*, ii, 9, has 'crowd' in place of 'number'.

[2] Friedrich Josias, prince of Sachsen-Coburg-Saalfeld (1737–1815), defeated in the Netherlands in 1794 (*Allgemeine deutsche Biographie*).

[3] Karl Joseph de Croix, Graf von Clerfait (1733–98). In 1795 Jourdan crossed the Rhine in the face of Clerfait's forces. (Ibid.)

*beside this!* This sublime spectacle concluded the *ballet*, but why must I give it so poor a name! After this there followed a ballet which one might call so, but even this was totally different from what they used to be. The National Guards were introduced again and, instead of dancing, at least three fourths of the exhibition were military evolutions, which it should seem are more now to the French taste than allemandes and minuets and pas de deux—so best! It is curious now to consider at what rate one may see all this. I paid for my seat, in the boxes, 150 livres in assignats, which at the present rate is very nearly 6 pence sterl[in]g. The highest priced seats were but 200#,[1] which is 8*d*.! I mention this principally to introduce a conjecture which struck me at Havre, but which seems much more probable here, that the Government supports the theatres, privately; and in France it is excellent policy where the people are so much addicted to *spectacles* of which there are now about twenty in Paris, and all full every night. What would my dearest love have felt at the *Offrande à la liberté*!

## 14 Feb. 1796

Dined at a tavern in a room covered with gilding and looking glasses down to the floor. Superb beyond anything I had seen. It was the hotel of the Chancellor to the Duke of Orleans.[2] There went much misery of the people to the painting and ornamenting that room and now it is open to any one to dine for 3*s*. '*Make aristocracy laugh at that*.'[3] But Paris now yields so many thousand instances of a similar complexion that nobody minds them. *Comédie ballet* (improperly so called). The *Chant du départ*.[4] A battalion under arms, with their knapsacks at their backs ready to march, with their officers and a representative of the people (whom P.P. would call a tyrant) at their head; on one side of the stage a group of venerable figures representing the parents of the warriors; on the other a band of females who, I can venture to say, were not selected for their ugliness, appeared as their wives and their lovers, and a number of beautiful children were scattered over the stage. The representative began the song, which was answered by the soldiers. The next verse was sung by the women, and I leave it to any man with a soul capable of feeling what the effect of such a song from such beautiful beings must be; the next was sung by the old men, and at the end of it the little boys and girls ran in among the soldiery, who caught them up in their arms and carressed them; some of the little fellows pulled off the grenadiers' caps and put them on their own heads, while others were strutting about with great sabres, longer than themselves; at length the battalion was formed again, and filed off, the representative and the officers saluting the audience as they passed, while the women and children were placed on an eminence and waved their hands to them as they

[1] Spelt out '200 livres' in *Life*, ii, 11.

[2] Louis Philippe Joseph, duke of Orleans (1747–93), descendant of Louis XIII; leader of the opposition to the court at the beginning of the revolution; took the name of Égalité in 1792 and at the king's trial voted for death; executed, 1793 (*Dict. parl. franç.*).

[3] Source of quotation not identified.

[4] Music by Étienne Méhul (1763–1817).

passed along. Nothing could exceed the peals of applause when the ensign passed with the Tricolor flag displayed. *Here was no fiction*; and that it is what gave it an interest which drew the tears irresistibly into my eyes. From all this it is evident that the French are a nation of canibals, incapable of human feeling, and that John[1] will just begin at the banks of the Waal, and never stop till he has driven them into the Mediterranean.

## 15 Feb. 1796

Went to Monroe's, the ambassador's, and delivered in my passport and letters.[2] Received very politely by Monroe who inquired a great deal as to the state of the public mind in America, which I answered as well as I could, and in a manner to satisfy him pretty well as to my own sentiments.[3] He asked me particularly whether people did not think his situation a painful one.[4] I told him they certainly did. He interrupted me by assuring me that it was most extremely so, and spoke with a good deal of emphasis; he then asked me what people in America thought would be the conduct of France on the treaty with England and the manifest bias of the American gov[ernmen]t in favor of the latter country? I answered that the public opinion seemed to be that France, however justly provoked, would not manifest any open discontent at the late measures. He did not make any observation on this. He then enquired how the President[5] bore the outcry against the Treaty?[6] I told him with a great deal of what himself and his friends would call firmness. He then asked me did the President hold his ground with the people as formerly? I answered that he still retained a great share of his popularity, but undoubtedly it was considerably diminished, and I instanced the alteration made by the House of Rep[resentative]s in their answer to his speech.[7] He asked me did I think he would be re-elected, if he wished it? I answered I thought he would, undoubtedly; but that, if he was wise he would, in my opinion, never suffer himself to be proposed again. He then enquired how Pickering[8] and Wolcott[9] stood with the people? I answered they were looked

[1] Expanded in *Life*, ii, 12, to 'John Bull'.

[2] The 'passport' was probably a travel document issued by the American government. Tone states in his diary for 17 Feb. that he brought only one letter to Monroe. This is obviously Beckley to Monroe, 14 Dec. 1795 (above, pp 35–6).

[3] What follows, as far as 'read it with impartiality', is omitted from *Life*.

[4] Monroe was expected to defend the Jay treaty between the United States of America and Great Britain signed in Nov. 1794 (see above, p. 2, n. 1) and to protest against French interference with American commerce, but in the opinion of his own government he showed excessive sympathy for France (*D.A.B.*).

[5] Washington.

[6] The Jay treaty (see above, n. 4).

[7] When the draft reply of the house of representatives to the address delivered by Washington to Congress on 8 December, at the beginning of the session, was being debated it was decided to omit the words that 'he possessed the undiminished confidence of the people' (*The debates and proceedings of the congress of the United States* . . . (42 vols, Washington, 1834–56), fourth congress, first session, pp 144–55).

[8] Timothy Pickering (1745–1829), secretary of state, 1795–1800. An uncompromising 'federalist', he had a deep loathing for the French revolution. (*D.A.B.*)

[9] Oliver Wolcott (1760–1833), secretary of the treasury, 1795–1800 (*D.A.B.*).

upon as mere puppets danced by Mr Hamilton[1] and that the President himself was completely under the same influence. He asked me then was it thought that [he] himself was any wise influenced by that party? I said, by no means, but very much the reverse, and that, among other reasons, might make his situation unpleasant. 'No', said he, 'they would cut my throat.' He then, adverting to Adet's letter,[2] asked me what was his opinion of the American Government? I answered I could not pretend to say, but I did believe it was very bad, for that he seemed to me to be extremely disgusted. 'I believe so too', answered he, 'do you know that he has applied to be recalled?'. He then asked me what effect Randolph's vindication[3] (which I had brought in my pocket and given him) had on the public mind? I evaded answering this by saying it had only appeared a day or two before I sailed and of course I could not tell. He then asked what I thought, myself, would be the effect? I answered him that I thought it would only confirm both parties in the present way of thinking, for neither would read it with impartiality.[4] I enquired of him where I was to deliver my dispatches;[5] he informed [me] at the Minister for Foreign Affairs,[6] and gave me his address. I then rose and told [him] that when he had read Beckley's letter[7] (which was in cypher) he would I hope find me excused in taking the liberty to call again; he answered he would be happy at all times to see me, and after enquiring after Mr Hamilton Rowan, how he liked America, &c., I took my leave and returned to his office for my passport. The secretary smoked me for an Irishman directly. *A la bonheur!*[8]

Went at 3 o'clock to the Minister for Foreign Affairs, Rue du Bacq, 471; delivered my passport and enquired for someone who spoke English. Introduced immediately into an inner appartment[9] to the chef de bureau, Lamare,[10] a man of an exceedingly plain appearance. I shewed my letter and told him I wished for an opportunity to deliver it into the Minister's hands. He asked me would it not do if he took charge of it? I answered he undoubtedly knew the official form best, but if it was not irregular I should consider myself much obliged by being allowed to deliver it in person. He then brought me into a magnificent antichambre, where a general officer and another person were waiting and after a few minutes delay I was introduced to the Minister, Charles De la Croix, and delivered my letter, which he opened, and seeing it in cypher he told me in French he was much obliged to me for the trouble I had taken, and that the Secretary would give

[1] Alexander Hamilton (1757–1804), secretary of the treasury, 1789–95; a leading 'federalist' (*D.A.B.*).

[2] Perhaps Adet's letter to the Committee of Public Safety introducing Tone (above, pp 34–5).

[3] Edmund Randolph, *A vindication of Mr Randolph's resignation as secretary of state* (Philadelphia, 1795). See above, p. 35, n. 3.

[4] At this point the text is resumed in *Life* (see above, p. 52, n. 3).

[5] Including the letter Adet had given him addressed to the Committee of Public Safety (above, pp 34–5).

[6] Delacroix.

[7] Above, pp 35–6. In the MS 'Beckley's' is inserted in a different pen; in *Life*, ii, 12, it is given as 'B——'s'.

[8] Corrected in *Life*, ii, 12, to '*A la bonne heure*!', meaning 'Well done!'.

[9] Last four words omitted from *Life*.

[10] According to the *Almanach national de France An 4*, Lamare was 'secrétaire en chef, deuxième bureau, secrétaire général'.

me a receipt[1] acknowledging the delivery. I then made my bow and retired with the Secretary, the Minister seeing us to the door. He is a respectable looking man, I should judge near sixty, and has very much the air of a bishop. The Secretary then gave me a receipt, of which the following is a translation—

I have received from Mr James Smith a letter addressed to the Committee of Public Safety, and which he tells me comes from the Citizen Adet, minister plenipotentiary of the French Republic at Philadelphia. At Paris the 26th Pluviôse the 3d year of the French Republic.

The Secretary General of
Foreign Affairs
Lamare.

I have thus broken the ice. In a day or two I shall return for my passport. I am perfectly pleased with my reception at Monroe's; and at the Minister's I can form no possible conjecture as to the event. The letter being in cypher, he could form no guess as to who I might be or what might be my business. All I can say is that I found no difficulty in obtaining access to him; that his behavior was extremely affable and polite, and, in a word, that if I have no ground to auger anything good, neither have I reason to expect anything bad. All is *in equilibrio*. I have now a day or two to attend to my private affairs, and the first must be the affair of Mr W[illia]m Browne.[2]

Opera in the evening. The *Chant du départ* again. I lose three fourths of the pleasure I should otherwise feel for the want of my dear love, or my friend P.P., to share it with. How they would glory in Paris just now! And then the Burgundy every day at the Restaurateur's! Poor P.P! He is the only possible bearable companion except the Boys. *Well ''Tis but in vain &c.'*.[3]

—This book is used up![4]—

## Receipt from secretary general for external relations for Adet's letter of 13 December 1795, 15 February 1796

Tone (Dickason) papers.

J'ai reçu de Monsieur James Smith une lettre adressée au Comité de Salut public[5] et qu'il m'a dit venir du Citoyen Adet, ministre plénipotentiaire de la République Françoise à Philadelphie.

À Paris ce 26 pluviôse l'An 3e[6] de la République Françoise

Le Secrétaire Général
des relations extérieures
Lamare

[1] Below.
[2] *Life*, ii, 13, adds in parentheses: 'my brother Matthew'. See above, pp 10–11.
[3] See above, p. 43, n. 6. [4] Last five words omitted from *Life*. [5] Above, pp 34–5.
[6] *Recte* 4e.

# Diary, 16–21 February 1796

T.C.D., Tone papers, MS 2048, ff 1r–5v; *Life*, ii, 13–19.

## No. 2
## At Paris

### 16 Feb. 1796

Walked out alone to see sights. The Thuilleries, the Louvre, Pontneuf &c. Superb. Paris more magnificent a thousand times than London, but less convenient for those that go afoot. Saw two companies of Grenadiers[1] in the garden of the Thuilleries, the first I have met. All very fine fellows, but without the *air militaire* of private sentinels; many in the ranks have the appearance of gentlemen in soldiers' coats and on the whole they exactly resembled two companies of Irish Volunteers as I have seen them in that country in the days of my youth and innocence. These are the '*Youth of the first requisition*'.[2] Their uniform blue, faced white, red cape and cuffs, red shoulder-knots and plumes in their hats, white belts, vests and breeches, black stocks[3] and gaiters. I think them equal in figure to any men I have ever seen of their number. *The women*! only to think what a thing *fashion* is! The French women have been always remarkable for fine hair, and therefore at present they all prefer to wear *wigs*. They actually roll and pin up their own beautiful tresses so that they become invisible, and over them they put a little shock periwig! Damn their wigs! I wish they were all burnt! but it is the *fashion*, and that is a solution for every absurdity. In the evening walked the Palais Royal; filled with the military, most of them superb figures; I do not mean as to dress, but in their air, their manner and gait. I now perceive the full import of the expression '*an armed nation*' and I think I know a country that for its extent and population could produce as many and as fine fellows as France. Well, all in good time. It will be absolutely necessary to adopt measures similar to those which have raised and cherished this spirit here, if ever[4] God almighty is pleased in his goodness to enable us to shake off our chains, or at least to attempt it. I think Ireland would be formidable as an '*armed nation*'.

[1] The Grenadiers of the Legislature, a corps 1,200 strong, were formed in 1795; the Guard of the Directory was formed in 1796. These corps were later absorbed in Napoleon's guard. (Henry Lachouque, *The anatomy of glory* (London, 1961), pp 4–6).

[2] The youth of the first requisition ('la jeunesse de la première réquisition') were conscripts, unmarried men aged 18 to 25, recruited into the army by Carnot's decree passed by the Convention on 23 Aug. 1793. This *première réquisition* provided over 400,000 recruits who, together with volunteers, satisfied the needs of the republic's army for the next five years. (N. H. Gibbs, 'Armed forces and the art of war' in *The new Cambridge modern history*, ix (Cambridge, 1965), pp 62–3).

[3] Close-fitting neckcloths.

[4] Erroneously 'every' in MS.

## 17 Feb. 1796

Went at one o'clock to the Minister's[1] *bureau* for my passport. A clerk tells me that a person had called yesterday in my name and got it. I assured him I knew nobody in Paris and that I had not sent anyone whatever to demand it; and I reminded him that it was on this day he had desired me to call; he looked very blank at all this, and just then the Principal Secretary coming up, I informed him of what had happened; he recollected me immediately and told me the Minister wished to see me, and had sent to the ambassador's[2] to learn my address. I answered I should attend him whenever he pleased to appoint; he replied, 'Instantly'; and accordingly I followed him into the Minister's cabinet, who received me very politely. He told me (in French) that he had had the letter I brought decyphered and laid instantly before the *Directoire Exécutif*, who considered the contents as of the greatest importance; that their instructions were that I should go immediately to a gentleman whom he would give me a letter to, and, as he spoke both languages perfectly and was confidential, that I should explain myself to him without reserve; that his name was Madgett. I answered that I knew him by reputation and had a letter of introduction to him, but that I did not consider myself at liberty to make myself known to any person whatever without his approbation. He answered me that I might communicate with Madgett without the least reserve. He then sat down and wrote a note to Madgett which he gave me, and I took my leave, the Minister seeing me to the door. I mention the minute circumstances of my reception, not that I am a man to be too much elevated by the attentions of any man in any station, at least I hope so, but that I consider the respect shewn to me by De La croix as really shewn to my mission, and of consequence[3] the readiness of access and the extreme civility of reception that I experience I feel as so many favorable circumstances of presage.[4] I have been at the bureau but twice and both times I had been admitted to the Minister's cabinet without a minute's delay. Surely all this looks well. The *costume* of the Minister was singular.[5] I have said already that he had the presence of a bishop. He was dressed today in a grey silk robe de chambre, under which he had a kind of scarlet cassock of sattin, with rose-coloured silk stockings & scarlet ribbands in his shoes. I believe he has as much the manners of a gentleman as Lord Grenville. I mention all these little circumstances because I know they will be interesting to her whom I prize above my life ten thousand times. There are about six persons in the world who will read these detached memorandums with pleasure; to everyone else they would appear sad stuff—but they are only for the women of my family, for the Boys,[6] if ever we meet again, and for my friend P.P.[7] Would to God he were here just now! Well, '*If wishes were horses, beggars would ride*',[8]

[1] Delacroix's. [2] Monroe's. [3] *Life*, ii, 15, has 'course' instead of 'consequence'.

[4] *Life*, ii, 15, has 'presages' instead of 'circumstances of presage'.

[5] A minister's official costume consisted of a black mantle, red coat and trousers, a white sash round his waist and a black hat with a red plume (*Lois de la république française*, An IV, loi 1208).

[6] His sons or his brothers? [7] Russell. [8] A proverb?

and there is another curious quotation, equally applicable, on the subject of wishing, which I scorn to make.

Set off for Madgett's and delivered my letter. Madgett delighted to see me; he tells me that he has the greatest expectation that our business will be taken up in the most serious manner; that the attention of the French government was now turned to Ireland, and that the stability and form it had assumed gave him the strongest hopes of success; that he had written to Hamilton Rowan about a month since to request that I might come over instantly in order to confer with the French government and to determine on the necessary arrangements, and that he had done this by order of the French executive. He then asked me had I brought any papers or credentials? I answered him that I had brought to Paris merely the letter of Adet to the Executive,[1] and one to our ambassador;[2] that I had destroyed a few others on the passage, including one from Mr Rowan to himself, we having been chased by a Bermudian; that as to credentials, the only ones I had, or that the nature of the case would permit, I had shewn to Adet on my first arrival in Philadelphia in August last; that these were the vote of thanks of the General Committee of the Catholics of Ireland for my services as their Agent, signed by Mr Edw[ar]d Byrne and the two secretaries, Rich[ar]d McCormick and John Sweetman, and dated in April 1793,[3] a second vote of thanks from the Catholics of Dublin, signed by the Chairman & Secretary,[4] and the resolution of the Belfast Regiment of Volunteers, electing me an honorary member in testimony of their confidence and signed by the officers of the regiment.[5] These I had offered to Adet to bring[6] with me to France, if he thought it would be necessary, but that he said it was sufficient that I had satisfied him, and as they were large papers it would be running an unnecessary risque of discovery in case we were stopped by British cruisers, that he would satisfy the French executive, and that the fewer papers of any kind I carried the better, and consequently that I had brought only those I mentioned. Madget[t] then said that was enough, especially as he had the newspapers &c. containing the resolutions I mentioned and that the French executive were already fully apprised who I was. He then said we should have ten sail of the line, any quantity of arms that were wanted and such money as was indispensable, but that this last was to be used discreetly inasmuch as the demands for it on all quarters were so numerous and urgent; he added that he thought a beginning might be made thro' America so as to serve both Ireland and France; that is to say that military stores might be brought[7] from France to

[1] Above, pp 34–5. In fact the letter was addressed by Adet to the Committee of Public Safety, which in November 1795 was replaced by the Executive Directory.

[2] John Beckley to James Monroe, 14 Dec. 1795 (above, pp 35–6). In *Life*, ii, 15, the last clause reads: 'that I only brought the letter of Adet to the Executive, and one to the American Ambassador'.

[3] See above, vol. I, p. 443. In fact it was signed by Byrne, who was chairman, and only one secretary, McCormick.

[4] See above, vol. I, p. 529. It was signed by John Sweetman, chairman, and Richard McCormick, secretary, and dated 9 Apr. 1795.

[5] See above, vol. I, pp 203–4.

[6] Followed in MS by redundant 'these', omitted also from *Life*.

[7] *Life*, ii, 16, has 'might be sent through this channel' instead of 'might be brought'.

Ireland, purchased there by proper persons, and provisions, leather, &c., returned in neutral bottoms. I answered this last measure was impracticable on account of the vigilance of the Irish Government and the operation of the Gunpowder Act,[1] which I explained to him. I then gave him a very short sketch of what I considered the state of Ireland, laying it down as a *positum* that nothing effectual ever would[2] be done there unless by a landing; that a French army was indispensably necessary as a *point de ralliement* and I explained to him the grounds of my opinion. He then told me it was necessary we should arrange all the information we possessed and for that purpose fixed me to breakfast with him tomorrow, when we could go at length into the business; and so we parted.

I shall in all my negociations here press upon them the necessity of a landing being effectuated. If it is not, the people will never move, but to the destruction of a few wretches, and we have had already but too much of that in Ireland. A French army with a general of established reputation at their head is a *sine quā non*. Pichegru to choose, but if not, Jourdan. Their names are known in Ireland, and that is of great consequence.

## 18 Feb. 1796

Breakfast at Madgitt's. Long account on my part of the state of Ireland when I left it, which will be found substantially in such memoirs as I may prepare. Madgitt assures me again that the Government here have their attention turned most seriously to Irish affairs; that they feel that unless they can separate Ireland from England, the latter country is invulnerable; that they are willing to conclude a treaty offensive and defensive with Ireland, and a treaty of commerce on footing of reciprocal advantage; that they will supply ten sail of the line, arms and money, as he had told me yesterday, and that they were already making arrangements in Spain and Holland for that purpose. He asked me did I think anything would be done in Ireland by her spontaneous efforts? I told him most certainly *not*; that if a landing were once effected everything would follow instantly, but that *that* was indispensable, and I begged of him *to state my opinion to be so* to such persons in power as he might communicate with; that if twenty thousand French were in Ireland, we should in a month have an army of 1, 2, or if necessary, 300,000 men but that the *point d'appui* was indispensable. He said it appeared so to him also. He then returned to the scheme of importing stores &c. thro' the medium of America. I again mentioned the difficulty from the Gunpowder Act and the risque of alarming the Irish Government.[3] He said he thought still it would be possible and mentioned as a reason that eighteen brass cannon had to his knowledge lately been smuggled into Ireland thro' Belfast. *If this be true it surprises me a little,*[4] *but I rather judge Madgitt is misinformed.* I answered that if the landing were once effected, the measure would be unnecessary, as in that event

[1] See above, vol. I, p. 409, n. 2.
[2] *Life*, ii, 16, has 'nothing effectual could' instead of 'nothing effectual ever would'.
[3] See Diary for 17 Feb. (above).
[4] *Life*, ii, 17, has 'it surprises me not a little'.

we should[1] have all the stores of the kingdom in our hands; and if the landing were not effected, it would be also unnecessary, as the people would not move, unless in local riots and insurrections, which would end in the destruction of the ring-leaders. He seemed struck with this and said he saw that part of the scheme was useless. I then mentioned the necessity of having a man of reputation at the head of the French forces and I mentioned Pichegru or Jourdan, both of whom are well known by character in Ireland. He then told me that there[2] was a kind of coolness between the Executive and Pichegru. (☞ *This* I suspected—vide memorandum book No. 1)[3] but that if the measure were adopted that he might still be the general, adding that he was a man of more talents than Jourdan. I answered, either would do. He then desired me to prepare a memorial in form for the French executive as soon as possible which he would translate and have delivered in without delay. We fixed to dine together at his lodgings and so parted. ☞ *There is one thing here I wish to observe*. Madget[t] shewed me the Minister's note, which appeared to me completely confidential and in which he mentions his own desire to forward the business as much as possible, '*as a friend to liberty and to humanity*'. The Minister also desired me to explain myself to Madget[t] 'without reserve'. Am I too sanguine in believing what I so passionately wish—*that the French executive will seriously assist us*?

## 18, 19, 20 Feb. 1796

At work in the mornings at my memorial[4] (which buy). Call on Madgett once a day to confer with him.[5] He says there will be a person sent to Ireland immediately with whom I shall have conference, and that it would be desirable he should bring back an appointment for me of Minister Plenipotentiary in order to conclude an alliance, offensive and defensive, with the republic, in which case I would be acknowledged as such by the French Government. Certainly nothing could be more flattering to me. However, I answered him that such appointment could not be had without communicating with so many persons in Ireland as might endanger the betraying the secret to the Irish Government; that I only desired credit with the *Directoire Exécutif* so far as they should find my assertions supported by indisputable facts; that the information I brought was the essential part, and the credentials, tho' highly gratifying to my private feelings, would in fact be but matter of form; that when a government was formed in Ireland it would be time enough to talk of embassies, and then if my country thought me worthy, I should be the happiest and proudest man living to accept the office of

[1] *Life*, ii, adds 'soon'. [2] Erroneously 'were' in MS.

[3] See Diary for 13 Feb. (above, p. 49). [4] Below, pp 61–70.

[5] On 19 Feb. 1796, Madgett wrote to Charles Delacroix informing him that he had had several conversations with Tone, who stated that all the Irish needed was a French force between 10,000 and 12,000 strong, commanded by a general with a 'grande réputation', to serve as a nucleus for the 'troupes sans nombre' which they could field. The letter continues: 'je l'ai engagé à mettre toutes ses idées par écrit afin que je puisse les traduire et vous les présenter'. (Archives des Affaires Étrangères, Corresp. Politique Angleterre, cote 589, f. 154).

embassador from Ireland; in the meantime I besought him not to mention it.[1] So '*there was an end of my very good friend, the Athenian*'.[2] I must wait for my appointment[3] until the war is at least commenced, if ever it commences, or perhaps until it is over, if I am not knocked in the head meantime. I should like very well to be the first Irish ambassador, and if I succeed in my present business, I think I will have some claim to the office. '*O, Paris is a fine town and a very charming city*.'[4] If Ireland were independant I could spend three years here with my family, especially my dearest Love, very happily. I dare say P.P. would have no objection to a few months in the year *à l'Hôtel d'Irlande*. He is a dog. Indeed we would discuss several bottles of diplomatic Burgundy—but all this is building castles in Spain. Let me finish my memorial, which Madgett tells me, this day (20th), the minister has written to him about. I am glad of that impatience. He (Madgett) says if we succeed, it is part of the plan (but I believe he means *his* plan) to demand Jamaica for Ireland by way of indemnity. I wish we had Ireland, without Jamaica. My memorial filled with choice facts. Dine alone every day. D'aucourt has left me pretty much to myself, of which I am glad. Military in the Palais Royal superb figures (but this I said already).[5] Many fine lads of twenty years of age who have sacrificed an arm and[6] a leg to the liberty of their country. I could worship them. '*The Baronet can ca' for aught he needs, but he is not yet quite maistre of the accent*.'[7] Very wise memorandums for a minister plenipotentiary planning a revolution. 'Dangerous men' Oh Lord! Oh Lord! Well, ''*Tis but in vain*'.

## 21 Feb. 1796

Bought the *Constitution Française* at the shop of J. B. Louvet in the Palais Royal,[8] and received it from the hands of his wife so celebrated under the name of 'Lodoïska'.[9] I like her countenance very much; she is not handsome but very interesting. She resembles Mrs Sinnot[10] a good deal, excepting her beauty.[11] Louvet is one of those who escaped the 31st of May,[12] and after a long concealment and a thousand perils, in which Lodoïska conducted herself like a heroine, he returned on the fall of Robespierre,[13] whom he had been the first to denounce,

[1] The preceding eleven words and the following sentence are omitted from *Life*.

[2] Source of quotation not identified.

[3] The preceding three words omitted are from *Life*.

[4] Cf. 'O London is a fine town, a very famous city' (George Colman, *The heir at law* (1797), i, 2).

[5] See Diary for 16 Feb. (above, p. 55).

[6] *Life*, ii, 19, has 'or' instead of 'and'.

[7] 'He can caw for aught that he need, but he is na quite maister of the accent' (Samuel Foote, *The Englishman return'd from Paris* (1756), act 1).

[8] There was in the possession of Mrs Katherine Dickason a copy of *La Constitution française* which has the following inscription in Tone's hand: 'Feb. 20th, 1796, Bought this book at the shop of J. B. Louvet, a member of the Conseil de cinq cents and received it from the hands of Lodoïska'.

[9] Mme Cholet, Louvet's mistress whom he married, served as a model for Lodoïska in his novel, *Une année de la vie du chevalier de Faublas* (1787) (*Dict. parl. franç.*).

[10] Possibly Catherine Nolan (d. 1824), wife of Pierce Synnott (*Burke's Irish family records* (London, 1976)).

[11] *Life*, ii, 19, omits 'She resembles Mrs Sinnot a good deal, excepting her beauty'.

[12] i.e. 31 May 1793, when the Girondins were ousted by Robespierre.

[13] Maximilien François Marie Isidore de Robespierre (1758–94), member of the Constituent Assembly,

and resumed his place in the Convention. He is now a distinguished member of the *Conseil de[s] Cinq-cens*, supports a newspaper, *La Sentinelle*, and keeps a bookseller's shop in the Palais Royal. I am glad I have seen Lodoïska. I wish my dearest love could see her. I think she would behave as well in similar circumstances; her courage and her affection have been tried in some, very nearly as critical Well, I must go finish my Memorial.[1] Stone[2] has been acquitted in England, I believe very justly. He never will set the Thames in a blaze!

## First memorial to the French government on the present state of Ireland, 22 February 1796

Archives Nationales, AF IV, carton 1671, ff 88ʳ–92ᵛ; *Life*, ii, 181–92.

The version in *Life*, which is only slightly different, was presumably printed from an earlier draft. Only significant variants have been noted.

A very free French translation by Nicholas Madgett, dated '7 Ventôse an 4' (26 Feb. 1796), is in Archives des Affaires Étrangères. Corresp. Politique Angleterre, cote 589, ff 162–8, most of which is printed in Édouard Guillon, *La France et l'Irlande pendant la Révolution* (Paris, 1888), pp 449–62.

For the exact date of this document, see above, pp 59, 60, below, p. 70.

### First Memorial on the present state of Ireland, delivered to the French Government, February 1796[3]

The genius of the English nation, their manners, their prejudices and their government are so diametrically opposite to those of the French Republic in all respects that it is unnecessary to dwell upon this subject. I assume it as an axiom that there is an irreconcilable opposition of interests between the two nations. Since the French Revolution there is one still more irreconcilable between the governments, so that neither can be said to be in safety while the other is in existence.

Convention, and the Committee of Public Safety, becoming a virtual dictator until deposed and guillotined in the coup d'état of 9–10 Thermidor Year II (27–8 July 1794).

[1] Below, pp 61, 70.

[2] William Stone was tried at the Old Bailey in Jan. 1796 on a charge of high treason, it being alleged that he had conspired with his brother, John Hurford Stone (see below, p. 246), to promote a French invasion. Tone's name was mentioned in evidence and his 'Statement on the situation of Ireland' as apparently amended by Rowan (above, vol. I, pp 506–8) was read. The defence argued that Stone was 'a weak enthusiast who was desirous of bringing about a peace', and that he had advanced money to the Revd William Jackson without being aware he was a French agent. Stone was found not guilty, and shortly afterwards went to France. (Joseph Gurney, *The trial of William Stone for high treason at the bar of the court of king's bench on Thursday the twenty-eighth and Friday the twenty-ninth of January, 1796* (London, 1796); *Annual Register*, 1796, appendix to chronicle, pp 111–15).

[3] MS lacks a heading. This heading is as supplied in *Life*.

The war, hitherto however glorious to France, has not been unprofitable to England; her fleets were never more formidable and, in the true spirit of trade, she will console herself for the disgrace of her arms by land in the acquisition of power and territory and commerce by sea; but these very acquisitions render it, if possible, incumbent not merely on France but on all Europe to endeavour to reduce her within due limits and to prevent that enormous accumulation of wealth which the undisturbed possession of the commerce of the whole world would give her; and this reduction of her power can be alone, as I presume, accomplished with certainty and effect by separating Ireland from Great Britain.

The French Government cannot but be well informed of the immense resources, especially in a military point of view, which England draws from Ireland. It is with the beef and the pork, the butter, the tallow, the hides and various other articles of the first necessity which Ireland supplies, that she victuals and equips her navy and in a great degree supports her people and garrisons in the West Indies. It is with the poor and hardy natives of Ireland that she mans her fleets and fills the ranks of her army. From the commencement of the present war to June 1795 not less than 200,000 men were raised in Ireland for the land and sea service, eighty thousand of which were for the navy alone. It is a fact, undeniable though carefully concealed in England, that two thirds of the British navy are manned by Irishmen; a circumstance which if it stood alone should be sufficient to determine the French Government to wrest, if possible, so powerful a weapon from the hands of her implacable adversary. I shall not dwell longer on the necessity of the measure which I shall propose, but will endeavour to show how it may best be executed, and on what grounds it is that I rest my confidence of success, if the attempt be but once made.

For the better elucidation of the plan, it is necessary to take a review of the actual state of Ireland. I shall condense the facts as much as possible, as I trust the French Government is already in possession of those which are most material.

The people of Ireland consist of about four million five hundred thousand persons, distributed under three different religious sects, of whom the Protestants, whose religion is the dominant one and established by law, are four hundred and fifty thousand, or one tenth of the whole; the Dissenters, or Presbyterians, about nine hundred thousand, or one fifth; the Catholics form the remaining three million one hundred and fifty thousand. They may also be considered with regard to property, which is necessary in some degree to explain the political situation of the country.

The Protestants, who are almost entirely the descendants of Englishmen, forming so very small a minority as they do of the whole people, have yet almost the whole landed property of the country in their hands; this property has been acquired by the most unjust means, by plunder and confiscation during repeated wars, and by the operation of laws framed to degrade and destroy the Catholics, the natives of the country. In 1650 the people of three entire provinces were driven by Cromwell into the fourth, and their property divided amongst his officers and soldiers, whose descendants enjoy it at this day.

In 1688,[1] when James II was finally defeated in Ireland, the spirit of the Irish people was completely broken, and the last remnant of their property torn from them and divided amongst the conquerors. By these means the proprietors of estates in Ireland, feeling the weakness of their titles to property thus acquired, and seeing themselves, as it were, a colony of strangers forming not above one tenth part of the population, have always looked to England for protection and support; they have, therefore, been ever ready to sacrifice the interests of their country to her ambition and avarice, and to their own security. England, in return, has rewarded them for this sacrifice by distributing among them all the offices and appointments in the church, the army, the law, the revenue and every department of the state, to the utter exclusion of the two other sects and more especially of the Catholics. By these means the Protestants, who constitute the aristocracy of Ireland, have in their hands all the force of the Government; they have at least five sixths of the landed property; they are devoted implicitly to the connection with England, which they look upon as essential to the secure possession of their estates; they dread and abhor the principles of the French Revolution, and, in case of any attempt to emancipate Ireland, I should calculate on all the opposition which it might be in their power to give.

But it is very different with regard to the Dissenters, who occupy the province of Ulster, of which they form at present the majority. They have among them but few great landed properties; they are mostly engaged in trade and manufactures, especially the linen, which is the staple commodity of Ireland and is almost exclusively in their hands. From their first establishment, in 1620, until very lately, there has been a continual animosity between them and the Catholic natives of the country, grounded on the natural dislike between the old inhabitants and strangers, and fortified still more by the irreconcilable difference between the genius of the religions of Calvinism and Popery, and diligently cultivated and fomented by the Protestant aristocracy, the partizans of England, who saw in the feuds and dissensions of the other two great sects their own protection and security.

Among the innumerable blessings procured to mankind by the French Revolution arose the event which I am about to mention, and to which I do most earnestly entreat the particular attention of the French Government, as it is in fact the point on which the emancipation of Ireland may eventually turn.

The Dissenters are, from the genius of their religion and the spirit of inquiry which it produces, sincere and enlightened republicans; they have ever, in a degree, opposed the usurpations of England, whose protection, as well from their numbers and spirit as the nature of their property, they did not, like the Protestant aristocracy, feel necessary for their existence. Still, however, in all the civil wars of Ireland, they ranged themselves under the standard of England and were the most formidable enemies to the Catholic natives, whom they hated as Papists, and despised as slaves. These bad feelings were, for obvious reasons,

[1] *Recte* 1691.

diligently fomented by the Protestant and English party. At length, in the year 1790, the French Revolution produced a powerful revulsion in the minds of the most enlightened men amongst them. They saw that whilst they thought they were the masters of the Catholics, they were in fact but their gaolers, and that, instead of enjoying liberty in their own country, they served but as a garrison to keep it in subjection to England; the establishment of unbounded liberty of conscience in France had mitigated their horror of Popery; one hundred and ten years[1] of peace had worn away very much of the old animosity which former wars had raised and cherished. Eager to emulate the glorious example of France, they saw at once that the only guide to liberty was justice, and that they neither deserved nor could obtain independence whilst their Catholic brethren, as they then, for the first time, called them, remained in slavery and oppression. Impressed with these sentiments of liberality and wisdom, they sought out the leaders of the Catholics, whose cause and whose suffering were in a manner forgotten; the Catholics caught with eagerness at the slightest appearance of alliance and support from a quarter whose opposition they had ever experienced to be so formidable, and once more, after lying prostrate for above 100 years, appeared on the political theatre of their country. Nothing could exceed the alarm, the terror and confusion which this most unexpected coalition produced in the breasts of the English Government and their partizans, the Protestant aristocracy of Ireland. Every art, every stratagem, was used to break the new alliance and revive the ancient animosities and feuds between the Dissenters and Catholics. Happily such abominable attempts proved fruitless. The leaders on both sides saw that they had but one common interest, as they had but one common country; that while they were mutually contending and ready to sacrifice each other, England profited of their folly to enslave both; and that it was only by a cordial union and affectionate co-operation that they could establish their common liberty and establish the independence of Ireland. They therefore resisted and overcame every effort to disunite them, and in this manner has a spirit of union and regard succeeded to 250 years of civil discord, a revolution in the political morality of the nation of the most extreme importance, and from which, under the powerful auspices of the French Republic, I hope and trust her independence and liberty will arise.

I beg leave again to call the attention of the French Government to this fact of the national union, which from my knowledge of the situation of Ireland I affirm to be of importance equal to all the rest. Catholics and Dissenters, the two great sects, whose mutual animosities have been the radical weakness of their country, are at length reconciled and the arms which have been so often imbrued in the blood of each other are now ready for the first time to be turned in concert against the common enemy.

I come now to the third party in Ireland, the Catholics, who are the Irish properly so called and who form almost the entire body of the peasantry of the

[1] *Recte* ninety-nine.

country. The various confiscations produced by the wars of five centuries and the silent operation of the laws for 150 years have stripped the Catholics of almost all property in land; the great bulk of them are in the lowest degree of misery and want, hewers of wood and drawers of water; bread they seldom taste, meat never, save once in the year; they live in wretched hovels; they labour incessantly, and their landlords, the Protestant aristocracy, have so calculated that the utmost they can gain by this continual toil will barely suffice to pay the rent at which these petty despots assess their wretched habitations; their food the whole year round is potatoes, their drink sometimes milk, more frequently water; those of them who attempt to cultivate a spot of ground as farmers are forced, in addition to a heavy rent, to pay tythes to the priests of the Protestant religion, which they neither profess nor believe; their own priests fleece them. Such is the condition of the peasantry of Ireland, above 3,000,000 of people. But though there be little property in land, there is a considerable share of the commerce of Ireland in the hands of the Catholic body; their merchants are highly respectable and well informed; they are perfectly sensible as well of their own situation as that of their country. It is of these men, with a few of the Catholic gentry whose property escaped the fangs of the English invaders, that their General Committee, of which I shall have occasion to speak by-and-by, is composed, and it is with their leaders that the union with the Dissenters, so infinitely important to Ireland and, if rightly understood, to France also, has been formed.

I have now stated the respective situation, strength and views of the parties of Ireland; that is to say: *First*, the Protestants, 450,000, comprising the great body of the aristocracy, which supports and is supported by England. Their strength is entirely artificial, composed of the power and influence which the patronage of Government gives them. They have in their hands all appointments in every department, in the church, the army, the revenue, the navy, the law, and a great proportion of the landed property of the country, acquired and maintained as has been stated; but it cannot escape the penetration of the French Government that all their apparent power is purely fictitious; the strength they derive from Government results solely from opinion; the instant that prop is withdrawn, the edifice tumbles into ruins; the strength of property acquired like theirs by the sword continues no longer than the sword can defend it, and numerically the Protestants are but one tenth of the people.

*Second*. The Dissenters, 900,000, who form a large and respectable portion of the middle ranks of the community. These are the class of men best informed in Ireland; they formed the bulk of what was called the volunteer army in Ireland in 1782, during the late war,[1] which extorted large concessions from England and would have completely established their liberty had they been then, as they are now, united with their Catholic brethren. They are all to a man sincere Republicans and devoted with enthusiasm to the cause of liberty and France; they would

[1] The war of American independence, 1775–83.

make perhaps the best soldiers in Ireland and are already in a considerable degree trained to arms.

*Third.* The Catholics, 3,150,000. These are the Irish, properly so called, trained from their infancy in an hereditary hatred and abhorrence of the English name, which conveys to them no ideas but those of blood and pillage and persecution. This class is strong in numbers and in wretchedness and misery, which makes men bold; they are used to every species of hardship; they can live on little; they are easily clothed; they are bold and active; they are prepared for any change, for they feel that no change can make their situation worse. They[1] have their eyes fixed most earnestly on France, whom they look upon, with great justice, as fighting their battles as well as those of all mankind who are oppressed. Of this class, I will stake my head, there are five hundred thousand men who would fly to the standard of the Republic if they saw it once displayed in the cause of liberty and their country.

From what has been said, it appears that all the artificial strength of Ireland is implicitly devoted to England and decidedly adverse to France, that all the natural strength is equally devoted to France and adverse to England, for this plain reason that in the one they look for a deliverer, in the other they see a tyrant. It is now necessary to state the organization of the people of Ireland; and here I must be allowed to observe that even if there were no previous organization, the measures which I shall submit would not be the less advisable and practicable. Organization, like machinery, may be necessary to enable a small force to raise a great weight; but a whole people can act by their natural strength. The Republic may rely with confidence to meet support from the Dissenters, actuated by reason and reflection, from the Catholics, impelled by misery and inflamed by detestation of the English name. These are the actual force of Ireland, and in addition to their strength they are organized also.

In the year 1791, the Dissenters of Belfast, which is the principal city in Ulster and, as it were, the metropolis of that great body, framed the first club of United Irishmen, so called because in that club, for the first time in Ireland, Dissenters and Catholics were seen together in harmony and union. A similar club was immediately formed in Dublin which became speedily famous for its publications and the sufferings of its members, many of whom were thrown into prison by the Government, whose terror at this rising spirit of union amongst the people may be estimated from the severity with which they persecuted those who were most active in promoting it. This persecution, however, far from quelling the spirit, only served to make the people more cautious and guarded in their measures. Means have been adopted to spread similar clubs throughout Ulster, the seat of the Dissenting power, whose object is to subvert the tyranny of England, to establish the independence of Ireland and to frame a free republic on the broad basis of liberty and equality. These clubs were rapidly filled and extended in June last[2]

[1] In *Life*, ii, 187, this sentence begins: 'For these five years they . . .'.

[2] i.e. when Tone left Ireland.

over about two thirds of that province. I am satisfied that by this time they embrace the whole of it and comprise the activity and energy of the Dissenters of Ireland, including also numbers of the most spirited and intelligent of the Catholic body. The members are all bound by an oath of secrecy and could on a proper occasion, I have not the smallest doubt, raise the entire force of the province of Ulster, the most populous, the most warlike and the most informed quarter of the nation.

For the Catholics, from what has been said of their situation it will appear that little previous arrangement would be necessary to ensure their unanimous support of any measure which held out to them a chance of bettering their condition; yet they also have an organization, commencing about the same time with the clubs last mentioned but composing Catholics only. Until within these few months, this organization baffled the most active vigilance of the Irish Government, unsuccessfully employed to discover its principles, and to this hour they are, I believe, unapprized of its extent. The fact is that in June last it embraced the whole peasantry of the provinces of Ulster, Leinster and Connaught, three fourths of the nation; and I have little doubt but it has since extended into Munster, the remaining province. These men, who are called Defenders, are completely organized on a military plan, divided into their respective districts and officered by men chosen by themselves. The principle of their union is implicit obedience to the orders of those whom they have elected for their generals and whose object is the emancipation of their country, the subversion of English usurpation and the bettering the condition of the wretched peasantry of Ireland. The eyes of this whole body, which may be said, almost without a figure, to be the people of Ireland, are turned with the most anxious expectation to France for assistance and support. The oath of their association recites 'that they will be faithful to the united nations of France and Ireland' and several of them have already sealed it with their blood. I suppose there is no instance of a conspiracy, if a whole people can be said to conspire, which has continued for so many years as this has done where the secret has been so religiously kept and where in so vast a number so few traitors have been found.[1]

The organization of the Defenders embraces the whole peasantry of Ireland, being Catholics. There is also a further organization of the Catholics which is called the General Committee[2] and to which I have already alluded. This is a representative body chosen by the Catholics at large and consisting of the principal merchants and traders, the members of professions and a few of the remaining Catholic gentry of Ireland. This body, which has sat repeatedly in the capital at the same time with the Parliament, has twice within these four years sent ambassadors to the King of England, possesses a very great influence on the

[1] Charles Hamilton Teeling considered that Tone, 'a man of warm and ardent mind', was mistaken in asserting that in 1796 the Defenders were looking to France for help. Strong catholics, 'they had not then imbibed those democratical sentiments which subsequently became almost universal throughout Ireland'. (C. H. Teeling, *Observations on the history and consequences of the battle of the Diamond* (Belfast, 1838), pp 8–14).

[2] i.e. the Catholic Committee.

minds of the Catholics throughout the nation and especially decides the movements of the city of Dublin, a circumstance whose importance when well directed it is unnecessary to suggest to men so enlightened as those who compose the Government of France. It is true that by a late act of the Irish legislature[1] this body is prevented from meeting in a representative capacity, but the individuals who compose it still exist, and this act, without diminishing their power or influence, has still more alienated their minds from the British Government in Ireland, against which they were already sufficiently, and with great reason, exasperated. It is but justice to the General Committee, in whose service I had the honour to be during the whole of their activity and whose confidence I had the good fortune to acquire and retain, to say that there is nowhere to be found men of purer patriotism, more sincerely attached to the principles of liberty, or who would be more likely in an arduous crisis to conduct themselves with abilities and firmness. I can add, from my personal knowledge, that a great majority of those able and honest men who compose it are sincere republicans, warmly attached to the cause of France and as Irishmen and as Catholics doubly bound to detest the tyranny and domination of England, which has so often deluged their country with their best blood.

I have now stated the three modes of organization which exist in Ireland—

1st. The Dissenters, with some of the most spirited and enlightened of the Catholics under the name of *United Irishmen*, whose central point is Belfast, the capital of Ulster.

2d. The Defenders, forming the great body of the Catholic peasantry, amounting to 3,000,000 of people and who cover the entire face of the country.

3d. The General Committee of the Catholics, representing the talents and property of that body, possessing a very great influence everywhere in Ireland and especially deciding the movements of the capital.

I hazard nothing in asserting that these three bodies are alike animated with an ardent desire for the independence of Ireland, an abhorrence of British tyranny and a sincere attachment to the cause of the French Republic; and, what is of very great consequence, they have a perfect good understanding and communication with each other (that is to say, their leaders) so that on any great emergency there would be no possible doubt of their mutual co-operation. Many of the most active members of the General Committee, for example, are also in the clubs of the United Irishmen; many of the officers of the Defenders, particularly those at the head of their affairs, are also either members of those clubs, or in unreserved confidence and communication with those who regulate and guide them. The central point of all this is undoubtedly Belfast, which influences, and which deserves to influence, the measures of all the others, and, what I consider as extremely singular, the leaders of the Defenders in Ulster, who are all Catholics, are in more regular habits of communication and are more determined by the Dissenters of Belfast than by their Catholic brethren of Dublin, with whom they hold much less intercourse.

[1] See above, vol. I, p. 477, n. 3.

I shall add a few words on the military force of Ireland and on the navy, and then I shall conclude.[1]

In the month of June 1795 last, when I left Ireland, the army, as I believe, amounted to about 30,000 men, of which 12,000 were troops of the line[2] and 18,000 militia; a great proportion of the former, viz. the cavalry and artillery, and all the latter, being Irish. I believe a considerable number have been since detached to the West Indies[3] and elsewhere; if so, the relative proportion of Irish must be increased, as the militia cannot be ordered on foreign service. For the cavalry and artillery, which taken together may make 3,000 men or upwards, I cannot speak with certainty; but my belief is that if they saw any prospect of permanent support they would not act against their country. For the remaining 9,000 men of the troops of the line and fencibles, they are a wretched assemblage of old men and boys, incapable of the duties of active service; any resistance they could make, if they were inclined to resist, could be but trifling, and I have reason to believe they would not be so inclined, several of the fencible regiments being Scotch and already more than half disaffected to the Government. For the militia, they consisted, at the time I mention, of about 18,000 men, as fine troops as any in Europe. Of these at least 16,000 were Catholics and of those a very great proportion were actually sworn Defenders who were compelled to enter the service to avoid prosecution. I learn[4] that since my departure from Ireland Defenderism has spread rapidly among them and that numbers have been imprisoned on that account. I have not a shadow of doubt on my mind but that the militia would in case of emergency to a man join their countrymen in throwing off the yoke of England provided proper measures were taken and that they saw a reasonable prospect of support.

For the navy, I have already said that Ireland has furnished no less than 80,000 seamen and that two thirds of the English fleet are manned by Irishmen. I will here state the grounds of my assertion. First, I have myself heard several British officers, and among them some of very distinguished reputation, say so. Secondly, I know that when the Catholic delegates whom I had the honour to attend were at St James' in January 1793 in the course of the discussion with Henry Dundas, principal Secretary of State, they asserted the fact to be as I have mentioned, and Mr Dundas admitted it, which he would most certainly not have done if he could have denied it. And lastly on my voyage to America our vessel was boarded by a British frigate[5] whose crew consisted of 220 men, two hundred and ten of whom were Irish, as I found on inquiry. I humbly submit the importance of this fact to the particular notice of the French Government.

From all which has been said I trust it will appear that it is the interest of France to separate Ireland from England; and that it is morally certain that the

[1] *Life*, ii, 490, adds 'this memorial, which, in spite of all my efforts to condense it, I feel growing under my hand'.

[2] *Life*, ii, 490, adds 'or fencibles'.

[3] Cf. the letter written very probably by Thomas Russell, 21 Sept. 1795: 'twenty-five thousand men of the best are going to the West Indies' (above, pp 21–2).

[4] Probably from the letters written in Sept. 1795 by friends in Ireland (above, pp 17–23).

[5] See above, p. 1, and below, p. 335.

attempt, if made, would succeed for the following reasons: 1st that all the Dissenters are disaffected to England, attached to France and sufficiently organized; 2d that the whole peasantry of Ireland, being Catholics and constituting above 3,000,000 of people, are to a man eager to throw off the English yoke, that they also are organized and that part of the fundamental oath by which they are bound as Defenders is to be true as well to France as to Ireland; 3d that there is a certainty of a sufficient[1] harmony and co-operation between these two great bodies, which constitute nine tenths of the population of Ireland; 4th that the British Government cannot reckon on any firm support from the army, above two thirds of which are Irishmen and of that number nearly 10,000 being, as I am informed and believe, actually sworn Defenders; 5th that it is at least possible that by proper measures to be adopted relative to the Irishmen now serving in the navy of England her power at sea might receive such a shock as it has never yet experienced; and 6th, and lastly, that if these facts be as I have here stated them, it would be impossible for the Protestant aristocracy in Ireland to make any stand whatsoever, even for an hour, in defence of the connection with England.[2]

## Diary, 22–5 February 1796

T.C.D., Tone papers, MS 2048, ff 6$^r$–14$^r$; *Life*, ii, 20–31.

### 22 Feb. 1796

Finished my memorial,[3] and delivered a fair copy, signed, to Madgett for the Minister of Foreign Relations.[4] Madgett in the horrors; he tells me he has had a discourse yesterday for two hours with the Minister, and that the succours he expected will fall very short of what he thought; that the Marine of France is in such a state that Government will not hazard a large fleet, and consequently that we must be content to '*steal a march on them*'; that they will give 2,000 of their best troops and arms for 20,000; that they cannot spare either Pichegru or Jourdan; that they will give any quantity of artillery and, I think he added, what money might be necessary. He also said they would first send proper persons among the Irish prisoners of war to sound them and then exchange them the very first opportunity. To all this (*at which I am not disappointed*) I answered that as to 2,000 then they might as well send 20; that with regard to myself, I would go if they would send but a corporal's guard, but that my opinion was that 5,000 was as little as could be landed with any prospect of success, and that *that* number would leave the matter doubtful; that if there could be an imposing force sent in

[1] *Life*, ii, 192, has 'perfect' in place of 'sufficient'.

[2] In *Life*, ii, 192, there is an additional paragraph: 'Having now submitted the actual situation of Ireland to the notice of the French Government, I shall offer, in a second memorial, the plan which I conceive most likely to effectuate the separation of that country from Great Britain'.

[3] Above, pp 61–70. [4] Delacroix.

the first instance it would overbear all opposition, the nation would be unanimous, and an immense effusion of blood and treasure would be spared; the law of opinion would at once operate in favor of the Government which in that case would be instantly framed, and I pressed particularly the advantages resulting from that circumstance. He seemed perfectly satisfied with all this, but equally satisfied that it would not, or rather could not, be done. I bid him then remember that my plan was built on the supposition of a powerful support in the first instance; that I had particularly specified so in my memorial and I begged him to apprise the Minister that my opinion was so; that nevertheless with 5,000 men the business might be attempted, and I did believe would succeed, but that in that case we must fight hard for it; that tho' I was satisfied how the Militia and Army would act in case of a powerful invasion, I could not venture to say what might be their conduct under the circumstances he mentioned; that if they stood by the Government, which it was possible they might, we should have hot work of it; that if 5,000 were sent they should be the very flower of the French troops, and a considerable proportion of them artillery men with the best General they could spare. He interrupted me to ask me who was known in Ireland after Pichegru & Jourdan? I answered him Hoche,[1] especially since his affair at Quiberon. He said we might, he was sure, have Hoche. I also mentioned that if they sent but 5,000 men, they should send a greater quantity of arms, as in that case we could not command at once all the arms in the nation, as we should if they were able to send 20 or even 15,000. I added that as to the prisoners of war, my advice was to send proper persons among them, but not to part with a man of them until the landing was effected, and then to exchange them as fast as possible. He promised to represent all this, and that he hoped we would get 5,000 men at least and a greater quantity of arms. We then parted.

Now what is to be my plan? Suppose we get 5,000 men and 30 or even 20,000 stand of arms, and a train of artillery. I conceive, on the first view, the embarkation must be from Holland; but in all events the landing must be in the North as near Belfast as possible. Had we 20,000, or even 15,000, in the first instance, we should begin by the capital, the seizing of which would secure everything, but as it is, if we cannot go large, we must go close hauled, as the saying is. With 5,000 we must proceed entirely on a revolutionary plan I fear—that is to say to reckon only on the *sansculottes*,[2] and if necessary to put every man, every horse, every guinea, every potatoe in Ireland in requisition. I should also conceive it would be our policy at first to avoid an action, supposing the Irish army stuck to the Government; every day would strengthen & discipline us, and give us opportunities to work upon them. I doubt whether we could, until we had obtained some advantage in the field, frame any body that would venture to call itself the Irish

[1] Lazare Hoche (1768–97) rose from the ranks to command the army of the Moselle but was imprisoned, 1794. On his release he commanded and reorganised the armies of the west, deploying them successfully against the royalists. He was appointed to the command of the army of the Sambre-et-Meuse, 24 Jan. 1797. (*Dict. biog. franç.*).

[2] The disaffected poorer classes.

Government, but if we could, it would be of the last importance. '*Hang those that talk of fear!*'[1] With 5,000 men and very strong measures we should infallibly[2] succeed. The only difference between that number and 20,000 is that the first[3] would preclude all fighting and in the first's case we may have some hard knocks. '*Ten thousand hearts are great within my bosom.*'[4] I think I will find a dozen men who will figure as soldiers. O Good God, good ggod! [*sic*] What would I give tonight that we were safely landed and encamped on the Cave hill?[5] If we can find our way thus far, I think we shall puzzle John Bull to work us out. Surely we can do as much as the Chouans, or the people of La Vendeé![6]

## 23 Feb. 1796

Looked over Paine's *Age of reason*, 2d part.[7] Damned trash. His wit is without exception the very worst I ever saw. He is discontented with the human figure, which he seems to think is not well constructed for enjoyment. He lies like a dog. Ask P.P.[8] whether it is not possible to be most exquisitely happy, even under the incumbrance of the human shape, so awkward in Mr Paine's eyes. I beg the gentleman may speak for himself. I suppose he includes the female shape also. He seems to have some hopes that he shall enjoy immortality in the shape of a butterfly.[9] '*Say little foolish fluttering thing.*'[10] Damn his nonsense! I wish he was a butterfly with all my soul. He has also discovered that a spider can hang from the ceiling by her web, and that a man cannot; and this is philosophy! I think Paine begins to dote.[11] But, damn his trash, as I said with great eloquence already, and let me mind my business. I must now write my own credentials to the French Government. Awkward enough for a man to trumpet himself. However, it must be, and so ''*Tis but in vain &c.*'.[12] That is an invaluable quotation and wears like steel; for it, among other obligations, I am indebted to the witty and ingenious lucubrations of my friend P.P. Apropos! I never wanted the society, assistance, advice, comfort and direction of D° P.P.[13] half so much as at that moment. I have a pretty serious business on my hands, with a grand responsibility, and here I am, alone, in the middle of Paris, without a single soul to advise or consult with, and with nothing in fact to support me but a good intention. Sad, sad! Well, hang fear. ''*Tis but in vain*'. Da capo.[14]

[1] *Macbeth*, v, iii. [2] *Life*, ii, 21, has 'ultimately' instead of 'infallibly'.

[3] *Recte* 'latter', as corrected in *Life*, ii, 21.

[4] *Recte* 'A thousand hearts . . .' (*Richard III*, v, iii).

[5] See below, p. 333. [6] Counter-revolutionaries in western France.

[7] Thomas Paine, *The age of reason*, pt II (London, 1795). [8] Thomas Russell.

[9] In chapter 2, part II (the section dealing with St Paul) of his *Age of reason* (1795), Paine expresses the hope that in the future life he will have a better body and refers to winged insects as the most beautiful part of creation.

[10] Isaac Bickerstaffe, *The padlock* (1768), I, ii.

[11] For Tone's meeting Paine in Paris, see Diary for 3 Mar. 1797 (below, vol. III).

[12] See above, p. 43, n. 6. [13] This could also read 's[ai]d P.P.'. *Life*, ii, 22, has 'the said P.P.'.

[14] 'Da capo' is a direction at the end of a piece of music to repeat from the beginning.

## 23 Feb. 1796[1]

A busy day. Called on Madgett in order to explain to him that all I had said relative to the support to be expected from the people in Ireland, and the conduct of the Army, was on the supposition of a considerable force being landed in the first instance. This I had pressed upon him yesterday, but I cannot make it too clear for my own credit. My theory, in three words, is this. With 20,000 men, there would be no possibility of resistance for an hour and we should begin by the capital. With 5,000 I would have no doubt of success; but then we should expect some fighting and we should begin near Belfast. With 2,000 I think the business utterly desperate, for let them land where they would they would be utterly defeated before anyone could join them, or in fact before the bulk of the people could know that they were. This would be a mere Quiberon business[2] in Ireland and would operate but as a snare for the lives of my brave and unfortunate countrymen, to whose destruction I do not wish, God knows, to be accessary. Nevertheless I concluded, that if they sent but a serjeant and 12 men, I would go, but I wished them to be fully apprised of my opinion, that in case of a failure they might not accuse me of having deceived them. He agreed with me in every word of the statement and desired me to insert part of it in my letter to the Minister. He also promised me positively to have a letter written from the proper office to Guise to enquire after Mr W[illia]m Browne,[3] tho' he assures me the order for his liberation was expedited about the 1st of May last. If we can find the said Mr Browne, he may be very serviceable among the prisoners of war, both soldiers and seamen, being Irish. I have not pressed my enquiries about him, as my wishes prompt me lest I should appear to prefer the dearest affections of my heart, which God and my dearest love know I do not, to the public business with which I am charged. Quit Madgett, whom I believe *honest*, and whom I feel *weak*. Go to Monroe. Received very favorably. He has had my letter[4] decyphered and dropt all reserve. I told him I felt his situation was one of considerable delicacy, and therefore I did not at all wish to press upon him any information relative either to myself or my business further than he might desire. He answered that the letters had satisfied him, particularly that from James Thomson,[5] of whom he spoke in terms of great respect, and that, as he was not responsible for what he might hear but for what he might do, I might speak freely. I then opened myself to him without the least reserve and gave him such detail as I was able of the actual state of things, and of the grounds of my knowledge, from my situation. I also informed him what I had done thus far. He then addressed me, in substance, as follows. 'You must change

[1] This is the second entry for this date and apparently was written later on during the day.

[2] See above, p. 19, n. 1.

[3] *Life*, ii, 23, adds in parentheses: 'my brother Matthew'. Tone believed he was imprisoned at Guise (see above, p. 10).

[4] The letter from John Beckley to James Monroe, 14 Dec. 1795 (above, pp 35–6). See also Diary for 15 Feb. 1796 (above, pp 52–3).

[5] i.e. Hamilton Rowan. In *Life*, ii, 23, William Tone substitutes 'H. R.' for 'James Thomson'. Rowan himself states that he used the pseudonym James Thomson when in France (see above, p. 14, n. 2).

your plan! I have no doubt whatsoever of the integrity & sincerity of the Minister (De La Croix) nor even of Madgett, whom I believe to be honest. But in the first place, it is a subaltern way of doing business; and in the next, the vanity of Madgett will be very likely to lead him, in order to raise his own importance in the eyes of some of his countrymen who are here as Patriots, and of whom I have by no means the same good opinion as to integrity as I have of him, to drop some hint of what is going forward. Go at once to the *Directoire Exécutif* and demand an audience. Explain yourself to them, and as to me, you may go so far as to refer to me for the authenticity of what you may advance and you may add that you have reason to think that I am in a degree apprised of the outline of your business.' I mentioned Carnot,[1] of whose reputation we had been long apprised & who I understood spoke English. He said nobody fitter, and that Larevillière Lepaux[2] also spoke English; that either would do. I then expressed a doubt whether, as I was already in the hands of Charles Delacroix, there might not be some indelicacy in my going directly to the *Directoire Exécutif*, and if so, whether it might not perhaps be of some disservice. He answered by no means; that, in his own function, the proper person for him to communicate with was Delacroix, but that nevertheless when he had any business of consequence to transact, he always went at once to the fountain head.[3] He then proceeded to mention that in all the changes which had taken place in France, there never was an abler nor a purer set of men at the head of affairs than at present, that they were sincere friends to liberty and justice, and in no wise actuated by a spirit of conquest; that consequently, if they took up the business of Ireland on my motion, I would find them perfectly fair and candid; that not only the Government but the whole people was most violently exasperated against England; and that there was no one thing that would at once command the warmest support of all parties so much as any measure which promised a reduction of her power. He then examined me pretty closely as to the state of Ireland, on which I gave him complete information as far as I was able; and we concluded by agreeing that tomorrow I should go boldly to the Luxembourg and demand an audience, either of Carnot or of Larevillière Lepaux. Monroe tells me Barrere[4] (for I enquired) is yet in France, and he thought would not quit it. I told him Barrere would be very acceptable in Ireland as a deputy with the army. He answered that he did not at all doubt but

[1] Lazare Nicolas Marguerite Carnot (1753–1823), capt. in the corps of engineers before the revolution; member of the Committee of Public Safety, 1793–5; member of the Directory from 1795 until his flight to Switzerland in 1797; known as the 'organiser of victory' (*Dict. biog. franç.*; M. R. Reinhard, *Le grand Carnot* (Paris, 1952)).

[2] Louis Marie de La Révellière-Lépeaux (1753–1824), member of the Convention and Council of Ancients; member of the Directory, 1795–9 (*Dict. biog. franç.*; *Dict. parl. franç.*).

[3] According to Talleyrand, who was his successor, while Delacroix was minister of foreign affairs all important matters concerning his department were settled by the Directory (*Memoirs of the prince de Talleyrand*, ed. duc de Broglie (5 vols, London, 1891–2), i, 190–1).

[4] Bertrand de Barère de Vieuzac (1755–1841), advocate; member of the States General, the Convention and the Committee of Public Safety; after Thermidor condemned to transportation but escaped by flight and remained for five years in hiding; elected to the Council of Five Hundred but could not take his seat; amnestied after Brumaire (*Dict. parl. franç.*).

it might so happen that he should be the man;[1] that he would not advise me to begin by bolting out the name of Barrere, but that I might take an opportunity to mention him. I remarked to him that it had fallen to Barrere's lot to make some of the most splendid reports in the Convention, which made him well known to us, and that the people were used in a degree to associate the ideas of Barrere & victory, which, trifling as it was, was of some consequence. On the whole I am glad to find my lover Barrere as I hope in no danger. *It would be a most extraordinary thing if I should happen to be an instrument in restoring his talents to the cause of liberty.* I have always had a good opinion of him. He tells me the ground of the coolness between Pich[e]gru and the Government is that he is supposed to be attached too much to the party of the *Modérés*. I am glad of this; not that there is a coolness, but that the Government is not of that party. We talked of the resources of France & England. I mentioned that, in my judgement, France had one measure which sooner or later she must adopt and the sooner the better, and that was a *bankruptcy*, that she would then start forth with her immense resources against England staggering under 400,000,000 of debt. Monroe took me by the hand and said, 'You have hit it; and I will tell you that it is a thing decided upon'. If it be so, look to yourself Mr John Bull, '*Look to your house, your daughter and your ducats*'.[2] Took my leave of Monroe, with whom I am extremely pleased; there is a true republican frankness about him, which is extremely interesting. *And now* am I not a pretty fellow to go to the *Directoire Exécutif*? It is very singular that so obscure an individual should be thrown into such a situation! I presume I do not write these memorandums to flatter myself, and I here solemnly call God to witness the purity of my motives and the uprightness with what I shall endeavour to carry myself thro' this most arduous and critical situation. I hope I may not ruin a noble cause by any weakness or indiscretion of mine; as to my integrity I can answer for myself. What shall I do, for the want of P.P.? I am in unspeakable difficulty for the want of his advice and consolation. Well, if ever we meet again, it will amuse him to read these hints; but he is a dog, and so ''*Tis but in vain &c., &c*'.

## 24 Feb. 1796

Went at 12 o'clock in a fright to the Luxembourg,[3] conning speeches in execrable French all the way. What shall I say to Carnot? Well, '*whatsoever the Lord putteth in my mouth, that surely shall I utter*'.[4] Plucked up a spirit, as I drew near the Palace and mounted the stairs like a lion. Went into the first bureau that I found open, and demanded at once to see Carnot. The clerks stared a little, but I repeated my demand with a courage truly heroic, on which they instantly submitted, and sent a person to conduct me. This happened to be his day for giving audience, which each member of the Executive Directory does in his turn.

[1] *Life* omits 'that he should be the man'.
[2] 'My daughter! o my ducats! o my daughter!' (*Merchant of Venice*, II, viii).
[3] The Palais du Luxembourg was the seat of the Directory.
[4] Source of quotation not identified.

Introduced by my guide into the antichambre, which was filled with people, the officers of state, all in their new *costume*.[1] Wrote a line in English and delivered it to one of the *huissiers*, stating that a stranger just arrived from America wished to speak to Citizen Carnot on an affair of consequence. He brought me an answer in two minutes that I should have an audience. The folding doors were now thrown open, a bell being previously rung to give notice to the people that all who had business might present themselves, and Citizen Carnot appeared, in the *petit costume* of white sattin, with crimson robe, richly embroidered.[2] It is very elegant and resembles almost exactly the draperies of Vandyck.[3] He went round the room receiving papers, and answering those who addressed him. I told my friend the *huissier*, in marvellous French, that my business was too important to be transacted there, and that I would return on another day when it would not be Carnot's turn to give audience, when I should hope to find him at leisure. He mentioned this to Carnot, who ordered me instantly to be shewn into an inner apartment, and that he would see me as soon as the audience was over. That I thought looked well, and I began accordingly to con my speech again. In the apartment were five or six personages, who, being like myself of great distinction, were admitted to a private audience. I allowed them all precedence, as I wished to have my will of Carnot, and while they were in their turns speaking with him, I could not help reflecting how often I had wished for the opportunity I then enjoyed, what schemes I had laid, what hazards I had run; and when I looked round and saw myself actually in the Cabinet of the Executive Directory, vis-à-vis with Citizen Carnot, the '*Organiser of Victory*', I could hardly believe my own senses, and felt as if it were all a dream. However, I was not in the least degree disconcerted, and when I presented myself, after the rest were dismissed, I had all my faculties, such as they are, as well at command as on any occasion in my life. Why do I mention these trifling circumstances? It is because they will not be trifling in her eyes, for whom they are written. I began the discourse by saying, in horrible French, that I had been informed he spoke English. He answered, 'A little, Sir, but I perceive you speak French, and if you please we will converse in that language'. I answered, still in my jargon, that if he could have the patience to endure me I would endeavour, and I only prayed him to stop me whenever I did not make myself understood. I then told him I was an Irishman, that I had been Secretary and Agent to

[1] Henry Swinburne, a British agent in Paris, who in November 1796 witnessed a member of the Directory (Reubell) receiving petitions, writes that the huissiers were 'dressed in short black cloaks with red caps and feathers, very like Crispin's habit in the play and quite as ludicrous'. He explains that a bar across the middle of the room divided 'the simply curious from those who have petitions to present'. 'The room was filled', he writes, 'with tagrag and bobtail, a crowd of women presenting memorials, soldiers, etc., whilst aides-de-camp, secretaries and well dressed fellows stood about the first place.' (Henry Swinburne, *The courts of Europe* (London, 1841), ii, 155–6).

[2] On ordinary occasions a member of the Directory wore an orange red cloak, a white doublet with gold embroidery, a long white coat, white trousers, a blue sash round the waist and a black hat turned up at the side with a tricolour plume (*Lois de la République Française*, An IV, loi 1208).

[3] Antoon Van Dyck (1599–1641), Flemish painter (*D.N.B.*). Another visitor to the Luxembourg in 1796 found the director's 'grand costume' to be '*à la Vandyke*, superb and extremely costly' (A Lady, *A sketch of modern France in a series of letters . . . written in the years 1796 and 1797* (London, 1798), p. 158).

the Catholics of that country, who were above 3,000,000 of people; that I was also in perfect possession of the sentiments of the Dissenters, who were at least 900,000, and that I wished to communicate with him the actual state of Ireland at the present moment. He stopped me here to express a doubt as to the numbers being so great as I represented. I answered a calculation had been made within these few years grounded on the number of houses which was ascertained for purposes of Revenue; that by that calculation the people of Ireland amounted to 4,100,000, and it was acknowledged to be considerably under the truth.[1] He seemed a little surprised at this, and I proceeded to state that the sentiments of all those people were unanimous in favor of France, and eager to throw of[f] the yoke of England. He asked me then what they wanted. I said an armed force in the commencement for a *point d'appui*, until they could organise themselves, and undoubtedly a supply of arms and some money. I added that I had already delivered in a memorial[2] on the subject to the Minister of Foreign relations, and that I was preparing another,[3] which would explain to him in detail all I knew on the subject better than I could in conversation. He then said, 'We shall see the memorials'. The '*Organiser of Victory*' proceeded to ask me were there not some strong places in Ireland? I answered I knew of none but some works to defend the Harbour of Cork. He stopped me here, saying, 'Ay, Cork, but might it not be necessary to land there?', by which I perceived he had been *organising* a little already in his own mind. I answered I thought not; that if a landing in force were attempted, it would be better nearer the capital, for obvious reasons; if with a small army, it should be in the North of Ireland rather than the South for reasons which he would find in my memorials. He then asked me might not there be some danger or delay in a longer navigation? I answered it would not make a difference of two days, which was nothing in comparison of the advantages. I then told him that I came to France by the direction and concurrence of the men who (and here I was at a loss for a French word, with which, seeing my embar[r]assment, he supplied me, which satisfied me clearly that he attended to and understood me) *guided* the two great parties I had mentioned; that I had presented myself in August last in Philadelphia to Citizen Adet and delivered to him such credentials as I had with me; that he did not at that juncture think it adviseable for me to come in person but offered to transmit a memorial,[4] which I accordingly delivered to him; that about the end of November last I received letters[5] from my friends in Ireland repeating their instructions in the strongest manner that I should if possible force my way to France and lay the situation of Ireland before the Government; that in consequence I had again waited on Adet, who seemed eager to assist me and offered me a letter to the *Directoire Exécutif*,[6] which I accepted with

[1] Tone is thinking of the calculation of Ireland's population made by Gervase Parker Bushe on the basis of hearth tax returns (see above, vol. I, p. 115, n. 1, and below, p. 95, n. 2).

[2] Above, pp 61–70.   [3] Below, pp 88–97.   [4] Above, pp 34–5.   [5] Above, pp 17–23.

[6] In fact to the Committee of Public Safety, the predecessor of the Directoire Exécutif, i.e. the Directory. A version of Adet's letter, which was dated 24 Frimaire an IV (14 Dec. 1795), is printed above, pp 34–5.

gratitude; that I sailed from America in the very first vessel; that I was arrived about a fortnight; that I had delivered my letter to the Minister for Foreign Affairs, who had ordered me to explain myself without reserve to a Citizen Madgett, which I had accordingly done; that by his advice I had prepared and delivered one memorial[1] on the actual state of Ireland, and was then at work on another[2] which would comprise the whole of the subject; that I had the highest respect for the Minister, and as to Madgett that I had no reason whatsoever to doubt him, but nevertheless I must be permitted to say that in my mind it was a business of too great importance to be transacted with a mere *commis*; that I should not think I had discharged my duty, either to France or Ireland, if I left any measure unattempted which might draw the attention of the Directory to the situation of the latter country, and that in consequence I had presumed to present myself to him and to implore his attention to the facts contained in my two memorials; that I would also presume to request that, if any doubt or difficulty rose in his mind on any of those facts, he would have the goodness to permit me to explain. I concluded by saying that I looked upon it as a favorable omen that I had been allowed to communicate with *him*, as he was already perfectly well known by reputation in Ireland and was the very man of whom my friends had spoken. He shook his head and smiled, as if he doubted me a little. I assured him the fact was so, and as a proof I told him that in Ireland we all knew three years ago that he could speak English, at which he did not seem displeased. I then rose and after the usual apologies I took my leave, but I had not cleared the antichamber when I recollected a very material circumstance, which was that I had not told him in fact *who*, but merely *what*, I was. I was therefore returning on my steps, when I was stopped by the centry demanding my card, but from this dilemma I was extricated by my lover the *huissier* and I was again admitted. I then told Carnot that as to my situation, credit and the station I had filled in Ireland, I begged leave to refer him to James Monroe, the American Ambassador, who would satisfy him.[3] He seemed struck with this and then, for the first time, asked my name? I told him I had, in fact, two names, my real one and that under which I travelled and was described in my passport. I then took a slip of paper, and wrote the name 'James Smith, citoyen américain', and under it I wrote 'Theobald Wolfe Tone', which I handed him, adding that my real name was the undermost. He took the paper and looking over it said, 'Ha, Theobald Wolfe Tone', with the expression of a man who has just recollected a circumstance, from which little movement I augur good things. I then told him I would finish my memorial as soon as possible and I hoped he would permit me in the course of a few days after to present myself again to him; to which he answered, 'By all means', and so I again took my leave.

Here is a full and true account of my first audience of the Executive Directory of France, in the person of Citizen Carnot, the Organiser of Victory. I think I came off very clean. What am I to think of all this? As yet I have met no difficulty

[1] Above, pp 61–70. [2] Below, pp 88–97. [3] *Life* omits 'who would satisfy him'.

nor check; nothing to discourage me; but I wish with such extravagant passion for the emancipation of my country, and I do so abhor and detest the very name of England, that I doubt my own judgement lest I see things in too favorable a light. I hope I am doing my duty. It is a bold measure! After all if it should succeed and my visions be realised! Huzza! *Vive la République*! I am a pretty fellow to negotiate with the Directory of France, to pull down a monarchy and establish a republic, to break a connexion of 600 years standing, and contract a fresh alliance with another country! '*By'r lákin, a parlous fear*.'[1] What would my old friend Fitzgibbon say if he was to read these wise memorandums? '*He called me Dog, before he had a cause*.'[2] I remember he used to say that '*I was a viper in the bosom of Ireland*'.[3] Now that I am in Paris I will venture to say he lies and that I am better Irishman than he and his whole gang of rascals, as well as the gang of rascals who are opposing him, *as it were*, including Mr Grattan who, indeed, will '*stand and fall with England*'. I should like to give him an opportunity of keeping his word. I think if England falls, Ireland will rise, even tho' Mr Grattan should tumble with his ally.[4] But this is all castle building. Let me finish my *mémoire*, and deliver it to the Minister. Nothing but *ministers*, and *Directoires Exécutifs*, and *revolutionary memorials*! Well, my friend Plunkett[5] (but I have sincerely forgiven him) and my friend Magee[6] (whom I have not yet forgiven) would not speak to me in Ireland, because I was a republican! Sink or swim, I stand today on as high ground as either of them. My venerable friend, Old Capt[ai]n Russell,[7] always had hopes of me in the worst of times. I believe he was a wise old man.[8] *Huzza!* I would give five louis dor's for one day's conversation with P.P. What shall I do for want of his advice and assistance? Not but I think I am doing pretty well, considering I am quite alone, with no papers, no one to consult or advise with, and shocking all Christian ears with the horrible jargon which I speak, and which is properly no language! I see I have grand diplomatic talents, and by and bye I hope to have an opportunity to display my military ones and to shew that I am equally great in the Cabinet and the field. This is sad stuff, except for my love, who will laugh at it, or for P.P., who would enjoy it.

I have to add to all this day's Journal that I saw yesterday at the Luxembourg, besides my friend Carnot, Citizens Letournerer, the President, Barras,[9] and

[1] *A midsummer-night's dream*, III, i. [2] *Merchant of Venice*, III, iii. [3] Source not identified.

[4] The phrase in which Ireland promised 'to stand and fall with the British nation' occurred in the address of the Irish house of commons to the crown moved by Grattan on 27 May 1782 (*Parl. reg. Ire.*, 2nd ed., i (Dublin, 1784), p. 357). The words 'including Mr Grattan' as far as 'with his ally' are omitted from *Life*.

[5] William Conyngham Plunket.

[6] Tone and William Magee, contemporaries at T.C.D., had once been on friendly terms. In 1791 Magee, newly ordained in the Established Church, officiated in Tone's home at the christening of Tone's son William (b. 29 Apr.); Plunket's brother and another friend, George Knox, were also present (Matilda Tone-Wilson to Eliza Fletcher, 29 Apr. 1827 (Tone (Dickason) papers), cited in Elliott, *Tone*, pp 164, 440). For an earlier instance of friendly relations between Tone and Magee, see Autobiography (below, p. 277, n. 4).

[7] John Russell (*c.*1720–92), father of Thomas Russell. [8] This sentence is omitted from *Life*.

[9] Paul François Jean Nicolas Barras (1755–1829), member of the Directory, 1795–9 (*Dict. biog. franç.*).

Larepillern Lepaux. Barras looks like a soldier, and put me something in mind of James Bramston,[1] Larevillière Lepaux is extremely like Dr Kearney.[2] Mem: I saw two *poissardes*[3] admitted to speak to Carnot (who gave them money) when a general officer in his uniform was obliged to wait for his turn.[4] Bravo! I like all this business mightily! 'Damn me, it is *life*, however!' Oh Lord, oh Lord! shall I ever get to finish my memorial? But when I begin to write these ingenious memorandums, I feel just as if I were chatting with my dearest Love, and I know not when to leave off. By the bye, there is a good deal of vanity in this day's journal! No matter, there is no one to know it; and I believe that wiser men[5] than I am, if they would speak the truth, would feel a little elevated to be in my situation, hunted from my own country as a traitor, living obscurely in America as an exile, and received in France by the Executive Directory *almost* as an ambassador. Well, murder will out. I am as vain as the Devil; and one thing which makes me wish so often for P.P. (not to mention the benefit of his advice) is to communicate with him the pleasure I feel at my present situation. I know how sincerely he would enjoy it, and also how he would plume himself on his own discernment for he always foretold great things. So he did, sure enough! But will they be verified? Well if all this be not vanity, I should be glad to know what is? But nobody is the wiser, and so I will go finish my memoir. (Sings) '*Allons, enfans de la Patrie &c.*'[6]

### 25 Feb. 1796

Finished the draft of my second memorial and read it over with Madgett.[7]

## To Charles Delacroix, 26 February 1796

T.C.D., Tone papers, MS 2050, ff 1$^r$–2$^v$.

There is a translation in good French in another hand in Archives des Affaires Étrangères, Corresp. Politique Angleterre, cote 589, ff 169–70.

Paris, Feb$^y$ 26th, 1796 V.S.

Citizen Minister,

In pursuance of your orders communicated to me by Citizen Madgett, I have delivered to him a memorial[8] on the present state of Ireland and I request that if any point therein contained requires further elucidation, you

[1] James Yorke Bramston seems to have been a relation of Richard Griffith, whose first wife was Charity Yorke Bramston (see above, vol. I, pp 103, 234).

[2] John Kearney (1742–1813), fellow of T.C.D., 1764; provost, 1799–1806; bishop of Ossory, 1806–13 (*D.N.B.*).

[3] Meaning 'fishwives'.

[4] The following thirteen words are omitted from *Life*.

[5] The following three words are omitted from *Life*.

[6] Opening line of *La Marseillaise*.

[7] In fact Tone had not quite finished it. See his Diary entries for 27, 28 and 29 Feb. 1796 (below, pp 87, 97). The second memorial is given below (pp 88–97).

[8] Above, pp 61–70.

may have the goodness to mention your doubts and I shall to the best of my power explain them.

Particular circumstances rendering it in a degree impossible for me to bring my credentials, I am reduced to the disagreeable necessity of speaking of myself. If my own interests were alone concerned I should be silent; but in justice as well to France as to my own country, whose independance is now at stake, I feel it my duty to state to you the grounds on which I presume to expect credit from the French government for the facts which I have advanced in my memorials.

In the year 1792[1] I was invited to Belfast in order to frame the first club of United Irishmen, mentioned in my memorial, a measure whose importance can be justly appreciated by those alone who know the politics of Ireland intimately, and which was the first step to the reconciliation of the two great sects, the Catholics and Dissenters, by whose dissention the power of England in that country has been hitherto preserved. In consequence of this service, and some arguments which I had published in favor of their cause,[2] I was, tho' a Protestant, appointed to the office of Agent to the Catholics of Ireland and one of the secretaries to their General Committee.[3] In this station I continued during the existence of that body and had the honor to attend two separate deputations which they sent to the King of England in 1793 and 1795. I composed all their public acts and manifestoes, all their confidential and official business passed thro' my hands, and I had by these means an opportunity of thoroughly knowing the sentiments of the Catholics of Ireland, as my connexion with Belfast enabled me to collect the opinions of the Dissenters and I also became acquainted personally with the most active and intelligent men of both parties, in effecting whose reconciliation I had the good fortune to be an instrument. I received two unanimous votes of thanks from the Catholics of Ireland,[4] the last one when I was actually under the persecution of the Irish government for the part which I had taken in the affair of the late Citizen William Jackson. I was also elected an honorary member of the regiment of Belfast Volunteers in testimony of the confidence they reposed in me, the Certificate[5] of which, signed and authenticated by characters well known in Ireland, as well as the two votes of thanks of the Catholics signed by their President and Secretaries, I submitted to Citizen Adet on my arrival in Philadelphia in the month of August last. When it was agreed that I should come to France I offered to bring those documents with me, but Citizen Adet observed that I had satisfied him as to my credit, and that he would take on himself to satisfy the French government, especially as the certificates

[1] *Recte* 1791.

[2] Especially a pamphlet, *An argument on behalf of the catholics of Ireland*, first published in Aug. 1791 and reprinted above (vol. I, pp 108–28). Several of Tone's writings published in the first half of 1792 and reprinted above (vol. I) are also highly favourable to the catholics.

[3] This appointment, which was to the post of assistant secretary, was made in June or July 1792 (see above, vol. I, p. 226, n. 5).

[4] Above, vol. I, pp 443, 529.

[5] Probably the certificate of Tone's election as an honorary member of the Belfast regiment of National Volunteers, 10 June 1792 (above, vol. I, pp 203–4).

I have mentioned, being written on large sheets of parchment, were too bulky to be easily concealed in case of my being searched by British cruisers, and if they were found the consequence would be the certain forfeiture of my life and, what was of much more consequence, the total failure of a communication on Irish affairs, which he considered as highly material to the interests of his government.

When the trial and death of the late Citizen William Jackson rendered it impossible for me to remain in Ireland, I determined to go into exile in America. Before my departure, which was on the 20th of June last, I had interviews with all my confidential friends of both parties,[1] as well as with the leaders of those who are called Defenders,[2] and I received from them all the most positive instructions to communicate without reserve with the French minister in Philadelphia, and, if possible, to make my way to Paris and supplicate the attention of the French government to the situation of Ireland. In consequence I did instantly on my arrival wait on the Minister and after some conversation I prepared and delivered a memorial,[3] which he transmitted and which has been received here; he did not however seem to think my coming at that time likely to produce any effect and in consequence I did not press it. Subsequent to that period, in November last, I received letters[4] from my friends in Ireland, who, I beg leave to repeat, are among the most active and intelligent men in the country, renewing in the strongest manner their instructions, already mentioned, and informing me that the state of Ireland was growing more critical than even I could believe. These letters I brought to Citoyen Adet and satisfied him as to the situation of the writers by reference to Irish citizens then in Philadelphia who knew them well. In consequence of this he gave me the letter of introduction[5] which I had the honor to deliver to you, Citizen Minister, and which I trust you will see from the facts which I have now mentioned was the only credential the nature of my situation would admit. I sailed in the very next vessel which [de]parted for France.

I ask pardon for troubling you with this detail, which I should not do were it not necessary to satisfy you that I do not speak on the subject of Irish affairs without having sufficient grounds from my situation in that country to form an opinion and also to assure you that in making the present application to the government of France I act by the advice, direction and concurrence of the men who in case of a revolution would to a certainty direct the public sentiment in Ireland.

I entreat, Citizen Minister, you will do me the justice to believe that nothing but a conviction that it may be necessary for the success of measures in a high

[1] For some details of 'interviews' with United Irish leaders, see Autobiography (below, pp 330–31, 332, 333). There seem to be allusions to a similar conversation with John Keogh, a leading member of the Catholic Committee, in Keogh to Tone, 3 Sept. 1795 (above, pp 19, 20); there is mention of such a conversation with Richard McCormick, another member of the Catholic Committee, in Tone's Diary for 7 Nov. 1796 (see below, p. 368).

[2] Tone alludes in his Autobiography to having been authorised in some way to speak for the Defenders (see below, p. 334).

[3] Above, pp 7–10. [4] Above, pp 17–23. [5] Above, pp 34–5.

degree important both to France and Ireland could induce me to dwell so long upon a subject so uninteresting and obscure as myself.

I am with great respect &c., &c.
T.W.T.

Citizen Charles De la Croix
Minister for Foreign Relations, &c., &c., &c.
(Copy)

## Diary, 26–8 February 1796

T.C.D., Tone papers, MS 2048, ff $14^r$–$18^r$; *Life*, ii, 31–6.

### 26 Feb. 1796

This morning finished an awkward business, that is to say I wrote a long letter to the Minister,[1] all about myself—very proper in an ambassador to frame his own credentials. '*My commission was large, for I made it myself*.'[2] Read it over carefully; every word true and not exaggerated. Resolved to go at once to the Minister and deliver my letter, like a true Irishman, with my own hands. Went to his bureau and saw Lamare, the secretary, whom I sent in to demand an audience. Lamare returned with word that the Minister was just engaged with Neri Corsini,[3] ambassador from the Grand Duke of Tuscany, and the moment he was at leisure he would see me. Waited accordingly in an antichamber. A person came in and, after reconnoitring me some time, pulled out *an English newspaper* and began to read it. Looked at him with the most interesting indifference, as if he was reading a chapter in the Koran. Did the fellow think I would *rise* at such a bait as that? Neri Corsini having departed, I was introduced, leaving my friend in the antichamber to study his newspaper. I began with telling the Minister that tho' I spoke execrable French, I would, with his permission, put his patience to a short trial. (*Once for all, I am thus minute for the sake of my wife, whom I love ten thousand times more than all the universe and who will consider every circumstance, even the most trifling, which relates to me of consequence.*) I then told him that in obedience to his orders I had finished a memorial[4] on the actual state of Ireland, which I had delivered to Madgett, that I had finished the draft of another,[5] which I would deliver tomorrow, on the means necessary to accomplish the great object of my mission, the separation of Ireland from England and the establishing her as an independent republic in alliance with France. De la Croix interrupted me here by say[in]g substantially (for I do not pretend to quote his words, tho' I am perfectly clear as to their import) 'that I might count upon it, there was no object

[1] Above, pp 80–83. [2] Source of quotation not identified.
[3] Neri Corsini (1771–1845), Tuscan ambassador to France, 1796 (*Enciclopedia italiana* (Rome, 1949)).
[4] Above, pp 61–70.
[5] Below, pp 88–97. He put the finishing touches to it on 27, 28 and 29 Feb.

nearer the heart of the Executive Directory; that they had that business at that moment before them; and that they would leave no means consistent with their utmost capacity untried to accomplish it'; and he repeated again, with earnestness, that I might 'count upon it'. These are strong expressions from a man in his station! I then said that the information gave me the most sincere pleasure, not only on acount of my own country but of France, to whom the independence of Ireland was scarce less an object than to Ireland herself. He answered me, 'We know that perfectly, and for myself I can assure you that for the sake of both countries, as well as for the sake of liberty and humanity, you may depend on my most sincere and hearty co-operation in every measure likely to accomplish that end'. I then returned to the business which brought me to him, that is to say my credentials. I told him, in as few words as possible, the station I had filled in Ireland, and I added that I had thrown a few facts relating to myself on paper, which I delivered to him,[1] and added that as to my credit or veracity I could refer him to James Monroe, who had allowed me to mention his name, as a voucher for my integrity. He said it was unnecessary, and as to applying to Monroe, he would not wish to take any step relating to the business which could in the least, by possibility, take wind; that Madget was the only person whatsoever to whom he confided the affair; that his principal secretary and those who were most confidential with him knew nothing whatsoever of it, and he recommended to me to be equally cautious. I assured him, as the fact was, that I kept the most rigid guard on myself; that I did not know a soul in Paris, nor desire to know anyone; that I formed no connexions nor intended to form any, and that in short I kept myself purposely in solitude that I might escape notice as much as possible. He said I was very right, and asked me then did I know the person I saw in the antichamber. I answered I did not. He said he was an Irish Patriot named 'Duchet'[2] (as he pronounced it) who was persecuted into exile for some writing under the signature of Junius Redivivus.[3] I answered it might be so, but I knew nothing either of him, or the writings, and that if such an event had taken place it must be since June last when I left Ireland; I then mentioned the circumstance of his pulling out an English newspaper and setting a trap for me therewith, and how I avoided falling into his snare. The Minister said again I was quite right; but that that person had delivered in several memorials[4] on the state of Ireland. This is very odd! I never saw the man in my life, and yet I rather imagine he knew my person. Who the Devil is Junius Redivivus, or who is Duchette, if his name be 'Duchette'? I must

[1] Above, pp 80–83.

[2] William Duckett (1768–1841) was born at Killarney but lived in France from the age of 17; after the execution of the king he went to London to spread propaganda at the request of Pierre Le Brun, the minister of foreign affairs; he was a French agent in Hamburg, 1797–8, and later taught English at the Collège de Sainte-Barbe in Paris (*D.N.B.*; *Dict. biog. franç.*; P.R.O., FO 33/15).

[3] A letter emphasising the extent of the French successes in the war signed Junius Redivivus appeared in the *Morning Chronicle*, 17 Nov. 1794, and in the *Northern Star*, 1 Dec. 1794. According to the British resident at Hamburg, an effort was made early in 1795 to arrest Duckett as the author of this letter (Sir James Craufurd to ——, 13 July 1798, P.R.O., FO 33/15).

[4] There are memoranda by Duckett in the Archives Nationales, Paris, AF III 186[b], dossiers 858–9, and also in the Archives des Affaires Étrangères, Corresp. Politique Angleterre, cote 589, ff 156–8.

talk a little to Madgett of this resurrection of Junius, of whom to speak the truth I have no good opinion.[1] The Minister then asked me what we wanted in Ireland. I answered that we wanted a force to begin with, arms ammunition and money. He asked me what quantity of each would I think sufficient? I did not wish to go just then into the detail, as I judged from Madgett's discourse that the Minister's plan was on a smaller scale than mine, and I did not desire to shock him too much in the outset; I therefore took advantage of my bad French, and mentioned that I doubted my being able sufficiently to explain myself in conversation, but that he would find my opinions at length in the two memorials[2] I had prepared, and when he had considered them, I hoped he would allow me to wait on him and explain any point which might not be sufficiently clear. He then proceeded to give me his own ideas, which were, as I suspected, on a small scale. He said he understood Ireland was very populous and her people warlike so as soon to be made soldiers, and that they were already in some degree armed. I answered, not so much as to be calculated upon, in estimating the quantity of arms wanted, as most of the guns which they had were but fowling pieces. He then said he knew that they had no artillery nor cannoniers and that consequently it would be necessary to supply them with both; that field pieces would be sufficient, as we had no strong places; that we should have thirty pieces of cannon (*une trentaine*), half 8 pounders and half 16 pounders, properly manned and officered, and twenty thousand stand of arms. I interrupted him to say, twenty thousand at least, as the only limitation to the numbers we could raise would be the quantity of arms we might have to put in their hands. He then went on to say that these should be landed near Belfast, where he supposed they would be most likely to meet with early support. I answered, certainly, as that province was the most populous and warlike in the kingdom. He then produced a map of Ireland and we looked over it together; I took this advantage to slide in a little of my own ideas here, by say[in]g that if we were able to begin in considerable force, we should commence as near the capital as possible, the possession of which, if once obtained, would, I thought, decide the whole business; but if we began with a smaller force, we should commence as near Belfast as we could, and then push forward so as to secure the Mountains of Mourne and the Fews, by means of which, and of Lough Erne, we could cover the entire province of Ulster,[3] and maintain ourselves until we had collected our friends in sufficient force to penetrate to Dublin. He liked my plan extremely, which certainly appears to be the only feasible one in case of a small force being landed. He then mentioned the Irishmen serving in the British navy, and asked me what I thought of sending proper persons among them to insinuate the duty they owed to their country,

[1] Tone's suspicions of Duckett, expressed again and again in later entries in his Diary, were unfounded. See Paul Weber, *On the road to rebellion: the United Irishmen and Hamburg, 1796–1803* (Dublin, 1997), pp 43–6, 88–90, 110–13.

[2] Above, pp 61–70, and below, pp 87–97. The second memorial was not finally completed until 29 Feb.

[3] The Mourne Mountains are in south Down; the Fews Mountains are in south Armagh; Lough Erne traverses Fermanagh.

and whether in such case they would act against us or not? This is Madgett's scheme, and if it is not followed by very different measures is *nonsense*. I answered that undoubtedly the measure was a good one, if accompanied properly; but to give it full effect it was absolutely necessary there should be a government established in Ireland for reasons which he would find detailed in my memorials and of which I gave him an imperfect abstract. I think he seemed satisfied on that head. I added that great caution ought to be used as to sending those persons lest it might take wind in some shape and alarm the British Government. On the whole I fancy the scheme of sending apostles among the Irish seamen will be given up; for certainly, if there be once a government established in Ireland, it would in my mind be unnecessary, and if there be not, it would be useless. The Minister then repeated in the plainest and most unequivocal terms his former assurances, as well of his personal support, as of the positive and serious determination of the Executive Directory to take up the business of Ireland in the strongest manner that circumstances would possibly admit. He added that he hoped if France made the sacrifices she was inclined to do of men and money to enable us to establish our freedom, and even delayed to make peace on our account, we would in return manifest more gratitude and principle than America had done.[1] I interrupted him with great eagerness to assure him he would find us a different nation from America, and I took the opportunity to utter a short eulogium on the latter country in the strongest terms which contempt and indignation could supply. I became downright eloquent, and I must say the Minister appeared to concur most heartily in every word I uttered. The Minister then desired me, as to any part of the business whose preparation might rest with me, not to lose a minute; he also desired me to press Madgett to expedite the translations as much as possible, and on the whole he certainly appeared to me to be nearly as earnest and anxious in the business as myself. I then took my leave.

The result of this conversation, the principal circumstances of which I have substantially related, is that the Executive Directory at present are determined to take us up, but on a small scale; that they will give us 30 pieces of cannon, properly manned, and 20,000 stand of arms, with some money of course, to begin with, but I did not collect from the Minister that they had an idea of any definite number of troops, at least he mentioned none; and I did not press him on that head, as I wish they should first read and consider my memorials. *Perhaps what is said in them may induce them to reconsider the subject, and if so I shall have done a most important service both to France and Ireland.* If they act on the plan mentioned to me by De la Croix as above related, I, for one, am ready and willing most chearfully to stake my life on the hazard, but the measure is against my judgement, not from any doubt of the people at large, but from the difficulty, perhaps the impossibility, of having a proper organized government. Do I say therefore that the measure ought not to be attempted on the present scale? *By no means!*

[1] *Life*, ii, 34–5, has 'than other nations had done in similar cases' instead of 'than America had done'. What follows, as far as 'every word I uttered', is omitted.

I am clear it ought. As to France, it is but the risque, as to her, of the outfit which is nothing, and as to Ireland, she is in that situation that she ought to hazard everything on the chance of bettering her condition. I speak of the people at large and not of the aristocracy. For one then I am decided. We have at all events the strength of numbers, and if our lever be too short, we must only apply the greater power. If the landing be effected on the present plan, we must instantly have recourse to the strongest revolutionary measures and put, if necessary, man, woman and child, money, horses & arms, stores and provisions in requisition. '*The King shall eat, tho' all mankind be starved*.'[1] No consideration must be permitted to stand a moment against the establishment of our independence. I do not wish for all this, if it can be avoided but liberty must be purchased at any price, so '*Lay on Macdoff, and damned be he that first cries, hold, enough!*'.[2] We must strike the ball hard, and take the chance of the tables. I think P.P.[3] will shine in the character of a 'youth of the first requisition'.[4]

I should have observed that in the course of the conversation De la Croix mentioned that on the receipt of Adet's letter[5] inclosing the memorial[6] which I had delivered on my arrival in Philadelphia in Aug[us]t last, he had written to him that the subject was too important to be discussed at 3,000 miles distance and therefore desired I should come over. I was very glad to hear this, and answered that I was happy to have anticipated his desire. So it seems I was written for as Madgett said. I should be glad now to see that memorial, for I remember it was written in the burning summer of Pen[n]sylvania, when my head was extremely deranged by the heat. Bad as I dare say it is, it caught the attention of people here. Well, vanity again!

## 27 Feb. 1796

At work at my memorial,[7] which begins to look very spruce on paper.

## 28 Feb. 1796

Do. Went to Monroe's about my passport,[8] and had about an hour's conversation with him. I like him very much; he speaks like a sincere republican. How came he to be an American?[9] He praises the Executive Directory to the skies, and De la Croix. All for the better! Carnot, he tells me, is a military man and one of the first engineers in Europe. (Vide my observation touching his *organising* about

[1] Henry Carey, *Chrononhotonthologos* (1734). [2] *Macbeth*, v, vii. [3] Russell.

[4] See above, p. 55, n. 2. [5] Above, pp 23–4.

[6] Probably the document printed above, pp 7–10. [7] Below, pp 87–97.

[8] Tone had arrived in France with a travel document issued apparently by the American government which he delivered to Monroe on 15 Feb. 1796. It seems that he was now seeking to retrieve this document, probably endorsed by Monroe, in order to obtain a residence permit from the French government. See also above, p. 52.

[9] *Life* omits 'How came he to be an American?'.

Cork harbour.)[1] Le Tourneur is also a military man, so that, with Barras, there are three soldiers in the *Directoire. I am very glad of that!*

# Second memorial to the French government on the present state of Ireland, 29 February 1796

Archives Nationales, AF IV, carton 1671, ff 93ʳ–98ʳ; *Life*, ii, 193–204.

The version printed in *Life* appears to be the earlier of the two. Significant variants have been noted.

A free French translation by Madgett, dated '10 Ventôse an 4' (29 Feb. 1796), is in Archives des Affaires Étrangères, Corresp. Politique Angleterre, cote 589, ff 173–81, and is printed in a compressed form in Édouard Guillon, *La France et l'Irlande pendant la Révolution* (Paris, 1888), pp 179–83.

See above, pp 80, 83, below, p. 97.

## Second memorial on the present state of Ireland delivered to the French government, February–March 1796[2]

Having stated in a former memorial[3] the actual situation and circumstances of Ireland, I shall now submit to the consideration of the French government[4] those means which, in my judgement, will be most likely to effectuate the great object of separating that country from England and establishing her as an independant republic in strict alliance with France. I shall first mention those measures whose execution depend[s] on the French republic; and next those which will be to be executed by the people of Ireland.

In the first place, I beg leave to lay down as indispensable that a body of French troops should be landed in Ireland with a general at their head of established reputation whose name should be known in that country, a circumstance of considerable importance, and I must be permitted to observe here that if humbling the pride and reducing the power of England be an object with the French Republic, I know no place where the very best general in their service could be employed either with more reputation to himself or benefit to the public cause.

With regard to the strength of this army, it is my duty to speak with candor to the Government. It ought, if possible, to be of 20,000 men, at least 15,000 of which should land as near the capital as circumstances would admit, and 5,000 in the North of Ireland, near Belfast. If an imposing force such as I have mentioned

[1] See above, p. 77.
[2] MS lacks a heading. The heading given here is as supplied by William Tone in *Life*.
[3] Above, pp 61–70.
[4] Preceding seven words not in *Life*.

could be sent in the first instance it would save a great effusion of blood and treasure. By having possession of the capital we should in fact have possession of the whole country. The Government in existence there would fall to pieces without a possibility of effort. We should have in our hands at once the Treasury,[1] the Post Office,[2] the Banks, the Custom House, the seat of the Legislature and particularly, what is even of still more consequence, we should have the reputation which would result from such a commencement. If we could begin by the capital I should hope we should obtain possession of the entire country without striking a blow, as in fact there would in that case be no organised force to make resistance. But for this 20,000 men would be necessary. If, however, the other indispensable arrangements of the French Government[3] should render it impossible to send such a force, I offer it as my opinion, and I entreat it may be remembered, that 5,000 is the very lowest number with which the attempt could be made with anything like certainty of success, in which case it would be necessary to land[4] in the North of Ireland, where the people are in the greatest forwardness as to military preparation. It is unnecessary to observe here that commencing our operations at one hundred miles distance from the capital, of which the enemy would be in full possession, would give them very great advantages over us at first. They would still have, in a degree, the law of opinion in their favor and they would, at least for some time, retain the Treasury, the Post Office and all the other advantages which an established organisation would naturally give them. Nevertheless, with 5,000 men, an able general and the measures which I shall hereafter mention I should have no doubt of our success ultimately; but then we should have to fight hard for our liberties and we should lose many great advantages which a sufficient force in the commencement would give us, particularly that of disorganising at once the existing government of Ireland.

Supposing the number to be 5,000, a large proportion should be artillerists, of which we are quite unprovided. They should be the very best troops that France could furnish, men who had actually seen hard service and who would be capable of training and disciplining the Irish army. The necessity of this is too obvious to need any further comment. I do not go here into military detail on the conduct of the war; if the measure be adopted, I shall hope to be admitted to a conference with the general who may be appointed to the command and then, with the map of the country before us, I will submit with great deference my ideas on that head.

Before I quit the subject of the force necessary, I wish to observe that in my first memorial I have always said that the army, and especially the militia, would, I was satisfied, declare for their country if 'they saw a reasonable prospect of support', by which I would be understood to mean an imposing force in the first instance. I cannot commit myself as to what might be their conduct in case but

[1] Situated in Dublin Castle (*Gentleman's and Citizen's Almanack*, 1796, p. 70).

[2] Situated in College Green (*Wilson's Dublin Directory*, 1795, p. 10).

[3] *Life*, ii, 194, has 'French Republic'.

[4] Ibid. has 'the landing should be effectuated'.

5,000 men were landed. I hope and I believe, but cannot I positively affirm, that they would join the standard of their country. But even if they were, contrary to my expectations, to adhere to the British Government, the only difference would be that in that event we should have a civil war, which I would most earnestly wish if possible to avoid. As to the people at large, I am perfectly satisfied that whether there were 20,000 or 10,000 or 5,000[1] men landed it would make no manner of difference. I know they would flock to the Republican standard in such numbers as to embarrass the general.[2] It would be just as easy in a month's time to have an army in Ireland of 200,000 men as of 10,000, and therefore it is that, reckoning on this disposition of the people, I say and repeat that I would not have a shadow of doubt of our ultimate success, *provided* we had a body of 5,000 disciplined troops to commence with; a smaller number would, I apprehend, be hardly able to maintain themselves until they could be joined by the people, as the British Government in Ireland[3] would be able instantly to turn against them such a body of troops (who in that case would, I fear, adhere to them) as would overwhelm them,[4] the consequence of which would be, besides the loss to France of the men and money, the bringing Ireland under the yoke of British tyranny even more than she is at present, the breaking for ever the hopes and spirits of her people and the rendering all prospect of her emancipation at any future period impracticable and desperate.

As to arms and ammunition, I can only say that the more there is of both the better. If the Republic can send to Ireland 100,000 stand of arms, there are hands ready to put them in or treble the number.[5] A large train of artillery (that is to say field-pieces, as we have no fortified places) is absolutely indispensable together[6] with a considerable proportion of experienced cannoniers; engineers used to field practice are also highly necessary. As to money, I am at a loss to determine the sum. If 20,000 men were sent, I should say that pay for 40,000 for three months would be amply sufficient, as before that time was expired we should have all the resources of Ireland in our hands. If 5,000 men be sent, I humbly submit the *quantum* necessary to the wisdom and liberality of the French government, observing only that we could not in that case calculate at once on the immediate possessions of the funds which in the other instance we could seize directly.

Very much would depend upon the manifesto to be published on the first landing. I conceive the declaration of the object and intentions of the Republic should contain, among others, the following topics:

*First.* An absolute disavowal of all idea of conquest and a statement that the French come as friends and brothers with no other view than to assist the people in throwing off the yoke of England.

[1] *Life*, ii, 195, has 'or even 5,000'. [2] Ibid. has 'the General in Chief'.
[3] Ibid. has 'the Government of Ireland'. [4] Ibid. has 'as would swallow them up'.
[5] *Life*, ii, 195, has 'there are double the number of hands ready to put them in'.
[6] This word is not in MS but is in *Life*, ii, 195, and is retained here for clarity.

*Second.* A declaration of perfect security and protection to the free exercise of all religions without distinction or preference and the perpetual abolition of all ascendancy or connection between church and state.

*Third.* A declaration of perfect security and protection of property[1] to all who should demean themselves as good citizens and friends to the liberties of their country, with strong denunciations against those who should support or countenance the cause of British tyranny and usurpation.

*Fourth.* An invitation to the people to join the Republican standard and a promise to recommend to the future Legislature of their country every individual who should distinguish himself by his zeal, courage and ability.

*Fifth.* An invitation to the people immediately to organise themselves and form a national convention for the purpose of framing a government and of administering the affairs of Ireland, until such government could be framed and put in activity.

Other topics will naturally suggest themselves; but these seem to me, from my knowledge of Ireland, to be among the most likely as well to raise the people as to remove the fears and anxieties, especially on the great heads of religion and property of many who might otherwise be neutral or perhaps adverse but who would gladly support the independence of their country when satisfied as to these points. It is with the most sincere pleasure that I can assure the French Government that their singular moderation with regard to Holland[2] when that country lay at their mercy had an inconceivable effect on the mind of every independent man in Ireland and removed almost entirely the reluctance which many felt to put themselves to the hazard and uncertainty of a revolution.

To recapitulate, what I humbly[3] conceive would be *indispensably necessary* to be furnished on the part of the French Republic would be:

*First.* An armed force not exceeding 20,000 men, nor less than 5,000. If 20,000, to be landed as near Dublin as possible; if a smaller number, in the North of Ireland, near Belfast.

*Second.* A general whose name and character should be well known in Ireland.

*Third.* Arms and ammunition, as much as can be spared; a train of artillery, with an adequate number of experienced cannoniers and engineers.

*And lastly.* Such a sum of money as the French government might feel necessary and could grant consistently with their other arrangements.

On the part of the people of Ireland, the measures which I conceive would be most immediately necessary to ensure success and establish our independance would be as follow:

*First*, of course, to raise as many soldiers as we had arms to put in their hands, which would be the only limitation as to numbers.

[1] *Life*, ii, 22, has 'persons and property'.

[2] Having declared war on Holland in Feb. 1793, France occupied that country in the winter of 1794–5 and Dutch 'patriots' proclaimed a 'Batavian republic'.

[3] This word not in *Life*.

*Second.* To call a national convention, for which a basis is laid in the General Committee of the Catholics mentioned in my first memorial who, when joined by delegates to be chosen by the Dissenters, would be the actual representatives of nine tenths of the people. The first act of the Convention thus constituted should be to declare themselves the representatives of the Irish people, free and independant, and in that capacity to form an alliance, offensive and defensive, with the French republic, stipulating that neither party should make peace with England without the other and until the two republics were recognised, and also a treaty of commerce on terms of mutual advantage.

As the *immediate formation* of a national convention is of the last importance, I wish earnestly to press on the notice of the French Government the unspeakable advantage of having, if possible, an imposing force in the first instance for this reason—that the men of a certain rank in life and situation as to property (for instance the actual members of the Catholic Committee), who must be those who would naturally form the convention, would in that case at once declare themselves and begin to act, which I cannot venture to ensure that they would do, at least for some time, if they saw but a small force landed. For the great body of the people whom I have mentioned as being organised under the name of Defenders, and a great proportion of the Dissenters, the number to be landed is of little consequence as to them, for my firm belief is that if but 1,000 French were landed it would be impossible to prevent the peasantry of Ireland from rising as one man to join them; but then we should lose the inestimable advantages which would result from the *immediate organisation* of a body which could call itself the *Government of Ireland* and as such instantly assume the legislative and executive functions, raise money, grant commissions and, especially, conclude the alliance with France, the éclat of which must naturally produce the most beneficial and important consequences. Without such an arrangement, our commencement would have more the air of an insurrection than a revolution; and tho', I again repeat, I would have no doubt of the ultimate success of the attempt, yet the difficulties at first would be multiplied in proportion to the smallness of the force which might be landed. The measures which I am now about to mention, which can only be executed with effect by an actual Irish Government,[1] will shew at once the indispensable necessity of a national convention being organised, that not an hour should be lost in framing it, and of course that every possible effort should be made to send such force as would ensure its accomplishment in the first instance.

The convention being once formed should proceed to publish among others the following proclamations, from every one of which I have no manner of doubt there would result the most powerful effects.

*First.* One to the people of Ireland[2] notifying their independance and their alliance with the French Republic, forbidding all adherence to the British

[1] *Life*, ii, 198, has 'can only be effectually executed by a body which can, with some appearance of justice, call itself the Irish Government'.

[2] *Life*, ii, 198, has 'the people at large'.

Government under the penalties of high treason, ordering all taxes and contributions to be paid only to such persons as should be appointed by them[1] to receive them, and in the meantime making all collectors and public officers responsible with life and property for all monies in their hands &c. This would at once set the law of opinion on their side and give a spirit to every individual embarked in the cause. It would then be a war, not an insurrection; and even that circumstance, as operating on the minds of the soldiery, I consider as of great consequence.

*Second.* One to the militia of Ireland recalling them to the standard of their country, paying the value of their arms and granting an immediate discharge to all who should demand it, and ensuring a preference in all military promotion and a provision in land or otherwise at the end of the war, according to the rank[2] of each, to those who should enter into the service of their country. I am convinced, as I am of my existence, that this single proclamation would bring over the entire militia of Ireland, which is in fact the only formidable force in the country; but I must be permitted to add at the same time that this proclamation can only be published with effect by a national government.

*Third.* One addressed to all Irishmen now serving in the navy of England recalling them directly from that service, reminding them that they are a majority in the proportion of two to one and therefore exhorting them to seize on the vessels and bring them into the Irish ports; engaging the faith of the nation to purchase the ships at their value as prizes, to give, as in the case of the militia, an immediate discharge to all who should desire it; ensuring promotion in preference to all who should remain in the service; stating the hardships to which they are subjected in the British service into which they have been forced either by hunger or the press-gang; dwelling particularly on the unjust distribution of their prize money, stating the enormous disproportion between the share of an admiral or a captain and that of a common seaman; assuring them an equitable rate in that respect to be established in the future Irish navy; and reminding them of the immense wealth to be made by captures on the prodigious expanse of the British commerce, which now embraces that of the whole world.

From such a proclamation issuing from an Irish government I am sanguine enough to expect the most powerful effects. Let it never be forgotten that *two thirds* of the British seamen, as they are called, are in fact Irishmen. I will not say that this proclamation would bring one ship into the Irish harbours, but this I say, that if human nature be human nature it would raise such a spirit of distrust and jealousy in the naval service of Great Britain as must most essentially[3] serve the cause of the Republic. Will any English admiral leave Portsmouth with confidence with such a proclamation as that hanging over his head, against which too he has nothing to oppose but the mere force of discipline? How much will that discipline be necessarily relaxed from the fear lest by enforcing it strictly the

[1] *Life*, ii, 198, has 'by the convention'.

[2] *Life*, ii, 198, has 'rank and services'.

[3] *Life*, ii, 199, has 'materially'.

majority of the crew should instantly mutiny and carry the ship where they would meet with protection and support, among their friends and connexions, their wives and children—in one word, in their native country? Will any English captain be very fond[1] to tye up an Irish seaman for a trifling offence and flog him before the face of the crew, two thirds of whom are Irish, with the terror of such a proclamation before his eyes? And especially, what weapons has the English Government to oppose in return? I supplicate the attention of the French Government to this point, which is in my judgement of the very highest importance. It would be in her navy that England would be, then, first found vulnerable. If there were no other object proposed but this single one, I affirm with confidence it is of magnitude by itself sufficient to decide the French Government on making every effort to obtain it, which can only be effected thro' the medium of a national government to be established in Ireland. It would be easy to add a thousand arguments on this topic, but I trust, knowing as I do the superior information and talents of those whom I address, that what I have said will be sufficient to open the subject; and I do again most earnestly entreat them to follow in their own minds the long chain of consequences which must flow, as to the naval power of England, from the measure which I have mentioned, supposing it to have that success which I am satisfied it must.[2]

*Fourth.* A proclamation recalling in general terms all Irishmen from the dominions of Great Britain, whether in the land or sea service, or otherwise, within a certain time under pain of being treated as *emigrants*. The effect of this will appear when I come to speak of the actual and casual resources of Ireland.

*Fifth.* An address to the *people* of England and Scotland, as distinguished from the *Government*, stating the grounds of the conduct of the Irish nation and declaring their earnest desire to avoid the effusion of blood; that they wish merely for independance, which at all hazards they are determined to maintain; warning them by the examples of the revolutions in America and France how impossible it is to conquer a whole people determined to be free; shewing them by calculation[3] the expense of the war and applying to their interests as a commercial people contrasted and opposed to the personal views of their King and Government; shewing them how little they could possibly gain in the most prosperous event, how much blood and treasure they must necessarily expend; and, finally, pointing out the certain consequences to England if she should fail in the contest. If this proclamation were published I apprehend, as its principles are just, it might embarrass the British Minister a good deal[4] in his operations so as perhaps to render it impossible for him to continue the war. But as I do not at all calculate on the good sense or spirit of the British people, who seem to me for some years to have totally renounced that share of both which they once possessed, I will submit that if it totally failed in its object and the English nation

[1] *Life*, ii, 200, has 'be found' instead of 'be very fond'.
[2] *Life*, ii, 200, has 'I cannot myself for a moment doubt but' instead of 'I am satisfied'.
[3] *Life*, ii, 201, has 'demonstrating by calculation'.
[4] *Life*, ii, 201, has 'considerably' instead of 'a good deal'.

were so infatuated as to support the Minister in the war, this proclamation should be followed by the next[1] measure which I shall propose, that is to say,

*Sixth.* The immediate confiscation of every shilling of English property in Ireland, moveable or fixed, of every species, and appropriating it to the national service, which would then be an act of strict justice, as the English people would have made themselves parties in the war. In this manner I submit that one of two things must happen: either the English people would decidedly oppose the war, and if so peace and the establishment of the independence of Ireland would directly follow, or they would support the war, in which case they lose at once an immense property in Ireland, which is instantly transferred and becomes a weapon against them in the hands of their enemies, not to speak of the discontents which the loss of such a vast property in land, in money lent on mortgages, in goods and in debts must produce among all ranks and more especially among the merchants and traders in England.

I will not trespass longer on the time of the French Government but hasten to give a brief sketch of the actual and casual resources of Ireland and then conclude. First, her population, which has been established by incontestible calculations to be four million five hundred thousand people.[2] But tho' she is populous, she is poor! We are, thanks to the ruinous connexion with England, almost without trade or manufactures, and while that connexion holds we shall continue so, for this among other reasons that a wretched Irish peasant is tempted even by the scanty pay and subsistance of a foot soldier, from which a well-fed and well-clothed English artizan turns with contempt. The army of England is supported by the misery of Ireland.

Ireland would, however, in case of a revolution possess among others the following resources: *First.*[3] Her actual revenues, which amount at present to above £3,000,000 sterling, or 72,000,000 livres tournois. The army expences alone for last year amounted to £2,000,000 sterling, making 48,000,000 livres. *Second.* The church, college and chapter lands, whose exact value I do not know but which are of a vast amount. *Third.* The property of absentees who never visit the country at all, amounting at least to £1,000,000 ster[lin]g, or 24,000,000 livres, p[er] annum. *Fourth.* The casual property of emigrants, which would amount to a very

[1] *Life* lacks the following nine words.

[2] See G. P. Bushe, 'An essay towards ascertaining the population of Ireland' in *R.I.A. Transactions*, iii (1790), science, pp 145–55. In *Life*, ii, 201, this sentence reads: 'First, her population, 4,500,000'. The paragraph continues: 'It is necessary to state on what grounds I assert this: in 1788 there existed a tax on hearths in Ireland, by which means the number of houses was known with sufficient accuracy to those who administered the revenue. The number of people in Ireland, allowing six to a family, was in that year calculated by one of the commissioners, who of course had perfect information, at 4,100,000, and it was allowed to be under the truth, as well because some houses must necessarily have been omitted, as that the proportion of six to a family was less than what was usually found in Ireland, where the people are naturally prolific. I speak here from memory, but the calculation is to be found in the transactions of the Royal Academy of Ireland, which may perhaps be in the National Library, and it will justify my assertion that the people of Ireland amount to 4,500,000.'

[3] In *Life*, ii, 202, the following sentence reads: 'Her actual revenues, amounting at present to about £2,000,000 per annum, making 48,000,000 livres'.

great sum but which, as depending on circumstances, cannot be reduced to calculation. *Fifth.* The property of Englishmen in Ireland, whether vested in land, mortgages on land, trade, manufactures, bonds, bills, book debts or otherwise, to be confiscated and applied to the discharge of the obligations incurred in the acquisition of the independence of Ireland. I cannot say what the amount of this might be, but I know from circumstances it must be immense.[1] I leave it to the judgement of the French Government to determine what unspeakable confusion a measure of this kind would be likely to produce in England and what a staggering blow the separation of Ireland would be to her power even in a commercial point of view, not to speak of the military or, which is of far more importance, the naval part of the question.[2]

I have now done.[3] I humbly submit that England is the implacable, inveterate, irreconcilable enemy of the republic, which never can be in perfect security while that nation retains the dominion of the sea; that in consequence every possible effort should be made to humble her pride and reduce her power; that it is in Ireland, *and in Ireland only*, that she is vulnerable—a fact of the truth of which the French Government cannot be too strongly impressed; that by establishing a free republic in Ireland they attach to France a grateful ally whose cordial assistance, in peace and in war, she might command and who, from situation and produce, could most essentially serve her; that at the same time they cut off from England her most firm support, in losing which she is laid under insuperable difficulties in recruiting her army and especially in equipping, victualling and manning her navy, which unless for the resources she draws from Ireland she would be absolutely unable to do; that by these means and, suffer me to add, *by these means only*, her arrogance can be effectually humbled and her enormous and increasing power at sea reduced within due bounds, an object essential not only to France but to all Europe; that it is at least possible that by the measures mentioned not only her future resources as to her navy may be intercepted and cut off at the fountain head, but that a part of her fleet may be transferred to the Republic of Ireland; that the Irish people are prepared and united, and want nothing but the means to begin; that, not to speak of policy or the pleasure of revenge, in humbling to the dust[4] a haughty and implacable rival, it is in itself a great and splendid act of justice[5] worthy of the Republic to rescue a whole people[6] from a slavery

[1] *Life*, ii, 202, omits 'I know from circumstances'. It adds: 'One English nobleman, Earl Mansfield, formerly Ambassador at Paris under the name of Lord Stormont and an implacable enemy of France, has £300,000 sterling, or 7,200,000 livres, lent on mortgages in Ireland; another English gentleman, Mr Taylor, has £150,000 sterling, or 3,600,000 livres, lent in like manner.' The Earl Mansfield referred to was David Murray (1727–96), the second earl, British ambassador in Paris, 1772–8 (*D.N.B.*). Taylor has not been identified.

[2] In *Life* this sentence begins: 'I mention these instances to point out to the French Government what unspeakable confusion the measure I propose would be likely to produce in England . . .'; it omits 'to her power'.

[3] In *Life* the following sentence begins: 'I submit to the wisdom of the French Government that England . . .'.

[4] *Life* lacks 'to the dust'.

[5] *Life*, ii, 203, has 'generosity and justice'.

[6] *Life*, ii, 203, has 'whole nation'.

under which they have groaned for more than[1] six hundred years; that it is for the glory of France, after emancipating Holland and receiving Belgium into her bosom, to establish one more free republic in Europe; that it is for her interest to cut off, *as she now may do*, one half of the resources of England and lay her under extreme difficulties in the employment of those which remain. For all these reasons, in the name of justice, of humanity, of liberty, of my own country, of France,[2] I supplicate the French Government[3] to take into their consideration the state of Ireland; and by granting her the powerful aid and protection of the Republic to enable her at once to demonstrate her gratitude,[4] to vindicate her liberty, to humble her tyrant and to assume that independant station among the nations of the earth for which her soil, her productions and her position, her population and her spirit, have designed her.

## Diary, 29 February–11 March 1796

T.C.D., Tone papers, MS 2048, ff 18r–24v; *Life*, ii, 30–46.

### 29 Feb. 1796

Finished my second memorial[5] and delivered it to Madgett for translation.[6] Madgett has the slowness of age and at present of the gout about him. Judge, oh ye gods! how that suits with my impatience. Well, the Minister gave me directions to expedite him, so, please God, I will levee him at least once a day. We have not a minute to spare for this reason, that in a little time the Channel Fleet[7] will probably be at sea, and also the camps[8] may be formed in Ireland and of course the Gov[ernmen]t there would have the advantage of having their force ready concentered and prepared to act instantly, and perhaps they might happen to take the wrong side, which would be very bad. Mem. *To insense Carnot upon this head!* I must allow two or three days for translation, and two or three more for reflection on the subject of my memorials, before I go again to the Luxembourg. It is very singular!—in cool blood I can hardly frame a single sentence in French, and both with Carnot and De La Croix, I run on without the least difficulty. I screw my mind up, and I do not know how it [is], but expressions flow

[1] *Life* lacks 'more than'. [2] *Life*, ii, 204, has 'and of France herself'.

[3] *Life*, ii, 204, has 'Directory' instead of 'French Government'.

[4] *Life* lacks 'to demonstrate her gratitude'. [5] Above, pp 88–97.

[6] Madgett, writing to the minister of foreign affairs, Delacroix, on 2 Mar. 1796, states: 'Wolf Tone vient de me remettre un second mémoire dont je sais m'occuper. Le premier est trop long pour que vous ayez le tems de lire en entier. Vous trouverez en marge le mot récapitulation aux articles qu'il suffit de lire pour être au fait de tout le mémoire.' (Archives des Affaires Étrangères, Corresp. Politique Angleterre, cote 589, ff 182–2v).

[7] The British Channel fleet.

[8] The forces in Ireland would probably be concentrated in camps at strategic points in the summer.

upon me. I dare say I give them abundance of '*bad language*' but no matter for that. They understand me, and that is the main point. I have now six days on my hands and nothing to do. Huzza! Dine every day at Beauvilliers'[1] for about half a crown, including a bottle of choice Burgundy, which I finish regularly. Beauvilliers has a dead bargain[2] of me as to water; I do not think I consume a spoonful in a week. A bottle of Burgundy is too much, and I resolve every morning, regularly, to drink but the half, and every evening, regularly, I break my resolution. I wish I had P.P.[3] to drink the other half and then perhaps I should live more soberly. Oh Lord, oh Lord!—soberly! '*Wanted a miller, &c.*' Yes, we should be a sober pair! 'Patriots!', as Matty says. Well, '*it is the Squire's custom every afternoon, as soon as he is drunk*',[4] to begin thinking of his wife and family. I have, to be sure, sometimes most delightful reveries! If I succeed in my business here and ever return to Ireland (and am not knocked in the head) there will not be on earth so happy a circle as that round my fireside. Well, Huzza! '*I hope to see a battle yet before I die!*'[5] The French have an abominable custom of adulterating their Burgundy with water. '*Mem. Mr Nisby's opinion thereon.*'[6] I cannot but respect the generous indignation which P.P. would feel at such a vile deterioration of that noble liquor and the glorious example he would hold up for their imitation! He would teach them how, and in what quantities, generous Burgundy ought to be drank. I would gladly pay his reckoning today *en numéraire*[7] (which would be no small sum) for the pleasure of his company! Well, ''*tis but in vain &c.*'[8] I think it right for my credit to mention that all these wise reflections are written *before dinner*. So now I will go to Beauvilliers'. (Sings) '*When generous wine &c.*'.

## 1 Mar. 1796

This day I got an English newspaper from Madget dated the 2d of last month in which there is a paragraph alluding to the death of the 'late unfortunate Major Sweetman' in a duel.[9] I do not think I ever received such a shock in my life! Good God, if it should be my friend! The only chance I have is that there may be

[1] Antoine Beauvilliers (1754–1817) opened in the Palais Royal before the revolution a restaurant which became celebrated. He had to close in 1793 and when he reopened after the revolution he was not so successful. In 1814 he published *L'Art du cuisinier*. (*La Grande Encyclopédie*).

[2] i.e. an absolute bargain.

[3] Thomas Russell.

[4] 'It was Mr Western's custom every afternoon, as soon as he was drunk, to hear his daughter play on the harpsichord' (Fielding, *Tom Jones* (1749), bk IV, ch. 5).

[5] Source of quotation not identified.

[6] *Spectator*, no. 317 (4 Mar. 1712).

[7] In legal tender.

[8] See above, p. 43, n. 6.

[9] Edward Sweetman quarrelled at the opera with Brereton Watson, a captain in the 115th foot. One account of their quarrel states it arose because one trod on the other's toe. According however to a letter in the *Oracle*, Major Sweetman was behind a lady whose head-dress of fashionable feathers impeded his view. He stood up and incommoded her and, his apology being regarded as insufficient, Watson told him he was not a gentleman. Sweetman was killed in the duel at Cobham which followed and Watson badly wounded. At the next assizes Watson was tried for murder and acquitted. (*St James' Chronicle*, 5–7 Jan. 1796; *Oracle*, 8, 12 Jan. 1796; *True Briton*, 25 Mar. 1796; *New Annual Register*, 1796, occurrences, p. 16).

another person of that name, but I fear the worst. I had the sincerest and most affectionate regard for him; a better nor a braver heart blood never warmed. I have passed some of the pleasantest hours of my life in his society. If he be gone, my loss is unspeakable; but his country will have a much severer one. He was a sincere Irishman, and if ever an exertion was to be made for our emancipation he would have been in the very foremost rank. I had counted upon his military talents and had amused myself often in making him a general. Poor fellow! If he be gone there is a chasm in my short list of friends that I will not find it easy to fill. After all, it may be another, but I fear, I fear. I cannot bear to think of it.

## 6 Mar. 1796

I have not had spirits since the news of poor Sweetman's death to go on with my memorandums. As it happens I have had no serious business, and I am glad of it, for my mind has been a good deal engaged on that account. It seems the quarrel arose about treading on a lady's gown coming out of the Opera. A worthy cause for two brave men to fight about! They fought at four yards distance, which was Sweetman's choice; they were both desperately wounded, but Cap[tai]n Watson[1] (an Irishman also) is likely to recover. My poor friend is gone. When he received the shot, which went thro' his body, he cried out to Watson, 'Are you wounded?'. 'Yes', replied the other, 'I believe mortally.' 'And so am I', replied Sweetman. He fell instantly. I certainly did not think I could have been so much affected on his account as I have been. Independant of my personal regard for him, I reckoned much on his assistance in case of the French Government affording us any aid. His courage, his eloquence, his popular talents, his sincere affection for his country, would have made him eminently serviceable. All that is now lost. We must supply his place as we can. I will write no more about him, but I shall ever remember him with the most sincere regret.[2]

Madgett has not yet finished the translation.[3] Hell, Hell? However he tells me he has written to the Minister on the subject of Beurnonville's[4] being appointed

[1] Probably Brereton Watson, commissioned ensign in the 95th foot, Apr. 1793; 2nd lieut., 23rd foot, 1797; lieut., 20th foot, 1799; retired as capt., 56th foot, 1810; he was probably a son of John Watson of Brook Watson, Co. Tipperary, who in 1765 married Mary Brereton of Clonanihy, Co. Tipperary, and was perhaps the Thomas Brereton Watson who by 1810 had acquired Clonanihy (*Army list*; *Burke's landed gentry of Ireland* (1912), p. 70; see also above, p. 98, n. 9).

[2] Edward Sweetman had been a member of the Dublin Society of United Irishmen and a member of the Catholic Committee; he had been in the French army before the revolution and in the early 1790s a captain in the British army; he had been a catholic but conformed to the established church (see above, vol. I, esp. pp 291, 314, 401–3).

[3] But see above, p. 88, headnote 3.

[4] Pierre de Riel Beurnonville (1752–1821), army officer before the revolution; general, 1792; served with distinction at Valmy; handed over by Dumouriez to the Austrians, 1793; released, 1795; commanded army of Sambre-et-Meuse, 1796–7; commanded army of the North, 1797; then commanded troops in Batavia (*Dict. biog. franç.*).

to the command in case the expedition takes place. I have been reading the report of Camus,[1] and it has satisfied me that I could not have wished for a general fitter for the station. I hope in God[2] we may get him. One thing I see—Madgett must appear to do everything himself. He pleases himself with the idea that it was *he* who thought of Beurnonville. A la bonheur![3] I am sure, at present, I care little who has the credit of proposing any measure, provided the business be done; but the truth and fact is that it was I who mentioned him. Madgett has lost two or three days in hunting for maps of Ireland. Certainly maps are indispensable but not in this stage of the business. He had been much better employed in translating. His slowness provokes me excessively, but I keep it all to myself. This day however he promises me he will have finished and given in my last memorial to the Minister. If he does, I will see De la Croix the day after tomorrow, and Carnot, if possible the day after that. In the meantime I am idle.

I have been at the Museum,[4] where there is, I suppose, the first collection of paintings in the world. All France and Flanders have been ransacked to furnish it. It is a school where the artists are permitted to go and copy the best works of the best masters. The day I called it was not open to the public, but when the porter perceived I was a foreigner he admitted me directly. It would not be so in England. I like the works of Guido[5] the best; there are some portraits incomparably executed by Vandyck, Rubens, Rembrandt and Raphael; but the *Magdalen* of Le Brun[6] is, in my mind, worth the whole collection. I never saw anything in the way of painting which came near it. I am no artist, but it requires no previous instruction to be struck with the numberless beauties of this most enchanting piece. It is a production of consummate genius. I have likewise been at the Hotel des Invalides, where I had the pleasure to see the veterans at their dinner. They are very well accom[m]odated, and it was a spectacle which interested me very much. It put me in mind of the Royal Hospital,[7] and my old friend Captain Russell,[8] and that brought a thousand other ideas into my mind. Well, I hope I shall get back to Ireland yet! *Utinam!*[9]

[1] Armand Gaston Camus (1740–1804), lawyer and expert on canon law; supported the revolution; taken prisoner by Dumouriez when he deserted to the Austrians; released in 1795 and placed in charge of the republic's archives (*Dict. biog. franç.*).

[2] *Life* omits 'in God'.

[3] Corrected in *Life*, ii, 39, to 'A la bonne heure', meaning 'Well done!'.

[4] The museum (picture gallery) of the Louvre was opened in August 1793. The exhibits included pictures from the royal collection and from suppressed churches. After Belgium was overrun in 1794, pictures taken from there were added. (C. H. M. Gould, *Trophy of conquest* (London, 1965), pp 1–40).

[5] Guido Reni (1575–1642), 'one of the most admired artists of the period of incipient decadence in Italy' (*Encyclopaedia Britannica* (11th ed., 29 vols, Cambridge, 1910–11), xii, 688).

[6] Charles Le Brun (1619–90). 'The repentant Magdalen', which Tone so admired (see also Diary for 9, 10 Mar. 1796, below, p. 103), is reproduced in MacDermot, *Tone*, facing p. 196.

[7] The Royal Hospital, Kilmainham, near Dublin.

[8] John Russell, who seems to have been a captain of invalids at the Royal Hospital, Kilmainham. He was the father of Thomas Russell.

[9] 'Would that!'

## 7 Mar. 1796

Spent this day with Du Petit Thouars,[1] an ex-lieutenant of the Marine who came over with me in the *Jersey*, and with Roussillon,[2] an ex-lieu[tenan]t also. They are both of the *ci-devant noblesse*. Du Petit Thouars is a great original; he has a good deal of talent, and still more humour, and is the most complete practical philosopher I ever saw; nothing can ruffle him; but it is his temperament. Roussillon is a young man of very elegant manners, and adversity I am sure has improved him. It is a pity they should be aristocrats, yet I can hardly be angry with them. Aristocracy has been most terribly humbled in France and the reverse of fortune is too much for them. It is not only their own downfall but the exaltation of others, whom they were accustomed to despise, which mortifies them; and in fact, when I come to analyse their complaints there is so much fanciful grievance mixed with severe actual suffering that it abates a good deal of the compassion I should otherwise feel for them; and I must add that much of what they regret they are deprived of most meritoriously, and many of the pleasures they have lost were the pleasures of the most depraved luxury, splendid indeed but most abominably vicious. It is not fair however to judge too hardly of them, now they are down, but I confess I should be most sincerely sorry to be a witness of their resurrection; there is however no great danger of that event taking place, and they seem to be sufficiently sensible of that. They had quit the service some time back, I dare say in great disdain, and now they are suing, unsuccessfully, to be re-admitted. I cannot blame the Republic for being doubtful of the ancient marine since the affair of Toulon.[3] Apropos! of Toulon. Roussillon tells me that Trogoff,[4] the admiral who betrayed the French fleet and delivered it into the hands of Lord Hood,[5] died in an hospital at Leghorn, where the English generously paid *one shilling* a day for his maintenance! The scoundrel! it was just one shilling too much. And Dumouriez, an exile on the face of the Earth, ordered to quit England in six hours after his arrival, expelled from Brabant by the Emperor whom he had served, or endeavoured to serve, by his treachery![6] If men had common sense, not to say common honesty, they would not be traitors,[7] with such examples before their eyes. But I am preaching about aristocracy and God knows what! To return, I pity sincerely my two *ci-devant* ex-lieutenants, for

[1] Aristide Dupetit-Thouars (1760–98) served in the war of American independence and later commanded an expedition to search for La Peyrouse. The Directory gave him the command of the *Tonnant*, 80. He was killed at Aboukir. (*Biographie nouvelle des contemporains*; *Dict. biog. franç.*).

[2] Not identified.

[3] In Aug. 1793, after some hesitation, Trogoff, the French naval commander at Toulon, sided with the royalists and handed the port of Toulon over to the British fleet.

[4] Jean Honoré, comte de Trogoff de Kerlessy (1751–94), French admiral. He died on board ship off Porto Ferrago. (Six, *Dict. des généraux & amiraux*).

[5] Samuel Hood, 1st Baron Hood (1724–1816), British admiral; commander-in-chief in the Mediterranean, 1793–4 (*D.N.B.*).

[6] Dumouriez, victor at Valmy and Jemappes, and conqueror of the Austrian Netherlands, was defeated at Neerwinden on 18 Mar. 1793 and defected to the Austrians; he died in England (*Dict. biog. franç.*; see above, vol. I, p. 301).

[7] *Life*, ii, 40, adds 'to their country'.

'*God knows I have had afflictions and trouples enough upon my own pack, and as for a gentleman in distress, I lofe him as I lofe my own powels*'.[1]

We spent the day in seeing sights, viz. the Pantheon,[2] which will be most superb when it is finished but very far inferior to St Paul's, either in size or magnificence; we descended into the Catacombs where were the cenotaphs of Voltaire[3], Rousseau[4] and, what interested me much more, of Dampierre,[5] who was killed at Famars. Certainly nothing can be imagined more likely to create a great spirit in a nation than a repository of this kind, sacred to everything that is sublime and illustrious and patriotic. The French however have a little overshot the mark, for they have had occasion already to displace two, at least, of their Mighty Dead; I mean Marat, whom I believe to have been a sincere enthusiast incapable of feeling or remorse, and Mirabeau, whom I look upon to have been a most consummate scoundrel.[6] If we have a republic in Ireland, we must build a Pantheon, but we must not, like the French, be in too great a hurry to people it. We have already a few to begin with: Roger O'Moore[7], Molyneux, Swift, Lucas,[8] all good Irishmen. Mounted to the top of the Pantheon, from whence we could see all Paris, as in a ground plan, together with the country for several leagues round. It was the most singular spectacle I had ever seen.[9] Went from thence to the Botanic Garden,[10] where there was not much vegetation to be seen, there being a foot deep of snow on the ground; walked however thro' the green houses, where there is a vast collection of curious exotics. I felt '*my ancient propensities begin to revive*', for I love botany, tho' I do not understand it; it reminded me of my walks round Chateau Boue[11] with my dearest love and our little babies when I used to be gathering my *vetches*. Well, I hope I shall be there yet before I die. Crossed the Seine and saw the Place Royal[e],[12] formerly the principal square of Paris and built by Richelieu;[13] his hotel

Lucas

[1] Tobias Smollett, *Roderick Random* (1748), ch. 25.

[2] The replacement for the abbey church of Sainte-Geneviève, begun in 1756, had not been consecrated when in 1791 the national assembly decreed that it should be the sepulcre of citizens who had deserved well of the country (Amédée Boinet, *Les églises parisiennes* (Paris, 1964), iii, 273–317).

[3] François Marie Arouet, known by his pseudonym of Voltaire (1694–1778).

[4] Jean Jacques Rousseau (1712–78), moralist.

[5] Auguste Marie Henri Picot, marquis de Dampierre (1756–93), appointed general of division, 1793, was killed in action defending the camp at Famars near Valenciennes. The Convention decreed that he should be buried in the Pantheon. (Six, *Dict. des généraux & amiraux*).

[6] Mirabeau (d. 1791) was buried in the church of Sainte-Geneviève which was converted into the Pantheon. But after it was discovered he had been in correspondence with the royal court his ashes were removed and replaced by those of Jean Paul Marat (d. 1794), which in turn were removed in 1795. For Mirabeau and Marat, see above, vol. I, p. 120, n. 3, and p. 324, n. 3.

[7] Rory O'More (1620–52), Confederate commander (*D.N.B.*).

[8] Charles Lucas (1713–71), known as 'the Wilkes of Ireland' (*D.N.B.*).

[9] Some 200 metres to the south-south-east of the Pantheon lay the Collège des Irlandais, which however Tone nowhere mentions.

[10] The Jardin des Plantes, founded during the reign of Louis XIII, was protected during the revolution by Bernardin de Saint-Pierre (Gustave Pessard, *Nouveau dictionnaire historique de Paris* (Paris, 1904), pp 760–62).

[11] Note by William Tone: 'My father's cottage in County Kildare'.

[12] The square now known as the Place des Vosges; it was built, 1605–12.

[13] Armand Jean du Plessis, cardinal de Richelieu (1585–1642), principal minister of Louis XIII, 1624–42; he built in fact the Palais Cardinal, now known as the Palais Royal.

is in one side of the quadrangle. It is now a park of artillery for the Republic and filled with cannon. *Saw the spot where the Bastille once stood*, and where there is now a statue of Liberty! Traversed that great lyceum of French politics, the Fauxbourg St Antoine;[1] arrived at the Temple,[2] where Louis 16th was imprisoned, from whence Marie Antoinette was led to execution, and where Louis 17th (if I may so call him)[3] died. Nothing can be imagined more gloomy than the appearance of this prison. It made me melancholy to look at it.

## 8 Mar. 1796

Went to Madgett in consequence of a report which I saw in the papers relative to a general peace. He assures me there is nothing in it. A peace would ruin all. He tells me also that he has finished and delivered (yesterday) my second memorial[4] to the Minister, who had read the first with great attention and was extremely edified thereby, as may be well imagined. Madgett assures me that De la Croix assures him that the Executive Directory are determined on the measure, that is to say on the principle of it. All that is very good, but please God I will have it from the Minister's own mouth, after which I will indulge myself with a short interview with Carnot. I have not seen him since Feb[ruar]y 24th, that is to say a fortnight this day; but that has not been my fault, and the time has been employed in writing and copying and translating my memorials. The day after tomorrow I will see the Minister, and the day after I will go again to the Luxembourg. Madgett tells me Beurnonville is named to the army in Holland;[5] that is bad. Nevertheless, from the idea I have formed of his character, I should hope that if he was properly *insensed* on the subject of Irish affairs, he would prefer that command, supposing the expedition to be once undertaken. There would be glory; and if we succeeded, which I cannot for a moment doubt, the Irish are a generous people, even to a fault, and would reward his services most liberally. Desired Madgett, if he had an opportunity and could do it with security as to secresy, to explain all this to Beurnonville. Dined at the Restaurateur's[6] with Roussillon, whom I like very much. In the evening the Théâtre Italien. Saw Lodoïska,[7] &c., &c.

## 9, 10 Mar. 1796

Blank! Strolling about. The Museum[8] again, and the inimitable Magdalen of Le Brun. Spent near an hour looking at it.

[1] The Faubourg St Antoine, in north-east Paris, an area with many small workshops, was 'the traditional focal point of popular agitation' (George Rudé, *The crowd in the French revolution* (Oxford, 1959), p. 116).

[2] A group of buildings which had belonged to the Knights Templar and which from the 14th century had been used as a prison. From 13 Aug. 1792 the royal family was imprisoned there.

[3] Louis Charles (1785–95), eldest surviving son of Louis XVI.

[4] Above, pp 88–97. Tone means that Madgett has finished translating the second memorial.

[5] *Life*, ii, 42, has: 'Beurnonville is appointed to the command of the army in Holland'.

[6] Probably Beauvilliers' (see above, p. 98).

[7] Louvet's wife, known as Lodoïska (see above, p. 60, n. 9).

[8] Musée du Louvre. For Tone's previous visit, see Diary for 6 Mar. (above, p. 100).

## 11 Mar. 1796

Went to the Minister, De la Croix, and had a long conversation. He began by saying he had read my two memorials[1] carefully, and that I seemed to insist upon a considerable force as necessary to the success of the measure; that, as to that, there were considerable difficulties to be surmounted, arising from the superiority of the English fleet. That, as to 20,000 men, they could not possibly be transported, unless the French were masters of the Channel, in which case they could as easily send 40,000, or 60,000, and march at once to London. ☞ In this De la Croix is much mistaken. It would be in my mind just as impossible for France to conquer England as for England to conquer France. He does not know what [it] is to carry on a war in a country where every man's hand is against you; and yet his own country might have given him a lesson. However, it was not my business to contest the point with him, so I let him go on.[2] That as to 20,000 men it was out of the question; as to 5,000 there would be even there great difficulties; they would require, for example, 20 ships to convey them; it would not be easy to equip 20 sail in a French post without the English having some notice, and in that case they would instantly block up the port with a force double of any that could be sent against them. To this I answered that I was but too sensible of the difficulty he mentioned; that, however, all great enterprises were attended with great difficulties, and I besought him to consider the magnitude of the object; that as to 5,000, when I mentioned that number it was not that I thought it necessary for the people at large, but that it was for the men of some property, whose assistance was so essential in framing a government in Ireland without loss of time and who might be deterred from coming forward at first if they saw but an inconsiderable force to support them; that I begged leave to refer to my second memorial, where he would find my reasons on this subject detailed at length; that I had written those memorials under a strong sense of duty, not with a view either to flatter or mislead him, or to say what might be agreeable to the French Government, but what I thought essential for them to know, and that as to the truth of the facts contained in them I was willing to stake my head on their accuracy. He answered he had no doubt as to that; that he saw as well as I the convenience of an immediate government, but was it not feasible on a smaller scale than I had mentioned? For example, if they gave us a general of established reputation, an État-Major, 30 pieces of artillery, with cannoniers, &c., and 20,000 stand of arms, would not the people join them, and if so, might we not call the clubs that I had mentioned in my memorials (meaning the Catholic Comm[itt]ee and the United Irishmen of Belfast, &c.) and frame of them a provisory government until the national convention could be organised? I answered that as to the people joining them, I never had the least doubt; that my only fear was lest the men who composed the clubs of which he spoke might be at first backward from a doubt of the sufficiency of the force; that I hoped they would act with spirit and

[1] Above, pp 61–70, 88–97.

[2] In the MS the preceding four sentences are underlined.

as became them, but that I could not venture to commit my credit with him on any fact of whose certainty I was not positively ascertained. 'Well then', replied he, 'supposing your Patriots should not act at first with spirit; you say you are sure of the people; in that case you must only chuse delegates from the army and let them act provisorily until you have acquired such a consistence as will give courage to the men of whom you make mention.' I answered that by that means we might undoubtedly act with success; that a sort of military government was not what I should prefer to commence with if I saw any other; but that the necessity of the case must justify us in adopting so strong a measure in the first instance.

☞ N.B. In this I lied a little, for my wishes are in favor of a very strong or, in other words, a military government in the outset, and if I had any share or influence in such government, I think I would not abuse it; but I see the handle it might give to demagogues, if we had any such among us. It is unnecessary here to write an essay on the subject, but the result of my meditations is that the advantages, *all circumstances considered*, outweigh the inconveniencies and the hazard, and I, for one, am ready to take my share of the danger and the responsibility. I was consequently glad when De la Croix proposed the measure.[1] I added that the means which he then mentioned, undoubtedly weakened my argument as to the necessity of numbers considerably. He then said that from Madgett's representations he had been induced to think that men were not at all wanting. I answered, that was very compatible with my theory, for that certainly, if there were any idea of resistance, 5,000 might be said to be no force at all for conquest. I then shifted the discourse by saying that as to the embarkation, on whatever scale, it might be worth consideration whether it could not be best effectuated from Holland; that their harbours were, I believed, less closely watched than the French; and that at any rate England had no port for ships of war to the northward of Portsmouth, so that even if she had a fleet off the coasts of Holland, it must return occasionally to refit, and during one of these intervals the expedition might take place.

He asked me was I sure England had no port to the northward of Portsmouth? I said certainly. Not in Scotland? I referred him to the map. (I was a little surprised that he did not know this.) This brought on the old subject of debauching the Irish seamen in the British navy, which seems a favorite scheme of De la Croix's, and is, in my mind, *flat nonsense*. He questioned me as before, whether by preparing a few of them, and suffering them to escape, they might not rouse the patriotism of the Irish seamen, and cause a powerful revulsion in the navy of England. I answered, as I had done already, that the measure was undoubtedly good if properly followed up; at the same time that there was great hazard of alarming the British Government; that he would find my plan on the subject in my second memorial, where he would see that an Irish gov[ernmen]t was, in my mind, an indispensable requisite; that I had not built on the patriotism of the Irish seamen, but on their passions and their interest; that we could offer them the whole English commerce as a bribe, while England had nothing to oppose in

[1] In the MS the preceding part of this paragraph is underlined.

return but the mere force of discipline and I pressed this as strongly on the Minister as my execrable French would permit. He then mentioned that it would be necessary to send proper persons into Ireland to give notice to the people there of what was intended. I answered one person was sufficient. He asked me did I know one Duckett (the fellow who pulled out the English newspaper to decoy me)? I answered I knew nothing at all about him.

He then asked me did I know one Simon[1], a priest. I answered I had some recollection of one Fitzsimon,[2] a priest in Ireland, but that I was not personally acquainted with him. I also added that I had a strong objection to letting priests into the business at all; that I had the very worst opinion of them, and that in Ireland especially they were very bigotted and very ignorant, slaves to Rome and of course enemies to the French Revolution;[3] that if it were possible to find a military man, he would be the properest person to send into Ireland, the more so as it would encourage those to whom he might address himself, by shewing them that the French Gov[ernmen]t were serious in their intentions. He then said he would look out for such a person. I took this occasion to observe that there was not an hour to lose; that the season was approaching fast when the British Channel fleet would be at sea, and the various encampments formed in Ireland, which generally took place about the middle of May or beginning of June. He said the necessary preparations on the smallest scale could not be ready sooner than a month. I replied that *one* month would be time enough, but I added again that there was not a minute to lose. I then took my leave, having been closeted near an hour and a half.

On the whole, I do not much glory in this day's conversation. If I have not lost confidence, I certainly have not gained any. I see the Minister is rooted in his narrow scheme, and I am sorry for it. Perhaps imperious circumstances will not permit him to be otherwise, but if the French Gov[ernmen]t have the power effectually to assist us, and do not do it, they are miserable politicians. It is now one hundred and three years since Louis 14th neglected a similar opportunity of separating Ireland from England,[4] and France has had reason to lament it ever since. He too went upon the short-sighted policy of merely embar[r]assing England, and leaving Ireland to shift as she might. I hope the Republic will act on nobler motives and with more extended views. At all events I have done my duty in submitting the truth to them, and I shall continue so to do, and to press it upon them in all possible modes that I can compass. '*If they will give us 5,000 men, so!*

[1] *Recte* Fitzsimons. Dominick Fitzsimons was aged about 36 and had been guardian of the Irish Capuchin monastery at Bar-sur-Aube; he had been imprisoned during the Terror but later recommended by Prieur de la Marne as an excellent patriot (Madgett to General Clarke, 12 Fructidor an IV (29 Aug. 1796), Archives Nationales, Paris, AF III 186 B; Liam Swords, *The green cockade: the Irish in the French revolution, 1789–1815* (Dublin, 1989), pp 91, 100).

[2] See Diary for 18 July 1792 (above, vol. I, p. 224). He was not the same person.

[3] *Life* omits 'I had the very worst opinion of them, and that in Ireland especially they were very bigotted and very ignorant, slaves to Rome and of course enemies to the French Revolution' and substitutes 'most of them were enemies to the French Revolution'.

[4] During Williamite wars in Ireland (1689–91), the French gave military support to James II, who naturally was not in favour of separating the crowns of Ireland and England.

*if not, let the sheriff enter, if I become not the gallows as well as another, a plague of my bringing up.*'[1]

Seriously, I would attempt it with *one hundred men*. My life is of little consequence and I should hope not to lose it neither. '*Please God, the dogs shall not have my poor blood to lick*.'[2] In that case, as I have pleasantly said already, if our lever be short we must apply the greater power. Requisition, requisition! Our independence must be had at all hazards. If the men of property will not support us, they must fall; we can support ourselves by the aid of that numerous and respectable class of the community, *the men of no property*.

## Diary, 12–22 March 1796

T.C.D., Tone papers, MS 2049, ff $1^r$–$18^v$; *Life*, ii, 46–63.

Number 4
From March 12th to the 27th inclusive[3]
*Nil desperandum*
Paris
1796

'Mes premières vues iront toujours au grand, et je ne reviens au médiocre que lorsque je suis convaincu que le grand est impossible.'

Le Maréchal de Villars,[4] *Memoirs*, Vol. 2, p. 393.[5]

Paris
No. 4
1796[6]

### 12 Mar. 1796

Called on Madgett. He tells me that the business is going forward, but that the French Government is in the greatest difficulty for want of money; that the Executive Directory was within these few days on the point of resigning; and that

[1] Cf. *1 Henry IV*, II, v: 'If you will deny the sheriff, so! If not, let him enter. If I become not a cart as well as another man, a plague on my bringing up.' In this scene, however, there is no allusion to 5,000 men.

[2] Tobias Smollett, *Humphry Clinker* (1771), ii.

[3] The entries in the Diary for 23–7 Mar. are given as a separate document (below, pp 124–9).

[4] Claude Louis Hector, duc de Villars (1653–1734).

[5] *Vie du maréchal duc de Villars . . . écrite par lui-même* (4 vols, Paris, 1784), ii, 393.

[6] The preceding headings and verse, which were obviously written later than 12 Mar., are omitted from *Life*.

they had signified to the Legislature that they would do so if they were not properly supported. I should be sincerely sorry if they were to do so, as well for the sake of France as of Ireland, for I believe they are both able and honest. Madgett told me further that he expected we were on the eve of some considerable change, not of principles but of men; that the party who wanted to come in were throwing difficulties in the way of the present administration in order to force them to resign; that if the change took place, it would not extend to the Directory but to the Ministers; that with regard to the affairs of Ireland, they would be bettered, rather than injured, by the alteration; that it was the Jacobin party who expected to come in, not the Terrorists but the true original Jacobins who had made[1] the Revolution; that if they were in power he was sure they would give us 10,000; that, however, as to Beurnonville, he was obnoxious to them and, of course, would not be appointed to the command—that is bad.[2] If there is to be a change I confess I should be glad the Jacobins were to come again into play, for I have always had a leaning to that party and[3] I think a little more energy just now would do the French Gov[ernmen]t no harm. On the whole I am not much delighted with my[4] present prospects.

## 13 Mar. 1796

Went as usual to the Opera. *Serment de la Liberté*. The scene represented the Champ de Mars on the day of the confederation.[5] As usual the spectacle all military. In the procession was a band of young men in regimentals but without arms. At a particular verse of the Hymn, which was chanted before the altar of liberty,[6] they approached the grenadiers, who were under arms, and received from them their firelocks, which they shouldered, and took their places in the line. Several evolutions, and the manual exercise was then performed by the whole body, for as I have already remarked, these are the ballets of the French nation at present. At the conclusion a band of beautiful young women, equal in number to the young men, entered carrying drawn sabres in their hands, and ranged themselves on one side of the stage, the young men being drawn up in line on the other. Each of the youths advanced in his turn to the centre of the stage, where he was met by his mistress, who presented him with his sabre with one hand, and with the other pointed to the altar of liberty; the youth kissed the hilt of his sabre and returned it to the scabbard; they then fell back into their places and were succeeded by the next pair, until they had all received their arms and saluted their mistresses; the whole then joined in a grand chorus, and the

[1] *Life*, ii, 46, has 'begun' instead of 'made'. [2] *Life* omits 'that is bad'.

[3] *Life* omits 'I have always had a leaning to that party and'.

[4] *Life*, ii, 47, has 'our' instead of 'my'.

[5] On 14 July 1790 delegates of the National Guard from all over France assembled at the Champ-de-Mars to commemorate the fall of the Bastille.

[6] Probably the 'Marseillaise', since 1795 'l'hymne national français'.

soldiery filed off, as for the Frontiers, the women being placed on an eminence to view them as they passed. I do not know what Mr Burke[1] may think, but I humbly conceive, from the effect all this had on the audience, that the age of chivalry is not gone in France.[2] I can imagine nothing more suited to strike the imagination of a young Frenchman than such a spectacle as this, and indeed, tho' I am no Frenchman, not at present over and above young, it affected me extremely. I am sure nothing on Earth has such an influence on me as my wife's opinion; every action of my life has a reference more or less to that, and in the very business I am now engaged in, if I succeed, I look for and I shall find the reward dearest to my heart in her commendation. It is inconceivable (I lie, I lie; it is not at all inconceivable) the effect that the admiration or contempt of a woman has on the spirit of a man. Hector, when he is balancing in his mind whether he shall stand or fly before Achilles, is determined by the consideration of what the Trojan ladies will say of him. '*Troy's proud dames, whose garments sweep the ground*.'[3] From which I infer that human nature is pretty much now what it was 3,000 years ago, and that Homer[4] knew it well. So did Shakespeare,[5] and so did Fielding,[6] who has hit off the same point admirably, when Lady Bellaston is working upon Lord Fellamore.[7] To return. I owe so much to my wife for her incomparable behaviour on ten thousand different occasions that I feel myself bound irresistibly to make every effort and at every hazard, and with every personal sacrifice,[8] to place her and our dear little babies in a situation in some degree worthy of her merit, and suitable to my sense of it. I am not without ambition, nor without vanity, God knows; I love fame and I suppose I should like power, but I declare here most solemnly that I prefer my wife's commendation to that of the whole world. Well, if I succeed here, I shall stand on high ground, and I must be allowed to say I shall deserve it, and then she will be proud of me, as I am of her; and with that sentiment I conclude this day's journal.

## 14 Mar. 1796

Went this day to the Luxembourg. I have the luck of going on the days that Carnot gives audience and of course is most occupied. I waited however till the last, when only one person remained besides myself. Carnot then called me over and said 'you are an Irishman?'. I answered I was. 'Then', said he, 'here is almost a countryman of yours, who speaks English perfectly. He has the confidence of

[1] Edmund Burke (1729–97), M.P., orator and political writer (*D.N.B.*).

[2] 'But the age of chivalry has gone. That of sophisters, economists and calculators has succeeded.' (Edmund Burke, *Reflections on the revolution in France* (London, 1790)).

[3] Alexander Pope, *The Iliad of Homer* (1760), bk VI, line 563.

[4] Homer (8th century B.C.?), author of *Iliad* and *Odyssey*.

[5] William Shakespeare (1564–1616), dramatist (*D.N.B.*).

[6] Henry Fielding (1707–54), novelist (*D.N.B.*).

[7] In Fielding's *Tom Jones* (1749).

[8] The words 'to make every effort and at every hazard, and with every personal sacrifice' are omitted from *Life*.

Government. Go with him and explain yourself without reserve.' I did not much like this referring me over; however, there was no remedy, so I made my bow, and followed my new lover[1] to his hotel. He told me on the way that he was Gen[era]l Clark,[2] that his father[3] was an Irishman, that he had himself been in Ireland and had many relations in that country. He added (God forgive him if he exaggerated) that all the military arrangements of the Republic passed thro' his hands and in short gave me to understand that he was at the head of the War department. By this time we arrived at the hotel where he kept his bureau, and I observed in passing thro' the office to his cabinet an immense number of boxes labelled '*Army of the North, Army of the Pyrenees, Army of the Rhine, &c., &c.*',[4] so that I was pretty well satisfied that I was in the right track. When we entered the cabinet, I told him in three words who and what I was, and I then proceeded to detail at considerable length all I knew on the state of Ireland, which, as it is substantially contained in my two memorials[5] (to which I referred him), I need not here recapitulate. This took up a considerable time, I suppose an hour and a half. He then began to interrogate me on some of the heads in a manner which shewed me he was utterly unacquainted with the present state of affairs in Ireland, and particularly with the great internal changes which have taken place there within the last three or four years, which however is no impeachment of his judgement or talents. There were however other points on which he was radically wrong. For example, he asked me would not the aristocracy of Ireland, some of whom he mentioned, as the Earl of Ormond,[6] concur in the attempt to establish the independance of their country? I answered, most certainly not, and I begged him to remember that if the attempt were made, it would be by the people, and the people only; that he should calculate on all the opposition that the Irish aristocracy could give; that the French revolution, which had given courage to the people, had in the same proportion alarmed the aristocracy, who trembled for their titles

[1] Meaning here 'wellwisher'.

[2] Henri Jacques Guillaume Clarke (1765–1818), born in French Flanders; officer in the Irish brigade before the revolution; protégé of the Orleans family, on whose recommendation he was promoted lieut. col., 1792; took part in campaigns of 1792–3; in retirement, 1793–4; general of division, 1795; head of the 'Cabinet historique et topographique militaire du Directoire Exécutif' (the military section of the secretariat of the Directory), 1795–6; sent to Italy at the end of 1796 to represent the Directory at Bonaparte's headquarters; duc de Feltre, 1809; marshal, 1816. A skilful tactician and a highly competent and upright administrator, brusque with inferiors and very respectful to superiors; intensely interested in his family history. (A. Dry, pseud. Adrien Fleury, vicomte, *Soldats et ambassadeurs sous le Directoire* (2 vols, Paris, 1906), ii, 1–23; M. R. Reinhard, *Le grand Carnot* (Paris, 1952); *Dict. biog. franç.*). Tone's spelling of Clarke's name varies.

[3] Thomas Clarke, born in 1727 at Courtnaboula, near Callan, Co. Kilkenny; son of James Clarke of Aharney, Queen's Co.; he served in the French army and in the 1760s held an important position at Landrecies in French Flanders; married daughter of another French army officer, William Shee, formerly of Camas, Co. Limerick (Genealogical Office, Dublin, MS 96, p. 191, MS 171, pp 433–4).

[4] *Life*, ii, 49, has 'Armée du Nord, Armée des Pyrenées, Armée du Rhin'.

[5] Above, pp 61–70, 88–97.

[6] The Ormond peerage was held in 1796 by Walter Butler (1770–1820), who was M.P. for Co. Kilkenny from 1790 until he succeeded as 18th earl of Ormond on 25 Dec. 1795. He was the eldest son of John Butler (1740–95), M.P. for Kilkenny city from 1783 until he succeeded in 1791 as 17th earl (G.E.C., *Peerage*).

and estates; that this alarm was diligently fomented by the British Minister, who had been able to persuade every man of property that their only security was in supporting him implicitly in every measure calculated to oppose the progress of what were called French principles; that consequently, in any system he might frame in his mind, he should lay down the utmost opposition of the aristocracy as an essential point; at the same time I added that in case of a landing being once effected in Ireland, their opposition would be of very little significance, as their conduct had been such as to give them no claim on the affections of the people; that their own tenants and dependants would, I was satisfied, desert them, and they would become just so many helpless individuals, devoid of power and influence. He then mentioned the Volunteer convention in 1783 seemed to be an example against what I now advanced; the people then had acted thro' their leaders. I answered they certainly had and their leaders had betrayed them; and that very convention was one reason why the people had for ever lost all confidence in what was called *leaders*. He then mentioned the confusion and bloodshed likely to result from a people such as I had described and he knew the Irish to be breaking loose, without proper heads to control and moderate their fury. I answered it was but too true; that I saw as well as he that in the first explosion it was likely that many events would take place which might be in their nature very shocking; that revolutions were not made without much individual suffering; that however in the present instance there would be, supposing the worst, a kind of retributive justice, as no body of men on earth were more tyrannical and oppressive in their nature than those who would be most likely to suffer in the event he alluded to; that I had often in my own mind (and God knows the fact to be so) lamented the necessity of our situation, but that Ireland was so circumstanced that she had no alternative but unconditional submission to England, or a revolution, with a chance of all the concomitant sufferings; and that I was one of those who preferred difficulty and danger, and distress to slavery, especially when I saw clearly there was no other means. 'It is very true', replied he, 'there is no making an omelette without breaking of eggs.' He still however seemed to have a leaning towards the co-operation of our aristocracy, which is *flat nonsense*. He asked me was there no one man of that body that we could make use of, and again mentioned, for example, the Earl of Ormond? I answered, not one; that as to Lord Ormond he was a drunken beast, without a character of any kind but that of a blockhead;[1] that I did believe, speaking my own private opinion as an individual, that perhaps the Duke of Leinster might join the people if the revolution were once begun, because I thought him a good Irishman; but that for this opinion I had merely my own conjecture and that at any rate if the beginning were once made it would be of very little consequence what part any individual might take. I do not know how Fitzgibbon's name happened to come in here, but he asked me would it not be possible to make something of him? Any one who knows Ireland will readily believe that I did not find it easy to make a serious answer to this

[1] It seems likely that Clarke and Tone were thinking of the recently deceased earl of Ormond.

question. Yes, Fitzgibbon would be very likely, from his situation, his principles, his hopes and his fears, his property and the general tenor of his conduct, to begin a revolution in Ireland![1] At last I believe I satisfied Clark on the subject of the support to be expected from our aristocracy. He then asked me what I thought the revolution, if begun, would terminate in? I answered, undoubtedly, as I thought, in a republic allied to France. He then said what security could I give that in twenty years after our independance we would not be found engaged as an ally of England in a war with France. I thought the observation a very foolish one and therefore answered that I could not venture to foretel what the combinations of events for twenty years might produce, but that in the present posture of affairs there were a few things which presented themselves to my view under a more improbable shape. He then came to the influence which he seemed to think the Catholic clergy might have over the minds of the people and the apprehension lest they might warp them against France. I assured him, as the fact is, that it was much more likely that France should turn the people against the clergy than that the clergy should turn the people against France;[2] that within these last few years, that is to say since the French Revolution, there had an astonishing change taken place in Ireland with regard to the influence of the priests. I mentioned to him the conduct of that body, pending the Catholic business in Ireland, and how much and how justly they had lost character on that account; I told him the anecdote of the Pope's Legate in Ireland, who is also Archbishop of Dublin, being superseded in the actual management of his own chapel, of his endeavoring to prevent a political meeting therein, and of his being forced to submit and to attend the meeting himself;[3] but particularly I mentioned the circumstance of the clergy excommunicating all Defenders,[4] and even refusing the Sacraments to some of the poor fellows *in articulo mortis*, which to a Catholic is a very serious affair, and all to no purpose. This last circumstance seemed to strike him a good deal. He then said that I was not to augur anything either way from anything that had passed on that day; that he would read and consider my memorials very attentively, but that I must see that a business of that magnitude could not be discussed in one conversation, and that the first; that I was not however to be discouraged because he did not at present communicate with me more openly. I answered [that] I understood all that; that undoubtedly it was my turn to speak on that occasion and his to hear, as I was not to get information but to give it. I then fixed with him to return in six days,[5] and having requested him to get the

[1] It has been suggested that Clarke was confusing Lord Fitzgibbon with Lord Edward Fitzgerald (see below, p. 251) or even with Lord Fitzwilliam (see above, vol. I, pp 522–4) (Frank MacDermot, *Theobald Wolfe Tone: a biographical study* (London, 1939), p. 190). See, however, below, pp 154–5.

[2] *Life* omits 'than that the clergy should turn the people against France'.

[3] At the close of 1791 parochial meetings were being held by the Dublin catholics who supported the General Committee against the seceders. According to Drennan, 'Troy wanted to refuse the chapel in his parish for their meeting and, it being said that a sledge would remove that difficulty, it was left open for them' (*Drennan letters*, p. 64).

[4] See above, p. 18, n. 5.

[5] In *Life*, ii, 52, William Tone inserts in parentheses: 'on the 1st of Germinal'. For this meeting between Tone and Clarke, see Diary for 21 Mar. (below, pp 117–21).

original memorials,[1] as he was perfect master of the English, and I could not answer for a translation which I had never seen, I took my leave.

I see clearly that all Clark's ideas on Irish politics are at least thirty years behind those of the people, and I took pains to impress him with that conviction as delicately as I could. We should, according to his theory, have two blessed auxiliaries to begin with, the Noblesse and the Clergy. I hope however I have beat him a little out of that nonsense, and that when he reads the memorials in cool blood, he will be satisfied of its absurdity. By the bye, my memorials have never I find been laid before the Executive.[2] That is bad! I trust they are now in a train. When I mentioned that De la Croix had referred me to Madgett, which I looked upon as a bad sign,[3] I found with some little surprise that Clark did not know Madgett! To hear the latter speak, one would suppose it impossible that could be the case. This comes of being a stranger. I must grope my way here as well as I can. Carnot has positively referred me to Clark, and if he be as confidential as he gives me to understand he is, I have no reason to complain—but suppose he is not, where is my remedy? and how am I to ascertain that fact? I know nobody here of whom I can enquire. If I rest in the hands of the subalterns, I risque the success of my plans, and I act against my wishes and my judgement. If I go back to the principals, I risque the making an enemy of the sub., and there is no animal so mean but it has the power to do mischief. I would rather stick to Carnot, but at present what can I do, when he has handed me over to Clark? '*Suffolk, what remedy?*'[4] At any rate I must let things go on in the present track until I see some open, or until I conceive myself neglected. As yet I have certainly no reason to complain '*A pize upon thee for a wicked lawyer, Tom Clarke!*'.[5] I would rather deal with your master, but that can't be for the present, and so ''*tis but in vain, &c.*'. We will see what the first of Germinal will produce, and in the mean I will, as Matty says, '*let the world wag*'.

It is unnecessary to observe that I only give the outlines of the various conversations recited in these memorandums. There are a thousand collateral points which it is impossible to detail. The general tenor of my discourse was grounded on the facts contained in my two memorials, which I endeavoured to state and support in the strongest manner I could, dwelling particularly on the Defenders, the Dissenters, the recent union between the sects, which I mentioned as a circumstance of the last importance, the probable consequences to the naval power of England, and the effects to be hoped for from the proclamations mentioned in my second memorial, which seemed to strike Clarke very forcibly, tho' he combatted them at first, until I asked him how he would like to be an English admiral leaving Portsmouth under the circumstances I had described, on which he submitted, as became him. I do not detail all this for in fact it would be but amplifying my memorials. One thing I must observe here. Tho' I told Carnot I had been

[1] Above, pp 61–70, 88–97. [2] i.e. the Executive Directory.

[3] The words 'which I looked upon as a bad sign' are omitted from *Life*. [4] *1 Henry VI*, v, iii.

[5] Tobias Smollett, *Sir Launcelot Greaves* (1762), ch. 7.

with the Minister, I never told the Minister I had been with Carnot. In like manner Clarke knows I have seen Madgett, but Madgett does not know I have ever been at the Luxembourg. There is something like duplicity in this. Is there? If there be, my situation must excuse it. I am acting to the best of my judgement and I have not a soul to advise with. P.P.![1] P.P.! What would I give that you were here today! Mem. Beauvilliers' Burgundy, &c. *** Kakieldesmos kai Ophieldismos![2] &c., &c., &c. Patriots &c., &c.!—

## 15 Mar. 1796

Went to breakfast with Madgett in consequence of a note which I received from him. Madgett in high spirits; he tells me everything is going on as well as possible; that our affair is before the Directory; that it is determined to give us 50,000 stand of arms, artillery for an army of that force, 672 cannoniers and a demibrigade, which he tells me is from 3 to 4,000 men; that the Minister[3] desires to have our opinion in writing as to the place of landing &c. All this is very good and precise. I told him, with that force we must land near Belfast &c., push on immediately to get possession of the Fews Mountains, which cover the Province of Ulster,[4] until we could raise and arm our forces; that if it was possible there could be a second landing, it should be in the Bay of Galway, which army should as soon as possible cover itself by the Shannon, breaking down most of the bridges and fortifying the remainder; that we should thus begin with the command of one half the Nation, and that the most discontented part; that as to the port of embarkation, which the Minister had also mentioned, I suggested some of the Dutch ports for two reasons, first that I believed they were less watched than the French ports, and next that England having no harbour where she could refit a fleet to the N[orth]ward of Portsmouth, even if there were a fleet in the North Seas, they must return occasionally to refit, and in the interval the expedition might take place; if however the Dutch ports were too closely watched, then we might go from any of the French harbours on the Ocean[5] and coast round by the West of Ireland into the Lough of Belfast and so proceed as before. Madgett reduced this to writing (in French) and we went together to the Minister's where he delivered it to him before my eyes. Madgett tells me that Prieur de la Marne[6] is in the secret, and has recommended and guaranteed a Capuchin fryar of the name of Fitzsimons[7] to go to Ireland. I told Madgett I had the most violent dislike to letting any priest into the business at all. He said he did not like it neither, but that Prieur[8] had known this man for twenty years and would stake his

[1] Thomas Russell.

[2] The meaning of these words has not been satisfactorily established. 'Kaki-' has the sense of 'evil'; 'kai' means 'and'; 'ophi-' has the sense of 'serpent'. They and the rest of the paragraph are omitted from *Life*.

[3] Delacroix. [4] The Fews are in fact confined to south Armagh. [5] i.e. the Atlantic Ocean.

[6] Pierre Louis Prieur de la Marne (1756–1827), member of the Constituent Assembly, the Convention and the Committee of Public Safety; he had by 1796 retired from politics and was in practice at the bar (*Grand Larousse encyclopédique*).

[7] See above, p. 106, n. 1. [8] *Life*, ii, 54, gives this name in full: Prieur de la Marne.

life on his honesty. I do not care for all that. I will give my opinion plump against his being sent. Madgett mentioned to me that the fellow has some notion of a resumption of the forfeited lands.[1] That would be a pretty measure to begin with! Besides he has been out of the country for 20 or 30 years and knows nothing about it, and I dare say hates a Presbyterian like the Devil. No, no! If I can help it, he shan't go. If I can't, why I can't. I want a military man. For example, as I must see whoever is sent (I presume), how can I commit the safety of my friends in Ireland to a person in whom I have no confidence myself? And indeed I have had some doubts whether I have any right to commit the safety of any person but myself. However, the way I answer that objection is that it is absolutely necessary; that there is no engaging in a business of this nature without risque,[2] that I am acting by their advice and direction and with their concurrence; that I have not shrunk back myself from either trouble or labour or danger; that it is but just they should take their share, especially when it is essential to the success of the measure; and finally that I rely very much on their discretion to avoid all unnecessary hazard and to conduct themselves properly thro' this arduous business. These reasons are with me of sufficient weight to decide me in giving the names of five or six men in Ireland in order that whoever is sent, if any one is sent, by the French Gov[ernmen]t may see them. At the same time I will give my advice that the messenger shall see but *one* of them and leave it to him to communicate with the others, and that one shall be P.P. I will put him, tho' I love him like a brother, in the post of danger and of honor. I wish Ireland to come under obligations to the aforesaid P.P.

And now I must observe here that it is very odd, if the business be, as Madgett mentions, before the Directory and so far advanced, that Clarke should know nothing about it. Carnot did not appear to me yesterday to have even seen my memorials,[3] and I rather believe that to be the case. Madgett is much more sanguine than I am, for I preserve in all this business a phlegm which is truly admirable. I have resolved never to believe that the expedition will be undertaken until I see the troops on board, nor that it will succeed until I have slept one night under canvas in Ireland; *then* I shall have hopes. At present I keep my mind under a strict regimen, and without affectation, I think it must be an extraordinary circumstance which would much elevate or depress me. All which is truly edifying, and extremely philosophic! Madgett tells me that Reubell[4] is the member of the Directory who is most sanguine and earnest in support of the measure. Well, the first of Germinal[5] I suppose I shall know more of the matter. Clarke after all must be better authority than Madgett. One thing I see, that Madgett wishes to keep me out of sight as much as possible, which is very natural, and I am sure I am not

[1] An allusion to the possibility of the property of Irish Jacobites confiscated after their defeat in 1691 being restored to their descendants.

[2] *Life*, ii, 54, omits 'that there is no engaging in a business of this nature without risque'.

[3] Above, pp 61–70, 88–97.

[4] Jean François Reubell (1747–1807), member of the Directory, 1795–9 (*Dict. parl. franç.*).

[5] i.e. 21 Mar. 1796.

angry with him for it. Nevertheless I will smuggle an odd visit now and then to the Luxembourg, just to see things a little, &c., &c. '*Wheels within wheels*.'[1] '*Business, business, said I, Mr Secretary, must be done!*'[2] &c., &c. Wise memorandums! I had like to have forgotten. I have not neglected Mr W[illia]m Browne's affair.[3] Lamare has written to Guise by this day's post on that subject, having received no answer to a letter which he wrote on the same head about a fortnight since. I wish the said Mr Browne were here for a vast multiplicity of reasons too tedious to insert.[4]

## 16 Mar. 1796

Blank! Dined alone in the Champs-Élysées, a most delicious walk. The French know how to be happy, or at least to be gay, better than all the world besides. The Irish come near them; but the Irish all drink more or less (except P.P. who never drinks) and the French are very sober. I live very soberly at present, having retrenched my quantity of wine one half. I fear however that if I had the pleasure of P.P.'s company tomorrow, being Patrick's day, we should indeed '*take a sprig of watercresses with our bread*'.[5] Yes, we should make a pretty sober meal of it! Oh Lord! oh Lord! &c.

## 17 Mar. 1796

Patrick's day. Dined alone in the Champs-Élysées. Sad! Sad!—

## 18 Mar. 1796

Blank! ————. Theatre in the evening. ————

## 19 Mar. 1796

Madgett called on me this morning to tell me that the Directoire had resolved to give as an entire brigade (viz. 8,000 men) instead of 4,000. He told me also that the Minister had asked him whether I had ever been at the Directory and that he had said he was sure I had not. (*Mem. I rather believe that honesty is always the best policy in every affair, public and private; for tho', I am sure from the purest motives, I had not told Madgett of my visits to the Luxembourg, yet I felt very awkward at the question.*) I answered that in consequence of the extreme anxiety which I felt for the success of the business, as well as[6] of the directions I had received to omit nothing likely to bring the state of Ireland before the French Govern[men]t,

[1] Ezekiel, 1: 16. [2] Goldsmith, *The good-natur'd man* (1768), act II.

[3] 'William Brown' was a *nom de guerre* for Tone's brother Mathew (*Life*, ii, 55). He had in fact been released in May 1795 (see above, p. 10, and below, pp 264–5).

[4] *Life* omits 'too tedious to insert'. [5] Source of this quotation not identified.

[6] In the MS two words are intentionally obliterated here. *Life*, ii, 56, adds for clarity 'in pursuance'.

I had thought it my duty to go in person to the executive[1] and to obtain, if possible, an audience; the more so, as Carnot, who was now one of the Directory, was well known by reputation in Ireland, and I was particularly charged, if possible, to find him out. Madgett seemed quite satisfied at this and, having fixed to breakfast with him tomorrow, we parted.

## 20 Mar. 1796

Breakfast with Madgett. The Minister wants to know our plan of conduct supposing the landing effected. This has been already detailed in my memorials, but it is necessary to go over the same ground again and again. '*Put it to him in other words*', viz. the Catholic Committee is already a complete representation of that body, and the Dissenters are so prepared that they can immediately chuse delegates, that these two bodies, when joined, will represent numerically nine tenths of the people, and of course, under existing circumstances, are the best government that we can form at the moment, &c., &c. This Madgett reduced to writing, but I have no copy, which is of the less consequence as the paper is short, and, in fact, nothing but a paraphrase of part of my last memorial.[2] Desired Madgett to explain to the Minister that my visit to the Luxembourg was in consequence of positive directions I had received to communicate with Carnot, whether in or out of power; that I had the highest respect for his (the Minister's) talents and patriotism and that, if there was any irregularity in my applying to Carnot it was merely an error in judgement, as he must be convinced that, circumstanced as I was, I could dread nothing more than doing anything which might be disagreeable to a person in his high station,[3] &c., &c. I believe this will satisfy De la Croix, but I fancy, between friends, that it is Madgett who is a little piqued, rather than the Minister; for, with great sincerity and I am sure an honest anxiety for the success of the measure, I can see a little desire in his mind of doing everything himself &c. &c., for which, as I have already said with a laudable magnanimity, I am not at all angry with him; nevertheless, I shall take the liberty, under the rose, to follow my own plan a little—I do not think I have made e'er a blunder yet, unless (which I do not think) my going to Carnot without informing the Minister was one. '*Business tomorrow!*'[4] Took a delightful walk, alone,[5] in the Champs-Élysées and dined, by myself as usual, at a very retired restaurateur's. I live here in Paris absolutely like a hermit.

## 21 Mar. 1796

Went by appointment (this being the 1st Germinal) to the Luxembourg to Gen[era]l Clarke. Damn it and rot it for me! He has not yet got my memorials![6]

[1] i.e. the Executive Directory. [2] Above, pp 88–97.

[3] *Life*, ii, 57, has 'I could never dream of doing anything which might be disagreeable to a person in his station'.

[4] *Life* omits 'Business tomorrow!' [5] *Life* omits 'alone'. [6] Above, pp 61–70, 88–97.

Only think how provoking! I told him I would make him a fair copy, as I had the rough draft by me. He answered it was unnecessary, as he had given a memorandum in writing to Carnot to send for the originals, and he would certainly have them before I could make the copy. We then went into the subject, as before, but nothing new occurred. He dwelt a little on the nobles and the clergy, and I replied as I had done in the former conversation of the 14th.[1] He said he was satisfied that nothing was to be expected from either. I told him he might expect all the opposition they could give, if they had the power to give any, but that, happily, if the landing were once effected, their opinion would be of little consequence. He then asked me, as before, what form of government I thought would be likely to take place in Ireland in case of the separation being effected, adding that as to France, tho' she would certainly prefer a republic, yet her great object was the independance of Ireland under any form. I answered I had no doubt whatsoever but, if we succeeded, that we would establish a republic, adding that it was my wish, as well as that of all the men with whom I co-operated. He then talked of the necessity of sending some person to Ireland to examine into the state of things there, adding, 'You would not go, yourself?' I answered, certainly not; that in the first place I had already given in all the information I was possessed of, and for me to add anything to that would be in fact only supporting my credit by my own declaration; that he would find even in the English papers, and I was sure much more in the Irish, if he had them, sufficient evidence of the state of the country to support every word I had advanced, and evidence of the most unexceptionable nature, because it came out of the mouths of those who were interested to conceal it and who would conceal it, if they could; that for me to be found in Ireland now would be a certain sacrifice of my life, to no purpose; that if the expedition were undertaken I would go in any station; that I was not only ready and willing, but that I should most earnestly supplicate and entreat the French Government to permit me to take a part, even as a private volunteer, with a firelock on my shoulder, and that I thought I could be of use to both countries. He answered as to that there could be no difficulty or doubt on the part of the French Government; he then expressed his regret at the delay of the memorials, and assuring me he would use all diligence to procure them and would not lose a moment after they came to his hands. I entreated him to consider that the season was now advancing fast when the Channel fleet would be at sea, and the camps in Ireland formed, and of course that every hour was precious, which he admitted. I then took my leave, having fixed to return in five days, viz. on the 6th Germinal. I apologized for pressing him thus, which I assured him I should not do in a business of my own private concern, and so we parted. And now, is it not extremely provoking that in a business of such magnitude seven days have been lost! The papers are lying in the Minister's hands, ready and finished, and nothing to do but to send for them, yet they are not got! Well, if ever I come to be a Citizen Director, or a Citizen Minister, I hope I shall do better than that. I am in a rage! Hell, hell!

[1] *Life* omits 'of the 14th'. For Tone's conversation with Clarke on that date, see above, pp 109–14.

> Fury, revenge, disdain and indignation
> Tear my swol'n breast, while passions, like the wind,
> Rise up to Heav'n, and put out all the stars![1]

As I have nothing to add more outrageous, I will here change the subject.

Went to see *Othello*, not translated but only 'taken from the English'.[2] Poor Shakespeare! I felt for him. The French tragedy is a pitiful performance, filled with false sentiment. The Moor whines most abominably, and Iago is a personage of a very pretty morality. The author apologizes for softening the villainy of the latter character, as well as for saving the life of Desdemona, and substituting a happy termination in place of the sublime and terrible conclusion of the English tragedy, by saying that the *humanity* of the French nation, and their *morality*, would be shocked by such exhibitions. '*Marry come up, indeed! People's ears are sometimes the nicest part about them.*'[3] I admire a nation that will guillotine sixty people a day for months, men, women and children, and cannot bear the catastrophe of a dramatic exhibition. Yet certainly the author knows best, and I have had occasion repeatedly to observe that the French are more struck with any little incident of tenderness on the stage a thousand times than the English, which is strange! In short the French are a human people, when they are not mad, and I like them with all their faults, and the guillotine at the head of them, better a thousand times than the English, and I like the Irish better than either, and as no one can doubt my impartiality I expect my opinion will be received with proper respect and deference by all whom it may concern. '*I have nothing to add.*'[4]

Upon further recollection I have something to add. In the course of the conversation when I desired Clarke to count upon all the opposition the Irish aristocracy could give whether Protestant or Catholic, he said he believed I was in the right, for that since he saw me last he had read over a variety of memorials on the subject of Irish affairs which had been given in to the French Government for 40 years back, and they all supported my opinion as to that point. I answered I was glad of it; at the same time I begged him not to build much on any papers above a very recent date; that the changes even in France were not much greater than in Ireland since the year '89; that what was true of her ten years ago, or seven years ago, was not true now, of which there could not be a stronger instance than this, that if the French had landed during the last war,[5] the Dissenters to a man, and even the Catholics, would have opposed them; but then France was under the yoke of popery and despotism, both which[6] she had since broken; that all the changes in the sentiment of the Irish people flowed from the Revolution in France,

[1] Nathaniel Lee, *The rival queens* (1677), act III.

[2] Probably the verse adaptation made in 1792 by Jean François Ducis in conformity with the norms of French tragedy (Peter France, *New Oxford companion to literature in French* (Oxford, 1995)).

[3] '"Marry-come-up", cries Slipslop, "people's ears are sometimes the nicest part about them"' (Henry Fielding, *Joseph Andrews* (1742), i, ch. 8).

[4] Cf. 'As I have no will of my own, I have nothing to add' (George Colman, *Two to one: a comic opera* (1785), act II). In the MS at this point there is a change of pen.

[5] The war of American independence, 1775–83.

[6] *Life* omits 'of popery and despotism both which'.

which they had watched very diligently, and that being *the* case, he would I hoped find reason to believe that my opinion as to the influence of the nobles and clergy was founded in fact, as those two idols had been levelled with the dust in France.[1] I then went on to observe that about an hundred years ago Louis the 14th[2] had an opportunity of separating Ireland from England during the war between James 2d and William 3d;[3] that partly by his own miserable policy and partly by the interested views of his minister Louvois,[4] he contented himself merely with feeding the war by little and little until the opportunity was lost; and that France had reason to regret it ever since, for if Ireland had been made independant then, the navy of England would never be what it is[5] at this day. He said that was very true, and he added that, even in the last war, when the Volunteers were in force, and a rupture between Ireland and England seemed likely, it was proposed in the French council to offer assistance to Ireland, and overruled by the interest of the Count de Vergennes,[6] then prime minister, who received for that service a considerable bribe from England & that he was informed of this by a principal agent in the paying the money. So it seems we had a narrow escape of obtaining our independance fifteen years ago; it is better as it is, for then we were not united among ourselves, and I am not clear that the first use we should have made of our liberty would not have been to have begun cutting each other's throats; so, out of evil, comes good. I do not like this story of Vergennes, of the truth of which I do not doubt. How if the Devil should put it into anybody's head here to serve us so this time? Pitt is as cunning as Hell, and he has money enough, and we have nothing here but assignats! I do not like it at all. However it is idle speculating on what I cannot prevent. I can answer for myself at least. I will do my duty. But to return. Clarke asked me had I thought of subsisting the French troops after the landing in case the Executive decided in favor of the measure. I answered I had not thought in detail on the subject, but there was one infallible mode which presented itself, which was requisition in kind of all things necessary, adding that he might be sure whoever wanted, the army should not want, and especially our allies, if we were so fortunate as to obtain their assistance. He asked me might not that disgust the people of property in Ireland? I answered the revolution was not to be made for the people of property; that as to those of them who were our friends, the spirit of enthusiasm would induce them to much greater sacrifices, and as to those who were our enemies, it was fit they should suffer; and I referred him for a proof of what sacrifices the enthusiasm of a revolution will lead to, to his own experience of what had happened in France, and what I knew to have been the case in America, where during the contest for their liberties it was a scandal

[1] *Life* omits 'as those two idols had been levelled with the dust in France'.

[2] Louis XIV (1638–1715), king of France, 1643–1715.

[3] i.e. the war in Ireland between James II and William III, 1689–91. Louis XIV's aim was, however, not to separate Ireland from England but to restore both kingdoms to his protégé James II.

[4] François Michel Le Tellier (1639–91), minister for war, 1672–91.

[5] *Life*, ii, 60, has 'never have grown to what it is'.

[6] Charles Gravier, comte de Vergennes (1717–87), minister for foreign affairs, 1774–87.

to enjoy the luxuries and almost the conveniencies of life, insomuch that the people of the first properties and situations went in old and patched[1] clothes &c. He admitted this, but observed that this enthusiasm would subside in time, and that it was already the case in France. I admitted that, but observed that I hoped our revolution, if attempted, would be completed long before the spirit of enthusiasm had cooled. I do not recollect any other circumstance material in our conversation.

## 22 Mar. 1796

I have worked this day like a horse. In the morning I called on Madgett to tell him that Carnot wanted to see the memorials,[2] and I begged of him to expedite it. He boggled a good deal, and I got almost angry. However, I am growing so much of a statesman that I did not let him see it. It would be a most extraordinary thing indeed if one of the Executive Directory could not command a paper of that kind out of the pocket of Citizen Madgett. I resolved, however, not to contest the point with him, but quietly to make a copy of the two memorials and give them myself to Clark[e]. It is only the trouble, and I have nothing else to do, and it is very good business for me, and I do not understand people being idle and giving themselves airs, and wanting to make revolutions while they are grumbling at the trouble of writing a few sheets of paper. I therefore dropped the business of the memorials, and Madgett then told me that he sets off tomorrow on a pilgrimage to root out the Irish prisoners of war, and especially Mr W[illia]m Browne,[3] who is to be sent to Ireland, if he can be found out, or if he has not been long since discharged; that he (Madgett) is to go to Versailles, Compiègne, Guise, &c., &c., and to propagate the faith among the Irish soldiers and seamen. This is his favorite scheme and is, in my mind, not to mince the matter, *damned nonsense*. What is 500 or a 1,000 Irishmen, more or less, to the success of the business? Nothing. And then there is the risque of the business taking wind. I do not like it at all, and I surmise the real truth to be that it is a small matter of job *à l'Irlandoise*, and that there is some cash to be touched &c., &c. Madgett's scheme is just like my countryman's that got on horseback in the packet[4] in order to make the more haste. He is always hunting for maps, and then he thinks he is making revolutions. I believe he is very sincere in the business, but he does to be sure, at times, pester me most confoundedly. With regard to Mr W[illia]m Browne,[5] I wish to God, if he be still in France, that Madgett may be able to find him; and yet I dread his going to Ireland. If he be caught there, his life is gone,[6] and tho' I am willing to hazard my own, I have some doubts as to his. The best of it is that if Madgett proposes it to him, he will go,

[1] *Life*, ii, 61, has 'tattered' instead of 'patched'. [2] Above, pp 61–70, 88–97.

[3] Mathew Tone. [4] i.e. boat.

[5] *Life*, ii, 62, inserts in parentheses 'my brother Matthew'.

[6] This did happen, in 1798. Mathew Tone went to Ireland as a member of Humbert's expedition; he was captured, tried for high treason and, on 29 Sept., hanged. Some documents relating to this episode are to be printed in vol. III.

*bon gré, mal gré.*[1] Well, let him. If he escapes and Ireland is freed, she will reward him, and he will deserve it. He certainly would be the fittest person to go from this, as he is known to all my confidential friends, and I could communicate with him and he with them much better than any stranger whatsoever. On the whole, if he is found, he must go, and I hope God almighty will protect him, poor fellow, for I love him most affectionately. Perhaps while I am writing this, he is at Princeton with Matty and the children.[2] I have sent one brother[3] to Ireland already on this business. It is pretty early to entrust a matter of high treason to a boy of 14; however I have no doubt of him, and, if we succeed, I hope to see him yet a flag officer in the Irish navy. Well, I have made great sacrifices in this business. But to return. Madgett tells me that the Minister[4] is quite satisfied as to my having seen Carnot and that he would be very glad if I would take an opportunity artfully to insinuate to Carnot that Prieur de la Marne would be a very acceptable person in Ireland (which I dare say he would, as his name is well known there), which I may fairly do, as I am here the representative of the Irish people. So, '*Citizen Simonville is accredited*!'.[5] I will certainly mention Prieur to Carnot, as the Minister desires it; and I recollect Rowan told me in Philadelphia that when he was leaving Brest on his way up to Paris, after his escape from Ireland, Prieur, who was then deputy on mission, shook hands with him, observing that he hoped they would land in Ireland together.[6] It is not impossible but they may meet there. So I am to become an *intrigant*, I find, and to procure appointments for ex-deputies and God knows what![7] '*Hey day, what doings, what doings are here!*'[8] It is very laughable to think of the Minister of Foreign Affairs desiring me to recommend a member of the National Convention to the Executive Directory of France. Having done with Madgett, I returned home and set doggedly to copying my two memorials,[9] finished the first, and made a practicable breach in the second; then wrote the eight foregoing pages in my journal.[10] And now it is ten o'clock at night, and I am as tired as a dog, and my fingers are cramped and I cannot see out of my eyes. Tomorrow I will finish my second memorial. I expect time enough to go to the Luxembourg and give it either to Carnot or Clarke. '*Business, business, said I, Mr Secretary, must be done.*' I quoted that once already,[11] but a good thing cannot be done too often, and it is a choice quotation, and I learned it from P.P., who quotes better than anybody except my dearest love. I am but a fool

[1] Meaning 'willy-nilly'.

[2] Tone's wife and children were living at Princeton, New Jersey (see Autobiography, below, p. 338).

[3] Arthur (see above, p. 37, n. 1, and below, p. 340).

[4] Delacroix.

[5] This appears to be a literary quotation; its source has not been identified. Instead of 'Citizen Simonville is accredited!', *Life*, ii, 62, has 'I am accredited'.

[6] Rowan states in his autobiography that Prieur de la Marne, as *député en mission* at Brest, ordered his liberation from prison and sent him to Paris, 'for which place we set out . . . in a *berline à quatre chevaux* with the tricolour flag flying' (Rowan, *Autobiography*, p. 232).

[7] Instead of 'God knows what!', *Life*, ii, 62, has 'I know not what'.

[8] Cf. Sir Robert Howard, *The surprisal* (1665), III, iii.

[9] Above, pp 61–70, 88–97.

[10] T.C.D., MS 2049, ff 14–17[v] (printed above, pp 119–22).

[11] See above, p. 116.

to them, only sometimes I make a lucky hit. Oh Lord, oh Lord, what wise memorandums I am making, and I am as tired as a devil, for I have written *nine hours* today, which is more than ever I did in my life. '*What do I not suffer, oh Athenians, that you may speak well of me?*'[1] Pretty and modest! Comparing myself, by craft, to Alexander the Great![2] Well, the vanity of some people is most unaccountable! When I get into this track of witty and facetious soliloquy, I know not how to leave off, for I always think I am chatting to my dearest life and love, and the light of my eyes. Well, I will not begin another page, and that is flat.

After all, I must begin another page, for with my nonsense I had like to forget the most important part of the business. The Minister[3] is in daily expectation of three millions of livres in specie, one million of which he destines for our expedition. If this be so, it looks like business at last. The moment he receives the money he will begin his preparations; but then Clark, who is certainly at the head of the military correspondence, knows nothing of all this. I am '*lost in sensations of troubled emotion*'.[4] What am I to think? '*Hey ho! Hey day! I know not what to do, nor what to say!*'[5] I have made a very wise rule for myself, and I will keep it; that is, never to be elevated by appearances; and indeed to say the truth, as yet I see no great appearances to elevate me. Well, I am blind with the sleep, and yet I am bound in honor to finish this page as I have begun it. Now for a quotation!

*There's thirteen lines gone thro' driblet by driblet,*
*'Tis done; count how you will, I warrant there's fourteen.*[6]

## To General Henri Jacques Guillaume Clarke, 23 March 1796

Archives Nationales, AF IV, carton 1671, f. 66.

See Diary for 23 Mar. 1796 (below, p. 125).

Tridi,[7] 3 Germinal

Dear Sir,

As I apprehend the delay in the other bureaux, I have made copies of the two memorials for your perusal. I wish they were shorter, as I know the value of your time. The copies I leave with you differ in one or two trifling circumstances from the originals which I delivered to the Minister, but in none of any importance.

[1] The source of this quotation has not been identified.
[2] Alexander the Great (356–323 B.C.). [3] Delacroix.
[4] Source of quotation not identified. [5] George Villiers, *The rehearsal* (1672), II, vi.
[6] 'A sonnet imitated from the Spanish of Lopez de Vega Menagiana' in *Miscellanies and collections, 1660–1750: a collection of poems* (1763).
[7] 'Tridi' is the third day in the *décade* in the republican calendar.

I shall call on you the day after tomorrow at one o'clock, and I hope you may be able in the meantime to find leisure to look over the memorials.

I am, Dear Sir, with great respect
Your very humble servant
James Smith

Gen[era]l Clark, &c., &c.

## Diary, 23–7 March 1796

T.C.D., Tone papers, MS 2049, ff 19r–24r; *Life*, ii, 64–70.

### 23 Mar. 1796

Madgett sent for me this morning to tell me, as usual, that everything is going on well; but for my part I think everything is going on very slowly; however, I did not say so, and he went on that he was going express to look among the prisoners for Mr W[illia]m Browne[1] by the Minister's directions and if he found him that he would be sent off instantly to Ireland after I had given him his instructions. So that affair is settled if Mr Browne be to be found. It is a perilous business, but he must take his chance, and as he will have no papers I hope he may come clear. He then consulted me as to the old scheme (which I am more and more satisfied is some kind of *job*) concerning debauching the Irish prisoners. His idea is now that they should be put aboard privateers and landed in different parts of Ireland to *prepare* the people for what was to happen, tho' neither they nor the people were to be in the secret. How they were to communicate what they did not know is not very clear; however, let that pass! I answered I should be very glad to see them all in Ireland on a proper occasion, but that I conceived it would be hazarding the whole measure to part with one of them until the landing was first effected, as the enemy might surmise something of the business and so take effectual measures to prevent it; and as to *preparing* the people, he might take my word that they were sufficiently *prepared* already. This is the six and fiftieth time that I have given my opinion on this head, and yet he still returns to the charge. I know the Irish a little; the way to manage them is this. If they intend to use the Irish prisoners let them be marched down, under other pretences, to the port from whence the embarkation is to be made. When everything else is ready, let them send in a large quantity of wine and brandy, a fiddle and some French *filles*, and then, when Pat's heart is a little soft with love and wine, send in two or three proper persons in regimentals and with green cockades in their hats to speak to them, of whom I will very gladly be one. I think, in that case, it would be not very hard to persuade him to take a trip over once more to Ireland, just to see his *people* a little. At least I am

[1] Changed in *Life*, ii, 64, to 'Matthew'. In fact Mathew Tone had already been released from prison.

sure if that scheme does not answer that nothing will. It may also be right to make the first man who offers a captain on the spot and one or two more subalterns &c., &c. To return. Madgett spoke to me again about Prieur with great commendation and, I dare say, justly of his talents and patriotism, adding that he had come out of power as poor as Job and literally drank water to save the expence of wine, which he could not afford. This in a member of the late Salut Public[1] is strong *presumptive proof* at least of his honesty. He added that Prieur was almost a stranger to him, but it was the Minister's desire, and that I should in mentioning it to Carnot use some little address. I answered I certainly would do my best and, if I succeeded and that we went together to Ireland, I believed if Prieur continued to drink water it would be out of preference for that liquor, for we would put him in a state to drink what he liked. I always keep up the idea, and in fact it is my opinion, that liberal provision should be made in case we succeed for those Frenchmen who might be in high station in Ireland as the generals and the *commissaire civil* &c. I am sure it would be money well laid out and agreeable to the native generosity of the Irish people. In fine, I should like Prieur very well, from what I hear of him, and I will certainly push that affair as far as it will go. Madgett then told me that the Minister desired I would draw up such a memorial as I thought the French commander ought to publish on the landing.[2] *That is not quite so easy!* I wished to evade it by saying the style of French eloquence was so different from ours that I doubted my abilities to do it. He answered it was precisely for that reason it was necessary I should write it; that when I had done the Executive Directory would make such alterations and additions as they might see necessary but the ground work must be mine. I then said I would try, and we parted. He is to be seven or eight days on his tour, apostolizing among the Irish prisoners, which once for all, as he is conducting it, I do not like.

For the manifesto, I had never in my life less appetite for composition than just now. It is a serious business, and I have no assistance. I wish to God P.P.[3] was here; or Gog.[4] What shall I do? I am in damned fright! Well tomorrow we will see. At present my idea is to make it as plain as a pikestaff, but how will the French like that? They love metaphors, but I think in the present case I will stick to plain English.

> Well, if we must, we must; and since 'tis so,
> The less that's said, the better![5] ————

Apropos! I should have observed that I finished the copies of my two memorials and left them at Clarke's bureau with a note[6] that I would call the day after but one.

[1] Expanded in *Life*, ii, 65, to '*Comité de salut public*'.
[2] See below, p. 126, n. 1. [3] Thomas Russell.
[4] John Keogh. [5] Sheridan, *The critic* (1781), II, i. [6] Above, pp 123–4.

## 24 Mar. 1796

Begun my French manifesto.[1] It drags a little heavy or so, but there is no remedy. I wish they would write it themselves.

## 25 Mar. 1796

At work in the morning at my manifesto. I think it begins to clear up a little. I find a strong disposition to be scurrilous against the English Government which I will not check. I will write on pell-mell and correct it in cool blood, if my blood will ever cool on that subject. Went at one o'clock to Clark[e]. Damn it! He has had my memorials and never looked at them! Well, this is my first mortification! God knows I do not care if the memorials were sent to the Devil, provided the business be once undertaken. It is not for the glory of Gen[era]l Clark[e]'s admiration of my compositions that I am anxious. He apologized for the delay by alledging the multiplicity of other business, and perhaps he had reason; yet I think there are few affairs of more consequence than those of Ireland if well understood, but how can they be understood if they will not read the information which is offered them? Well, '*'tis but in vain, &c.*'.[2] Clarke fixed with me to call on him the day but one after, at two o'clock. The delay, to be sure, is not great, nevertheless I do not like it. There was something too in his manner which was not quite to my taste, not but he was extremely civil. Perhaps it is all fancy, or that I was out of humour. Well, the 27th I hope we shall see, and till then let me work at my manifesto. Heigho! I have no great stomach for that business today, but it must be and so, *allons*! But first I will go, gingerly, and dine alone in the Elysian fields.[3] It is inconceivable the solitude I live in here. Sometimes I am most dreadfully out of spirits, and it is no wonder. Losing the society of a family that I doat upon and that loves me so dearly, and living in Paris among utter strangers, like an absolute Chartreux.[4] '*Well, had honest Sam Crowe been within hail—but what signifies palavering?*'[5] I will go to my dinner. Evening lounged about. Did no good. '*I cannot write this self-same manifesto, said I despairingly.*'[6] No opera. Went to bed at eight o'clock.

## 26 Mar. 1796

At work at the manifesto like a vicious mule, kicking all the way. However I am getting on; but I declare I know no more than my Lord Mayor whether what I am

[1] The 'memorial' or 'manifesto' mentioned in the preceding entry of his Diary. It is mentioned again in the entries for 25, 26 and 27 Mar., 2, 9, 10, 11 and 12 May, 3, 6, 9, 10, 11 and 19 June and 8 and 23 July. From 9 May, Tone usually refers to it as a 'proclamation'. On 6 June General Clarke, having received a draft from Tone, asked him to 'curtail it considerably', which Tone did on 9 and 10 June. The abridged version is given below (pp 196–8).

[2] *The buck's bottle companion* (1775).

[3] i.e. the Champs-Élysées.

[4] Carthusian.

[5] Tobias Smollett, *Sir Launcelot Greaves* (1762), ch. 22.

[6] Laurence Sterne, *A sentimental journey* (1768), i.

writing is good, bad or indifferent. '*Fair and softly goes far in a day.*'[1] I am going '*fair and softly*', but I cannot say I go '*far in a day*'. I have been writing now above five hours without intermission and I am surprised to find how little I have done, but I write two lines and blot out three, so it is easy to see how I get on. Well, now I think it is time for me to go to my dinner,[2] and the walk will do me good, and so *Allons*, as the French say. I am to dine with my friend Petit Thouars,[3] who has, I am heartily glad to find, re-entered the service. He has at present the rank of commodore and, if the war continues some time longer, may probably be an admiral. I hope and believe he will do his duty, tho' he is a damned aristocrat, but then he hates the English cordially and that '*covereth a multitude of sins*'.[4]

Evening. Petit Thouars prevented by business, but to make me amends he left a very troublesome French boy to keep me from being low spirited I suppose. Got rid of him as well as I could. At night sent one[5] for a bottle of Burgundy, intending to drink just *one glass*; began to read (having opened my bottle) *Memoirs of the reign of Louis the 14.*[6] After reading some time found my passion at a particular circumstance kindled rather more than seemed necessary, as I flung the book from me with great indignation; turned to my bottle to take a glass to cool me; found to my great astonishment that it was empty. *Oh, ho!* got up and put everything in its place exactly; examined all my locks; saw that my door was fast, as there may be rogues in the hotel; peeped under my bed, lest the enemy should surprise me there. It is the part of a wise man to be cautious, and I found myself inclined just then to be extremely prudent. Having satisfied myself that all was safe, '*I mounted the wall of my castle, as I called it, and having pulled the ladder up after me, I lay down in my hammock and slept contentedly*'.[7] That is vilely misquoted, but no matter for that; it is just like one of P.P.'s quotations. Slept like a top all night.

## 27 Mar. 1796

On looking over my manifesto[8] this morning, I begin to suspect it is *damned trash*. God forgive me if I judge uncharitably, but it seems to me to be pitiful stuff; at any rate, it certainly is not a *French manifesto* at all, and I foresaw the difficulty in the outset of my writing in the character of a French general. I am sure I shall never be able to make anything of it.[9] If it were to compose a manifesto for the Irish convention, and that I had good advisers, I might get on, but as to this here affair, I see I shall have to *give it up for hard work*, as they say in Galway. Went at two o'clock to Gen[era]l Clark at the Luxembourg[10] and had a long conversation.

[1] Daniel Bellamy, *The rival nymphs* (1739), IV, v.
[2] *Life* omits remainder of sentence.
[3] Corrected in *Life*, ii, 67, to 'Dupetit-Thouars'.
[4] 'Charity shall cover the multitude of sins' (1 Peter, 4: 8).
[5] *Life* omits 'one'.
[6] Possibly a volume of C.F.X. Millot's *Mémoires politiques et militaires pour servir à l'histoire de Louis XIV* (6 vols, Paris, 1779), or Voltaire's *Le Siècle de Louis XIV* (1751).
[7] Robinson Crusoe, Defoe's hero, built for himself a stockade, entered it by a removable ladder and slept inside in a hammock.
[8] See above, p. 126, n. 1.
[9] In *Life* this sentence is omitted.
[10] In *Life* 'at the Luxembourg' is omitted.

He told me that he had read my two memorials,[1] and without flattery could assure me that they were extremely well done (*that, of course*); that he had made a favorable report in consequence to Carnot, who had endeavoured to read them also, but finding a difficulty in reading English manuscript, he, Clark, was to translate them for him; that all he could at present tell me was that the Executive[2] was determined to send a person directly to Ireland, and that he had in consequence written to an ex-officer[3] of the Irish brigade to know if he would go, but that he had declined, on the score of his health. I told him I was sorry for that, as a military man, if one could be found proper in other respects, would be what I would prefer. He asked me did I know any person myself fit to go? I answered, I did not, having no acquaintance and industriously avoiding having any in France; that I did not know, however, but that at that moment I had a brother[4] lying in the prison of Guise. I then gave him a short history of Mr W[illia]m Browne's[5] affair, concluding by saying that if he was yet in France, and no other more proper person could be found, he might do; at the same time I did not at all mean to propose him, first because it was a service of danger in which I did not wish to hazard his life, and next that I would avoid recommending a person so nearly connected with me to the French Gov[ernmen]t, lest I might appear to act on interested views. Clarke then, after some civilities in reply, asked me what I thought of some of the Irish priests yet remaining in France? I answered he knew my opinion as to priests of all kinds, and especially Irish priests;[6] that they had all along acted execrably in Ireland; that they hated the very name of the French revolution; and that I feared, and indeed was sure, that if one were to be sent from France he would immediately, from the *esprit du corps*, get in with his brethern in Ireland, who would misrepresent everything to him, and of course that any information he might collect would not be worth a farthing. I added that the state of Ireland might be much better collected from the debates of their Parliament, even mutilated as he would find them in the English newspapers which I saw on his table, than from the report of any individual just peeping into the country and returning, supposing that he was lucky enough to escape; and I observed that those debates furnished the very strongest evidence because they were extorted from the mouth of the enemy who was so interested to conceal the facts and who would conceal them if he was able. (*This I had mentioned in a former conversation, but I thought it right to press it, and it seemed to strike Clarke very forcibly.*) I then went on to observe that I hoped, if the measure were adopted by the French executive, that they did not mean to delay it until the return of the emissary, if one were sent, especially as his business would be to give information in Ireland, not to bring any thence. Clarke answered, supposing the measure to be adopted, certainly not; that all preparations would be

[1] Above, pp 61–70, 88–97. [2] i.e. the Executive Directory.

[3] Perhaps Henry Shée (see below, p. 310, n. 2) who was authorised by the Directory on 30 July 1796 to accompany Hoche to Ireland 'en qualité d'agent civil' (Debidour (ed.), *Recueil des actes du Directoire Exécutif*, iii, 224).

[4] Mathew Tone. [5] In *Life*, ii, 68, William Tone inserts in parentheses 'my brother Matthew's'.

[6] In *Life* the words 'and especially Irish priests' are omitted.

going on in the meantime, but I must see it would be necessary to send a person to apprise the people in Ireland. I replied, by all means, but that whoever was sent must carry no papers, nor speak to above 4 or 5 persons, whom I would point out, for fear of hazarding a discovery which might blast all, in which Clark agreed. We then fell into discourse on the detail of the business, being in fact a kind of commentary, *vivā voce*, on the memorials. I began by saying that as I presumed the number of troops would not be above 5, or 6,000 men, I hoped and expected they would be the best that France could spare us. Clarke replied, they would undoubtedly be sufficiently disciplined. I answered that it was not merely disciplined troops but men who were accustomed to stand fire that we wanted, some of the old battalions from Holland or the Rhine, for as to raw troops we should soon have enough of them. Clark answered he could not promise that we should have the pick and choice of the French army, but that, if any were sent, they would be brave troops 'that would run on the enemy as soon as they saw them'. I answered as to the courage of the French army it was sufficiently known, and I would venture to engage that wherever they would lead, the Irish would follow. (*I see however we shall not get veterans, if we get any, which is bad, but we must do as well as we can.*) I then said, at least as to the cannoniers, of which we had none, it would be indispensable that they should be perfectly trained and disciplined, in which he agreed. I then came to the general and said that it would be of the greatest consequence, if the thing were possible, that he should be an officer of reputation whose name were known in Ireland, where names were things of weight. He replied that it would not be easy to get an officer such as I described to undertake the enterprise with so small a force. (*This I was all along afraid of!*) I replied, none such would, unless some dashing, fighting fellow, with a good deal of enthusiasm in his character; adding that Beurnonville, whom I knew only by his reputation and Camus's report, seemed to me to be precisely such a man as we wanted. *Clark's reply thereto is to be found in book No. 5, which I am just going to begin!*[1]

## Diary, 27 March–4 April 1796

T.C.D., Tone papers, MS 2049, ff 25$^r$–39$^r$; *Life*, ii, 70–85.

Number 5
From March 27th to April 9th inclusive[2]
*Nil desperandum!* ——
Paris
1796

[1] The preceding sentence is omitted from *Life*.

[2] Part of the Diary entry for 4 Apr. and the entries for 5–9 Apr. are given as a separate document (below, pp 145–51).

O fiers Anglais! gens toujours trop hardis,
Le ciel un jour à son tour en colère,
Se lassera de vos façons de faire.—
Voltaire, *La Pucelle*, Chant 11$^{me}$[1]

## 27 Mar. 1796[2]

Clarke replied, as to Beurnonville, he was already appointed to the army in Holland and it was not to be supposed he would quit the command of 60,000 men to go command 6,000. I answered he knew best, but that my opinion was there was more glory to be expected in Ireland, even with that force, and also more profit, if profit were any object, as he must suppose the Irish nation would reward those amply who were instrumental in establishing their liberties, adding that we were generous even to prodigality. He said he was sure that Beurnonville would prefer his present situation. *So there is an end of that expectation, for which I am sorry.* Clarke then said there were some Irish officers yet remaining in France who might go, and he mentioned Jennings,[3] who used to call himself Baron de Kilmaine, God knows why. I answered that in Ireland we had no great confidence in the Irish,[4] so many of them had either deserted or betrayed the French cause; that as to Jennings, he had had the misfortune to command after Custine and had been obliged to break up the famous *Camp of Cæsar*; that tho' that might probably have been no fault of his, it had made an impression, and as he was at any rate not a fortunate general, I thought it would be better have a Frenchman. This naturally introduced the Irish Brigade,[5] in which Clarke served for two years (in Berwick's), and I gave him an account of the various slights and mortifications they had undergone, both in England and Ireland—how they had been obliged to accept the King's pardon for high treason for having been in the French service, how those who were able were obliged to pay the fees, and those who were not were obliged to accept it *in formā pauperis*, a circumstance so excessively degrading as nothing could be worse; how the Lord Lieutenant had applied on

[1] This verse and the preceding headings, which were obviously added later than 27 Mar., are omitted from *Life*.

[2] MS reads 'March 27th (continued from No. 4)'. This line is omitted from *Life*. The continuation is from above, p. 129.

[3] Charles Édouard Saul Jennings de Kilmaine (1751–99), born in Dublin; capt. of hussars, 1788; general, 1797; imprisoned, 1793–4; served in Italy, 1795–9; commander of the 'armée d'Angleterre', Mar.–Dec. 1798 (Six, *Dict. des généraux & amiraux*).

[4] In *Life*, ii, 70, this clause reads 'we had no great confidence in the officers of the old Irish Brigade'.

[5] There were three Irish regiments in the French service during the eighteenth century, Dillon's, Berwick's and Walsh's. In 1791 the foreign regiments in the French army were placed on the same footing as other line regiments. In 1794 the British government decided to raise a corps of four (later six) regiments to be known as the Irish Brigade in which commissions would be given to emigrant officers who had served in the Irish Brigade in the French service. These officers might have been obliged under the aliens act (33 Geo. III, c. 1) to receive a licence from the secretary of state or his majesty's pardon. Irish radicals were contemptuous of the efforts to recruit men for the brigade. (P.R.O., WO 1/766; Portland to Camden, 29 May 1795, P.R.O., HO 100/54; *Army list*; *D.E.P.*, 6 Aug., 15 Sept., 13 Oct. 1795).

their behalf to the Catholic Comm[itt]ee and had been refused; how the very mob despised them, as an instance of which I mentioned the anecdote of the État Major intending to go to Mass on Christmass day[1] in grand costume and how they were obliged to give it up for fear of being *hustled* by the populace, who had given Dr Troy warning that they would treat them as *crimps*, with all which Clark was exceedingly delighted. He spoke of O'Connel[2] with some respect as a good *parade officer* to prepare troops for service, but no extent of genius for command. (He would do for us, as Baron Steuben[3] did in America, and if matters go forward I, for one, will be for his being employed, for I know he hates England, and my poor friend Sweetman,[4] whom I shall ever deeply regret, had an excellent opinion of him.) He also said that Col[one]l Moore[5] was the best officer among them, and as for all the others they were to be sure brave men, but none of them of any reputation. We then returned to our own affairs. I said we would want a few engineers. He asked me for what, where we had no fortifications? I replied for field practice, redoubts, &c. He replied that was always done by the adjutant generals. I then observed I had one thing to mention entirely personal as to myself; that I had exerted myself a good deal, that I had risqued my safety on more than one occasion, and had had a very narrow escape for my life; that if this business went forward, I hoped and expected the French Government would allow me to take a part in the execution, and that I was sure, if he would excuse the vanity of the assertion, that I could be of material service; that I was willing to encounter danger as a soldier, but that I had a violent objection to being hanged as a traitor; that consequently what I had to expect and desire was a commission in the French service;[6] that as to the rank it was indifferent to me, my only object being a certainty of being treated as a soldier, in case the fortune of war should by any accident throw me into the hands of the enemy, who I knew[7] would otherwise shew me no mercy, and that I hoped, under all the circumstances of the case, that my request would not be considered as unreasonable. He answered, as to that he could see no possibility of difficulty; that undoubtedly I had a claim, at the least, for so much, and he was sure it would be done, and that in the manner most agreeable to my feelings. So I am in hopes, if the business goes forward, that that affair will be settled. We then began to *chat* rather than talk seriously, and to moot points of war. First, as to Dublin. I told him I did not

[1] Probably in 1794.

[2] Daniel Charles O'Connell (1745–1833), colonel of the Royal Swedes and of the Salm-Salm regiment; emigrated, 1792; commissioned as colonel in the Irish brigade raised by the British government in 1794 (M. J. O'Connell, *The last colonel of the Irish brigade* (2 vols, London, 1892)).

[3] Friedrich Wilhelm Ludolf Gerhard Augustin, Baron von Steuben (1730–94), a German professional soldier who acted as military adviser to the Americans during the war of independence (*D.A.B.*).

[4] Edward Sweetman.

[5] James Moore (or O'Moore) (1741–*c.*1814) joined regiment of Berwick as ensign, 1763; major, 1780; lieut. col., 1789; left the regiment, 1791. In 1789 he was regarded as one of the best majors in the French service. He was lieut. col. in the first regiment of the Irish brigade in the British service, 1794, and was promoted colonel, 1800. (Archives de la Guerre, Y[b] 452; *Army list*).

[6] In *Life*, ii, 71, this line reads: 'that consequently, I desired a commission in the French army'.

[7] In MS followed by redundant 'so'.

expect, with the force we had to expect, that much would be done there at first; that there always was a strong garrison of at least 5,000 men, and that the Government, taking the advantage of the momentary success of the coalised despots,[1] had disarmed the people, taken their cannon, and passed the gunpowder & convention bills, &c.,[2] whose nature and operation I explained to him; that, however, if the landing were once effected one of two things would happen: either the Government would retain the garrison for their security, in which case there would be 5,000 men idle on the part of the enemy, or they would march them off to oppose us, in which case the people would rise and seize the capital; and I added that, if they preferred the first measure, which I thought rather the most likely, whenever we were strong enough to march southward, if we were as I had no doubt we should be, superior in the field, we could starve Dublin in a week without striking a blow. I then mentioned the great advantages that would result from a diversion in Connaught, if it were possible, from the discontents prevailing in that province, and the strong line of defence which the Shannon affords, and this I pressed upon him as strongly as I could. He saw all the advantages of it as clear as I did, for indeed they are self-evident, but I cannot say he gave me any violent hopes that it would be attempted in the first instance. *But*, what is to hinder our doing it ourselves in a week by way of Sligo &c.? *Mind this and examine the map!* We then spoke of Cork, of which I know nothing. He tells me the Harbour is admirably situated for defence against any attack by sea, but if you are superior at land, you can, by taking possession of a hill which supplies the town with water, force it to surrender without striking a blow. I then mentioned my scheme as to the Irish now prisoners in France, and I made him laugh immediately as to my mode of recruiting (which is however admirably adapted to the gentlemen whom I should have to address). Seeing that he was tickled with the business, I exerted myself and made divers capital *hits*, at the expense of poor Pat, concerning '*Women and wine, which compare so well, that they run in a perfect parallel*',[3] as the poet hath it. To be sure, it is in vain to deny it, but the poor fellow is a little exposed on those two sides, and the foul fiend, who knows it right well, always judiciously chuses one or the other, and sometimes both, to defeat him. God knows I have been buffetted by Satan as well as another in my time.[4] '*With women and wine I defy every care &c., &c.!*' (sings) ————.[5] I should be glad to know what P.P. would say as to my doctrine concerning the fallibility of poor Pat's judgement, when the '*wine looks red in the glass*'[6] and ***** Kakieldismos

[1] During 1793 the war had on the whole gone in favour of the coalition against France. *Life*, ii, 71, has 'coalesced despots'.

[2] See above, vol. I, p. 409, n. 2, and p. 477, n. 3.

[3] Charles Dibdin, *The deserter* (1774), II, iv.

[4] In the MS at this point a line is crossed out beyond recognition, the line which follows here being inserted by Tone in a smaller hand below.

[5] In the MS at this point one and a half lines are crossed out beyond recognition and the asterisks and Greek words which follow here are interlined in Tone's hand.

[6] *Life*, ii, 73, has (indented): 'The wine looks red in the glass, And the bright eyes of beauty are beaming'. The second line is possibly what is crossed out in the MS. *Life* omits '****Kakieldismos kai Ophieldismos*****seduces all mankind'.

Kai Ophieldismos[1] ******* seduces all mankind &c. &c.! Yes, yes! He is proof to all that; and so is P. P. and another person that shall be nameless! Well, we are all men and so let us say no more about the matter. Clarke asked me might not they serve us as the French prisoners did the British at Quiberon?[2] I answered there was this most material difference that the French were brought back to fight *against their country*, and the Irish would be brought back to fight not against their country but *against the English*, and that I had no doubt but they would do their duty. I then begged him to keep me in Carnot's recollection, and having fixed to call on him regularly once a week to see how things were going on, I took my leave, his last words being 'I wish most sincerely *and I hope*' (which he marked) 'the business will be seriously taken up by the Executive'.

I like this day's business very well. I see I was wrong the day before yesterday in thinking Clarke's manner cold. I fancy it was myself that was out of temper because forsooth he had not read my memorials. That was not unnatural on my side neither; but, *indeed*, it was much more my anxiety about the business than my *amour propre* or any attachment to my own compositions. I hope I am above all that, for I have a very pretty opinion of the purity of my motives. I have protested again and again in these memorandums that I am acting to the best of my judgement, seeing I have no advisers, which is a great loss, and on the very fairest principles. Have I no selfish motives? Yes, I have! If I succeed here I feel I shall have strong claims on the gratitude of my country and, as I love her, and as I think I shall be able to serve her, I shall certainly hope for some honorable station that will reward me for the sacrifices I have already made and the dangers I have incurred, and those which I am ready, and shall have, to make and incur in the course of the business. Why not? If it were the case of any other person I am sure I should have the same opinion. *I hope* (but I am not sure) my country is my *first object*; at least, she is *my second*. If there be one before her (*as I rather believe there is*) it is my dearest Life and Love, and the light of my eyes and the spirit of my existence. I wish more than for anything on earth to place [her] in a splendid situation. There is no situation so elevated that she would not adorn and that she does not deserve, and I will believe that not I only but everyone who knows her will agree as to that. Truth is truth. She is my first object but would I sacrifice the interests of Ireland to her elevation? No, that I would not; and if I would, she would despise me, and if she were to despise me, I would go hang myself, like Judas. Well, there is no regulator for the human heart like the certainty of possessing the affections of an amiable woman, and, if so, what unspeakable good fortune do I enjoy![3] Well, I do love my wife dearly, and that is the God's truth of the matter, and she is a thousand times too good for me, and I am not very bad

[1] The meaning of these words has not been satisfactorily established. 'Kaki-' has the sense of 'evil'; 'kai' means 'and'; 'ophi-' has the sense of 'serpent'.

[2] Prisoners of war enrolled in the royalist ranks after the émigré forces landed at Quiberon proved untrustworthy (J. H. Rose, *Pitt and Napoleon* (London, 1912), p. 51).

[3] In the MS 'enjoy' is interlined in substitution for another word, which has been deleted indecipherably. *Life*, ii, 74, reads 'do I not enjoy!'.

neither; but then she is so infinitely better that it throws my great merit into the shade. For all that I have said of her and myself here, I will be judged by Whitley Stokes and Peter Burrowes and P. P., who are three fair men; and I have now done this day's journal and shall only observe on looking over it that I think I am as pretty a negotiator as a man would wish to see of a summer's day. But then this damned manifesto sticks in my stomach. Well, ''*Tis but in vain &c., &c.*'

## 28 Mar. 1796

Went to the Opera, as usual, like a fine gentleman. I always go to that theatre because I understand music, as yet, better than French. *Panurge.*[1] Superb spectacle! Laïs[2] the best singer of the men, Madame Maillarde[3] of the women; Madame Ponteuil[4] extremely pretty with something foolish in the expression of her countenance. Madamemoiselle [*sic*] Gavaudan[5] a *coquine*, an *accrocheuse*, but[6] an excellent comic actress; Dufresne[7] an admirable actor and sings tolerably. All the others middling enough. Dansers. Vestris certainly first, then Nivelon,[8] then Deshayes,[9] then Goyon &c.[10] Females. Clotilde a fine figure with an infinity of grace and execution but wants, as the French tell me, the *plomb*, as they call it, that is that immobility of posture after executing a difficult passage; for my part I did not observe it till it was pointed out to me, but now I am beginning to grow something of a judge myself. Perignon & Chevigny admirable dansers and of merit so exactly equal that I know not which to prefer. They are both ordinary both in face and figure, but they manage themselves with such dexterity that nothing can appear more graceful than they do in all their movements. Duchemin pretty and dances very well, Millier as ugly as a mortal sin but a most charming danser. I believe I like her the best. The Parisians prefer Chevigny. Nothing could be executed with more taste, or, as I may say, more classically than the 'Pas russe' was tonight by Nivelon and Millier. Once for all, the King's Theatre in the Haymarket is no better than a barn of strollers, beside the Théâtre des Arts,[11] as to scenery, machinery, dresses and decorations, but in revenge their

[1] *Panurge dans l'Isle des Lanternes*, a comic opera, with music by Grétry and words by Morel de Chédeville and the comte de Provence (Lajarte, *Bibliothèque musicale du théatre de l'opéra*, i, 346–7).

[2] François Laïs or Lays (*c.*1757–1831), a leading opera singer and a fervent exponent of revolutionary views, 1793–4 (*Biographie universelle ancienne et moderne*, supplément).

[3] Mademoiselle Marie-Thérèse du Voux or Davoux, later Madame Maillard (1766–1818), was noted for beauty of voice, fine figure and quick intelligence (F. J. Fétis, *Biographie universelle des musiciens* (2nd ed., 10 vols, Paris, 1860–84)).

[4] Not identified.

[5] Mademoiselle Gavaudan (d. 1810), possibly the elder sister of Jean-Baptiste Gavaudan, the actor. There were also two actresses of this name at the Théâtre Feydeau in 1796. (Fétis, *Biog. des musiciens*, iii, 428).

[6] The words 'a *coquine*' (meaning 'strumpet'), 'an *accrocheuse*' (meaning 'fighter' or 'vixen') and 'but' are omitted from *Life*.

[7] Not identified.

[8] Not identified.

[9] A. J. J. Deshayes became a professor at the Conservatoire (Fétis, *Biog. des musiciens*).

[10] Goyon and the following performers named have not been identified.

[11] See above, p. 49, n. 5.

singers (being Italians) are far before the French, who on the other hand excel the Italians and all the world[1] in their dances. It is impossible to conceive anything in its kind more perfect than a grand ballet at the Opera in Paris; and indeed in all their theatres there is an attention paid to the preservation of the *costume* even in the minutest points very far beyond the English theatres, where I have seen myself Macbeth, a Scotch chief of eight centuries ago, dressed in a very spruce suit[2] of scarlet regimentals and a bag wig in which he need not have been ashamed to shew his face at St James's, and where to this hour Hamlet the Dane, the son of Horwendillus, is exhibited, even by Kemble,[3] from whom I would expect better things, in a fine black velvet full-trimmed suit, with the ribbon of the Order of the Elephant over his shoulders; where King John is habited after the fashion of 1160 and his antagonist King Philip confronts him in a cocked hat and feather and a coat and waistcoat of the last court fashion. These are absurdities the eye is never shocked with in France, and they are as attentive to the appearance of the meanest domestic as of the hero of the piece. All the minutiæ of the scene are equally correct; for example, in a Grecian tragedy they would not introduce a pair of handsome plated candlesticks &c. They have carefully studied the antique, and whatever is graceful among the Moderns, and profited accordingly. I believe I have now said enough of the Opera &c., to which the French are devoted *à la folie*. All the theatres are as full every night as they can hold and I have never seen an instance of what we call in England a *bad* or even a *middling* house.

## 29 Mar. 1796

Blank!

*My time, oh ye muses, was happily spent,*
*When Phœbe went with me wherever I went!*[4]

Am I not to be sincerely pitied here? I do not know a soul! I cannot speak the language but with great difficulty I live in taverns, which I detest! I cannot be always reading; and I find by experience that when one reads *perforce*, there is not much of either profit or pleasure to be derived from it, from which I infer, philosophically, that the nature of man is adapted to liberty and that all restraint beyond what is necessary—. Oh Lord! Oh Lord! Metaphysics! I return to my apartment, which is notwithstanding a very neat one, as if I was returning to gaol, and finally I go to bed at night as if I was mounting the Guillotine. I do lead a dog's life here that is the truth of it. My sole resource is the Opera.

[1] *Life*, ii, 75, has 'all other nations' instead of 'all the world'.

[2] Ibid. has 'vest' instead of 'suit'.

[3] John Philip Kemble (1757–1823), well known as an actor, especially in Shakespearian parts. He many times played the part of Hamlet including appearances at the Smock Alley theatre, Dublin, in Nov. 1781. (*D.N.B.*).

[4] Opening lines of 'Colin and Phoebe' (1714), a popular, playful pastoral poem by John Byrom (1692–1763) (*D.N.B.*).

## 30 Mar. 1796

Went today to the Church of St Roch,[1] to the *Fête de la Jeunesse*. All the youth of the district who have attained the age of *sixteen years* were to present themselves before the Municipality and to receive their arms; and those who were arrived at *twenty-one* were to be enrolled in the list of citizens in order to ascertain their right of voting in the assemblies, &c. The church was decorated with the national colours and a statue of liberty with an altar blazing before her. At the foot of the statue the Municipality were seated and the sides of the church were filled with a crowd of spectators, the parents and friends of the young men, leaving a space vacant in the centre for the procession, which consisted of the État-major of the sections composing the district, of the National Guards under arms, of the officers &c., of the sections, and finally of the young men who were to be presented. The guard was mounted by veterans of the troops of the line, and there was a great pile of musquets and sabres before the Municipality. When the procession arrived, the names of the two classes were enrolled, and in the meantime the veterans distributed the arms among the parents and friends and mistresses of the young men. When the enrollment was finished an officer pronounced a short address to the youths of sixteen on the duty which they owed to their country and the honor of bearing arms in her defence, to which they were about to be admitted; they then ran among the crowd of spectators and received their firelocks and sabres, some from their fathers, some from their mothers and many, I could observe, from their lovers. When they were armed, their parents and their mistresses embraced them and they returned to their station. It is impossible to conceive anything more interesting than the spectacle was at that moment, the pride and pleasure in the countenances of the parents, the *fierté* of the young soldiers, and above all the expression in the features of so many young females, many of them beautiful and all of them interesting from the occasion. I was in an enthusiasm. I do not at all wonder at the miracles which the French Army has wrought in the contest for their liberties. When I looked at the spectacle before me and recalled to mind the gangs of wretched recruits I had seen in Ireland marching in their fetters and handcuffed,[2] I was no longer surprised at anything. Yet the poor Irish are a brave people, and I think it would not be impossible to bring them up to the enthusiasm of the French. At least, if we have an opportunity, we will try. I am more and more satisfied of the powerful effects of public spectacles, properly directed, in the course of a revolution. I should have observed that during the

[1] Built between 1653 and 1740, it was closed in 1793 and reopened in June 1795 (Amédée Boinet, *Les églises parisiennes* (3 vols, Paris, 1958–64), ii, 344–81).

[2] A comparable scene was observed in northern France a few months later by an English traveller who on her way to Montreuil 'passed four or five military waggons and a number of good-looking young men belonging to the first requisition tied two and two, with their knapsacks on their backs and escorted by some Gens d'Armes or Cavaliers de maréchaussées on horseback'. They were said to have 'been sent to reinforce the army of the Rhine' but 'instead of doing their duty they had deserted their colours and returned home'. (A Lady, *A sketch of modern France in a series of letters written in the years 1796 and 1797* (London, 1798), p. 49).

ceremony all the civic hymns were chanted accompanied by a full band and joined in the chorusses by the young men. I wish my dearest love had heard the burst of '*Aux armes, Citoyens!*'.[1] It is impossible to conceive the effect of that immortal hymn, unless by those who have heard it at a festival in France. It is absolute enchantment. This was a good day.

## 31 Mar. 1796

Blank! Not knowing what to do with myself I lounge[2] about the book stalls and pick up military books dog cheap. If I had money to spare I could make up a famous French library for a trifle. There are very expensive editions here just now, if one chuses to lay out money on fine types, paper and binding; but on the other hand there are most excellent editions of excellent works for half nothing. The ordinary price I pay for a duodecimo bound is 50#[3] in assignats, which at the present rate of the louis is about two pence. Mary, I know, will laugh at my collection of *État militaires*, as she calls them. No matter for that. '*By God's provi-dinch, they may be yused some time or other*.'[4] I laugh at them myself sometimes; but I am tempted because they are bargains, in spite of poor Richard. 'Never', says he, 'buy what you don't want because it is a bargain. I have known many a man ruined by buying bargains.'[5] ——————

## 1 Apr. 1796

Lounged about '*cheapening old authors at a stall*'.[6] Saw a superb battalion of infantry and a squadron of cavalry inspected at the Tuilleries by a general officer. The French are very fine troops, such of them as I have seen; they are all of the right military age, with scarcely any old men past service, or boys not grown up to it. They are not very correct in their evolutions; not near equal even to the British,[7] much less, as I suppose, to the German troops. This has a little shaken my faith in the force of discipline, for they have certainly beaten both British and Germans like dogs. But after the spectacles which I see daily why need I wonder at that? The *Fête de la Jeunesse*, for example, of yesterday[8] explains it at once. Discipline will not stand against such enthusiasm as I was a witness to and, I may say, as I felt myself. I remember P.P.[9] was always of that opinion, tho' I doubted it, which shews the superiority of his judgment and his more accurate knowledge

[1] Opening words of the chorus of 'La Marseillaise'.

[2] *Life*, ii, 77, has 'stroll' instead of 'lounge'.

[3] i.e. fifty francs, as spelt out in *Life*, ii, 77.

[4] Cf. 'With the blissing of Heaven they may be yused some time or other' (Tobias Smollett, *Humphry Clinker* (1771), ii).

[5] 'Poor Richard says "Buy what thou hast no need of and ere long thou shall sell thy necessaries . . . The bargain by straitening thee in thy business, may do thee more harm than good"' (Benjamin Franklin, *Political, miscellaneous and philosophical pieces* (London, 1779), pp 30–31).

[6] Swift, *Horace, epist. I, vii: imitation of Horace to Lord Oxford* (1713), line 6.

[7] *Life*, ii, 78, substitutes 'English' for 'British'.

[8] *Recte* of two days before (see Diary for 30 Mar., above).

[9] Thomas Russell.

of the human character. He used to instance in Tom Macabe and he could not have found a better.[1] If we go on in Ireland, we must move Heaven and Earth to create the same spirit of enthusiasm which I see here; and, from my observation of the Irish character, which so nearly resembles the French, I think it very possible. The Devil of it is that poor Pat is a little given to drink, and the French are very sober. We must rectify that as well as we can. He is a good man that has no fault, and I have a sort of sympathetic feeling that makes me the more indulgent on the score of ebriety. *Quere?* Would it have a good effect to explode corporal punishment altogether in the Irish army and substitute a discharge with infamy for great faults and confinement and hard diet for lesser ones? I believe there is no corporal punishment in the French army,[2] and I would wish to create a spirit in our soldiers, a high point of honor, like that of the French. When one of their generals (Maréchal Richelieu)[3] was beseiging a town,[4] he was tormented with the drunkenness of his army. He gave out in orders that any soldier who was seen drunk should not be be suffered to mount to the assault, and there was not a man to be seen in liquor afterwards. Drunkenness then induced a suspicion of cowardice, which kept them effectually sober. It is a choice anecdote and pregnant with consequences. To return. There is a great latitude in dress allowed both to the French officers and soldiers, which has demolished, or at least very much circumscribed, another of my prejudices, for I was on that score a great martinet. I fancy truth may lie between P.P.'s opinion and mine, so let us compound as follows. If there be a high point of honor and a spirit of ardent enthusiasm, then discipline (I mean the discipline which makes men machines) may be in a great degree suffered to relax, and *a fortiori* the minutiae of dress to be neglected; but if that point of honor and spirit of enthusiasm do not exist, their absence must be supplied by the force of discipline, and then as part of the system even the article of dress becomes of some consequence. The French cavalry are armed only with sabres and pistols *without carbines*. I am glad of that, for I always thought carbines useless. The fire of infantry seems to me to have very little effect in comparison of the noise it makes, and the fire of cavalry I am sure is *nonsense*. The *arme blanche* is the system for the French and I believe for the Irish—at least, if our affair goes forward, it will be what I shall recommend, for poor Pat is very furious and savage, and the tactics of every nation ought to be adapted to the national character. Platooning at forty yards[5] may answer very well with the English and German phlegm, but as we have rather more animal spirits, I vote for the bayonet. I do not love playing at *long bullets*. To conclude. I wish to study the

[1] *Life* omits the preceding sentence.

[2] In 1789 a French soldiers' petition requested the National Assembly to abolish corporal punishment in the army and under the military code of 1791 corporal punishment was not employed to enforce discipline but a number of offences were punished by death or imprisonment in irons (*Lettre des soldats composant les troupes françaises adressée à l'assemblée nationale* ([Paris], 1789); *Journal gratuit: Code militaire, armée de terre*... ([Paris, 1791]).

[3] Louis François Armand de Vignerot du Plessis, duc de Richelieu (1696–1788), in 1756 captured Port Mahon.

[4] Note by William Tone: 'Port Mahon in Minorca'.

[5] *Life*, ii, 79, inserts 'distance'.

character of the French soldiery, and if possible to create the same spirit in Ireland and, in a word, to make the French army our model in preference to[1] the Prussian. I think P.P. will allow that that is candid in me, after all the disputes he and I have had on the subject of discipline &c., &c. In the afternoon went for the first time to the *Conseil de[s] Cinq-Cens*, or the French House of Commons. It is certainly the first assembly in Europe and the worst accom[m]odated. The room is mean and dirty and ill contrived; the system of speaking from a tribune is in itself bad, and they have made it worse by placing it at the feet of the President (to whom the orator's *back* is turned) at one end of a very oblong room, so that those at the lower end cannot possibly hear the half of what is said.[2] They are likewise very disorderly, which I wonder at the more as they have had now six years' experience of public assemblies, but it is the same impetuosity that makes them redoubtable in the field and disorderly in the Senate. As to their appearance, it was extremely plain. Nobody was what I would call *dressed*, many without powder, in pantaloons and boots. From the figure of the room and the appearance of the Assembly, they put me strongly in mind of my old masters, the General Committee, at their famous meeting in Back Lane.[3] The resemblance was very striking, with this difference that I must say the General Committee looked more like gentlemen and were ten times more regular and orderly, or, in a word, like a legislative body, than the *Conseil de[s] Cinq-Cens*.[4] They were only on business of course, and as I found nobody to point out to me the most celebrated members, I did not remain above half an hour. On the whole they looked more like their countrymen who broke into the Roman Senate than like the Senators assembled in their ivory chairs to receive them; nor can I say, as some ambassador[5] did of the Senators of Rome, that they looked like an assembly of demigods. But it is very little matter what they look like. They have humbled all Europe thus far with their blue pantaloons and unpowdered locks, and that is the main point. The rest is of little consequence.

## 2 Apr. 1796

Went today to Clark, to the Luxembourg. He tells me he has been hunting for a proper person to go to Ireland in vain; that he had a Frenchman[6] tampering with who was educated from a child in England and who spoke the language perfectly; that at first he had agreed to go, but afterwards, on learning the penalties of the English law against high treason, his heart failed him and he declined. *This is bad*; however, there is no remedy. Clarke went on to tell me that if the measure was pursued (*without saying whether it would or not*) the Executive was

[1] In ibid. 'instead of' replaces 'in preference to'.

[2] The Cinq-Cents met in a chamber constructed in the west wing of the Tuileries.

[3] Where the Catholic Convention met, in the Tailors' Hall, in December 1792; it runs from Cornmarket to Patrick St.

[4] *Life* omits 'than the *Conseil de Cinq Cens*'.

[5] *Life*, ii, 80, has 'the ambassador of Pyrrhus' instead of 'some ambassador'.

[6] Not identified.

determined that I should be employed in the French service in a military capacity, and that I might depend on finding everything of that kind settled to my satisfaction. I answered it was the great object of my ambition,[1] and, as to my own personal feelings, I had nothing more to demand. He then said that he wished I would give him a short plan for a system of *chouannerie*[2] in Ireland, particularly in Munster, for, he would tell me frankly, the Government had a design, before anything more serious were attempted, to turn in a parcel of renegades (or, as he said, 'blackguards') into Ireland in order to distress and embarrass the Government there, and to distract them in their motions. I answered I was sorry to hear it; that if a measure of that kind was adopted with a view to prepare the minds of the people it was unnecessary, for they were already sufficiently prepared; that it would only produce local insurrections, which would soon be suppressed, because the Army (including the Militia) would in that case to a certainty support the Gov[ernmen]t and every man of any property whatsoever,[3] even those who otherwise[4] wished for the independence of their country, would do the same from the dread of an indiscriminate plunder, which was but too likely to ensue from such a measure as he described; that there was another thing very much to be apprehended in that case, and which, if I was Minister of England, I should not hesitate a moment about and in which the parliaments of both countries would instantly concur, viz. to pass two acts repealing those clauses which enact that the militia shall only serve in their own country, and directly to shift the militia of Ireland into England and replace them by the English militia, which would serve to awe both countries and most materially embarrass us. That if all this was so, and those insurrections were suppressed, the inevitable effect grounded upon all historical experience would be to strengthen the existing government; that England would take that opportunity to reduce Ireland again to the state of subjection, or even a worse one, that she had been in before 1782, and would bind her hand and foot in such a manner as to make all future exertion impossible, in which she would be supported by the whole Irish aristocracy, who compose the legislature and who would sacrifice everything to their own security; that if France had nothing in view but to distress England for the moment, undoubtedly what he mentioned, however ruinous to Ireland, might have that effect; but if the Republic went on more enlarged views and a sounder policy, she ought not for a moment to give consideration to the scheme; that if the main force were once landed, undoubtedly it would be right to set Ireland in a blaze at the four corners and burn out the English Gov[ernmen]t; but that I was satisfied it would be ruinous to make the measure he described *precede* the landing. Finally I added that, as to myself, I was ready to be one of ten men, if the French Government were determined to send no more.[5]

[1] In *Life*, ii, 80, 'it was the great object of my ambition' is omitted.

[2] Guerrilla warfare waged by the royalist peasantry in western France against the republic. It began in Lower Maine in 1793 under the influence of Jean Cottereau (known as Jean Chouan) and spread to Normandy and Brittany.

[3] *Life* omits 'whatsoever'. [4] *Life* omits 'otherwise'.

[5] In the MS two lines are crossed out here.

I also begged him to remember that I gave this, with all deference, as my opinion[1] on a point which I had considered in consequence of an idea of the same kind having been started to me by Madgett from the Minister. Clarke began by saying that as to my being sent, it was not the idea of the French Gov[ernmen]t to risque my safety in that stage of the business; that the objections I had mentioned were of considerable weight, and that he would give them serious consideration; he then desired to see me in four or five days, and, after demanding my address, which I gave him, I took my leave. (Vide No. 4, March 22d and 23d, No. 2, Feb^y^ 2d,[2] on this head,[3] which I am sorry to see has got ground among them.) This conversation explains what Madgett (who is returned from his mission) told me this morning; that he had got 51 Irish prisoners who would fight blood to the knees against England, and that it would he thought be very serviceable if they were dispersed thro' the country. I referred him for my opinion to our former conversations on that head; that I thought undoubtedly if the business were once begun the wider the flame was spread the better but that the grand blow of the landing near Belfast should precede all others, and that being once effected, as many others as he pleased. I see clearly my opinion will not be followed and I fear it will be found to be so much the worse. I have however discharged my conscience. I cannot blame France for wishing to retaliate on England the abominations of La Vendée and the Chouans, but it is hard that it should be at the expence of poor Ireland. It will be she, and not England, that will suffer, and the English will be glad of it, for they hate us next to the French. If these ragamuffins are smuggled into the country, local insurrections will ensue; the militia will obey their officers, the bravest of our poor peasants will stand to be cut down, and of those who run away, numbers will be hanged, and many more sent aboard the fleet to fight the battles of England and the Government will be so much the stronger; not to mention the mischief which will be unprofitably done, even to the aristocracy. I dislike all this very much, if I could help myself, but I fear I shall not be able to prevent it. At all events I have given my opinion honestly. Poor Pat! I fear he is just now in a bad neighbourhood. Madgett tells me that Mr W[illia]m Browne[4] left Guise with his passport eight months ago, so there is an end of that business. I hope in God he is, by this, safe with the girls[5] at Princeton. How happy shall we be, if ever we have the good fortune to meet again! I suffer a good deal in this business; however "*'Tis but in vain &c.*' ———

## 3 Apr. 1796

Called on Madgett this morning by appointment. He is always full of good news. He tells me the marine force will be 17 ships of war, great and small; arms and artillery, &c., for 50,000 men; that many of the officers are already named, but, he believes, not the *general en chef*. All this is very good, but '*I would I could*

[1] *Life*, ii, 81, has 'fixed opinion'. [2] *Recte* 'Feb^y^ 22d'.
[3] See above, pp 121–2, 124–5, 70–72, respectively. [4] Mathew Tone.
[5] Tone's wife, Matilda, and his sister, Mary.

*see it, quoth blind Hugh*'.[1] We then came to my business as to procuring a commission in the service of the Republic. He asked me, as I was here the representative of the Irish people, would I not feel it beneath the dignity of that character to accept of a commission? This he mentioned as to my own private feelings,[2] for with regard to the French Government they would give me any rank I pleased to demand. I answered that I considered the station of a French officer to be one that would reflect honor on anyone who filled it; that consequently on that score I could have no possible objection; that besides my object was to ensure protection, in case the fortune of war, by any one of the infinite varieties of accidents likely to happen should throw me into the hands of the enemy; that I was very willing to risque my life in the field, but not to be hanged up as a traitor; that as to rank, it was indifferent to me, as I did not doubt but as soon as things were a little reduced into order in Ireland, I should obtain such a station in that service as they might think I merited; that in the meantime I should wish to be of the family[3] of the *general en chef*, as I could be of use there, speaking a little French, to interpret between him and the natives; unless the Government here thought proper to raise a corps of the Irish prisoners, in which case I hoped they would entrust me with the command. Madgett asked me how many might be necessary to form[4] a corps? I answered if we could muster 150 it would be sufficient, and as soon as we got to Ireland we would mount them as hussars. Just then we were interrupted by the arrival of Fitzsimons, the priest, who has been recommended by Prieur de la Marne to go to Ireland. Madgett began to speak without reserve, but for my part I kept myself in generals, because '*Dolus versatur in universalibus*.'[5] I was soon very glad I did so, for I see that he is a damned fool, not fit to deliver a common message. He may be honest for aught I know, and may have the courage necessary, but he has not a grain of talents. I never was more provoked in my life; and the fellow was pinning himself on me, tho' my manner was as cold and dry as possible; but he seems to have a reasonable assurance, resulting partly from his extreme ignorance. Curse on him, for a bladdering[6] idiot! What shall I do with him? How can I explain myself to such a damned dunce? Or entrust the safety of my friends, not to speak of the measure itself, to a blockhead that has not sense enough to keep his mouth shut, or to count five on his fingers? Where the Devil in hell did Prieur lick him up? And what sort of a fellow must Prieur be himself to recommend him? If he judges him capable, he is a fool; if not, he is worse. Damn him to hell! I wish he was dead. '*I would fain have him die, split me!*'[7] Is not this most terribly provoking? for it seems to be a thing settled that he shall go. What am I to do in this cursed dilemma? And how came Madgett not to interfere in time? I objected all along to priests as the worst of all possible agents, and here is one who is the worst of all possible priests. How the Devil can I communicate with such an ass? It is impossible to conceive anything more vulgar and

[1] Swift, *Polite conversation* (1738), dialogue 1.
[2] The nine preceding words are omitted from Life.
[3] i.e. staff.
[4] *Life*, ii, 83, inserts 'the *cadre* of'.
[5] 'Treachery is all around us.'
[6] *Recte* 'blattering', meaning 'prating volubly'.
[7] Source of this quotation not identified.

ignorant and stupid. If he goes to Ireland, the people there will suppose we are laughing at them, to send such a fellow. What will Gog[1] think? Yes, Gog will open his heart very fast[2] to Mr Fitzsimons, the priest.[3] God rot him! I am in such a rage I know not how to leave off abusing him. Well, I am to dine today with Madgett, and please the Lord I will tell him a piece of my mind. Perhaps I may be able to put a spoke in Mr Fitzsimons's wheel, if it be not, as I fear it is, too late. To give a specimen of his talents (because he amuses me). There happened to be some Portuguese dispatches taken aboard a vessel going to Brasil. Sullivan[4] (Madgett's nephew) was carrying them to the office to be translated, and Mr Fitzsimons made the following remark. 'You will have fine fun making out what these Portuguese fellows say; are all those papers, pray, *wrote in English*?' The dispatches of the Portuguese Minister to the Governor of Rio Janeiro *written in English*! Oh Lord! Oh Lord! I thought I should have been choked endeavouring to smother the irresistible propensity I felt to laugh in his face. Yes, he is a pretty devil of an agent. I suppose he will talk Portuguese to the Irish by way of keeping the secret. Damn him sempiternally! What the devil brought him across me? Dinner with Madgett; after dinner I began my remarks on Fitzsimons, and after relating the anecdote of the Portuguese dispatches written in English, I told him plump, I would not hazard the safety of my friends in Ireland, nor of the measure, by communicating with such an eternal blockhead. Madgett at first seemed inclined to make some defence for him, but the cause was too bad, and I was too determined, so he gave him up, and assured me he should not go to Ireland, and there the matter rests; but I think I will go tomorrow to the Minister and tell him a piece of my mind touching this said Mr Fitzsimons. I must leave nothing to chance. I cannot conceive how Prieur could be mistaken in him. The fellow was fawning on me too, but I was as cold as ice and as stiff as a Spaniard, and would not understand the broadest hints. Hang him, I have taken up too much of my paper about him and his Portuguese written in English. Is it not strange however that Prieur and Delacroix and Madgett should be satisfied to let him pass on a business of such magnitude? I think I must go to the Minister and make it a point that he shall be stopped. At all events *I* will not communicate with him; *that is flat!* After dinner walked with Sullivan for two hours in the Tuilleries, talking red hot Irish politics. Sullivan is a good lad, and I like him very well. Bed early.

## 4 Apr. 1796

Called on Madgett at nine in order to give him in cool blood my determination as to Mr Fitzsimons, who indeed does not understand Portuguese. Madgett gone

[1] John Keogh. [2] *Life*, ii, 84, has 'readily' instead of 'fast'. [3] *Life* omits 'the priest'.

[4] Sullivan (Christian name not ascertained) was employed, like Madgett, in the translation section ('bureau des traductions') of the ministry of foreign affairs; in 1794, as an inspector of prisoners-of-war, he discovered Hamilton Rowan in prison at Brest and secured his release; in 1798 he was, under the *nom de guerre* La Roche, aide-de-camp to Humbert (Rowan, *Autobiography*, p. 232; Archives des Affaires Étrangères, Personnel, Sullivan dossier).

out of town *recruiting*. That is another scheme that, as they are managing it, I do not like. I will go to Clarke again tomorrow and protest against it, for I will not be accessary to spilling the blood of my brave and unfortunate countrymen, poor fellows! And it would be the best and bravest of them whose lives, if they must be sacrificed, should be reserved for a better occasion. I will not, on my part, leave anything undone to prevent the infinite mischiefs which I see in every point of view resulting from introducing the spirit of *chouannerie* in Ireland. I think I will go now and put my reasons against it on paper, in order to give to Clark[e] tomorrow—xxx.

## Memorandum to General Henri Jacques Guillaume Clarke on the encouragement of *chouannerie* in Ireland, 4 April 1796

Archives Nationales, AF IV, carton 1671, ff $65^{r}$–$67^{v}$.

This document, though dated 14 Germinal an IV (3 Apr. 1796), is referred to in a part of the Diary dated 4 Apr. as having been written that day (see below, p. 145).

Paris $14^{p}$ Germinal l'an $4^{me}$

I beg leave to submit, with all deference, the following objections to the measure of dispatching emissaries to Ireland, previous to the landing of the French Troops, in order to raise a spirit of what is called *chouannerie* in that country.

$1^{st}$ That it is unnecessary, if intended to prepare the people, because the people are already sufficiently prepared.

$2^{d}$ The only effect it would produce would be to raise local insurrections, of which we have had but too many already; in which case the Army and the Militia would to a certainty support the Government, as well as every man of property of every party, even those who are the most zealous for the independence of their country, from the dread of an indiscriminate plunder, which would be but too likely to ensue.

$3^{d}$ That if the attempt succeeded so far as to raise those insurrections, it would be the most forward and ardent of the peasantry, the best and bravest of them, who would fall a sacrifice; that of the rest, numbers would be hanged, and much greater numbers sent to serve on board the fleet; thereby in fact strengthening instead of weakening the enemy.

$4^{th}$ That an insurrection suppressed, as this would certainly be, always leaves the existing government stronger than before; and it is to be apprehended that England, taking the advantage of the alarm and terror raised in the minds of the men of property in Ireland, might seize that opportunity to reduce her once more to the situation of a dependant province, and even to enslave her worse than before the year 1782, and to render all hope of her emancipation impossible.

5th That tho' France has every right and every provocation to retaliate on England the horrors of the war in La Vendée, yet it is submitted that in case this measure were adopted it would be Ireland, and not England, that would suffer more. Ireland has never concurred willingly in any measure to distress France, and consequently it would be scarcely just to make her suffer for the crimes of her oppressors; and as to England, she hates Ireland, next to France and not a man in that country would eat, drink, or sleep one jot the worse, if the Irish were employed in cutting each other's throats; if indeed, it be not a circumstance that would give them pleasure.

6th That the British Government might take the advantage of the alarm such insurrections would produce to prevail on the legislatures of both countries to pass acts transferring the Irish militia to England and the English militia to Ireland, which would most materially strengthen their hands in both countries, as is too evident to require elucidation.

7th That Ireland, having no great woods or forests, appears to be a country not adapted to support for any time a system of insurrection like that of the Chouans in the Vendée in France.

T. Wolfe Tone

# Diary, 4–9 April 1796

T.C.D., Tone papers, MS 2049, ff 39r–44r; *Life*, ii, 85–91.

In the MS there is a change of pen for that part of the Diary for 4 Apr. given below. It is clear from this, and from other internal evidence, that it was written later in the day than the part given above (pp 143–4).

## 4 Apr. 1796 (contd)

Wrote my reasons (which are to be found [in] the memorandums of the 2d inst.) in the shape of five or six short propositions[1] and set off to give them to Clarke. Called in my way at the Rue de Bacq and saw the Minister.[2] I told him that it was not a pleasant thing to speak hardly of anybody, but that my duty compelled me to tell him that Fitzsimons, whom I had seen and conversed with, was absolutely unfit for the mission on which it was proposed to send him; that as to his principles or his honesty I had no reason to doubt them, but as to his talents, he was a downright blockhead (*un imbécile*); that consequently I could not commit myself or my friends, or the cause, to a person whom I found to be absolutely incapable. The Minister replied that he did not know him at all. He asked me then had I no person myself to recommend? I told him that I knew not a soul in Paris. He then desired me to look out for a proper person (*which I will not do, for*

[1] Above, pp 144–5. [2] Delacroix.

*in the first place I know nobody, and in the next I will not make myself responsible by a recommendation*), for that it was absolutely necessary the Government should be informed of the actual state of things in Ireland. He then asked me had I not seen Gen[era]l Clarke? I told him I had, by the orders of Carnot. Well, said he, I suppose he told you that the affair is in train, that preparations are making '*et j'espère que ça ira!*'. I told him I was very happy to hear it from him and so I took my leave. This short conversation happened in the court of his hotel, where I met him coming out of his bureau. From the Minister I went to Clarke, whom I saw for two minutes, he being engaged with a general officer and his aid du camp [*sic*]. I gave him my '*reasons*' and he told me the plan was *given up*, which I am very glad to hear; he also said he had not yet been able to find a proper person to go to Ireland. I then mentioned that I had been with the Minister about Fitzsimons, that he was utterly incapable and that I mentioned it to him lest he might be taken by surprise as to his appointment. He then desired me to call on him every three or four days, and so we parted. I am heartily glad the system of *chouannerie* is knocked in the head and I hope it is partly owing to my representations against it. I am now absolutely idle for three or four days and I am truly weary of this life. '*Fie upon it! I want work!*'[1] Well, if ever I get to Ireland I shall have work enough to make me amends for this. Strolled as usual to the Champs-Élysées and dined alone. Delicious weather, and all the world out diverting themselves except me. '*Poor moralist! and what art thou—a solitary fly!*'[2] I declare I am as much alone here as if I were in the deserts of Arabia, and that is hard in such a city as Paris. In the evening the Comédie Italienne &c. No great things. The Opera is the only spectacle for me. Bed at ten. '*Well, God's blessing be about the man*', quoth Sancho Panza, '*that first invented sleep! It covers a man all over like his cloak!*'[3]

## 5, 6 and 7 Apr. 1796

Blank! Blank! Blank! This is sad!

## 8 Apr. 1796

Strolled to the Palais de Justice, the Westminster Hall of Paris, because I have a sneaking kindness for the profession of the law of which I was so distinguished a member in my own country. Saw a man tried for stealing a plank.[4] He told his own story very well and he had a counsel who made a very good defence for him and spoke extremely well. I understood every word of his speech, which I think

[1] 'Fie upon this quiet life! I want work.' (*1 Henry IV*, II, iv).

[2] Thomas Gray, 'Ode on the spring' (1768), ll 43–4.

[3] These words are quoted from Laurence Sterne rather than from Cervantes (*Don Quixote*, pt ii, chap. 68). Sterne, in his *Tristram Shandy* (1759), vol. iv, chap. 15, reads: 'God's blessing, said Sancho Pancha, be upon the man who first invented this self-same thing called sleep—it covers a man all over like a cloak'.

[4] Tone seems to have been present at a sitting of the departmental criminal tribunal (Jacques Godechot, *Les institutions de la France sons la Révolution et l'empire* (Paris, 1951), pp 120–21, 416).

is evidence that it was a good one. The jury made a respectable appearance; they retired to consider of their verdict but I did not stay for the event. I suppose from what I heard the man was acquitted. The judge charged them with great moderation and exactly in the language of the English law told them it was their verdict, not his; that the point for them to consider was the intention of the culprit, as the fact was admitted; that if they believed he had no criminal intent but acted merely thro' ignorance, they were bound to acquit him, &c. All which I liked very well. I did not think they had so much notion of criminal law in France; but the reason of that was that I grounded my opinion on that consummation of all iniquity and horror, the Revolutionary tribunal. The judges (five in number) were dressed in black, à la Vandyke, with hats decorated with the national feathers, and a tricolor ribband round their necks, like the collars of the orders of knighthood in England, to which were suspended the fasces and axes, in silver, the emblem of their functions; the public accuser, or attorney general, was habited pretty much after the same fashion; the lawyers had no discrimination of dress, which shews their good sense. It is the same in America; the judges alone are distinguished by their habits, and they are not disguised by that most preposterous and absurd of all human inventions—the long full-bottomed wig. Altogether I liked the appearance of the French *tribunal criminel* and the manner in which the trial was conducted [pleased me][1] extremely. Certainly every justice was done to the prisoner. I was astonished at the purity of his diction and the politeness of his manner in a short discussion he had with the public accuser, who on his part shewed great lenity and candour. I am afraid an Irish thief would hardly conduct himself with the same talents, or at least the same manners; but let that pass. Poor Pat is not to be despised because he is not as polished as a Frenchman, and besides who knows what we may make of him yet?—he has very pretty capabilities.

Went[2] in the evening to see *Le Déserteur*,[3] at the Théâtre des Italiens. Disappointed—a very poor performance. I speak as to the actors, for the piece itself is inimitable. Even Chenard,[4] who in general is admirable, was very indifferent in Montauciel. His manner was dry and hard. The fact is the French do not know how to represent a man drunk, which is owing to a defect in their education, for as they never drink hard, they have no archetypes, so they form some vague notions of the manner in which a drunken man walks and speaks, &c., but this is all from the imagination and the perfection of acting is to copy nature. If Chenard had the great advantage to spend two or three afternoons with P.P.[5] and another person who shall be nameless, I think he might very much enlarge and improve

[1] In the MS a word or words are missing from this sentence and so suitable wording has been supplied as in *Life*, ii, 87.

[2] Preceded in MS by redundant 'in'.

[3] *Le Déserteur*, a three-act play by Michel Jean Sedaine (1719–97), was first performed in Paris in 1769. One of the characters, Montauciel, a dragoon, at the end of the second act declares 'Buvez et chantez'. (*Grand Larousse encyclopédique*).

[4] Simon Chenard (1738–1832), well-known opera singer. During the revolution he sang the 'Marseillaise' at official ceremonies. He became master of the chapel under Napoleon I. (*Dict. biog. franç.*).

[5] Thomas Russell.

his ideas as to the manner of acting Montauciel. By the bye the character of Montauciel, which is so inimitably characteristic of the *French soldier* in the original, is miserably disguised on the English theatre; they have carefully preserved and I must say improved his drunkenness, which is but a subordinate and accidental trait in France, and they have suffered his gai[e]ty, his fierté, his carelessness of manner and his high spirit totally to evaporate. There is no character on earth more appropriate or better discriminated than that of a French dragoon, as I have myself had one or two opportunities to observe. In that view Montauciel is inimitably drawn. Skirmish, the Montauciel of England, is nothing but a drunkard; take away his bottle and you take away his existence. Montauciel can maintain himself without it. But I believe there is enough of criticism for the present, and besides I am sleepy, &c., &c.

## 9 Apr. 1796

Sullivan called on me this morning with an English paper[1] of the 31st of March (viz. 10 days ago) in which is an article on Ireland wherein mention is made of Sir Edw[ar]d Bellew of Bellewstown being arrested as being connected with the Defenders. That is a little surprising, for he is a confirmed aristocrat, and he and all his family have been devoted to the Government so extremely as even to have the meanness to oppose the Catholics.[2] Such is the gratitude of the Irish Government! But this piece of news is accompanied with another which gives me the most sincere anxiety on every possible account, public and private; it is the arrest of John Keogh, a man to whom I am indebted much, and his country much more.[3] This is no place to write his panegyric. Poor fellow! I have not got such a shock this long time. If we lose him, I know not where to look for a man to supply his place. I have differed with him at one time, and I am sure now I was in a great degree wrong.[4] His services to Ireland have been eminent indeed, more especially to the Catholics, and in all probability they will prove his ruin, for from the state of his health confinement in the unwholesome air of a prison will be to him death as certain as the Guillotine. I am inexpressibly concerned on his account. That infernal government of Ireland! It is of a long time they have been on the watch for his destruction, and I am sure they will stick at no means, however atrocious, to accomplish their ends. I can scarcely promise myself ever to see him again, and I can sincerely say that one of the greatest pleasures I had proposed to myself, in case of our success, was the pleasure of the society of Mt Jerome, where I have spent so many happy days, and some of them serviceable to

[1] Not identified.

[2] i.e. to oppose the Catholic Committee. For the Bellew family, who were catholics but had seceded from the Catholic Committee in 1791, see above, vol. I, p. 309. The report about Sir Edward Bellew (who had succeeded as baronet in 1795) may have arisen because of his youngest brother having been charged with being a leader of the Defenders four years earlier (*Trial of Francis Bellew, Esq., youngest son of Sir Patrick Bellew, Bart, for appearing in arms with a mob of Defenders on the 26th of December, 1792* (Dublin, 1792)).

[3] The preceding thirteen words are omitted from *Life*.

[4] The preceding twelve words are omitted from *Life*.

the country. It was there that he and I used to frame all our manifestoes and papers. It was there that we drew up the Petition[1] and Vindication of the Catholics,[2] which produced such powerful effects in England and Ireland. I very much fear we shall never labour together again for the good of our native country. Poor fellow![3] If that abominable crew succeed in their designs upon his life, he will be an irreparable loss to Ireland. This is the second of my friends, and what is of far more consequence, friends to their country, that I fear I shall have to lament. Poor Sweetman[4] is gone irrecoverably. For Keogh there is yet a chance, but I dread the villainy of the Government, who hate and fear him worse than hell. I am sure he has been too wise and too cautious to put himself in their power, but what wisdom or caution is proof against forged and suborned testimony, which I know they will never stick at procuring, and in the state affairs are in now in Ireland any evidence will be received. Well! a day will come for all this! If we cannot prevent his fall, at least I hope we shall be able to revenge it; *and I for one promise if it be in twenty years from this not to forget it*. My heart is hardening hourly, and I satisfy myself now at once on points which would stagger me twelve months ago. The Irish aristocracy are putting themselves in a state of nature with the people, and let them take the consequences. They shew no mercy and they deserve none. If ever I have the power I will most heartily concur in making them *a dreadful example*. I am to meet Madgett today on this business. See what the consequence of delay is! We have already lost perhaps the two *most useful* men in their respective departments in Ireland.[5] Unhappy is the man and the nation whose destiny depends on the will of another! This blow has deranged my system terribly. The Government here insist on sending somebody to Ireland. Keogh was the very principal person whom he ought to see; he is confined in a prison. I observe in the same paper several other persons have been obliged to abscond to avoid imprisonment. I have no doubt but the most useful and active of my friends are in the number. This is a gloomy day![6] How will John Keogh's sons[7] take their father's imprisonment? *How will the people take it?* What if this indiscriminate persecution were to provoke a general rising as in 1641? The thing is not impossible. Oh France, France! What do you not deserve to suffer, if you permit this crisis to escape you! Poor Ireland! Well, it does not signify whining or croaking and I am sworn never to despair; but the slowness of people here, if they really have the means to act, is beyond all human suffering; if they have not the means, we must submit, but it is dreadful to think of.[8] What would I not give to have poor

[1] See above, vol. I, pp 361–71. [2] See above, vol. I, pp 371–88.

[3] From 'Poor fellow!' to 'than hell' five lines down is omitted from *Life*. John Keogh in fact was not arrested at this time and was not prominent in politics during the next nine years.

[4] Edward Sweetman, who was killed in a duel three months earlier (see above, pp 98–9).

[5] *Life*, ii, 89, inserts their names (Sweetman and Keogh).

[6] In ibid., p. 90, the following two sentences are omitted.

[7] Keogh had sons named Cornelius, George Drew, John and Michael.

[8] In the MS faint ink marks half-encircle the word that follows, and also the word 'country' several lines below, as if to set apart the intervening three sentences. In *Life*, ii, 90, these sentences are omitted.

Keogh with me today in Paris! I have often wished for him since my arrival, but now I have a reason stronger ten thousand fold. Well, once more *I swear*, if his death ensues from this horrible persecution, that I for one will revenge his fall, without pity or remorse, as well from the sincere regard I feel for him as for the gratitude which I owe him for many acts of private friendship, and especially as an Irishman I shall ever consider him as the victim of the great services he has rendered his country.

Dined today in the Elysian Fields[1] with Madgett and a person of the name of Ahern,[2] a physician who is to be sent to Ireland. Explained to him my sentiments as to the conduct he should adopt there, and particularly cautioned him against writing a syllable, or carrying a single scrape of a pen with him; pointed out to him the persons whom he is to see and speak to, at the same time that I fear many of the most useful are now either in prison or concealing themselves. This comes of delays, but that is no fault of mine. I like Ahern very well. He seems a cool man, with good republican sentiments. He has been already employed in Scotland. Apropos of Scotland! There is some scheme going on there, as I collected from hints which dropped from him and Madgett, but what it is I know not, nor did I enquire. My opinion is that nothing will ever be done there, unless we first begin in Ireland. If we succeed, John Bull will have rather a troublesome neighbour of us. We shall be within eighteen miles of him.[3] Ahern is to call on me tomorrow morning in order to talk over the business of his mission at length, and I am to give him some memorandums, which I will advise [him] to commit to memory first, and then by all means to burn them. I should have observed in its place that I went at twelve o'clock to Clarke and brought him the newspaper containing the account of Keogh's being arrested, with a translation of the article in French for Carnot which I got Sullivan to make. Clarke was just going off to the Directory, so I had hardly time to speak a word to him. I wished to speak to Carnot myself, and I could see Clarke was not at all desirous that I should have an opportunity. Damn such pitiful, jealous vanity! Every man here must do everything himself. I have found this unworthy sentiment in every one of them except Carnot. First the Minister is disobliged because I go to Carnot; then Madgett would be huffed, if he durst, because I go to Clarke; and now Clarke truly wants to thrust himself in between me and his principal. Please God he shall not tho'! If I want to see Carnot, I will see him, or I will be refused. I am to call on Clarke again tomorrow

[1] i.e. the Champs-Élysées.

[2] Eugene Ahern, who in Dec. 1793 was sent on a secret mission to Scotland (Archives des Affaires Étrangères, 'Personnel', Ahern dossier). He was very probably the 'Aherne' (Christian name not stated) who was the subject of a lengthy but inaccurate note in a suspects book in the Rebellion papers (Nat. Arch. (Ire.), 620/1/216). This 'Aherne' was said to have been born in Co. Kerry in the mid-1760s and to have gone to study medicine in Edinburgh 'where he acted as a delegate from the Irish to the Scotch societies'. Eugene Ahern may be the same as the John Ahearn mentioned by Miles Byrne as having been appointed captain in Napoleon's Irish legion on 7 Dec. 1803 and died at Metz in 1806 on a march to Mayence (Miles Byrne, *Memoirs* (3 vols, Paris, 1863), iii, 174).

[3] The minimum distance between Ireland and Great Britain (from Torr Head to the Mull of Kintyre) is in fact 12½ English miles, or 20 km.

at one. I think I will then, with all possible deference and politeness, give him to understand my opinion on this point, which, as they manage it, is most excessively provoking, especially at a period when every minute is precious and my anxiety is so great. Madgett tells me the Minister[1] has been superseded in the business these fifteen days, and that it has been given entirely into the hands of Carnot. I am most heartily glad of that, because he is given to *organising* a little. He is the man I want, and I hope the measures being given to his management is partly at least, if not entirely, owing to my going directly to himself and to the discourse we had together, *malgré* my execrable jargon, which is neither French nor English. If that be so, as I hope it is, I may say that in this instance I have deserved well of my country. I hope I shall deserve still better yet. *Nous verrons!*

## Diary, 10–21 April 1796

T.C.D., Tone papers, MS 2049, ff 45$^{r}$–51$^{v}$; *Life*, ii, 91–8.

Number 6
From April 10th to May 16th [1796] inclusive[2]
*Nil desperandum!*
Paris
1796

La Renommée, à qui dans tous les tems
Le plus modeste a donné quelques encens
Le sage dit que son coeur la méprise
Qu'il haït l'éclat que lui donne un grand nom
Que la louange est pour l'âme un poison
Le sage ment, et dit une sottise!

*La Pucelle*, Chant 6[3]

### 10 Apr. 1796

Ahern called on me this morning and I gave him a list of the persons whom he is to see, viz. Gog, Magog, P. P., C. T., the Tanner, and S. N., O. B., J. McN.[4] with

[1] Delacroix.

[2] The Diary entries for 22–5 Apr., 26 Apr.–2 May, 7–11 May, 12–13 May, 14 May, 15 May and 16 May are given as separate documents (below, pp 160–64, 169–76, 177–9, 181–2, 183, 184, 185).

[3] *La Pucelle* by Voltaire (1755). In *Life* this verse and the preceding headings, obviously added later than 10 Apr., are omitted.

[4] i.e. John Keogh, Richard McCormick, Thomas Russell, Charles Hamilton Teeling, Robert Simms, Samuel Neilson, Oliver Bond and William James MacNeven.

a quere as to J. P.[1] and T. E.[2] I also gave him some trifling anecdotes, known only to ourselves, which will satisfy them that he has seen and conversed with me. When we had done I went to Clarke, who was for the first time denied to me. However, I waited for a few minutes and caught him coming out of his bureau. He seemed, and probably was, in a great hurry. He said that he had shewed the newspaper[3] to Carnot, who was very sorry that the gentleman was arrested; but what could he do? I looked at him very earnestly and repeated, 'What could he do?'. I then shrugged up my shoulders and repeated twice, in French, '*Mauvaise augure!*'. 'No', replied Clarke, 'you must not look on it in that light, you must not infer anything bad from that'. We then walked on towards the Directory, where he was going, and I was pressing him, if the business were at all attempted, on the necessity of not losing a moment. He interrupted me by asking me, 'How do you know that we are losing a moment?'. I replied that was enough, and so we parted. I am to see him again in a few days. From all this I infer, for I ask him no questions, that preparations are actually going forward somewhere, and indeed I hear it indirectly from other quarters, and I am sorry for it; not that the business is doing, but that they talk so much of it. I wish they would be as reserved to others as Clarke is to me; but what do I care for his reserve? Let them once do the business and treat me as they like.

## 11 Apr. 1796

Sullivan called on me this morning (for it is he that brings me my secondary intelligence) to tell me that D'Albarade,[4] the late Minister of the Marine, is to command in the naval department of our expedition and that a confidential person told him yesterday that he might look for good news soon for his country, for that there was something at that moment doing for her in Holland, by which I presume that it is there preparations are making. I am glad of that. I mentioned Holland myself to Carnot, to Clarke and to the Minister. By the bye, the Minister is on the eve of being turned out;[5] but as the business is now in the hands of Carnot himself, I am in hopes that will make no difference as to us. I do not glory at all in the present aspect of things.

## 12 Apr. 1796

Blank! How my life stagnates just now! Well, ''*Tis but in vain &c.*'

[1] Probably James Plunkett. In *Life* he is not identified.

[2] Thomas Addis Emmet, as identified in *Life*, ii, 91.

[3] See Diary for 9 Apr. (above, p. 148).

[4] Jean Dalbarade (1743–1819), a naval officer before the revolution; minister of the marine, 1793–4 (Six, *Dict. des généraux & amiraux*).

[5] Delacroix continued as minister for foreign affairs until 19 July 1797.

## 13 Apr. 1796

Ahern called on me this morning to tell me that yesterday he was to see Clarke, to whom he was introduced by Ysabeau,[1] one of the *chefs de bureaux* under the Minister for Foreign Affairs. He seems egregiously disgusted with both of them and especially with Clarke, who I find has been talking sad stuff with him. They did not conclude anything, but he collected from them that the idea was that he should go to Ireland and that one or two persons should come from that country here in order to *insense* the French Government on the state of affairs. Ahern mentioned the loss of time which this would produce and also that I was on the spot ready and competent to give them every information on the subject. Clarke replied, after speaking handsomely of my abilities &c., that I had been now several months out of the country and things might have changed since my departure. He also observed that I seemed so earnest in the business that probably my zeal might make me a little heighten the picture without any intention to deceive the French Government, to which Ahern replied that all I had advanced was supported by the recent accounts in the papers relative to Irish affairs. Clarke, however, did not seem satisfied and so the affair rested as to him. As to Ysabeau, who knows not one syllable with regard to the situation of Ireland, he has thrust himself into the business and is to frame the instructions which are to govern Ahern. How he will contrive to adapt them to a subject of which he is utterly ignorant is more than I can possibly conceive. This is most intolerably provoking! Here is the liberty of Ireland shuffled back and forward between two French *commis*, one of whom is under gross prejudices and the other absolutely ignorant. What is to be done? As to me, how shall I satisfy Clarke that I am not the dupe of my own enthusiasm in the cause, supposing he is gracious enough to give me credit for being sincere? The more earnestness I shew to convince him, the more enthusiasm I manifest, so here I am in an unfortunate circle! By the bye, Clarke is just as competent to regulate this affair as I am to be made Lord Chancellor of England, and for my fitness for that station I appeal to all who ever knew me in the capacity of a lawyer. I have not forgot his nonsense about gaining over some of the Irish aristocracy to our side to begin with, such as Lord Ormond for example; neither have I forgot his asking me might we not be able to *make something of Fitzgibbon*?[2] Good God! Is it not enough to set me mad to be obliged to listen and to keep my temper, not to say my countenance, at such execrable trash? And yet the fate of Ireland is in a certain degree in this man's hands! Well, well! Wretched, I again repeat, is the nation whose independance hangs on the will of another. Clarke has also some doubts as to my report on the influence of the Irish priests, which he dreads a good deal; and this is founded on his own observation in a visit he paid

[1] Ysabeau, chief secretary, premier bureau, secrétaire intime, ministry of foreign affairs. A report sent to Grenville in May 1796, based on information from an agent in France, described Ysabeau as being the most important official in the ministry. It added that he was ambitious, loved money and might be a source of information. (*Almanach nationale*, An 4; P.R.O., FO 27/47).

[2] See Diary for 14 Mar. 1796 (above, pp 111–12).

to Ireland in the year 1789.[1] That is to say, a Frenchman who just peeps in the country for an instant *five years ago*, and those five the heat of the Revolution, sets up his opinion against mine, who have been on the spot, who have attentively studied and been confidentially employed and to whom nothing relating to Catholic affairs could possibly be a secret. That is reasonable and modest in my friend Clarke. He likewise catechised Ahern as to the chance of our preferring monarchy as our form of government in case of a successful revolution, adding that in that case we would of course consult the French Government in our choice. That is selling the bear's skin[2] with a vengeance! I wonder does he seriously think that if we succeeded we would come post to Paris to consult him, Gen[era]l Clarke, a handsome, smooth-faced young man, as to what we should do? I can assure him we would not. When he spoke to me on this head he was more reasonable, for he said it was indifferent to the French republic what form of government we adopted, provided we secured our independence. It seems now he is more sanguine; but I for one will never be accessory to subjecting my country to the control of France merely to get rid of England. We are able enough to take care of ourselves if we were once afloat; or if we are not, we deserve to sink. So much for Clarke! As to his confrère, the other *commis*, Ysabeau, who has got into this business, God knows how, for I do not, it is still more provoking. Ahern tells me he is a blockhead, but if he had ever such talents, how the devil can he give instructions on a subject of which he is utterly ignorant? I suppose he will hardly be inspired on the occasion. Well, poor Ireland, poor Ireland! Here you are at the mercy of two clerks, utterly incapable, supposing them honest; it they be not (and who knows?) it is still worse.[3] And what can I do? I could tear my flesh with rage and fury. Well, Ahern is gone to Ysabeau (to whom by the bye Madgett gave in a draft of instructions which he never shewed me, I know not why, and which Ysabeau never condescended to read) to settle about his instructions. I will stop here for the present and see what this conversation will produce.[4]

Ysabeau is *turned out*! A pretty time they chose to entrust him with the secret! Is not this folly incredible? Ahern saw the minister himself and spoke his opinion without reserve of Clarke, whom he thinks *not honest*. I do not know but he is right. I remember he told me in our first conversation[5] that he was related to Lord Cahir and the Butler family in Ireland.[6] Lord Cahir is married to Fitzgibbon's niece.[7] Will this explain his anxiety about the aristocracy and his wish to hook in

[1] No more on this has been found. [2] i.e. selling the bear's skin before catching the bear.

[3] *Life* omits the following words as far as and including 'Well'.

[4] In the MS at this point there is a large asterisk and the pen changes.

[5] On 14 Mar. 1796 (see above, pp 109–14).

[6] Richard Butler (1775–1819) succeeded as 12th Baron Caher in 1788 and inherited Caher Castle in Co. Tipperary; he was created earl of Glengall, 1816. The only family connexion traced to Clarke is through his mother, Sarah (née Nichols) of Knockeenglass, Co. Kilkenny, whose sister Susannah seems to have been related by marriage in some way to the Shees and Clarkes (G.E.C., *Peerage*; 'O'Shea of Munster', B.L., Add. MS 45576).

[7] In Aug. 1793, Lord Caher married Emily (1767?–1836), youngest daughter of James St John Jefferyes of Blarney Castle by his wife Isabella, sister of Lord Fitzgibbon (see above, vol. I, p. 24, n. 8).

Lord Ormond, the head of the Butlers? and the monstrous extravagance of his question about Fitzgibbon? It has a very odd appearance. I am very much afraid he will turn out a scoundrel, and I see now I was right in thinking his manner towards me was changed. Well, if it be so, I will see what is fit for me to do, and if it is necessary to punish him personally I will do it, for I begin to dislike him mortally.[1] It seems he told Ahern that he should apprise the people in Ireland to be on the look out for assistance by September, or it might be November next, viz. in six or seven months; and this he guarded by saying 'unless something should happen in the course of the campaign to prevent it'. That is a pretty general exception! When Ahern told this to the Minister, he seemed astonished, for the fact is he is utterly unacquainted with the business. He therefore got rid of it by giving Ahern a few queries in writing on the subject of Ireland, the answers to which are already in my memorials, but it was merely to gain time, and he said he would see Clarke himself and let Ahern know the result tomorrow at one o'clock, and then give him his final instructions. Altogether things cannot look much worse. If Clarke be a rascal,[2] we are blown up. I have determined as to what I will, myself, do. I will first learn the result of the Minister's conversation with Ahern tomorrow, and what Clark[e] has said to him. I will then go to Clarke myself and have an explanation with him, and I will insist upon being in a certain degree informed of what is going forward, which hitherto I have not done at all. In short I will endeavour to bring him to something definite. If I find that impossible, I will write to Carnot my opinion fully, as well of the mode of doing business here in general as of Clarke's conduct in particular, without the least reserve, and the grounds on which I found that opinion. I will likewise demand that all my future communication shall be directly with himself and that I shall look on the refusal of this request as a sympton that the measure is abandoned; and if General Clarke is offended at all this, let him take his remedy. I suspect most violently that he is secretly counteracting the business to save his noble connections in Ireland, and if so, I should be heartily glad to have an opportunity to punish him *personally*. After all it is possible he may be innocent, and I will not proceed but upon good grounds such as will satisfy my conscience. Ahern is *acharné* against him and so is Sullivan. I am much cooler than either of them. Ahern will denounce him again to the Minister tomorrow, especially for what he said as to our consulting France relative to the choice of a monarch, which is, to be sure, most unaccountable in Clarke. Sullivan will set Prieur and Laignelot[3] on his back. For my part I know nobody, and of course I have not the power, if I had the wish, to intrigue against him, which I disdain to do. If I find him, or have satisfactory reasons to suspect him, to be a traitor in the business, I will denounce

[1] In *Life*, ii, 94, this and the preceding sentence are conflated as: 'If he should turn out a scoundrel, I will see what is fit for me to do, and if it is necessary . . .'.

[2] *Life*, ii, 95, has 'not honest' instead of 'a rascal'.

[3] Joseph François Laignelot (1750–1829), member of the Convention and deputy on mission; he was implicated in Babeuf's conspiracy and after its failure in May 1796 was arrested and imprisoned (*Dict. parl. franç.*).

him at once to Carnot, and let him then act as he pleases. Ahern and Sullivan, who know the pavé better than I do, are satisfied he is betraying us; for my part, I am not convinced, tho' I see appearances strong against him. I will wait for further proof and if I am once decided, I will then do what is right in the premisses. Let us see what the next three or four days will produce, and in the mean time do nothing rashly. Dined at Ahern's lodgings, with Madgett, Sullivan, &c. Choice champaigne! Got half tipsy, partly with rage and vexation at the prospect before me. Have I risqued my life, ruined my prospects, left my family and deserted my country to be baffled by a scoundrel at last? If he prove one, woe be to him!

## 14 Apr. 1796

Breakfast with Ahern and Sullivan; they still hold their opinion as to Clarke. I will wait for further evidence. Ahern is to see the Minister[1] today and that will be one step in the demonstration. Fixed to dine together. Dinner. Ahern could not see the Minister, so nothing is done.

## 15 Apr. 1796

Went with Ahern to the Minister's and met a most gracious reception. He had nothing to tell us, but that he had seen Clarke, to whom the military part of the business had been entrusted, and that Clarke had assured him that preparations were actually making in the interior of Holland. With regard to Ahern, he said his instructions would be ready in three or four days; then we shall see something of the plan. I mentioned to him the arrestation of Keogh,[2] and the embar[r]assment it must produce in our affairs. He observed it would only inflame the people's minds the more. I answered, as to them it was unnecessary, they were sufficiently inflamed, but when I saw the difficulty was in the imprisonment of him and others, in as much as they could be of such service in framing a provisional government, I observed likewise as to myself, and I begged him to remember it, that the very men I had pointed out as my friends, and as the proper persons to speak to in Ireland, were the very persons now imprisoned and persecuted by the British Government. I also took the opportunity to apologize for my not seeing him oftener, that I knew the value of his time too well to take it up in visits of ceremony, &c. We parted the best friends in the world, he assuring me that in every part of the business where he was engaged I might depend on his utmost exertions. I must now wait till I see Ahern's instructions.

## 16, 17 Apr. 1796

Blank! Damn it!

[1] Delacroix. [2] See Diary for 9 Apr. 1796 (above, pp 148–9).

## 18 Apr. 1796

Called on Clarke, who is very reserved of late—let him! He had *nothing to tell me* of our expedition, but he said they had some scheme of introducing *chouannerie*[1] into England, and he desired I would write a paper fit to be distributed in case of a landing on that scheme being effected. I told him I was sure I could not do it; that I did not know the grievances of England and that I could not write in the character of a Frenchman. He said he was sure I could if I would try. So to get rid of the business I said I would make the attempt, but I won't. He is plaguy fond of *chouannerie*!

## 19 Apr. 1796

Blank! ——

## 20 Apr. 1796

This being the first Floréal, I left the Hôtel des Étrangers, where I have been fleeced like ten thousand devils, and removed to the house where Ahern lodges, where I hope I shall live much cheaper and more comfortable.[2] Went with Ahern at one o'clock to the Minister's[3] in order to see after his instructions. At last there is a prospect of something like business. The Minister read the draft of the instructions, in which there is a great deal of trash mixed with some good sense. Only think of one of the articles wherein they say that if Ireland continues devoted to the House of Stuart, one of that family can be found who will be agreeable to all parties! Who the devil is this Pretender *in petto*? It is all one to us, however, for we will have nothing to do with him. I made one or two observations to the Minister on the instructions. He acted very fairly, for he gave me them and desired me to make what observations struck me, and as to Ahern, he said that he must only be guided by such of them as might apply to the state of things[4] and disregard those which did not—all which is candid. I see the instructions are written by Clarke, for I find in them his trash about monarchy, the noblesse and the clergy. There is one thing however which reconciles me to all this absurdity, which is that the French government promise us 10,000 men and 20,000 stand of arms. With that force I have not the shadow of doubt of our success. It is to be escorted by 9 sail of the line (Dutch I believe) and 3 frigates, and will be ready about the middle or towards the end of May, which is not more than six weeks off. *If this be so*! But let me not be sanguine. Went to Madgett to communicate this good news, and fixed to dine together, Ahern, he and I, in the Champs-Élysées. Dined accordingly and

[1] Meaning here irregular warfare. For its origins, see above, p. 140, n. 2.

[2] Henry Swinburne, the British agent, who in 1796 stayed for a short time in the Hôtel des Étrangers, also left it because it was too expensive (Henry Swinburne, *The courts of Europe* (London, 1841), ii, 144, 171).

[3] Delacroix's.

[4] *Life*, ii, 97, inserts 'he found there'.

drank *rather enough*. Walked out and saw the French soldiery dancing in groupes [*sic*] under trees with their wives and mistresses. Judge in the humour I was in, with near two bottles of Burgundy in my head, whether I did not enjoy the spectacle. How often did I wish for my dearest love! Returned to the *cabaret*[1] and indeed drank another bottle of wine, which made three, and walked home in a state of considerable elevation, having several delightful visions before my eyes. Well '*wine does wonders, does wonders every day*'.[2] Bed. Slept like a top.

### 21 Apr. 1796

Walked about Paris diverting myself innocently. '*I 'gin to be aweary of the sun.*'[3] I wish I could once more see the green sod of Ireland! Yet Paris is delightful! But then '*Home is home*'. Well, who knows? I may be there yet.

## Tone's 'Observations' on 'Instructions' intended for Eugene Ahern, 22 April 1796

T.C.D., Tone papers, MS 2050, ff 13ʳ–13ᵛ.

For the dating of this document, see Diary for 22 Apr. 1796 (below, p. 160).

Eugene Ahern's instructions, copied by Tone (T.C.D., MS 2050, ff 11ʳ–12ᵛ), directed him on his arrival in Ireland to get in touch with the 'principaux chefs' of the Defenders and to ascertain the aims and resources of the organisation. If the Defenders were all catholics he was to find out whether they were led by their priests, by their 'seigneurs' or by 'marchands', and whether they were in contact with the northern presbyterians. If there was an alliance between the two groups he was to find out whether the catholics were influenced by the presbyterians, who were republicans, or were under the domination of their priests, whose aim would be to throw off the English yoke and establish the catholic religion with its 'institutions fanatiques'. Ahern was to endeavour to alter Irish opinion, but if he could not do so he should try and discover whether the Defenders intended to make one of their 'seigneurs' king of Ireland. If the future monarch was already selected, Ahern was to convince him that he was bound to be dependent on French support. If the Defenders had not a candidate in mind, he was to persuade them to consult France about their choice. Ahern was to urge the Defenders to organise themselves in geographical sub-divisions; to make arrangements for keeping in close touch with France; to secure information about their opponents' activities by building up a network of agents; and to collect suppliers

[1] *Life*, ii, 98, substitutes 'Restaurateur' for 'cabaret'.

[2] Wine does wonders ev'ry day,
Makes the heavy light and gay

(*The buck's bottle companion* (London, 1775), p. 65).

[3] *Macbeth*, v, v.

in anticipation of a French landing. The French, he could tell them, intended to send to Ireland 10,000 men with arms for 20,000.

A copy of the 'Instructions' and a French translation of Tone's 'Observations' are in Archives des Affaires Étrangères, Corresp. Politique Angleterre, cote 589, ff 267r–269v and 270r–271r). Ahern did not, however, go to Ireland. Another Irishman, Richard O'Shée, was to go in his place and apparently was given the 'Instructions' and Tone's 'Observations' (see below, p. 163, n. 3, p. 174, n. 1, p. 362, n. 1).

## Observations on the instructions delivered to ——[1]

[On] 3d paragraph[2]

The Defenders are all Catholics. They are *not led* by their priests. On the contrary their priests have exerted themselves to the utmost to prevent Defenderism. The Pope's Legate in Ireland, who is also Archbishop of Dublin,[3] has fulminated a general excommunication from the altar against them without effect; and their priests even refuse the Sacraments of the Romish church to those unfortunate men who have been condemned to be executed as Defenders, unless they would recant and betray their principals [*sic*]; there appears no instance of any one of them having done so; on the contrary they have preferred dying without the Sacraments. It is presumed these facts will sufficiently prove not only that they are not guided by their priests but that they become Defenders in spite of all the opposition of their clergy and in the teeth of a general excommunication. The truth is that within these five years the Romish clergy have lost almost totally the influence they had over the people, and the English party is heartily sorry for it, for thereby they have lost one of their most useful instruments for governing the peasantry of Ireland.

Neither have their nobility any influence over them at present. On the contrary their houses have been plundered of arms indiscriminately with their Protestant neighbours—in a word, religion makes no part whatsoever of the question of Defenderism. It is not because they are Catholics, but because they are poor and wretched and oppressed, that the peasantry of Ireland are Defenders. The distinction of religion is merely accidental.

There can be little doubt but that if the business were fairly commenced the Presbyterians must have a commanding influence from their superior knowledge and information. It would require some address in the chiefs on both sides at first to prevent any possible misunderstanding; but as they perfectly understand each other, there is very little apprehension of any difference of sentiment between the parties.

As to the idea of Royalty, there is nobody in Ireland would entertain it for a moment. If there is a revolution there, it most assuredly will never terminate in kingly government. As to the Stuart family, they are held in contempt by the

[1] The name is omitted in the French translation also.

[2] This paragraph begins 'Si les Deffenders ne sont composés que de catholiques . . .'.

[3] Troy.

Catholics, and as to the last of that race who was in Ireland (James 2d), his memory is despised and they have ever marked him by a name expressive in their language of the very lowest degree of contempt and disgrace.[1]

The number of 10,000 men is amply sufficient, but it is much to be desired that the number of spare arms should be increased to 30, 40, or even 50,000 stand instead of 20,000 mentioned in the instructions. Sabres and pistols for cavalry, suppose at least 1,000, or rather if possible 2,000 would be extremely necessary. It is adviseable that the landing should if possible be at Carrickfergus; but if not, Galway seems preferable to Londonderry, which is colonised in a great degree by the descendants of English settlers.

There is no definite time mentioned in the instructions at which the Irish people may expect the arrival of the French fleet.

All the other observations in the instructions are highly important and useful; but much, depending on local and temporary circumstances, must be left to the spirit and ability of those who have hitherto conducted Irish affairs, who will undoubtedly execute every part of them which the nature of things and the posture of affairs will permit.

## Diary, 22–5 April 1796

T.C.D., Tone papers, MS 2049, ff 51$^{v}$–54$^{r}$; *Life*, ii, 98–101.

### 22 Apr. 1796

Copied Ahern's instructions and wrote my observations,[2] which are very short. I barely mention what is necessary, and for the rest I say that it is all very right and that when he arrives in Ireland I have no doubt but the people there will execute every part of them which circumstances will admit, &c. Gave them to Madgett to translate. Went to Clarke to apprise him of my having changed my lodging. Asked him had he any news for me? He answered, not. I replied that hitherto he had not found me very pressing for information, but that nevertheless I expected and relied upon it that, when the time came, I should be properly apprised of everything. He answered, certainly. I also said that as to my own affairs, which I had scarcely mentioned, I hoped and expected that the request which I had suggested once already to him, of being employed in the expedition as an officer in the French service, would not be refused. He answered as to that I might depend upon it. I then mention'd the old subject of the necessity of losing no time, to which he replied, with an air of great significance, that *if* the affair were undertaken it would be within *two years* at any rate. He is a puppy, that is the truth of it. This good-humoured irony I dare say he thought was extremely diplomatic, but I can assure him he acts the statesman very poorly. He is much

[1] James II was nicknamed in Irish 'Séamus an Chaca'.

[2] Above, pp 158–60.

fitter to figure away at Ranelagh[1] than in a *bureau diplomatique*, for he is a handsome lad. I then mentioned Pichegru to him, observing that any old woman would make an ambassador for Sweden (where they are sending him) whereas our expedition required a man of great talents and military reputation. He replied he was sure Pichegru would not undertake it. I said I was not so sure of that; that if glory was an object with him, as doubtless it was, the dismemberment of the empire of England, the destruction of her power and the establishment of a new republic in Europe of 4,500,000 people were not ordinary occurrences; that if he was a man to be influenced by interested considerations there was no doubt but in case of our success he would be rewarded by Ireland to the utmost extent of his wishes, as well as every person who was instrumental in effectuating her emancipation. This hint I threw in for the Citizen Clarke himself. He made me some vague indefinite answer, which signified nothing, so I dropt the subject and I shall not renew it with him, but I have a little scheme in my head[2] in that score which a few days may develope. He then attacked me about his proclamation for *chouannising* England, mentioned in our last conversation.[3] I replied I had done nothing in it and that, if he would permit me to give my opinion, the measure was unwise, if not impracticable; that the peasantry of England were not at all in that situation which rendered it likely they would take any part in such a business, for several reasons which I enumerated; that perhaps in Scotland, which I was not however sure of, it might succeed, but I was satisfied in England never. He pressed me however to write the manifesto. I replied, as before, that I did not know their grievances, and that I had much rather write one for Ireland, which I did know. He desired me to do that also, *and without loss of time*. I promised him I would, and so we parted. He is a strange fellow. Does he know that the Minister[4] has told me everything that he is apprised of relative to the business? And if so, why all this prodigious reserve on his part? I suppose he has heard that secresy is a necessary quality in a great statesman, and so he is acting this part to impress me with an idea of his diplomatic talents. He is very much out I can tell him. Standing as I do here I confess I do not see the policy of concealing the measure from me more, especially when I hear it directly from the Minister and indirectly (which I am very sorry for) from a dozen different quarters. Well, let him go to the dogs, tho' he is a pretty gentleman. I believe I am at least as much interested in the success of the measure as he is, and perhaps a little more—confound him! I do not like him.

## 23 Apr. 1796

Blank! The blanks are very thick sown latterly in these memorandums, but that is not my fault. '*Can I make men live, whether they will or no?*'[5]

[1] Ranelagh in Chelsea was a place of public entertainment, the principal room being a large Rotunda where there was music and promenading (H. B. Wheatley, *London past and present* (London, 1891), iii, 190–91).

[2] *Life* omits 'in my head'.

[3] See above, p. 157. *Life* omits 'mentioned in our last conversation'.

[4] De la Croix.

[5] *2 Henry VI*, III, iii. This quotation is omitted from *Life*.

## 24 Apr. 1796

Called on Madgett to get my observations[1] which I gave him to translate.[2] He tells me he has not them. Hell and the Devil! Sure he has not lost them! It would be a pretty paper to set afloat just now in Paris where there are for aught I know a thousand English spies. If it be gone, I do not know what may be the consequence—perhaps the blowing up the whole expedition. Left Madgett in a rage, which I could hardly conceal.

*Evening.* He has found the paper![3] '*Ah, je respire!*' If he had lost it, I never should have forgiven him. Got Sullivan to translate it.[4] Tomorrow we go to the Minister's. '*Time, time!*' The French have begun the campaign by a splendid victory in Italy.[5] The *entamour*[6] of a negotiation between Wickham[7] and Barthélemi[8] has produced nothing, and the cry now is '*Guerre aux Anglais!*'. All this is *very good.* Théâtre de la République.[9] Macbeth, by Ducis.[10] Much better than his Othello. Talma,[11] Macbeth, a most excellent actor. Lady Macbeth, Madame Vestris,[12] very good, if I had not seen Mrs Siddons,[13] before whom all the actresses here vanish. A good ridiculous farce supported entirely by Dugazon,[14] who represents *five* different characters. '*Affairs look so well in the North, that it is impossible to displease me.*'[15]

[1] Above, pp 158–60.

[2] Tone seems to mean 'which I had given him to translate'.

[3] *Life*, ii, 100, has 'papers' and employs the plural throughout.

[4] Sullivan's translation is in Archives des Affaires Étrangères, Corresp. Politique Angleterre, cote 589, ff 270ʳ–271ʳ.

[5] The battle of Montenotte, on 12 Apr. 1796.

[6] *Recte* 'entamure', meaning here 'opening'.

[7] William Wickham (1761–1840), British minister to the Swiss cantons, 1795–7 (*D.N.B.*).

[8] François Barthélemy (1747–1830), French minister at Berne during 1796; replaced Letourneur as a member of the Directory, 1797; after Fructidor deported to Guiana; peer of France, 1814 (*Dict. biog. franç.*).

[9] In 1791 some actors and actresses including Talma left the Comédie Française (founded in 1680) and started to work in a theatre in the Rue de Richelieu (subsequently known as the Théâtre de la République). In September 1793 the Comédie Française company, being suspected of having counter-revolutionary sympathies, were arrested. On the fall of Robespierre they were released and, finding their old theatre in the Faubourg St Germain occupied, early in 1795 they migrated to the vast Théâtre Feydeau which was close to the Théâtre de la République. (H. F. Collins, *Talma* (London, 1964), pp 36, 66–70, 88–92, 99).

[10] Jean François Ducis (1733–1817), French dramatist and adapter of Shakespeare for the French theatre (*Dict. biog. franç.*).

[11] François Joseph Talma (1763–1826), tragedian.

[12] Françoise Marie Rosette Vestris (1743–1804), famous actress and sister of Gourgaud Dugazon (see below, n. 14); she strongly supported the revolution (Lyonnet, *Dict. des comédiens*, ii, 704–5).

[13] Sarah Siddons née Kemble (1755–1831), Shakespearean actress (*D.N.B.*).

[14] J. B. Gourgaud Dugazon (1746–1809), brother of Madame Vestris. Along with Talma, he was an enthusiastic supporter of the revolution; he was aide-de-camp to Santerre. (Lyonnet, *Dict. des comédiens*, i, 596–8).

[15] Cf. 'Affairs look so well in the North that I was never in a better humour' (Henry Fielding, *Tom Jones* (1749), i, ch. 4).

## 25 Apr. 1796

Went with Ahern to the Minister's[1] and gave him my observations,[2] which he read and liked very well. He struck out in consequence all the stuff about royalty, &c., and returned the instructions to Ahern in order to his copying them, but he kept my observations in order to shew them to Citizen Carnot. He tells us that Ahern will be dispatched in a few days (*dans quelques jours*),[3] and that he has every reason to think the expedition will be ready by the latter end of May (*vers la fin du mai*). I begin to speak French like a nabob. I astonished the Minister with a volubility of diction. On leaving De la Croix (who by the bye has had a narrow escape of being turned out, but is now, I fancy, pretty safe)[4] I met Sullivan who gave me an English paper with the quarters of the army in Ireland for this year. I was very glad to get it. I see but nine regiments of dragoons and two of troops of the line; the rest all fencibles or militia. There is to be a camp in the North of about 2,500 men, and two near Dublin which with the garrison will make about 6,500 men. The whole force is about 30,000 men, as I guessed, but I am sure is not above 20,000 effectives. I have not the least doubt of success if we can land with ten thousand French. Apropos, of the French! Two days after the victory mentioned on the other side,[5] called the affair of Montenotte, they had a second action at Millesimo[6] with the Austrian and Sardinian armies, whom they utterly defeated, taking everything that was takeable, including a lieutenant general, God knows how many officers, colours, cannon, standards and stores, together with 8,500 men—a pretty moderate victory, being the second in two days! I give up discipline forever, after this, *provided always* that we can raise such a spirit of enthusiasm (which I hope and believe is very possible) among the Irish. The French general is Buonaparte,[7] a Corsican. Two French generals[8]

[1] Delacroix. [2] See above, pp 158–60, 162.

[3] Ahern did not go to Ireland. Carnot, on behalf of the Directory, stated in a letter to Delacroix dated 8 Prairial an 4 (27 May 1796) that owing to money difficulties Ahern had not yet left for Ireland and proposed as a substitute 'C$^{n}$ Richard O'Shée, chef de bataillon' (Archives des Affaires Étrangères, Corresp. Politique Angleterre, cote 589, ff 260–61). He also proposed that Tone should give O'Shée the names of the Defender leaders. Carnot refers in a letter to Charles Reinhard, the French minister at Hamburg, dated by a clerk 12 Germinal an 4 (1 Apr. 1796), obviously an error for 12 Prairial (31 May), to O'Shée being ready to leave Paris and to travel via Hamburg (ibid., f. 264). Clarke in a letter to Delacroix, misdated 13 Germinal and obviously 13 Prairial (1 June), also refers to O'Shée's mission (ibid., f. 266). 'Instructions pour le Citoyen O'Shée' together with Tone's 'Observations', both documents similarly misdated, are to be found with Clarke's letter (ibid., ff 267–71). A copy of the 'Instructions' is in the O'Shée 'dossier personnel' in the Archives des Affaires Étrangères. Richard O'Shée later informed General Hoche, prob. Nov. 1796, that he had been in touch with a 'comité central secret et révolutionnaire d'Irlande' (Archives de la Guerre, B$^{11}$ carton I; see also below, p. 362, n. 1).

[4] In fact he was replaced on 19 July 1797. [5] T.C.D. MS 2049, f. 53$^{r}$ (above, p. 162).

[6] The battle of Millesimo, on 13 Apr. 1796.

[7] Napoléon Buonaparte or Bonaparte (1769–1821), commander of the French army in Italy, 1795–8; First Consul, 1799–1804; emperor of the French, 1804–14, 1815. For Tone's meetings with him, see Diary for 18–21, 23 Dec. 1797 and 13 Jan. 1798 (below, vol. III).

[8] Their names were given as 'Banal and Quanin'. The first of these has been identified as Pierre Banel (1766–96) who joined the army as a private before the revolution and was made général de brigade, 1795 (*Annual Register*, 1796, p. 88; Six, *Dict. des généraux & amiraux*).

were killed, at the head of their columns, and a third desperately wounded, leaping with *seven grenadiers* into the Austrian works; but, as I have often told P.P.,[1] '*we are certainly the bravest nation in Europe*'. I cannot recall the names of many English generals who have fallen this war *within* or indeed *without* the enemy's lines. There was only one killed (Mansel)[2] and he was an Irishman. This piece of news from Italy will wonderfully regale John Bull, especially coming close on the heels of a second loan of 7,500,000 which he has cunningly borrowed from himself in order to put down French principles and preserve the regular governments of Europe. The regular government of Sardinia (*which island is in open revolt*) is in a hopeful way after this last battle. The atheists are now within 15 leagues of Turin, and only one strong place in their way; besides that they creep into your strong places like cats. '*Ah, John, thou'rt a deep one!*' I declare I am in as pleasant a humour as a man would wish to see of a summer's day. *One thing I wish to remark here*, because it may be of use. If we have any generals, &c., killed, leaping in or out of trenches, their families must be adopted *always* by the Republic! I know nothing (judging by my own feelings) so likely to make men fight with enthusiasm, as the consciousness that their wives and children will become the objects of the National gratitude in case of their falling in the public service. I like my new lodging very well, and especially I like being quit of that infernal, extorting mansion '*L'Hôtel des Étrangers, Rue Vivienne*'. The villains have hardly left me a louis! Well, ''*Tis but in vain, &c.*'.

## Memorandum on the number and position of the troops in Ireland, 26 April 1796

Archives de la Guerre, B[11] I, dossier 3.

See Diary for 25 and 26 Apr. (above, p. 163, and below, p. 169). Although Tone dated this memorandum 26 Apr., the date on which he composed it, he selected 1 May as the date to which it was to relate, sensibly enough, since the precise numbers must have continually fluctuated.

Paris, 7th Floréal an 4[me]

### Memorial relative to the number and position of the troops which appear to be in Ireland, May 1[st], 1796

By the report in the English gazettes it appears there are now in Ireland 9 Regiments of Dragoons, 2 Regiments of Troops of the line, 18 Regiments of Fencibles (12 of which are Scotch) and 37 Regiments of Militia.

[1] Thomas Russell.

[2] John Mansel, major-general, killed near Cambray when commanding a cavalry brigade, Apr. 1794; he belonged to a Northamptonshire family (E. P. Statham, *History of the family of Maunsell* (London, 1920)).

A Regiment of Cavalry consists of six troops of 30 men each, and including officers may be taken to be 200 men; there are consequently about 1,800 cavalry in Ireland.

The 2 Regiments of Troops of the line are most probably only skeletons who are there to recruit and it will be a fair average to suppose them to contain 500 each of raw troops—indy 1,000 men.

The Regiments of Fencibles I do not exactly know their force, but I am sure that, one with another, they do not exceed 500 men each, making in all 9,000 men for the 18 Regiments. It is impossible to conceive the wretched appearance that those Fencibles make; a great majority of them are either old men past service, or boys not grown up to it. Most of those which I saw appeared much fitter for the hospital than the camp. It is likewise to be remembered that many of the Scotch regiments are supposed to be highly disaffected to the British Government, and from this circumstance, if proper measures be adopted to take advantage of it, as well as from the despicable state of those regiments, there seems little reason to apprehend much from their opposition. I am sure they could not muster 500 men fit for the duties of active service.

For the Militia, who are, as well as the Cavalry above mentioned, to a man Irish, they are most excellent troops, probably equal to any in Europe. The strength of those Regiments differs exceedingly, varying between 10 companies, which is the highest establishment, to 4, which is the lowest, some being of 8, some of 6 and one or two of 5 companies, at about 60 men per company. I believe it will be a fair average to take them at 8 companies at 60 men each, making per Regiment 480 men. The 37 Regiments will consequently compose a corps of 17,760 men, all, as has been already observed, Irish, and of those vast numbers *sworn Defenders*. I am sure this calculation is above the truth, but it is an error on the safe side

The total Force in Ireland, then, is as follows:

| | |
|---|---|
| 9 Regiments of Dragoons @ 200 men each | 1,800 |
| 2 Reg^ts^ Troops of the Line @ 500 men each | 1,000 |
| 18 Reg^ts^ Fencibles @ 500 men each | 9,000 |
| 37 Reg^ts^ of Irish Militia, averaging one with another 480 men each | 17,760 |
| | 29,560 |

In this calculation there is no allowance made for non-effectives, for the sick, for deserters, for deficiencies, nor false musters; but the Regiments are taken as they appear *on paper*. Perhaps the number might be with truth diminished *one third*.

These Troops appear, by the English papers, to be distributed as follows:

IN ULSTER

The principle camp, probably at Lisburne, within 7 miles of Belfast, 5 Reg^ts viz.

| | | | |
|---|---|---|---|
| Limerick militia | 480 | men | 2,440 |
| Cavan do. | 480 | " | |
| Queen's county do. | 480 | " | |
| Fife Fencibles | 500 | " | |
| York Fencibles | 500 | " | |
| Total | 2,440 | | |

| | | | |
|---|---|---|---|
| In Belfast, the Ray Fencibles | 500 | men | 5,800 |
| In Carrickfergus, the Westmeath Militia | 480 | " | |
| In Armagh, the Caithness Fencibles | 500 | " | |
| the 24^th Light dragoons | 200 | " | |
| In Enniskillen, the Essex Fencibles | 500 | " | |
| In Monaghan, Leith's Fencibles | 500 | " | |
| In Dungannon, Clavering's Fencibles | 500 | " | |
| In Cavan, Frazer's Fencibles | 500 | " | |
| In Belturbet, the 4^th Dragoons | 200 | " | |
| In Newry, the Kerry Militia | 480 | " | |
| In Derry, the Limerick Militia | 480 | " | |
| In Coleraine, the Longford Militia | 480 | " | |
| In Ballyshannon, the Drogheda Militia | 580 | " | |
| Total | 5,800 | " | |
| | | Grand Total | 8,240 |

There are consequently in Ulster:

| | | |
|---|---|---|
| 2 Reg^ts Dragoons @ 200 each | 400 | |
| 8 Reg^ts Militia @ 480 each | 3,840 | |
| 8 Reg^ts Fencibles @ 500 each | 4,000 | |
| 18 Reg^ts | 8,240 | of which there are in and near Belfast 3,220 men.[1] |

[1] The numbers for Lisburn, Belfast and Carrickfergus (which is also near Belfast) add up to 3,420.

*26 April 1796*

IN CONNAUGHT

| | | | | |
|---|---|---|---|---|
| Athlone | 22[d] Dragoons | 200 | men | 3,820 |
| – | Angus Fencibles | 500 | " | |
| Galway | Cork (city) Militia | 480 | " | |
| – | Perthshire Fencibles | 500 | " | |
| Castlebar | 23[d] Dragoons | 200 | " | |
| Westport | Prince of Wales's Fencibles | 500 | " | |
| Sligo | North Cork Militia | 480 | " | |
| Roscommon | King's County Militia | 480 | " | |
| Carrick-on-Shannon | Tipperary Militia | 480 | " | |
| | | 3,820 | | |

There are consequently in Connaught

| | | | |
|---|---|---|---|
| 2 Reg[ts] | Dragoons @ 200 each | | 400 |
| 4 Reg[ts] | Militia @ 480 | " | 1,920 |
| 3 Reg[ts] | Fencibles @ 500 | " | 1,500 |
| | | | 3,820 men of which there are in Galway 980 |

Total in Ulster & Connaught 12,060

IN LEINSTER

| | | | |
|---|---|---|---|
| In Dublin 9th Dragoons | 200 | men | 1,660 now |
| – – Tyrone militia | 480 | " | |
| – – Kilkenny militia | 480 | " | |
| – – Elgin Fencibles | 500 | " | |
| In Laughlintown camp (six miles from Dublin) | | | |
| Kildare militia | 480 | " | 1,940 |
| Clare Do. | 480 | " | |
| Donegal Do. | 480 | " | |
| Inverness Fencibles | 500 | " | |
| In Ardfinnan Camp[1] | | | |
| Armagh militia | 480 | " | 2,420 |
| Antrim militia | 480 | " | |
| Louth militia | 480 | " | |
| Wexford militia | 480 | " | |
| Balfour's Fencibles | 500 | " | |

[1] Ardfinnan is in Co. Tipperary, 9 km south-south-east of Caher; it is in Munster, not Leinster.

| | | | |
|---|---|---|---|
| In Longford 7th Dragoons | 200 | men | |
| In Tullamore 5th Dragoons | 200 | " | |
| In Kilkenny 6th Foot | 500 | " | |
| In Wexford 89th Foot | 500 | " | |
| In Granard the Northamptonshire Fencibles | 500 | " | |
| In Kells the Breadalbane Fencibles | 500 | " | |
| In Trim the Carlow militia | 480 | " | 5,760[1] |
| In Drogheda, the Down militia | 480 | " | |
| In Dundalk, the Dublin (city) militia | 480 | " | |
| In Naas, the Mayo militia | 480 | " | |
| In Maryboro', the Monaghan Militia | 480 | " | |
| In Portarlington, the Wicklow Militia | 480 | " | |
| In Mullingar, the Waterford Militia | 480 | " | |

There are consequently in Leinster

| | | | | |
|---|---|---|---|---|
| 3 | Regts | Dragoons @ 200 men | 600 | |
| 16 | Regts | Militia @ 480 men | 7,200[2] | |
| 5 | Regts | Fencibles @ 500 | 2,500 | |
| 2 | Regts | Troops of the Line @ 500 | 1,000 | |
| 26 | | | 11,300 | of which there are in Dublin and the camps adjacent 3,600 men |

IN MUNSTER

| | | | | |
|---|---|---|---|---|
| Mallow, 1st Regt Fencible Cavalry | 200 | 400 | | |
| Clonmell, 2d Regt Fencible Cavalry | 200 | | | |
| In Ross Castle, Hall's Fencibles | 500 | | | |
| Cork Dunbar's Do. | 500 | | | 5,720 |
| Cork, Dublin (county) Militia | 480 | | Ardfinnan Camp | 2,420 |
| Clare Castle, South Cork militia | 480 | | | |
| Limerick, Derry militia | 480 | | | 8,140 |
| Waterford, Fermanagh militia | 480 | 5,320 | | |
| Macroom, Galway Militia | 480 | | | |
| Charles Fort,[3] Leitrim militia | 480 | | | |
| Youghall, Meath militia | 480 | | | |
| Cork, Roscommon militia | 480 | | | |
| Kinsale, Sligo militia | 480 | | | |

[1] In the MS the total for Leinster is given in a bracket as 9,360. This excludes the total for Ardfinnan Camp (2,420), which recurs below under Munster.

[2] *Recte* 7,680. The difference is 480, the complement of a militia regiment. The discrepancy is carried forward to the Leinster total, which should be 11,780.

[3] Charles Fort, near Kinsale.

There are consequently in Munster

| | | | |
|---|---|---|---|
| 2 | Reg^ts | Dragoons @ 200 men | 400 |
| 2 | Reg^ts | Fencibles @ 500 | 1,000 |
| 9 | Reg^ts | militia @ 480 | 4,320 |
| 13 | | | 7,720[1] |

Grand Total 29,560

The Irish Brigade,[2] which left the service of France, after the experience of two years' recruiting, has been able to raise but 1,000 men among 7 regiments. Three have been formed into two regiments of 500 each and sent to Gibraltar. The difficulty the officers of these corps have found in raising recruits marks very strongly the sentiments of the peasantry of Ireland.

On the whole it appears that the apprehension of the Irish Government is principally turned on Dublin and its neighbourhood where they are forming two camps, besides the garrison of the city; that in Ulster there is no extraordinary appearance of alarm or preparation, the single camp there being under 2,500 men; that in Con[n]aught there is no camp whatsoever, there being in that whole province, one of the most turbulent in Ireland, not 4,000 men, whereas in Leinster there are 12,000. These circumstances, it is apprehended, are decisive that the attempt should be made either in Ulster or Connaught, but if possible in Ulster, first because it is there we might be sure of meeting the most effectual and instantaneous support, a circumstance of infinite consequence when time is so precious; secondly because it is the seat of the Dissenters, who are by far the most enlightened men, and the best Republicans in Ireland; and lastly, which is of the highest importance, because we could in that province frame in the first instance an Irish army of soldiers of all religious persuasions, particularly Dissenters & Catholics, which at the outset would produce the most beneficial effect, whereas in the other provinces, and especially in Con[n]aught, the peasantry are to a man Catholics; the great advantage of having the army composed of the different religious sects, in order to remove all possibility of jealousies, is too obvious to need further observation.

T. Wolfe Tone

## Diary, 26 April–2 May 1796

T.C.D., Tone papers, MS 2049, ff 54ᵛ–59ᵛ; *Life*, ii, 102–8.

### 26 Apr. 1796

Wrote a short memorial[3] on the force and disposition of the army in Ireland as it appears in the English paper and gave it to Sullivan to translate. I think it is very

[1] *Recte* 5,720. [2] See above, p. 130, n. 5. [3] Above, pp 164–9.

prettily done, which is not the case with all my productions. Tomorrow I will give it to the Minister.[1] Went in the evening to the Théâtre Montansier,[2] in the Palais Royal. Mlle Ferton[3] a good actress and pretty.

## 27 Apr. 1796

Sullivan brought me my memorial[4] admirably translated. Went at one o'clock to the Minister, where I met Ahern by chance. The Minister tells us that the Directory is just now occupied by very important business, but in two or three days they will be disengaged, and then Ahern will receive his final instructions and be dispatched; he also told me that matters were so arranged and the combinations so made that in a month everything would be ready. All this is excellent, but I am sworn never to believe it till I see it. What makes these minutes valuable (*that is to say, to myself and my dearest life and Love*) is that they are a faithful transcript of all that passes in my mind, my hopes and fears, my doubts and expectations, in this important business. The Minister also said he would instantly have a copy made of my remarks[5] and have them given to Carnot, by which I see (or suppose at least) that the business is entirely in his hands, of which I am sincerely glad, for he is the man I have all along wished to fix my claws in. By the bye I must see the aforesaid *Organiser*, one of these odd come shortly's,[6] to wit, in three or four days, because I meditate a little stroke of politics (being my *first*). Let us see how it will succeed. I intend artfully to insinuate a thing or two to him. I want likewise to sound him about Pichegru. As he is a 'Shallow Pomona',[7] I foresee I shall overreach him. This day's paper gives an account of a *third* victory[8] by the army of Italy. It seems they were too confident—on the two former ones, which induced Beaulieu,[9] the Austrian general, tho' twice beaten to take the attack with the *élite* of his army, with which he surprised the French right wing, and it was it was not without the most vigorous efforts of the remainder of the army that he was at length repulsed, which however he was effectually, losing 2,500 men in prisoners only. The French loss must have been severe. In the three battles, *four* generals have fallen and *three* desperately wounded; very like the British generals in

[1] Delacroix.

[2] Mademoiselle Marguerite Brunet Montansier (1730–1820) had been a protégée of Marie Antoinette. In 1790 she founded a theatre in the Palais Royal. She was imprisoned, 1793–4. (Lyonnet, *Dict. des comédiens*).

[3] Not identified.

[4] Tone's 'memorial on the force and disposition of the army in Ireland' referred to in the preceding diary entry.

[5] Probably Tone's observations on the instructions intended for Ahern; they had been translated into French by Sullivan (see above, pp 158–60, 162).

[6] *Life*, ii, 102, substitutes 'shortly' for 'one of these odd come shortly's'.

[7] In John O'Keeffe's *The agreeable surprise* (1784), II, iv, and *Wild oats* (1792), III.

[8] At the battle of Dego, fought on 14 Apr. 1796. It followed victories at Montenotte and Millesimo on 12 and 13 Apr.

[9] Johann Peter Beaulieu (1725–1819), born at Namur in the Austrian Netherlands; commanded Imperial army in Italy, Mar.–July 1796 (*Allgemeine deutsche Biographie*).

Flanders,[1] as I have already remarked with great wit and severity.[2] The idea of attacking the French after being twice defeated does Beaulieu's talents great honor, and if it had not been for the invincible valor of the French soldiery, it seems very likely that he would have succeeded. As it was, it was a work of great difficulty to repulse him, the battle continuing from day break to 3 o'clock in the afternoon. Went in the evening to the Théâtre de la rue Feyd[e]au. These are the veterans of the French stage, the Drury Lane of Paris. Molé[3] is an excellent actor; in manner, in age, voice, figure and talents he put me strongly in mind of King.[4] Mademoiselle Contat[5] is a delicious woman; she is the Miss Farren[6] of the Rue Feydeau and in all respects just such another actress. She is forty years of age and she certainly does not appear to be five and twenty. She has been the mistress of the whole French (ci-devant) nobility, and of course bears no great devotion to the Revolution. She lives now, I am told, with Legendre,[7] the Deputy, who was, and for aught I know is, a butcher in Paris. I confess I am so much of an aristocrat that I do not glory in that circumstance. It is a scandalous fact, but I am afraid too true, that the[8] deputies have availed themselves of their situation to secure the possession of numbers of beautiful women, who submit to their embraces to secure their protection. If it be so, it is abominable. I do not like to see the Republic pimp for Legendre, but people here mind these things much less than I do, for on this topic I have perhaps extravagant notions of delicacy and refinement, and their manners here are horridly dissolute, by all I can learn. Well, give me my own countrywomen after all; they are the material to make wives and mothers. If I want a mistress I will[9] go to Paris or London. Protection! Legendre's *protection*! I like no protection, but that of the Law, that protects all. I find I am growing angry on this subject so I will quit it. Maybe I am jealous of Legendre? Oh Lord, oh Lord! jealous indeed! 'Marry come up.'[10] Well! I am sleepy now, so I will go to bed, and Mlle Contat may do the same, if she pleases.

[1] An allusion to the British expedition to the Low Countries in 1793 and 1794.

[2] See Diary for 25 Apr. (above, p. 164).

[3] François René Molé (1734–1802) played with success in a very wide variety of roles. In 1799 Mlle Contat declared 'il a soixante-cinq ans et il n'existe pas un jeune homme qui se jette aussi bien aux genoux d'une femme' (Lyonnet, *Dict. des comédiens*, ii, 437–9).

[4] Thomas King (1730–1805), actor and dramatist (*D.N.B.*).

[5] Louise Françoise Contat, aînée (1760–1813), a brilliant actress, was imprisoned, 1793–4, being suspected of having royalist sympathies. It was rumoured that before the revolution she had been the mistress of Maupeou, the count d'Artois and Louis de Narbonne. Later she was generally believed to be Legendre's mistress. In 1809 she married a cavalry officer. (Lyonnet, *Dict. des comédiens*, i, 382–6; *Dict. biog. franç.*).

[6] Elizabeth Farren (*c.*1759–1829), actress. In 1797 she married the 12th earl of Derby (*D.N.B.*).

[7] Louis Legendre (1752–97), member of the Convention and of the Council of Ancients (*Dict. parl. franç.*).

[8] *Life*, ii, 103, replaces 'the' by 'many'.

[9] *Life*, ii, 103, substitutes 'would' for 'will'.

[10] *Romeo and Juliet*, II, v.

## 28–9 Apr. 1796

Blank! Is not this cruel; but what can I do? I have not lost one minute by my own negligence since my arrival at Paris. Well, that is some comfort however! Madgett tells me that peace is as good as concluded with the King of Sardinia,[1] and that these late victories will give him a plausible excuse for cutting out of the party,[2] like the King of Spain.[3] He tells me also that a revolution is organised in Piemont and Sardinia; so that[4] it is highly probable the poor *Roi des Marmottes* may go keep company with the Stadtholder.[5] A pretty dialogue they would have on meeting! Voltaire's supper of the Six Kings (was it *six*?)[6] seems likely to be realised. This is sad, that I must be writing about revolutions in Piemont and Sardinia instead of—. Well, ''*Tis but in vain, &c.*'.[7]

## 30 Apr. 1796

Called on Clarke again. He is a sad puppy and I am fairly tired of him. Our dialogue is always the same. 'Well, General Clarke, I have called to know if you have anything to tell me?' Not a word. 'Well, I hope when there is anything going forward you will let me know.' Two or three words of commonplace discourse follow this, and so I take my leave as ignorant as a horse. I confess I cannot fathom General Clarke's policy in keeping me so totally in the dark—moreover today he was not over civil, for he spoke to me *en passant* in the porter's antichamber, being as he said in a hurry. If he was in twice as great a hurry he might have spoken to me in his cabinet. I will not forget it to him, that I can tell him. I filled a station once as honorable as his, and I hope yet perhaps to fill one far above it, and if I do, I must not give myself airs like General Clarke, The puppy! I am as angry as the Devil. One thing however I will do. As I have given him, by Carnot's orders, all the directions in my power, and as he will tell me nothing in return, but on the contrary evidently shews a disposition to avoid me, I will not call on him any more. I will very gingerly demand an audience of Carnot himself and see what that will produce. This is sad, and I am as melancholy as a gib cat, or a lugged bear,[8] and I cannot help myself.

## 1 May 1796

Blank! Thinking of my interview with Carnot. I declare I am tired of my life, literally.

[1] Victor Amadeus III (1726–96), king of Sardinia, 1773–96, was forced by Bonaparte's victories to agree to the armistice of Cherasco, 28 Apr. 1796.

[2] i.e. the war.

[3] Charles IV (1748–1819), king of Spain, 1788–1808.

[4] Erroneously 'is' in MS.

[5] William V of Orange (1748–1806), stadtholder, 1766–95. In 1795 when France invaded Holland, he fled to England.

[6] It was six (*Candide* (1759), pt I, chap. 26).

[7] *The buck's bottle companion* (London, 1775).

[8] *1 Henry IV*, I, ii.

## 2 May 1796

Went to the Luxembourg and saw Reubell give audience in his costume. I have now seen all the members of the Directory.[1] Wrote a note desiring to see Carnot, and was admitted. He recollected me perfectly. I began by saying (fluently enough) that in pursuance of his orders I had been several times with General Clarke, and that I had given him all the information I was possessed of, as well verbally as by memorials and other papers. He said he knew I had. I then observed that considering General Clarke as in an official station I had avoided pressing him to give me any information in return; but that at present when I learned directly from the Minister and indirectly from several[2] other quarters that preparations were in a considerable degree of forwardness for the expedition, I hoped, when he considered the efforts I had made, the risques I had run, the dangers I had escaped in endeavouring to lay the state of Ireland before the French Government, as well as the situation I had once the honor to fill in my own country, that he would not consider me as unreasonably importunate in requesting him to give me such information as he might judge proper as to the state of the expedition supposing it were to take place. He replied, my request was not at all unreasonable, *but that before measures were finally determined upon, it would be necessary that the French government should be satisfied as to the actual state of things in Ireland, and for that purpose a person should be sent to observe everything and make his report accordingly; for if the people there were amicable to the French republic, the attempt might be made, but if not, it would require a considerable force to conquer the country. This was a staggering blow to me, to find myself no further advanced at the end of three months than I was at my first audience.* However, I recollected myself, and said that undoubtedly the French Government were in the right to expect every possible information as to the actual state of the country; that I begged leave to observe that there were few individuals more competent, from their situation, to give them that information than myself, much more so than any stranger they might send, who would just slide into the country for a moment and return, if he were lucky enough to escape; that as to all I had advanced, I hoped he would find my assertions confirmed by the English gazettes; that nevertheless, if he doubted my information, or supposed that affairs might be altered since my departure from Ireland and so thought it necessary to send a confidential person there, I begged him to remember that the time was precious and that there was not a moment to lose. He said he understood I could not go myself. I answered I was too well known in that country to be there four and twenty hours without being discovered and seized; that consequently I was the most unfit person in the world; and I took that opportunity to mention that, if the expedition were undertaken, I hoped to be permitted to bear a part in its execution. He replied that the French Government would, in that case,

1 This sentence is omitted from *Life*. The members of the Directory were Carnot, Barras, La Révellière-Lépeaux, Letourneur and Reubell.

2 In *Life*, ii, 104, 'several' is replaced by 'many'.

certainly avail themselves of my courage and talents (*'profiter de votre courage et de vos talens'*), but still he did not say whether the expedition would take place or not, tho' this was the second push I made at him on that head. When I saw he would not give me any definite information[1] I observed that there was a subject on which I had received such positive instructions on leaving Ireland that I considered myself as bound to mention it to him, and that was the general who might be appointed to the command; that it was our wish if possible that it should be Pichegru; that if he remained at the head of the army of the Rhine I probably should not have mentioned him, but that at present when he was not employed in any military function, I hoped I was not irregular in praying him (Carnot) to turn his thoughts on Pichegru for the command, supposing, as before, that the expedition were to take place. Carnot replied that undoubtedly Pichegru was an officer of consummate talents, but at the same time there were many generals not inferior to him in abilities (*'aussi forts que lui'*). I replied I was satisfied the Republic abounded with excellent officers, but that in my country the prejudice as to Pichegru's character was so strong that I rated him equal to an army of twenty thousand men as to the effect his appointment would have on both parties in Ireland. He replied that he would give every consideration to what I said on that subject, and that at any rate I had done perfectly right in suggesting Pichegru to the notice of the Directory. I then observed that as to Pichegru himself, I thought the appointment would add a new lustre to his former glory; that if he desired fame, the assisting in creating a free republic of four million and a half of people was an object of no ordinary magnitude; and if he was studious of his own interest, which I did not suppose, he might rely on the gratitude of my country in its fullest extent, as well as every person who might be instrumental in establishing her liberties. Just at this moment Gen[era]l Clarke entered and I cannot say that he seemed highly delighted at the rencontre. I took my leave of Carnot and went over to speak to him. I told him in substance our conversation as it is above written, and when I mentioned Pichegru, he said, 'Pichegru! oh, he won't accept it'. I said I was sorry for it. He then asked me had I finished his proclamation for chouannising England?[2] I told him I found it impossible, but that I would finish one[3] I had begun for Ireland, whose grievances I know and with whose local circumstances I was acquainted, of both of which with regard to

[1] Three weeks after this conversation the Directory instructed the minister of foreign affairs to send Richard O'Shea (O'Shée) to Ireland, 'le citoyen Aherne' having been detained in Paris owing to 'des détails de comptabilité'. It wanted him to verify the information on Irish conditions communicated by 'le citoyen Wolfe-Tone' and information which could be gathered from English newspapers. O'Shea was to be given the instructions that had been given to Aherne with the addition of instructions that the Directory itself had prepared. It considered Tone to be highly intelligent (he had 'beaucoup d'esprit') and intended to employ him and to inform him about certain plans when it was opportune to do so. Tone appeared, however, to be a little too close to ('un peu lié avec') Aherne, which could have been prejudicial to the purpose of verifying his reports. (Executive Directory to Charles Delacroix, 27 May 1796, Archives Nationales, AF III, 373, dossier 1853, printed in Debidour, *Recueil des actes du Directoire Exécutif*, ii, 489–91).

[2] See Diary for 18 Apr. (above, p. 157). [3] See above, p. 126, n. 1.

England I was utterly unacquainted.[1] He desired me then to finish that one and bring it to him without loss of time. I said I would, in the course of four or five days, and so I took my leave. '*So, I have got much by my intended expostulation!*', as Sir Peter Teazle says.[2] In the first place I am utterly ignorant whether there is any design to attempt the expedition or not. I put it twice to Carnot and could extract no answer. My belief is that, as yet, there is no one step taken in the business, and that in fact *the expedition will not be undertaken*. What signifies what the Minister says? He is on the eve of being turned out every day, and is at this moment at open war with the Directory. They want him to resign and he will not, but says they may dismiss him, if they please. (By the bye, the Directory are too fond of changing their ministers, which shews either want of judgement in forming their choice, or of steadiness in adhering to it.) They are of course not very likely to trust him just now with their designs. I therefore must regard all he says, and Madgett from him, as of *no authority whatsoever*, and that being the case, it is impossible things can wear a more frosty appearance for our hopes. I am pretty sure Carnot has never read one line of my memorials, but has taken them on the report of Clarke, and God only knows what that report may have been. I cannot get it out of my head that that fellow is betraying the cause, or at least doing everything in his power to thwart and oppose it, and what can I possibly do to prevent him? Absolutely nothing! That is hard! I fear all my exertions and all my sacrifices and all my hopes will come to nothing at last. Well, if it should be so, I hope I shall be able to bear it, but it is cruel. I begin now to think of my cottage and my family again. I fancy it will be my lot at last to bury them and myself in the backwoods of America. My poor little Boys! I had *almost* begun to entertain hopes of being able to rescue them from that obscurity, and above all things to place my wife and our dear Maria in a situation more worthy of them; but if I cannot, I must submit. It is at least no fault of mine. I think I have left nothing on my part undone or untried or unhazarded. If I have to go back to the woods, I must see and inveigle P.P.[3] out with me. Otherwise I shall be in great solitude. Perhaps Mr W[illia]m Browne[4] is at home before me. *At home!* In America! And is that to be our home after all?

> Well, if it must, it must, and since 'tis so
> The less is said the better![5]

From this day I will gradually diminish the little hope I had begun to form. I suppose another month at most will decide our fate, and if that decision be adverse, I will then try the justice and generosity of the French Government in my own particular case; if they make me compensation, so! if not, I have nothing to do but submit and return in the first vessel for America. At least I shall be sure of happiness and tranquillity in the bosom of my family, especially if I can catch P.P. and

[1] In *Life*, ii, 107, 'ignorant' is substituted for 'unacquainted'.
[2] In Sheridan's *School for scandal* (1777), II, i.
[3] Thomas Russell.
[4] Mathew Tone.
[5] Sheridan, *The critic* (1781), II, ii.

Mr W[illia]m Browne. I will now wait to see what they will do with Ahern. If they dispatch him, promptly, the business may yet revive; if they delay him, or send a person of Clarke's choosing, I shall look on it as utterly desperate, and take my measures accordingly.

## To General Henri Jacques Guillaume Clarke, 7 May 1796

Archives Nationales, AF IV, carton 1671, ff 68–9.
See Diary for 7 May 1796 (below, p. 177).

18 Floréal An 4[me], Paris

Dear Sir,

As it is possible I may not be lucky enough to meet you today I bring this letter, which I beg you will consider at your leisure, and I shall call on you the day after tomorrow at eleven o'clock in order to talk it over with you for five minutes.

In the first place, it is with the greatest regret that I see the delays which attend the outfit of the expedition, *supposing it to take place*, of which I am not yet informed. Perhaps I might expect at least so much confidence in return for the efforts and sacrifices which I have made in the business, for the exile in which I now find myself, for the peril of my life, which I have hazarded more than once, and especially for the interest which I have in its success. I am here, it is true, unknown and almost unnoticed, but I can assure you that if my own country were free, there would be very few stations, political or military, to which I might not pretend and I should not be refused.

When I confess myself thus deeply interested, you will not suppose I can intend any indelicacy towards you, when I beg you to consider *whether you are not very deeply interested yourself?* The station you now hold is a very honorable one; but let me assure you that if Ireland were emancipated once, and her Government apprised that you were highly useful and instrumental in preparing and forwarding the measures to which she owed her liberty, you might rely upon her gratitude in its utmost extent. I, for one, should in that case be happy to bear witness to your zeal and ability and perhaps even my testimony might be of service to you. If the expedition be undertaken (of which, I must again repeat, I know nothing decisive) what is there to prevent your going yourself to Ireland in a military capacity? There will be glory and there will be profit to be reaped, and besides our cause is a just one. *I beg you may think seriously of what I have thrown out here for, be assured, it is worthy of your notice*.

There is one thing which I wish to observe to you. If this expedition is to be undertaken, you have already assured me that I shall be allowed to take my part in it. I will only remark that, in that case, the more attention that appears to be shewn to me by the French Executive, the more influence I shall naturally possess in Ireland on my return, and by consequence I shall be the better able to be of service, as well to the Republic of France as to those individuals here, to whom we shall be most obliged, and I assure you, once more, that if Ireland were once free, we should want neither the inclination nor the ability to be both grateful and generous.

This letter, you will see, is merely introductory to our next conversation, when I shall explain myself more fully. In the meantime consider that the best friends to France and Ireland are now most probably languishing in prison or concealment, and that every day that passes prolongs their sufferings and delays the liberty of our country.

Health, Fraternity and Respect
T. Wolfe Tone
dit
James Smith

Gen[era]l Clarke, &c., &c.

## Diary, 7–11 May 1796

T.C.D., Tone papers, MS 2049, ff 60$^{r}$–62$^{r}$; *Life*, ii, 108–10.

### 7 May 1796

What signifies my making daily journals when I have nothing to say? The Directory gives me no business, and I am not in spirits to write good nonsense, and I am tired of saying 'Blank! Blank!'. This day wrote an artful letter[1] to Clarke to see if I can list him on the score of his interest. It is also his duty. This is sad work, but what can I do?' '*Il faut hurler avec les loup*s.'[2] I will engage him £1,000 a year for his life, if we succeed, and I rely on the nation to make good my engagement.

### 9 May 1796

Saw Clarke. He told me that if he gave me no information it was because he was not permitted, that I might rely on receiving it as soon as it was necessary I should be informed, and that I might also depend on it that, *if the expedition were undertaken*, everything should be made as agreeable to me, personally, as I could desire. All this is civil however, but still it is not what I want to come at. I told him, as usual, that I did not mean to press him, and that I would wait, in submission, for the determination of the Directory. I then asked him had he read my letter?[3] He said he had, but as to any idea of reward, he was in the service of France, and it must be to her he should look for compensation. I replied certainly it was just that France should reward him, but that did not preclude Ireland also from

[1] Above, pp 176–7. [2] Literally, 'One must howl with the wolves'. [3] Above, pp 176–7.

manifesting her gratitude; that he might rely on it that every individual in France who was instrumental in establishing our independance would be amply rewarded at the conclusion of the war. He replied we would not have the means; that we had no money, and besides that he did not much count on the gratitude of nations. To this I answered that it was true we had little or no money, but that we had abundance of means besides, and as to the gratitude of nations I did not think quite so humbly of it as he seemed to do; that America was an instance against him, where every soldier and officer was rewarded on the establishment of her independance, and where La Fayette[1] had a provision of 30,000 acres of land, which was all he had to trust to at this moment on earth, and that I hoped we were as capable of gratitude as the Americans.[2] I stopped there, and the discourse turned on Ireland. I told him I had seen the Instructions,[3] and that there were two points on which I wished much to satisfy him, viz. the influence of the priests, and the question of royalty, neither of which I assured him were at all to be apprehended, and I adduced several arguments which, as they are recited already in these memorandums, I need not here repeat. I do not know whether I satisfied him or not, but the discourse rested there. He asked me had I finished the proclamation?[4] I said not, but that I would bring it to him in two or three days at farthest. I then took my leave. On the whole I made no great way in this day's conversation, yet I was better pleased with Clarke, I do not know why, than I have been of a long time. He has got my memorandum[5] on the number and disposition of the troops in Ireland. I also saw, among his papers relating to the expedition, one in the margin of which were the names of several towns in Holland and Dutch Flanders. What does that forebode? I cannot decypher; so let me go finish my proclamation. I have not looked at it since the 27th of March.[6] I see I was on a wrong track, so I will begin on a new plan. *Courage, mon ami! allons donc!*

## 10 May 1796

Madgett has got orders to find ten or a dozen intelligent prisoners who are to be sent *into England*! Into England of all places in the world! What can that mean? He tells me there is to be an expedition there contemporary with ours in order to cut out work for John Bull at home, and to prevent his distracting his poor head too much about his Irish affairs. He tells me also that Hoche is to command in England. If that be so, it looks serious, but Madgett is so terribly sanguine that

[1] Marie Joseph Paul Yves Roch Gilbert du Motier, marquis de La Fayette (1757–1834), French statesman and soldier (*Dict. biog. franç.*; *D.A.B.*).

[2] In 1784 Pennsylvania named one of its new counties after Lafayette. 'The erroneous rumour spread in both France and England that this was an estate that had been granted as a fresh mark of gratitude.' (L. R. Gottschalk, *Lafayette between the American and the French revolutions, 1783–1789* (Chicago, 1950), p. 74).

[3] Above, pp 158–9. [4] See above, p. 126, n. 1. [5] Above, pp 164–9.

[6] In MS 'April' is written above 'March' and *Life*, ii, 109, prints 'April'. Tone in his diary entry for 27 Apr. does not mention a proclamation but does refer to a 'damned manifesto' in an entry for 27 Mar. (see above, p. 134).

I know not what to think. I will say for the present, in the language of the gazettes, '*this news merits further confirmation*'. At work at my proclamation.

## 11 May 1796

At work furiously at my proclamation. I like it better than my first attempt. Madgett is gone in search of his imps, whom he has orders to send off to Hoche as soon as he has found them. That looks a little serious, but still, I am slow of faith. This day the Directoire Exécutif has denounced a grand plot to massacre themselves, the Legislative bodies, the État-Major of Paris, &c., &c., and to proclaim the constitution of 1793.[1] Above 40 persons have been arrested, and at the head of them Drouet[2] who stopped the King at Varennes in 1791, and who has lain for three years in a dungeon in Austria, from where he is returned not above six months. I am heartily sorry for him, for I believe him sincere in his principles and an undoubted republican. At the same time I would shew no mercy to any man, whatever might be his past merits, who would endeavour in the present position of France to subvert the existing government. If the plot had taken place, our business would have been in a hopeful way. I think in my conscience the French have at this moment an exceeding good form of government, and such as every man of principle is bound to support. It might possibly be better but the advantage which might possibly result from an alteration is not such as to warrant any honest man in hazarding the consequences of another bloody revolution. The people of this turbulent city seem of the same way of thinking. I do not imagine it would be easy, or indeed possible, from all that I can observe, to excite a serious insurrection in Paris. The Government is very strong; the *enragés* are but few, and the mass of the people seems disposed for tranquillity at any rate. As a friend to France and Ireland, and as an irreconcilable enemy to England, I am heartily glad of it, for I am not so completely *ultra-révolution[n]aire* as some to whom I speak here. As an Irishman I cannot but rejoice at the discovery of this *complot*. Had it suceeded, what would have become of us? *Au propos!*[3] There is a law passed today enjoining, among other things, all strangers to quit Paris in three days.[4] I must apply to the Minister[5] and see what he says on that head.

[1] In the early months of 1796 François Noël 'Gracchus' Babeuf (1760–97) and his associates planned to overthrow the Directory and replace it by a temporary dictatorship, their aim being to establish direct democracy and economic equality. On 10 May Babeuf and a number of his supporters were arrested. (*Dict. biog. franç.*; R. B. Rose, *Gracchus Babeuf* (London, 1978)).

[2] Jean-Baptiste Drouet (1763–1824) was largely responsible for preventing Louis XVI from escaping at Varennes. A member of the Convention, he was captured by the Austrians, 1793, and exchanged, 1795. He supported Babeuf and was arrested in 1796. (*Dict. biog. franç.*).

[3] Corrected in *Life*, ii, 110, to 'A propos'.

[4] On 21 Floréal an IV (10 May 1796) it was decreed that persons in a number of categories must leave Paris within 24 hours. These included all foreigners not resident there before 14 July 1789 or who did not belong to the corps diplomatique. On 12 May the Directory, using its powers under the law of 21 Floréal, decreed that twelve persons, including Tone, should be permitted to stay in Paris. (*Bulletin des lois de la République Française*, no. 45 [395]; Débidour, *Recueil des actes du Directoire Exécutif*, ii, 364).

[5] Delacroix. For Tone's letter to Delacroix asking him what he should do, see the following document.

## To Charles Delacroix, 12 May 1796

Archives Nationales, AF III 369, f. 50.

This is the earliest known letter that Tone wrote in French. He asks the foreign minister 'what I must do in consequence of yesterday's law ordering all foreigners to leave Paris in three days'.

It is endorsed 'sur l'arrêté du 23 fl[oré]al an 4' (12 May). The decree was in fact issued a day or two earlier (see Diary for 11 May, above, p. 179).

Tone refers to this 'short note' in his Diary for 12 May 1796 (below, p. 181).

Citoyen Ministre,

Je m'ai fait l'honneur de passer chez vous, pour vous rendre mes respects et de vous prier de me dire, s'il vous plaît, ce qu'il me faudra faire en conséquence de la loi d'hier[1] qui ordonne à tous les étrangers de quitter Paris dans trois jours. J'espère au moins que je ne serai pas compris dans l'ordre, vu la situation actuelle dans laquelle je me trouve, et les droits que je me flatte d'avoir acquis sur votre protection. Ayez la bonté d'excuser mon détestable français.[2]

Salut et respect,
Theobald Wolfe Tone
dit
James Smith

[Endorsed in top left-hand corner:]
A comprendre dans ceux qui peuvent rester à Paris

23 floréal an 4 rép.
Carnot

[Endorsed by Carnot in bottom left-hand corner:]
Theobald Wolfe Tone a été adressée
par le C[en] Adet. Il a donné des renseignemens
précieux sur l'Irlande dont il a été forcé de fuir.
Il seroit nécessaire de le conserver à Paris pour
l'objet dont le Directoire a déjà été entretenu.

## Extract from the register of the Executive Directory, 12 May 1796

Archives Nationales, AF III 369, f. 49.

[1] The decree was in fact issued on 10 May.

[2] Apart from erratic use of initial capitals and punctuation (silently standardised as usual by the editors), three errors occur: 'Je m'ai fait' (*recte* 'Je me suis fait'), 'rendre mes respects' (*recte* 'présenter mes respects'), 'et de vous prier' (*recte* 'et pour vous prier').

This is a printed document with certain words inserted by hand.

The Executive Directory authorises Tone ('Theobald-Wolfe-Jones') to stay in Paris. See above, p. 179, n. 4.

Égalité [crest] Liberté

Extrait
des Registres des Délibérations du Directoire Exécutif

Paris, le vingt-trois floréal l'an quatre
de la République française, une et indivisible

Le Directoire Exécutif, en vertu de l'art. quatre de la loi du vingt un floréal présent mois, autorise Théobald-Wolfe-Jones, réfugié d'Irlande, à séjourner à Paris.

Le présent arrêté ne sera point imprimé.

Pour expédition conforme
[signed] Carnot
par le Directoire Exécutif
Le Secrétaire général
Lagarde

# Diary, 12–13 May 1796

T.C.D., Tone papers, MS 2049, ff 62r–63v; *Life*, ii, 111–12.

## 12 May 1796

Finished my memorial and gave it to Clarke. I should say my proclamation.[1] It is too long, but let Carnot cut it down as he pleases. Went to the Minister[2] to apply for permission to stay in Paris *malgré* the law. The Minister occupied, so I wrote him a short note,[3] in very pretty French, which I left for him. In the evening the spectacle, as usual. The French comedians[4] are infinitely beyond the English. Even in the little theatres on the boulevards,[5] they perform admirably, and there is an attention to the *costume* never seen in England. All the theatres, too, are pretty, and some of them magnificent. The opera however continues to stand first in my opinion. It is a charming spectacle, and I never go there without wishing for my dearest Love. But matters are so uncertain here that I labour to prevent myself wishing for anything. I am a dog, I am a dog, and I lead a dog's life here, dancing attendance perpetually, and in a continual suspense; it is truly alarming.[6] '*I have, I know not why, foregone my usual amusements*.'[7] Sad, sad! '*Man*

[1] See above, p. 126, n. 1, and pp 174–5. For Clarke's comments, see Diary of 3 June (below, p. 193).
[2] Delacroix. [3] Above, p. 180. [4] i.e. actors.
[5] A 'théâtre de boulevard' provided light entertainment.
[6] *Life* omits 'it is truly alarming'. [7] *Hamlet*, II, ii.

*delights not me, nor woman neither!*'[1] What shall I do? The novelty of Paris is worn off, my anxiety about our affairs increases, and I get no satisfactory information. The Devil puts it in my head sometimes that I am like Hannibal at the court of Prusias,[2] supplicating his aid to enable Carthage to make war upon the Romans. There is a sort of analogy in the circumstances, *excepting* that I am not Hannibal, nor General Clarke Prusias. Well, politics are fine things, '*mais c'est quand on en est revenu*'. I declare I wish our revolution was effected, and that I was set down once more quietly in the bosom of my family, and that is not very strange, for I doat upon them, and I am here like a fish out of water, and everything frets me. Yet I admire the French of all things; the men are agreeable and the women enchanting; and if my mind were at ease (as it is not) I could make it out very well here for some time longer, but as it is—well, I can't help myself, and so what signifies complaining? Let me write nonsense, and I cannot even write good nonsense when I am not in spirits, and I am never in spirits now. The French women are before the English, far and wide. They are incomparably well made, almost without exception. The English women have as handsome faces, but for figure and fashion there is nothing which approaches the French women; and then they walk so incomparably, and their language is so adapted for conversation that they all appear to have wit. For their morality, it is, to be sure, '*a nice morality, split my windpipe*'.[3] Paris in that respect beats London hollow, and that is a bold word, after what I have seen in London. Well, give me Ireland, after all, for women to make wives and mothers of. For '*casual fruition*',[4] go to London, or indeed rather to Paris, but if you wish to be happy, chuse your companion at home. The more I see of this wide world, the more I prize the inestimable blessing I possess in my wife's affection, her virtues, her courage, her goodness of heart, her sweetness of temper; and besides she is very pretty, a circumstance which does not lessen her value in my eyes. What is she doing just now? What would I give to be with her and the little fanfans for half an hour?

## 13 May 1796

Called on the Minister[5] relative to the law enjoining all strangers to quit Paris in three days. The Minister very civil; he desires me to give myself no trouble, but, in case the Police should molest me, to apply directly either to himself or Carnot. That will do for the present. Dined with Madgett in the Elysian fields[6] and drank like a fish.

[1] *Hamlet*, II, ii.

[2] After his final defeat by the Romans, Hannibal (247 or 249 B.C. to *c.*183 B.C.) took refuge with Prusias, king of Bithynia. On hearing that Prusias intended to hand him over to the Romans he committed suicide.

[3] R. B. Sheridan, *A trip to Scarborough* (1777), V, ii.

[4] Cf. 'the bought smile of harlots, loveless, joyless, unindear'd; casual fruition' (John Milton, *Paradise lost* (1674), bk IV).

[5] Delacroix.

[6] i.e. the Champs-Élysées.

## To General Henri Jacques Guillaume Clarke, 14 May 1796

Archives Nationales, AF IV, carton 1671, f. 70.

See Diary for 14 May 1796 (below).

Dear General,

In consequence of the law which ordains to all strangers to quit Paris in three days, I called yesterday[1] on the minister for foreign affairs to secure his protection when he told me he had already made application to Carnot on my behalf and that I might rest tranquil. I beg however that when you see Carnot next, you may take the trouble to mention me again to him and to request an order for my stay or such written document as may be necessary, that I may have it to produce in case of my meeting any molestation from the Police.

I beg you will excuse this trouble and believe me
Yours very sincerely,
T. W. Tone

[P.S.] I presume the order, if one be necessary, will be made out in the name of *James Smith*, under which I am known here.
26th Floréal[2] an 4me

## Diary, 14 May 1796

T.C.D., Tone papers, MS 2049, f. 63v; *Life*, ii, 112.

### 14 May 1796

Wrote a letter[3] to Clarke and left it for him, praying him to apply to Carnot for a written order for my stay, for fear of accidents. Paris is growing more and more stupid on my hands, and this horrible suspense and delay kill me. There is a sad falling off in my journals, but that is not my fault,

## To General Henri Jacques Guillaume Clarke, 15 May 1796

Archives Nationales, AF IV, carton 1671, f. 72.

[1] See above, p. 182. [2] *Recte* 25th Floréal. [3] Above.

Dear Sir,

I have just now been at the Directory and have spoken to Citizen Carnot, to whom I am to present a short memorial[1] tomorrow praying permission to remain in Paris. You need not therefore take the trouble to mention me to him.

Yours very sincerely,
T. W. Tone

General Clarke &c., &c.
27[2] Floréal

# Diary, 15 May 1796

T.C.D., Tone papers, MS 2049, f. 63ᵛ; *Life*, ii, 112.

15 May 1796

Went to the Directory and saw Carnot, who desired me to write a short memorial desiring leave to stay, and to bring it to him tomorrow. Saw Ahern. Nothing done in his business yet! That looks very bad.

# To the Executive Directory, 16 May 1796

Archives Nationales, AF III 369, f. 51.

Tone seeks permission to remain in Paris.

Paris, le 28[3] Floréal, an 4ᵐᵉ de la République

Aux Citoyens composant le Directoire exécutif de
la République Française.

Citoyens Directeurs,

Le Citoyen Theobald Wolfe Tone (dit James Smith) vous rappelle qu'il est arrivé des États Unis d'Amérique depuis trois mois, chargé d'une mission de la plus haute importance auprès du Gouvernement François; que cette mission n'étant pas encore terminée, sa présence à Paris est indispensablement nécessaire.

En conséquence il vous prie d'user à son égard du droit que vous donne la loi et de lui accorder la permission de rester à Paris.

Salut et Respect
Theobald Wolfe Tone

[1] Below. [2] *Recte* 26. [3] *Recte* 27.

[Endorsed at top]: Accordé Carnot 29 f [l]o[réa]l an 4.[1]
[Endorsed in another hand]: La permission a été annullée.[2]

## Diary, 16 May 1796

T.C.D., Tone papers, MS 2049, ff 63v–64v; *Life*, ii, 112–13.

### 16 May 1796

Delivered my memorial[3] at the Luxembourg and received directions to apply at the Secretariat General for a *permission*[4] *en règle*; so that affair is settled. Lounged in the evening to the Théâtre d'Émulation, one of the little theatres of the boulevards. It was Easter Monday[5] and, being a fête, the house was filled with the *bonne bourgeoisie*, all dressed out and as gay and happy as possible. I was agreeably surprised to find the piece was the *School for Scandal*,[6] extremely well adapted to the French stage and very well represented. It had an effect on me which I cannot describe. I was alone, and it brought a thousand recollections into my mind. Shall I ever see the *School for Scandal* on an English theatre again? Well, that is the least of my grievances. The French comedians are incomparable; even on this little theatre of the suburbs they acted admirably, particularly Charles, Sir Oliver and Lady Teazel; they excel in the management of their bye play, but they have one fault: in their soliloquies they always address themselves too much to the audience with the expression as if they were telling them a secret. '*The soliloquy always to the pit, that is the rule!*'[7] The civic airs were applauded with something like sincerity, a circumstance which I have not remarked for some time. On the whole I was very well amused. How my life stagnates just now, when I have nothing to write of but the theatres of the boulevards! Sad!

## Diary, 17 May 1796

T.C.D., Tone papers, MS 2049, ff 65r–66r; *Life*, ii, 113.

1 See Decree of the Executive Directory, 18 May 1796 (below, p. 186).
2 Presumably because it had been made out in the wrong name.
3 Above, pp 184–5.
4 The following seven words are omitted from *Life*.
5 *Recte* Whit Monday.
6 By Richard Brinsley Sheridan.
7 Sheridan, *The critic* (1779), III, i.

Number 7
From May 17 to June 23d inclusive[1]
*Nil desperandum!*
Paris
1796
*Arma pia quibus, nisi in armis, spes nulla!*[2]

17 May 1796

Blank! A good beginning of my new journal![3]

## Decree of the Executive Directory, 18 May 1796

Archives Nationales, AF III 369, f. 48.

This is a printed document but with certain words inserted by hand. It is scored through.

The Directory authorises Tone to stay on in Paris. See Diary for 20 May 1796 (below p. 187).

POLICE GÉNÉRALE
MOTS
de
RECHERCHES

Minute d'Arrêté
Sommaire de l'Arrêté

Theobald Wolfe Jones

Paris, le 29 floréal an 4 de la République Française, une et indivisible

Reçu l'expédition
Le 29 floréal

T. W. Tone[4]

Le Directoire Exécutif, en vertu de l'art. 4 de la Loi du 21 floréal présent mois autorise Théobald Wolfe Jones, refugié d'Irlande, à séjourner à Paris.

Le présent arrêté ne sera point imprimé.

Carnot
Reubell L.M. Revellière Lépeaux

[1] The Diary entries for 18–29 May, 3–9 June, 10–12 June and 14–23 June are given as separate documents (below, pp 187–92, 193–6, 198–201, 202–11).

[2] 'War is just to those who have no other hope'. In *Life* this verse and the preceding headings, obviously inserted later than 17 May, are omitted.

[3] *Life* omits this line except for the word 'Blank!'.

[4] Signed thus by Tone.

# Diary, 18–29 May 1796

T.C.D., Tone papers, MS 2049, ff 66ʳ–71ʳ; *Life*, ii, 113–18.

## 18 May 1796

This day I had a *tift* with my lover[1] Carnot. In signing the memorial[2] which I delivered to him I had written my name 'Theobald Wolfe Tone (dit James Smith)'. The permission[3] was made out in the name of T. W. Tone and, of course, was refused to me when I applied for it in the name of J. Smith. I was therefore obliged, sore against my will, to apply again to Carnot, who spoke very chuff about the trouble I gave him to write a second memorandum &c. I was damnably vexed and told him, civilly but drily, that I was sorry for the mistake but that it was not my fault. He then wrote a second note to the Secretary, so I suppose tomorrow it will be made out properly. Men in high station ought never to speak short to people who do not deserve it. I take that to be a very pretty political maxim, and so I halt here for the present. I have not recovered my good humour yet.

## 19 May 1796

I learn today that Carnot was as cross as the Devil to everybody yesterday; so it seems I was not singular.

## 20 May 1796

Received, at last, my permission to stay in Paris, signed 'Tomkins, creditor',[4] or, indeed, 'Carnot, Pres[iden]t'. Only think of the folly of some people! The first permission that was made out (as I saw today) was for 'Le Citoyen Theobald Wolfe Tone, Refugié *Irlandais*!'. That was a pretty business to spread on a paper which was to be seen by Lord knows how many clerks and commis, as well at the Luxembourg as at the Municipalité. Well, it was no fault of mine, as I told Citizen Carnot ere[5] yesterday; and besides there is no harm done, as it happens, for the paper is *biffé*, as they call it here, or[6] cancelled; so that affair is off my hands and I have nothing to do but divert myself, for the Government give me no business. '*Fie upon this idle life; I want work*'.[7] It seems the plot[8] which was discovered by the Directoire Exécutif was dreadfully sanguinary. Among other features, all

[1] Meaning here 'wellwisher'. [2] Above, pp 184–5. [3] See above, p. 186.
[4] Sheridan, *The critic* (1779), III, i. [5] *Life* omits 'ere'. But see Diary for 18 May (above).
[6] *Life* omits the preceding seven words.
[7] More correctly 'Fie upon this quiet life! I want work.' (*1 Henry IV*, II, iv).
[8] For Babeuf's plot, see above, p. 179, n. 1.

strangers were to present themselves, in order to their being imprisoned, *voluntarily, under pain of death!* If that fact be so, it seems I have had, among others, a very good escape, for in times of revolution, it is a short journey sometimes from the prison to '*that undiscovered country from whose bourne no traveller returns*'.[1] Things are better as they are for France and for us. It is curious enough to observe how the enthusiasm of the Revolution is entirely abated here. Even the immortal victories of the army of Italy have not the smallest effect on their feelings. I observe it particularly at the spectacles, where they sing (by order of the Executive) *les chants civiques* every night, and they are received with the utmost phlegm, and sometimes worse. Enthusiasm is a passion which will not last for six years of a war which, however glorious beyond all historical example, has been attended with great individual suffering. I observe too the Young Men are the most disaffected part of the nation, which is caused by the dominion of the women (who are without exception aristocrats) over their minds; that is very natural and very abominable.[2] I did expect the rising generation would have been good Republicans, but I cannot say that the fact has justified my expectation. The *Jeunes Gens*[3] sculk as much as possible from the Requisition, which they evade by every means in their power. To see them in Paris, they are a race of wretched Sybarites, yet these very young men, when they are forced at last to join the armies, only see how they fight! This is a curious paradox. I believe if the Republic were to suffer a sudden reverse of fortune, for example if Brunswick were once more at the Pass of Biesme,[4] the old spirit of France would revive, but as it is, there is *no enthusiasm here*. There is however a good succedaneum[5] in a very well organised government, which, combined with the untamable courage of the French soldiery,[6] does the business sufficiently, as I believe Gen[era]l Beaulieu and the King of Sardinia will bear witness.[7] It is very lucky the new government was in function before this absolute decadence of public spirit in France. If the enthusiasm had failed before the present system was ready to supply its place, I know not what might have happened. At any rate, if the combined despots had, in that case, made any progress in France it would only have once more roused the energy of 1792 and the succeeding two years, so that at last it would have come to the same thing. It is the successes of France which have rebated her enthusiasm. I believe this is enough of politics for the present. I will only add that, if I were the Directory, I would forbid the singing of all political airs at the spectacles, without distinction, for a forced spirit is always a bad one.

[1] *Hamlet*, III, i. [2] *Life*, ii, 114, substitutes 'bad' for 'abominable'.

[3] Literally 'young people'. For the *jeunes gens de la réquisition*, see above, p. 55, n. 2.

[4] In Sept. 1792 the French army occupied Biesme, a strategic point in the eastern part of the *département* of the Marne, in order to halt the invasion of the allied armies of Prussia, the Emperor and French émigrés in the Argonne, as the district was called. After two weeks of confrontation a decisive victory was won by the French army at Valmy. William Tone substitutes 'passes of Argonne' for 'Pass of Biesme' (*Life*, ii, 114).

[5] Meaning here 'remedy'.

[6] William Tone substitutes 'armies' for 'French soldiery' (*Life*, ii, 114).

[7] See above, pp 170, 172, n. 1.

## 21 May 1796

This morning, on sallying out, the first thing I saw was an *affiche*[1] of a vessel to sail in ten days for New York. This knocked me in the head for the whole day. I have been planning a thousand schemes. Tomorrow I will see Madgett in order to take his opinion on one or two points. If I can do it with safety to my wife and our dear, dear Babies, I think I will settle in France—that is *if I can.*[2]

## 22 May 1796

Called on Madgett and took a serious walk with him in the Thuilleries. I told him that I had considered my situation maturely and the result was that I felt a strong inclination to settle in France; that by a rough calculation I supposed I could command about 400 louis d'or, with which I could do very little in America unless I went very far back[3] and then I should feel myself helpless, not being myself enured to labour and servants being not to be had; that I conceived property could be had very cheap now in France[4] and that it was my wife's wish, as well as my own, to fix here rather than in America, which we both detested, as well the people as the country. I therefore begged his advice on two points: first whether he apprehended (as I did *not*) that there was any actual danger of a counter-revolution, by which I meant the restoration of royalty, &c.; and next whether it would be more adviseable to purchase national or patrimonial property with the small sum which I could command? Madgett replied that as to a counter-revolution, he did not well know what to say, more than that it was an event far from being impossible;[5] that the Government was in the most extreme distress for money, being absolutely without any; that the *mandats* had failed in their operation[6] and what should be substituted he could not pretend to guess; that the approvisioning Paris was a work of immense difficulty, and if there once came an actual scarcity of food there, it was impossible to say what might be the result, from the fury of an enraged and starving populace, any one of whom might take it in his head to cry '*Vive le Roi*!' and perhaps the whole mass adopt it; that Pitt was moving heaven, earth and hell to ruin the finances; that the louis was today at 10,500#;[7] that things were driven now to that state that a very few days, five or six, must decide the business whether the Government could go on or not, and that for himself he wished he was well[8] out of it. He added that perhaps it would be preferable to buy patrimonial property and that with the sum I mentioned I might purchase an estate of ten times the value (viz. £4,000). We

[1] i.e. a public notice. [2] *Life* omits 'that is *if I can*'. [3] i.e. westwards.

[4] *Life* omits the remainder of the sentence. [5] *Life*, ii, 115, has 'far from improbable'.

[6] For a glossary of French currency in circulation up to this time, see above, p. 41, n. 5. By a decree of 18 Mar. 1796 *mandats territoriaux* were created as a substitute for *assignats* (*Bulletin des Lois de la République Française*, no. 34 [252]). Towards the end of May the Directory published a proclamation on the exchange of *assignats* for *mandats* (*Moniteur*, 28 May 1796).

[7] *Life*, ii, 115, spells out 'francs'.

[8] *Life*, ii, 116, substitutes 'fairly' for 'well'.

then fixed to meet in three or four days, and in the meantime he is to make inquiries and to turn the matter in his thoughts. So it rests.

For my own part, whether it is that I am younger and more sanguine than Madgett, or whether it is that I am less acquainted with circumstances, I know not; but so it is that I have not the smallest apprehension of a counter-revolution. The present government is one of extraordinary mildness, perhaps too much so; but if they are pressed by an invincible necessity, they must, and I have no doubt will, have recurrence to stronger measures; but what decides me is the excellent spirit of the army. The mutiny among the Légion de Police (which appears now to have been a ramification of Baboeuf's plot) was quelled in an instant by the other troops, and I see today a most excellent address to the Directory from the privates and non-commissioned officers of the 3d Dragoons, which compose a part of their guard. While the armies continue steady, and there is every appearance that they will do so, I fear nothing. I believe I can lay out the little money I can command to more advantage here than in America, supposing only the half of what Madgett says to be true, and there is no possible comparison between the two countries; besides I am on the spot; I am *à portée* of Ireland. I need not here recite my reasons; but, as at present advised, I think I will write an order by this vessel to my Love to convert everything possible into specie, to buy louis d'ors at the Bank in Philadelphia,[1] and set off for Havre with our family in the first ship that sails. Good God! how happy shall I be, if I can fix them in a comfortable cottage in France! For my schemes of ambition, I am almost worn out of hope. I act now without expectation, and merely that I may safely say that nothing on my part has been left untried or undone. If there comes a peace and I settle here, it will be but a step for P.P.[2] to come visit us, and to be sure we will not make him welcome, and there is no wine in France, &c., &c. I feel my ancient propensities revive *a little*.

## 26 May 1796

After ballancing these four or five days and turning the matter every way in my thoughts I have taken my resolution, and this day I have written to my dearest Love, to Rowan and to Reynolds,[3] acquainting them with my determination to settle in France, and desiring them to make preparations for the departure of my family with all possible haste. It is a bold measure but '*audaces fortuna juvat*'.[4] If my negociation here succeeds, still it will be best they should be in France; if it fails, I am satisfied it is more advisable for us to settle in France than in America. At all events the die is now cast. It is an epoch in my life. I have decided to the best of my judgement and if I fail, I fail. I am weary of floating about at the mercy of events. Let me fix myself, if possible at last.

[1] *Life*, ii, 116, has 'Bank of Philadelphia'.
[2] Thomas Russell.
[3] *Life*, ii, 116, has 'Doctor Reynolds'.
[4] 'Fortune favours the brave' (*Aeneid*, x, 28).

## 27 May 1796

Paris has been in a sort of smothered fermentation for several days, and I suppose a very few more must bring it to a crisis. Within a fortnight all the assignats in Paris will be called in and exchanged against their value in mandats,[1] which in other words is changing at once the currency of France. The small assignats of 100₶[2] and under will be allowed to circulate for the convenience of the poor. An hundred livres in assignats are worth today about 2½*d.*; their nominal value is £4 3[*s*]. 4[*d*]. That is a pretty reasonable depreciation! For my part, who am neither financier nor agioteur,[3] I do not pretend to understand the question, but I can clearly see it is no ordinary matter to annul, at a blow, the entire currency of the nation and to substitute another in its place; yet it has been done here once already in the case of the assignats, which superseded gold and silver, as the mandats will, I have no doubt, supersede the assignats.[4] Something or other must be done, or the finances here will tumble. I hope the Government will have firmness. They seem lately to be assuming a higher tone than formerly and I am glad of it, for I sometimes could not help thinking of King Log, when I saw them insulted with impunity.[5] If they stand bold, the enemies of the Republic will be put down, but if they go back, or even fluctuate, in my mind they are lost; it is certainly a most critical period. If the Govern[men]t holds out till the 1st Messidor,[6] which is now three weeks off, and if their new scheme of finance succeeds, to ascertain which nothing seems wanting but firmness on their part, the Republic will be established forever. As it is, we are '*walking on embers covered with unfaithful dust*!'.[7] *Courage!* A few days will settle the business, and I doubt not, for my part, prosperously. *Vive la République!* Yesterday I had a visit from the *commissaire de police* of my Section, by order of the Bureau Central of Paris, in order to bring me before my betters for remaining in town contrary to the law of the 21st Floréal[8] concerning strangers. However, I *jumped suddenly upon him and deprived him of the use of his weapon* by producing my permission to remain,[9] signed Carnot, pres[iden]t, and countersigned Lagarde,[10] secretary, on which he begged my pardon, &c. He then dressed a *procès verbal*[11] of the business, which I signed, and so we parted the best friends possible. This visit is owing to some blunder in the Bureau Central, where I went the day after I received my permission to have it viewed by the proper officer, who omitted, I suppose, to make the proper entry. I am glad however to find the Government serious in compelling the strangers to leave Paris; they are a pest to France, speculating in her funds, and

[1] See above, p. 41, n. 5, p. 189, n. 6. [2] *Life*, ii, 117, spells out 'francs'.

[3] Meaning speculator. [4] See above, p. 189, n. 6.

[5] An allusion to Æsop's fable of frogs asking for a king. Jupiter first throws them down a log of wood, but they grumble at a spiritless king; he then sends them a stork, who devours them.

[6] i.e. 19 June 1796. [7] Source of this quotation not identified.

[8] See above, p. 179, n. 4. [9] See Diary for 20 May (above, p. 187).

[10] Joseph Jean Lagarde (1755–1839), secretary general to the Directory from Nov. 1795. He had been secretary general of a department and had reorganised the central administration of Belgium. He was created baron of the empire, 1809. (*Biographie universelle ancienne et moderne*; *Dict. biog. franç.*).

[11] i.e. a statement.

ruining her currency. I am told that there is an exception in favor of the Americans,[1] who are precisely those who should not be suffered to remain, not merely on account of their own demerits, tho' they are bad enough, but because of the multitudes of English agents and spies, who all pass here for Americans. If I was the Government I would not suffer a man of them to remain for whom the Ambassador would not engage personally, and perhaps not even then.

### 29 May 1796

Went to the *Fête de Victoire*[2] which was celebrated today in the Champ de Mars.[3] The Directory, the Ministers, the Corps Diplomatique, &c., &c., assisted, all in grand costume. Incense was burned before the statue of Liberty and the usual civic hymns were chanted, with two or three new ones composed for the occasion, alluding to the successes of the army of Italy.[4] It was a superb spectacle, and the spirit of the people much better than I expected, under all the circumstances of the case. There were about 6,000 troops under arms, divided into 14 battalions, representing the 14 armies of the republic, each of whom received from the hands of Carnot, the President, a standard and a garland of oak, the emblem of victory, which was borne by the handsomest grenadier of the corps. The troops made a very fine appearance, all young healthy men, fit for active service. I was placed at the foot of the altar in the middle of my brethren of the Corps Diplomatique, but for particular reasons I chose to remain *incognito*. Altogether I was exceedingly pleased with the exhibition, and the tears ran down my cheeks when Carnot presented the wreaths and the standards to the soldiers. It was a spectacle worthy of a great republic, and I enjoyed it with transport. '*Vive la République!*'

## To General Henri Jacques Guillaume Clarke, 3 June 1796

Archives Nationales, AF IV, carton 1671, f. 73.

See Diary for 3 June (below, p. 193).

General,

I have this moment received your note, and am extremely flattered by the approbation contained in it. I will, in pursuance of your direction, call at your bureau *the 18th at eleven o'clock*. If that hour be inconvenient to you,

[1] For the remainder of the paragraph *Life*, ii, 118, substitutes the following: 'If I was the Government, I would not suffer one of them to remain for whom the Ambassador would not engage personally, because of the multitude of English agents and spies who all pass for Americans'.

[2] Corrected in *Life*, ii, 118, to 'Fête des victoires'.

[3] For the programme of the fête, see *Moniteur*, 29 May 1796.

[4] See above, pp 162, 163, 170–71.

you will be so good as to leave directions with the Porter at what hour you will be at leisure.

Health & Fraternity,
J. Smith

Le 15th Prairial An 4me &c.

## Diary, 3–9 June 1796

T.C.D., Tone papers, MS 2049, ff 71v–73v; *Life*, ii, 119–21.

### 3 June 1796

A faint ray of hope has broke today across the almost impenetrable gloom which has for some time enveloped my prospects. I called on Clark, *pro formâ*, not expecting to find him, in which in fact I was not disappointed. I found however a note informing me that he had read my proclamation (No. 6, May 12th)[1] and liked it very well, that however it would be necessary to curtail it somewhat, and that he desired to see me for that purpose any time after this day and tomorrow. *It is the first time he has desired to see me*. Well, that is something however! I wrote an answer immediately, appointing the 18th Prairial (June 6), by which I leave him, out of respect, one day clear. Will anything come of this? I am glad Clarke likes my proclamation, which I found too long myself. I see he has a correct taste in these things. If the expedition takes place, it will be something to boast of to have written the proclamation. But let me not be '*running before my horse to market*'.[2] I have kept my hopes under a strict regimen all along, and latterly God knows on a very low diet. I will not let this little breeze tempt me to spread a deal of canvas merely to have it to furl again. Things however are better today than they were yesterday.

### 5 June 1796

A French lover[3] of mine, Mons[ieu]r Degas,[4] took me today in his cabriolet to Versailles. It is a pleasant drive of 12 miles from Paris,[5] the environs of which are certainly before those of London, but far inferior to those of Dublin, which are beautiful beyond description owing to the two grand features, the sea and the Wicklow mountains. The Château of Versailles is truly magnificent and the Gardens of a vast extent but of a most tiresome uniformity; all in the old school, strait alleys, clipt hedges, round basins, marble statues, and systems of terrasses. It is a detestable style. There are some admirable paintings yet remaining, particularly one of Charles 1st of England by Vandyck which has been engraved

[1] See above, p. 181. [2] Cf. 'I run before my horse to market' (*Richard III*, I, i).
[3] Meaning here 'friend' or 'wellwisher'. [4] Not identified.
[5] Versailles is 23 km from Paris.

by Strange,[1] and one of Charles 12th of Sweden,[2] which is a striking resemblance of Lord Landaff.[3] All the furniture has been removed or sold, excepting a most magnificent cabinet which belonged to Marie Antoinette[4] and in which she kept her jewels. Nothing can exceed the extravagant flattery displayed in the ceilings, which are all painted in allegories alluding to the different events in the reign of Louis 14th,[5] who is represented one time as Hercules, another time as Mars, and again as Jupiter; what makes it still better is that all those paintings were executed by his order. I was particularly struck with one where there is a group of four figures, Louis, his brother Orleans,[6] the Grand Condé[7] and Turenne,[8] certainly not ordinary men. Portraits of illustrious characters are the style of painting which I like best. There is also a good portrait of Madam Maintenon.[9] It would take I think a week to examine the Palace and Gardens, and I did not remain much above an hour. I saw however enough to satisfy me that the King of France was magnificently lodged, but for my part I should die of the spleen in a week if I were confined to the Château de Versailles. It is the same with all the palaces I have ever seen, which are not many. Hampton Court, in England, is magnificent but it would be lost in Versailles. From the Château we walked to Trianon which is about half a mile distant. The Pavillon is beautiful (viz. the outside, which is all I saw), being all built of coloured marble; the gardens are like those of Versailles, equally monotonous, but less extensive. It is an abominable style. We then went to Le Petit Trianon, the favorite retreat of Antoinette, '*the bower of wanton Shrewsbury, and love*'.[10] It is a most delicious spot, completely finished in the English style. After the dreary regularity of the other two gardens, I was enchanted, and even the French folk acknowledged the infinite superiority of taste manifested in the laying out the grounds. Trianon would be beautiful in England, but in France it is like fairy ground. There have been some pretty frolics executed here[11] by the late Queen[12] and her favorites. I could not help making many profound reflections, while I walked thro' it, *de vanitate mundi et fuga sæculi*.[13] I do not wonder

[1] Robert Strange (1721–91), engraver, published in 1784 his engraving of the Van Dyck portrait of Charles I which was at Versailles (*D.N.B.*).

[2] Charles XII (1682–1718), king of Sweden, 1697–1718.

[3] Francis Mathew (1744?–1806), M.P. for Co. Tipperary, 1768–83; created Baron Landaff of Thomastown, 1783; viscount, 1793; earl of Landaff, 1797; he was noted for his good looks (G.E.C., *Peerage*).

[4] Marie-Antoinette (1755–93), queen of France, 1774–92.

[5] Louis XIV (1638–1715) reigned 1643–1715.

[6] Philippe, duc d'Orléans (1640–1701).

[7] Louis de Bourbon, prince de Condé (1621–86), known as Le Grand Condé.

[8] Henri de la Tour d'Auvergne, vicomte de Turenne (1611–75), marshal of France.

[9] Françoise d'Aubigné, marquise de Maintenon (1635–1719), usually known as Madame de Maintenon, was the second wife of Louis XIV.

[10] Apparently a confused conflation of *1 Henry IV*, III, i, where there is mention of Shrewsbury and where there appear the lines:

> Upon the wanton rushes lay you down
> And rest your gentle head upon her lap.

Tone's quotation is omitted from *Life*.

[11] In *Life* the remainder of the sentence is omitted.

[12] Marie-Antoinette, executed in 1793.

[13] 'On the vanities of the world and the passing of time'.

that the Queen regretted to fall from the station that she once held. Altogether it made me melancholy.

## 6 June 1796

Called this morning, by appointment, on Gen[era]l Clarke. Found him more cordial in his manner than ordinary. He told me he had read my proclamation[1] and found it extremely well done; that however it would be necessary to curtail it considerably, for the first point in these compositions is to ensure their being read, and for that it is necessary that they should be short; that there would be a longer one prepared for those who studied politics, but that mine was intended for the people and the soldiery. I thought there was good sense in all this, and I can safely say that in all the public papers I have ever written I am above the personal vanity of an author, as I believe Gog[2] will witness. I therefore told him I would '*mince it, sans remorse*'.[3] He then told me I might rely on it that they had not lost sight either of the business itself or of my share in it. We then talked for a few minutes of the gigantic successes of the army of Italy, and so, having fixed to return, with my proclamation cut down to a reasonable size, in a few days, I took my leave. I liked Clarke very well today. On my return I met Sullivan in the horrors. Madgett has told him that affairs were reduced to such a crisis that the Directory and legislative bodies were actually thinking of removing to Fontain[e]bleau for their personal security. Madgett has always news either extravagantly good or extravagantly bad. I told Sullivan plump that I did not believe it; but that if they took such a pusillanimous step as that, they were undone for ever. I added many fine observations, stolen from Shakespeare, on the folly of fearing death in public situations, and made on the whole a most eloquent harangue by which I convinced Sullivan and myself that there was no danger. I do not however like these reports. After all there may be something in them, and if the Government here were to blow up, it would be terrible.

I have been ever since as melancholy as a cat. I think it is growing my prevailing habit. '*Hope long deferred*', saith the scripture, '*maketh the heart of a man sick*'.[4] I am sure mine just now is not in rude health, but I am sworn never to despair. *Courage, donc, allons!*

## 8 June 1796

Called today on Monroe, whom I have not seen for above two months. Found him extremely civil. Staid and chatted with him above an hour. All American politics. He had the delicacy not to mention my business, for which I was obliged to him. He also told me that Beckly[5] had written him word[6] that they had heard

[1] See Diary for 12 May and 3 June (above, pp 181, 193). [2] John Keogh.
[3] *Timon of Athens*, IV, iii. [4] Proverbs, 13: 12. [5] Abbreviated in *Life*, ii, 121, to 'B.'.
[6] The letter alluded to, John Beckley to James Monroe, 2 Apr. 1796, is in the Monroe papers (New York Public Library).

in Philadelphia of my safe arrival in Havre, so that my family is out of all anxiety on that account. I am heartily glad of that circumstance.

### 9 June 1796

At work cutting and slashing my proclamation.[1] I will bring it to something at last. I am just like Jack in the *Tale of a Tub* altering his coat, &c., &c.[2]

## Proclamation to the people of Ireland, 9–10 June 1796

Archives Nationales, AF IV, carton 1671.

This document is in Tone's hand and has every appearance of being of his composition. It is identifiable as the abridged version of the 'memorial', 'manifesto' or 'proclamation' that is continually referred to in his Diary between 24 Mar. and 6 June 1796 (see above, p. 126, n. 1). The abridgement was requested by Clarke on 6 June ('curtail it considerably'), worked on by Tone on 9 June ('cutting and slashing my proclamation') and completed on the following day. When Tone called on Clarke on 19 June he found his aide-de-camp making a copy and, at Clarke's request, made a copy himself, which took him 'about half an hour'. Evidently a copy reached General Lazare Hoche, appointed on 20 June to command the French military expedition to Ireland, for, in his Diary for 23 July, Tone wrote 'Hoche shewed me my proclamation printed and signed by himself. It is the one intended for distribution.' No copy of the printed version has been found. The copies intended for distribution on a landing being made in Ireland were probably on board Hoche's flagship, the *Fraternité*.

Liberty Equality Union Fraternity

People of Ireland!

The French Republic, actuated by an earnest desire to bring to a speedy termination a bloody and destructive war, as well as to restore a brave and suffering nation to the enjoyment of her long lost rights, has thought proper to send to Ireland a powerful and well appointed military force, and has entrusted me with the command. The principles which govern the conduct of France, and which have been unvaryingly manifested since her revolution, are so well known that it is unnecessary here to repeat them. Nevertheless, as it is my earnest wish to avoid the possibility of doubt on some important topics, I feel it my duty explicitly to declare that our sole object is the establishment of your independence, solemnly disclaiming all idea whatsoever of conquest, and to this I pledge the good faith of

[1] Below, pp 196–8.

[2] Swift, *Tale of a tub* (1704), section VI.

my country. We come amongst you, not as enemies to invade, but as brothers to assist you; not to reduce you to a state of dependance upon France, but to break the chains which have so long bound you in subjection to England, and to raise you from the abject situation of a province to the rank and dignity of a free nation. The army which I have the honour to command, in unison with the sentiment of the French people, will preserve the most inviolable respect for persons and property; they will protect the free and uncontrolled exercise of all religions, without distinction or preference, and they will in all respects manifest towards the people of Ireland, the same spirit of affection, moderation, and fraternity which has signalised their brothers in arms who emancipated Holland from the British yoke. To those who know the characteristic spirit of a French soldier, by which any individual under my command is equally actuated, it is unnecessary to say more. Our conduct and our actions will better speak for the honour of the Republic than any engagements.

People of Ireland, now is your time! The hour of your emancipation is at length arrived. We bring you arms, ammunition, artillery, stores, everything of which your tyrants have industriously deprived you, and the want of which alone has kept your indignant spirit so long in fetters. Strike for the honour of your country, for the destruction of tyranny and the freedom and happiness of mankind. Swear with us eternal war against the ambition and the avarice of England, to which your liberty, your property and your blood have been so long sacrificed. Join the standard of your allies, your friends and your brothers. We desire no more than to combat with you side by side or to shew you the way to glory. It will not be the first time. The plains of Fontenoy and Lawfeld,[1] the rocks of Eustatia,[2] have already witnessed the prostration of English pride before the valour of France and Ireland. Who are our antagonists? Are they the troops which we have seen so often fly before the invincible arms of the Republic over the plains of Flanders and the ice of Holland? The contest will be short between the satellites of British despotism and the soldiers of the United Nations, animated by their characteristic courage, by a deep sense of past wrongs, by the unconquerable hatred of oppression and an ardent passion for liberty. Is there to be found an Irishman so base as to remain in the service of the common enemy, to wear the livery and to fight the battles of England, the implacable oppressor of his native land? If there be, let him take his fate! Let him fall, denied by his country, disowned by his friends, and despised by the very tyrants who traffic in his blood. But Frenchmen, judging of you by themselves, will not believe that so degraded a being can exist in a country, whose honor is recognised throughout Europe. We rely with confidence that those of you whom the pressure of circumstances may have forced into the service of Britain,

[1] On which the battles of Fontenoy and Laifeld were fought (1745 and 1747).

[2] Dillon's and Walsh's regiments in the French service were employed at the capture of St Eustache in Nov. 1781 ('A brief historical sketch of the Irish infantry regiment of Dillon' in *Royal United Services Institute Journal*, xlix (1905), p. 829).

will fly to the standard of their native soil, the moment they see it once displayed in defence of the liberties of Ireland.

For us, we have no friends but your friends, no enemies but your enemies. We wish not to interfere in your domestic concerns. Frame your own organisation; regulate for yourselves your properties, your religion and your laws. We ask nothing of you but your friendship. Remember America who, with not the thousandth part of your wrongs to inflame her, did not hesitate to embark in the contest, in order to sever herself from the possibility of a tyranny which she did not feel, and under which you actually groan. Look to the unexampled prosperity she enjoys at this hour, the fruit of her independance and the just reward of her courage and her patriotism. France, which emancipated her from the yoke of British usurpation, now offers to you the same glorious opportunity. And are Irishmen less sensible of disgrace and injury, or do they love their country less than Americans? Are their bodies less framed to encounter hardship, or their minds less fortified against the fear of death? Rise then; assert your liberties and the independance of your native land. Let Ireland become a nation and yourselves a people. Forget for ever all past animosities. Be united among yourselves. Mark that man as the agent of your enemies who endeavours by word or action to revive among you the memory of religious differences. Remember that you are all Irishmen alike, with one common interest and one common foe. Unite and conquer! Let it be your maxim and your oath. One grand effort and your fetters are broken, the sceptre of your tryant is wrested from his hand, and Ireland is for ever free, independant and happy.

# Diary, 10–12 June 1796

T.C.D., Tone papers, MS 2049, ff 74$^{r}$–76$^{r}$; *Life*, ii, 121–4.

## 10 June 1796

Madgett tells me today an odd piece of news. One of the clerks in his bureau assures him that the landing of the French in Ireland has been effected, and that he has it from a member of the Legislative body, who has it immediately from one of the Directory. If it be so,[1] it is most extraordinary that neither Madgett nor I were favored with the smallest information on the subject. Madgett has been with the Minister[2] to enquire about it. The Minister said he did not believe it, and that the news must be *premature*. That however leaves it possible that it may be true. I do not well know what to think. I have finished my proclamation,[3] which is cut down to a frigate, and I will go with it to Clarke tomorrow. If there be anything in this report, he will probably mention it to me, and if he does not, I will conclude it is unfounded.

[1] It was not. [2] Delacroix. [3] Above, pp 196–8.

## 11 June 1796

Called on Clarke, whom I met running to his Bureau in a violent hurry to Gen[era]l Lacuée,[1] who was waiting for him. I had just time to give him the paper[2] and he did not say one word about the landing, so I presume the story is, as the Minister said, *premature*.

*Evening*. Madgett with me again. The report seems to be growing more serious. It stands now as follows. Grandjean,[3] chef de bureau in the Foreign Affairs, told him this day that the French were landed in Ireland to the number of 15,000 men, that they had been perfectly well received by the people who were flocking about them in thousands when the dispatches were sent off; that he had this from Beffroy,[4] a member of the Cinq-cens, who had it directly from one of the Directory. All that is very circumstantial and precise and I confess staggers me extremely. There must be something in it, or how would Beffroy and Grandjean come to think of Ireland at all? There has also certainly a frigate arrived at Brest (the *Atalanta*) within these few days after accompanying a fleet of transports, &c., somewhere or other. After all, if it should be to Ireland? *Madgett is as sure of it as of his existence*, and is most terribly chagrined at its being kept a secret from him. For my part the main point to me is that the landing should be effected; my concern in the business is the least part of it. Yet I should be mortified to the last excess not to bear a part in it. '*Quoi! Les François en Irlande, et Montauciel n'y est pas!*'[5] I am '*lost in sensations of troubled emotion*'.[6] On the whole I think it very unlikely that the report should be true, yet it is certainly possible, and there are strong circumstances in its favor. Among others, it is now a month since Madgett sent off 15 Irish prisoners to Hoche, by Clarke's orders, who said they were intended for England, which by the bye I did not believe (*No. 6, May 11th*).[7] But then on the other hand why should the Directory conceal such a piece of good news from the public, and why should Clarke conceal it from me? If the report be true they have not kept faith with me, for both Carnot and Clarke assured me, if the expedition were undertaken, I should be of the party and Clarke repeated it in our last conversation, and I confess it would give me great pain to be left out of the business here, after having laboured successfully thus far. Notwithstanding all that, I would to God that the report were true. That is the main point. My interests are of little consequence, and besides in the long run the truth will come out, and justice be done to all parties. Madgett is a thousand times more enraged than I am, tho' I think with less reason, for he has neither done nor suffered as

[1] Jean Gérard Lacuée (1752–1841), army officer before the revolution; general of brigade, 1795; member of the Council of Ancients; count, 1808; noted as an administrator and writer on military subjects (Six, *Dict. des généraux & amiraux*; *Dict. parl. franç.*).

[2] Tone's proclamation.

[3] Grandjean was 'chef du dixième bureau des dépenses' (*Almanach National de France*, An 4).

[4] Louis Étienne Beffroy de Beauvoir (1755–1825), member of the Convention and of the Council of Five Hundred (*Dict. parl. franç.*).

[5] See below, p. 232, n. 1.

[6] Source of this quotation not identified.

[7] He wrote he was 'slow of faith' (above, p. 179).

much in the business as I have. Once for all, *I do not yet believe it*. A very few days however must ascertain the truth or falsehood of the report, and in the meantime I think I will take no step whatsoever. The Directory have received today the news of two victories. One in Italy being I believe the tenth at least this campaign, in which Beaulieu has been again totally routed before Mantua with the loss of all his baggage, cannon, stores, &c., and his whole État-Major prisoners. That I think will settle the affair in Italy. The other is on the Rhine, being the second. (The first was gained two or three days before,[1] but I forgot to insert it.) I have not seen the details, but I learn it is a complete victory. The Emperor is like to make a worthy campaign of it. To be sure the military exertions of the French are beyond all belief. Only think of the Government maintaining fourteen armies, near a million of men, absolutely without money or credit! It is inconceivable! It is true Buonaparte has raised a little cash in Italy, for he has given notice to Citizen Carnot to draw on him for seven millions at sight, payable at the Bank of Genoa. I wonder how John Bull would like to discount his bill?[2] I remember two Patriots[3] in the worst of times who sometimes used to draw bills and to walk in fear of the attorney for the plaintiff. '*I've seen a bill of his signed Tomkins, creditor*'[4] which '*seared mine eyeballs*.'[5] Those were fine times! '*Fine times, Mr Rigmarol!*'[6] I have more than once thought '*our sepulchres would be the maws of kites*'.[7] However, after all, here I am at Paris in a most critical period, and in a state of anxiety which baffles all description, writing nonsensical memorandums. I wonder where is P.P. this day.[8] If the French are in Ireland, I can give a guess where he is. Confusion! *Tête! ventre! sang! milles bombes!* Are the *sansculottes* in Ireland, and I here? Hell! hell, hell![9] O Citizen Carnot, can it be that you have broke faith with me? '*White cat, white cat, thou has deceived me! and instantly he felt the scratch of a cat's paw on his hand*.'[10] Well, if the worst comes to the worst, my friends in Ireland will not forget me.

## 12 June 1796

Drank punch last night with Madgett. He is come off his confidence a little as to the landing. '*Goodman Verges speaks a little of the matter; an old man and his wits are not so blunt as heaven help I could desire they were*.'[11] He does bore me sometimes most confoundedly. Moreover I think I see by his discourse that he has his

[1] On 12 June the *Moniteur* published a despatch from Bonaparte dated 1 June 1796 reporting the battles of Borgetto (29 May) and Peshiera (Castelnova). On 11 June it had published a despatch from Kléber, commanding the left wing of the army of the Sambre-et-Meuse, dated 4 June reporting the French victory on the Sieg on 1 June.

[2] In *Life* what follows up to and including 'maws of kites' is omitted.

[3] Probably Tone himself and Thomas Russell. Cf. 'two wise patriots, Mr Hutton and P.P.' (*Journals and memoirs of Thomas Russell, 1791–5*, ed. C. J. Woods (Dublin, 1991), pp 73–4).

[4] R. B. Sheridan, *The critic* (1779), III, i.

[5] *Macbeth*, IV, i.

[6] Oliver Goldsmith, *Essays* (1765).

[7] *Recte* 'Our monuments shall be the maws of kites' (*Macbeth*, III, iv).

[8] Erroneously 'way' in MS.

[9] Preceding three words omitted from *Life*.

[10] Source of quotation not identified.

[11] *Much ado about nothing*, III, v.

eye on the ambassadorship of Ireland that is to be. He has not talents for that station and besides age is beginning to make inroads on his faculties; yet Madgett is a good fellow and has undoubtedly strong claims on the gratitude of his country if she succeeds; but he is not to be her ambassador to the French Republic. His misfortune is that he thinks it is he does everything and moves everything, and knows everything, and I can see that he knows no more of what is going forward than my boot. It is laughable enough to see him sometimes hiding his ignorance and want of importance under a veil of great mystery and reserve, in which I always indulge him by telling him, like a dog as I am, that I do not wish to press on his official delicacy, &c., &c., '*which makes me for to laugh and sneer*'[1] when I leave him. He tells me today that *in consequence of a memorial he gave in some months [ago] containing what passed in the Privy Council of England with his remarks thereon*, Spain will have a fleet at sea and will break with England in fifteen days. '*Would I could see it, quoth blind Hugh*.'[2] I quoted that already,[3] but no matter. *Nous verrons*, as the French say. It would be a great point gained if Spain would declare against the common enemy of the liberties of mankind.

## To General Henri Jacques Guillaume Clarke, 14 June 1796

Archives Nationales, AF IV, carton 1671, f. 75.

This letter is among others addressed to Clarke. Tone, in fact, saw him on 14 June but may have written the letter in anticipation of not being able to secure an interview.

Dear Sir,

I have heard within these three days a report, which I do not believe, that a landing has been effected in Ireland to the number of 15,000 men.[4] I am satisfied it must be premature, and if so, it is highly indiscreet in whoever set afloat. I wish very much to see you for five minutes and I promise not to detain you longer. I shall call on you, for that purpose the 1st Messidor[5] at eleven o'clock, at which time if you be not at leisure, I beg you will have the goodness to leave word when it will be convenient for you to see me.

Yours very sincerely
J. Smith

26th Prairial An 4me.

[1] The first six words between quotation marks are to be found in Goldsmith's *She stoops to conquer* (1773), act III; the word 'sneer' occurs as a noun at a much earlier point in the same act.
[2] Swift, *Polite conversation* (1738), dialogue I.
[3] In his Diary for 3 Apr. 1796 (see above, pp 141–2).
[4] See above, pp 198–9.
[5] i.e. 19 June 1796. See below, pp 205–6.

# Diary, 14–23 June 1796

T.C.D., Tone papers, MS 2049, ff 76v–84r; *Life*, ii, 124–34.

## 14 June 1796

Called on Clarke this morning for want of other idleness. Saw him for two minutes. Mentioned Madgett's report of the landing, adding that I never believed it. He assured me it was utterly unfounded. '*So there is an end of my very good friend the Athenian.*'[1] I observed that it was dreadfully indiscreet in whoever had set it going. He agreed but observed it was impossible to prevent the indiscretion of people sometimes; he also told me he had not yet had time to read my proclamation as cut down.[2] I fixed to call on him the 1st Messidor, viz. in four or five days, and so we parted. Clarke was civil enough. I want to consult him as to what I am to do concerning *trade affairs*.[3] My finances are reduced to a state that is truly deplorable. I am worth today about 13 louis d'or, which will not last me much more than a month, and I must not let myself be run to the last *sous*. '*I sit here at ten pounds a week*.'[4] I might have been perhaps something more economical, but not much, all things considered,[5] for the commerce is terribly against the stranger. I do not blame them for it, seeing how the French are fleeced without remorse in America. Paris is after all much more reasonable than Philadelphia, and I presume I need not say a million of times more pleasant. Yet it is absolutely impossible to lead a more comfortless life than I do here. It is dreary; it is pitiful. All my habitudes are domestic, and here I am isolated in the midst of Paris, in which there is not a single soul interested in my well or ill being. At home or abroad it is all one, and I cannot express how this sinks my spirits. I am as much in a desert, for all purposes of happiness, as if I were in the middle of Caffraria.[6] The opera is my only resource, and that will not do at all times. I always go alone, and I have nobody to communicate the pleasure I sometimes feel, or the observations which strike me. After the friendship of P.P.[7] and the inestimable happiness of my dearest love's society, judge how I feel here, where neither man nor woman cares if I were in the moon. '*Oh sad, oh sad! I declare I pity the poor Draper! after this he goeth and saith*.'[8] The only thing that consoles me (and it is a powerful consolation) is the unparallelled success of the French arms. *I think England must tumble, and if so, we rise!* I see in the *Morning Chronicle* (which I get from time to

[1] *Life*, ii, 124, substitutes 'that business' for 'my very good friend the Athenian'. The source of the quotation has not been identified.

[2] The proclamation that in his Diary for 9 June he states he is 'cutting and slashing' (see above, p. 196).

[3] i.e. money. For this explanation, see T. W. Tone to Matilda Tone, 2 June 1798 (below, vol. III).

[4] *Merry wives of Windsor*, I, iii. This quotation is omitted from *Life*.

[5] The remainder of this sentence and the whole of the sentence that follows are omitted from *Life*.

[6] In southern Africa. [7] Thomas Russell. [8] Source of quotation not identified.

time from Sullivan) that the journey of Lady Bute[1] to Madrid, where her husband[2] is ambassador, is suspended until it is known what turn affairs will take in Spain. I see likewise that there is a camp forming at St Roch and a levy of 60,000 men ordered. *That looks warlike!* It is also certain that Beaulieu is flying before Buonaparte, who gives him no respite; that the French are making a progress nearly as rapid on the Rhine as in Italy; that the Austrian armies are in the greatest disorder and utterly dispirited and sick of the war, a circumstance of the last importance; that the Emperor has sent Count Metternich[3] to London, most probably to announce his determination to make peace instantly, and if so the battle will remain to be fought out between France and England. *Alors nous verrons!* Madgett (but he is no great authority, as appears from divers parts of these entertaining and instructive memorandums), Madgett, I say, always informs me that we are waiting on the Dutch. Carnot tells me nothing; Clarke tells me nothing, and for the Minister,[4] he knows, I am sure, no more than Madgett. Nic Frog[5] is always, to be sure, plaguy slow in his motions, yet he contrived to steal a march on John Bull already. Would to God he were after stealing a second! My very soul is sick with expectation. I cannot think it possible but England must tumble, and I have the greatest faith in the talents of the Government here and in their *acharnement* against the English. It is said today that two deputies from the Emperor are actually arrived *incognito* to treat of a peace. That young gentleman[6] has made prodigious acquisitions on the French territory in virtue of his alliance with John Bull. It is said likewise that Richéry[7] has sailed from Cadiz with his seven sail, and twelve sail of Spanish ships of the line under Solano,[8] but nobody knows where. If they fall in with the British that will bring matters probably to a crisis; but John will thrash them both at sea to the end of time if they do not inveigle Pat out of his hands. I wish to God Carnot was as sensible of this as I am. Well, here I am, and here I must remain, and I am as helpless as if I were alone, swimming for my life in the middle of the Atlantic. 'Tis terrible. However, ''Tis but in vain, &c., &c.'.

## 15 June 1796

Got a parcel of English newspapers from Sullivan. Strolled out into the fields, all alone, and lay down under a hedge to read them. Melancholy as ten thousand

[1] Charlotte Jane Stuart *née* Windsor (1746–1800), marchioness of Bute (G.E.C., *Peerage*).

[2] John Stuart, 4th earl and 1st marquis of Bute (1744–1814), British ambassador to Spain, 1795–6 (ibid.).

[3] Franz Georges Charles de Metternich-Winneburg (1746–1818) (*Biographie nouvelle des contemporains*).

[4] Delacroix. [5] The Frenchman.

[6] The emperor, Francis II, was aged 28, having been born on 12 Feb. 1768.

[7] Joseph de Richéry (1757–99), admiral; captured a British convoy bound for the Levant, 1795; raided the Newfoundland fisheries, 1796; blockaded in Mohifit, he sallied out and joined Bouvet at Brest (Six, *Dict. des généraux & amiraux*).

[8] José Solano y Bote, marqués del Socorro (1726–1806), Spanish admiral (*Enciclopedia universal ilustrada europeo-americana* (70 vols, [Barcelona], 1907?–30).

devils, and no wonder! I see the Americans have ratified the English treaty[1] after all by a majority of 51 to 48. Damn them![2] The Dutch fleet, which gave John Bull the slip, put into Teneriffe in bad condition, March 26th, to look for provisions. They are two 64, a 50, four frigates and two sloops of war. They are bound for the Cape of Good Hope. I wish they were well there and after driving the English out,[3] but I fear it. Quere, are the troops on board French or Dutch? Because on that circumstance the event will probably turn. I see Combe[4] is returned for the City of London and Fox is first, the 7th of June, for Westminster. He is opposed by Adm[ira]l Gardner,[5] who is within a dozen of him. Horne Tooke[6] is the third candidate and is above a thousand behind both of them. Fox and Tooke make admirable speeches from the hustings. From the little I can observe, being nearly uninformed, the new parliament will probably be as hollow with Pitt as the old. I mean the counties, for, as to the boroughs, there is no doubt of them. There are three War members for example returned for the City of London.[7] So best! The more warlike they continue the better. Reading these papers has left me as dull as ditchwater and I did not want that. Hell, Hell, Hell!

## 17 June 1796

Called today, for the first time God knows when, on the Minister.[8] He was busy and could not see me. That is no good sign, neither is it very bad. I do not on the whole much glory in it. The news today is that the King of Naples[9] has made his peace, paying 30,000,000# *en numéraire*,[10] and withdrawing his cavalry from Beaulieu, and five sail of the line from the British admiral in the Mediterranean.[11] That will strengthen the Emperor and John Bull prodigiously. This news however is not yet confirmed, but if it has not yet happened, it soon must, for the petty princes of Italy are, as the French say '*en queue pour faire la paix*'. It is an excellent metaphor taken from a crowd who stand one behind another in order to be served in their turn, as the poor of Paris, for example, at the bakers. There cannot be a more ridiculous image.[12]

[1] See above, pp 1–2. [2] *Life* omits 'Damn them!'.

[3] A British fleet had taken possession of the Dutch colony in 1795 by authorisation of the stadtholder who had taken refuge in England after having been driven out of Holland by the Patriots.

[4] Harvey Christian Combe (1752–1818), brewer; M.P. for London, 1796–1817; Foxite whig (R. G. Thorne (ed.), *The history of parliament: the house of commons, 1790–1820* (5 vols, London, 1986), iii, 488–9).

[5] Sir Alan Gardner (1742–1809), created baronet for services in Howe's victory of the 'glorious first of June', 1794; M.P. for Westminster, 1796–1806; created baron in Irish peerage, 1800 (*D.N.B.*).

[6] John Horne Tooke (1736–1812), a radical allied to Fox, was unsuccessful (*D.N.B.*).

[7] They were John William Anderson (1736?–1813), M.P. for London, 1793–1806, William Curtis (1752–1829), M.P. for London, 1790–1818, and William Lushington (1747–1823), M.P. for London, 1795–1802 (R. G. Thorne (ed.), *The history of parliament: the house of commons, 1790–1820* (5 vols, London, 1986), ii, 263–4, iii, 65–7, 545–8, iv, 475–6).

[8] Delacroix. [9] Ferdinand IV (1751–1825), king of Naples from 1759.

[10] i.e. livres in specie.

[11] In fact an armistice between France and Naples was signed on 5 June 1796 and peace was concluded between the two powers on 10 Oct. 1796.

[12] *The Oxford English dictionary* for its first example of the use of the word 'queue' to describe persons

## 19 June 1796

Called on Clarke by appointment. Found his aid du camp[1] copying my proclamation as abridged.[2] Clarke seemed glad to see me, and begged me to make a copy myself, *as he wanted it immediately*. I accordingly sat myself down at his desk, and he went about his lawful occasions. In about half an hour I had finished, and he returned. I told him in three words the position of my affairs; that I had gone on thus far entirely on my own means; and that I calculated I had about as much as would enable me to carry on the war for another month, in which time I should be *à sec*,[3] as the French say; finally I asked his advice on the premises. He answered me friendly enough. He said they must provide for me in the military line, for which I had expressed an inclination, and in the cavalry where the pay was the most considerable; but he added the pay of all ranks was below their necessities. He then asked me had I ever served. I answered not; that I had been a Volunteer in the Belfast Regiment, which I considered as no service; but that I was fond of a military life, and, in case of anything being done for Ireland, it would be the line I should adopt. He then said it might make some difficulty, my not having served, but that he would see about it and let me know the result in three or four days, adding that I might be sure something should be done. He then took me in his carriage to the Minister's, with whom he had business. On the way I told him it was extremely painful to me to apply to the Republic for any pecuniary assistance, but that circumstances compelled me; that I was not a man of much expence, and that a moderate supply would of course satisfy me; and I added that being engaged here on the service of my country, any sum advanced to me was to be considered as advanced on her account and as such to be repaid, with the other expences, at the conclusion of the business. He laughed at this and said we would have no money. I said that was true, at least we should not have much, but we would have means, and I instanced in the quantity of English property which would be forfeited in that event to the State; and I assured him we would have enough to pay our debts of justice, of honor, and of gratitude. As to want of money, which I observed to him he seemed to dwell on a little, France had given, and was at that hour giving, a splendid example of what could be done, even without money, when people are in earnest. The conversation then turned on the expedition. He said it would be absolutely necessary the general *en chef* should speak English. I said it would undoubtedly be convenient, but not absolutely necessary. He then said it would be hard to find an Irishman

ranged in a line quotes Carlyle referring in 1837 to how 'that talent . . . of spontaneously standing in queue distinguishes . . . the French people'.

[1] Jean Louis Cuviller-Fleury (b. 1774), volunteer, 1793; promoted to be sergeant-major and acted as secretary to three generals in succession; appointed aide-de-camp to Clarke, 1796; sub-lieut., 10th chasseurs à cheval; lieut., 1797; received permission to retire in 1798 on the ground that his aged parents required him at home (Archives de la Guerre, dossier).

[2] See Diary esp. for 24 Mar., 12 May 1796, 3, 6, 9, 11 June (above, pp 126, 181, 193, 195, 196, 199). The proclamation is given above (pp 196–8).

[3] Meaning here 'broke'.

qualified for the command. I answered I[1] would prefer a Frenchman, on account of the effect it would have on public opinion, and especially a general whose name had figured in the gazettes. (*This is a circumstance I never omit to suggest when an opportunity offers.*) He then mentioned three or four names, as Kilmaine, Harty,[2] Lynch[3] and O'Keeffe,[4] with his opinion on their situation and talents in very few words. I repeated I would wish to see a French general at the head of the business, and that the officers he mentioned might be employed under him. He seemed at length to be of my opinion. In the course of the discussion, I asked him why he might not command the expedition himself? He answered that if he were to make the offer, the Directory he was sure would not accept it, as they could not spare him from the department where he was placed.

This discourse brought us to the Minister's, where we parted, and I am to return in four[5] days. In the meantime he is to see into my affair and to let me then know the result. And now, what is to be the end of this? When I made the offer or request of being employed in a military capacity I certainly limited it, in my own mind, to the expedition; but here it is generalised. If I were a single man I should not hesitate an instant, as I look upon the situation of an officer in the service of the French republic to be the most honorable in the world; and besides it is my passion, the army.[6] But when I think of my wife, and our three children (and perhaps by this a fourth),[7] depending on my life for their existence, it staggers my resolution, and I know not what to determine. I have written to her to come with my family to France, and am I to leave her and them to chance and to go and perhaps be knocked on the head at the frontiers? If I were an officer, it would be only my duty and I would have no choice; but as it is in the service of my own country, I hope I would avoid no danger which came fairly in my way, and, if I fell, I would leave my family to the public gratitude, which would I have no doubt preserve them from want; but here I have no such prospect. I am extremely embarrassed. I will take these four days to consider. After all, if I were to turn out a captain of French dragoons it would be droll. '*It is a life I have desired; I will thrive.*'[8] Assuredly, if I were single, I would embrace the offer, upon the instant, but my fears for my wife and my poor little babies perplex me in the extreme. This offer makes no part of my original system, nor does it come in the strict line of my duty. I declare I know no more what to determine than a horse. Certainly

> To give a young gentleman right education,
> The army's the only good school in the Nation.[9]

[1] *Life*, ii, 128, substitutes 'we' for 'I'.

[2] Olivier Harty (1746–1823), born at Knocklong, Co. Limerick; officer in the Irish brigade before the revolution; general, 1793; baron, 1812 (Six, *Dict. des généraux & amiraux*).

[3] Isidore Lynch (1755–1838) was an officer in Clare's regiment before the revolution; served in the American and revolutionary wars (ibid.).

[4] Patrick O'Keeffe (1740–1809), born at Castlekelly, Co. Kilkenny; served in Dillon's regiment; lieut, 1777, capt., 1787, lieut-col., 1792, general of brigade, 1795 (ibid.).

[5] *Life*, ii, 128, substitutes 'a few' for 'four'.

[6] *Life* omits 'the army'.

[7] Just before leaving America in Dec. 1795 Tone received a letter from his wife informing him that she was pregnant (see Autobiography, below, p. 340).

[8] *Merry wives of Windsor*, I, iii.

[9] Swift, *The grand question debated* (1729), lines 162–3.

But then Matty[1] and the Daffs![2] Well, I am '*lost in sensations of troubled emotion*'.[3] Besides I must do something and that speedily, because '*money, money, money is your friend*'. What would I give that my family were here today? Well, let the world wag. I have four days yet to reflect. I fancy I will state my difficulties to Clarke, and hear what he says. *Allons!*[4]

## 20 June 1796

Today is my birthday. I am thirty-three years old. At that age Alexander had conquered the world; at that age Wolfe[5] had completed his reputation and expired in the arms of victory. Well, it is not my fault if I am not as great a man as Alexander or Wolfe. I have as good dispositions for glory as either of them, but I labour under two (at least) small obstacles, want of talents and want of opportunities, '*neither of which I confess I can help*'. *Allons! Nous verrons!* If I succeed here, I may make some noise in the world yet, and, what is better, the cause to which I am devoted is so just that I have not one circumstance to reproach myself. I will endeavor to keep myself as pure as I can as to the means; the end is sacred. The liberty and independance of my country first; the establishment of my wife and our darling babies next; and last, I hope, a well earned reputation. I am sure I am doing my very best here, as indeed I have endeavored to do all along.

> I am not idle, but the ebbs and flows
> Of Fortune's tide cannot be calculated.[6]

I will push everything here as far as I can make it go. I have taken it in my head today that our expedition will not take place (*if at all*) until the winter because of the Channel fleet. Howe[7] is to have the command with 28 sail of the line and they are moving heaven and earth to man them. I should not be surprised if our business were the cause of these great exertions. I cannot doubt but Pitt is informed of everything which passes here and of course of my arrival, obscure as I am.[8] Perhaps it may be fear of Spain, with whom it seems likely the Republic is about to form a treaty of alliance? At all events, if the Channel fleet be once at sea there is an end of our expedition for the summer, as I told the Minister long since.[9] Well, there is no remedy but patience. John[10] will thrash them all at sea to

[1] Matilda, his wife. [2] Their nickname for their children. In *Life*, ii, 129, 'darlings' is substituted.

[3] The sources of this and the following quotation have not been identified.

[4] In *Life*, ii, 129, the word 'Courage!' is added.

[5] James Wolfe (1727–59), conqueror of Quebec (*D.N.B.*).

[6] John Home, *Douglas* (1757), act III.

[7] Richard Howe (1726–99) had commanded the British fleet on the 'Glorious first of June' (1794) and was nominally in command of the Channel fleet, 1795–7 (*D.N.B.*).

[8] But a month or two later the under-secretary for Ireland reported that a letter had been received in Dublin 'from Mr Napper Tandy in America. The substance reported to me by a gentleman whom I can rely on is . . . Tone keeps quite retired; study is his object and he is preparing a work for the press.' (Edward Cooke to ——, [late July 1796], P.R.O., HO 100/62).

[9] Cf. Diary for 29 Feb. and 21 Mar. 1796 (above, pp 97, 118). [10] i.e. John Bull.

the end of time while he is able to press poor Pat into the service, and this is what I labour (God knows with what success) to impress on them here. If we were independant[1] once, all parties, friends and enemies, would soon feel the difference.

## 21 June 1796

I walk, every day almost, to the Thuilleries to see the Guards[2] relieved. There are about 400 infantry and from 50 to 80 dragoons The grenadiers attached to the national representation are, I am satisfied, for appearance and, I have no doubt, for courage the first corps in Europe. I am more and more pleased with the French soldiery notwithstanding the slovenliness (to speak out) of their manoeuvres and their dress. Everyone wears what he pleases; it is enough if his coat be blue and his hat cocked, and even that I have seen dispensed with. The essential part is that they all seem in high health and spirits, young, active and fit for immediate service. Their arms they keep in *tolerable* order, but there is nothing of the brilliant polish of arms and accoutrements that I have seen in England. Their bayonets are too short, which is a fault, and their musquets seem[3] much lighter that ours. Their grenadiers are noble fellows and luckily Jourdan has 22,000 of them in one corps on the Rhine. They are fond of ornamenting themselves, particularly with flowers. One scarce sees a sentinel without a little bouquet in his hat or his breast, and most frequently in the barrel of his firelock. I like that, and I do not know why, but it pleases me. I believe I have a small prejudice in favour of the French, especially the army, which is the flower of the nation. Their dragoons are fine fellows, but ill mounted, which is a pity. Both themselves and their horses are slovenly like the infantry, but that does not prevent [them] fighting like tygers, for the truth of which I appeal to the slaves of the Despots, whom they are driving before them (thank God) in all quarters. It is said today that the Emperor sent commissaries, as it were, to negotiate with the Directory in order to amuse them and to gain time, but the Directory smoked the foul[4] contrivance and refused all suspension of arms. They were quite right. Beat him well and he will negotiate in good earnest. '*Si vis pacem, para bellum.*'[5] John has been defeated in his first attempt this campaign in the West Indies.[6] He sent 4,000 men to take Leogane but it seems they came back without their errand. Much good may it do his poor heart, because I have a regard for him.

[1] In *Life*, ii, 130, the words 'in Ireland' are inserted here.

[2] See above, p. 55, n. 1.

[3] *Life*, ii, 131, substitutes 'are' for 'seem'.

[4] *Life* omits 'foul'.

[5] 'If you wish for peace prepare for war.'

[6] In March 1796 a British attack on Leogane in Santo Domingo was repulsed (J. W. Fortescue, *A history of the British army* (13 vols, London, 1899–1930), iv, pt 1, p. 471).

## 22 June 1796

Bad news today! Jourdan has received a check,[1] and I fancy a pretty serious one, which has compelled him to repass the Rhine, and Kléber[2] to fall back on the Sieg. He says it is but an affair of posts, but an affair of posts would not lead to such consequences. We have lost men, cannon, ground and character, which is worse than all. I fear this will force Moreau,[3] whose advanced guard is under the walls of Manheim, to retreat also. Bad, bad! Well, ''*Tis but in vain &c.*'[4] One thing however; it will encourage John Bull in his warlike propensities, and the King will meet his new parliament with the successes of the Emperor in his mouth; so, out of evil comes good! Madgett shewed me today a private letter which he just received indirectly from London informing him that a rupture with Spain was looked upon there as inevitable and that the Admiralty were actually issuing letters of marque against the Spaniards. I hope in God it is true! Clarke has likewise applied to him for the names of such persons as he would wish to [have] employed on our business, and Madgett concludes, from circumstances, that there will be two embarkations, one from Holland and one from Britanny. I do not however build much on Madgett's inferences, which he takes up often upon very slight grounds.

## 23 June 1796

Called on Clarke this morning and found him in high good humor. He tells me that he has mentioned my business to Carnot and that within a month I may expect an appointment to a situation in the French army.[5] That is glorious! He asked me would I chuse to serve in the cavalry or infantry? I said it was equal to me and I referred it to him to fix me in the most eligible station. I fancy it will be in the cavalry, '*for a captain of horse never takes off his hat*'.[6] He then told me that he was at liberty to acquaint me so far as that the business, and even the time, were determined on by the Directory, and the manner only remained under discussion. There is good news at last! I observed to him, after expressing the

[1] The archduke Charles had concentrated on Jourdan's army and compelled him to fall back, Kléber's force, which formed the left wing, being badly mauled.

[2] Jean Baptiste Kléber (1753–1800), architect; officer in the Bavarian army, 1777–85; joined national guard in 1789 and by 1793 was general of division; in command of the advance guard of 'l'armée d'Angleterre', Jan.–Apr. 1798; served with Bonaparte in Egypt (Six, *Dict. des généraux & amiraux*).

[3] Jean Victor Moreau (1763–1813), general of division, 1794; conspired against the First Consul and emigrated to the United States, finally serving with the Russians in 1813 (ibid.).

[4] *Life*, ii, 131, inserts '*for soldiers to complain*'. For the source of this quotation, see above, p. 43, n. 6.

[5] The Directory informed Hoche in a letter dated 5 Messidor An IV (23 June 1796): 'La place de chef de brigade restera à la disposition du Directoire, qui la destine à un Irlandais député par les Defenders d'Irlande et qui vous sera envoyé aussitôt que vous le jugerez convenable. C'est l'auteur du manifeste qui vous a été adressé pour l'Irlande. Il a beaucoup de moyens et peut rendre de grands services. Il connaît le pays, le génie des habitants et le caractère des principaux personages de l'Irlande. Il peut contribuer très fortement à assurer le succès de l'expédition dont la conduite vous est confiée.' (Debidour, *Recueil des actes du Directoire Exécutif*, ii, 697–9).

[6] Swift, *The grand question debated* (1729).

satisfaction I sincerely felt at this information, that I wished to remind him of the great advantages to be derived from the landing being effectuated in the North, particularly from the circumstance of framing our first army of the different religious persuasions, which I pressed upon him, I believe with success. I then asked him had he many Irish prisoners remaining unexchanged, as I thought they might be usefully employed in case of the landing being effected. He laughed at this and said, 'I see you want to form your regiment'. I said I should like very well to command two or three hundred of them, who might be formed into a corps of hussars to serve with the advanced guard of the army not only as soldiers (which I knew they would and with sufficient courage) but as *éclaireurs*[1] to insense the country people. He seemed to relish this a good deal, and I went on to say that in that case they should be as an *Irish corps*, in green jackets, with green feathers, and a green standard with the Harp, surmounted with the Cap of Liberty. He bit at this, and made me draw a sketch of the devise, and also a description which he took down himself in French, from which I infer the standard will be made directly.[2] All the world, viz. Matty and Mary and P.P.,[3] will laugh heartily at this council of war, because it savours of the *État militaire*, and P.P. in his wisdom will remind me of my famous button for the National Volunteers, which did such mischief in Ireland;[4] but I will jump suddenly upon him and deprive him of the use of his weapon,[5] by reminding him that I swore solemnly then never to quit until I saw that button upon every soldier's coat in Ireland, in which declaration, '*clenching a fist something less than the knuckle of an ox, Mr Adams declared he would support me*'.[6] After that I think he will be reduced to a state of silent mortification which will be truly deplorable. To return to Clarke. He desired to see me regularly every fifth morning and, assuring me again that he would charge himself with my business, we parted. I fancy in the upshot I shall be sent to Lisle[7] to recruit; and in that event I will make '*reeling Bacchus call on Love for aid*',[8] or in the language of the vulgar I will attack Pat with '*Women and wine which defy every care*'[9] and because I know he has an ear for music, I will also bring a fiddle with me. I understand that John Doyle's *Irish Heroes* (the 87th)[10] are there to a man, and as many of them are from Prosperous in my own county,[11] and many more from Glasmanogue,[12] and not a few from Mutton Lane and Crooked

[1] i.e. scouts.

[2] For the uniform of a proposed Irish regiment in the French service, see F. W. Van Brock 'A proposed Irish regiment and standard, 1796' in *Irish Sword*, xi (1973–4), pp 226–33.

[3] i.e. his wife, sister and friend Russell.

[4] See above, vol. I, p. 321, n. 2.

[5] These words appear to be a quotation (cf. above, p. 191).

[6] Henry Fielding, *Joseph Andrews* (1742), ch. 7.

[7] Lille, in northern France.

[8] Sheridan, *The rivals* (1775), epilogue.

[9] Source not identified.

[10] The 87th regiment in the British army was raised in 1793 by John Doyle (1750?–1834). In 1795, when forming part of the garrison of Bergen-op-Zoom, it was captured. Early in 1796 the prisoners-of-war belonging to the regiment were released. (*D.N.B.*; M. F. Cunliffe, *The Royal Irish Fusiliers, 1793–1950* (London, 1952), pp 8–9).

[11] County Kildare.

[12] Now called Constitution Hill, a street in north Dublin (C. T. McCready, *Dublin street names dated and explained* (Dublin, 1892)).

Staff,[1] I think I shall be able to make something of them. I will make I hope as good a colonel as John Doyle, tho' he is a brave man and a tolerable officer. While I was with Clarke, Madgett called on him and I stepped into the next room while he gave him audience. It is to recommend Ahern to be employed as a military man in this business. Clarke seemed, I thought, disinclined; he asked me did I know Ahern? I answered I knew him merely officially, by the Minister's orders, but that I knew nothing whatsoever to his prejudice, and that as to Madgett I had a very good opinion of him and of course supposed he would not recommend an improper person, but I could say nothing from myself, for or against him, further than what I had then mentioned. I do not wish to hurt Ahern, but I had rather he were not employed in Ireland at first, for he is outré and extravagant in his notions; he wants a total *bouleversement* of all property, and he has not talents to see the absurdity and the mischief, not to say the impossibility, of this system, if system it can be called. I have a mind to stop his promotion, and I believe I will do it. It would be terrible doctrine to commence with in Ireland. I wish all possible justice to be done to Ahern, but I do not wish to see him in a station where he might do infinite mischief. I must think of this. I told Clarke I had written [for][2] my family and was determined, at all events, to settle in France.

## Diary, 24–9 June 1796

T.C.D., Tone papers, MS 2049, ff 85ʳ–93ʳ; *Life*, ii, 134–42.

No. 8
From June 24 to July 17th[3]
*Nil desperandum!*
Paris
1796

Epicharis, *Tragédie*

Dans cette entreprise, où j'ose m'engager,
J'envisage la gloire, et non pas le danger.[4]

[1] Mutton Lane and Crooked Staff (now Ardee St.), streets in the Coombe district of Dublin (ibid.).

[2] Corner of MS missing. *Life*, ii, 134, has 'for'.

[3] The Diary entries for 1–3, 4–5, 6–11, 12–14 and 15–17 July are given as separate documents (below, pp 220–22, 222–5, 226–32, 232–7, 237–9).

[4] In *Life* this verse and the preceding headings, obviously added later than 24 June, are omitted.

## 24 June 1796

'*I've now not fifty ducats in the world*';[1] but hang it, that does not signify. Am I not going to be an officer in the French service? I believe I might have been a little more economical, but I am sure not much.[2] The commerce here (as I know it is in America and, I presume, everywhere) is terribly against the stranger. I brought with me an hundred louis to France, and they will have lasted me just six months, by the time they are run out,[3] '*be the same more or less*'. After all that is no great extravagance. Besides that '*a fool and his money is soon parted*',[4] and poor Pat was never much noted for his discretion on that point, and I am in some things as arrant an Irishman as ever stood on the Pont Neuf. I think I have made as good a defence as the nature of the case will admit. And I leave it to all the world whether I am not fairly excusable for any little *dédommagement* that I can lay hold on, seeing the sacrifices I have made therefore, the services which I hope I shall at last have rendered my country, and especially the dreary and tristful solitude to which I have devoted myself in Paris, where I have not formed a single connexion but with the persons indispensably necessary to the success of my business[5] and where my only relaxation is the *spectacles*, &c., &c.

## 25 June 1796

There has been a damned lie in circulation these two days that the advanced guard of Buonaparte's army in Italy has been cut in pieces to the number of 15,000 men; and there are scoundrels in Paris base enough to seem not sorry for it! However today it is contradicted formally by a letter of Buonaparte's just published, which bears date *thirteen days* after the date mentioned and which makes no allusion to any check whatsoever.[6] My heart was sunk down to my heels at the bad news, and I was as melancholy as a cat, for I have everything dear to me embarked on the fortune of the republic, and I would as lief they would put rat's bane in my mouth as come croking to me with their evil tidings. I am now '*a little better, but very faint still*'.[7] I wish I was after getting my brevet, &c. Madget tells me today that he has orders from Clarke to find him twenty-five recruits[8] in fifteen days, to be sent after the first fifteen to Hoche; and, in our last conversation, Clarke told me they were *not* for Ireland. Where the Devil are they for then?

1 Arthur Murphy, *The apprentice* (1756), II, iii.
2 *Life* omits the following sentence.
3 The following quotation seems to have no function in the sentence and is omitted from *Life*. Its source has not been identified.
4 Arthur Murphy, *The citizen* (1763), I, ii, II, i.
5 In *Life*, ii, 134, 'my business' is rendered as 'our business' and the remainder of the sentence is omitted.
6 Bonaparte's latest published dispatches, those of 3 and 15 June (*Moniteur*, 14, 17, 26 June 1796), do not mention a setback.
7 John O'Keeffe, *Wild oats* (1792), act V.
8 Irish prisoners-of-war to be recruited for the French service.

## 26 June 1796

I go regularly every day at twelve o'clock to the Thuilleries to see the guard relieved. It is one of my greatest relaxations. I take pride in the French troops tho' they are neither powdered nor varnished like those of the other states of Europe. I frequently find the tears gush into my eyes while I am looking at them. It is impossible to conceive a body of finer fellows than the guards of the Legislative body,[1] who are by the bye perfectly well dressed and appointed in all respects. They are all handsome young men, six feet high and well proportioned. They have (as I believe I remarked already) the air of officers in soldiers' coats and look as if they were *set up* by the dancing master rather than the drill serjeant. As to the courage of the French soldiery, I believe it is now pretty well understood in Europe. Nevertheless, '*one Englishman is always able to beat five Frenchmen*',[2] which is very consoling to John Bull. I wonder what figure poor Pat will make upon the sod? I fancy he will be not much amiss. Well, let me but once see myself in Ireland, buckled to a long sabre, and with a green coat on my back and a pair of swinging epaulets on my shoulders. '*Alors, nous verrons, Messieurs de la cabale.*' The Whig Club, I see, are taking up the condition of the labouring poor.[3] The scoundrels! They are getting frightened; their guilty conscience is flying in their faces and will not let them sleep.[4] I suppose they will act like the gentry of Meath, who for fear of the Defenders raised their workmen's wages p[er] day from eight pence to a shilling, but took care at the same time to raise the rent of their hovels and the grass of their cows in the same proportion, so that at the end of the year the wretched peasant was not a penny the richer. There is the honesty of the *squirarchy* of Ireland! No, no! It is we that will better the condition of the labouring poor, if ever we get into that country; it is we that will humble the pride of that execrable and contemptible corps, *the country gentlemen of Ireland*. Rascals, whom I know not whether I most hate or despise; the tyrants and the slaves of the people and the Government.[5] Well, I must not put myself in a passion about them. I have not forgot the attack made on my honor by Mr Grattan, nor that intended on my life by Mr Geo[rge] Ponsonby.[6] I fancy I shall stand as high one day as either of these illustrious Whigs. If I do, I hope I shall act as becomes me. I am in a good humour today, I do not know why. Huzza, generally! *Vive la République!*

[1] Footnote by William Tone (*Life*, ii, 135): 'This corps was the nucleus of Napoleon's *Vieille garde*'.

[2] 'The knight, in the triumph of his heart, made several reflections on the greatness of the British nation, as that one Englishman could beat three Frenchmen' (*Spectator*, no. 383 (20 May 1712)).

[3] On 10 June 1796 the Whig Club of Ireland resolved that from the information it had already received it was clear that in some counties 'the price of labour is not adequate to the necessary support of the labouring poor' (*D.E.P.*, 12 June 1796). In the following month it published a long report, suggesting schemes for assisting the poor (*Memoirs of the life and times of . . . Henry Grattan*, ed. Henry Grattan junr (5 vols, London, 1839–46), iv, 245–9).

[4] 'The scoundrels!' and 'is flying in their faces and' omitted from *Life*.

[5] *Life*, ii, 135, has 'the tyrants of the people and slaves of the Government'.

[6] Referring to his position after his relations with William Jackson had been discovered (see above, vol. I, pp 504–23).

Went in the evening to the Theatre, Rue Feydeau,[1] to see the *Festin de Pierre.*[2] Incomparably well performed. I remember P.P. was delighted with Don Juan, who is the archetype, as he observed, of Lovelace.[3] Fleury,[4] who played Don Juan, is an admirable actor. He is the Lewis[5] of the Rue Feydeau, but Lewis is not worthy to be his valet-de-chambre. D'azincourt[6] is the Sganarelle[7] and a most excellent one. I saw this piece once already at the Théâtre de la République, with Baptiste[8] and Dugazon in the same characters. It is hard to say which is best. I believe I prefer Fleury to Baptiste, and Dugazon to D'azincourt. They are all four inimitable actors. The English comedians are beasts beside the French, but this I have said a thousand times already. I have likewise seen the *Barbier de Séville*,[9] with Fleury the Count,[10] D'azincourt Figaro, and Mlle Lange[11] Rosine. It is not possible to conceive better acting. Mlle Lange is a charming woman who has ruined several young fellows; one in particular twice over. D'azincourt is the original Figaro of Beaumarchais.[12] I have also seen at the Théâtre de la République, *Robert, Chef de Brigands*, a translation of the *Robbers* of Schiller.[13] It acts very well, and Baptiste is admirable in Robert. I am writing here, like a *Muscadin*,[14] about the theatres and all that kind of thing. But what can I do? I must write something to amuse me, and I have nothing more serious. When I have, I will not be found to neglect it for the *spectacles*. After all, give me the opera.

## 27 June 1796

A sad rainy day, and I am not well, and the blue devils torment me. Hell, hell!—'*Allah, allah, allah!*' Tomorrow I will go see Clark[e] about my commission.

[1] *Life*, ii, 135, has 'Theatre Feydeau'.

[2] *Le festin de pierre* (1677), an adaptation by Thomas Corneille (1625–1709) of Molière's *Dom Juan* (1665).

[3] Lovelace is the principal male character, a selfish voluptuary, in Samuel Richardson's novel, *Clarissa Harlowe* (1747–8).

[4] Abraham Joseph Bernard Fleury (1750–1822), an outstanding actor. Being suspected of having royalist sympathies, he was imprisoned, 1794–5. (Lyonnet, *Dict. des comédiens*, ii, 58–60).

[5] William Thomas Lewis (1748?–1811). He began his stage career in Dublin and specialised as a comedian. (*D.N.B.*).

[6] Joseph Jean Baptiste Albouy Dazincourt (1747–1809). In 1784 Beaumarchais, on the advice of Préville, selected him for the role of Figaro which established his reputation. Dazincourt was imprisoned, 1793–4. (Lyonnet, *Dict. des comédiens*, i, 444–8).

[7] A comic character in several of Molière's plays.

[8] Nicholas P. Baptiste Anselme Baptiste, aîné (1761–1835) created the principal role in *Robert, chef de brigands* in 1792. It was rumoured that his first brigand then was Gouvion Saint-Cyr, the future marshal of France. (Lyonnet, *Dict. des comédiens*, i, 71).

[9] By Pierre Augustin Caron de Beaumarchais (1732–99) (*Dict. biog. franç.*).

[10] *Life*, ii, 136, has 'with Fleury in Almaviva'.

[11] Mlle Anne Françoise Elisabeth Lange (1772–1816) had been imprisoned for some months in 1793 and 1794 (Lyonnet, *Dict. des comédiens*, ii, 283–4).

[12] The character Figaro appears in three of Beaumarchais's dramas: *Le barbier de Séville* (1775), *Le mariage de Figaro* (1784) and *La mère coupable* (1792).

[13] A French translation of Schiller's *Die Räuber* by La Martelière, entitled *Robert, chef de brigands: drame en cinq actes, en prose*, was published in Paris in 1793.

[14] *Life*, ii, 136, inserts in parentheses: 'N.B. Dandy'. The Muscadins were fashionable young men, dressed extravagantly and hostile to the Jacobins.

Will it not be extraordinary to see me in the service of the Republic? That will console me for the exile I lie under from my native country. It is raining now like ten thousand devils.

## 28 June 1796

Called on Clarke by appointment. I told him I had two things to mention; the first was that, as we had the Pope now in our grasp,[1] I wished him to consider whether we might not artfully seduce him into writing to his legate, Dr Troy, in order to secure at least the neutrality if not the support of the Irish Catholic clergy. He objected that this would be recognising the authority of the Pope, and said he was sure the Directory would make no public application of the sort; besides that it would be making the matter known in Italy. I replied that undoubtedly it was not a matter for an official application, but for private address, and, as to making it known, it need not be applied for until the last stage of the business; nevertheless, I threw it out merely as a hint for his consideration, without pressing it, as I expected no formidable opposition from the priests in Ireland. The other thing I had to mention was that Madgett told me last night there was a person going to London officially as commissary of prisoners,[2] and pressed me very much to write to my friends by that opportunity; that I had only said I would think of it, as I did not consider myself at liberty to take such a step without his (Clarke's) approbation; that I came now to know whether I should write or not, and if I were to write what line I should follow; that, if I were to allude to our business, I must beg of him to give me such information as he might think fit to communicate, without at all wishing to press him on the subject; that, if I were not, I thought it best not to write at all, as I was in general disinclined to writing, even when it was absolutely necessary, [and] much more in the present instance when all I would have to say would be that I was alive and well at Paris. Clarke answered, 'As to that, your friends know it already'. I replied, not that I knew of. He answered, 'Ay, but I know it, but I cannot tell you at present how'. He then went on to tell that he did not know how to explain himself further, 'for', added he, 'if I tell you ever so little you will guess the rest'. So it seems I am a cunning fox without knowing it. He gave me however to understand that he had a communication open with Ireland, and he shewed me a paper, asking me did I know the handwriting?[3] I did not. He then read a good deal of it. It stated very briefly that

[1] Bonaparte's latest published dispatch, dated from his headquarters at Tortonne, reported the submission of the duke of Modena (*Moniteur*, 26 June 1796). Tone was anticipating the submission of the papal states. For his views on the papacy, see Diary entries for 4 July 1796 and 1 Mar. 1798 (below, p. 223 and vol. III).

[2] Probably Joseph Niou who in 1798 was commissary for French prisoners-of-war in Britain (see below, vol. III). On 26 June 1796 the minister of the interior in a report to the Directory referred to the services rendered to French prisoners-of-war by Citizen Brun who had been resident in London from before the revolution (Debidour, *Recueil des actes du Directoire Exécutif*, ii, 721–2).

[3] Apparently a statement on the situation in Ireland by Lord Edward Fitzgerald (see below, p. 251, n. 3) or Arthur O'Connor (see above, p. 25); Fitzgerald had arrived in Hamburg on 14 May 1796, O'Connor on

fourteen of the counties (including the entire North) were completely organised for the purpose of throwing off the English yoke and establishing our independance; that in the remaining eighteen the organisation was rapidly advancing and that it was so arranged that the inferiors obeyed their leaders without examining their orders, or even knowing who they were, as everyone knew only the person immediately above him; that the militia were about 20,000 men, 17,000 of whom might be relied on; that there were about 12,000 regular troops, wretched bad ones, who would soon be settled in case the business were attempted. Clarke was going on, but he stopped here, and said, laughing, 'there is something there which I cannot read to you or you will guess'. I begged him to use his discretion, without ceremony. He then asked me did I know of this organisation? I replied that I could not with truth say positively I *knew it*, but that I had no manner of doubt of it; that it was now twelve months exactly since I left Ireland, in which time I was satisfied much must have been done in that country, and that he would find in my Memorials[1] that such an organisation was then begun, was rapidly spreading and I had no doubt would soon embrace the whole people.

It is curious the coincidences between the paper he read me and those I have given in here; tho' upon second thoughts it is not at all curious, for as truth is uniform it would be more extraordinary if they should vary. I am delighted beyond measure with the progress which has been made in Ireland since my banishment; I see they are advancing rapidly and safely; and, personally, nothing can be more agreeable to me than this coincidence between what I have said and written, and the accounts which I see they receive here. The paper also stated, as I had done, that we wanted arms, ammunition and artillery, &c. In short it was as exact in all particulars as if the same person had written all. This ascertains my credit in France beyond a doubt. Clarke then said, as to my business, he was only waiting for letters from Gen[era]l Hoche in order to settle it finally; that I should have a regiment of cavalry, and it was probable it might be fixed that day; that the arrangement of the forces intended for the expedition was entrusted to Hoche, by which I see we shall go from Britanny [*sic*] instead of Holland. '*All's one for that*',[2] provided we go at all. I returned Clarke my acknowledgements, and he went on to desire me not to mention this to Madgett, of whose discretion he had no opinion (*in which he is very right*) but rather to train him off the scent by appearing to think the business not likely to be attempted, which I promised him I would take care to do. We then had some good-humoured laughing at Madgett, who is, literally, the greatest P.P.[3] I ever saw. In fact the *Cinq*[4] are but five puppets which he dances and Carnot a soft youth who never opens his mouth but to utter the words which he puts into it. He amuses me often by this, as I have already

5 June, and had communicated with the French minister, Charles Reinhard. From Hamburg they travelled to Basle to negotiate with the French minister to Switzerland, François Barthelémy. O'Connor eventually entered France and met General Lazare Hoche at Angers, *c.*15 Aug. 1796. (Marianne Elliott, *Partners in revolution: the United Irishmen and France* (New Haven, 1982), pp 98–103; Elliott, *Tone*, pp 301–2).

[1] Above, pp 61–70, 88–97. [2] *Richard III*, v, iii, and *1 Henry IV*, II, iv.

[3] Thomas Russell. [4] The five members of the Directory (see above, p. 173, n. 1).

remarked in these witty and engaging memorandums.[1] Clarke then said he supposed they would see me again here as ambassador. I replied that, if the business were undertaken, I should be ready to serve my country where and in what manner she thought I could be most useful; that if my services were necessary in France, I should undoubtedly be highly honored by the station, but I rather thought, from the circumstance of my being perhaps the only man so intimately connected with both Catholics and Dissenters from the station I held with the one and the friendship which I might say the others bore me, that I would be detained in Ireland in order to cultivate and ensure that spirit of harmony and union so essential to the success of our affairs. I took this opportunity to mention to Clarke that on my departure I should have a request to propose to the Directory, viz. that if they were satisfied with my conduct here they would be pleased to signify it by a letter addressed to me from the President, or a resolution or such means as they might think proper, in order that I might have on my return a testimonial to shew my countrymen that I had to the best of my power executed their instructions. Clarke said he was sure the Directory would readily accede to my request, which was but reasonable, and in fact I think it is but reasonable.

> Such services rendered, such dangers incurred,
> He, himself, thinks he ought to be better preferred.[2]

I have a fine spot of ground here, clear before me for castle building, but I will not be in too great a hurry to lay the first stone. I have not got my commission yet, and it will be time enough, when I am a colonel, to begin dreaming of being an ambassador. *A colonel of horse in the service of the Republic!* Is it not most curious? Well, after all I begin to believe my adventures are a little extraordinary. Eighteen months ago it was a million to one that I should be hanged as a traitor and now I am like to enter the country in which I was not thought worthy to live at the head of a regiment of horse. It is singular. P.P. used always to be foretelling great things, and I never believed him, yet a part of his prophecy seems likely to be verified. He said I would make a greater figure, and that I had more talents than Plunkett[3] or Burrowes; for the talents, *Negatur*; but for the figure, the Devil puts it in my head sometimes that he was right.

I am very well pleased with myself this morning, as I believe the track of these memorandums will prove. My name may be spoken of yet, and I trust there is nothing, thus far, attached to it of which I need be ashamed. If ever I come to be a great man, let me never forget two things. The honor of my masters of the General Committee[4] who refused to sacrifice me to the requisition of Mr Grattan;[5] and the friendship I may say of the whole town of Belfast in the moment of my departure into exile. They are two instances of steadiness and spirit under

[1] Possibly he has in mind the Diary entries of 23 Feb. and 6, 15 and 22 Mar. (above).

[2] Christopher Anstey, *The new Bath guide; or memoirs of the B[lunde]r[hea]d family in a series of poetical epistles* (1766).

[3] William Conyngham Plunket.

[4] i.e. the Catholic Committee.

[5] See above, vol. I, pp 522–3.

circumstances peculiarly trying which do honor to them, to me, and to our common nature. *I never will forget them!* Affairs look rather well in the North today, and Moreau has passed the Rhine on three points near Strasbourg and I cannot foresee the consequences, for Madgett tells me *he* has organised a revolution in Suabia, and if the poor Emperor Francis loses that after Brabant and the Milanese, what will he have left? To be sure the French are going on miraculously this campaign. It must be Providence itself which guides them for the common liberty of man. Surely, surely our poor country cannot be fated to remain much longer in slavery to England! The Milanese have three commissioners now in Paris to negotiate the establishment of a republic and the subversion of the Austrian tyranny.[1] Well, poor Ireland has a sort of a commissioner too at Paris, on pretty much a like business. Oh, if the British were once chased from Ireland, as the Austrians from Milan! Well, who knows? But their damned fleet torments me, and it is we ourselves, miserable rascals that we are, that are fighting the battles of the enemy and rivotting our own fetters with our own hands! It is terrible! There is a report today that the Piedmontese are in open insurrection, that the King of Sardinia has been forced to fly from Turin and to take shelter under the French flag at Coni, one of his ci-devant fortresses. It is by no means improbable. Thus all the world are emancipating themselves but Ireland, notwithstanding which, as I have always told P.P., we are undoubtedly the bravest nation in Europe. I wish I could see a little more of it, tho'. Well perhaps I may, by and bye. '*I hope to see a battle yet before I die.*'[2] But I am running on with nonsense. Let me return to Gen[era]l Clarke. I mentioned to him that it would be highly necessary that somebody should be sent to Ireland without delay to apprise the people there of what was going forward. He said he was surprised Ahern did not go. I answered it was because he had not the means, the Government not having yet paid up his arrears.[3] Clarke said as to that he knew nothing, but as to the sum necessary for his departure, he could have it at once. I observed it seemed to me highly indiscreet to trust a man so far as the Minister had trusted Ahern, even to giving him his instructions, and afterwards to break with him, in which Clarke concurred. And certainly it is strange conduct in De la Croix, tho' I am not sorry upon the whole that Ahern does not go for Ireland. From an expression of Clarke's I am led to suppose it possible that he may be himself of the expedition. He has relations here in the French service, one of whom at least will go for Ireland, and he observed that he had some doubts how others of them who remained in Ireland would act; 'but I believe', added he, 'when they see Elliot[4] (his cousin) with me, they will most probably join us'. The words 'with me' struck me, but I did not ask him for any explanation; the thing will soon explain itself. He told me

[1] On 7 June 1796 the *Moniteur* reported that the Milanese were considering sending a deputation to Paris with the aim of obtaining a republic under French protection.

[2] Source of quotation not identified. [3] See above, p. 158, headnote.

[4] Andrew Elliott (d. 1796), born in Co. Kilkenny; captain in Dillon's regiment before the revolution; aide-de-camp to Bonaparte in Italy; killed at the battle of Arcole, Nov. 1796 (Richard Hayes, *Biographical dictionary of Irishmen in France* (Dublin, 1949)).

Moreau's plan for crossing the Rhine has been arranged for six months back in the Directory, and the secret kept all the time. That is surprising. As for our business, it is what the French call '*le secret de la Comédie*', but I cannot help that.

## 29 June 1796

Madgett tells me today that he has heard from Duckett (who is I understand a great blackguard), who has heard from a Mons[ieu]r Morin[1] (who is God knows[2] what) that there are to be two expeditions into Ireland, one from Flushing commanded by Gen[era]l MacDonnell,[3] an Irishman, and the other from Brest, commanded by Gen[era]l Hoche. Madgett added that he had endeavoured to put Duckett off the scent by saying that he did not believe one word of the story, but that Duckett continued positive. The fact is it seems likely enough to be the truth, and probably is so, but it is most terribly provoking to have the subject bandied about for table talk by such a fellow as this Duckett, to whom, by the by, Charles De la Croix revealed in confidence all that he knew three months ago, for which he ought to be damned; happily at present he knows nothing, as I believe, so I presume he will keep the secret. I took this opportunity to train off, myself, a little from Madgett, in consequence of the hint which Clarke gave me yesterday, by saying that I was weary and sick of expectation when I saw nothing done, and that my belief was that nothing would be done; that I wished I had my family in France, and that I were settled quietly on some little spot and well quit of the business. He exhorted me not to despair, at which I only shook my head significantly, like Lord Burleigh,[4] and so we parted. I am today on my last five louis, which is a circumstance truly amusing. My regiment, *if I get it*, comes just in the nick of time. But hang money. I hate to think of it, and yet there is no doing without it in this vale of tears. *Effodiuntur opes, irritamenta malorum*,[5] as the learned Lilly saith in his grammar.[6] If that be so, I shall soon be in the high road to virtue, for I am like to be quit of all temptation to vice; but hang it for one, as I have said, archly enough, above. (Sings) '*Oh, money, money, money, is your friend*'.[7] '*Passion of my heart and life; I have a greater mind for to cry*.'[8] (Sings) '*When as as [*sic*] I sat in Pabilon; and a thousand vragrant posies &c.*'[9]

[1] François Antoine Morin (1749–1810) was a member of the Council of Five Hundred (*Dict. parl. franç.*). He may be the Morin referred to.

[2] *Life*, ii, 141, substitutes 'I know not' for 'God knows'.

[3] Étienne Jacques Joseph Alexandre Macdonald (1765–1840), son of a Scottish Jacobite. He was an army officer before the revolution and served in the Irish brigade. He was appointed general of brigade, 1793, general of division, 1794, marshal and duke of the empire, 1809. (Six, *Dict. des généraux & amiraux*).

[4] In Sheridan's *The critic* (1779).

[5] 'Riches are dug out, those spurs to crime' (Ovid, *Metamorphoses*, i, 140).

[6] William Lilly or Lily (1468–1532) (*D.N.B.*). Tone is probably referring to his *A short introduction of grammar*, of which there were a number of eighteenth-century editions.

[7] Source of quotation not identified.

[8] Probably a confused recollection of the words of the Welsh parson in Shakespeare's *Merry wives of Windsor*, III, i: 'Got's will, and his passion of my heart! I had as lief you would tell me of a mess of porridge.' About forty lines above occurs the sentence 'I have a great dispositions to cry'.

[9] Cf. 'Whenas I sat in Pabylon—; and a thousand vagram posies' (*Merry wives of Windsor*, III, i).

# To General Henri Jacques Guillaume Clarke, 30 June 1796

Archives Nationales, AF IV, carton 1671, f. 78.

Dear Sir,

I have called agreeably to your directions, and am sorry to find you indisposed. I hope however a day or two will re-establish you completely, and I shall in consequence take the liberty to call on you the day after tomorrow.

I am Dear Sir Yours very truly
J. Smith

General Clarke
12 Messidor An 4^me &c.

# Diary, 1–3 July 1796

T.C.D., Tone papers, MS 2049, ff 93^r–94^r; *Life*, ii, 142–3.

## 1 July 1796

(Sings, with great courage) '*Oh, July the first, in Oldbridge town, there was a grievous battle*'.[1] We made no great figure that day; that is the God's truth of it. Well, no matter—what is past, is past. We must see and do better the next time—besides we pulled up a little the year after at Aughrim[2] and made a most gallant defence at Limerick[3]—but I am writing a history of the Wars in Ireland instead of minding my business. Suffice it to say (God forgive me for lying) that '*We are undoubtedly the bravest nation in Europe*'. There are however some brave men scattered here and there thro' the French army, but let that pass. '*I hope to see a battle yet, before I die.*'[4] Huzza, generally.[5] I am in a middling good humour today. Huzza!

## 2 July 1796

Clarke has been confined to his room and I believe his bed these four days. He is cut down by continual labour in his bureau. This delays my affair a little. I saw

[1] Opening lines of 'The Boyne Water', a ballad commemorating the battle between forces led by William III and James II fought on 1 July 1690 Old Style at the Boyne near Oldbridge, Co. Meath.

[2] On 12 July 1691 Old Style. The Jacobite army had the advantage until its commander, Saint Ruth, was killed, after which it was routed.

[3] Limerick was besieged in 1690 and 1691 by a Williamite force and eventually surrendered on terms favourable to the Jacobite defenders.

[4] Source of this quotation not identified.

[5] In *Life* the remainder of the paragraph is omitted.

his aid du camp[1] today who told me, by his orders, that he hoped to be able to see me the day after tomorrow; that he wished to consult me on an affair of great importance, on which he must also see another person besides; and that when we met we would arrange certain matters, &c., &c. This is a flourish to amuse the aid du camp, or perhaps he has translated Clark into his own language; '*else why do we wrap the gentleman in our rawer breath*'.[2] My friend Osric[3] however is a fine lad and I have no doubt would fight like a tyger. Apropos! I desire my readers (viz. P.P.,[4] Miss Mary[5] and my dearest love) to take notice that I recant every word I have said heretofore in these memorandums to the prejudice of General Clarke. '*No! I lie, I lie! He is a tall, handsome, proper young man, with a face like a cherubim.*'[6] I would blot out all the passages which reflect upon him, but upon second thoughts I will keep them as a memento to prevent my forming hasty judgements of people. In fact it was Ahern and Sullivan and even Madgett (but particularly the two first) that turned me against him, for I am myself '*magnanimous, artless, and credulous*', as P.P. used to say, whereas they have been used, I will not say to intrigue, but at least to look at people intriguing here, of a long time, which is some excuse for them. However I have now made him the only recompense in my power by retracting on the same ground where I gave the offence, for my remarks to his disadvantage have not travelled beyond my memorandum book. I think that is handsome.

## 3 July 1796

I see today in '*The Thun*'[7] (will P.P. remember that hit, which is a choice one, and I learned it from himself?)[8] that the Channel fleet is preparing at Spithead to the number of 21 sail of the line (damn and sink them!) with God knows how many admirals;[9] that the camps are not yet formed in Ireland, but that vast quantities of arms and ammunition are daily imported into that country from London and Liverpool, as also tents and camp equipage. I am very glad of that, because I hope it will appear in the event that it is for us that the worthy John Bull is putting himself to all this expense and trouble. I see likewise that the British have taken three of our best frigates,[10] being the entire of a flying squadron sent to cruise in the chops of the channel. That is damned ball! But then again the French are defending themselves in St Lucie like devils incarnate.[11] That is good. There is

[1] Jean Louis Cuviller-Fleury (see above, p. 205, n. 1). [2] *Hamlet*, v, ii.

[3] A courtier in *Hamlet*. William Tone substitutes 'Fleury' for 'Osric' (*Life*, ii, 142).

[4] Thomas Russell. [5] Mary Tone. [6] Source of quotation not identified.

[7] Not identified.

[8] The preceding nineteen words are omitted from *Life*. '*The Thun*' has not been identified.

[9] The *Gazetteer*, 23 June 1796, lists British ships at Spithead. There were 21 ships of the line, commanded by four admirals.

[10] *La Tamise*, *La Tribune* and *La Prosperine* (*London Gazette*, 18 June 1796).

[11] At the end of April 1796 a British force under Abercromby landed on St Lucia and after a month's hard fighting captured the island (J. W. Fortescue, *A history of the British army* (14 vols, London, 1899–1930), iv, pt 1, pp 487–92).

also news today of another victory on the Rhine by Moreau,[1] '*but this gentleman will tell you the perpendiculars*',[2] which are not yet published. I hope it is true. *Vive la rép[ublique]!*

## To Henri Jacques Guillaume Clarke, 4 July 1796

Archives Nationales, AF IV, carton 1671, f. 67.
For the dating of this letter, see Diary for 4 July 1796 (below).

Dear Sir,

I am happy to find that your health is nearly re-established I beg to call to your recollection that the time I mentioned to you is nearly elapsed and I hope you will take the necessary steps to prevent my falling into any difficulties. In two or three days I trust I shall have the pleasure to see you in person and am, Dear Sir

Yours very sincerely,
J. Smith

General Clarke

## Diary, 4–5 July 1796

T.C.D., Tone papers, MS 2049, ff 94ᵛ–97ʳ; *Life*, ii, 143–6.

### 4 July 1796

Called today on Clarke. He has not yet left his room, so I did not see him, but I saw Fleury, his aid du camp, who brought me word, as before, that the General expected to see a person in order to arrange my business, and begged I w[ould] call the day after tomorrow. I wrote him a polite and tender note,[3] praying him to lose no time, &c., which I gave Fleury, and so we parted. Confound these delays! I am sick of them. I want to change my domicil. I am lodged in the house of a little *bossue* (anglice, a hunchback) and she wants me to go to bed to her, and I won't, for my virtue forbids it, and so she is out of humour and very troublesome sometimes. To tell the God's truth, I have no great merit in my resistance, for she is as crooked as a *ram's horn* (which is a famous illustration) and as ugly as sin besides. Rot her, the dirty little faggot, she torments me! '*I will not march thro' Coventry with her, that's flat!*'[4] Moreover I see today official news (viz. Buonaparte's

[1] On 3 July 1796. [2] R. B. Sheridan, *The rivals* (1775), v, i. [3] Above.
[4] 'I'll not march through Coventry with them, that's flat' (*1 Henry IV*, iv, ii).

letter) that the King of Naples has concluded an armistice,[1] withdrawing all his troops from Beaulieu's army, which will impugn the latter gentleman considerably, particularly in the article of cavalry; he likewise withdraws his ships from Hotham[2] in the Mediterranean, which will tend somewhat to the edification of John Bull; and finally he sends Prince Pignatelli[3] to Paris to negociate a peace with the Directory. I like that dearly! The French always oblige the enemy to come to Paris to negociate, which, besides the triumph, gives them prodigious advantages. I hope they may make as good and as haughty a peace with him, as they have done with the King of Sardinia. Imprimis, I hope they will take care to secure the fleet. *That* is what they want. I see likewise His Holiness[4] has at last been obliged to submit, and Buonaparte has granted him an armistice, and *he* also sends an ambassador to Paris to negociate. There is a pretty batch of Italian ambassadors just now here. Salicetti[5] mentions in his letter to the Directory that, in the conditions accorded provisionally to the Pope, he did not neglect to avail himself of the terror which the French arms have inspired thro' all Italy.[6] I dare say not, indeed! Who doubts him? I am heartily glad that old priest is at last laid under contribution in his turn. Many a long century he and his predecessors have been fleecing all Europe, but the day of retribution is come at last, and besides I am strongly tempted to hope that this is but the beginning of his sorrows. Well, I must see if we cannot make something out of him touching our affair, as I hinted to Clarke already (June 28th).[7] It is also said with confidence that the French have taken possession quietly of Leghorn.[8] I hope in God that is true for fifty reasons; among others, John Bull, I know, has generally a bale or two of broad cloth and a few cases of hardware stored up there, and the Republic perhaps has occasion for them; and as he has passed sundry wise and humane laws touching French and Dutch property, I want to see how he will like a little confiscation in his turn. I do not see where he will victual and water his Mediterranean fleet now, unless it be in his Kingdom of Corsica,[9] which by all accounts is in a fair way to be speedily reduced to the circumference of Bastia and its environs. Sir Gilbert Elliot,[10] the viceroy, has found that the *air of Corsica* disagreed with him, so he is gone to

[1] Dated 8 Messidor An 4 (*Moniteur*, 5 July 1796).

[2] William Hotham (1736–1813), admiral; commanded the British Mediterranean fleet, 1794–5; relieved by Jervis, Nov. 1795 (*D.N.B.*).

[3] Antonio Pignatelli, principe di Belmonte, Neapolitan minister to France, July–Nov. 1796 (*Repertorum der diplomatischen Vertreter aller Länder* (Graz and Köln, 1965)).

[4] Giannangelo Braschi (1717–99), pope, 1775–99, as Pius VI.

[5] Jean Jacques Bernardin Coland de Salicette (1759–1834), commandant of Lombardy, 1797; baron of the empire, 1811 (Six, *Dict. des généraux & amiraux*).

[6] On 23 June 1796 an armistice was concluded at Bologna between the French republic and the pope. The pope was obliged to pay an indemnity and to close his ports to the enemies of the republic.

[7] See above, p. 215.

[8] The French entered Leghorn at the end of June, but the British merchants resident there with much of their property and the British ships in the harbour escaped under the protection of the *Inconstant* (36) commanded by Thomas Francis Fremantle (1765–1819) (*London Gazette*, 25 July 1796).

[9] Since 1794 Corsica had been a British possession. See above, p. 27, n. 3.

[10] Gilbert Elliot (1751–1814), viceroy of Corsica, 1794–6; created Baron Minto, 1797 (*D.N.B.*).

England *for his health*! It would not, to be sure, be decent for the King's representative to fall into the hands of Republicans and Rebels. What would I give that *another* of his sacred Majesty's representatives found himself suddenly attacked with the same complaint! Well, all in good time; we shall see. I hear nothing of Moreau's victory, mentioned in yesterday's memorandum, so I suppose it is *premature*.

## 5 July 1796

''*Twas a sad rainy night, but the morning is fine*.'[1] I think it rains as much at Paris as in Ireland, and that kills me. I am devoured this day with the spleen, and I have not settled with Clarke yet, and everything torments me. '*Time, time!*' I never felt the *tædium vitæ* in my life till the last two or three months I have spent here, but at present I do suffer dreadfully, that is the truth of it. Only think! There is not at this moment man, woman nor child in Paris that cares one farthing if I were hanged; at least, for my sake. I may say the Executive Directory are my nearest connexions, Charles De la Croix my chosen of ten thousand, and General Clarke the friend of my bosom. Certainly I respect them all and wish them sincerely well on every account; but I would rather spend an hour talking nonsense with P.P.[2] than a week with any one of them, saving, at all times, their order and my business here. I do not speak of the loss of the society of my dearest love and our little family, for that is not to be replaced. Well, if ever I find myself at Paris as ambassador from Ireland, I will make myself amends for all my present privations. '*I will, by the god of war!*',[3] and I will have P.P. here too, and I will give him choice burgundy to drink *ad libitum*, and Matty and Miss Mary and he and I will go the opera together, and we will be as happy as the day is long. '*Visions of glory, spare my aching sight!*'[4] This is choice castle building, but what better can I do just now to amuse myself? Trifling as these memorandums are, they are a great resource to me, for when I am writing them I always fancy I am chatting with P.P. and my dearest love. I wish I had my commission tho'—I long to see myself in regimentals. (Sings) '*Zounds, I'll soon be a brigadier!*'.[5] That is *choice*.

*Evening. 5 o'clock*. It was not for nothing that I have been in the horrors all the forenoon. On the 26th of May last I wrote to my wife, to Rowan and Reynolds, relative to the immediate removal of my family to France;[6] and today I see in an English paper given me by Sullivan that the vessel which carried my letter[s] (an American, the *Argus*, Capt[ai]n Fanning), was carried into Plymouth on the 25th of June last and is detained.[7] *That is pleasant*. This event throws my private affairs

[1] Swift, *The grand question debated* (1729). [2] Thomas Russell.

[3] Probably an inaccurate recollection of 'by the god of war we will' (John O'Keeffe, *Love in a camp* (1785), I, iii).

[4] Thomas Gray, *The bard* (1757), III, i, line 11. [5] John O'Keeffe, *Love in a camp* (1785), I, ii.

[6] See Diary for 26 May (above, p. 190).

[7] It was reported at the end of June 1796 that the *Argus* of New York, commanded by Captain Fanning,

into unspeakable confusion, and I am too angry now to see how to rectify them. I was this very morning counting that my dearest love would have my letters in about a fortnight. Was there ever anything so distressing? These are the fruits of the American treaty![1] The scoundrels, I mean the Americans! They richly deserve it.[2] But it is hard my poor little family should suffer. See how their *Fifteen stripes* is respected by England! I am infinitely embarrassed by this event. One thing consoles me. In all my letters I have hardly mentioned a word of politics or of my business here, and the little I have said is calculated to mislead them, for at the time I wrote appearances were as gloomy as possible. Well, this is the second time in my life I am indebted for a serious evil to Master John Bull. He hunted me out of my own country first, and now he is preventing my bringing my family to France. And does he think I will forget all that? No, that I won't; no more than I will forget his attempt to press me for a sailor on my passage out to America.[3] Well it does not signify cursing or swearing;[4] but, if ever I have an opportunity to revenge myself of the English nation and do not avail myself of it, I hope the next time they catch me they may hang me up at once. I am in too great a fury to write any longer. God knows now when my family will get my letters, or whether they will ever get them.

## To General Henri Jacques Guillaume Clarke, 6 July 1796

Archives Nationales, AF IV, carton 1671, ff 77ʳ–77ᵛ.

This is the 'note' mentioned in the Diary for 6 July (below, p. 226).

Dear General,

As the arrival of the person you mentioned[5] is uncertain, or at least the *time* of his arrival, and as I have not more money remaining than will last me four or five days, I request you will apply on my behalf to Citizen Carnot for such a sum as he may think proper to grant me for my immediate occasions. I presume you will see the necessity of my not being left in my difficulty here, especially as I am here on the business of the republic, that I have not hitherto made the smallest application for assistance, and that I am an utter stranger in Paris. I beg leave to mention that any money advanced to me is to be considered as advanced on account of my business, *and to be repaid accordingly at the conclusion*. I am sure I need not intreat

laden with salt and bound for New York from Havre-de-Grâce, had been detained in the English Channel by a sloop of war and sent into Plymouth (*Morning Chronicle*, 28 June 1796; *Gazetteer*, 28 June 1796; *True Briton*, 28 June 1796).

[1] The Jay treaty (see above, pp 1–2).

[2] *Life*, ii, 146, omits: 'The scoundrels, I mean the Americans! They richly deserve it.'

[3] See T. W. Tone to Thomas Russell, 7 Aug. 1795 (above, p. 1), and Autobiography (below, p. 335).

[4] *Life* omits the remainder of the sentence.

[5] Hoche.

you not to neglect this, as you must see the unpleasant situation in which I shall otherwise find myself. I shall call, agreeable to your directions the day after tomorrow, by which time I hope you will have this affair arranged for me.

I am, Dear General
Yours very sincerely
J. Smith

18 Messidor An 4
Au Général Clarke
(pour lui seul)

## Diary, 6–11 July 1796

T.C.D., Tone papers, MS 2049, ff 97ʳ–102ʳ; *Life*, ii, 146–52.

### 6 July 1796

Saw Clarke this morning. He is almost recovered. He tells me that my business is delayed solely by the absence of *Gen[era]l Hoche, who is coming up with all possible privacy to Paris to confer with the Directory*; that on his arrival everything will be settled; that I must be introduced to him and communicate with him, and most probably return with him to the army, where my presence would be necessary. All this is very good. I shall be glad to be introduced to Hoche. It looks like serious business. Clarke also told me that he wanted to have my commission expedited instantly by the Minister at War, but that Carnot had decided to wait for Hoche. I told him it was equal to me; I also begged to know what time he expected Hoche? He replied, every day. I then took occasion to mention the state of my finances, that in two or three days I should be run out, and that I relied upon him to prevent my falling into difficulties. He asked me could I not carry on the war for some little time longer? I answered I could not, for that I did not know a soul in Paris but the Government. He seemed a little taken aback by this, by which I see that money is not their *forte* at present. Damn it for me! I am sure, I wish there was not a guinea in the world. So here I am, with exactly two louis in my exchequer, negociating with the French Government and planning revolutions. I must say it is truly original. '*Crescit amor nummi, quantum ipsa pecunia crescit.*'[1] That is not true, as to me, for my passion increases as my funds diminish. I reckon I am the poorest ambassador today in Paris; but that gives me no great concern. Huzza! *Vive la République! 'When Christmass comes about again, Oh, then I shall have money.*'[2] To be sure I am writing most egregious nonsense; *mais c'est égal*! I also told Clarke of the miscarriage of my letters, as mentioned in yesterday's memorandum, by way of precaution against certain unknown

[1] 'Love of money grows as wealth increases'.
[2] Henry Carey, *The ballad of Sally in our alley* (1729).

apprehensions which I felt. How lucky it was that I hardly mentioned one word of my business to any one! Well, Lazarus Hoche, I wish you were come with all my soul. Here I am, '*in perplexity and doubtful dilemma*',[1] waiting your arrival. Sad, sad! I am gnawing my very soul with anxiety and expectation. And then I have a vision of poverty in the background, which is truly alarming. '*O cives, cives, querenda pecunia primum.*'[2] I think I will stop for the present with that pathetic appeal to the Citizen Directors. I had like to forget that after leaving Clarke I sat down in an outside room and wrote him a note[3] desiring him to apply to Carnot on my part[4] for such assistance in the premises as he might think fit, adding that any money advanced me was to be considered as advanced on the public account, and that I would call on him the day after tomorrow. In the meantime I will devour my discontents, '*and in this harsh world draw my breath in pain*'.[5] Maybe my friend Lazarus, who is '*not dead but sleepeth*',[6] may make his appearance by that time. It is, to be sure, most excessively ridiculous, *vu les circonstances actuelles*, that I should be run out of money. Clarke told me that Jourdan had recrossed the Rhine at Neuwied and gained another victory. Moreau's victory is confirmed; he is now beyond Offemburgh,[7] and has cut off the communication between Wurmser[8] and the Archduc Charles.[9] *Vive la République!*

## 7 July 1796

In order to divert myself and to get rid of a little of my superfluous cash I went last night to the Opera, where by the bye I go most frequently. I am more and more pleased with that spectacle. Nothing can be more perfect in its kind that the representation of *Œdipe à Colonne*.[10] It is a complete Greek tragedy represented in music; Adrien[11] is Œdipus, Rousseau[12] Polynices, Laïs Theseus, and Madame Chéron Antigone. I have seen it now I believe a dozen times and every time I am more pleased with it, which is a rare thing to be able to say of an opera. I am not sure that the Œdipus of Adrien is not the first piece of acting I ever saw on any theatre *without exception*. He reminds me in many passages of Kemble, but Adrien is superior. Mad[a]me Chéron is a delightful woman; without being handsome she is excessively interesting. *Le Déserteur* was the ballet which I have

1 *Merry wives of Windsor*, IV, v.

2 'O citizens, citizens, money must first be sought!' (Horace, *Epistles*, I, i, 53).

3 Above, pp 225–6.

4 *Life* omits 'on my part'.

5 *Hamlet*, V, ii.

6 Jesus's words 'not dead but sleepeth' refer in fact not to Lazarus but to the daughter of Jairus (St Luke, 8: 41–52; cf. St John, 11).

7 *Recte* Offenburg.

8 Dagobert Sigmund, Graf von Wurmser (1724–97), born in Alsace; served first France, then Austria; commanded Austrian army on Upper Rhine, 1793, 1795–6; appointed commander-in-chief in Italy, May 1796 (*Allgemeine deutsche Biographie*).

9 Karl Ludwig, archduke of Austria (1771–1847), commander-in-chief on the Rhine, 1796–7 (ibid.).

10 *Œdipe à Colone*, with music by Sacchini and words by Guillard, an immensely popular opera (Lajarte, *Bibliothèque musicale du théâtre de l'opéra*, i, 354–6).

11 Martin Joseph Adrien (1766–1822), better as an actor than a singer (Fétis, *Biog. des musiciens*, i, 24–5).

12 J. Rousseau (1761–1800) (ibid., vii, 337).

also seen I know not how often;[1] it is the triumph of Goyon in Montauciel, and of Millot[2] in 'Le grand cousin'. It is a charming delusion, that of the theatre. It '*soothes my soul to mortal anguish*',[3] as P.P.[4] says. If it were not for that, what should I do at Paris? I think I will go now and scold Monroe about the capture of the *Argus*, and the consequent miscarriage of my letters. Sat with Monroe for above an hour. I like him very well. Drank a bottle of wine and prosed[5] with Madgett in the evening at the Champs-Élysées. Stupid enough, God knows.

## 8 July 1796

Called on Clarke. He tells me my commission will be made out in two or three days. I returned him my acknowledgements. As soon as I receive it I must wait on Carnot to thank him, &c. Fixed with Clarke to call on him, regularly every two days (*les jours pairs du décade*).[6] Lazarus is not yet arrived, and be hanged! The moment he comes Clarke is to let me know. I am surprised at the *sang froid* with [which] I view this affair of my regiment; but it is my temper. I am sure if I were made an emperor it would not in the least degree elevate my spirits, tho' I am susceptible enough on some points. Is that in my favor or not? for I'll be hanged if I know. No matter. *Je suis, comme je suis*, and that is enough about myself for the present. Moreau has had what other nations would call another *victory*, but what we content ourselves with calling an *advantage*. The French troops scaled the highest of the Black Mountains and stormed a redoubt on the summit, the General, '*whose name I know not, but whose person I reverence*',[7] being the first man to leap down into the fossé.[8] Remember that, Mons[ieu]r le Colonel! If a man will conmand French troops, he must be rather brave, and besides I shall have '*the Honor of the Sod*' to support. Well, I will do my best. Horne Tooke had good reason to say on the hustings[9] that the French generals not only gave the soldiers the *command* but the *example*. They are noble fellows, that is the truth of it. Pray God we may imitate their glorious example. But I have no doubt but we will. Why not? The Irish are a very brave people, and we have a famous good cause to support us. I see in the papers that Lady Elliot[10] is ordered by her physicians to the baths of Lucca, the air of Corsica disagreeing with her also, as well as with her spouse. These removals bode ill for the King of Corsica.[11] I see also that the poor Emperor

[1] For instance, on 8 Apr. 1796 at the Théâtre des Italiens (see above, pp 147–8).
[2] Neither Goyon nor Millot has been identified.
[3] Cf. 'fills my soul with mortal anguish' (Alexander Dow, *Sethona* (1774), act 1).
[4] Thomas Russell. [5] i.e. chatted.
[6] On even days of the *décade*, the ten-day period in the republican calendar.
[7] Cf. 'Whose profession I honour, but whose person I know not' (Dryden, *The Spanish fryar* (1681)).
[8] The French success at the Black Mountain was described in Moreau's despatch of 3 July 1796, printed in the *Courier Universel*, 8 July 1796. General Laroche was the first to leap into the ditch.
[9] See Diary, 15 June 1796 (above, p. 204). *Life* omits 'on the hustings'.
[10] Anna Maria Elliot (1752–1829), daughter of Sir George Amyand and wife of Sir Gilbert Elliot (G.E.C., *Peerage*, viii, 714).
[11] i.e. George III, king of Great Britain and Ireland, who was offered and accepted the crown of Corsica in 1794. In *Life*, ii, 149, 'kingdom' is substituted for 'king'.

has made an application to the Empress of Russia for assistance, and what assistance, in God's name, do you think she has given him? *A declaration*,[1] addressed to the petty princes of Germany, calling on them, poor devils, to assist the head of the Empire, and telling them that it is *a shame for them* not to support him better and that she is quite surprised at them for her part, &c., &c. After all it is a more decent declaration than Brunswick's[2] but I do not believe it will have a prodigious effect on the Army of the Rhine, or that of the Sambre and Meuse. But to return to our own affairs. I reminded Clarke about the Pope, and told him that the Legate for Ireland was Cardinal Antonelli,[3] and that if we could artfully get a line from him to Dr Troy, it might perhaps save us some trouble. Clarke promised to think of it. He also told me that my proclamation[4] had been translated into French to be laid before the Directory. If they adopt it, it will be a decisive proof of the integrity of their principles as to Ireland, for I have worded everything as strongly in our favour as I knew how, and have made no stipulations for any return as to France, but left everything to the justice, honour and gratitude of the Irish people. I am sure it is, as with regard to France, the wisest course, and therefore I hope they may adopt my proclamation.

## 9 July 1796

By dint of perseverance I am getting thro' the remainder of my cash. When I am near being run out, I am always more extravagant, and, like the Old Batchelor,[5] '*I run into the danger to avoid the apprehension*'. Last night, I was at the Théâtre des Vaudevilles, one of the *petits spectacle[s]*, where I was exceedingly amused by *Hazard, fils de son père*, a parody of *Oscar, fils d'Ossian*. Laporte,[6] who played Hazard, imitated Talma in Oscar incomparably. He beats Jack Bannister[7] for mimickry all to nothing, and that is a bold word. But I am always alone at these spectacles and that kills me. I wish my dearest love were here, and P.P. Today I scaled Montmartre, *all alone*, and had a magnificent view of Paris at my feet; but it is terrible to have nobody to speak to, or to communicate the million of observations which '*rise and shine, evaporate and fall*'[8] in my mind. Money, money, money! I declare for my part I believe it is gone clean under the ground! I have this day six crowns in silver, being '*of dissipated wealth the small*

[1] The emperor having asked the empress of Russia for assistance, Catherine II informed the imperial diet that she trusted that the emperor would have the zealous support of all the German princes (*Moniteur*, 10 July 1796).

[2] Published in July 1792 when he was preparing to march on Paris.

[3] Leonardo Antonelli (1730–1800), cardinal, 1775; prefect of Sacra Congregatio de Propaganda Fide, 1780; he was against a peace with France, 1797; arrested by the French, 1798 (*Dizionario biografico degli Italiani* (29 vols, Rome, 1966–83)).

[4] Above, pp 196–8.

[5] Heartwell, chief character in Congreve's *The old bachelor* (1693).

[6] Jacques François Claude Rozière Laporte (1775–1841) was often, on account of his gracefulness ('*gentillesse*') and playfulness ('*espièglerie*'), compared to a young cat. He imitated well-known actors. (Lyonnet, *Dict. des comédiens*, ii, 289).

[7] John Bannister (1760–1836), comedian (*D.N.B.*).

[8] Samuel Johnson, *The vanity of human wishes* (1749).

*remains*'.[1] Sad, sad! I hope Citizen Carnot may '*bid his treasurer disburse six pounds to pay my debts*'.[2] Otherwise the consequences I fear will be truly alarming. In the evening lounged, *all alone as usual*, to the Champs-Élysées, and drank coffee by myself. It is dismal, this solitude. For society I might just as well be in Arabia Deserta, not Arabia Felix. Well, as Kite says, '*it is all for the good of the service*'.[3] If I have not passed almost six tedious months in France, I wonder at it! I am sure my country is much my debtor, if not for what I have done, at least for what I have suffered on account of her liberty. Well, I do not grudge it to her, and if ever she is able, she will reward me, and I think I will by that time have deserved it at her hands. Tomorrow I will go see Clarke, and hear what he has to say for himself. He assures me (for I asked him a second time for greater certainty) that my friends in Ireland know I am here. I am heartily glad of it. I was dreaming all last night of Plunkett,[4] and Peter Burrowes and Geo[rge] Knox, and I believe it is that which has thrown me into the *blue devils* all this day. I remember Swift makes the remark, with respect to dreams, that their complexion influences our temper the whole day after, and I believe he is right.[5] Perhaps the marvellous state of my finances may a little contribute to plunge me into a state of tender melancholy, for Shenstone says there is a close connexion between the animal spirits and the breeches pocket.[6] Aristotle[7] has many fine things on that subject. Oh Lord, oh Lord, these are but sickly jokes! It won't do! '*Croker is a rhime for joker. Poor Dick!*'[8] I find I have '*a prodigious affection for the louis*'.[9] That is not so bad! I think I will leave off while I am well. I have made '*divers ineffectual efforts to sing*' in this day's journal, all for the amusement of Matty and Miss Mary and P.P.[10] What are they doing this way?[11] Oh that I had them all with me tonight, and everything arranged to my mind! I wish I had my commission tho'. (Sings)

*Says this frog, I will go ride,*
*With sword and pistol by my side*
*Cock ma Kary, Kitty alone, Kitty alone and I.*[12]

That quotation I take to be inimitable![13] I do not recollect anything from P.P. which exceeds it. I know green envy will gnaw his soul at the perusal.

[1] Samuel Johnson, *London: a poem in imitation of the third satire of Juvenal* (1738).
[2] 'Bid *our* treasurer disburse six pounds to pay *their* debts' (Henry Fielding, *Tom Thumb* (1731), III, x).
[3] George Farquhar, *The recruiting officer* (1706), V.
[4] William Conyngham Plunket.
[5] Possibly Tone has in mind *Tale of a tub* (1704), section IX.
[6] The work of William Shenstone in which this statement appears has not been identified.
[7] Aristotle (384–322 B.C.), philosopher.
[8] Goldsmith, *The good-natur'd man* (1768), I.
[9] Samuel Foote, *The Englishman return'd from Paris* (1756), II.
[10] His wife, sister and Thomas Russell.
[11] Obviously an error for 'this day'. *Life*, ii, 151, has 'this evening'.
[12] Expanded in *Life*, ii, 151, as follows:

Oh, says this Frog, I will go ride, Kitty alone, &c.
Oh, says this Frog, I will go ride, Kitty alone and I.
Oh, says this Frog, I will go ride, with sword and pistol by my side.
Cock ma Kary, Kitty alone, Kitty alone and I.

[13] Its source has not been identified.

## 10 July 1796

It is in vain to deny it, my journal of yesterday is as dull as a post. I think I have not seen anything more stupid, and there is a sort of pert affectation of being witty, for which I deserve to be kicked. '*Gentle dullness ever loved a joke!*'[1] Well, let me mind my business. It is raining all this blessed day like ten thousand devils, so I could not go to Clarke till an hour and a half after the proper time, and then he was gone out. I saw Fleury, however, who had nothing to tell me but that the citadel of Milan had surrendered,[2] with 2,800 prisoners and 150 pieces of cannon. Mantua alone remains to the Austrians and it is closely besieged by 60,000 men. We are certainly (viz. the French) in Leghorn, but the official dispatches are not yet arrived, and this is all the news. I left word I would call tomorrow and so took my leave. I am as sick as a dog of these delays.

## 11 July 1796

Called on Clarke, who took down my name and the day and place of my birth, in order to have my commission filled up, which he expects to have done tomorrow; he was very civil, and mentioned that if it rested merely with him, the business should have been done long since. He then asked me did I know one Duckett? I answered I did not, nor did I desire to know him. He asked me, why? I answered I understood from Madgett and others that he was a blackguard. He seemed a little taken aback at this and said, 'Ay, but he is clever'. I answered I knew nothing more about him; that it was disagreeable to me to speak ill of anybody, especially a person whom I knew merely by report, but in a business of such consequence as ours I felt it my duty to speak without the least reserve. Clarke said undoubtedly, and so the matter rested. I am to call the day after tomorrow, at which time I hope my eternal commission will be ready. Bought the *Règlement pour le service de la Cavalerie*[3] and sat down to study it. I must get a sensible *sous officier*[4] to drill me a little before I join the regiment. I am tired now of tactics so I think I will go walk a little to refresh me.

*Evening*. Tactics, tactics! I wish I was as good an officer of cavalry as Maréchal Schweidnitz.[5] I may say (or sing) with my friend Montauciel,

*Maudit l'infernal faiseur de grimoire,*
*Dont l'esprit fatal, mit dan[s] sa mémoire*
*Tout ce bac[c]hanal!*
*Sans cette écriture, et sans la lecture*

[1] Alexander Pope, *The Dunciad variorum* (1729), bk II, line 30.

[2] The citadel of Milan surrendered at the end of June 1796.

[3] Possibly *Règlement provisoire sur le service en campagne des troupes à cheval du 12 août 1783* (Paris, 1793), or *Manuel de la cavalerie concernant l'exercice et les manoeuvres des troupes à cheval au service de la République* (Paris, 1793).

[4] *Life*, ii, 152, adds in parentheses: 'non-commissioned officer'.

[5] Possibly Tone was thinking of Field-Marshal Christopher count de Schiverin (1684–1757) (*Biographie universelle ancienne et moderne*).

*Ne peut-on, morbleu!*
*Manger, rire, et boire, marcher à la gloire,*
*Et courir au feu?*—.[1]

I glory in these lines; they are the veritable sentiments of a French dragoon. Huzza! I shall be a dragoon myself one of these days. (Sings)

*Oh, there was a captain of Irish Dragoons,*
*Was quartered in the town of Kilkenny, oh!*[2]

## From General Henri Jacques Guillaume Clarke, 12 July 1796

Tone (Dickason) papers.

See Diary for 12 July 1796 (below).

Paris, le 24 messidor l'an 4[e]
de la République française, une
et indivisible

H. Clarke, Général de Division, Directeur du Cabinet Historique
et Topographique Militaire du Directoire Exécutif

To C[itize]n Wolfe Tone

The person I expected is here. I would wish to see you today at one o'clock precise.

G. Clarke

You will call for my aid de camp.

## Diary, 12–14 July 1796

T.C.D., Tone papers, MS 2049, ff 102[v]–106[r]; *Life*, ii, 152–7.

### 12 July 1796

Battle of Aughrim![3] As I was sitting in my cabinet, studying my Tactics, a person knocked at the door who on opening it proved to be a dragoon of the

[1] Lines sung by Montauciel, a dragoon, in *Le Déserteur, drame en trois actes* (1769) by Michel Jean Sedaine (1719–97), act III, scene 4.

[2] Source of this verse not identified.

[3] On 12 July 1691 Old Style at Aughrim, Co. Galway, the Jacobite forces were destroyed by those of William III.

3d Regiment. He brought me a note[1] from Clarke informing me that the person he mentioned was arrived and desired to see me at one o'clock. I ran off directly to the Luxembourg and was shewed into Fleury's cabinet, where I remained in waiting till three, when the door opened and a very handsome, well-made young fellow in a brown coat and nankin pantaloons entered and said, 'Vous êtes le citoyen Smith?'. I thought he was a *chef de bureau*. I replied, 'Oui, Citoyen, je m'appelle Smith'. He said, 'Vous vous appellez aussi, je crois, Wolfe Tone'. I replied, 'Oui, Citoyen, c'est mon véritable nom'. 'Eh bien', replied he, 'je suis le Général Hoche'. At these words I mentioned that I had for a long time been desirous of the honor I then enjoyed, to find myself in his company.

*Into his arms I soon did fly,*
*And there I embraced him tenderly.*[2]

He then said he presumed I was the author of the memorials which had been transmitted to him.[3] I said I was. 'Well', said he, 'there are one or two points I want to consult you upon'. He then proceeded to ask me, in case of the landing being effectuated, might he rely on finding provisions and particularly *bread*? I said it would be impossible to make any arrangements in Ireland *previous to the landing*, because of the *surveillance* of the Government; but if that were once accomplished there would be no want of provisions; that Ireland abounded in cattle, and as for bread, that I saw by the gazettes that there was not only no deficiency of corn, but that she was able to supply England in a great degree during the late alarming scarcity in that country; and I assured him that, if the French were once in Ireland, he might rely on it that, whoever might want bread, they should not want it. He seemed satisfied at this, and proceeded to ask me, might we count upon being able to form a *provisory government*, either of the Catholic Committee, mentioned in my memorials, or of the chiefs of the Defenders? I thought I saw an open here, to come at the number of troops intended for us, and replied that *that* would depend on the force which might be landed; if that force were but trifling, I could not pretend to say how they might act, but if it were considerable, I had no doubt of their co-operation. 'Undoubtedly', replied he, 'men will not sacrifice themselves when they do not see a reasonable prospect of support; but if I go, you may be sure I will go in sufficient force'. He then asked did I think *ten thousand men* would decide them? I answered *undoubtedly*; but that early in the business the Minister had spoken to me of *two thousand*, and that I had replied that number could effect nothing.[4] 'No', replied he, 'they would be overwhelmed before anyone could join them'. I replied I was glad to hear him give that opinion, as it was precisely what I had stated to the Minister, and I repeated that with the force he mentioned I could have no doubt of support and co-operation sufficient

[1] The preceding document.
[2] Source of this quotation not identified. [3] Above, pp 61–70, 88–97.
[4] The minister of foreign affairs, Delacroix, in discussing with Tone on 26 Feb. and 11 Mar. the military resources France was prepared to invest in an Irish expedition was reticent about numbers of men (see above, pp 85–6, 104–5).

to form a provisory government. He then asked me what I thought of *the priests*, or was it likely that they would give us any trouble? I replied that I certainly did not calculate on their giving us any assistance, but that neither did I think they would be able to give us any effectual opposition; that their influence over the minds of the common people was exceedingly diminished of late, and I instanced in the case of the Defenders, so often repeated in my memorials and these memorandums. I explained all this at some length to him and concluded by saying that, in prudence, we should avoid as much as possible shocking their prejudices unnecessarily, and that with common discretion we might, I thought, at least secure their neutrality if not their support. I mentioned this merely as my opinion, but I added I was satisfied that, in the contrary event, it would be absolutely impossible for them to take the people out of our hands, even if they were so inclined.[1] We then came to *the army*. He asked me how I thought they would act? I replied, for the regulars I could not pretend to say, but that they were wretched bad troops; for the militia, I hoped and believed that when we were once organised they would not only not oppose us, but would come over to the cause of their country *en masse*. Nevertheless I desired him to calculate on their opposition and make his arrangements accordingly; that it was the safe policy, and if it became unnecessary, it was so much gained. He said he would undoubtedly make his arrangements so as to leave nothing to chance that could be guarded against; *that he would come in force*, that he would bring great quantities of arms, ammunition, stores and artillery, and that for his own reputation he would see that all the arrangements were made on a proper scale. *I was very glad to hear him speak thus; it sets my mind at ease on divers points*. He then said there was one important point yet remaining on which he desired to be satisfied, and that was *what form of government* we would adopt in the event of our success?

I was going to answer him with great earnestness, when Gen[era]l Clarke entered to request we would come to dinner with Citizen Carnot. We accordingly adjourned the conversation to the apartments of the President, where we found Carnot and one or two more. Hoche after some little time took me aside and repeated his question. I replied, 'most undoubtedly a republic'. He asked me again, was I sure? I said as sure as I could be of anything; that I knew nobody in Ireland who thought of any other system, nor did I believe there was anybody who dreamt of monarchy. He asked me was there no danger of the Catholics, for example, setting up one of their chiefs for king? I replied, 'not the smallest', and that there were no chiefs among us of that kind of eminence. This is the old business again, but I believe I satisfied Hoche; it looks well to see him so anxious on this topic on which he pressed me more than on all the others. Carnot joined us here, with a pocket map of Ireland in his hand, and the conversation became pretty general between Clarke, Hoche and him, everyone else having left the room. I

[1] *Life* omits preceding six words.

said nothing scarcely, as I wished to listen. Hoche related to Carnot the substance of what had passed between him and me. When he mentioned his anxiety as to bread, Carnot laughed and said, 'There is plenty of beef in Ireland; if you cannot get bread, you must eat beef'. I told him they would find, I hoped, enough of both, adding that within these last twenty years, Ireland had become a great corn country, so that at present it made a considerable article in her exports. They then proceeded to confer, but I found it difficult to follow them, as it was in fact a *suite* of former conversations, at which I had not assisted,[1] and besides they spoke with the rapidity of Frenchmen. I collected however (if I am right) that there will be *two landings*, one from Holland near Belfast, and the other from Britanny in Connaught; that there will be (I suppose in *both* embarkations) *not less than ten*, nor more than *fifteen thousand men*—twelve thousand was also mentioned; but I did not hear any *time* specified. Carnot said, 'it will be, to be sure, a most brilliant operation!'. And well may he say so, if it succeeds.

We then went into dinner, which was very well served, without being luxurious. We had two courses and a desert. There were present about 16 or 18 persons. M[a]d[am]e Carnot,[2] her sister,[3] and sister-in-law, Carnot, his brother,[4] Hoche, the Minister of the Marine, Truguet,[5] Clarke, two or three officers, and Lagarde, the *secrétaire général*. I sat beside Hoche. After coffee was served, we rose, and Carnot, Hoche, Truguet, Lacuée and Clarke retired into a cabinet and held a council on Irish affairs, which lasted from six till nine o'clock. In the meantime I walked with Lagarde in the garden,[6] where we listened to a symphony performed in the apartments of Lerevillière-Lépaux,[7] who is lodged over Carnot. Lagarde tells me Lerevillière has concerts continually and that music is his great resource after the fatigues of his business, which are immense. I was glad of that, because I love music very much myself.[8] At nine o'clock the council broke up, and I walked away with Clarke. He said everything was now settled and that he had, himself, much trouble to bring everything to bear, but that at last he had succeeded. I wished him joy most sincerely and, having fixed to call on him tomorrow at twelve, we parted. This was a good day. I dined with the President of the Executive Directory of France, beyond all comparison the most illustrious station in Europe. I am very proud of it, because it has come fairly in the line of my duty and I have made no unworthy sacrifices to obtain it. I like Carnot extremely, and Hoche I think yet better.

[1] Tone seems to mean 'at which I had not been present'.

[2] Before her marriage in 1791 Sophie Du Pont de Lierdt (M. R. Reinhard, *Le grand Carnot* (2 vols, Paris, 1950–52), i, 177–82).

[3] Probably Adélaïde. She also had a sister named Gaëtane. (Ibid.).

[4] Carnot had seventeen siblings. The most likely brother is Claude Marie Carnot-Feulins (1755–1836), appointed général de brigade, 4 June 1796; he lost his employment in the army, Sept. 1797, after Lazare Carnot's fall (*Dict. biog. franç.*).

[5] Laurent Jean François Truguet (1752–1839), naval officer before the revolution; minister of the marine, 1795–7; count of the empire, 1814; peer of France, 1819 (Six, *Dict. des généraux & amiraux*).

[6] In *Life*, ii, 155, this is expanded to 'gardens of the Luxembourg'.

[7] *Recte* La Révellière-Lépeaux.

[8] In *Life* this sentence is omitted.

## 13 July 1796

I cannot help this morning thinking of Gil Blas when he was secretary to the Duke of Lerma.[1] Yesterday I dined with Carnot, and today I should be puzzled to raise a guinea. I am almost on my last louis, and my commission is not yet made out, tho' Clarke tells me it is done; but I never will believe him till I have it in my hand. I will push him today, that is positive. *Allons!* Saw Clarke. Nothing new; my commission not yet come. '*Damn it, for me, Lord pardon me for swearing!*'[2] I charged Clarke with great vigour, and he promised me positively for after tomorrow at farthest; so I must wait, and I am tired waiting. Hoche called for a moment on Clarke to say that he had no further questions to propose to me, and so matters rest. I wish however I was after studying a little the *language of the birds*.

## 14 July 1796

Taking of the Bastile 1789. No business. Yesterday[3] Hoche praised Sir Sidney Smith,[4] now prisoner in Paris, as a gallant officer; he said he had '*une rude réputation en Bretagne*', and that there was hardly a cape or headland on the coast which was not marked by some of his exploits. I like to hear one brave man praise another. Carnot said that they would take care of him for some time and that he should certainly *not be exchanged*. I am glad of that for one or two reasons. Hoche also spoke of the ignorance of the Bretons; he says they know no more of the real state of the Revolution than the inhabitants of Tartary, that they always call the government the *Convention*, and they had a report when he set off that the Convention had ordered the Pope to the bar. I think there is no part of Ireland more ignorant, by his account. Carnot said he was satisfied that Babœuf's plot was the work of an Orleans faction. When I walked in the garden with Lagarde, whom I found very conversible [*sic*], we spoke of the astonishing successes of the armies, particularly of the Army of Italy. He assured me that before the opening of the campaign he trembled for the event; that the reluctance of the *jeunesse*[5] to join their colours was almost insurmountable; that the Government was obliged to employ the most rigorous measures, even to tying them neck and heels and transporting them on carts in that manner to the army; 'and yet', said he, 'you see how they fight, after all that'. It is to be sure most astonishing. Hoche yesterday told Clarke, speaking of me, that 'he had got me by heart'. Was that by way of compliment? '*Ha, there may be two meanings in that!*'[6] Either that he had studied my memorials diligently, which is good, or that he had fathomed me in one conversation, which is not quite so flattering. I fear he '*does spy into the bottom of this*

[1] Cf. book VIII of *Gil Blas* by Alain René Le Sage (1668–1747).

[2] Source of quotation not identified.

[3] In MS preceded by redundant 'he'.

[4] Sir (William) Sidney Smith (1764–1840) showed great skill in harassing the French coast until he was captured off Le Havre in April 1796; he made a sensational escape from the Temple in 1798 and distinguished himself at the defence of Acre (*D.N.B.*).

[5] See above, p. 55, n. 2.

[6] Possibly a confused recollection of 'I moralize two meanings in one word' (*Richard III*, III, i).

*Justice Shallow*'.[1] No matter; no matter. Let us see and get the business done. If that is once effected, it is of very little consequence whether I have any talents or not. Huzza! I am in good humour to day.

## To General Henri Jacques Guillaume Clarke, 15 July 1796

Archives Nationales, AF IV, carton 1671, f. 79.

27 Messidor an 4

Dear General,

I am exceedingly mortified at the trouble which I am forced so often to give you, but you know my situation perfectly, and I leave it to you to judge whether it is for the honor of the republic that I should be left in difficulties here under the circumstances of the case. I am sure I need not press you further than to tell you, that my resources are *absolutely exhausted* and that I shall be in arrear for my lodging, &c., in *two* days. I shall take the liberty to call tomorrow at twelve, by which time I hope you will have made such arrangement as you may think fit to extricate me. It is exceedingly painful to me to make this application but I hope it may be *the last*.

Yours very sincerely
J. Smith

## Diary, 15–17 July 1796

T.C.D., Tone papers, MS 2049, ff 106ᵛ–108ʳ; *Life*, ii, 157–9.

### 15 July 1796

Blank! Dull as a post all day. ——

### 16 July 1796

Saw Clarke. He tells me the *arrêté* of the Directoire for my commission will be signed today;[2] and that he will write to the Minister at War[3] to send back the brevet to him, so that I shall have it by tomorrow at twelve o'clock. All that is very good, but still, as I have said already six and fifty times, '*Would I could see it, quoth*

[1] *Recte* 'I do see the bottom of Justice Shallow' (*2 Henry IV*, III, ii).

[2] By a decree of the Directory, dated 28 Messidor an IV (16 July 1796), 'Le citoyen Théobald Wolfe Tone' was promoted to the rank of 'chef de brigade d'infanterie' from 1 Messidor (Debidour, *Recueil des actes du Directoire Exécutif*, iii, 111–12).

[3] Claude Pétiet (1749–1806), member of the Conseil des Anciens; minister of war, 1796–7.

*blind Hugh*'.[1] He tells me also there is a change in the arrangement, viz. the cavalry of the ci-devant Légion de Police has been formed into a regiment of dragoons, the 21st.[2] The Colonel had given the Directory to understand there were supernumeraries of men and horses enough to form a second regiment, which was intended for me. It has, however, appeared on inspection that the contrary is the fact, for the 21st is even ten men short of its compliment [*sic*]. In consequence of this I am to serve in the infantry with the rank of *chef de brigade*, which answers to that of colonel, and Clarke tells me the pay, &c., is the same, and so is the rank, with less trouble. One must not look a gift horse in the mouth, so I said of course I was perfectly satisfied, and we parted the best friends in the world, and I am to return tomorrow at twelve for this weary brevet.

Called on Madgett in my way home to desire him to find me two louis d'ors in two days at farthest, for I am just run out and I shall have my lodging to pay in three days from this, which is most fearful, for I dread my little *bossue* of a landlady more than the enemy a thousand times; but Madgett has promised to supply me, and so '*Hang those that talk of fear,*[3] *our castle's strength will laugh a siege to scorn*'.[4] I forget to mention in its place that Hoche has a famous cut of a sabre down his forehead, eyebrow and one side of his nose. He was pretty near the enemy when he got that, and luckily it does not at all disfigure him. He is but two and thirty, Jourdan five and thirty, Buonaparte twenty-nine, Moreau about thirty and Pichegru, who is the oldest of all, about six and thirty. The French have no old generals in service; it is their policy to employ young men, and the event has shewed they are right. Moreau and Jourdan continue to drive the Austrians before them in all quarters. Every gazette brings new victories, so that now we are beginning not to mind them.

In the evening the Opera. *Tarare*,[5] which I have seen twenty times. It is brilliant, but the music by Salieri[6] very inferior to that of Gluck.[7] Adrien in the Sultan was magnificently dressed in the Indian costume—everything, down to his slippers, was completely Indian; but I have already remarked fifty times the scrupulous attention the French actors pay to the costume. Rousseau in Calpigi and Mlle Gavaudan in Spinette are inimitable; they are the originals of Beaumarchais.[8] Lainez,[9] Tarare; Mme Ponteuil[10] Astasie. Altogether it is a charming

[1] Swift, *Polite conversation* (1738), dialogue I.

[2] On 23 June 1796 the Directory informed Hoche that a regiment was to be formed from the supernumaries of the 'Légion de police à cheval' and that it was intended it should be commanded by 'un Irlandais député par les Deffenders d'Irlande et qui vous sera envoyé aussitôt que vous le jugerez convenable' (Archives de la Guerre, Registre B5* 97, ff 77v–78r; F. W. Van Brock, 'A proposed Irish regiment and standard, 1796' in *Irish Sword*, xi (1973–4), pp 227–8).

[3] *Macbeth*, v, iii.

[4] *Macbeth*, v, v.

[5] *Tarare*, with music by Salieri and words by Beaumarchais (Lajarte, *Bibliothèque musicale*, i, 357–9).

[6] Antonio Salieri (1750–1825), Italian composer.

[7] Christophe Willibald Gluck (1714–87), German composer.

[8] For Beaumarchais, see above, p. 214.

[9] Etienne Lainez or Lainé (1753–1822), well known as an actor and singer; he was a strong royalist who in *Iphigénie en Aulide* in 1791 sang with enthusiasm 'Chantons, célébrons notre reine' (Fétis, *Biog. des musiciens*).

[10] Madame Ponteuil and the three dancers mentioned in the next sentence but one have not been identified.

spectacle. In one of the ballets there is a charming *pas de trois* by Nivelon, Duchemin and Coulon to the air of the *Follies d'Espagne*. It is almost as good as the 'Pas russe' by Nivelon and Miller[1] in *Panurge*.

## 17 July 1796

Called as usual on Clarke. My eternal brevet not yet come from the war office, but he gave orders to Fleury to write again to the Minister to have it sent directly, so one way or other I shall get it.[2] He tells me Hoche will leave town in two or three days and that he will endeavour to give me a corner in his carriage if possible. I answered it would be highly flattering to me to have the honor of travelling with him; at the some time I said I hoped he would give me a few days' notice, as I had no clothes but *habits b[o]urgeois*. He said he could not be sure to give me four and twenty hours' notice, and as to my regimentals, &c., I could get them made up at Quarters. I replied, as to myself, I was ready at a moment, and the sooner the better. He then desired me to call every day at twelve and we parted. So here I am at single anchor, ready to cut and run. As to money matters I am exceedingly embarrassed. I have not a guinea. I think I must write to Carnot and demand a supply. I am sure I have reason to expect that much from the French government; at the same time God knows whether I shall get it or not, and at any rate it is cursed disagreeable to be obliged to make the application, but what can I do? Damn the money for me; I wish it was in the bottom of the sea! This embarrassment is a drawback on the pleasure I should otherwise feel at the promising appearance of our business. Sat down and wrote two pages of a letter to my dearest life and love, informing her very obscurely of my success here, and of my having obtained the rank of *chef de brigade*; desiring her to sell off everything and embark in the first vessel for Havre de Grâce. I will not finish my letter for a day or two till I see how things turn out on one or two topics. I do not write to Rowan nor Reynolds because, as my last letters were intercepted and carried into England,[3] I do not like to run any more risques.

I forgot to mention in its place a trifling anecdote. The day I dined with Carnot, Hoche's aid du camp[4] came up to me, and asked me how I liked my reception in France. I vented some compliments on the nation. 'Yes', replied he, 'but you have been well received particularly?' I answered the French were ever remarked for their politeness and hospitality to strangers. He then struck at me directly. 'Yes', said he, 'but you are here on some private negociation. You are accredited?' I looked up in his face with infinite good humour and did not reply *one word*. He repeated his question, and I continued to smile on him with all possible stupidity. So he found he could make nothing of it and, turning on his heel, left me. He was, I thought, a sad impudent fellow.

[1] See above, pp 134, 256. [2] *Life* omits preceding nine words.
[3] See above, p. 224. [4] Perhaps Jean François Privat (see below, pp 317, 358).

# From Claude Pétiet, 17 July 1796

Tone (Dickason) papers.

The minister of war notifies Tone that he has been 'raised to the rank of *chef de brigade* in the infantry' as from 19 June 1796. See Diary, 18 July (below).

*LIBERTÉ [Crest] ÉGALITÉ*

4e Division
3e Subdivision

Paris, le 29 Messidor an 4[e] de la
République française, une et indivisible

Bureau
du Personnel
de l'Infanterie

---

Nota. Les réponses à
faire au Ministre doivent
porter en marge l'indication ci-dessus
du Bureau, afin d'éviter tout retard
dans l'expédition des affaires

---

Le Ministre de la Guerre
Au Citoyen Theobald Wolfe Tone à Paris

Je vous préviens, Citoyen, que le Directoire Exécutif par son arrêté du 28 de ce mois vous a élévé au grade de chef de brigade d'Infanterie à dater du premier Messidor dernier, et vous a autorisé à jouir à Paris du traitement et des rations affectés au grade. D'après cette disposition je viens de donner les ordres nécessaires pour vous faire jouir du rang et des appointements de ce grade à la suite d'un corps employé à Paris; vous pouvez en conséquence vous adresser au Général en chef de l'Armée de l'Intérieur qui vous indiquera celui des corps sous ses ordres à Paris dans lequel il croira pour le bien du service devoir vous employer avec ce grade dont vous recevrez incessamment le brevet.

Salut et Fraternité
Le Ministre de la Guerre
. . . . .
[Claude Pétiet]

# To Lazare Nicolas Marguerite Carnot, 18 July 1796

Archives Nationales, AF IV, carton 1671, f. 81.

Tone tells Carnot that he is 'absolutely penniless' and asks him for assistance.

He wrote this letter early in the day and did not learn until after midday of Pétiet's letter of 17 July notifying him of his appointment as an army officer—which by implication promised a solution to his money problems. See Tone to Clarke, 18 July 1796 (I), and Diary for 18 July (below, pp 242, 243, 245).

Au Citoyen Carnot, Président du Directoire Exécutif

Citoyen Président,

J'ai l'honneur de vous exposer que je suis venu d'Amérique à Paris, il y a six mois, par les ordres conjonctifs du Ministre de la république à Philadelphie, et du Ministre des relations extérieures, pour une affaire de la plus haute importance, dont vous êtes parfaitement instruit.

Jusqu'ici je me suis soutenu par mes propres moyens, sans faire application[1] à personne; mais les dépenses inévitables de mon voyage et d'un séjour de six mois en France (montant à une somme de cent cinquante louis) les ont totalement épuisés, et je me trouve à présent *absolument sans argent*.

Dans ces circonstances je suis forcé de m'addresser à vous, Citoyen Président, pour m'obtenir du Directoire exécutif telle assistance que vous jugerez convenable à mes services, et aux sacrifices que j'ai déjà fait[s] et que je suis prêt à faire encore. Je me repose avec confiance sur la générosité et la justice de la République, et surtout je me recommande à votre protection et support.

C'est avec la peine la plus grande que je fais cette application[2], mais les circonstances actuelles l'ont rendu[e] indispensable, vû que j'attends chaque jour un ordre de quitter Paris et de me rendre ailleurs sur la service de la République. Très reconnaissant des attentions dont vous m'avez déjà honoré, j'attends de votre bonté de me débarasser de la situation pénible où je me trouve actuellement, et de m'accorder tel secours que vous jugerez raisonnable et que les circonstances actuelles vous semblera d'exiger.

Salut et respect
James Smith

Paris, 30 Messidor, An 4$^{me}$

[1] Tone's expression 'sans faire application' is an anglicism. He might have written 'sans faire une demande'.

[2] *Recte* 'demande'.

# To General Henri Jacques Guillaume Clarke, 18 July 1796 (I)

Archives Nationales, AF IV, carton 1671, f. 82r.

It appears that Tone wrote this letter soon after the preceding one in anticipation of not being able to see Clarke when calling on him at 12 noon. See Diary for 18 July (below).

Dear General,

I have written a short letter[1] to Carnot, which he will doubtless shew you, mentioning the expence I have been at, and praying the Directory to accord me such assistance as he may think reasonable. I hope you will see that it will not be for the dignity of the Republic to leave me in any difficulties, especially when my request is moderate. You must see that some money is indispensably necessary for my equipment, &c., and as I am here a kind of ambassador *incognito*, I consider any sum advanced to me as given on account of my country and as such to be repaid. I return you a thousand thanks for the trouble you have had about my commission. I hope you will continue to serve me in my present application, and in return, if I ever reach my own country, there is no service which I can render to any friend of yours that you may not readily command.

Health and Fraternity
J. Smith

# To General Henri Jacques Guillaume Clarke, 18 July 1796 (II)

Archives Nationales, AF IV, carton 1671, f. 86r.

This letter was written after the conversations Tone had with Clarke and then Carnot on 18 July (see below, p. 245).

Dear General,

I am just come from seeing Citizen Carnot and shewing him the enclosed memorial.[2] He desired me to give it to you and that you would report it to him. In consequence I leave it, and I request on this occasion, as on all others, a continuation of your friendship & good offices.

Health & Fraternity,
J. Smith

[1] Above, p. 241. [2] As n. 1.

# Diary, 18–20 July 1796

T.C.D., Tone papers, MS 2049, ff 109ʳ–114ʳ; *Life*, ii, 159–64.

No. 9
From July 18th to September 27th inclusive[1]
*Nil desperandum!*
Paris
1796

Heis olōnos aristos amunesthai peri patrēs!
Homer[2]

—His sword the brave man draws
And asks no omen but his country's cause—.
Pope[3]

## 18 July 1796

Rose early this morning and wrote a threatening letter[4] to Citizen Carnot, telling him '*if he did not put five pounds in a sartin place!!*—'.[5] It is written in French and I have a copy. God forgive me for calling it French, for I believe properly speaking it is no language; however, he will understand that *money* is the drift of it and that is the main point. Called at twelve on Clarke. At last he has got my brevet from Pétiet, the Minister at War.[6] It is for the rank of *chef de brigade* and bears date the 1st Messidor (June 19th v.s.[7]). It remains now to be signed by Carnot and Lagarde, which will be done today and tomorrow at nine I am to pass muster.

*Tomorrow I swear, by nine of the clock,*
*I shall see Sir Andrew Barton, Knight.*[8]

Clarke embraced me, on giving me the brevet, and saluted me as a brother officer; so did Fleury, and my heart was so full I could hardly reply to either of them. I am as proud as Punch! Who would have thought this the day I left the Lough of Belfast? *I* would have thought it, *and I did think* it. That is '*manly and decided*', as

[1] The Diary entries for 21 July–6 Aug., 8 Aug.–2 Sept., 5–9 Sept., 12–16 Sept. and 17–27 Sept. are given as separate documents (below, pp 249–60, 306–10, 310–11, 313–14, 314–20).

[2] Homer, *Iliad*, xii, line 243. Tone uses Greek characters.

[3] Alexander Pope, *The Iliad of Homer* (1760), bk XII, lines 283–4. These verses and the preceding headings, obviously inserted in the MS later, are omitted from *Life*.

[4] Above, p. 241. [5] Source of quotation not identified.

[6] It is mentioned in Pétiet to Tone, 17 July 1796 (above, p. 240). [7] i.e. vieux style.

[8] Thomas Percy, *Reliques of ancient English poetry* (1765), ii, bk I.

P.P.[1] used to say. I now write myself *chef de brigade*, '*in any bill, bond, quittance or obligation, armigero*!'.[2] Huzza! Huzza! Let me have done with my nonsense and huzzaing and mind my business. Clarke asked me would we consent in Ireland to let the French have a direct interference in our government? adding that it might be necessary, as it was actually in Holland, where, if it were not for the continual superintendance of the French, they would suffer their throats to be cut again by the Stadtholder. I answered that undoubtedly the French must have a very great influence on the measures of our government, in case we succeeded, but that I thought if they were wise, they would not expect any direct interference, adding that the most effectual way to have power with us would be to appear not to desire it. I added that for that reason I hoped whoever was sent in the civil department would be a very sensible cool man, because a great deal would depend on his address. Clarke replied, 'We intend to send nobody but you'. That stunned me a little. What could he mean? Am I to begin by representing the French Republic in Ireland, instead of representing the Irish Republic in France? I am '*puzzled in mazes and perplexed with errors*'.[3] I must have this explained in tomorrow's conversation. Clarke then went on to say that they had no security for what form of government we might adopt, in case of success. I replied I had no security to offer but my decided opinion that we would establish a republic. He objected we might establish an aristocratic republic like that of Genoa. I assured him the aristocracy of Ireland were not such favorites with the people that we should ever spill our blood to establish their power. He then said, perhaps, after all, we might chuse a king; that there was no security against that but information, and that the people of Ireland were in general very ignorant. I asked him in God's name who would we chuse, or where would we go look for a king? He said, maybe the Duke of York?[4] I assured him that he, or his aid du camp, Fleury, who was present, had full as good [a], and indeed a much better, chance than his Royal Highness; and I added that we neither loved the English people in general, nor his Majesty's family in particular, so well as to chuse one of then for our king, supposing, what was not the case, that the superstition of royalty yet hung about us. As to the ignorance of our peasantry, I admitted it was in general too true, thanks to our execrable government, whose policy it was to keep them in a state of barbarism, but I could answer for the information of the Dissenters, who were thoroughly enlightened, and sincere republicans, and who, I had no doubt, would direct the public sentiment in framing a government. He then asked was there nobody among ourselves that had any chance, supposing the tide should set in favor of monarchy? I replied, *not one*. He asked, would the Duke of Leinster, for example? I replied, *not*, that everybody loved and liked the Duke, because he was a good man and always resided and spent his fortune in Ireland, but that he by no means possessed that kind of character or talents which would elevate him to that station. He then asked me again could I think of nobody? I replied I could not; that Lord Moira was the only person I could recollect who could have had the least chance, but that

[1] Thomas Russell. [2] *Merry wives of Windsor*, I, i. [3] Joseph Addison, *Cato* (1713), I, i.
[4] Frederick, duke of York (1763–1827), second son of George III (G.E.C., *Peerage*).

he had blown his reputation to pieces by accepting a command against France, and after him there was nobody. 'Well', said Clarke, 'maybe after all you will chuse one of your leaders—who knows but it may be yourself?' I replied we had no leaders of a rank or description likely to arrive at that degree of eminence, and as to myself I had neither the talents nor the desire to aspire so high.[1] Well, that is enough of royalty for the present. We then, for the hundredth time, beat over the old ground about the priests, without however starting any fresh ideas, and I summed up all by telling him that as to religion my belief was we would content ourselves with pulling down the establishment without setting up any other; that we would have no State religion, but let every sect pay their own clergy voluntarily; and that as to royalty and aristocracy, they were both odious in Ireland to that degree that I apprehended much more a general massacre of all the gentry and a distribution of the entire of their property than the establishment of any form of government which would perpetuate their influence; that I hoped this massacre would not happen and that I for one would do all that lay in my power to prevent it, because I did not like to spill the blood even of the wicked;[2] at the same time that the pride and cruelty and oppression of the Irish aristocracy were so great that I apprehended every excess from the just resentments of the people. The conversation ended there. Clarke gave me Hoche's address, and desired me to call on Fleury tomorrow at 9 and that he would introduce me at the War Office, where I must pass review.

From Clarke I went to the Luxembourg, where I had an audience of Carnot. I told him I was come, in the first place, to return him my acknowledgements for the high honor conferred on me by the Directory in giving me the rank of *chef de brigade* in the armies of the republic; and I mentioned that, as Gen[era]l Clarke had told me that I should probably be ordered to join my regiment at a day's notice, and as my resources were entirely exhausted, I had taken the liberty to address a short memorial[3] to him requesting a supply. He asked me had I spoken to Clarke? I said not explicitly on that subject. He then ran his eye over my letter and desired me to give it to Clarke and that he would report upon it to him, and see what was to be done. I then took my leave. Carnot's manner was very friendly, but I see no great certainty of the cash. I returned to Clarke's and wrote him a note,[4] inclosing my memorial and requesting his good offices &c., adding that if ever I reached my own country and had it in my power to render a service to any friend of his, he might command me. That is a little stroke of intrigue. '*I have a thing in me that you want; you do me, I do you &c.*', as Lofty says.[5] All fair, all fair!

Went in the evening boldly to the opera, as usual. Pleasant enough. *Renaud*[6] and the ballet of *Psiché*. Rousseau excellent in *Renaud*, as he is in everything. Poor little Chevigny fell in the ballet and strained her ancle. I was in a fright, like a good

[1] In the MS at this point three lines are crossed out illegibly.

[2] *Life*, ii, 162, substitutes 'guilty' for 'wicked'.

[3] Above, p. 241.

[4] Above, p. 242.

[5] Goldsmith, *The good-natur'd man* (1768), act III.

[6] *Renaud*, a lyric tragedy in three acts, with music by Sacchini and words by Le Boeuf (Lajarte, *Bibliothèque musicale*, i, 333–4).

soul as I am, for I thought she struck her breast against the steps of the altar, and that would have been a thousand pities, for she is a charming dancer.

## 19 July 1796

I am writing these memorandums at four o'clock in the morning, for I can't sleep sometimes. I missed a famous quotation yesterday, in the manner of P.P. Where I say that Carnot will collect that *money* is the object of my letter, I should have said that '*I made him an harangue, of which the waiter understood not a single word but brandy, on which he disappeared and returned in an instant with the noggin*'.[1] That I take to be truly witty and instructive.[2]

Called[3] on Fleury at nine o'clock, and walked with him to the War Office; when we arrived there found, like a couple of wise heads, that we had forgot my commission, so that business is postponed till tomorrow. He tells me the pay p[er] month is 35#[4] in cash and 600# in mandats, with three rations of meat—1½ lb, three do. of bread—4½ lb, besides haricots, salt and wood to I know not what amount. But in God's name what shall I do with bread and meat? After all I fear I must consult Madgett and that is what I do not wish to do. Well, I will wait at all events till tomorrow, when I will see what impression I can make on Clarke concerning trade affair.[5] '*Oh, if the States General would but pay me what they owe me &c.*'[6] I am exceedingly embar[r]assed with my rations. Went muzzing[7] with Madgett in the evening; as we were walking thro' the Thuilleries met my old friend Stone[8] of Hackney full plump, walking with Helen Maria Williams,[9] authoress of the *Letters on France*, &c.[10] I was fairly caught, for I have avoided Stone ever since my arrival; not that I know anything to his prejudice, but that I guard the incognito. He made me promise to call on him tomorrow, and as he is already acquainted with almost the whole of my history, I will tell him that I am here memorializing the French government for some compensation for what I have suffered in their cause, and that if I succeed I mean to settle in France. That is the truth but not the whole truth. Went on with Madgett and drank punch—told him of my commission, having first sworn him to secresy. What shall I do with my rations? Tomorrow I will see Clarke

[1] Tone may be thinking of a passage in ch. 17 of Tobias Smollett's *Sir Launcelot Greaves* (1762): 'the waiter . . . understood no part of this address but the word *brandy*, at mention of which he disappeared'; the words 'noggin' and 'returned' occur several lines below this passage.

[2] This sentence is omitted from *Life*.

[3] In the MS this word and what follows are in a different pen. This and the content indicate that it was written later.

[4] Spelt out '35 francs' in *Life*, ii, 163.

[5] i.e. money.

[6] Source of this quotation not identified.

[7] i.e. strolling aimlessly.

[8] John Hurford Stone (1763–1818), British radical; emigrated to France and was imprisoned during the Terror; he had a liaison with, or was secretly married to, Helen Maria Williams (*D.N.B.*).

[9] Helen Maria Williams (1762–1827), poetess and writer on French affairs; she resided in France from 1788 and was a friend of Madame Roland (*D.N.B.*).

[10] *Letters written in France in the summer of 1790* (London, 1790); *Letters containing a sketch of the politics of France from the thirty-first of May 1793 till the twenty-eighth of July 1794* (2 vols, London, 1795); *Letters from France containing many new anecdotes relative to the French revolution and the present state of French manners* (4 vols, London, 1792–6).

and learn what report he makes on my letter to Carnot. If they would pay me that £150 it would set me at my ease, but I doubt it very much. I want money sadly.

## 20 July 1796

Called at Clarke's and saw Fleury who gave me my brevet signed by Carnot, &c., so now I am to all intents and purposes *chef de brigade* in the service of the republic. Fleury is to bring me tomorrow at nine to the *commissaire ordonnateur* to pass review, and from that I go [to] the Treasury to receive a month's pay, so *vogue la galère*![1] Fleury also told me another thing not quite so agreeable, by Clarke's orders, viz. that Carnot's answer to my memorial was that he thought a month's pay in advance was a handsome compensation; nevertheless if I thought otherwise, he desired I might signify to Clarke what I thought reasonable. I desired Fleury to tell Clarke that I would consider of it, and let him know the result tomorrow or the day after. I do not think it at all a compensation. What is a month's pay? £3 2[*s*]. 6[*d*]. ster[lin]g. It is absolutely nothing. I will put it to Carnot as a debt of honor, and let him pay it or not, as he pleases. As to my rations, I am quite at a loss to know how I shall manage with them. A Frenchman would soon settle it, but it is a different thing with a foreigner.

# Extract from the register of the Executive Directory, 21 July 1796

Archives de la Guerre.

This is an official record of Tone's appointment to the rank of 'chef de brigade', to take effect from the preceding 1 Messidor (19 June 1796). It is a printed document with certain words and a message added by hand.

4^e^ Division<br>
3^e^ Subdivision *LIBERTÉ* [crest] *ÉGALITÉ*<br>
Bureau de l'Infanterie *DÉPARTEMENT DE LA GUERRE*

Paris, le 3 Thermidor an 4^e^ de la République française

Ampliation

Extrait des Registres du Directoire exécutif,

Du 28 Messidor de l'an 4^e^ de la République française, une et indivisible.

Le Directoire exécutif arrête:

Le C^en^ Theobald Wolfe Tone est promu au grade de chef de brigade d'infanterie, à prendre date du premier messidor dernier.

Il jouira à Paris du traitement & des rations affectés à ce grade.

Pour ampliation<br>
Le chef de la 4^e^ Div[isi]on<br>
Davernoy[2]

[1] Meaning 'come what may!'. [2] Not identified.

# To General Henri Jacques Guillaume Clarke, 21 July 1796

Archives Nationales, AF III, cote $186^{B}$, dossier 858.

Paris, $3^{d}$ Thermidor An $4^{me}$

Dear General,

Your aid du camp[1] (if I understand him right) told me that the President's[2] answer to my memorial was that he thought a month's pay in advance was a reasonable compensation, but that if I thought otherwise, I should offer my reasons to you. I take the liberty in consequence to trouble you with this letter.

I will not speak of any services rendered, or sacrifices made, or risques run by me in the business thus far; but what I request you to consider is that, being as I am a foreigner, the commerce in everything is against me, as it is, I know, against the French in Philadelphia. In consequence the allowance, which would be ample for a Frenchman, who knows the *pavé* of Paris thoroughly, may not be so for me, who am in a great degree a stranger to the language, the customs, the prices, in short everything almost in the country. I shall therefore be in difficulties as to disposing of my appointment (I mean the rations &c.) and the utmost I can expect, if I succeed even so far, is a bare existence. I leave it to you to consider whether I have not merited something more than that. I beg leave to add that I am here in a situation approaching to an *official character*. I may say, I represent my country, under the actual circumstances, and of course any attention shewn by the French government is to be considered as shewn to the nation much more than to me as an individual.

I will not take up more of your time than to observe that I have stated the sum I have actually spent out of my own shattered property.[3] Whatever compensation, whether the whole or any part of that sum, may be thought reasonable, I humbly conceive is to be considered as a debt of honor on the part of the French government, and in that case I could not desire a better umpire than the President of the Executive Directory to ascertain the quantum. I submit myself therefore implicitly to his decision, intreating him only in forming his determination to consult his own feelings, as a gentleman, and the honor of the Republic, on whose good faith I have come thus far.

I take this opportunity to return you my sincere acknowledgements for the

[1] Fleury. [2] Carnot's.

[3] When Tone left Philadelphia for France seven months earlier he had with him *louis d'or* to the value of £100 sterling (see below, p. 340). On 13 July he wrote in his diary: 'I am almost on my last louis' (see above, p. 236).

favors I have already received at your hands; and I entreat you to believe that it is with the greatest reluctance I give you the trouble of this letter, which I should not do, did not the urgency of my situation render it unavoidable.

I have the honor to be, with great respect, Dear General,

Your most obliged
and obedient servant
J. Smith

General Clarke &c., &c.

## Diary, 21 July–6 August 1796

T.C.D., Tone papers, MS 2049, ff 114r–124r; *Life*, ii, 164–75.

### 21 July 1796

Went to pass my review with the *commissaire ordonnateur*. Obliged to return for an order from the minister at war to receive my pay, &c., at Paris. Wrote to Clarke[1] putting my compensation on Carnot as a debt of honor and gave my letter to Fleury.

### 22 July 1796

Called at Clarke's on Fleury. Coming out met General Hoche, who gave me his address and desired to see me tomorrow morning at seven o'clock, in order to talk over our business and to settle about my leaving Paris. *That looks like business!* Huzza! Huz–. I am always huzzaing, like a blockhead. Went to the commissaire's and passed my review, from that to the Treasury, where the forms are terribly slow. I received for my month's pay 35#[2] in cash, 600# in mandats, worth today 24#, and 300# in assignats, worth, I suppose, about 6*d*. It is no great things but hang the money. Dined very pleasantly with Stone and H. M. Williams. All our politics English. Stone was very hearty, but Helen Williams is Miss Jane Bull completely. I was quite *genteel and agreeable*. Wrote to Monroe to know if I might, in case of necessity, draw on him for £50. Bed very early, thinking of my interview with Hoche.

### 23 July 1796

Called on Hoche at seven and found him in bed talking with two generals whom I did not know. One of them is going to Italy, very much against the grain.

[1] Above, pp 248–9. [2] Spelt out '35 francs' in *Life*, ii, 164.

General Sherlock[1] (*un enfant*)[2] called in. I collect from what he said that he is to be of our expedition, and that he does not know it himself yet. After they were gone Hoche asked me when I would be ready to leave town? I answered I was at his orders but that I wished to have if possible four or five days to make some little arrangements,[3] and then I would be ready to march. He said, by all means; that he proposed leaving town in seven days himself and that if he could he would give me a seat in his carriage, but if not he would settle that I should travel with General Chérin[4] (I think was the name), his most particular friend, who was to have a command in our business, but to whom as yet he had not opened himself on the subject. I made my acknowledgements, and asked him at the same time whether my appearance at head quarters might not give rise to some suspicion from the circumstance of my being a foreigner? He replied he would settle me in a village near Rennes, his head quarters, where I should be incognito and at the same time within his reach. I asked him then was he apprised of the *Directoire's* having honored me with the rank of *chef de brigade*? He replied he was, and made me his compliments. I then observed to him that I presumed I should be of most service if I were placed in some situation near his person; that I spoke French, as he might observe, very imperfectly, nevertheless I could make myself understood, and that, as he did not speak English, I should be necessary in his communications with the people of Ireland. He replied, 'Leave all that to me. As soon as you join and that your regiment is formed, I will apply for the rank of adjutant general for you; that will place you at once in the État-Major,[5] and besides you must be in a situation where you may have a command if necessary.' I returned him a thousand thanks, and he proceeded to ask me did I think it was likely that the men of property, or any of them, wished for a revolution in Ireland? I replied *most certainly not*, and that he should reckon on all the opposition that class could give him; that however it was possible, and probably might happen, that when the business was once commenced, some of them might join us upon speculation, but that it would be sorely against their real sentiments. He asked me then did I know Arthur O'Connor? I replied I did, and that I entertained the highest opinion of his talents, principles and patriotism. He asked me did he not some time ago make '*an explosion*' in the Irish Parliament? I replied he made the ablest and the honestest speech,[6] to my mind, that ever was made in that house. 'Well', said he, 'will he join us?'. I answered I hoped, as he was *foncièrement Irlandois*,[7] that he

[1] Sauveur François Louis Sherlock or Scherlock (1771–1800), born at Lyons; grandson of an Irish refugee in France; son of a lieutenant colonel of an Irish regiment in the Irish brigade who was wounded at Fontenoy; he was a sous-lieutenant, 1788, lieutenant, 1791, adjutant general, 1797, chef de brigade, 1797; elected to Council of Five Hundred, 1798, and to the Senate, 1799 (Archives de la Guerre, dossier; *Dict. parl. franç.*).

[2] In *Life* 'un enfant' is omitted.

[3] In *Life* the remainder of the sentence is omitted.

[4] Louis Nicolas Hyacinthe Chérin (1762–99), chief of staff to Hoche, 1795. A genealogist and expert on the rights of the noblesse, he supported the revolution. (Six, *Dict. des généraux & amiraux*; *Dict. biog. franç.*). In *Life*, the words which follow in parentheses are omitted.

[5] i.e. the general staff.

[6] On 4 May 1795 (see above, p. 25, headnote).

[7] i.e. 'root-and-stock Irish'.

undoubtedly would. So it seems O'Connor's speech is well known here. If ever I meet him, as I hope I may, I will tell him what Hoche said and the character that he bears in France. It must be highly gratifying to his feelings.[1] Hoche then went on to say, 'There is a lord in your country (I was a little surprised at this beginning, knowing as I do what stuff Irish peers are made of). He is son to a duke. Is he not a Patriot?' I immediately smoked my lover,[2] Lord Edward Fitzgerald,[3] and I gave Hoche a very good account of him.[4] He asked me then about the Duke.[5] I replied that I hoped for his assistance, or at least his neutrality, if the business were once commenced. He then mentioned Fitzgibbon of all the men in the world! I endeavoured to do him justice, as I had to the others he spoke of, and I believe I satisfied Hoche that we will not meet with prodigious assistance from his Majesty's lord high chancellor of Ireland. He then asked me what quantity of arms would be necessary? I replied the more the better as we would find soldiers for as many firelocks as France would send us. He then told me he had demanded eighty thousand, but that he was sure of *fifty thousand. That is a piece of good news!* I answered with fifty thousand stand to begin with, we should soon have all the arms in the nation in our hands, adding that I had the strongest hopes that the Militia, who composed the only real force in Ireland, would give us no opposition. 'Oh', said he, as to opposition, '*Je m'en fouts!*',[6] which the reader will not expect me to translate literally, but it was as much as to say he disregarded it. He then asked me very seriously did I apprehend any royalism, or aristocratism, in Ireland? I assured him I did not; that in case of a change, we should most undoubtedly establish a republic, and I mentioned my reasons, which seemed to satisfy him. He observed however, as Clarke had done before, that even if monarchy in Ireland were to be the result, it would not alter the system on which France was proceeding, as her main object was the independance of Ireland, under any form of government, tho' undoubtedly she would prefer a republic. We then spoke of the aristocracy of Ireland and I assured him, as I had done Clarke, that what I

[1] Clearly Tone did not know that O'Connor was on the Continent, very probably in Switzerland and perhaps already contemplating entering France (see above, p. 215, n. 3, and below, p. 366, n. 5).

[2] Meaning here 'wellwisher' or 'friend'.

[3] Lord Edward Fitzgerald (1763–98), fifth son of the 1st duke of Leinster; served in army, 1780–92; M.P. for Co. Kildare 1790–97; joined United Irishmen and in 1796 went on a mission to France with Arthur O'Connor (*D.N.B.*; Frank MacDermot, 'Arthur O'Connor' in *I.H.S.*, xv, no. 57 (Mar. 1966), pp 52–5; Marianne Elliott, *Partners in revolution: the United Irishmen and France* (New Haven, 1982), pp 98–103).

[4] Though Tone was ignorant of Fitzgerald's mission, Fitzgerald knew of Tone's. The French minister in Hamburg, Charles Reinhard, wrote to Delacroix on 18 May 1796 reporting that Fitzgerald had said to him after arriving there 'que si j'allois à Paris, il me remettroit une lettre pour une personne au fait des affaires d'Irlande. Je lui ai demandé le nom de cette personne; il m'a dit qu'elle était revenue d'Amérique au mois de décembre passé.' The letter would bring Tone up to date on Irish affairs. (Archives des Affaires Étrangères, Corresp. Politique Angleterre, cote 589, ff 249–52). Tone does not mention any such letter and so presumably if it was ever written it did not reach him.

[5] The 2nd duke of Leinster, eldest brother of Lord Edward, was the leading whig politician in Co. Kildare.

[6] In *Life*, ii, 166, this is rendered 'pour l'opposition, je m'en f—', which is a vulgar expression implying 'I don't care'.

apprehended was not the aggrandisement but the massacre of that body, from the just indignation of the people whom they have so long and so cruelly oppressed, adding that it was what I sincerely deprecated, but what I feared was too likely to happen. He said certainly the spilling of blood was at all times to be avoided as much as possible; that he did conceive in such explosions as that which was likely to take place in Ireland it was not to be supposed but some individuals would be sacrificed, but the less of that the better and it was much wiser to secure the persons of those I mentioned or to suffer them to emigrate to England, as they would no doubt be ready to do, than to put them to death, in which I most sincerely agreed, for I am like Parson Adams, '*I do not desire to have the blood even of the wicked upon me*'.[1] Hoche also mentioned that mischief had been done to the principles of liberty, and additional difficulties thrown in the way of the French revolution by the quantity of blood spilt, 'for', added he, 'when once you guillotine a man, you get rid of an individual it is true, but then you make all his friends and connexions for ever enemies to the government', a sentence well worth considering. I am heartily glad to find Hoche of this humane temperament, because I hope I am humane myself, and by this means I trust we shall be able to prevent unnecessary bloodshed in Ireland, which I shall most sincerely exert my utmost endeavours to do. He then desired me to call on him every two or three days at seven o'clock, at which time I might be sure to find him disengaged, adding that he did not wish to mix me with the crowd, and after several expressions of civility and attention on his part, all which I set down to the credit of my country, we parted. I like Hoche more and more. He is one of the finest fellows I ever conversed with, with a fine manly mind, and a fine manly figure.

On my return, I found a very friendly and attentive answer from Monroe, inviting me to dinner for today, in order to settle about *trade affair*.[2] I should have mentioned that Hoche asked me whether the Defenders had ever sent anyone to France to make representations? I answered I could not positively say, but that I believed not, they being for the most part the peasantry of Ireland, and of course not having the means, nor proper persons to send.

At twelve I went and saw Clarke. We were both a little out of humour about my application for money, but our ill temper was pointed against the Directory rather than against each other. He said he was sure they w[oul]d give me nothing. I asked him then how I was to leave Paris in five or six days, as Gen[era]l Hoche had that morning given me orders to hold myself in readiness to do? This was 'Gr—gr—grimgribber'[3] to him. 'Well', said he, 'but you ask too much'. 'So far from it', said I, 'that I ask nothing. I barely state how much I have spent of my own money, and I leave it to Carnot's honor to determine what he thinks reasonable.' 'But I do not see', continued he, 'how it is to be done, or on what fund?' I answered I came by order of La Croix, the minister for foreign affairs, and of Adet, the ambassador of the Republic in America, which last had offered me

[1] Henry Fielding, *Joseph Andrews* (1742), bk II, ch. 9.
[2] An allusion to his money troubles.
[3] Jargon or learned gibberish.

money for my expences, an offer that I had refused, some proof that I did not want to extort on them; that the natural way therefore was to give an order to La Croix to make me such recompense as the Directory might think fit. Clarke then '*began to complain of the scarcity of silver, which I improved by complaining of the scarcity of gold, and we both agreed that money never was so scarce as at present*'.[1] Damn it, sempiternally, for money. I am sure I have wished a thousand times that there was not a guinea in the world! At last Clarke said he would speak again to Carnot, but I confess I see no great hopes, which is pleasant. I made many fine reflections in my own mind, during this *spar*, on the gratitude of nations, &c., &c. However, after all I am a *chef de brigade*, about to be an *adjutant general*. By what I see, however, we are like to reap more glory than profit in this business. '*I beseech you, Sir John, let me have five hundred of my thousand.*' '*That may not be Master Shallow!*'[2] Well, my own country will pay me sometime or other, so *allons*! I then took Clarke up on our conversation of the 18th relative to a direct interference on the part of France.[3] I said if he meant by that to admit a representative of the Republic into any part of our government, it was what France ought not to expect, nor we to grant; that France would certainly have great influence, but the surest way to have it would be not to assume it; that what he said of Holland did not apply to us. The French had conquered Holland, and they had a right, if they pleased, to throw it into the sea, but it was not so with Ireland. We rather resembled the situation of America in the last war.[4] Clarke seemed satisfied with all this, and I proceeded to ask him had they thought of a person to reside near the future Irish government? He said Gen[era]l Hoche would be there. I replied he would be moving about, but I meant a sort of *chargé d'affaires*, who should be stationary. Clarke replied undoubtedly a proper person would be sent. I said I hoped the French government would be very delicate in their choice, and send a man of great temper and discretion, as much would depend on his conduct. I then observed that Clarke had often asked me what security Ireland would give that, if her independance were once established, she might not, like America,[5] forget her obligations to France, and perhaps hereafter be found leagued with her enemies? To which I offered him, as the only security, our honor as gentlemen, and I begged leave in return to ask him what security he had to give us, that if England offered to renounce everything provided France would sacrifice us, France would not accept the offer? He answered in my own words 'Our honor as gentlemen', and he assured me in the strongest manner France would be (as I believe, myself, the fact to be) incapable of such conduct. I asked him then whether he thought, if our government were once organised, we should be able to borrow money either in Spain or Holland? He said he doubted it very much;

[1] Goldsmith, *The vicar of Wakefield* (1766), I, ch. 14.

[2] *2 Henry IV*, v, v. Tone misquotes these two lines slightly and gets them in the wrong sequence. Shallow's words 'I beseech you, good Sir John, . . .', are in fact preceded several lines above by Falstaff's words 'That can hardly be, Master Shallow', which are in reply to Shallow's previous remark.

[3] See above, p. 244.

[4] The war of American independence, 1775–83.

[5] *Life* omits 'like America'.

that Holland had no money, and Spain very little. If that be so we must only make *assignats* first, and then *mandats*, like our betters. It is now two o'clock and I must go dress for dinner at Monroe's. '*Fine times, Mr Rigmarol!*'[1] Nothing but generals and ambassadors! Well, I shall be one or other, and perhaps *both*, one of these *odd come shortlys*.

Dinner at Monroe's. Very pleasant. Mrs Monroe[2] a pretty little woman, with very white teeth, a rare circumstance in an American.[3] After dinner, went with Monroe into his cabinet. He tells me he is just now poor, but he offered to supply me to the amount of £50 in gales[4] of ten or fifteen, as I might want it; or else he desired me to go to Skipwith,[5] the Consul for the United States, and see if he would give me cash for my bill on Philadelphia, which he would guarantee, or for one to the same amount on himself at a short date, which he would accept; he offered me at the same time ten louis for my current expences. All this is very handsome in Monroe. After thanking him, I told him I would avail myself of his permission to try Skipwith and I told him at the same time that I was not in any difficulties for a few days to come, and consequently I refused, with many acknowledgements, the money he offered me. He goes out of town tonight for two days; on the third I am to call on him, and in the meantime to see the consul, so called, a *consulendo*, because I mean to consult him. Once for all, damn the money for me! I will make no more memorandums about it, that is flat. It degrades the dignity of my history. This is a long day's journal; nine pages[6] and it is now but six o'clock. I have run thro' a good deal of business today, besides writing those nine pages. I had like to forget that Hoche shewed me my proclamation printed and signed by himself.[7] It is the one intended for distribution, and I think it will be found to be an honest one.

## 24 July 1796

No business. In the evening the Opera as usual. *Œdipe* again.[8] More and more delighted with that piece, and especially with Adrien in Œdipe. *Psiché* the ballet with Duchemin, a charming little woman, in Psiché.[9] I do love the spectacles of Paris dearly, and how much more should I enjoy them if I had the society of my dearest love? Well, I hope I shall not die until I find myself in a loge[10] with her, and Miss Mary and P.P. That may happen yet!

[1] Goldsmith, *Essays* (1765), xix.
[2] Eliza Monroe née Kortright (d. 1830).
[3] In *Life* the preceding six words are omitted.
[4] i.e. instalments. *Life*, ii, 169, substitutes 'sums' for 'gales'.
[5] Fulwar Skipwith of Virginia, consul-general of the United States in France, 1795–1802 (*Writings of James Monroe*, ed. S. M. Hamilton (7 vols, New York, 1898–1903), ii, 67, n. 1).
[6] MS ff 114$^{v}$–119$^{r}$.
[7] Above, pp 196–8.
[8] Tone had already seen a performance of *Œdipe à Colone* on 7 July (see above, p. 227).
[9] He had already seen *Psiché* on 18 July (see above, pp 245–6).
[10] i.e. box.

## 25 July 1796

Running about all this morning on *trade affair* (damn it!).[1] Saw Clarke. He tells me I am to travel with Hoche and that we set off the 30th, viz. in five days. Huzza! to be sure I am not proud of that! Called at Monroe's. The secretary tells me there is a person[2] arrived within this week who has a letter for me. My heart is up in my mouth! Please God I will run off the minute I swallow my dinner. I am in a frenzy till I get my letter. I have had not one line since I left New York, now six months. How is my dearest life and soul, and our darling little babies? The little things! My life lies in those children. Well, I hope I shall have news of them this night. Poor little Will![3] and my Fantom![4] and the Daff,[5] that I doat upon, and their darling mother! Oh, that I had my letter, oh that I had my letter!

Evening. My lover[6] gone out. Left a note that I would call tomorrow about eleven and desiring him to leave the letter for me in case he should be obliged to go out before that time. I know nothing that agitates me so much as an incident of this kind. I am projecting all possible kinds of accidents and misfortunes. It is terrible. I will not torment myself any longer, that is flat. I will go walk in the Champs-Élysées to dissipate my chagrin. Home early. Bed.

## 26 July 1796

Up at six and called on Hoche at seven. He was gone out, so I had my walk for nothing. '*I hope my early rising may do me no harm!*'[7] I want to settle with him about our journey. Called at eleven on Col[one]l Fulton,[8] and got my letter (for there is but one), which is from Hamilton Rowan. It is dated March 30th, nearly four months since, at which time all my family were well. He tells me also that Matt[9] is arrived in America in December last. That gives me most unspeakable satisfaction, as he will be a protection for my wife and family during my absence, or in case of the worst happening to me in this contest wherein I am about to embark. My mind is now as much at ease as I can rationally expect it to be for some time. I look upon this letter as a good omen before my departure. Met Ahern for the first time God knows when. He tells me that rascal Duckett is telling all the world that there is to be an invasion of Ireland and that he has it from Clarke and General Hoche, with whom he is in confidence, &c., &c. Is not

[1] An allusion to his money troubles.

[2] Apparently the Samuel Fulton mentioned in the Diary for 26 July (see below).

[3] William Tone (1791–1828). [4] Francis Rawdon Tone (1793–1806).

[5] Maria Tone (1786–1803). In *Life*, ii, 170, 'my girl' is substituted for 'the Daff'.

[6] Meaning here 'wellwisher'. The allusion is to Fulton.

[7] Source of quotation not identified.

[8] Samuel Fulton, a native of North Carolina with 'a propensity to travel', was in Paris pressing George Rogers Clark's claims against the French government arising from a projected expedition against the Spanish colony of Louisiana. He was granted the rank of lieutenant colonel in the French army. (*American state papers: Indian affairs* (Washington, 1832), i, 463; *Annual report of the American Historical Association for the year 1896* (2 vols, Washington, 1897), i, 930–1107).

[9] Mathew Tone.

this most dreadfully provoking? Here I have doomed myself to a rigorous solitude for six months to avoid the possibility of alarm, and now a blackguard is sounding the trumpet before him and proclaiming the business to all the world! I will call on Clarke tomorrow and abuse him for his indiscretion in opening himself, as I know he has done (and I have reason to believe Hoche also), to such a scoundrel. It is vexations beyond all bearing. I am in a rage. Met my *compagnon de voyage* D'aucourt, with whom I lodged on my first arrival.[1] He was very civil, and tells me he is applying for the rank of *chef de brigade* and to be sent out again to the West Indies. Well, other people are *chefs de brigade* as well as he, but he does not know that. In the evening the opera as usual. *Iphigénie en Aulide* by Gluck. It is the best of the operas here. Mme Chéron is delightful in Iphigénie, but I have praised her already. *Télémaque* the ballet. Vestris took leave of Paris for some time, as he goes, I am told, to London. He exerted himself, of course, and was to be sure astonishing. Mme Gardel (ci-devant Miller), in Eucharis, made her first appearance after a long indisposition. She is incontestibly the first female dancer in the world. I am delighted with her, and she is as ugly as possible. Heigho! I shall soon bid '*Adieu to the village delights*'.[2] I know not how it is. I have spent five dreary months at Paris without forming one connexion, male or female, that I care a farthing about, or that cares a farthing about me, yet I find myself low-spirited now that I am about to quit it. That is curious enough, but I have often had occasion to remark the same sentiment. I am as dull tonight as a cat.

## 27 July 1796

Clarke tells me this morning the Directory have ordered me three months' pay. That is *tant pris sur l'ennemi*,[3] but I am forced to borrow £50 from Monroe, which grieves me sorely, for it is breaking in still more on the sacred funds of my little family. It is however unavoidable, and so, '*what can't be cured, &c.*'.[4] I cannot go down to quarters without some money in my pocket. Went to the Champ de Mars to see the *fête de la Liberté*.[5] Very superb, but I am not now in a humour to relish *fêtes*. I want to be off, and my impatience is growing greater the nearer the time approaches. Paris is as bad to me now as Havre was the first week of my arrival. '*Pardonnez, Princesse, à mon impatience!*'[6] I hate to be *going*. *Apropos*. It is extremely attentive of Hoche to take me with him. I believe I am not sufficiently sensible of it. The fact is, I am surprised, myself, at the *sangfroid* with which I

[1] See Diary entries for 3, 9 and 10 Feb. 1796 (above).

[2] First line of a song in Sheridan's *The glorious first of June* (1794). Its origin may be earlier.

[3] Literally 'so much taken on the enemy'. In *Life*, ii, 171, the French expression is corrected by William Tone to 'tant de pris sur l'ennemi'. The expression indicates smug satisfaction at having taken at least something from the enemy or rival party.

[4] Possibly Tone was recalling these words from George Colman, *Phormio* (1765), II, ii.

[5] There was a procession from the Place de la Bastille to the Carousel where symbols representing royalty and feudalism were burned and Carnot made a speech on the significance of 14 July 1789, 10 Aug. 1792 and 9 Thermidor. On 28 July far larger crowds than gathered on the previous day watched foot and horse racing. (*Moniteur*, 31 July 1796).

[6] Probably a literary quotation.

regard the progress of my business here, so infinitely beyond my expectations. I had very little expectation of success the day I left Sandy Hook,[1] and in fact I came merely to discharge a duty. Things have turned out miraculously, to be sure. Think of my being at a counsel of war, with Carnot and Hoche, and Clarke; of my rank of *chef de brigade*; of my travelling now with Hoche, besides what may yet follow! It is like a romance absolutely. There is one thing I must say for myself. On reviewing my conduct in France, I do not see one indiscretion with w[hi]ch I have to charge myself. I think, in my conscience, I have conducted myself very well. I have, to be sure, laboured very hard in this business. '*Damn me, I was none of your guinea pigs! I have served all offices aboard, from cook's shifter to the command of a vessel. Here you Tunley, there's the hand of a seaman, you dog!*'[2] There is another thing I wish to remark here. I owe unspeakable obligations, and such as I can never repay, to my masters of the General Committee. I have in consequence not lost sight of their honor or their interests here, as will appear from my memorials[3] delivered to the Executive Directory, in which I have endeavoured to make them the basis of the national legislature. If that succeeds, I shall have been instrumental in throwing a great game into their hands; and I hope (and I believe) they will have talents and spirit to support it. At any rate I have, I think, done my duty by them, and in part at least acquitted the debt of gratitude I owe them. Let me never forget their behaviour to me in the hour of my persecution, and their heroic refusal to sacrifice me to the requisition of Grattan and the Whigs.[4] If I contribute to seat them in the places of the aforesaid Whigs, it will be a proof that with parties (I may say with nations) as with individuals, honor and honesty will ever be found to be ultimately the true policy. But let me not be preaching so much about myself. I want to be off, I want to be off! '*I think there be six Richmonds in the field.*'[5] (I do not see what the duce that applys to, but no matter.) '*A horse, a horse, my kingdom for a horse*!'[6]

## 28 July 1796

Called on Hoche early, and saw him for one minute. I travel with him, and we set off the 31st, that is a day later than I hoped. I am to see him again the day after tomorrow. Saw Clarke. Nothing new there. I am to get the order for three months' pay tomorrow. Called at Skipwith's, the American consul, who gave me £50, for which I gave him a bill on Reynolds in Philadelphia for £55. I would have given one for £65 rather than go without the money. I am now ready to march. I see the Orange boys are playing the Devil in Ireland.[7] I have no doubt it is the work of the

[1] From where he left America. [2] Tobias Smollett, *Peregrine Pickle* (1751), chap. 2.

[3] Above, pp 61–70, 88–97.

[4] Referring to his position after his relations with William Jackson had been discovered (see above, vol. I, pp 504–23).

[5] *Richard III*, v, iv. [6] Ibid.

[7] On 12 July 1796, it was reported in the *Northern Star*, the 'Orange Boys, who have desolated the county of Armagh during the last year, paraded publicly in large bodies with orange cockades and colours flying thro' the towns of Lurgan, Waringstown, Portadown &c.'. These 'banditti', the report continued,

Government. Please God, if I get safe into that country, I will settle those gentlemen, and their instigators also, more especially.

*Fête de la Liberté* in the evening. The crowd most astonishing. I never saw anything like it, and I was heartily glad to remark that everyone seemed perfectly pleased and satisfied. It is the first *fête* I have seen into the spirit of which the people seemed fairly to enter.

## 29 July 1796

Running about all the morning making arrangements for my departure.

## 30 July 1796

Called on General Hoche. He tells me I am to travel with Gen[era]l Chérin, *chef d'État-Major*, and that we set off about the 12th of next month. I had rather set off this morning. He desired me to call on Chérin and present myself as the person of whom he had spoken, which I did accordingly but Chérin was gone out. Called at the War Office and got an order for three months' pay. Dined with Madgett and went in the evening to the Opera. *Castor*[1]—a dull piece, and very heavy music by Rameau.[2] I did not like it at all. I should have mentioned that I gave yesterday to Skipwith a pacquet, directed to Holmes & Rainey,[3] Philadelphia, containing two letters, one for Hamilton Rowan, and the other for my dearest love, in which I repeat my orders for the removal of my family and property with all possible speed to France.[4] Skipwith promised me to put them in a way of going with speed and security, so I am in hopes they will have better fortune than my last.

## 31 July 1796

Received my pay, '*and are all as drunk as so many swabbers*'. I insist upon it that is a very good quotation from Rigdum Funnidos.[5] The monotony of my life just now will appear from the stupidity of these memorandums, and especially from the dullness of my jokes. I cannot express how much I long to be *en route*.

'parade in open day under banners bearing the king's effigy and sanctioned by the magistrates' (*N.S.*, 15 July 1796).

[1] *Castor et Pollux*, lyric tragedy in five acts, with music by Rameau, and words by Gentil-Bernard (Lajarte, *Bibliothèque musicale*, i, 182–4).

[2] Jean Philippe Rameau (1683–1764), the most famous 18th-century French musician. *Castor et Pollux* (1737) has been considered his best work. (Fétis, *Biog. des musiciens*).

[3] Hugh Holmes and Robert Rainey, merchants, of 36 South Front St., Philadelphia (*Stephens's Philadelphia Directory for 1796* (Philadelphia, n.d.)).

[4] Earlier letters from Tone to Hamilton Rowan and to Matilda Tone had gone astray (see Diary for 5 July, above, p. 224).

[5] Rigdum Funnidos, a character in Henry Carey's burlesque, *Chrononhotonthologos* (1734).

## 1 Aug. 1796

(Sings) *Oh, merry be the first, and merry be the last,*
*And merry be the first of August!*

That is a sprightly beginning, however! I am plaguy musical this morning; but God knows the heart. Called on Clarke from mere idleness. Did not see him, but coming out met General Hoche, who took me in his carriage to General Chérin, with whom I am to travel. On the way I told Hoche that I hoped the glory was reserved for him to amputate the right hand of England for ever, and I mentioned the immense resources in all respects, especially men and provisions, which Ireland furnished to that country, and of which I trusted we were now on the eve of depriving her. Hoche observed that his only anxiety was about finding subsistance for the troops. I replied that as to *that* I hoped there would be no difficulty; that it was Ireland which victualled the navy, the West Indies and the foreign garrisons of England, and I reminded him of what I had before told him, that in the late scarcity, so far from finding any difficulties at home, she exported vast quantities of corn to that country. I might have added, but it did not occur, that we are now on the eve of harvest, so I am sure we shall find abundance of everything. I went on to say that *my* difficulty was not how *to subsist* but how *to get* there, for that I dreaded that eternal fleet. Hoche laid his hand on my arm and said, '*Ne craignez rien; nous y irons; vous pouvez y compter; ne craignez rien*'.[1] I answered, that being so, I had not a doubt of our success. Hoche then asked me who were these Orange boys?[2] I explained it to him, adding that as to them, it was an affair of no consequence, which we would settle in three days after our arrival. 'Oh', said he, 'ce n'est rien'. I then told him I hoped he would take care to have a sufficiency of cannoniers and artillery, of which we were quite unprovided. 'You may depend upon it', said he, 'that I will bring enough, and of the best, particularly the *Artillerie Légère*.' He then asked me had we many great plains in Ireland? I said not, that in general the face of the country was intersected with fences, and I described the nature of an Irish ditch and hedge to him. By this time we arrived at Chérin's, who was indisposed and in bed. I was introduced by Hoche, and I remember now he is one of the generals with whom I dined at Carnot's.[3] After a short conversation, in which it was fixed that we set off from the 7th to the 10th, I took my leave, Hoche and Chérin desiring me in the meantime to call on them without the ceremony of sending up my name, which is civil of them. So now I have *les grandes entrées*.[4]

## 2–3 Aug. 1796

Blank! My time drags just now most horribly.

[1] 'There is nothing to be afraid of; we are going; you can count on it; there is nothing to be afraid of.'
[2] See above, p. 257, n. 7. [3] See Diary for 12 July (above, p. 235).
[4] *Life*, ii, 175, has '*les petites entrées*'.

## 4 Aug. 1796

Called on Gen[era]l Hoche. No news. He tells me that it may be the 16th or 17th before we set off, which is desolation to me. '*My soul's in arms, and eager for the fray*.'[1] He tells me also that when we get to Rennes he and I will settle the proclamation. I mentioned to him that as we would arrive in the middle of harvest there could be no doubt about our finding subsistance. He answered he had thought of that himself. Called on Chérin twice and saw him for about a moment. I cooled my heels in his anti-chamber for above an hour, but that is only a petty mortification. I always find the subalterns greater men than the principals. One thing is in my favour.[2] As I have begun by dancing attendance on others, if ever I arrive at any situation, I must remember the anxiety and vexation I suffered in my march,[3] and not give myself airs. Called on Clarke. I am out of luck today. He was engaged and could not see me, so I left my name. Altogether I am out of humour. I believe it is the delay of our departure which has vexed me. Chérin told me we should set off the 16th or 17th. *Damn it!*

## 5 Aug. 1796

Blank! Terrible, terrible! I fret[4] myself absolutely sick at these delays. Dined with Madgett and three other Irishmen in the Elysian fields.[5] Stupid as a horse. Everybody is talking of our business. I hear of it from fifty different quarters. That is most terribly provoking.

## 6 Aug. 1796

Blank! Damn it! I am weary of complaining that I am weary. I will not make another memorandum until something happens, that is flat.[6] It is eleven days still to my departure! How shall I get over them?

# Autobiography (1763–92), 7 August–8 September 1796

T.C.D., Tone papers, MS 2046, ff $1^r$–$47^v$; *Life*, i, 11–58. A facsimile of f. $6^r$ is printed above as the frontispiece.

Writing this autobiography was Tone's response to the question posed in the closing lines of his Diary for 6 Aug. 1796: 'it is eleven days still to departure! How shall I get over them?'. His Diary entries for the following weeks are fewer and thinner than usual. In that for 24 Aug. he complains of further delay (see below, p. 309). In that for 2 Sept. he states: 'to divert the spleen which is

[1] Colley Cibber's adaptation of Shakespeare's *Richard III* (1700), v, iii.
[2] *Life*, ii, 175, has 'One thing I must keep in mind'.
[3] *Life* substitutes 'time' for 'march'.
[4] *Life* substitutes 'feel' for 'fret'.
[5] Amended in *Life* to 'Champs-Élysées'.
[6] In *Life* the remainder of the paragraph is omitted.

devouring me I have been these some days back throwing memorandums of my life and opinions on paper from recollection. They are very ill done and probably inaccurate in the dates, but they are better than nothing. I have already filled nearly two books.' (see below, p. 309). Six days later he writes: 'Scribbling now and again at my memoirs, which I have brought down to the beginning of 1792' (see below, p. 311).

## [Volume the First][1]
## [Memorandums relative to my life & opinions, 1796]
## [*Nil desperandum!*]
## Paris, August 7th, 1796

AS I shall embark in a business within a few days, the event of which is uncertain, I take the opportunity of a vacant hour to throw on paper a few memorandums relative to myself and my family which may amuse my boys, for whom I write them in case they should hereafter fall into their hands.

I was born in the city of Dublin on the 20th of June 1763. My grandfather[2] was a respectable farmer near Naas in the county of Kildare. Being killed by a fall of[f] a stack of his own corn in the year 1766, his property being freehold leases descended to my father[3], his eldest son, who was at that time in successful business as a coachmaker. He set, in consequence, the lands which came thus into his possession to his youngest brother,[4] which eventually was the cause of much litigation between them and ended in a decree of the Court of Chancery that utterly ruined my father's affairs;[5] but of that hereafter.[6] My mother,[7] whose name was Lamport, was the daughter of a captain of a vessel in the West India trade[8] who, by many anecdotes she has told me of him, was a great original. She had a brother who was an excellent seaman and served as first lieutenant on board of the *Buckingham*, commanded by Admiral Tyrrel,[9] a distinguished officer in the British service.[10]

[1] This and the following two headings are supplied to range with the volume headings below (p. 285 and p. 321).

[2] William Tone (1705?–66) was described as 'gentleman' when he leased land in Co. Kildare (later mortgaged for £100) from Andrew Nash in 1755. He died on 24 Apr. 1766 aged 60. (William Sherlock, 'Bodenstown graveyard' in *County Kildare Archaeological Society Journal*, vi, no. 3 (1910), p. 227; Registry of Deeds, Dublin, 488/296/310911).

[3] Peter Tone (d. 1805) was in business as a coachmaker as early as 1763, living in Liffey St. By 1768 his address was Stafford St., where he seems to have erected a dwelling house; he had some land at Drumcondra. (*Wilson's Dublin Directory*; Registry of Deeds, Dublin, 225/38/144986, 315/399/213962, 348/572/235501).

[4] Jonathan Tone (1754?–92).

[5] *Life*, i, 11, reads 'ruined my father'.

[6] See below, pp 281–2.

[7] Margaret Tone (d. 1818).

[8] Possibly James Lamport (d. 1747/8) of Dublin, mariner (Genealogical Office, Dublin, MS 808, p. 3).

[9] Richard Tyrrell (d. 1766), captain, 1743; rear-admiral, 1762; commanded the *Buckingham*, 1757–9; distinguished himself in an engagement with the *Florissant* (74 guns). The only Lamport or Lambert serving on the *Buckingham* under Tyrrell was Richard Lambert who entered the ship as a private of marines in 1759, became an able seaman, was discharged, Sept. 1760, and re-entered as able seaman, Oct. 1760 (John Charnock, *Biographia navalis* (6 vols, London, 1794–8); *The commissioned sea officers of the Royal Navy, 1660–1815* (3 vols, n.p., [1955?]); P.R.O., Adm. 33/548).

[10] The following paragraph is omitted from *Life*.

Both my father and mother were of ordinary understandings, which I mention because all their children, without exception, have had a certain degree of talents and particularly a romantic spirit of adventure, which I know not whence they inherited. My mother was a shrewd woman, and I think we rather copied her.[1] My father was extremely addicted to his pleasures, and in that all his sons, as yet, have faithfully followed his example.

I was the eldest,[2] but before I come to my history I must say a few words of my brothers. William, who was born in August 1764, was intended for business, and was in consequence bound apprentice at the age of 14 to an eminent bookseller. With him he read over all the voyages he could find, with which, and some military history, he heated an imagination naturally warm and enthusiastic so much that at the age of 16 he ran off to London and entered as a volunteer in the East India Company's service.[3] But his first essay was very unlucky, for instead of finding his way out to India, he was stopped at the island of St Helena, on which barren rock he remained in garrison for six years, when, his time being expired, he returned to Europe. It is highly to his honor that, tho' he entered into such execrable society as the troops in the Company's service must be supposed to be, and at such an early age, he passed thro' them without being affected by the contagion of their manners or their principles. He even found means, in that degraded situation and remote spot, to cultivate his mind to a certain degree, so that I was much surprised, at our meeting in London[4] after a separation of, I believe, eight years, to find him with the manners of a gentleman and a considerable acquaintance with the best parts of English literature. He had a natural turn for poetry, which he had much improved, and I have among my papers a volume of his poems, all of them pretty, and some of them elegant. He was a handsome, well-made lad, with a very good address, and extremely well received among the women, whom he loved to excess. He was brave as Cæsar, and loved the army. It was impossible for two men to entertain a more sincere and, I may say, enthusiastic affection for each other than he and I; and at this hour there is scarcely anything on earth I regret so much as our separation.

Having remained in Europe for three or four years, my father being as I have above alluded to utterly ruined by a lawsuit with his brother,[5] Will took the resolution to try his fortune once more in India, from which, my own affairs being nearly desperate, I did not attempt to dissuade him. In consequence he re-entered the Company's service in the beginning of the year 1792[6] and arrived at

[1] In 1771, Mrs Margaret Tone was granted a bishop's certificate testifying that she had conformed to the Church of Ireland (*The convert rolls*, ed. Eileen O'Byrne (Dublin, 1981), p. 169). Tone never mentions that his mother was born a catholic and so presumably her religious background was not emphasised in the family.

[2] *Life*, i, 12, has 'their eldest son'.

[3] In the list of troops embarked on the *Northumberland* for Madras in 1780 there appears the entry: name, William Tone; quality, private; county, Dublin; occupation, labourer; age, 15 (India Office Library, Mil/9/90, Embarkation lists, vi, 194).

[4] In the spring of 1788 (see below, p. 277).

[5] See also above, vol. I, p. xxvii.

[6] In one of his notebooks Tone recorded 'Will sailed to London on his way to India Feb^y 20, 1790'

Madrass towards the end of the same year.[1] With an advantageous figure, a good address, and the talents I have described, he recommended himself so far to the colonel of the battalion in which he served that he gave him his discharge, with letters to his friends at Calcutta and a small military command, which defrayed the expences of his voyage and procured him a gratification from the Company of £50 for his good behaviour on his arrival. The service he performed was quelling, at some hazard, a dangerous mutiny which arose among the black troops who were under his command and had formed a scheme to run away with the ship. He had the good fortune to recommend himself so far to the persons at Calcutta to whom he had brought letters that they introduced him with strong recommendations to a Mons[ieu]r Marigny,[2] a French officer, second in command in the army of the Nizam,[3] who was then at Calcutta purchasing military stores for that prince. Marigny in consequence gave him a commission in the Nizam's service, and promised him the command of a battalion of artillery (the service to which he was attached) as soon as they should arrive at the army. The stores, &c., being purchased, Will marched with the first division, of which he had the command, and arrived safely at the Nizam's camp. After some time Marigny followed him, but by an unforeseen accident all my brother's expectations were blown up. A quarrel took place between Marigny and the Frenchman first in command,[4] in which my brother with an honorable indiscretion engaged on the side of his friend. The consequence was that Marigny was put in irons, as would have been Will also, if he had not applied for protection as a British subject to the English Resident at the Nizam's court.[5] This circumstance, together with the breaking out of the war between England and France,[6] utterly put an end to all prospects of his advancement, as all the European officers in the Nizam's service were French, and he determined in consequence to return to Calcutta.

On his journey, having travelled 400 miles, and having yet 200 to travel, he alight[ed] off his horse and went to shoot in a jungle, or thick wood, by the road side. On his return he found his servant and horses in the hands of five ruffians who were plundering his baggage. He immediately ran up and fired on them, by

(T.C.D., MS 3805, f. 38ʳ). However, he must not have re-embarked in London for India, as Tone recorded on the next page '14th Feb^y, 1792, Will sailed for England on his way to India' (ibid., f. 38ᵛ).

[1] In the list of troops embarked on the *Melville Castle* in 1792 for Bengal appears the entry name, William Henry Tone, where enlisted, Town; County, Dublin; occupation, labourer (the occupation of the man named above is given as labourer. Tone is given as 'do', stroked through); Age, 24; Height, 5, 6 (India Office Library, Embarkation lists Mil/9/94/, xii, p. 84).

[2] It is possible that Marigny was the French gentleman in Raymond's corps in the nizam's service 'who had been an officer in the regiment at Pondicherry, but, openly professing his attachment to royalty', was dismissed (*The despatches . . . of the marquess Wellesley*, ed. M. Martin, i (London, 1836), pp 63–9).

[3] Ali Khan (d. 1803), nizam of Hyderabad, 1761–1803 (Hastings Fraser, *Our faithful ally, the nizam* (London, 1865), pp 30–32).

[4] François de Raymond (1755–98), who from 1786 commanded a large corps in the service of the nizam (Herbert Compton, *A particular account of the European military adventurers of Hindustan* (London, 1892), pp 382–6).

[5] Sir John Kennaway (1758–1836), soldier and diplomatist; aide-de-camp to Cornwallis, 1786; British Resident in Hyderabad, 1788–94; created baronet, 1791 (*D.N.B.*).

[6] On 1 Feb. 1793. The news would have taken some weeks to reach India.

which he shot one of them in the belly; another returned the fire with one of his pistols which they had seized and shot him thro' the foot; they then made off with their booty, and in this condition my brother had to travel 200 miles in that burning climate, at the commencement too of the rainy season, badly wounded and without resources. His courage, however, and a good constitution supported him, and he arrived at length at Calcutta, where he got speedily cured. His friends there had not forgot him, and after some time an opportunity offering of Major Palmer[1] going up to Poonah as Resident at the court of the Peishwa of the Mahrattahs,[2] they procured him strong recommendations to that court, and he set off with Major Palmer in high health and spirits, with expectation of the command at least of a battalion of artillery.[3] Such is the substance of the last letter which I received from him dated [ ].[4] Since that time I am utterly ignorant of his fate. I hope and trust the best of him; he has a good constitution, unshaken courage, a fluent address, and his variety of adventures must by this time have sufficiently matured his mind and given him experience. I look therefore with confidence to our meeting again, and the hour of that meeting will be one of the happiest of my life.[5]

My second brother, Mathew,[6] was of a temper very different from that of William; with less of surface[7] he was much more solid; he spoke little but thought a great deal; in the family we called him 'the Spectator', from his short face and his silence. But tho' he had not Will's volubility, and could not, like him, make a great display, with frequently little substance, and tho' his manner was reserved and phlegmatic, so as to be frequently absent in company, he had a rambling, enthusiastic spirit stronger than any one of us. He loved travelling and adventures for their own sakes. In consequence before he was twenty-four[8] he had visited England twice or three times, and had spent twelve months in America, and as much in the West Indies.[9] On his return from this last place, he mentioned to me his determination to pass over to France, and enter a volunteer in the service of the Republic, in which I encouraged and assisted him. This was in the month of

[1] William Palmer (1740–1816), lieut. col., 1794; British Resident at Lucknow, 1782–97, and at Sindhia's court, 1797–8 (V.C.P. Hodson, *List of the officers of the Bengal army, 1758–1834* (4 pts, London, 1927–47), iii, 452).

[2] The peishwa at that time was Mahdoo Rao (1774–95) (J. G. Duff, *History of the Mahrattas* (2 vols, Bombay, 1878)).

[3] William Henry Tone served in Boyd's corps in the service of the peishwa of Poona, 1796–1801. Captured at the siege of Sonda, he entered Holkar's service and was killed, 1802. He was the author of a work on the Mahrattas. (P. R. Butler, 'William Henry Tone' in *Studies*, xxxv (1946), pp 259–62).

[4] In the MS a gap of 5 cm is left here. *Life* omits 'dated'.

[5] For more on William Henry Tone, see W. H. Tone to Peter Tone, 1 and 25 June 1797 (Madden, *United Irishmen*, 3rd series (1846), i, 179–82), Diary for 1 May 1798 (below, vol. III) and W. H. Tone to Matilda Tone, 2 Jan. 1800 (*Life*, ii, 560–62).

[6] Mathew Tone (1771–98). In *Life* his name is spelt 'Matthew' throughout.

[7] In *Life*, i, 14, 'fire' is substituted for 'surface'.

[8] *Life*, i, 14, has 'twenty-five'.

[9] In one of his notebooks Tone recorded: 'Matt left Ireland 23d March 1789, returned July 17, 1790'; 'Matt sailed for England, Sept. 7, returned 30, 1790'; 'Matt sailed for England May 6, 1791, returned June 15th, 1791'; '24th [Feb^y^ 1792] Matt sailed for England on way to America, March 1st, 1793, returned to Ireland' (T.C.D., MS 3805, ff 38^r^–38^v^); 'Aug^t^ 3d, 1793, M. T. sailed for Liverpoole' (ibid. f. 42^r^).

August 1794. In consequence he crossed over to Hamburg whence he passed to Dunkirk, and presenting himself as an Irishman desirous of the honor of serving in the French armies, he was immediately thrown into prison on suspicion. There he remained until May 1795, when he was discharged by order of the Committee of Public Safety, and going on to Havre de Grâce he took his passage to America, where he arrived in safety, for the second time, about Christmass, at which time I was actually at New York, waiting for my passage to France; so that we were together in America without knowing of each other, a circumstance which I regret most exceedingly, as, in the present situation of my affairs, it is at least possible that we my never meet again;[1] but I am not of a very desponding temper. The variety of adventures we have both gone thro', and the escapes we have had in circumstances of great peril, have made me a kind of fatalist, and therefore I look with confidence to the day, and I hope not a very remote one, when the whole of my family shall be reunited and happy, by which time I think the spirit of adventure will or at least ought to be pretty well laid in all of us.

My brother Mathew, like Will, is something of a poet, and has written some trifles in the burlesque style that are not ill done. He is a brave lad, and I love him most sincerely. His age, at the time I write this, is about 26 or 27 years. Mathew is a sincere and ardent republican and capable, as I think, of sacrificing everything to his principles. I know not what effect his lying so long in a French prison may have had on him, but if I do not deceive myself it has made no change in his sentiments.[2] He is more temperate in all respects than William or myself, for we have both a strong attachment to pleasures and amusements, and a dash of coxcombry from which he is totally free; and perhaps a little, at least, of the latter foible would be of no prejudice to him, nor render him less agreeable.

My third brother, Arthur, is much younger than any of us, being born about the year 1782; of course he is now 14 years of age.[3] If I can judge, when he grows up, he will resemble William exactly in mind and person. He is a fine smart boy, as idle as possible (which we have all been, without exception) with very quick parts and as stout as a lion. My father was bent on making him an attorney, for which no boy on earth was ever in all respects[4] so unfitted. He wished himself (having the true vagrant turn of the family) to go to sea; his father was obstinate, so was he, and the boy was in a fair way to be lost, when I prevailed, with some difficulty, on his father to consent to his going at least one voyage; in consequence he sailed with a Captain Meyler[5] to Portugal, being then about twelve years of age. On his return he liked the sea so well that he was bound regularly apprentice

[1] In fact they did meet again, probably in Jan. 1798 (see Diary for 1 Feb. 1798, below, vol. III).

[2] Mathew Tone joined Humbert's expedition to Ireland in 1798, was captured near Ballinamuck, tried by court martial for 'having acted traitourously, rebelliously and hostilely against his majesty's government' and hanged in Dublin on 29 Sept. 1798 (see below, vol. III).

[3] For more on Arthur Tone, see above, p. 37.

[4] *Life* omits 'in all respects'.

[5] Possibly Captain Philip Myler of the *Lovely Mary* (*H.J.*, 5 Jan. 1789; *Lloyd's List*, 16 May 1794).

to Captain Meyler, under whom he made a voyage to London, and a second voyage to Portugal. On his return from this last[1] in June 1795, he found me at Belfast on my stop[2] for America and he determined to accompany me. I was extremely happy to have him with us, and in consequence he crossed the Atlantic with me, and remained until I decided on coming to France, when I resolved to dispatch him to Ireland to give notice to my friends there of what I was about. I put him in consequence on board the *Susannah*, Cap[tai]n Baird, at Philadelphia on the 10th December 1795,[3] since which time, from circumstances, it has been impossible for me to have heard of him, but I rely with confidence that he has arrived safe and discharged his commission with ability and discretion.[4]

My sister, whose name is Mary, is a fine young woman; she has all the peculiarity of our disposition, with all the delicacy of her own sex. If she were a man, she would be exactly like one of us; and as it is, being brought up among boys, for we never had but one more sister, who died a child,[5] she has contracted a masculine habit of thinking, without however in any degree derogating from that feminine softness of manner which is suited to her sex and age. When I was driven into exile in America, as I shall relate hereafter, she determined to share my fortunes, and in consequence she also, like the rest of us, has made her voyage across the Atlantic.[6]

I have said,[7] my father and mother were pretty much like other people; but from this short sketch, with what I have to add concerning myself, I think it will appear that their children are not at all like other people, but have had, every one of them, a wild spirit of adventure, which, tho' sometimes found in an individual, rarely pervades a whole family, including even the females. For my brother William has [*sic*] visited Europe, Asia and Africa before he was thirty years of age. Mathew has been in America twice, in the West Indies once, not to mention several trips to England and his voyage and imprisonment in France, and all this before he was 27. Arthur, at the age of 14, has been once in England, twice in Portugal, and has twice crossed the Atlantic, going to and returning from America. My sister has crossed the same ocean and I hope will soon do the same on her return. I do not here speak of my wife and our little boys and girl, the eldest of whom was about 8, and the youngest two years old, when we sailed for America, And by all I can see it is by no means certain that our voyages are yet entirely finished.

1 *Life*, i, 16, inserts 'trip'.

2 In ibid. 'departure' is substituted for 'stop'.

3 The *Susanna*, 300 tons burden, Captain William Baird master, took 28 days on the passage from Philadelphia to Belfast. After her arrival in Belfast fourteen passengers published a notice recording their thanks to the captain for a pleasant passage. (*N.S.*, 21, 25 Jan. 1796).

4 He did so. See Margaret Tone to Thomas Russell, prob. 26 Jan. 1796 (above, pp 37–8).

5 Fanny, born *c.*1784, died of consumption before Tone left Ireland for America (*Life*, ii, 561).

6 Mary Tone was to accompany Matilda Tone back to Europe and to marry a Swiss merchant, Jean Frédéric Giauque (see T. W. Tone to Matilda Tone, 13 Jan. 1797, below, vol. III).

7 Above, p. 262. The preceding three words are omitted from *Life*.

I come now to myself. I was, as I have said, the eldest child of my parents and a very great favorite. I was sent at the age of eight or nine to an excellent English school, kept by Sisson Darling,[1] a man to whose kindness and affection I was much indebted, and who took more than common pains with me. I respect him yet. I was very idle, and it was only the fear of shame which could induce me to exertion. Nevertheless at the approach of our public examinations, which were held quarterly and at which all our parents and friends attended, I used to labour for some time, and generally with success, as I have obtained six or seven premiums in different branches at one examination, as Mathematics, Arithmetic, Reading, Spelling, Recitation, Use of the Globes, &c. In two branches I always failed, Writing and the Catechism, to which last I never could bring myself to apply. Having continued with Mr Darling for about three years, and pretty nearly exhausted the circle of English education, he recommended strongly to my father to put me to a Latin school, and to prepare me for the University, assuring him that I was a fine boy, of uncommon talents, particularly for the Mathematics; that it was a thousand pities to throw me away on business, when by giving me a liberal education, there was a moral certainty I should become a fellow of Trinity College, which was a noble independance besides the glory of the situation. In these arguments he was supported by the parson of the parish, Doctor Jameson,[2] a worthy man, who used to examine me from time to time in the *Elements* of Euclid. My father who, to do him justice, loved me passionately, and spared no expence on me that his circumstances would afford, was easily persuaded by these authorities.

It was determined I should be a fellow of Dublin College.[3] I was taken from Mr Darling, from whom I parted with regret, and placed about the age of twelve under the care of the Revd Will[ia]m Craig,[4] a man very different in all respects from my late preceptor. As the school was in the same street (Stafford St.) where we lived, and as I was under my father's eye, I began Latin with ardor, and continued for a year or two with great diligence, when I began Greek, which I found still more to my taste; but about this time, whether unluckily for me or not the future colour of my life must determine, my father,[5] who had for some years

[1] Sisson Putland Darling (1737–1817) had a mercantile academy at 35 and 36 Mabbot St., Dublin, until *c.*1785 and from *c.*1792 at the Strand; he became in the early 1790s a senior employee of the Grand Canal Co.; a fine penman, he engrossed documents for Dublin corporation. According to John Binns (1772–1860), who attended the school, it had a high reputation; he remarks that it was Darling's practice every quarter day to read out publicly in the school 'the name of every scholar whose bill for schooling was more than one quarter unpaid'. (*Wilson's Dublin Directory*; John Binns, *Recollections* (Philadelphia, 1854), p. 20; J. T. Gilbert (ed.), *Calendar of ancient records of Dublin* (19 vols, Dublin, 1889–1944), xv, 39, 123; Genealogical Office, Dublin, MS 177, p. 416; see above, vol. I, p. 443).

[2] Thomas Jameson (d. 1789) entered T.C.D., 1763; graduated B.A., 1768; M.A., 1772; curate of St Mary's, Dublin, 1774–87 (*Alumni Dubl.*; Representative Church Body Library, Dublin, J. B. Leslie's list of Dublin diocesan clergy).

[3] i.e. Trinity College, Dublin.

[4] William Craig (d. 1780) entered T.C.D., 1764; graduated B.A., 1769; ordained, 1769; schoolmaster in Castle St., Dublin (*Alumni Dubl.*; Representative Church Body Library, Dublin, J. B. Leslie's list of Dublin diocesan clergy).

[5] The following clause, as far as 'dissipated and irregular life', is omitted from *Life*.

entirely neglected his business and led a very dissipated and irregular life, meeting with an accident of a fall down stairs, by which he was dreadfully wounded in the head, so that he narrowly escaped with life, found on his recovery his affairs so deranged in all respects that he determined on quitting business and retiring to the country,[1] a resolution which he executed accordingly, settling with all his creditors and placing me with a friend near the school, whom he paid for my diet and lodging, besides allowing me a trifling sum for my pocket. In this manner I became, I may say, my own master before I was sixteen, and as, at this hour, I am not remarkable for my discretion, it may well be judged I was less so then. The superintendance of my father being removed, I began to calculate that, according to the slow rate chalked out for me by Craig, I could very well do the business of the week in three days, or even two if necessary, and that consequently the other three were lawful prize. I therefore resolved to appropriate three days at least in the week to my amusements, and the others to school, always keeping in the latter three the day of repetition, which included the business of the whole week, by which arrangement I kept my rank with the other boys of my class. I found no difficulty in convincing half a dozen of my schoolfellows of the justice of this distribution of our time, and by this means we established a regular system of what is called 'mitching'; and we contrived, being some of the smartest boys at school, to get an ascendancy over the spirit of the master, so that when we entered the school in a body after one of our days of relaxation, he did not chuse to burn his fingers with any one of us, nor did he even once write to my father to inform him of my proceedings, for which he most certainly was highly culpable. I must do myself and my schoolfellows the justice to say that, tho' we were abominably idle, we were not vicious; our amusements consisted in walking to the country, in swimming parties in the sea, and particularly in attending all parades, field days and reviews of the garrison of Dublin in the Ph[o]enix Park. I mention this particularly because, independant of confirming me in a rooted habit of idleness, which I lament most exceedingly, I trace to the splendid appearance of the troops, and the pomp and parade of military shew, the untameable desire I have ever since had to become a soldier, a desire which has never once quit me, and which after sixteen years of various adventures, I am at last at liberty to indulge.

Being at this time approaching seventeen years of age, it will not be thought incredible that woman began to appear lovely in my eyes, and I very wisely thought that a red coat and cockade with a pair of gold epaulettes would aid me considerably in my approaches to the objects of my adoration. This, combined with the reasons above mentioned, decided me. I began to look on classical learning as nonsense, on a fellowship of Dublin College as a pitiful establishment; and, in short, I thought an ensign in a marching regiment was the happiest creature living. The hour when I was to enter the university, which now approached, I looked forward to with horror and disgust; I absented myself more and more

[1] i.e. to Bodenstown, Co. Kildare.

from school, to which I preferred attending the recruits on drill at the Barracks, so that at length my schoolmaster, who apprehended I should be found insufficient at the examination for entering the College and that he, of consequence, would come in for his share of the disgrace, thought proper to do what he should have done at least three years before and wrote my father a full account of my proceedings. This immediately produced a violent dispute between us. I declared my passion for the army and my utter dislike to a learned profession, but my father was as obstinate as I, and as he utterly refused to give me any assistance to forward my scheme, I had no resource but to submit or to follow my brother William's example, which I was too proud to do. In consequence I sat down again, with a very bad grace, to pull up my lost time; and, at length, after labouring for some time, sorely against the grain, I entered a pensioner of Trinity College in February 1781,[1] being then not quite eighteen years of age.

My tutor was the Revd Mathew Young,[2] the most popular in the University, and one of the first mathematicians in Europe. At first I began to study logic courageously, but unluckily, at my very first examination, I happened to fall into the hands of an egregious dunce, one Ledwich,[3] who instead of giving me the premium which, as best answerer, I undoubtedly merited, awarded it to another, and to me very indifferent judgements.[4] I did not stand in need of this piece of injustice to alienate me once more from my studies. I returned with eagerness to my military plan; I besought my father to equip me as a volunteer, and to suffer me to join the British army in America, where the war[5] still raged. He refused me, as before, and in revenge I would not go near the College, nor open a book that was not a military one. In this manner we continued for above a twelvemonth, on very bad terms, as may be well supposed, without either party relaxing an inch from their determination. At length, seeing the war in America drawing to a close, and being beset by some of my friends who surrounded me, particularly Dr Jameson, whom I have already mentioned,[6] and a Mr G. J. Brown,[7] who had been sub-master at Mr Darling's academy and was now become a lawyer, I submitted a second time and returned to my studies, after an interval of above a year. To punish me for my obstinacy I was obliged to submit to *drop a class*, as it is called in the University; that is, to recommence with the students who had entered a year after me. I continued my studies at College as I had done at school, that is, I idled until the last moment of delay; I then laboured hard for

[1] See above, vol. I, p. 1.

[2] Matthew Young (1750–1800), fellow of T.C.D., 1775–98; bishop of Clonfert, 1798–1800, and author of several works (*D.N.B.*).

[3] The fellows were the examiners at the quarterly examinations, but the T.C.D. Term and Examination Book gives 'Mr Ledwich' as examining a division of Junior Freshmen at the Easter examination of 1781. He was probably Edward Ledwich who graduated B.A. in 1774 (*Alumni Dubl.*).

[4] Tone's level of answering at the quarterly examinations was high. See below, p. 270, n. 1.

[5] The war of American independence, 1775–83.

[6] See above, p. 267.

[7] George Joseph Brown (d. 1793), called to the Irish bar, 1784; member of the Dublin Society of United Irishmen (R. B. McDowell, 'The personnel of the Dublin Society of United Irishmen' in *I.H.S.*, ii, no. 5 (Mar. 1940), p. 22).

about a fortnight before the public examinations, and I always secured good judgements, besides obtaining three premiums in the three last years of my course.[1]

During my progress thro' the University I was not without adventures. Towards the latter end of the year 1782, I went out as second to a young fellow of my acquaintance of the name of Foster who fought with another lad, also of my acquaintance, named Anderson, and had the misfortune to shoot him thro' the head.[2] The second to Anderson was William Armstrong,[3] my most particular friend, who is now a very respectable clergyman & settled at Dungannon. As Anderson's friends were outrageous against Foster and me, we were obliged at first to withdraw ourselves, but after some time their passion abated, and I returned to College, whence this adventure was near driving me a second time and for ever. Foster stood his trial, and was acquitted; against me there was no prosecution. In this unfortunate business the eldest of us was not more than twenty years of age.[4]

After one or two fugitive passions,[5] about the beginning of the year 1783 I fell in love with a woman who made me miserable for near two years. She was the wife of Richard Martin of Galway,[6] a member of parliament & a man of considerable fortune in that county.[7] Martin was passionately fond of acting and had fitted up a theatre on which he had several dramatic representations. Mrs Martin, independent of a thousand other attractions, was one of the first actresses I ever saw, and as I lived in the house with her and, being myself somewhat of an actor, was daily thrown into particular situations with her, both in rehearsals and on the stage, and as I had an imagination easily warmed, without one grain of discretion to regulate it, I very soon became in love to a degree almost inconceivable. I have never never met in history, poetry or romance a description that comes near what I actually suffered on her account for two years that our acquaintance continued, in which time I made three visits to her house of four or five months each. As I was utterly unable, and indeed unwilling, to conceal my passion from her,

[1] Although he dropped three successive terms during 1782–3 and did not take his final examination until Michaelmas 1785, Tone's academic record was excellent; he almost always received the highest 'judgement' in all subjects and was awarded three premiums (T.C.D., MUN V/27/3).

[2] Neither Anderson nor Foster (or Forster) seems to have been an undergraduate at T.C.D. (*Alumni Dubl.*).

[3] William Jones Armstrong (1764?–1827?), educated at Craig's school; entered T.C.D., 1781; graduated B.A., 1786; curate of Dungannon, Co. Tyrone, 1793; rector of Termonfechin, Co. Louth, 1805–27?; married Margaret, daughter of Alderman John Tew, sometime lord mayor of Dublin (*Alumni Dubl.*; J. B. Leslie, *Armagh clergy and parishes* (Dundalk, 1911), p. 419).

[4] In an account of Tone's early career in *Faulkner's Dublin Journal*, 22 Nov. 1798, signed 'P. H.', there is a reference to Tone 'being concerned in a duel between two of his school-fellows which terminated badly for one of them, a boy of fourteen years of age'.

[5] The whole of this paragraph and the following one are omitted from *Life*.

[6] Elizabeth Martin (d. 1796?), daughter of George Vesey of Lucan, Co. Dublin, and from 1777 until 1793 the wife of Richard Martin of Dangan, Co. Galway (Shevawn Lynam, *Humanity Dick: a biography of Richard Martin* (London, 1975)).

[7] According to 'P. H.', during his forced absence from Trinity College Tone was 'tutor in the family of Mr Martin of Dangan' (*Faulkner's Dublin Journal*, 22 Nov. 1798).

she very soon detected me, and as I preserved, as well as felt, the profoundest respect for her, she supposed she might amuse herself innocently in observing the progress of this terrible passion in the mind of an interesting young man of twenty. But this is an experiment no woman ought to make. As Martin neglected her a good deal, and as I was continually on the spot, she could not avoid making daily comparisons between our behaviour towards her, and not at all to the advantage of her husband. In short, without any art on my side, for I was too sincerely in love to be capable of it, I insensibly engaged her affections, so that at length she became at least as much in love with me as I was with her, nor did she attempt to conceal it from me. I was the proudest man alive to have engaged the affections of a woman whom even now I recognise to have had extraordinary merit and who then appeared in my eyes more divine than human. In this intercourse of sentiment, which alternately pained and delighted me almost beyond bearing, we continued for about two years, keeping up a regular correspondence by letters in the intervals of my absence, without however in a single instance overstepping the bounds of virtue, such was the purity of the extravagant affection I bore her. At length a quarrel took place between Martin and me. He wanted me to swear an affidavit against two ruffians who had broke into his apartment, armed with pistols, and arrested him in my presence. This I considered as derogatory to my character, and in consequence I refused. A smart altercation by letter ensued in which he tried every means, not excepting pretty direct menaces (as he was a famous duellist), to bend me to his purpose. But tho' I was very young, tho' I adored his wife beyond all human beings,[1] and knew well that my refusal was in effect a sentence of banishment from her presence for ever, I had the courage to persist in my refusal. In consequence I wrote Martin a peremptory letter which finished our correspondence and sealed, as I expected, our separation for ever. And thus at the age of twenty I sacrificed a passion of the most extravagant violence to what I considered my duty as a man of honor, an effort which cost me then very, very dear, and for which I now applaud my resolution. I have never seen Mrs Martin since.

As I am on this subject, tho' it makes no part of my own history, I think right to insert that, eight or nine years after, Martin and his wife being at Paris, and he treating her with his usual neglect, she formed a connection with an Englishman of the name of Petrie,[2] with whom at length she eloped. Martin brought an action against Petrie in Westminster Hall and recovered £10,000 damages.[3] In this business I am satisfied, from my own observation and knowledge of the characters of both parties during my residence for many months in their family, that the fault

[1] In the MS half a line is crossed out and 'all human beings' inserted above.

[2] John Petrie of Essex, a merchant.

[3] The case was heard on 14 Dec. 1791. It was asserted on Martin's behalf that for fourteen years he and his wife had lived together most happily. But when in 1790 he had had to return to Ireland because of the general election, leaving her in Paris, she had been seduced by John Petrie, 'a man of very general gallantry'. In the action Martin obtained £10,000 damages and in June 1793 the marriage was dissolved. (*Ten thousand pounds !!!: trial between Richard Martin, Esq., . . . and John Petrie, Esq., . . . for criminal conversation* . . . (Dublin, 1792); *Journals of the house of lords*, xxxix, 715).

was originally Martin's. Nevertheless it opened my eyes on many little circumstances which had passed between her and me, and perhaps (as I now think) had my passion for her been less pure, it might have been not less agreeable. But the truth is I loved her with an affection of a seraphic nature; the profound respect I bore her, and my ignorance of the world, prevented my availing myself of opportunities which a man more trained than I was would not have let slip. And now that at this distance of time I review the affair coolly,[1] I cannot regret that my inexperience prevented me from wronging a man to whom I was indebted for many civilities, or from profiting, as I might have done, of the affections of a woman, at that time undoubtedly virtuous, whom I adored as a deity and who, I am sure, returned my affection with an ardour equal to my own. But if I suffered, as I did most severely, by this unfortunate passion, I also reaped some benefit from it: the desire to render myself agreeable to a woman of elegant manners and a mind highly cultivated induced me to attend to a thousand little things and to endeavour to polish myself in a certain degree, so that after the first transports of rage and grief at her loss had subsided, I considered myself as on the whole considerably improved; and as no human passion is proof against time and absence, in a few months I recovered my tranquillity.[2]

At length, about the beginning of the year 1785, I became acquainted with my wife. She was the daughter of William Witherington,[3] and lived at that time in Grafton St. in the house of her grandfather, a rich old clergyman of the name of Fanning.[4] I was then a scholar of the house in the University, and every day after Commons[5] I used to walk under her windows with one or other of my fellow students. I soon became passionately fond of her, and she also was struck with me, tho' certainly my appearance, neither then nor now, was much in my favor; so it was however that before we had ever spoken to each other, a mutual affection had commenced between us. She was at this time not sixteen years of age, and as beautiful as an angel. She had a brother[6] some years elder than herself, a most egregious coxcomb;[7] nevertheless as it was necessary for my admission to the

[1] In the MS at this point one line is crossed out. [2] End of omission from *Life*.

[3] William Witherington (d. 1793?) of 68 or 69 Grafton St., Dublin, was a woollen draper, 1774–84, and a wine merchant or merchant, 1785–93; he represented the merchants' guild on the Dublin Common Council (*Wilson's Dublin Directory*, 1774–94; H. F. Reynolds, 'Witherington of Dublin' in *Notes and Queries*, 12th ser., ix, no. 170 (16 July 1921), p. 43).

[4] Edward Fanning (1709?–91), vicar of Dungiven, Co. Londonderry, 1751–91. In his will dated 9 July 1790 he mentions his daughter Catherine Witherington and granddaughter Matilda Tone (H. F. Reynolds, 'Fanning of Dublin' in *Notes and Queries*, 12th ser., vii, no. 131 (16 Oct. 1920), p. 307; J. B. Leslie, *Derry clergy and parishes* (Enniskillen, 1937), p. 119). In one of Tone's notebooks there is, in Tone's hand, a recipe, 'To distil whiskey from wheat', followed by 'Rev[d] Edw[d] Fanning, July 1, 1790' (T.C.D., MS 3805, f. 23).

[5] The evening dinner in Trinity College dining-hall.

[6] Edward Witherington (1765–1832), eldest child of William Witherington; entered T.C.D., 1779; graduated B.A., 1784; lieut, 5th dragoons, 1785; capt., 9th dragoons, 1791; major, 1797; lieut col., 1802; died of cholera. Thomas Reynolds junior, a man of strong family feeling, asserts in his life of his father that Witherington behaved badly to his brother-in-law, Thomas Reynolds senior, also that Witherington, after retiring from the army, speculated on the stock exchange. (*Gent. Mag.*, cii (1832), pt II, p. 190; Thomas Reynolds, junr, *Life of Thomas Reynolds* (2 vols, London, 1839), i, 114–33, ii, 246–7, 453–5).

[7] *Life* omits 'a most egregious coxcomb' and substitutes 'and' for 'nevertheless'.

family that I should be first acquainted with him, I soon contrived to be introduced to him, and as he played well on the violin (his only talent),[1] and as I was myself a musical man,[2] we soon grew intimate, the more so as, it may be well supposed, I neglected no fair means to recommend myself to him and the rest of the family, with whom I soon grew a favorite. My affairs now advanced prosperously; my wife and I grew more passionately fond of each other, and in a short time I proposed to her to marry me, without asking consent of any one, knowing well it would be in vain to expect it. She accepted the proposal as frankly as I made it, and one beautiful morning in the month of July we ran off together and were married.[3] I carried her out of town to Maynooth for a few days, and when the first *éclat* of passion had subsided, we were forgiven on all sides, and settled in lodgings near my wife's grandfather's.

I was now, for a very short time, as happy as possible in the possession of a beautiful creature that I adored, and who every hour grew more and more upon my heart. The scheme of a fellowship, which I never relished, was now abandoned, and it was determined that when I had taken my degree of Batchelor of Arts, I should go to the Temple,[4] study the law, and be called to the Bar. I continued in consequence my studies in the University, and obtained my last premium two or three months after I was married. In February 1786 I commenced Batchelor of Arts,[5] and shortly after I resigned my scholarship and quit the University. I may observe here that I made some figure as a scholar and should have been much more successful if I had not been so inveterately idle, partly owing to my passion for a military life, and partly to the distractions to which my natural disposition and temperament but too much exposed me. As it was, however, I obtained a scholarship, three premiums, and three silver medals from the Historical Society, a most admirable institution, of which I had the honor to be Auditor and also to close the session with a speech from the chair,[6] the highest compliments which that society is used to bestow. I look back on my College days with regret, and I preserve and ever shall a most sincere affection for the University of Dublin.

But to return. The tranquil and happy life I spent for a short period after my marriage was too good to last. My wife's brother,[7] jealous of the affection which her grandfather bore her and of the esteem he was beginning to entertain for me, notwithstanding my irregular introduction into the family, contrived by a thousand indirect means to sow feuds and dissensions between us, and at length succeeded so far that we were obliged to break off all connexion with my wife's family, who began to treat us with all possible slight and disrespect. We removed

[1] *Life* omits 'his only talent'.

[2] According to Madden, 'Tone was passionately fond of music, though a very indifferent performer on his favourite instrument—the flute' (R. R. Madden, *The United Irishmen*, 2nd ed. (4 vols, London, 1857–60), ii, 25).

[3] On 21 July 1785 at St Ann's Church, Dublin (see above, vol. I, p. 3).

[4] The Middle Temple in London.

[5] The degree of B.A. was conferred on Tone on 28 Feb. 1786 (T.C.D., Registry of degrees, 1743–1834). See above, vol. I, p. 4.

[6] Above, vol. I, pp 18–22.

[7] From 'my wife's brother' to 'so far that' is omitted from *Life*.

in consequence to my father's, who then resided near Clain[1] in the County of Kildare, and whose circumstances could at that time but ill bear such an addition to his family. It is doing him, however, but justice to mention that he received and treated us with the greatest affection and kindness, and as far as he was able endeavoured to make us forget the grievous mortifications we had undergone from my wife's family.[2] After an interval of a few months my wife was brought to bed of a girl,[3] a circumstance which, if possible, increased my love for her a thousandfold; but our tranquillity was again broken in upon by a most terrible event.[4] On the 16th[5] of October 1786 the house was broke open by a gang of robbers to the number of six, armed with pistols and having their faces blacked. Having tied the whole family, they proceeded to plunder and demolish every article they could find, even to the unprofitable villainy of breaking the china, looking glasses, &c. At length after two hours, a maidservant whom they had tied negligently having made her escape, they took the alarm and fled with precipitation, leaving the house such a scene of horror and confusion as can hardly be imagined. With regard to myself, it is impossible to conceive what I suffered. As it was early in the night, I happened to be in the courtyard, where I was seized and tied by the gang, who then proceeded to break into the house, leaving a ruffian sentinel over me, with a case of pistols cocked in his hand. In this situation I lay for two hours, and could hear distinctly the devastation which was going forward within. I expected death every instant, and I can safely and with great truth declare that my apprehension for my wife had so totally absorbed the whole of my apprehensions,[6] that my own existence was just then the least of my concern. When the villains, including my sentry, ran off, I scrambled on my feet with some difficulty and made my way to a window, where I called but received no answer. My heart died within me. I proceeded to another and another, but still no answer. It was horrible! I set myself to gnaw the cords with which I was tied in a transport of agony and rage, for I verily believed that my whole family lay murdered within, when I was relieved from my unspeakable terror and anguish by my wife's voice, which I heard calling on my name at the end of the house. It seems that as soon as the robbers fled, those within had untied each other with some difficulty, and made their escape thro' a back window; they had got a considerable distance from the house before, in their fright, they recollected me, of whose fate they were utterly ignorant, as I was of theirs. Under these terrible circumstances my wife had the courage to return, alone and in the dark, to find me out, not knowing but she might again fall into the hands of the villains from which she had scarcely escaped, or that I might be lying a lifeless carcase at the threshold. I can imagine no greater effort of courage; but of what is not a woman capable for him she truly

[1] At Bodenstown, about 3 km south of Clane. Peter Tone's house was situated opposite the ruined parish church.

[2] *Life* omits the preceding four words.

[3] Maria Tone (1786–1803).

[4] A report of the event described by Tone in the following appeared in *H.J.*, 30 Oct. 1786, and is reprinted above, vol. I, pp 4–5.

[5] *H.J.*, 30 Oct. 1786, gives the date as 'Thursday the 19th of October'.

[6] In *Life*, i, 23, 'mind' is substituted for 'apprehensions'.

loves? She cut the cords which bound me, and at length we joined the rest of the family at a little hamlet within half a mile of the house, whither they had fled for shelter. Of all the adventures wherein I have been hitherto engaged, this undoubtedly was the most horrible. It makes me shudder even now to think of it. It was some consolation that none of us sustained any personal injury, except my father, whom one of the villains scarred on the side of the head with a knife. They respected the women, whose danger made my only fear, and one of them had even the humanity to carry our little daughter from her cradle where she lay screaming and to place her beside my wife on the bed whereon she was tied with my mother and sister. This terrible scene, besides infinitely distressing us otherwise by the heavy loss we sustained and which my father's circumstances could very ill bear, destroyed in a great degree our domestic enjoyments. I slept continually with a case of pistols at my pillow, and a mouse could not stir that I was not on my feet and thro' the house from top to bottom. If anyone knocked at the door after nightfall, we flew to our arms, and in this manner we kept a most painful garrison thro' the winter. I should observe that two of the ruffians, being taken in an unsuccessful attempt within a few days after our robbery, were hanged, and that my father's watch was found on one of them.[1]

At length when our affairs were again reduced into some little order, my father supplied me with a small sum of money, which was however as much as he could spare,[2] and I set off for London, leaving my wife and daughter with my father, who treated them during my absence with great affection.[3] My wife's family, tho' they were in great affluence and well knew our embarrassments, refused to give us the least assistance. I was more than once tempted to give her brother,[4] who was now become a captain of dragoons, a severe caning, and indeed I spoke to him more than once in a manner that indicated as much; however, he was of a peaceable disposition, and the reflection of his near affinity to my wife tying my hands, the business came to nothing.

After a dangerous passage to Liverpool, wherein we ran some risque of being lost, I arrived in London in January 1787, and immediately entered my name as a student at law on the books of the Middle Temple;[5] but this I may say was all the progress I ever made in that profession. I had no great affection for study in general, but that of the law I particularly disliked, and to this hour I think it an illiberal profession both in its principles and practice. I was likewise amenable to nobody for my conduct; and, in consequence, after the first month I never opened a law book nor was I ever three times in Westminster Hall in my life. In

[1] Michael Casey and John Walsh were arrested in Lucan on 25 Oct. 1786 for breaking into a shop in Leixlip and were lodged in Kilmainham jail. Among articles found in their possession was a silver watch. At the Kildare autumn assizes of 1787 Thomas Casey was convicted of having in company of others robbed 'the house of Mr Tone near Sallins' of articles worth £450 and sentenced to death. (*H.J.*, 1 Nov. 1786, 20 Aug. 1787).

[2] It was said that Tone's wealthy neighbour, Richard Griffith, made up the deficiency (see above, vol. I, p. 502, n. 1).

[3] In *Life* the words which follow up to and including 'the business came to nothing' are omitted.

[4] Edward Witherington.

[5] On 3 Feb. 1787 (see above, vol. I, p. 5).

addition to the reasons I have mentioned, the extreme uncertainty of my circumstances, which kept me in much uneasiness of mind, disabled me totally from that cool and systematic habit of study which is indispensable for attaining a knowledge of a science so abstruse and difficult as that of the English code. However, one way or other I contrived to make it out. I had chambers in the Temple (No. 4 Hare Court)[1] on the first floor, and, whatever difficulties I had otherwise to struggle with, I contrived always to preserve the appearance of a gentleman and to maintain my rank with my fellow students, if I can call myself a student. One resource I derived from the exercise of my talents, such as they were. I wrote several articles for the *European Magazine*,[2] mostly critical reviews of new publications. My reviews were but poor performances enough; however they were in general as good as those of my brother critics, and in two years I received, I suppose, about fifty pounds for my writings, which was my main object, for as to literary fame I had then no great ambition to obtain it. I likewise, in conjunction with two of my friends, named Jebb[3] and Radcliff,[4] wrote a burlesque novel, which we called 'Belmont Castle', and was intended to ridicule the execrable trash of the circulating libraries. It was tolerably well done, particularly Radcliff's part, which was by far the best; yet so it was that we could not find a bookseller who would risque the printing it, tho' we offered the copyright *gratis* to several. It was afterwards printed in Dublin, and had some success, but I believe after all it was most relished by the authors and their immediate connexions.[5]

At the Temple I became intimate with several young men of situation and respectability, particularly with the Hon[ble] George Knox, son of Lord Northland, with whom I formed a friendship of which I am as proud as of any circumstance of my life. He is a man of inappreciable merit, and loved to a degree of enthusiasm by all who have the happiness to know him. I scarcely know any one person whose esteem and approbation I covet so much; and I had, long after the commencement of our acquaintance, when I was in circumstances of peculiar

[1] Charles Lamb describes Hare Court, some years after Tone resided there, as 'a gloomy churchyard-like court . . . with three trees and a pump in it' (H. B. Wheatley, *London past and present* (3 vols, London, 1891), ii, 191).

[2] The *European Magazine and London Review* ran from Jan. 1782 to June 1826. It has not been found possible to identify positively Tone's articles. A cautious attempt to do so has been made by Marion Deane in the introduction to her edition of *Belmont Castle* (Dublin, 1998), pp 6, 23–4, 29, where a likely attribution to Tone is the review of Charlotte Smith's *Emmeline* (1788) which appeared in the *European Magazine*, Nov. 1788, p. 348.

[3] Richard Jebb (1766–1834) entered T.C.D., 1781; B.A., 1786; called to the Irish bar, 1789; justice of the king's bench, 1818–34 (*D.N.B.* art. on John Jebb; F. E. Ball, *The judges in Ireland* (2 vols, London, 1926), ii, 340).

[4] John Radcliffe (1765?–1843) entered T.C.D., 1782; B.A., 1787; called to the Irish bar, 1789; judge of the prerogative court (*Gent. Mag.*, new ser., xx (1843), pt II, p. 333; *Alumni Dubl.*).

[5] *Belmont Castle, or suffering sensibility; containing the genuine and interesting correspondence of several persons of fashion* (Dublin: P. Byrne, 1790). It was advertised in the *Freeman's Journal*, 13 Dec. 1790. Part of it is reprinted above (vol. I, pp 7–9). The *Universal Magazine*, Nov. 1790, praised the book for its 'wit, humour and playful ingenuity' (Francis O'Kelley, 'Wolfe Tone's novel' in *Irish Book Lover*, xxiii (1935), pp 47–8). In a critical edition by Marion Deane (Dublin: Lilliput, 1998) 18 of the 36 chapters are attributed to Tone, the work is characterised as a '*roman-à-clef*' and its completion is dated to shortly before its publication.

and trying difficulty, and deserted by many of my former friends, the unspeakable consolation and support of finding George Knox still the same and of preserving his esteem unabated. His steady friendship on that occasion I shall mention in its place;[1] it has made an indelible impression of gratitude and affection on my heart. I likewise renewed an old college acquaintance with John Hall,[2] who by different accessions to his fortune was now at the head of about £14,000 a year. He had changed his name twice for two estates, first to that of Stevenson, and then Wharton, which is his present name. He was then a member of the British Parliament, and to his friendship I was indebted for the sum of £150 at a time when I was under great pecuniary difficulties. Another old college friend I recall with sentiments of sincere affection, Benjamin Phipps[3] of Cork. He kept a kind of batchelor's house, with good wine and an excellent collection of books (*not law books*), all which were as much at my command as at his. With some oddities, which to me only rendered him more amusing, he had a great fund of information, particularly of political detail, and in his company I spent some of the pleasantest hours which I passed in London.

At length, after I had been at the Temple something better than a year, my brother William, who was returned a few months before from his first expedition to St Helena, joined me and we lived together in the greatest amity and affection for about nine months, being the remainder of my stay in London. At this distance of time (now eight years) I feel my heart swell at the recollection of the happy hours we spent together. We were often without a guinea, but that never affected our spirits for a moment; and if ever I felt myself depressed by any untoward circumstance I had a never-failing resource and consolation in his friendship, his courage, and the invincible gaiety of his disposition, which nothing could ruffle.[4] With the companionable qualities he possessed, it is no wonder that

[1] See below, pp 292–3.

[2] John Hall (1765–1843) entered T.C.D., 1781; graduated LL.B., 1785; M.P. for Beverley, 1790–96, 1802–26; a Foxite whig and later a radical. His grandfather took the suffix Stevenson; Hall himself took the name of Wharton in 1788 in compliance with the will of his great-great-aunts. (*Alumni Dubl.*; *Burke's landed gentry of Great Britain* (1952), p. 2692; R. G. Thorne (ed.), *History of parliament: the house of commons, 1790–1820*, v (London, 1986), pp 521–4).

[3] Benjamin Phipps (1766–1825?) of Cregg, Fermoy, Co. Cork; entered T.C.D., 1780; graduated B.A., 1785; called to the Irish bar, 1789 (*Wilson's Dublin Directory*, passim; *Alumni Dubl.*; *Burke's landed gentry of Ireland* (1958), p. 578).

[4] An anecdote concerning Tone's brother William in London is given by James Wills in *Lives of illustrious and distinguished Irishmen* (6 vols, Dublin, 1840–47), vi, 356. After Tone's Trinity College friend William Magee (see above, vol. I, p. 25, n. 1) was elected to a fellowship in June 1788, Magee's uncle and guardian wished him to go to the bar, to which he only reluctantly agreed. 'Arrangements were in progress for his terms at the Middle Temple. These were entrusted to the care of Theobald Wolfe Tone, then saving terms for himself in London, and Mr Magee was to have been represented in the needful qualifying law dinners by Tone's brother. Among other documents relative to this period for which we have not space in this memoir', Wills continues, 'we have before us an amusing letter from Wolfe Tone himself in which he urges the immediate remittance of a sum of money for the purpose of lulling the vigilance and purchasing the integrity of the cook, chief butler and their subordinates'. But the provost of Trinity refused to recommend Magee for a dispensation from the obligation to take holy orders and so he did not proceed to read for the bar. Magee's name does not appear in the printed records of the Middle Temple or of any other London inn of court.

he recommended himself to Ben Phipps, so that he was soon I believe a greater favorite with him than even I was. They were inseparable. It fills my mind now with a kind of tender melancholy, which is not unpleasing, to recall the many delightful days we three have spent together, and the walks we have taken, sometimes to a review, sometimes to see a ship of war launched, sometimes to visit the Indiamen at Deptford, a favorite expedition with Phipps. Will, besides his natural gaiety, had an inexhaustible fund of pure Irish humour; I was pretty well myself; and Phipps, like the landlord of the Hercules Pillars, was '*an excellent third man*'.[1] In short we made it out together admirably.

As I foresaw by this time that I should never be Lord Chancellor, and as my mind was naturally active, a scheme occurred to me, to the maturing of which I devoted some time and study. This was a proposal to the Minister[2] to establish a colony in one of Cook's newly discovered islands in the South Sea, on a military plan (for all my ideas ran in that track), in order to put a bridle on Spain in time of peace, and to annoy her grievously in that quarter in time of war. In arranging this system, which I think even now was a good one for England, I read every book I could find relating to South America, as Ulloa,[3] Anson,[4] Dampier,[5] Woodes Rogers,[6] Narborough,[7] and especially the bucaniers [*sic*], who were my heroes and whom I proposed to myself as the archetypes of the future colonists. Many and many a delightful evening did my brother, Phipps and I spend in reading, writing and talking of my project, in which, if it had been adopted, it was our firm resolution to have embarked. At length when we had reduced it into a regular shape, I drew up a memorial on the subject, which I addressed to Mr Pitt[8] and delivered with my own hands to the porter in Downing Street. We waited, I will not say patiently, for about ten days, when I addressed a letter[9] to the Minister, mentioning my memorial and praying an answer, but this application was as unsuccessful as the former. Mr Pitt took not the smallest notice[10] of either memorial or letter, and all the benefit we reaped from our scheme was the amusement it afforded us during these[11] months wherein it was the subject of our

[1] Squire Western when he sat down in his Piccadilly lodgings with a parson friend over a bottle of wine said that the landlord of the Hercules Pillars at Hyde Park Corner 'would make an excellent third man and could inform them of the news of the town' (Fielding, *Tom Jones* (1749), bk XVI, chap. 2).

[2] 'Proposal submitted to William Pitt for the establishment of a military colony in the Sandwich Islands, August 1788' (above, vol. I, pp 10–16).

[3] *Relación histórica del viage a la América meridional* (2 vols, Madrid, 1748) by Antonio de Ulloa (1716–95), Spanish admiral. It was translated into English as *A voyage to South America* (London, 1758).

[4] *A voyage round the world* (London, 1748) by George Anson (1697–1762), British admiral (*D.N.B.*).

[5] *A new voyage round the world* (London, 1697) by William Dampier (1652–1715), pirate, capt., R.N. and hydrographer (*D.N.B.*).

[6] *A cruising voyage round the world* (London, 1712) by Woodes Rogers (d. 1732), commander of two private men-of-war fitted out by Bristol merchants to cruise in the Pacific (*D.N.B.*).

[7] Sir John Narbrough (1640–88), commander of a ship detained by the Spaniards on the coast of Chile, 1670–71; he later commanded a squadron sent against Tripoli and Algerine corsairs (*D.N.B.*). His journal is printed in *An account of several late voyages and discoveries to the south and north* (London, 1694).

[8] William Pitt, the prime minister.

[9] Above, vol. I, pp 14–16.

[10] The MS has a redundant 'either' between 'notice' and 'of'.

[11] *Life*, i, 27, has 'three' instead of 'these'.

constant speculation. I regret those delightful reveries which then occupied my mind! It was my first essay in what I may call politics, and my disappointment made such an impression on me as is not yet quite obliterated. In my anger I made something like a vow that if ever I had an opportunity I would make Mr Pitt sorry, and perhaps fortune may yet enable me to fulfil my resolution.

It was about this time that I had a very fortunate escape. My affairs were exceedingly embar[r]assed, and just at a moment when my mind was harassed and sore with my own vexations, I received a letter from my father filled with complaints, and a description of the ruin of his circumstances, which I afterwards found was much exaggerated. In a transport of rage, I determined to enlist as a soldier in the India Company's service, to quit Europe for ever, and to leave my wife and child to the mercy of her family, who might, I hoped, be perhaps[1] kinder to her when I was removed. My brother combated this desperate resolution by every argument in his power, but at length, when he saw me determined, he declared I should not go alone, and that he would share my fate to the last extremity. In this gloomy state of mind, deserted as we thought by gods and men, we set out together for the India House in Leadenhall Street, to offer ourselves as volunteers. But on our arrival there we were informed that the season was passed, that no more ships would be sent out that year, but that, if we returned about the month of March following, we might be received. The commis[2] to whom we addressed ourselves seemed not a little surprised at two young fellows of our appearance presenting ourselves on such a business, for we were extremely well dressed, and Will, who was the spokesman for us both, had an excellent address. Thus were we stopped; and I believe we were the single instance, since the beginning of the world, of two men absolutely bent on ruining themselves who could not find the means. We returned to my chambers, and, desperate as were our fortunes, we could not help laughing at the circumstance that India, the great gulph of all undone beings, should be shut against us alone. Had it been the month of March instead of September we should most infallibly have gone off, and in that case I should most probably at this hour be carrying a brown musquet on the coast of Coromandel. Providence however decreed it otherwise, and reserved me, as I hope, for better things.[3]

At the age of four and twenty, with a tolerable figure and address and in an idle and luxurious capital, it will not be supposed I was without adventures with the fair sex. The English men neglect their wives exceedingly in many essential circumstances; I was totally disengaged and did not fail to profit, as far as I could, of their neglect, and the English women are not naturally cruel. I formed in consequence several delightful connexions in London; and as I was extremely discreet, I have the satisfaction to think that not one of those to whom I had the good fortune to render myself agreeable ever suffered the slightest blemish in her reputation on my account. I cherish yet with affection the memory of one

[1] *Life* omits 'perhaps'. [2] i.e. clerk, the word substituted in *Life*, i, 28.
[3] The next paragraph is omitted from *Life*.

charming woman to whom I was extremely attached, and I am sure she still remembers me with a mutual regard.

I had been now two years at the Temple, and had kept eight terms; that is to say, I had dined three days in each term in the Commons Hall. As to law I knew exactly as much about it as I did of necromancy. It became however necessary to think of my return, and in consequence I made application, thro' a friend, to my wife's grandfather[1] to learn his intentions as to her fortune. This gentleman[2] exerted himself so effectually on our behalf that the old gentleman consented to give us £500 immediately and expressed a wish for my immediate return. In consequence I packed up directly, and set off with my brother for Ireland. We landed at Dublin the 23d of December and on Christmass day, 1788, arrived at my father's house at Blackhall,[3] where I had the satisfaction to find all my family in health, except my wife, who was grown delicate principally from the anxiety of her mind on the uncertainty of her situation. Our little girl[4] was now between two and three years old, and was charming. After remaining a few days at Blackhall, we came up to Dublin [and] were received as at first in Grafton St. by my wife's family. Mr Fanning paid me punctually the sum he had promised, and my wife and I both flattered ourselves that all past animosities were forgotten, and that the reconciliation was as sincere on their part as it most assuredly was on ours,[5] an expectation in which it soon appeared we were rather too sanguine. I now took lodgings in Clarendon St., purchased about an hundred pounds worth of law books, and determined in earnest to begin and study the profession to which I was doomed. In pursuance of this resolution, I commenced Batchelor of Laws in February 1789[6] and was called to the Bar in due form the Trinity term following,[7] shortly after which I went my first (the Leinster) circuit, having been previously elected a member of the Bar club. On this circuit, notwithstanding my ignorance, I pretty nearly cleared my expences, and I cannot doubt, if I had continued to apply sedulously to the law, but I might have risen to some eminence. But whether it was my incorrigible habits of idleness or the sincere dislike I had to the profession, which the little insight I was beginning to get into it did not tend to remove, or whether it was a control[l]ing destiny, I know not, but so it was that I soon got sick and weary of the law. I continued, however, for form's sake, to go to the courts and wear a foolish wig and gown for a considerable time, and I went the circuit, I believe in all, three times; but as I was, modestly speaking, one of the most ignorant barristers in the Four Courts, and as I took little, or rather no, pains to conceal my contempt and dislike of the profession, and especially as I had neither the means, nor the inclination, to treat Messieurs the Attornies, and to make them drink (a sacrifice of their respectability which even the most

1 Edward Fanning. 2 i.e. the friend. *Life*, ii, 28, substitutes 'he' for 'this gentleman'.

3 More precisely at Bodenstown, Blackhall being the adjacent townland, the demesne of the Wolfes of Blackhall.

4 Maria Tone. 5 The remainder of the sentence is omitted from *Life*.

6 On 24 Feb. 1789. See above, vol. I, pp 16–17. 7 Very probably some time in June 1789.

liberal minded of the profession are obliged to make), I made, as may be well supposed, no great exhibition at the Irish Bar.[1]

I had not been long a counsellor when the *coup de grâce* was given to my father's affairs by a decree in Chancery which totally ruined him; this was in a lawsuit between him and his brother,[2] who was lieutenant of grenadiers in the 22d Regiment. During the whole of this business, in which my father was undoubtedly in the wrong,[3] I obstinately refused to take any part, not thinking it decent to interfere where the parties were both so nearly allied to me. When, however, he[4] was totally ruined I thought it my duty, as it was most certainly my inclination, to distress myself even, to assist him, a sacrifice which the great pains and expence he had bestowed on my education well merited. I in consequence strained every nerve to preserve a remnant of his property, but his affairs were too desperate, and I was myself too poor to relieve him effectually; so that after one or two ineffectual efforts, by which I lost considerably with reference to my means, without essentially serving him, we were obliged to submit, and the last of his property, consisting of two houses, one in Stafford St. and one on Summer Hill, were sold much under their value to men who took advantage of our necessities as is always the case.[5] I had not even the satisfaction to see that my father was content with the efforts I made on his behalf, tho' they were in fact far beyond my abilities; but I

[1] Tone's friend George Knox, when he decided to cease practising at the bar, wrote: 'I retire from a profession the study and practice of which I have never relished, but yielding to necessity endeavoured to combat or at least conceal my disgust—as a science it is uncertain and contracted—as a trade it is precarious and laborious and exposes who follow it to constant anxiety and frequent mortification'. He also, it should be added, accepted that he had to face stiff competition from a number of 'adventurers to whom I must yield the superiority in talents and knowledge'. (George Knox to Lord Abercorn, 2, 20 July 1793, P.R.O.N.I., Abercorn papers, D/623/A).

[2] Jonathan Tone (see above, vol. I, pp xxvi–xxvii, 274). He entered the army as an ensign in the 22nd regiment on 6 Dec. 1778 and presumably served with it in America; promoted lieut, 6 Sept. 1781; he still appeared in the *Army list* shortly before his death, which occurred in Sept. 1792, as an officer on full pay. In an army inspection return for 1792 he was said to be aged 38 and to have served for 14 years (P.R.O., WO 27/73).

[3] In *Life* the preceding nine words are omitted.

[4] In ibid., i, 29, 'my father' is substituted for 'he'.

[5] Tone himself purchased the two properties and resold them not long afterwards. There were two deeds of assignment dated 1 July 1789 from Peter Tone to his son Theobald, 'to whom the Stafford Street premises passed for a consideration of £140, to hold from the date thereof for the remainder of a term of 46 years "subject to the rent and covenants therein contained", and to whom also the Summer Hill premises passed for a consideration of £151 11*s.* 8*d.* for the residue of 41 years from the 25th of March, 1777, subject to a rent of £20 a year and a mortgage of £46 6*s.* 0*d.*'. The price paid was not unreasonable and, it has been suggested, Tone may have paid it 'as a speculation, or acting on trust for others'. Whatever the reason, on 14 Nov. 1789 he transferred the Stafford Street house to 'John Cash, of Dublin, gent.', and on 1 Apr. 1790 the Summer Hill house to 'Patrick Byrne, bookseller', for an unknown price. (J. F. Fuller, 'The Tones, father and son' in *Cork Historical and Archaeological Society Journal*, 2nd ser., xxix (1924), pp 93–101). John Cash (d. 1833), Capel St., also a bookseller, was lord mayor of Dublin, 1813–14 (*Wilson's Dublin Directory*; Jacqueline R. Hill, *From patriots to unionists: Dublin civic politics, 1660–1840* (Oxford, 1997), p. 336). Patrick Byrne was the printer of Tone's burlesque novel and three of his pamphlets (see above, vol. I, p. 7). Tone's reason for purchasing the properties may have been to relieve his father of the financial embarrassment inevitably caused by litigation while at the same time keeping the houses within the family. He may have sold them afterwards in order to be able to relieve his father. See also above, vol. I, p. xxvii.

have always observed that money transactions are fatal to friendship, and even to natural affection.[1] Soon after he had the good fortune to obtain a place under the Paving Board,[2] which he yet retains and which secures him a decent, tho' moderate, independance.[3]

As the law grew every day more and more disgustful, to which my want of success contributed, tho' in that respect I never had the injustice to accuse the world of insensibility to my merit, as I well knew the fault was my own, but being, as I said, more and more weary of a profession for which my temper and habits so utterly disqualified me, I turned my attention to politics, and as one or two of my friends had written pamphlets with success, I determined to try my hand on a pamphlet. Just at this period the Whig Club[4] was instituted in Ireland, and the press groaned with publications against them on the part of Government. Two or three *Defences* had likewise appeared, but none of them extraordinary. Under these circumstances, tho' I was very far from entirely approving the system of the Whig Club, and much less their principles and motives, yet, seeing them at the time the best constituted political body which the country afforded, and agreeing with most of their positions, tho' my own private opinions went infinitely farther, I thought I could venture on their defence without violating my own consistancy. I therefore sat down and in a few days finished my first pamphlet, which I entitled *A review of the last session of parliament*.[5] To speak candidly of this performance, it was barely above mediocrity, if it rose so high; nevertheless, as it was written evidently on honest principles, and did not censure or flatter one party or the other without assigning sufficient reason, it had a certain degree of success. The Northern Whig Club[6] reprinted and distributed a large impression at their own expence, with an introduction highly complimentary to the author, whom at that time they did not even know; and a very short time after, when it was known that the production was mine, they did me the honor to elect me a member of their body, which they notified to me by a very handsome letter,

[1] The preceding sentence is omitted from *Life*.

[2] He was described in 1803 as 'one of the inspectors of globes' (*Wilson's Dublin Directory*).

[3] Peter Tone lost the lands in Co. Kildare obtained from his brother some 20 years previously. On 7 Mar. 1790 he granted and released to Jonathan Tone the land in Castlesize (Casumsize?) which belonged to William Milton, 43 acres in Sallins and all the lands of Whitechurch called Wellfield, Churchfield and Hither Churchfield. T. W. Tone was a witness to the deed. (Registry of Deeds, Dublin, 419/287/273989).

[4] The Whig Club of Ireland was founded in Dublin in July 1789 during the parliamentary struggles which followed the regency crisis. Its membership included peers and M.P.s and it had a programme of moderate administrative reform. (R. B. McDowell, *Irish public opinion, 1750–1800* (London, 1944), pp 133–4). William Drennan, a northern radical, complained that 'the whig club is literally an eating and drinking aristocratical society without any fellow feeling with the commonalty' (Drennan to Samuel McTier, 21 May 1791, P.R.O.N.I., Drennan papers, D 591/300).

[5] It was entitled in fact *A review of the conduct of administration during the seventh session of parliament*. It was signed 'An Independent Irish Whig' and published in Dublin by Patrick Byrne on or about 6 Apr. 1790. It is reprinted above, vol. I, pp 26–49.

[6] The Northern Whig Club was founded in Feb. 1790. It supported the principles and programme of the Whig Club of Ireland, in addition emphasising the need for parliamentary reform. (R. B. McDowell, *Irish public opinion, 1750–1800* (London, 1944), p. 134).

signed by their secretary, Henry Joy Jun[io]r, of Belfast, and to which I returned a suitable answer.[1]

But this was not all. The leaders of the Whig Club, conceiving my talents, such as they were, might be of service to their cause, and not expecting much intractability from a young lawyer who had his fortune to make, sent a brother barrister to compliment me on my performance and to thank me for the zeal and ability I had shewn. I was in consequence introduced to George Ponsonby, a distinguished member of the body and who might be considered as the leader of the Irish opposition; with him however I never had any communication further than ordinary civilities. Shortly after the barrister above mentioned spoke to me again; he told me the Ponsonbies were a most powerful family in Ireland; that they were much pleased with my exertion, and wished in consequence to attach me to them; that I should be employed as counsel on a petition then pending before the House of Commons,[2] which would put an hundred guineas in my pocket, and that I should have professional business put in my way from time to time that should produce me at least as much per annum. He added that they were then, it was true, out of place, but that they would not be always so, and that, on their return to office, their friends when out of power would naturally be first considered. He likewise observed that they had influence, direct or indirect, over no less than two and twenty seats in Parliament, and he insinuated pretty plainly that when we were better acquainted it was highly probable I might come in on one of the first vacancies. All this was highly flattering to me, the more so as my wife's fortune was now nearly exhausted, partly by our inevitable expences, and partly by my unsuccessful efforts to extricate my father. I did, it was true, not much relish the attaching myself to any great man, or set of men; but I considered, as I have said before, that the principles they advanced were such as I could conscientiously support *so far as they went*, tho' mine went much beyond them; I therefore thought there was no dishonor in the proposed connexion, and I was certainly a little dazzled with the prospect of a seat in Parliament, at which my ambition began to expand. I signified in consequence my readiness to attach myself to the Whigs, and I was instantly retained on the petition for the Borough of Dungarvan on the part of James Carrigue Ponsonby, Esqr.[3]

I now looked upon myself as a sort of political character, and began to suppose that the House of Commons, and not the Bar, was to be the scene of my future exertions; but in this I reckoned like a sanguine young man. Month after month elapsed without any communication on the part of George Ponsonby, whom I looked upon as most immediately my object. He always spoke to me, when we

[1] See Diary for 14 Oct. 1791 (above, vol. I, p. 133).

[2] On 2 July 1790 a petition was lodged against the return of Marcus Beresford and Chambré Brabazon Ponsonby for the borough of Dungarvan on the grounds that the returning officer had been irregularly appointed and had acted with gross partiality. On 8 Feb. 1791 a select committee was appointed to hear the petition which reported in favour of the sitting M.P.s on 18 Feb. (*Commons' jn. Ire.*, xiv, 11, 28–9, 85–6, 168).

[3] *Recte* Chambré Brabazon Ponsonby-Barker (1762–1834) of Kilcooley, Co. Tipperary; M.P. for Dungarvan, 1790–97 (*Burke's peerage* (1912), p. 230).

met by chance, with great civility, but I observed that he never mentioned one word of politics. I therefore at last concluded that he had changed his mind, or that, on a nearer view he had found my want of capacity. In short I gave up all thoughts of the connexion and determined to trouble myself no more about Ponsonby or the Whigs; and I calculated that, as I had written a pamphlet which they thought had served them, and as they had in consequence employed me professionally in a business which produced me eighty guineas,[1] accounts were balanced on both sides, and all further connexion was at an end.

But my mind had now got a turn for politics. I thought I had at last found my element, and I plunged into it with eagerness. A closer examination into the situation of my native country had very considerably extended my views, and as I was sincerely and honestly attached to her interests, I soon found reason not to regret that the Whigs had not thought me an object worthy of their cultivation. I made speedily what was to me a grand discovery, tho' I might have found it in Swift or Molyneux, that the influence of England was the radical vice of our Government, and consequently that Ireland would never be either free, prosperous or happy until she was independent, and that independance was unattainable while the connexion with England existed. In forming this theory, which has ever since unvaryingly directed my political conduct, to which I have sacrificed everything, and am ready to sacrifice my life if necessary, I was exceedingly assisted by an old friend of mine, Sir Laurence Parsons,[2] whom I look upon as one of the very, *very* few honest men in the Irish house of commons. It was he who first turned my attention on this great question, but I very soon ran far ahead of my master. It is in fact to him I am indebted for the first comprehensive view of the actual situation of Ireland; what his conduct might be in a crisis I know not, but I can answer for the truth and justice of his theory. I now began to look on the little politics of the Whig Club with great contempt, their peddling about petty grievances instead of going to the root of the evil; and I rejoiced that, if I was poor, as I was actually, I had preserved my independance, and could speak my sentiments without being responsible to anybody but the law.

An occasion soon offered to give vent to my newly received opinions. On the appearance of a rupture with Spain, I wrote a pamphlet[3] to prove that Ireland was not bound by the declaration of war, but might, and ought, as an independant nation, to stipulate for a neutrality.[4] In examining this question I advanced the question of separation with scarcely any reserve, much less disguise; but the

[1] There is a record of how Tone spent this money on a page of one of his notebooks (T.C.D., MS 3805, f. 20$^{v}$). Dated 'Feb$^{y}$ 15, 1791' and headed 'Received on the Dungarvan Comm[itt]ee', it states the amount received as £79 12*s.* 6*d.* and indicates that he repaid small debts (including £2 5*s.* 6*d.* to Sharkey and £1 2*s.* 9*d.* to Russell), lent his mother £8 10*s.* 7½*d.* and spent £1 2*s.* 9*d.* on a 'journey to Prosp[erou]s'.

[2] Sir Lawrence Parsons (1758–1841), 5th baronet (see above, vol. I, p. 91, n. 1).

[3] *Spanish war: an enquiry how far Ireland is bound, of right, to embark in the impending contest on the side of Great Britain*, signed 'Hibernicus' (Dublin: P. Byrne, 1790). It was published *a.*30 June 1790 and is reprinted above (vol. I, pp 50–63).

[4] At this point it should be pointed out that Tone's chronology is misleading. The Dungarvan petition could not have been contemplated until after the general election of Apr.–May 1790 and in fact was not decided until 18 Feb. 1791. Tone's pamphlet *Spanish war* appeared in June 1790.

public mind was by no means so far advanced as I was, and my pamphlet made not the smallest impression. The day after it appeared,[1] as I stood perdue in the bookseller's shop, listening after my own reputation, Sir Harry Cavendish,[2] a notorious slave of the House of Commons, entered, and throwing my unfortunate pamphlet on the counter in a rage exclaimed, 'Mr Byrne,[3] if the author of that work is serious, *he ought to be hanged!*'. Sir Harry was succeeded by a bishop, an English doctor of divinity with five or six thousand a year, laboriously earned in the Church. His Lordship's anger was not much less than that of the other personage. 'Sir', said he, 'if the principles in that abominable work were to spread, do you know that you would have to pay for your coals at the rate of five pounds a ton?' Notwithstanding these criticisms, which I have faithfully quoted against myself, I continue to think my pamphlet a good one, but apparently the publisher, Mr Byrne, was of a different opinion, for I have every reason to believe that he suppressed the whole impression, '*for which his own gods damn him*!'[4]

Vol 1st.

## Volume the Second
*Nil desperandum!*
Paris,
1796

### Memorandums relative to my life and opinions, 1796[5]

Shortly after the premature end of my second pamphlet which I have recorded and which did not, however, change my opinion or its merits,[6] for '*Victrix causa diei placuit, sed victa Catoni*',[7] we came to an open rupture with my wife's family. It is not my intention to record the petty insults and mortifications we submitted to for a long time;[8] one circumstance is sufficient to prove that the breach was not of our seeking, viz. that we had everything to lose and nothing to gain by a quarrel,[9] whereas by removing my wife from her grandfather's presence, who

[1] It was first advertised for sale on 30 June 1790 (*Hibernian Journal*, 30 June 1790).

[2] Sir Henry Cavendish (1732–1804), born in England; married an Irish heiress, 1757; succeeded as 2nd baronet, 1776; member of the British and Irish parliaments; receiver-general for Ireland, 1779–95 (*D.N.B.*; G.E.C., *Peerage*, xii, pt II, pp 426–7).

[3] Patrick Byrne of Grafton St.

[4] Tone may be recalling these words from John Hawkesworth, *Oroonoko* (1759), act v, final scene.

[5] A redundant 'Volume 2[d]' below this heading in the MS and a meaningless 'B' above 'Nil desperandum!' are omitted.

[6] *Life*, i, 33, has 'my opinion on its merit'.

[7] *Recte* 'Victrix causa deis placuit . . .' (Lucan, *Pharsalia*, bk I, verse 128). Lucan's meaning is 'The conquering cause was pleasing to the gods, but the conquered one to Cato'.

[8] In *Life*, i, 33, this reads: 'it is not my intention to enter into this subject'.

[9] In *Life*, i, 33, 'quarrel' is followed by asterisks and the remainder of the paragraph is omitted.

was very fond of her, any portion of his fortune which he might intend for her would naturally be divided among the rest. Of course it was their interest to provoke as it was ours to avoid hostilities. My wife's health was at this time in a very delicate state when her brother, the captain,[1] thought proper one day to insult her grossly and almost to strike her. I should not mention[2] this circumstance, if it were not to give me an opportunity of recording my brother William's behaviour on the occasion.[3] He took an opportunity to see Capt[ai]n Witherington the same evening and told him in three words that he must either come the next morning and apologize to his sister for his brutality or fight him. Witherington seemed inclined to do neither, and my brother left him, telling him he should hear from him the next day. Witherington however spared him the trouble, for he was with him the next morning by seven o'clock, and repeated an apology to my wife which my brother dictated; when he had finished his apology he added, from himself, that he thought still he was in the right, on which my brother told him that spoiled all, and that he must repeat the apology a second time, simply and without adding any qualification, which the Captain thought proper to do, and my brother dismissed him with a very severe rebuke, in which he made use of expressions such as no officer or gentleman ought to have submitted to. At the time of this event I was in the country, and on my return they told me all that had passed, and my wife declared her resolution never again to expose herself to similar treatment, in which I heartily concurred. Shortly after I met Captain Witherington in the street; he asked me, was I apprised of what had passed? I said I was. He asked me then what I thought of it? I replied that I approved of everything which my wife and brother had said and done, and that I condemned the whole of his conduct except his apology. I added that if he was any way dissatisfied at this, I was ready to explain with him in any manner he thought proper. He replied he was perfectly satisfied with his own conduct. I said in that case I had nothing further to say to him. All intercourse from hence forward ceased between us and the Captain had after all the satisfaction to intercept any addition which might have been made to my wife's fortune by her grandfather, as the old gentleman died shortly after[4] at a very advanced age without even seeing her. It is unnecessary to observe on the magnanimous behaviour of my brother on the occasion I have just recited, nor does it stand in need of the contrasted meanness of his adversary to set it off. I hope I should in similar circumstances manifest the same readiness to protect his wife and defend his honor.[5]

About this time it was that I formed an acquaintance with my invaluable friend Russell,[6] a circumstance which I look upon as one of the most fortunate of my life. He is a man whom I love as a brother. I will not here attempt a panegyric on his

[1] Edward Witherington. [2] In the MS 'mention' is substituted for 'record' which is crossed out.

[3] In the MS at this point two lines are crossed out illegibly.

[4] His will was proved on 7 July 1791 (J. B. Leslie, *Derry clergy and parishes* (Enniskillen, 1937), p. 119).

[5] At this point the text is resumed in *Life*, i, 34.

[6] In the MS these words in their original form are crossed out, only two groups of them remaining legible: 'About this time' and 'with my friend Russell'. For Thomas Russell, see above, vol. I, p. 77, n. 1.

merits. It is sufficient to say that to an excellent understanding he joins the purest principles and the best of hearts. I wish I had ability[1] to delineate his character with justice to his talents and his virtues. He well knows how much I esteem and love him, and I think there is no sacrifice that friendship could exact that we would not with chearfulness make for each other to the utmost hazard of life or fortune. There cannot be imagined a more perfect harmony, I may say identity, of sentiment than exists between us; our regard for each other has never suffered a moment's relaxation from the hour of our first acquaintance, and I am sure it will continue to the end of our lives. I think the better of myself for being the object of the esteem of such a man as Russell. I love him, and I honor him; I frame no system of happiness for my future life in which the enjoyment of his society does not constitute a most distinguishing feature and if I am ever inclined to murmur at the difficulties wherewith I have so long struggled, I think on the inestimable treasure I possess in the affection of my wife and the friendship of Russell, and I acknowledge that all my labours and sufferings are overpaid. I may truly say that, even at this hour, when I am separated from both of them, and uncertain whether I may ever be so happy as to see them again,[2] there is no action of my life which has not a remote reference to their opinion which I equally prize. When I think I have acted well, and that I am likely to succeed in the important business wherein I am engaged, I say often to myself, 'My dearest love and my friend Russell will be glad of this!'. But to return to my history. My acquaintance with Russell commenced by an argument[3] in the Gallery of the House of Commons.[4] He was at that time enamoured of the Whigs, but I knew those gentlemen a little better than he, and indeed he did not long remain under the delusion. We were struck with each other, notwithstanding the difference of our opinions, and we agreed to dine together the next day in order to discuss the question; we liked each other better the second day than the first, and every day since has increased and confirmed our mutual esteem.

My wife's health continuing still delicate, she was ordered by her physician to bathe in the salt water. I hired in consequence a little box of a house on the sea-side at Irishtown, where we spent the summer of 1790.[5] Russell and I were inseparable, and as our discussions were mostly political and our sentiments agreed exactly, we extended our views and fortified each other in the opinions to the propagation and establishment of which we have ever since been devoted. I recall with transport the happy days we spent together during that period, the delicious dinners, in the preparation of which my wife, Russell and myself were all engaged, the afternoon walks, the discussions we have had, as we lay stretched on

[1] In the MS 'ability' is substituted for 'talent', which is crossed out.

[2] Tone was reunited with his wife on 7 May 1797 (see Diary for that date, below, vol. III), but he never met Russell again.

[3] In MS 'an argument' is substituted for 'a dispute', which is crossed out.

[4] During 1790 the Irish parliament was in session 21 Jan.–5 Apr. and 2–24 July.

[5] They seem to have been still residing at Irishtown in September 1792 (see above, vol. I, p. 270, n. 2). It is on the south shore of Dublin Bay and about 3 km from College Green.

the grass. It was delightful! Sometimes Russell's venerable father,[1] a veteran of near seventy with the courage of a hero, the serenity of a philosopher and the piety of a saint, used to visit our little mansion and that day was a *fête*.[2] My wife doated on the old man, and he loved her like one of his children. I will not attempt, because I am unable, to express the veneration and regard I had for him, and I am sure that next to his own sons, and scarcely below them, he loved and esteemed me. Russell's brother John,[3] too, used to visit us, a man of a most warm and affectionate heart, and incontestibly of the most companionable talents I ever met. His humour, which was pure and natural, flowed in an inexhaustible stream. He had not the strength of character of my friend Tom, but for the charms of conversation he excelled him and all the world. Sometimes too my brother William used to join us for a week from the County Kildare where he resided with my brother Mathew, who had lately commenced a cotton manufactory at Prosperous in that county.[4] I have already mentioned the convivial talents he possessed. In short when the two Russells, my brother and I were assembled, it is impossible to conceive a happier society. I know not whether our wit was perfectly classical or not, nor does it signify. If it was not sterling, at least it passed current among ourselves. If I may judge, we were none of us destitute of the humour indigenous in the soil of Ireland; for three of us, I can answer they possessed it in an eminent degree; add to this, I was the only one of the four who was not a poet, or at least a maker of verses; so that every day produced a ballad, or some poetical squib, which amused us after dinner; and, as our conversation turned upon no ribaldry or indecency, my wife and sister never left the table. These were delicious days! The rich and great, who sit down every day to the monotony of a splendid entertainment, can form no idea of the happiness of our frugal meal, nor of the infinite pleasure we found in taking each his part in the preparation and attendance. My wife was the centre and the soul of all. I scarcely know which of us loved her best; her courteous manners, her goodness of heart, her incomparable humour, her never failing chearfulness, her affection for me and for our children rendered her an object of our common admiration and delight. She loved Russell as well as I did. In short a more interesting society of individuals, connected by purer motives and animated by a more ardent attachment and friendship for each other, cannot be imagined.

[1] John Russell (1720?–92).

[2] The 'little mansion' may have been 'Garristown'. In one of Tone's memorandum books under this heading a number of articles of furniture are listed, many of them in the following rooms: Russell's room, Boy's room, Study or office, dining room, Kitchen, Dairy (T.C.D., MS 3508, ff 11–12).

[3] For John Russell (1748?–*c.*1815?), see above, vol. I, p. 270, n. 10.

[4] 'An extensive cotton manufactory' had been started in the 1770s by Captain Robert Brook (d. 1802?) at a place near Clane in Co. Kildare to which he gave the name 'Prosperous'. However, in 1786 he failed badly. The trustees of his estate seem to have tried to retrieve matters by letting the buildings and machinery to persons willing to enter the industry. (*Commons' jn. Ire.*, xii, appendices, pp ccxiv–ccxvii, dccxlvii–dccxlviii; T. J. Rawson, *Statistical survey of the county of Kildare* (Dublin, 1807), p. 56; Lena Boylan, 'Prosperous: landlords and tenants' in *County Kildare Archaeological Society Journal*, xvi (1977–86), pp 242–63; James Kelly, 'Prosperous and Irish industrialization in the late eighteenth century' in ibid., pp 441–67).

During the course of this summer there were strong appearances of a rupture between England and Spain relative to Nootka Sound.[1] I had mentioned to Russell my project for a military colony in the South Seas, and as we had both nothing better to do, we sat down to look over my papers and memorandums regarding that business.[2] After some time, rather to amuse ourselves than with an expectation of its coming to anything, we enlarged and corrected my original plan, and having dressed a handsome memorial[3] on the subject, I sent it inclosed in a letter to the Duke of Richmond,[4] then Master of the Ordnance. I thought I should hear no more about it, but we were not a little surprised when, a few days after, I received an answer[5] from his Grace, in which, after speaking with great civility of the merits of my plan, he informed me that such business was out of his department, but that if I desired it, he would deliver my memorial and recommend it to the notice of Lord Grenville, Secretary of State for Foreign Affairs,[6] whose business it properly was. I immediately wrote him an answer[7] of acknowledgement intreating him to support my plan, and by the same post I wrote also to Lord Grenville.[8] In a few days I received answers from them both,[9] informing me that the memorial had been received by Lord Grenville and should be taken into speedy consideration, when, if any measures were to be adopted in consequence, I might depend on receiving further information. These letters we looked upon as leaving it barely possible that something might be done in the business, tho' very unlikely; and so indeed it proved, for shortly after a kind of peace, called a convention, was agreed upon between Spain and England, on which I wrote once more to Lord Grenville[10] enclosing a second memorial,[11] in order to learn his determination, when I received a very civil answer,[12] praising my plan, &c., and informing me that existing circumstances had rendered it unnecessary at that time to put it in execution, but that ministers would keep it in recollection. Thus ended, for the second time, my attempt to colonise in the South Seas, a measure which I still think might be attended with the most beneficial consequences to England. I keep all the papers relating to this business,[13] including the originals of the Minister's letters; and I have likewise copied the whole of them in

[1] See above, vol. I, p. 50. [2] Above, vol. I, pp 10–16.

[3] Above, vol. I, pp 70–74. This and other documents referred to in the remainder of this paragraph are given under the heading 'Renewed proposal for the establishment of a military colony in the Sandwich Islands, September–December 1790' (above, vol. I, pp 68–89).

[4] Tone to the duke of Richmond, 20 Sept. 1790 (above, vol. I, p. 69).

[5] Duke of Richmond to Tone, 24 Sept. 1790 (above, vol. I, p. 74).

[6] Tone's recollection is imprecise. Grenville was not raised to the peerage until 25 Nov. 1790; he was home secretary and did not become foreign secretary until 8 June 1791 (*D.N.B.*).

[7] Tone to duke of Richmond, 30 Sept. 1790 (above, vol. I, pp 74–5).

[8] Tone to W. W. Grenville, 30 Sept. 1790 (above, vol. I, pp 75–6).

[9] No such answers have been found. Three weeks later Tone did receive a letter, dated 23 Oct. 1790, from an under-secretary at the Home Office, Scrope Bernard (above, vol. I, p. 76).

[10] Tone to Lord Grenville, 7 Dec. 1790 (above, vol. I, pp 81–2). [11] Above, vol. I, pp 82–5.

[12] Lord Grenville to Tone, 17 Dec. 1790 (above, vol. I, p. 85).

[13] Not mentioned here by Tone are the letter he addressed to the duke of Richmond on 12 Nov. 1790 and Richmond's reply dated 25 Nov. (above, vol. I, pp 77–80).

a 4° book, marked [ ],[1] to which I refer for further information. It was singular enough, this correspondance, continued by two of the King of England's cabinet ministers at St James's on the one part and Russell and myself from my little box at Irishtown on the other. If the measure I proposed had been adopted, we were both determined on going out with the expedition, in which case instead of planning revolutions in our own country, we might be now perhaps carrying on a piratical[2] war (for which I think we have both talents) on the coasts of Spanish America. This adventure is an additional proof of the romantic spirit I have mentioned in the beginning of my Memoirs as a *trait* in our family, and indeed my friend Russell was in that respect completely one of ourselves. The Minister's refusal did not sweeten us much towards him. I renewed the vow I had once before made to make him, if I could, repent of it, in which Russell most heartily concurred. Perhaps the Minister may yet have reason to wish he had let us go off quietly to the South Seas. I should be glad to have an opportunity to remind him of his old correspondent, and if ever I find one I will not overlook it. I dare say he has utterly forgot the circumstance, but I have not. '*Everything however is for the best*', as Pangloss says, '*in this best of all possible worlds*'.[3] If I had gone to the Sandwich Islands in 1790, I should not be today *chef de brigade* in the service of the French Republic, not to mention what I may be in my own country, if our expedition thither succeeds. But to return.

Shortly after this disappointment, Russell, who had for two or three years revelled in the ease and dignity of [an] ensign's half pay, amounting to £28 a year, which he had earned before he was twenty-one by broiling in the East Indies for five years, was unexpectedly promoted by favor of the commander-in-chief to an ensigncy on full pay in the 64th Regiment of Foot,[4] then quartered in the town of Belfast. He put himself in consequence in battle array, and prepared to join. I remember the last day he dined with us in Irishtown, where he came, to use his own quotation, '*all clinquant all in gold!*',[5] we set him to cook part of the dinner in a very fine suit of laced regimentals. I love to recal[l] those scenes! We parted with the sincerest regret on both sides. He set off for Belfast and shortly after we returned to town for the winter, my wife's health being perfectly re-established, as she manifested by being in due time brought to bed of our eldest boy, whom we called William[6] after my brother.[7]

[1] MS blank. *Life* reads simply 'in a quarto book'. The book referred to, which is bound in T.C.D. MS 3086, has a pink cover which is, however, unmarked.

[2] In *Life*, i, 37, 'privateering' is substituted for 'piratical'.

[3] A summary of the views of Pangloss, the optimistic philosopher in Voltaire's *Candide* (1759).

[4] Thomas Russell is listed in the *Dublin Chronicle*, 28 Sept. 1790, as having been promoted from ensign on half pay in the late 100th foot to ensign on full pay in the 64th foot.

[5] *Henry VIII*, 1, i.

[6] William Theobald Wolfe Tone was born in Dublin on 29 Apr. 1791 (*Life*, ii, 674). He was not, however, Tone's first son. A son named Richard was born in 1787 or 1789 but died very young (Katherine Anne Tone-Maxwell, 'Tone of Bodenstown, Co. Kildare' in *Notes and Queries*, 12th series, vii (July–Dec. 1920), p. 432; MacDermot, *Tone*, p. 49).

[7] In the MS at this point the pen changes.

This winter I endeavoured to institute a kind of political club, from which I expected great things. It consisted of seven or eight members,[1] eminent[2] for their talents & patriotism, and who had already, more or less, distinguished themselves by their literary productions. They were John Stack, fellow of Trinity College; Dr W[illia]m Drennan, author of the celebrated *Letters*, signed Orellana;[3] Joseph Pollock, author of the still more justly celebrated *Letters of Owen Roe O'Nial*;[4] Peter Burrowes, a barrister, a man of a most powerful and comprehensive mind; William Johnson, a lawyer also, of respectable talents; Whitley Stokes, fellow of Trinity College, a man the extent and variety of whose knowledge is only to be exceeded by the number and intensity of his virtues; Russell (a corresponding member) and myself. As our political opinions at that time agreed in most essential points however they have since differed,[5] and as this little club most certainly comprised a great proportion of information, talents and integrity, it might naturally be expected that some distinguished publications should be the result. Yet I know not how it was. We did not draw well together; our meetings degenerated into downright, ordinary suppers. We became a mere oyster club, and at length a misunderstanding, or rather a rooted dislike to each other, which manifested itself between Drennan and Pollock (who were completely Cæsar and Pompey with regard to literary empire),[6] joined to the retreat of John Stack to his living in the North,[7] and the little good we saw resulting from our association induced us to drop off one by one, and thus after three or four months' sickly existence our club departed this life, leaving behind it a puny offspring of about a dozen essays on different subjects, all, as may be supposed, tolerable, but not one of any distinguished excellence.[8] I am satisfied any one of the members, by devoting a week of his time to a well chosen subject, would have produced a work of ten times more value than the whole club were able to shew from their joint labours during its existence. This experiment satisfied me that men of genius, to be of use, must not be collected in numbers. They do not work well in the aggregate; and indeed even in ordinary conversations I have observed that too many wits spoil the discourse. The dullest entertainment at which I ever remember to have assisted was one formed expressly to bring together near twenty persons, every one more or less distinguished for splendid talents, or great convivial qualities. We sat and prosed together in great solemnity, endeavouring by a rapid

[1] Twelve members of Tone's political club (including Tone himself) are named by William Tone (see above, vol. I, pp 90–91).

[2] In the MS 'eminent' is substituted for 'distinguished', which has been struck out.

[3] *Letters of Orellana, an Irish helot, to the seven northern counties* (Dublin, 1785).

[4] *Letters of Owen Roe O'Nial* (Dublin, 1779).

[5] In the MS the words 'at that time' and 'however they have since differed' are interlined.

[6] It was Drennan's opinion that 'Pollock, or rather Pendulum, . . . does not know his own mind half an hour' (Drennan to Samuel McTier, 24 Dec. 1791, P.R.O.N.I., Drennan papers, D 591/318).

[7] Stack was formally presented to the living at Derryvollen, Co. Fermanagh, on 23 Aug. 1791, having resigned his fellowship on 8 June (T.C.D. MS MUN; *Trinity College record volume* (Dublin, 1951), pp 42, 48).

[8] A list of these essays and their respective authors, and the text of the four by Tone, is printed above, vol. I, pp 90–91.

circulation of the bottle to animate the discourse; but it would not do; every man was clad in a suit of intellectual armour in which he found himself secure, it is true, but ill at his ease, and we all rejoiced at the moment when we were permitted to run home and get into our *robes de chambre* and slippers. Any two of the men present would have been the delight and entertainment of a well chosen society, but all together was, as Wolsey says, '*too much honor*'.[1]

In recording the names of the members of the club, I find I have strangely omitted a man, whom as well for his talents as his principles I esteem as much as any, and far more than most of them; I mean Thomas Addis Emmett, a barrister. He is a man completely after my own heart, of a great and comprehensive mind,[2] of the warmest and sincerest affection for his friends, and of a firm and steady adherence to his principles, to which he has sacrificed much, as I know, and would I am sure, if necessary, sacrifice his life.[3] His opinions and mine square exactly. In classing[4] the men of most esteem, I would place him beside Russell at the head of the list, because, with regard to them both, the most ardent feelings of my heart coincide exactly with the most severe decisions of my judgements. There are men whom I regard as much as it is possible. I am sure, for example, if there be on earth such a thing as sincere friendship, I feel it for Whitley Stokes, for George Knox, and for Peter Burrowes; they are men whose talents I admire, whose virtues I reverence, and whose persons I love,[5] but the regard which I feel for them, sincere and affectionate as it is, is certainly not of the same species with that which I entertain for Russell & Emmett. Between us three there has been, from the very commencement of our acquaintance, a coincidence of sentiment, a harmony of feeling on points which we all conscientiously consider as of the last importance, which binds us in the closest ties to each other. We have unvaryingly been devoted [to] the pursuit of the same object, by the same means, we have had a fellowship in our labours, a society in our dangers; our hopes, our fears, our wishes, our friends and our enemies have been the same. When all this is considered, and the talents and principles of the men taken into the account, it will not be wondered at if I esteem Russell and Emmett as the first of my friends. If ever an opportunity offers, as circumstances at present seem likely to bring one forward, I think their country will ratify my choice.

With regard to Burrowes and Knox, whom I do most sincerely and affectionately love, their political opinions differ fundamentally from mine; and perhaps it is for the credit of us all three that with such an irreconcilable difference of sentiment we have all along preserved a mutual regard and esteem for each other; at least I am sure I feel it particularly honorable to myself, for there are perhaps no two men in the world about whose good opinion I am more sollicitous; nor shall

[1] *Henry VIII*, III, ii. At this point William Tone has a lengthy footnote referring to Tone's letter to Thomas Russell of 9 July 1791 (*Life*, i, 39–40).

[2] In the MS the following ten words are interlined.

[3] In the MS at this point one line is crossed out illegibly.

[4] In the MS the following five words are substituted for a word that is crossed out illegibly.

[5] In the MS at this point one and a half lines are crossed out and the remainder of the sentence interlined.

I ever forget the steady and unvarying friendship I experienced from them both when my situation was to all human appearance utterly desperate, and when others, with at least as little reason to desert me, shunned me, as if I had the red spots of the plague out on me—but of that hereafter.[1] With regard to Whitley Stokes, his political opinions approach nearer to mine than those of either Knox or Burrowes. I mention this, for, in these days of unbounded discussion, politics unfortunately enter into everything, even into our private friendships. We however differ on many material points, and we differ on principles which do honor to Stokes's heart. With an acute feeling of the degradation of his country, and a just and generous indignation against her oppressors, the tenderness and humanity of his nature is such that he recoils from any measures to be attempted for her emancipation which may terminate in blood. In this respect I have not the virtue to imitate him. I must observe that with this, perhaps extravagant, anxiety for the lives of others, I am sure in any cause which satisfied his conscience no man would be more prodigal of his own life than Whitley Stokes, for he is an enthusiast in his nature; but '*what he would highly, that would he holily*',[2] and I am afraid that, in the present state of affairs, that is a thing utterly[3] impossible. I love Stokes most sincerely. With a most excellent and highly cultivated mind, he possesses the distinguishing excellence[4] of the best and most feeling heart; and I am sure it will not hurt the self-love of any one of the friends whose names I have recorded when I say that, in the full force of the phrase, I look upon Whitley Stokes as the *very best man* I have ever known. Now that I am upon this subject, I must observe that in the choice of my friends I have been all my life extremely fortunate. I hope I am duly sensible of the infinite value of their esteem, and I take the greatest pride in being able to say that I have preserved that esteem, even of those from whom I most materially differed on points of the last importance and[5] on occasions of peculiar difficulty; and this too without any sacrifice of consistency or principle on either side, a circumstance which however redounds still more to their credit than to mine.

But to return to my history, from this long digression, in which, however, I dwell with affection; exiled as I am from the inestimable friends I have mentioned, and from others whom I regard not less, of whom I am about to speak, it is a consolation to my soul to dwell upon their merits, and the sincere and animated affection I feel for them. God knows whether we shall ever meet, or, if we do, how many of us may survive the contest in which we are, by all appearance, about to embark.

[1] An allusion to the discovery by the Irish government of Tone's connexion with a French agent, William Jackson, and his authorship of a memorandum on the political situation in Ireland which may have been intended for the French government. Both Burrowes and Knox used their influence to secure a 'compromise' by which it was agreed that Tone, on engaging to make for the Irish government a statement of his communications with Jackson and to leave Ireland as soon as he could settle his private affairs, would not be prosecuted (*Life*, i, 113; above, vol. I, pp xxxvii–xxxix, 510–11). Tone does not, however, refer again in the Autobiography to this episode, as he was obliged by lack of time to pass over events of 1793 and 1794 (see below, p. 330).

[2] *Recte*: '. . . what thou wouldst highly, / That thou wouldst holily; . . .' (*Macbeth*, I, v).

[3] *Life* omits 'utterly'.

[4] *Life*, i, 41, substitutes 'character'.

[5] In the MS at this point one line is crossed out and the five words that follow here are interlined.

If it be my lot for me to fall, I leave behind me this small testimony of my regard for them written under circumstances which I think may warrant its sincerity.

THE French Revolution had now been above a twelvemonth in its progress. At its commencement, as the first emotions are generally honest, everyone was in its favour; but after some time the probable consequences to monarchy and aristocracy began to be foreseen, and the partizans of both to retrench considerably in their admiration. At length Mr Burke's famous invective[1] appeared, and this in due season produced Payne's reply,[2] which he called *The rights of man*. This controversy, and the gigantic event which gave rise to it, changed in an instant the politics of Ireland. Two years before the nation was in a lethargy. The puny efforts of the Whig Club, miserable and defective as their system was, were the only appearance of anything like exertion, and he was looked on as extravagant who thought of a parliamentary reform, against which, by the bye, all parties equally set their face. I have already mentioned[3] that in those days of apathy and depression, I made an unsuccessful blow at the supremacy of England by my pamphlet on the expected rupture with Spain,[4] and I have also fairly mentioned that I found nobody who ventured to second my attempt, or paid the least attention to the doctrine I endeavoured to disseminate. But the rapid succession of events, and above all the explosion which had taken place in France and blown into the elements a despotism rooted for fourteen centuries, had thoroughly aroused all Europe, and the eyes of every man, in every quarter, were turned anxiously on the French National Assembly. In England Burke had the triumph completely to decide the public. Fascinated by an eloquent[5] publication which flattered so many of their prejudices, and animated by their unconquerable hatred of France, which no change of circumstances could alter, the whole English nation, it may be said, retracted[6] from their first decision in favor of the glorious and successful efforts of the French people; they sickened at the prospect of the approaching liberty and happiness of that mighty nation; they calculated, as merchants, the probable effects which the energy of regenerated France might have on their commerce; they rejoiced when they saw the combination of despots formed to restore the ancient system,[7] and perhaps to dismember the Monarchy; and they waited with impatience for an occasion which, happily for mankind, they soon found, when they might, with some appearance of decency, engage in person in the infamous contest.

[1] Edmund Burke, *Reflections on the revolution in France* (London, 1790; 8th ed., Dublin, 1791).

[2] Thomas Paine, *The rights of man, being an answer to Mr Burke's attack on the French revolution* (London, 1791; Dublin, 1791).

[3] See Autobiography, above, pp 284–5.

[4] *Spanish war!: an enquiry how far Ireland is bound, of right, to embark in the impending contest on the side of Great Britain* . . . (Dublin, 1790). It is reprinted above (vol. I, pp 50–63).

[5] In the MS 'an' is substituted for 'his', which is crossed out, and 'eloquent' is erroneously 'eloquence'. It appears that Tone originally wrote 'fascinated by his eloquence', changed his mind to 'fascinated by an eloquent publication', but failed to alter 'eloquence' to 'eloquent'.

[6] In the MS this word is indistinct and could also read 'retreated'. *Life* has 'retracted'.

[7] In the MS 'system' is substituted for 'despotism' which is crossed out.

But matters were very different in Ireland, an oppressed, insulted and plundered nation. As we well knew, experimentally, what it was to be enslaved, we sympathised most sincerely with the French people, and watched their progress to freedom with the utmost anxiety; we had not, like England, a prejudice rooted in our very nature against France. As the Revolution advanced, and as events expanded themselves, the public spirit of Ireland rose with a rapid acceleration. The fears and animosities of the aristocracy rose in the same or a still higher proportion. In a little time the French revolution became the test of every man's political creed, and the nation was fairly divided into two great parties, the *Aristocrats* and the *Democrats* (epithets borrowed from France), who have ever since been measuring each other's strength and carrying on a kind of smothered war, which the course of events, it is highly probable, may soon call into energy and action.

It is needless, I believe, to say that I was a *Democrat* from the very commencement, and as all the retainers of Government, including the sages and judges of the law, were of course on the other side, this gave the *coup de grâce* to any expectation, if any such I had, of my succeeding at the Bar, for I soon became pretty notorious; but in fact I had, for some time, renounced all hope and I may say all desire of succeeding in a profession which I always disliked and which the political prostitution of its members (tho' otherwise men of high honor and of great personal worth) had taught me sincerely to despise. I therefore seldom went near the Four Courts, nor did I adopt any one of the means, and least of all the study of the law, which are successfully employed by those young men whose object it is to rise in their profession.

As I came, about this period, rather more forward than I had hitherto done, it is necessary for understanding my history to take a rapid survey of the state of parties in Ireland, that is to say, of the members of the established religion, the Dissenters and the Catholics.

The first party,[1] whom for distinction sake I call the *Protestants*, tho' not above the tenth of the population, were in possession of the whole of the Government and of five sixths of the landed property of the nation; they were, and had been for above a century, in the quiet enjoyment of the Church, the Law, the Revenue, the Army, the Navy, the Magistracy, the Corporations, in a word of the whole patronage of Ireland. With properties whose titles were founded in massacre and plunder, and being, as it were, but a colony of foreign usurpers in the land, they saw no security for their persons and estates but in a close connexion with England, who profited of their fears, and, as the price of her protection, exacted the implicit surrender of the commerce and the liberties of Ireland. Different events, particularly the revolution in America, had enabled and emboldened the other two parties, of whom I am about to speak, to hurry the Protestants into measures highly disagreeable to England and beneficial to their country, but in which, from accidental circumstances, they durst not refuse to concur. The spirit

[1] In the MS the eight words that follow here are interlined.

of the corps however remained unchanged, as they have manifested on every occasion since which chance has offered them. This party therefore, so powerful by their property and influence, were implicitly devoted to England, which they esteemed necessary for the security of their existence; they adopted in consequence the sentiments and the language of the British cabinet; they dreaded and abhorred the principles of the French revolution, and were, in one word, an *aristocracy* in the fullest and most odious extent of the term.

The Dissenters, who formed the second party, were at least twice as numerous as the first. Like them, they were a colony of foreigners in their origin, but being mostly engaged in trade and manufactures, with few overgrown landed properties[1] among them, they did not like them feel that a slavish dependance on England was essential to their very existence. Strong in their numbers and their courage, they felt that they were able to defend themselves, and they soon ceased to consider themselves as any other than Irishmen. It was the Dissenters who composed the flower of the famous Volunteer army of 1782, which extorted from the English Minister the restoration of what is affected to be called the Constitution of Ireland. It was they who first promoted and continued the demand of a parliamentary reform, in which, however, they were baffled by the superior address and chicanery of the aristocracy; and it was they finally who were the first to stand forward, in the most decided and unqualified manner, in support of the principles of the French Revolution.

The Catholics, who composed the third party, were above two thirds of the nation, and formed perhaps a still greater proportion. They embraced the entire peasantry of three provinces, they constituted a considerable portion of the mercantile interest, but, from the tyranny of the penal laws enacted at different periods against them, they possessed but a very small proportion of the landed property, perhaps not a fiftieth part of the whole. It is not my intention here to give a detail of that execrable and infamous code, framed with the art and the malice of demons, to plunder and degrade and brutalize the Catholics. Suffice it to say that there was no injustice, no disgrace, no disqualification, moral, political or religious, civil or military, that was not heaped upon them; it is with difficulty that I restrain myself from entering into the abominable detail, but it is the less necessary, as it is to be found in so many publications of the day. This horrible system pursued for above a century with unrelenting acrimony and perseverance had wrought its full effect, and had in effect reduced the great body of the Catholic peasantry of Ireland to a situation, morally and physically speaking, below that of the beasts of the field; the spirit of their few remaining gentry was broken, and their minds degraded; and it was only in the class of their merchants and traders, and a few members of the medical profession, who had smuggled an education in despite of the penal code, that anything like political sensation existed.

Such was pretty nearly the situation of the three great parties at the commencement of the French Revolution, and certainly a much more gloomy

[1] *Life*, i, 45, has 'proprietors'.

prospect could not well present itself to the eyes of any friend to liberty and his country. But as the luminary of truth and freedom in France advanced rapidly to its meridian splendor, the public mind in Ireland was proportionably illuminated; and to the honor of the Dissenters of Belfast be it said they were the first to reduce to practice their newly received principles, and to shew by being just that they were deserving to be free.

The dominion of England in Ireland had been begun and continued in the disunion of the great sects which divided the latter country.[1] In effectuating this disunion the Protestant party were the willing instruments, as they saw clearly that if ever the Dissenters and Catholics were to discover their true interests and, forgetting their former ruinous dissensions, were to unite cordially and make common cause, the downfal of English supremacy and of course of their own unjust monopoly, would be the necessary and immediate consequence. They therefore laboured continually, and for a long time successfully, to keep the other two sects asunder; and the English government had even the address to persuade the Catholics that the non-execution of the penal laws, which were in fact too atrocious to be enforced in their full rigour, was owing to their clemency, that the Protestants and Dissenters, but especially the latter, were the enemies, and themselves in effect the protectors, of the Catholic people. Under this arrangement the machine of government moved forward on carpet ground; but the time was at length come when the system of iniquity was to tumble in the dust and the day of truth and reason to commence.[2]

So far back as the year 1783 the Volunteers of Belfast had instructed their deputies to the Convention held in Dublin for the purpose of framing a plan of parliamentary reform to support the equal admission of the Catholics to the rights of freemen. In this instance of liberality they were then almost alone, for it is their fate, in political wisdom, ever to be in advance of their countrymen; it was sufficient however to alarm the Government, who immediately procured from Lord Kenmare, at that time esteemed the leader of the Catholics, a solemn disavowal, in the name of the body, of any wish to be restored to their long lost rights. Prostrate as the Catholics were at that period, this last insult was too much; they instantly assembled their General Committee and disavowed Lord Kenmare and his disavowal, observing at the same time that they were not framed so differently from all other men as to be in love with their own degradation. The majority of the Volunteer Convention, however, resolved to consider the infamous declaration of Lord Kenmare as the voice of the Catholics of Ireland, and in consequence the emancipation of that body made no part of their plan of reform. The consequence natural to such folly and injustice immediately ensued. The Government, seeing the Convention by their own art separate themselves from the great mass of the people, who could alone give them effective force, held them at defiance, and that formidable assembly, that under better principles might

[1] Note by William Tone: 'At least since the reign of Elizabeth and James I'.

[2] In the MS at this point there is a change of ink.

have held the fate of Ireland in their hands, was broken up with disgrace and ignominy; a memorable warning that those who know not to render their just rights to others will be found incapable of firmly adhering to their own.

The General Committee of the Catholics, of which I have spoken above, and which since the year 1792 has made a distinguished feature in the politics of Ireland, was a body composed of their bishops, their country gentlemen, and of a certain number of merchants and traders, all resident in Dublin but named by the Catholics in the different towns corporate to represent them. The original object of this institution was to obtain the repeal of a partial and oppressive tax, called quarterage, which was levied on the Catholics only, and the Government, which found the committee at first a convenient instrument on some occasions, connived at their existence.[1] So degraded was the Catholic mind at the period of the formation of their committee (about 1770)[2] and long after, that they were happy to be allowed to go up to the Castle with an abominable slavish address to each successive viceroy, of which, moreover, until the accession of the Duke of Portland in 1782,[3] so little notice was taken that His Grace was the first who condescended to give them an answer; and indeed for above twenty years the sole business of the General Committee was to prepare and deliver in these records of their depression. The effort which an honest indignation had called forth, at the time of the Volunteer Convention in 1783, seemed to have exhausted their strength, and they sunk back into their primitive nullity. Under this appearance of apathy however a new spirit was gradually arising in the body, owing principally to the exertion and the example of one man, John Keogh, to whose services his country, and more especially the Catholics, are singularly indebted. In fact the downfal of feudal tyranny was acted, in little, on the theatre of the General Committee; the influence of their clergy and of their barons was gradually undermined and the third estate, the commercial interest, rising in wealth and power, was preparing by degrees to throw off the yoke in the imposing, or at least the continuing, of which the leaders of the body, I mean the prelates and aristocracy, to their disgrace be it spoken, were ready to concur. Already had those leaders, acting in obedience to the orders of the Government which held them in fetters, suffered one or two signal defeats in the Committee, owing principally to the talents and address of John Keogh. The parties began to be defined and a sturdy democracy of new men, with bolder views and stronger talents, soon supersed[ed] the timid counsels and slavish measures of the ancient aristocracy. Everything seemed tending to a better order of things among the Catholics, and an occasion soon offered to call the energy of their new leaders into action.

The Dissenters of the North, and more especially of the town of Belfast, are from the genius of their religion and from the superior diffusion of political

[1] For the early history of the Catholic Committee and the quarterage dispute, see above, vol. I, p. 427, n. 1.

[2] *Recte* 1760.

[3] William Henry Cavendish-Bentinck, 3rd duke of Portland (see above, vol. I, p. 526), was lord lieutenant of Ireland from 8 Apr. until 15 Aug. 1782.

information among them, sincere and enlightened republicans; they had ever been foremost in the pursuit of parliamentary reform and I have already mentioned the early wisdom and virtue of the men[1] of Belfast in proposing the emancipation of the Catholics so far back as the year 1783. The French revolution had awakened all parties in the nation from the stupor in which they lay plunged from the time of the dispersion of the ever memorable Volunteer Convention, and the citizens of Belfast were the first to raise their heads from the abyss and to look the situation of their country steadily in the face. They saw at a glance their true object, and the only means to obtain it, conscious that the force of the existing government was such as to require the united efforts of the whole Irish people to subvert it; and long convinced in their own minds that to be free it was necessary to be just, they cast their eyes once more on the long neglected Catholics and profiting of past errors, for which however they had not to accuse themselves, they determined to begin on a new system, and to raise the structure of the liberty and independance of their country on the broad basis of equal rights to the whole people.

The Catholics on their part were rapidly advancing in political spirit and information. Every month, every day, as the Revolution in France went prosperously forward, added to their courage and their force, and the hour seemed at last arrived when, after a dreary oppression of above one hundred years, they were once more to appear on the political theatre of their country; they saw the brilliant prospect of success which events in France opened to their view, and they determined to avail themselves with promptitude of that opportunity which never returns to those who omit it. In this the active members of the General Committee resolved to set on foot an immediate application to Parliament praying for a repeal of the penal laws. The first difficulty they had to surmount arose in their own body; their peers, their gentry (as they affected to call themselves) and their prelates, either seduced or intimidated by Government, gave the measure all possible opposition, and at length after a long contest, in which both parties strained every nerve and produced the whole of their strength, the question was decided, on a division in the Committee, by a majority of at least six to one in favor of the intended application.[2] The triumph of the young democracy was complete; but tho' the aristocracy was defeated, they were [*sic*] not yet entirely broken down. By the instigation of Government they had the meanness to secede from the General Committee, to disavow their acts, and even to publish in the papers[3] that they did not wish to embarrass Government by advancing their claims of emancipation. It is difficult to conceive such a degree of political degradation; but what will not the tyranny of our[4] execrable system produce in time? Sixty-eight gentlemen, individually of high spirit, were found who

[1] *Life*, i, 48, has 'town' instead of 'men'.

[2] The debate took place on 17 Dec. 1791; ninety members were in favour of petitioning and seventeen against (R. Dudley Edwards (ed.), 'The minute book of the Catholic Committee, 1773–92' in *Archivium Hibernicum*, ix (1942), p. 141).

[3] e.g. *H.J.*, 28 Dec. 1791.

[4] In the MS this word is indistinct and could also be 'an'.

publicly and in a body deserted their party and their own just claims, and even sanctioned this pitiful desertion by the authority of their signatures. Such an effect had the operation of the penal laws on the mind of the Catholics of Ireland, as proud a race as any in all Europe!

But I am in some degree anticipating matters, and indeed, instead of a few memorandums relating to myself, I find myself embarking on a kind of '*history of my own times*'. Let me return and condense, as much as I can.[1]

The first attempts of the Catholic Committee failed totally. Endeavouring to accom[m]odate all parties, they framed a petition so humble that it ventured to ask for nothing, and even this petition they could not find a single member of the legislature to present. Of so little consequence, in the year 1790, were the great mass of the Irish people! Not disheartened however by this defeat they went on, and in the interval between that and the approaching session they were preparing measures for a second application. In order to add a greater weight and consequence to their intended petition, they brought over to Ireland Richard Burke, only son of the celebrated Edmund, and appointed him their Agent to conduct their application to Parliament.[2] This young man came over with considerable advantages, and especially with the éclat of his father's name, who the Catholics concluded, and very reasonably, would for his sake if not for theirs, assist his son with his advice and directions. But their expectations in the event proved abortive. Richard Burke, with a considerable portion of talents from nature, and cultivated as may be well supposed with the utmost care by his father, who idolised him, was utterly deficient in judgement, in temper and especially in the art of managing parties. In three or four months' time during which he remained in Ireland he contrived to embroil himself, and in a certain degree the committee, with all parties in Parliament, the Opposition as well as the Government, and finally, desiring to drive his employers into measures of which they disapproved, and thinking himself strong enough to go on without the assistance of the men who introduced and, as long as their duty would permit, supported him, in which he miserably deceived himself, he ended his short and turbulent career by breaking with the General Committee. That body however treated him respectfully to the last, and on his departure they sent a deputation to thank him for his exertions and presented him with the sum of two thousand guineas.

It was pretty much about this time that my connexion with the Catholic body commenced in the manner which I am about to relate. I cannot pretend to strict accuracy as to dates, for I write entirely from memory, all my papers being in America.

Russell had, on his arrival to join his regiment at Belfast, found the people so much to his taste, and in return had rendered himself so agreeable to them, that

[1] In the MS at this point there is a change of pen.

[2] On 15 Jan. 1792 the Catholic Committee ratified Richard Burke's appointment as its agent. He had arrived in Ireland on 3 Jan. (R. Dudley Edwards (ed.), 'The minute book of the Catholic Committee, 1773–92' in *Archivium Hibernicum*, ix (1942), p. 145; *The correspondence of Edmund Burke*, vii, ed. P. J. Marshall and John A. Woods (Cambridge, 1968), p. 13).

he was speedily admitted into their confidence and became a member of several of their clubs. This was an unusual circumstance, as British officers, it may well be supposed, were no great favorites with the Republicans of Belfast. The Catholic question was, at this period, beginning to attract the public notice, and the Belfast Volunteers, on some public occasion (I know not precisely what), wished to come forward with a declaration in its favour. For this purpose Russell, who by this time was entirely in their confidence, wrote to me to draw up and transmit to him such a declaration as I thought proper, which I accordingly did.[1] A meeting of the corps was held in consequence, but an opposition unexpectedly arising to that part of the declaration which alluded directly to the Catholic claims, that passage was, for the sake of unanimity, withdrawn for the present, and the declaration then passed unanimously. Russell wrote me an account of all this, and it immediately set me on thinking more seriously than I had yet done on the state of Ireland. I soon formed my theory, and on that theory I have unvaryingly acted ever since.

To subvert the tyranny of our execrable government, to break the connexion with England, the never failing source of all our political evils, and to assert the independance of my country—these were my objects. To unite the whole people of Ireland, to abolish the memory of all past dissensions, and to substitute the common name of Irishman in place of the denominations of Protestant, Catholic and Dissenter—these were my means. To effectuate these great objects I reviewed the three great sects. The Protestants I despaired of from the outset, for obvious reasons. Already in possession, by an unjust monopoly, of the whole power and patronage of the country, it was not to be supposed they would ever concur in measures, the certain tendency of which must be to lessen their influence as a party, how much soever the nation might gain. To the Catholics I thought it unnecessary to address myself, because that, as no change could make their political situation worse, I reckoned upon their support as a certainty; besides they had already begun to manifest a strong sense of their wrongs and oppressions, and finally I well knew that, however it might be disguised or suppressed, there existed in the breast of every Irish Catholic an inextirpable abhorrence of the English name and power. There remained only the Dissenters, whom I knew to be patriotic and enlightened. However the recent events at Belfast had shewed me that all prejudice was not yet entirely removed from their minds. I sat down accordingly and wrote a pamphlet, addressed to the Dissenters, and which I entitled *An Argument on behalf of the Catholics of Ireland*,[2] the object of which was to convince them that they and the Catholics had but one common interest, and one common enemy; that the depression and slavery of Ireland was produced and perpetuated by the divisions existing between them, and that consequently to assert the independance of their country and their own individual liberties, it was necessary to forget all former feuds to consolidate the

[1] Above, vol. I, pp 106–8.

[2] *An argument on behalf of the catholics of Ireland in which the present political state of that country and the necessity of a parliamentary reform are considered addressed to the people and more particularly to the protestants of Ireland* (Dublin: P. Byrne, 1791). It is reprinted above, vol. I, pp 108–28.

entire strength of the whole nation and to form, for the future, but one people. These principles I supported by the best arguments which suggested themselves to me, and particularly by demonstrating that the cause of the failure of all former efforts, and more especially of the Volunteer Convention in 1783, was the unjust neglect of the claims of their Catholic brethren. This pamphlet, which appeared in September 1791[1] under the signature of 'A Northern Whig', had a considerable degree of success. The Catholics (*with not one of whom I was at the time acquainted*)[2] were pleased with the efforts of a volunteer in their cause and distributed it in all quarters. The people of Belfast, of whom I had spoken with the respect and admiration I sincerely felt for them, and to whom I was also perfectly unknown, printed a very large edition[3] which they dispersed thro' the whole North of Ireland, and I have the great satisfaction to believe that many of the Dissenters were converted by my arguments. It is like vanity to speak of my own performance so much, and the fact is I believe I am somewhat vain on that topic; but as it was the immediate cause of my being made known to the Catholic body, I may be perhaps excused for dwelling upon a circumstance which I must ever look on, for that reason, as one of the most fortunate of my life.

As my pamphlet spread more and more, my acquaintance among the Catholics extended accordingly. My first friend in the body was John Keogh and thro' him I became acquainted with all the leaders, as Richard McCormick, John Sweetman, Edward Byrne, Thomas Braughall, in short the whole sub-committee and most of the active members of the General Committee. It was a kind of fashion this winter (1791) among the Catholics to give splendid dinners to their political friends, in and out of Parliament, and I was always a guest of course. I was invited to a grand dinner,[4] given to Richard Burke on his leaving Dublin, together with W[illia]m Todd Jones, who had distinguished himself by a most excellent pamphlet in favor of the Catholic cause,[5] as well as to several entertainments given by clubs and associations. In short I began to grow into something like reputation, and my company was, in a manner, a requisite at all the entertainments of that winter.

But this was not all. The Volunteers of Belfast of the 1st or Green Company were pleased, in consequence of my pamphlet, to elect me an honorary member of their corps,[6] a favor which they were very delicate in bestowing, as I believe I was the only person, except the great Henry Flood, who was ever honored with

[1] *Recte* August 1791 (C. J. Woods, 'The contemporary editions of Tone's *Argument on behalf of the Catholics*' in *Irish Booklore*, ii, no. 2 (1976), p. 218).

[2] Tone means catholics who were members of the Catholic Committee.

[3] Tone said earlier that it was of 'six thousand copies' (Woods, 'Tone's *Argument*', p. 225).

[4] On 2 April 1792 'a dinner was given by the Catholic Committee to R. Burke, Esq., previous to his departure for England. Several very respectable gentlemen of the Established Church and of the Dissenters were present. After dinner a great variety of national, loyal, patriotic and personal toasts were drank, and the evening's entertainment concluded with the utmost hilarity and concord.' (*D.E.P.*, 5 Apr. 1792).

[5] *A letter to the societies of United Irishmen of the town of Belfast upon the subject of certain apprehensions which have arisen from a proposed restoration of catholic rights* (Dublin, 1792).

[6] See above, vol. I, pp 203–4.

that mark of their approbation. I was also invited to spend a few days in Belfast in order to assist in framing the first club of United Irishmen and to cultivate a personal acquaintance with the men whom, tho' I highly esteemed them, I knew as yet but by reputation.

In consequence, about the beginning of October, I went down with my friend Russell, who had by this time quit the army and was in Dublin on his private affairs. The incidents of that journey, which was by far the most agreeable and interesting one I had ever made, I recorded in a kind of diary, a practice which I then commenced and have ever since, from time to time, continued, as circumstances of sufficient importance occurred. To that diary I refer.[1] It is sufficient here to say that my reception was of the most flattering kind, and that I found the men of the most distinguished public virtue in the nation, the most estimable in all the domestic relations of life. I had the good fortune to render myself agreeable to them, and a friendship was then formed between us, which I think it will not be easy to shake. It is a kind of injustice to name individuals, yet I cannot refuse myself the pleasure of observing how peculiarly fortunate I esteem myself in having formed connexions with Samuel Neilson, Rob[er]t Simms, William Simms, William Sinclair, Thomas Macabe. I may as well stop here, for in enumerating my most particular friends I find I am in fact making out a list of the men of Belfast most distinguished for their virtues, talents and patriotism. To proceed. We formed our club,[2] of which I wrote the declaration,[3] and certainly the formation of that club commenced a new epoch in the politics of Ireland.

At length, after a stay of about three weeks, which I look back upon as perhaps the pleasantest of my life, Russell and I returned to Dublin, with instructions to cultivate the leaders in the popular interest, being Protestants, and if possible to form in the capital a club of United Irishmen. Neither Russell nor myself were known to[4] one of those leaders; however we soon contrived to get acquainted with James Napper Tandy, who was the principal of them, and thro' him with several others, so that in a little time we succeeded and a club was accordingly formed,[5] of which the Hon[oura]ble Simon Butler was the first chairman and Tandy the first secretary; the club adopted the declaration of their brethren of Belfast, with whom they immediately opened a correspondence. It is but justice to an honest man who has been persecuted for his firm adherence to his principles to observe here that Tandy in coming forward on this occasion well knew that he was putting to the most extreme hazard his popularity among the corporations of the city of Dublin, with whom he had enjoyed the most unbounded influence for near twenty years; and in fact, in the event, his popularity was sacrificed. That did not prevent however his taking his part decidedly; he had the firmness to forego [*sic*] the gratification of his private feelings for the good of his country. The truth is Tandy was a very sincere republican and it did not require much

[1] Diary entries for 14–26 Oct. 1791 (above, vol. I, pp 133–7, 138–9, 141–2, 144–9).

[2] The first Society of United Irishmen of Belfast.

[3] Above, vol. I, pp 139–41.

[4] In the MS 'acquainted with' is crossed out and 'known to' interlined.

[5] On 9 Nov. 1791.

argument to shew him the impossibility of attaining a republic[1] by any means short of the united powers of the whole people; he therefore renounced the lesser object for the greater, and gave up the certain influence which he possessed (and had well earned) in the city for the contingency of that influence which he might have (and which he well deserves to have) in the nation. For my own part, I think it right to mention that at this time the establishment of a republic was not the immediate object of my speculations. My object was to secure the independance of my country under any form of government, to which I was led by a hatred of England so deeply rooted in my nature that it was rather an instinct than a principle. I left to others better qualified for the enquiry the investigations into the merits of the different forms of government, and I contented myself with labouring on my own system, which was, luckily, in perfect coincidence, as to its operation, with that of those men who viewed the question on a broader and juster scale than I did at the time I mention. But to return.

The club was scarcely formed before I lost all pretensions to anything like influence on their measures, a circumstance which at first mortified me not a little; and perhaps, had I retained more weight in their councils, I might have prevented, as on some occasions I laboured unsuccessfully to prevent, their running into indiscretions which gave their enemies but too great advantages over them. It is easy to be wise after the event. So it was however that I soon sunk [*sic*] into obscurity in the club,[2] which however I had the satisfaction to see daily increasing in numbers and consequence. The Catholics particularly flocked in, in crowds, as well as some of the Protestant members of corporations most distinguished for their liberality and public spirit on former occasions; and indeed I must do the society the justice to say that I believe there never existed a political body which included, for its numbers, a greater portion of sincere uncorrupted patriotism, as well as a very respectable proportion of talents. Their publications, most written by Dr Drennan, and many of them admirably well done, began to draw the public attention, especially as they were evidently the production of a society utterly disclaiming all party views or motives and acting on a broad original scale, not sparing those who called themselves patriots more than those who were the habitual slaves of the government, a system in which I heartily concurred, having long entertained a more sincere concept for what is called

[1] In the MS 'a Republic' is substituted for 'that object' which is crossed out.

[2] Tone may be understating his role in the Dublin Society of United Irishmen, which was formed on 9 Nov. 1791. Soon after its foundation, he opposed—together with Russell and Stokes—a proposal made by the steering committee and carried unanimously that candidates for admission should after election publicly pledge themselves to strive for the attainment of its objectives. Despite this rebuff and another rebuff over the same issue, he was prepared to be pro-secretary when Tandy was involved in a conflict with the house of commons (Feb.–Apr. 1792), he was one of eight members appointed to 'a committee of constitution or secrecy' (5 Oct.), and he was one of 'a committee of 21 members appointed to prepare a parliamentary reform' (Jan. 1793). He seems, however, not to have taken a prominent part in the proceedings of these committees and later his attendances at meetings of the society fell off. (R. B. McDowell, 'Proceedings of the Dublin Society of United Irishmen' in *Analecta Hibernica*, no. 17 (1949), pp 17–22, 34, 59, 132, 133, 138; *The Drennan–McTier letters, 1776–1793*, ed. Jean Agnew (Dublin, 1998), pp 370–74; see above, vol. I, pp 188–90, 191–2, 195).

*Opposition* than for the common prostitutes of the treasury bench, who want at least the vice of hypocrisy.

At length, the Solicitor General in speaking of the society, having made use of expressions in the House of Commons extremely offensive,[1] an explanation was demanded of him by Simon Butler, chairman, and Tandy, secretary. Butler was satisfied; Tandy was not, and after several messages, which it is not my affair to detail, the Solicitor General at length complained to the House of a breach of privilege, and Tandy was ordered in the first instance into custody. He was in consequence arrested by a messenger, from whom he found means to make his escape, and immediately a proclamation was issued offering a reward for retaking him.[2] The society now was in a difficult situation, and I thought myself called upon to make an effort, at all hazards to myself, to prevent its falling, by any improper timidity, in the public opinion. We were in fact committed with the House of Commons on the question of privilege, and having fairly engaged in the contest it was impossible to recede without a total forfeiture of character. Under these circumstances I cast my eyes on Archibald Hamilton Rowan, a distinguished member of the society whose many virtues, public and private, had set his name above the reach of even the malevolence of party, whose situation in life was of the most respectable rank, if ranks be indeed respectable, and above all whose personal courage was not to be shaken, a circumstance, in the actual situation of affairs, of the last importance. To Rowan therefore I applied; I shewed him that the current of public opinion was rather setting against us in the business, and that it was necessary that some of us should step forward and expose themselves at all risques, to shew the House of Commons and the nation at large that we were not to be intimidated or put down so easily. I offered, if he would take the chair, that I would, with the society's permission, act as secretary, and that we would give our signatures to such publications as circumstances might render necessary. Rowan instantly agreed, and accordingly, on the next night of meeting,[3] he was chosen chairman, and I pro-secretary in the absence of Tandy; and the society having agreed to the resolutions proposed, which were worded in a manner very offensive to the dignity of the House of Commons, and in fact amounted to a challenge of their authority, we inserted them in all the newspapers and printed 5,000 copies with our names affixed.[4] The least that Rowan and I expected in consequence of this step (which under the circumstances was, I must say, rather a bold one) was to be committed to Newgate for a breach of privilege, and perhaps exposed to personal discussions with some of the members of the House of Commons; for he proposed, and I agreed, that if any disrespectful language was applied to either of us in any debate which might arise on the

[1] In the house of commons on 20 Feb. 1792 the solicitor general, John Toler, referred scathingly to the Dublin United Irishmen and in particular to their secretary, 'Napper Tandy, lending his countenance', adding that 'it was rather odd that they could not contrive to set a better face on the matter' (*Parl. reg. Ire.*, xii, 202).

[2] On 22 Feb. 1792 (*Commons' jn. Ire.*, xv, 59–60).

[3] On 24 or 25 Feb. 1792.

[4] For the text of these resolutions, see above, vol. I, p. 188.

business, we would attack the person, whoever he might be, immediately and oblige him either to recant his words or give battle. All our determinations however came to nothing. The House of Commons, either content with their victory over Tandy, who was obliged to conceal himself for some time, or not thinking Rowan and myself objects sufficiently important to attract their notice, or perhaps, which I rather believe, not wishing just then to embroil themselves with a man of Rowan's firmness and courage, not to speak of his great and justly merited popularity, took no notice whatsoever of our resolutions, and in this manner he and I had the good fortune, I may say the merit, to rescue the society from a situation of considerable difficulty without any actual suffering, tho' certainly with some personal hazard on our part. We had likewise the satisfaction to see the society, instead of losing ground, rise rapidly in the public opinion by their firmness on the occasion. Shortly after, on the last day of the session,[1] Tandy appeared in public and was taken into custody, the whole society attending him in a body to the House of Commons. He was ordered by the Speaker to be committed to Newgate, whither he was conveyed, the society attending him as before; and, the Parlia[men]t being prorogued in half an hour after, he was liberated immediately and escorted in triumph to his own house. On this occasion Rowan and I attended of course and were in the gallery of the House of Commons. As we were not sure but we might be attacked ourselves, we took pains to place ourselves in a conspicuous situation, and to wear our Whig Club uniforms, which were rather gaudy, in order to signify to all whom it might concern that there we were. A good many of the members, we observed, remarked us, but no further notice was taken; our names were never mentioned; the whole business passed over quietly, and I resigned my pro-secretaryship, being the only office I ever held in the society, into the hands of Tandy, who resumed his functions. This was in Spring 1792.

I should observe that the day after the publication above mentioned, when I attended near the House of Commons in expectation of being called before them to answer for what I had done, and had requested my friend Sir Laurence Parsons to give me notice in order that I might present myself, the house took fire, by accident, and was burned to the ground.[2]

# Diary, 8 August–2 September 1796

T.C.D., Tone papers, MS 2049, ff 124$^{v}$–126$^{v}$; *Life*, ii, 175–9.

## 8 Aug. 1796

Saw Hoche and Chérin together this morning. Both very civil but no news. Hoche I believe sets off the 11th.

[1] On 18 Apr. 1792 (*Commons' jn. Ire.*, xv, 111).

[2] On 27 Feb. 1792 the roof of the house of commons was discovered to be on fire. The next day the Commons met in one of the adjoining chambers. (*Commons' jn. Ire.*, xv, 67).

## 10 Aug. 1796

*Fête* to celebrate the anniversary of the subversion of royalty in France. Foot racing, horse racing and running at the ring in the Champ de Mars. The Directory, the Ministers and the constituted authorities in grand costume attended with the foreign ambassadors &c. It was a delicious evening. The prizes were all military, sabres, pistols and carabines of the manufactory of Versailles. That is exactly as it should be. The concourse of people was immense, and I was very glad to observe that everybody seemed pleased and happy. When the Directory rose from their place in order to retire, the people forced the sentinels, and got into the center in order to see them. I was delighted to observe that circumstance, which I look on as by no means trifling. After the exercises in the Champ de Mars were over the people retired *en masse* to the Elysian fields,[1] where there was a most magnificent illumination and fireworks.[2] I never saw anything so brilliant in the way of *coup d'oeil*. The *Muscadins*[3] and the *elegant women* of Paris made it a point to stay away, but nobody missed them. The French enjoy these kind of spectacles better than any people on earth, and for my part I never was more amused or gratified than in observing the spectators. Altogether I spent a very pleasant, I may say[4] happy day.

## 13 Aug. 1796

Saw Chérin this morning. He tells me it may be *ten* days yet before we set off. Hell, Hell, Hell! How shall I get over these eternal delays? Hoche set off yesterday.

## 15 Aug. 1796

Put on my regimentals for the first time; as pleased as a little boy in his first breeches: foolish enough, but not unpleasant. Walked about Paris to shew myself. Huzza! Citizen Wolfe Tone, *chef de brigade* in the service of the Republic! Opera in the evening. *Panurge*.[5] Laïs incomparable in Panurge. Mme Guénet[6] a charming singer. Mme Gardel and Nivelon in the 'Pas russe' inimitable; it is worth a voyage from Ireland to America and from America to Paris to see that single dance. I think now I have got on regimentals, I begin to write like a very pretty gentleman. There is a strong report (and I believe true) that Hammond,[7] who was embassador from England to the United States, is now at Calais with

[1] i.e. the Champs-Élysées, as amended in *Life*, ii, 176.

[2] The programme for the Fête Nationale of 10 Aug. was published in the *Moniteur* for 10 Aug. It included horse and foot racing, tilting and an aerostatic exercise in the Champ de Mars and a concert, an illumination, fireworks, and a ball in the Champs-Élysées.

[3] See above, p. 214, n. 14.

[4] *Life*, ii, 176, has 'I almost say'.

[5] Cf. Diary for 28 Mar. 1796 (above, p. 134).

[6] Not identified.

[7] George Hammond (1763–1853), British minister at Philadelphia, 1791–5; under-secretary at the foreign office, 1795–1806, 1807–9 (*D.N.B.*).

some proposals for peace on the part of the English Ministry.[1] I do not at all apprehend that anything will come of it. It is a manoeuvre of Pitt's, in order to prepare for meeting the new Parliament with a declaration that he has been ready on his part to make peace, but that the pride and haughtiness of the French government would listen to no conditions but such as were dishonorable to England. John Bull is not yet at all beaten into his senses. For my part I do not see how it is possible for France and England to make peace, preserving their respective governments. I think one or other must go down. I do not speak of the nations, but merely of the governments.

## 20 Aug. 1796

The gaps in my journal will demonstrate how my time hangs on my hands. Called on Gen[eral]l Chérin this morning; found him very courteous. He tells me we shall certainly set off in ten days, viz. the 30th inst. Well, ten days more! However '*'Tis but in vain, for soldiers to complain*',[2] as the poet sweetly sings. He tells me also that a valet-de-chambre has presented himself to be hired with him who speaks English and has lately been thro' England, Scotland and Ireland; that he has not at all the appearance or manners of a domestic, and that he (Chérin) suspects that he may be an emissary slipt at him as a spy. It is very probable. He promises to send him to me on a message in two or three days in order that I may sift him as to his knowledge of England &c. *À la bonheure!*[3] I see in the papers (I hope it is true) that the French Admiral Richéry has sailed from Cadiz in company with a powerful Spanish squadron.[4] If that be so, it will probably bring matters between Spain & England to a crisis. If they pick up the Brest squadron and the Dutch fleet now lying in the Texel, I think they must be an overmatch for anything John Bull can produce against them. If that were so! Huzza! Huzza! (Sings) '*How merrily we live that soldiers be, that soldiers, soldiers be!*'[5] I am vastly musical and engaging this evening, methinks. Well, God knows the heart.

## 23 Aug. 1796

Met Chérin today, driving about in his cabriolet. He stopped me, and asked was I ready to set off. I answered, in five minutes, and that I waited only for his orders. He then desired me to call on him tomorrow at eleven in order to settle about our departure, so perhaps we may set off before the 30th.

The armies continue victorious in all quarters. The news of today is (I mean the report) that Richéry and the Spaniards are before Lisbon and that a French army

[1] In fact he was en route to Berlin via Hamburg. [2] *The buck's bottle companion* (London, 1775).

[3] Corrected in *Life*, ii, 177, to 'À la bonne heure!', meaning 'Well done!'.

[4] According to a letter from Cadiz dated 5 Aug. 1796, Richéry had sailed from that port (*Moniteur*, 22 Aug. 1796).

[5] Opening line in Henry Bate Dudley, *The flitch of bacon* (1779), act I.

[is] in full march across Spain in order to enter Portugal.[1] That would be a blow to Master John Bull fifty times worse than the affair of Leghorn. Why the unhappy Portuguese did not make their peace at the same time with Spain I cannot conceive, except it was, as is most probably the case, that they durst not consult their own safety for fear of offending the English. What an execrable nation that is! And how cordially I hate them! If this affair of Portugal be true, there will not remain one port friendly to England from Hamburgh to Trieste, and probably much farther both ways. It is impossible she can long stand this. Well, if the visitation of Providence be sometimes slow, it is always sure. If our expedition succeeds, I think we shall give her the coup de grâce, and make her pay dear for the rivers of blood she has made flow in our poor country, her massacres, her pillage & her fraud. '*Alors, ce sera mon tour!*'[2] We shall see, we shall see! Oh that I were, this fine morning, on the Cave Hill,[3] at the head of my regiment! Well, all in, good time.

## 24 Aug. 1796

Saw Chérin. Our departure fixed for the 1st September. '*The Devil take Henry of Lancaster and thee; patience is stale and I am weary of it!*'[4] He asked me to dine with him the day before we set off. Saw the servant of whom he spoke to me; found nothing suspicious about him, yet after all he may be a rogue. It is seven clear days yet, *at least*, to our departure. Damn it, for me!

## 25 Aug. 1796

The report today is that Spain has declared war against England,[5] and that the declaration, to speak technically, contains sixty-three *counts*. I hope in God it is true.

## 2 Sept. 1796

Here I am yet! Well, it does not signify swearing, so (sings) ''*Tis but in vain, for soldiers to complain*'. To divert the spleen which is devouring me, I have been these some days back throwing memorandums of my life and opinions on paper from recollection.[6] They are very ill done, and probably inaccurate in the dates, but they are better than nothing. I have already filled nearly two books as big as

[1] It was reported from London that France and Spain intended to invade Portugal (*Moniteur*, 26 Aug. 1796).

[2] Meaning 'Then it will be my turn!', though Tone probably means 'Then it will be our turn!'. In *Life*, ii, 178, William Tone substitutes 'notre' for 'mon'.

[3] About 6 km north-north-west of Belfast. Fourteen months previously, Tone had spent two days there with friends who were fellow members of the 1st Belfast regiment of Volunteers (see Autobiography, below, p. 333).

[4] *Richard II*, v, v.

[5] It was reported towards the end of August that Spain had declared war on England (*Courier Universel*, 25 Aug. 1796). In fact Spain declared war on 11 October.

[6] His autobiography (above, pp 260 et seq.).

this.[1] Saw Chérin today. He knows no more about our departure than I do, but he promised me faithfully to write a pressing letter to Hoche on the subject.

## To General Henri Jacques Guillaume Clarke, 5 September 1796

Archives Nationales, AF IV, carton 1671, f. 84.

See Diary for 5 Sept. 1796 (below).

Dear Sir,

I take the liberty to trouble you with this, by direction of General Chérin, with whom I had expectations of travelling to Rennes; but the time of his departure being utterly uncertain and my stay in Paris being attended with a considerable expence, which I can very ill afford, I entreat, if the request be not an improper one, that you will procure me *an order to depart with the first courier.* I should not give you this trouble did I not fear being reduced a second time to difficulties in money matters; and I think it right to inform you that since I received my commission I have not drawn a single ration of any kind, as I do not wish to put the Republic to expence, at a time when I am rendering her no service. I shall call tomorrow at twelve, in expectation of an answer, at which time, if you should be engaged, I request you will be so good as to leave it with your Aid du Camp. With many thanks for your past kindness

I am, Dear Sir, Yours very truly

J. Smith

## Diary, 5–9 September 1796

T.C.D., Tone papers, MS 2049, f. 127ʳ; *Life*, ii, 179.

### 5 Sept. 1796

Called on Chérin. He knows nothing further than that Colonel Shee,[2] a relation of Clarke's,[3] is gone down to Rennes.[4] He advised me to call on Clarke.

[1] The 'two books' are MS 2046, ff 1ʳ–47ᵛ, which bring the 'life and opinions' down to Feb. 1792 (above, pp 260–306).

[2] Henri Shée (1739–1820), born at Landrecies in French Flanders; son of William Shee, formerly of Camas, Co. Limerick, and his wife, a daughter of Pierre Preponier, a surgeon at Landrecies; he joined the French army and before the revolution had risen to the rank of colonel; under the empire he was prefect of the Bas-Rhin and a strong supporter of the regime; created a count, 1810; after the restoration he was created a peer of France and at Ney's trial voted for death (*Burke's landed gentry of Great Britain and Ireland* (London, 1858), pp 895–6; *Dict. parl. franç.*; *Biographie universelle ancienne et moderne*).

[3] Shée's sister Louise was Clarke's mother.

[4] On 30 July 1796 the Directory instructed Citizen Shée to accompany Hoche 'en qualité d'agent civil' (Debidour, *Recueil des actes du Directoire Exécutif*, iii, 224).

Came home in a rage and wrote a letter[1] to Clarke, supplicating an order for my immediate departure, which I delievered to his aid du camp, Fleury.

### 8 Sept. 1796

This evening received a note from Chérin informing me that he has received letters from Gen[era]l Hoche and desiring to see me in the morning. So at last, I hope, we are about to move; I never suffered so much *ennui* in all my life together as since Hoche's departure, which is now almost a month. Scribbling now and again at my memoirs, which I have brought down to the beginning of 1792.[2] Stupid enough, but when my mind is so agitated as it is at present, I can neither read, write, nor think. I hope in God I am at last going to *act*. It is high time; but it is no fault of mine that I did not begin long since. Well, better late than never!

### 9 Sept. 1796

Called on Chérin. He promises positively that we set off the 13th, and has desired me to call on him the 12th, in the morning, to receive his definitive orders; so at last I hope I am about to move.

## Matilda Tone to Thomas Russell, 11 September 1796

Nat. Arch. (Ire.), Rebellion papers, 620/25/136.

Tone's wife Matilda's authorship of this letter is evident from the contents and is confirmed by the signature 'M.T.'.

Sep$^{ber}$ ye 11$^{th}$–'96

My very dear Friend,

I have received several letters from you & am much concerned to find by y[ou]r last of the 3rd of June that you suffer any anxiety from my silence. I never wrote to *any one* since Arthur went home,[3] as I knew Reynolds wrote frequently. I trusted you w[oul]d hear *of us*. We are still in the same situation in which A[rthur] left us, indeed I cannot boast of our having enjoyed much health, happiness or comfort but the privations have been the order of the day with us, & I trust we have principles to support us under circumstances infinitely more trying than any we have met here.

[1] Preceding document (above). [2] See above, pp 305–6.

[3] Arthur Tone had joined Tone and Mrs Tone in Belfast in June 1795 and had accompanied them to America (see Autobiography, above, p. 266). On 10 Dec. 1795 he sailed from Philadelphia for Belfast on board the *Susannah* with instructions to inform Russell and others of Tone's plan to go to France (see Autobiography, below, p. 340). Arthur arrived after twenty-eight days' sailing (see above, p. 266, n. 3). Having visited Belfast he went to stay briefly with his parents in Dublin. By May 1796, thanks to assistance

I had a letter from Tone about a fortnight since.[1] We are all to join him in the Back Countries this fall.[2] This is an arduous undertaking, considering how dreadfully fatiguing travelling is in this country, particularly with children, but I am not discouraged.

I rec[eive]d Robert Simms's letter with £100 enclosed & another by the *Susannah*. I will not attempt to express my gratitude for his kindness & attention; his own benevolent & honest heart will tell him how I feel.

I have also rec[eive]d William S[imms]'s letter; it gave me infinite pleasure. How I delight in my cousins! Indeed, my dear & respected friends, it is not exaggeration to say, language can't express the love & admiration I feel for you all. I mean this letter for all my friends; it is the only one I will write. I am not fond of writing; when it is not *necessary* it is *idle*.

As for your part, my good friend, I must now fire at you a little. From my country, where you cou[l]d hardly mention a subject I w[oul]d not be warmly interested in, you write & send 3,000 miles a *few lines* stating that you have '*just* heard of a vessell which is *just* going off' dated the 3rd of June; you write on the 6th by the same vessell, & I get a letter from one of y[ou]r closest friends by it of the 20th of May. This is incivic. Next—you have never noticed my poor father & mother[3] since we left Ireland. Their situation is truly pitiable, & we relied on you to be great comfort to them—this is very incivic & I think the gov[ernmen]t much handsomer than you.[4]

As to the circumstance you allude to in y[ou]r two last, I am very delicate in giving my opinion, but as you have twice asked it I will give it to you like an honest republican. *I entirely disapprove of it.*[5] Friendship, honor & principle all forbid it unless you have the approbation of her family & prospects, which I confess I cannot foresee. Tho' a young man, you are not a boy & you have much experience. For my part I cannot conceive your being led away by passion (particularly at this time) to involve a lovely girl in inevitable ruin—for I will not one moment suppose your intentions are not serious. And now, my dear friend, I feel it necessary to appologize [*sic*] for the manner I have written to you in. I hope you will not attribute it to any want of regard; no I assure you the sincere affection I have felt for you these six years is this moment as ardent as ever, & nothing cou[l]d

from Russell and other friends of Tone, he was attending school in Belfast. (See Tone family letters in MacDermot, *Tone*, chap. 8; above, p. 37, n. 1).

[1] Very probably the one begun on 17 July (see Diary, above, p. 239).

[2] Ostensibly this meant that Matilda and her family were to join Tone in the undeveloped country further west a month or so later; in truth it meant that they were to join him in France, of which plan Russell would already have learnt from Arthur Tone.

[3] i.e. her parents-in-law, Peter and Margaret Tone. Her own father seems to have been dead by 1796 and her mother was probably comfortably off.

[4] An allusion to Peter Tone being employed by the Dublin paving, lighting and cleansing commissioners (see above, p. 37, n. 3).

[5] According to Madden, in 1795 or 1796 'Russell formed an attachment for Miss Simms, the sister of his friends William and Robert Simms of Belfast. In 1803, when he visited Belfast on his unfortunate and ill-advised mission, his companion, James Hope, says he spoke of Miss Simms in terms of sincere affection; and the impression left on Hope's mind was that Russell was strongly attached to her.' (R. R. Madden, *The United Irishmen*, 3rd ser. (London, 1846), ii, 148).

induce me to wound y[ou]r feelings but to save you from involving yourself & the woman you love in lasting misery & ruin. I shall say no more on this, as I trust you believe me that what I have said was dictated by the most affectionate regard.

For many reasons I advise you *not to place any confidence* in the friend[1] with whom you had the famous quarrell of 'yes, yes' & 'no, no'.

Remember us[2] with sincere affection to every man, woman & child in Belfast. You have not mentioned a word of Arthur. That boy gives me great uneasiness. I can't give you any idea of the unremitting kindness & attention we have received from Reynolds. Mention it to him. Napper Tandy is at present with us. He is an excellent old citizen & has had a harder struggle for his life lately.

Don't mention a word of the back countries to any of our family or they will come to us.

God Almighty bless you my dear Tom. We are all well & in great spirits to undertake our journey. Tell Will S[imms] I hope they will take good care of that charming old [*word illegible*]. Mary[3] & Maria[4] send their love to you. Maria sends her love to Arthur.

Ever aff[ectionate]ly y[ou]rs
M.T.

[on face]
Mr Tho^s Russell
Belfast[5]
[postmark:] Oc 28 96

# Diary, 12–16 September 1796

T.C.D., Tone papers, MS 2049, ff 127^r–127^v; *Life*, ii, 179.

## 12 Sept. 1796

Called on Chérin by appointment. He is gone to the country for two or three days! Hell, hell, hell!

## 15 Sept. 1796

At last I have brought Chérin to the point. He has received a courier last night from Gen[era]l Hoche and he tells me now I may set off with the first courier, or wait a few days for him, but I am tired waiting. I wrote therefore, by his direction, a note to the Minister at War,[6] praying an order to depart with the first courier for Rennes, and he has promised to get it for me by tomorrow. Huzza!

1 Not identified. 2 Interlined in substitution for 'me', which is struck out.
3 Her sister-in-law Mary Tone (later Giauque). 4 Her daughter.
5 'Belfast' is struck out in another hand and 'in prison in Dublin' substituted.
6 Pétiet. Tone's note has not been found.

16 Sept. 1796

Got my order, and presented it to the directors of the post. There is a courier for tomorrow, with whom I secured my place. Packed up my kit, &c. As gay as a lark.

## To Charles Delacroix, 17 September 1796

Archives des Affaires Étrangères, Corresp. Politique Angleterre, cote 589, f. 395.

Being about to leave for Rennes, Tone thanks Delacroix for his kindness.

Paris, le 1er jour complémentaire, An 4me

Au Citoyen Charles de la Croix, Ministre des relations extérieures de la République Française

Citoyen Ministre,

Étant sur le point de partir aujourd'hui pour le Quartier Général de Rennes, je prens la liberté de vous faire mes sincères remerci[e]mens de la bonté avec laquelle vous avez bien voulu me recevoir, et des services essentiels dont je suis persuadé que ma patrie est redevable à votre patriotisme et à votre zèle pour la cause de la liberté. Je sais trop combien votre tems est précieux pour vouloir en abuser par une visite de cérémonie ou par une longue épître. Je vous prie seulement d'accepter ma sincère reconnoissance de toutes vos bontés, dont je suis vivement pénétré et que je n'oublierai jamais.

Salut et respect
T. Wolfe Tone
dit
James Smith

## Diary, 17–27 September 1796

T.C.D., Tone papers, MS 2049, ff 127v–132v; *Life*, ii, 179–80, 205–10.

17 Sept. 1796

Took leave of Madgett, Ahern and Sullivan; wrote two letters of acknowledgement, to Carnot[1] and De la Croix,[2] thanking them for their kindness, &c., &c. *At three o'clock in the afternoon left Paris!*[3] It is now exactly seven months and five

[1] Not found. [2] Above.

[3] For Rennes and then Brest, in Brittany, in order to embark for Ireland.

days since I arrived there, and forms a very important era in my life. Whether it is for good or evil to my country and to myself, the event must determine; but I can safely say I have acted all thro' to the very best of my conscience and judgement, and I think I may say I have not conducted myself ill. I certainly did not expect on my arrival to have succeeded as well as I have done, and I have been under some difficulties at times, having not a soul to advise or communicate with. I have now done with Paris, at least for some time, and God knows whether I shall ever revisit it, but in all events I shall ever look back on the time I spent there with the greatest satisfaction. I believe there is no part of my conduct there, at least with regard to business, that I need wish to recall. As to pleasure or amusement, I had very little. I formed and endeavoured to form no connexions. I visited and was visited by nobody, French or foreigner, and left Paris after seven months without being acquainted with a single family; that is singular enough! The Spectacles[1] formed my grand resource against the monotony of my situation but on the whole I passed my time dull enough. Well, if ever I return I will make myself amends. I am now like the Turkish spy, '*who passed five and forty years at Paris without being known or suspected*'.[2] I dare say however Mr Pitt knows I was there, as close as I kept; if he did, it was by no fault or indiscretion of mine. It is singular enough that having passed my time in a manner so monotonous and not leaving behind me a single person whom on the score of personal regard I had reason to regret, I yet quit Paris with something like reluctance. But I made that remark before. *Allons!* I am now afloat again. Let us see what will come of this voyage!

## 18–19 Sept. 1796

On the road. No adventures. Passed the second day thro' the country of the Chouans.[3] It is delicious. It is as well wooded as New Jersey, of which it often put me in mind. The second night (for we travelled night and day) '*fear fell upon me*'. How if the Chouans were to stop the mail, as they have sometimes done? Looked at my sabre and pistols and was consoled. Determined to die hard in case of a battle, for I knew there was no quarter with these brigands. Luckily all quiet. Did not see a single Chouan. Huzza! Travelling a bad business. I hate it. Never made a tour completely to my satisfaction but with P.P.[4] He is indeed '*an agreeable companion in a post chaise*'.[5] I wish he were beside me in the mail, instead of this beast of a courier. Well, we may meet yet, and so ''*Tis but in vain*', &c.[6]

[1] *Life*, ii, 180, substitutes 'Theatres'.

[2] An allusion to *L'espion des grands seigneurs dans les cours des princes chrétiens*, a satirical piece published in Paris in 1684 by Giovanni Paolo Marana (1642–93), and translated into English as *Letters writ by a Turkish spy who lived five and forty years undiscover'd at Paris* (1694).

[3] For the *chouans* and *chouannerie*, see above, p. 140, n. 2.

[4] Thomas Russell.

[5] George Colman, *Tit for tat* (1786), act III.

[6] *The buck's bottle companion* (London, 1775).

## 20 Sept. 1796

At three this morning arrived at Rennes, having passed three nights agreeably without sleep, '*An hundred and twenty miles in thirty-four hours is pretty smart riding, but nothing to the fatigue of recruiting.*'[1] I do not think that quotation is any great things, myself; but let it pass. '*Well, now I am in Arden, the more fool I; when I was at home, I was in a better place.*'[2] Went to bed and slept like a dragon till eleven; rose and sent for[3] MacSheehy,[4] who has been here some days. He tells me all is going on, as he believes, prosperously. General Hoche is gone out fishing and does not return till night. I am glad Hoche is a fisherman, because I am one myself.

Wrote a note to Hoche to let him know I am arrived, and gave it to MacSheehy to deliver. Dined alone deliciously and drank a bottle of excellent claret, with divers patriotic and constitutional toasts. Thought of P.P. and my dearest Love ten thousand times. I am as pleased as Punch to find myself in quarters at last. '*Good apartments, Jack!*'[5] Went in the evening to the *Comédie.* Bitter bad! The piece was, to my great surprise, Addison's *Drummer*,[6] very tolerably translated, and I was glad to see the French enjoy it extremely, particularly Mr Vellum.[7] I remember Vellum used to be P.P.'s *grand cheval de bataille*, and furnished him with divers inimitable quotations: '*The gift is twofold, &c.*',[8] '*A thundering dog! &c., &c.*',[9] '*Ah, those were fine times, Mr Rigmarol!*'.[10] I delight to recall the nonsense that P.P. and I have vented together, and I would this night gladly give one half the contents of my purse, which indeed to speak candidly is no enormous sum, for the pleasure of his company. Well I do love the dog dearly, that is the truth of it. I am tired now, so I will go to bed and try to recover the arrear of sleep which is due to me.

## 21 Sept. 1796

Called on General Hoche and sat with him for about a quarter of an hour. Very civil, but no news as yet. I am to be for some time Mr Smith, an American. He asked me about Duckett, who is here, it seems. I said I neither knew nor intended

[1] George Farquhar, *The recruiting officer* (1706), I, i. Where Tone has 'thirty-four' the original has 'thirty'.

[2] *As you like it*, II, iv. In *Life*, ii, 205, 'Arden' becomes 'Ardenne'.

[3] *Life*, ii, 205, inserts 'my adjoint'.

[4] Bernard MacSheehy (1774–1807), born in Ireland; officier d'état-major, 1794; capitaine adjoint on Hoche's staff, 30 June 1796; adjutant commander, 1800; adjutant general, Irish legion, which he raised, 1803; killed at Preußisch-Eylau (Archives de la Guerre, dossier; F. W. Van Brock, 'Captain MacSheehy's mission' in *Irish Sword*, x (1971–2), pp 215–28; C. J. Woods, 'The secret mission to Ireland of Captain Bernard MacSheehy, an Irishman in French service, 1796' in *Cork Historical and Archaeological Society Journal*, 2nd ser., lxxviii (1973), pp 93–108).

[5] R. B. Sheridan, *The rivals* (1775), II, i.

[6] *The drummer, or the haunted house* (1716), by Joseph Addison (1672–1719). One French version was published in 1736 as *Le tambour nocturne, ou le mari divin*, and another (really an imitation) in 1737 as *La prétendue veuve, ou l'époux magicien*.

[7] Vellum is Sir George Truman's valet.

[8] *The drummer*, II, i. [9] Ibid., III, i. [10] Oliver Goldsmith, *Essays* (1765), xix.

to know him, and I mentioned his prating at Paris to all his acquaintance about his influence with General Clarke and with Hoche himself; so now if Hoche puts any confidence in that fellow, at least it is not my fault. Hoche spoke obscurely as if there were somebody here who knew and wished to see me, but I did not press him for an explanation, nor did he offer it. A few days may shew more. Called on Colonel Shee, uncle to General Clarke, who is here. He tells me he was stopped on this side of Laval at two o'clock in the day by seven Chouans who robbed him of every article of his property, except a box of papers relating to our business which he was bringing to Hoche, and which escaped their search as it were by miracle. It was most fortunate! This was but a few days since, so I have had a good escape. I doubt if I should be able, single handed, to conquer seven Chouans armed with firelocks, as he tells me his lovers were. They offered him no personal injury, and he has learned since that the favor was not intended for him, but for a commissary who was expected to pass with money to pay the troops. Dined at head quarters with the staff, Hoche, Hédouville,[1] Mermet,[2] &c., &c. All very slovenly and soldierlike; but nobody minds a dirty plate or thing of that kind here. '*On est à la guerre, comme à la guerre*', as the French say.

## 22 Sept. 1796

This being the 1st Vendémiaire, and of course the 1st day of the 5th year of the French Republic, one, indivisible and imperishable, we had a grand review of the troops in the Champ de Mars, with horse racing, &c., and speeches from the constituted authorities. After the review I met Hoche. He asked me did I hear the cannonade? I said I did. 'Ay', said he, 'you will soon hear enough of that'. I answered the sooner the better. In the evening at the Comédie, to see a new piece written by Privat,[3] one of Hoche's aid du camps [*sic*], on the termination of the war in La Vendée, in which he introduced some apposite and well-turned[4] compliments to the General and the Republic. The characters were filled by the young men of the État-Major, and it went off very well. The theatre was free for the ladies of the town (who by the bye seem to me villainous ugly)[5] and after the play there was a grand ball at the Town house[6] given by Hoche, for which I had a ticket, but unluckily I was not well, so instead of going to the ball I came home and went to bed, which was a pity for, '*with my hat so well cocked, and my hair so well curled, I*

[1] Gabriel Marie Théodore Joseph, comte d'Hédouville (1755–1825), a page to the queen and an army officer before the revolution; general of division, 1795; chief of staff to Hoche, 1796 (Six, *Dict. des généraux & amiraux*).

[2] Julien Augustin Joseph Mermet (1772–1837) rose from the ranks; general of brigade, 1796; baron of the empire, 1811 (ibid.).

[3] Jean François Privat (1759–1814) served in the ranks of the Gardes françaises before the revolution; sous lieutenant, 1792; captain, Oct. 1796; retired from the army, 1801, and entered civil service, becoming a revenue inspector (A. M. Chuquet, *Quatre généraux de la révolution* (2 vols, Paris, 1911), i, 273–4).

[4] *Life*, ii, 207, has 'well timed'.

[5] In *Life* the words in parentheses are omitted.

[6] In *Life*, ii, 207, 'Hotel de Ville' is substituted for 'Town house'.

*looked like a man of the very first world*'.[1] I believe that quotation is not correct, but no matter. It is as good as one of P.P.'s quotations at any rate.

## 23 Sept. 1796

At work all the morning with Col[one]l Shee making an analysis of the distribution of the troops actually in Ireland. The General called in and sat with us half an hour. Dined as usual with the État-Major. I am now to all intents one of the family and I like it of all things. (Sings) '*How merrily we live that soldiers be!*'[2] I have got rooms at head quarters and moved my *kit* accordingly. We are all lodged in the palace of the ci-devant Bishop of Rennes, a superb mansion but not much the better of the Revolution. The chapel, for example, is converted into a stable, and divers other changes of a like nature have taken place. I do not know but I sleep tonight in his Lordship's bedchamber. Col. Shee asked me today did I know Duckett? I said to him, as I had said to Hoche,[3] that I neither knew nor desired to know him, for that I believed him to be a blackguard. Shee answered, it was exactly his own resolution; that Duckett had made two or three sets at him, but that he had always avoided him. He added that Duckett has told several people here that he is *sent here by the Committee of Nine who manage the affairs of the Catholics as their plenipotentiary*! The impudence of this last stroke to be sure did astonish me! I answered Shee that Duckett was a scoundrel, and if he were to tell so outrageous a lie in my presence that I would knock him down on the spot. I also besought him to put Hoche on his guard, particularly as to this last story, offering at the same time to confront him before the General and to compel him to tell the truth. Shee answered that it was unnecessary, for that he was sure Hoche saw thro' him completely. But I am not yet quite satisfied, and I believe I will take an opportunity myself to set this matter on its right footing. Damn the impudence of the rascal! My brother ambassador! Marry, come up, indeed![4] I'll Duckett him, the scoundrel, if I can catch him fairly in my grip.[5]

## 24 Sept. 1796

Walked with Col[one]l Shee in the garden. He tells me that Hoche has selected the *élite* of the Army of the Ocean, which consisted of 117,000 men, for our

[1] Cf. 'my manners so well form'd, and my wig so well curl'd, I look like a man of the very first world' (Christopher Anstey, *The new Bath guide, or memoirs of the B[lunde]r[hea]d family* (1766)).

[2] Opening line of Henry Bate Dudley, *The flitch of bacon* (1779), act I.

[3] See Diary for 21 Sept. (above, pp 316–17).

[4] 'Marry, come up, I trow' (*Romeo and Juliet*, II, v).

[5] Note by William Tone: 'I wonder my father did not record a laughable incident which occurred at one of these dinners, and which he often mentioned to my mother. The conversation was running on the great Lord Chatham, and the funeral honors which he received at the national expense, which my father was explaining to General Hoche. Duckett thrust himself between them, and observed, that to receive such a recompense, had always been the highest object of his ambition. All stared at the modesty of the declaration, when Mr Shee gravely observed that he never saw anyone who was more likely to be gratified in such a wish—(a pause ensued, and every eye was cast with wonder upon him)—"for, wherever you die, the parish will surely have to bury you".'

expedition; that the arms and everything are ready and that we are waiting only on the Marine. He also spoke as if in a fortnight more we might put ourselves in motion, but I did not press him for specific information. The season is slipping away fast thro' our fingers; however, I believe they are doing their best.

## 25 Sept. 1796

Walked as usual in the garden with Colonel Shee. I turned the discourse upon my own situation and that which I had filled in Ireland. Shee told me that both the Executive Directory and Gen[era]l Hoche were perfectly satisfied as to who and what I was, by means of a channel which he was not at liberty to inform me of,[1] but that I might be perfectly easy on the score of my credit. I answered that I was extremely glad they had satisfied themselves as to my veracity, and that I dreaded no investigation or scrutiny into my character or principles. I added that I was the better pleased at this, inasmuch as I did not know but I might appear to them in the same light with that scoundrel Duckett, who is here. He assured me again that they were perfectly assured that I had said nothing of myself but the strict truth; he added that he had spoken to Hoche about Duckett, and that Hoche said he would send him back to Paris instantly, but that he desired him to keep the fellow here until the last moment, and then to dispatch him. I was very glad to hear this, because I disliked exceedingly the idea of such a rascally adventurer thrusting himself into our business. However, he is now I believe sufficiently known, and of course can do no mischief. We then spoke in general of our expedition, which is delayed entirely by the Marine. The General sets off tomorrow for Brest to hurry them, and, as he has extraordinary powers, I am in hopes he will work Messieurs the Commissaires. I collect from Shee's discourse that we will have 1,000 cavalry ready to mount, but the Irish must find horses. I do not yet know the number of infantry At dinner Privat, one of Hoche's aid du camps [*sic*], and author of the piece which was played the other night, told me that Hoche and he were private soldiers in the *Gardes Françaises* and were made corporals together on the same day. He also told me that Hoche's *coup de sabre* was received in a duel with a fellow soldier.[2] I *ennuye* myself[3] considerably at Rennes, but I had notwithstanding a thousand times rather be here than at Paris. I am pestered a little with MacSheehy, who is just such another as Sir William Browne,[4] whom I knew some years ago in London. I give him some hard rebukes at times, but he returns still to the charge. He has a vast inclination to be a coxcomb, and he wants the talents, and a would-be coxcomb is a poor animal.

[1] Possibly Arthur O'Connor, whom Hoche met at Angers in the middle of August (see above, p. 215, n. 3).

[2] In *Life* the remainder of the entry for this day is omitted.

[3] *Recte* 'je m'ennuie', meaning 'I am bored'.

[4] Sir William Augustus Brown (1764–1830) succeeded to a baronetcy, 1784; became insane, *c.*1790 (G. E. C[okayne], *Complete baronetage* (5 vols, Exeter, 1900–06), v, 73).

## 26 Sept. 1796

The General set off this morning at ten o'clock for Brest. I hope in God he may hurry those fellows. I dread the equinoctial gales passing over and finding us unprepared. By Shee's discourse I fancy it is intended that we make a race for it. Happy go lucky, in that case! I was in hopes the Spanish fleet would have joined us at Brest, but he tells me they are returned to Cadiz after escorting Richéry to some unknown latitude. Damn their foolish souls! They will be beaten, and the French also, in detail, whereas, if they were instantly to join, the united fleets in the Channel would be stronger than anything England could for some time oppose to them, and a week would be sufficient for our business. If they let this occasion escape them, as I fear they will, they need never expect to meet such another. I am in the horrors today. Well, let us see what Hoche's expedition will produce! He will be absent five or six days. Brest is 180 miles from this. '*Time, time!*' At all events, for me, the die is cast, and I am utterly desperate as to the event. Come what come may, I have done and am doing my duty, and if I fall, I fall. I have not on that score the smallest burthen on my mind. A short time now must (*I think*) put me at least out of uncertainty, and I am sure the worst event that can happen cannot be much more painful than the state of suspence and anxiety in which I have so long languished. Once again, *courage*! Let us see what Hoche will say on his return!

## 27 Sept. 1796

The report is that Thomas Grenville[1] is at Paris with some propositions for peace. I do not mind it. It is a fetch of Pitt's, if it be at all true that he is there.[2] Besides Col[one]l Shee has letters today from Gen[era]l Clarke which make no mention of his arrival, but assure us that everything is going on as fast as possible. '*As fast as possible*' is however too slow for my impatience. My life hangs terribly on my hands. After all however I had rather stagnate at Rennes than at Paris.[3]

# Autobiography (1792, 1795–6), *c.* 28 September 1796

T.C.D., Tone papers, MS 2046, ff 48$^{r}$–69$^{r}$; *Life*, i, 58–69.

Continued from above, p. 306. It is possible that this part of the Autobiography was begun before Tone left Paris (17 Sept.) or even on his journey west (17–20 Sept.). It is more likely he began it after arriving in Rennes (20 Sept.), for in his

[1] Thomas Grenville (1755–1846), M.P. and diplomat (*D.N.B.*).

[2] It was rumoured near the end of September that an English envoy had arrived in Paris to treat for peace. An official announcement stated that an envoy had not arrived and gave the terms on which the Directory was willing to treat. (*Courier Universel*, 27, 30 Sept. 1796; *Moniteur*, 1 Oct. 1796).

[3] *Life*, ii, 210, adds 'September 28, 29, 30. Blank.'

Diary for 27 Sept. he complains 'my life hangs terribly on my hands' (see above, p. 320). On finishing what he has to say about events of July 1792, he moves on to the early summer of 1795, dating his treatment of this period 'Rennes, Sep[r] 28th, 1796' (see below, p. 330).

## Volume the Third

## Memorandums relative to my life & opinions, 1796

THE Society of United Irishmen beginning to attract the public notice considerably in consequence of the events which I have mentioned,[1] and it being pretty generally known that I was principally instrumental in its formation, I was one day surprised by a visit from the barrister[2] who had, about two years before, spoken to me on the part of the Whig leaders, a business of which I had long since discharged my memory. He told me he was sorry to see the new line I was adopting in politics, the more so as I might rely upon it that the principles I now hold would never be generally adopted and consequently I was devoting myself without advancing any beneficial purpose; he also testified some surprise at my conduct and insinuated pretty directly, tho' with great civility, that I had not kept faith with the Whigs, with whom he professed to understand I had connected myself, and whom in consequence I ought to have consulted before I took so decided a line of conduct as I had lately done. I did not like the latter part of his discourse at all. However, I answered him, with great civility on my part, that as to the principles he mentioned, I had not adopted them without examination; that as to the pamphlet[3] I had written in the Catholic cause, I had not advanced a syllable that I did not conscientiously believe, and consequently I was neither inclined to repent nor retract; as to my supposed connexion with the Whigs I reminded him that I had not sought them; on the contrary, they had sought me; if they had, on reflection, not thought me worth cultivating, that was no fault of mine. I observed also that Mr Geo[rge] Ponsonby, whom I looked upon as principal in the business, had never spoken to me above a dozen times in my life and then merely on ordinary topics; that I was too proud to be treated in that manner, and, if I was supposed capable to render service to the party, it could only be by confiding in and communicating with me that I could be really serviceable, and on that footing only would I consent to be treated; that probably Mr Ponsonby would think that rather a lofty declaration, but it was my determination, the more as I knew he was rather a proud man. Finally I observed he had my permission to report all this, and that I looked on myself as under no tye[4] of obligation whatsoever; that I had written a pamphlet,[5] unsollicited [*sic*], in favor of the party; that I had consequently been employed in a business professionally, which

[1] See Autobiography, above, pp 303–6. [2] See above, p. 283.

[3] *An argument on behalf of the catholics of Ireland* (Dublin, 1791). It is reprinted above, vol. I, pp 108–28.

[4] Spelling modernised to 'tie' in *Life*, i, 59.

[5] *A review of the conduct of administration* (Dublin, 1790). It is reprinted above, vol. I, pp 26–49.

produced me eighty guineas; that I looked on myself as sufficiently rewarded, but I also considered the money as fully earned; that I had at present taken my party; that my principles were known, and I was not at all inclined to retract them. What I had done, I had done, and I was determined to abide by it.

My friend then said he was sorry to see me so obstinate in what he must consider an indiscreet line of conduct, and protesting that his principal object was to serve me, in which I believed him, he took his leave and this put an end completely to the idea of a connexion with the Whigs. I spoke rather haughtily in this affair, because I was somewhat provoked at the insinuation of duplicity, and besides I wished to have a blow at Mr George Ponsonby, who seemed desirous to retain me as a kind of pamphleteer in his service at the same time that he industriously avoided anything like communication with me, a situation to which I was neither so weak nor so mean as to suffer myself to be reduced; and as I well knew he was one of the proudest men in Ireland, I took care to speak on a footing of the most independant equality. After this discussion, I, for the second time, dismissed all idea of Ponsonby and the Whigs, but I had good reason a long time after to believe that he had not so readily forgot the business as I did, and indeed he was very near having his full revenge of me, as I shall mention in its place.[1]

I have already observed[2] that the first attempts of the Catholic Committee, after the secession of their aristocracy, were totally unsuccessful. In 1790 they could not even find a member of Parliament who would condescend to present their petition. In 1791 Richard Burke, then their agent, had prepared on their behalf a very well written philippic,[3] but which certainly was no petition, which, after considerable difficulties, resulting in a great degree from his want of temper and discretion, was, after being offered to and accepted by different members, at length finally refused; a circumstance which, by disgusting him extremely with all parties, I believe determined him to quit Ireland. After his departure another petition was prepared & presented by [ ],[4] but no unfortunate paper was ever so maltreated; the Committee in general, and its most active and ostensible members in particular, were vilified and abused in the grossest manner. They were called a rabble of obscure, porter-drinking mechanics, without property, pretention or influence, who met in holes and corners, and fancied themselves the representatives of the Catholic body, who disavowed and despised them. The independance and respectability of the sixty-eight renegadoes, who had set their

[1] In fact Tone did not do so, for lack of time, as he explains below, p. 330. For the episode Tone is referring to, see above, vol. I, p. 523, n. 1.

[2] See above, p. 300.

[3] Richard Burke, only son of Edmund Burke and a barrister, was agent in England to the (Irish) Catholic Committee. In Jan. 1792 he arrived in Ireland to assist the committee in preparing a petition to be presented to the Irish house of commons. Though the petition that he drafted was withdrawn at the end of Jan., it was printed as a pamphlet, *Petition of the Roman Catholics of Ireland intended to have been presented to parliament in February 1792, with a preface* (Dublin, 1792). At the end of June, Burke's services were politely dispensed with. (*Correspondence of Edmund Burke*, vii, ed. P. J. Marshall and John A. Woods (Cambridge, 1968), pp 12, 45–7; see also above, vol. I, p. 204).

[4] Blank in MS. This petition was presented on 18 Feb. 1792 by John Egan, M.P. for Tallow (*Parl. reg. Ire.*, xii, 15–16).

hands so infamously to their act of apostacy,[1] were extolled to the skies, while the lowest and most clumsy personalities were heaped upon the leaders of the Committee, particularly Edward Byrne and John Keogh, who had the honor to be selected from their brethern and exposed as butts for the small wit of the prostitutes of the Government. Finally the petition of the Catholics, three millions of people, was by special motion of David Latouche taken off the table of the House of Commons, where it had been suffered to lie for three days, and rejected.[2] Never was an address to a legislative body more unpitifully used. The people of Belfast, rapidly advancing in the career of wisdom and liberality, had presented a petition on behalf of the Catholics much more pointed than that which they presented for themselves; for their petition was extremely guarded, asking only the right of elective franchise and equal admission to grand juries, whereas that of Belfast prayed their entire admission to all the rights of citizens. This petition was also, on motion of the same member, taken of[f] the table and rejected,[3] and the two papers sent forth together to wander as they might.

There seems from this time out a special providence to have watched over the affairs of Ireland, and to have turned to her profit and advantage the deepest laid and most artful schemes of her enemies. Every measure adopted, and skilfully adopted, to thwart the expectations of the Catholics, and to crush the rising spirit of union between them and the Dissenters, has[4] without exception only tended to confirm and fortify both; and the fact I am about to mention is for one a striking proof of the truth of the assertion.

The principal charge, in the general outcry raised in the House of Commons against the General Committee, was that they were a self-appointed body, not nominated by the Catholics of the nation, and consequently not authorised to speak on their behalf. This argument, which in fact was the truth, was triumphantly dwelt upon by the enemies of the Catholics; but in the end it would have, perhaps, been more fortunate for their wishes if they had not laid such a stress upon this circumstance and drawn the line of separation so strongly between the General Committee and the body at large. For the Catholics throughout Ireland who had hitherto been indolent spectators of the business, seeing their brethren of Dublin, and especially the General Committee, insulted and abused for their exertions in pursuit of that liberty which, if attained, must be a common blessing to all, came forward, as one man, from every quarter of the nation with addresses and resolutions adopting the measures of the General Committee as their own, declaring that body the only organ competent to speak for the Catholics of Ireland, and condemning in terms of the most marked

[1] See above, vol. I, p. 166, n. 1.

[2] A petition of the committee acting for the Roman Catholics of Ireland requesting a further relaxation of the penal laws was presented to the house of commons on 18 Feb. 1792 and rejected on 20 Feb. by a majority of 208 to 25 (*Commons' jn. Ire.*, xv, 55–7).

[3] A petition of the inhabitants of the town of Belfast asking for the repeal of all penal and restrictive statutes against the Roman Catholics of Ireland was presented to the house of commons by John O'Neill on 8 Feb. 1792 and rejected on 20 Feb. (*Commons' jn. Ire.*, xv, 35, 57; *Parl. reg. Ire.*, xii, 82).

[4] Erroneously 'have' in MS. Corrected also in *Life*, i, 61.

disapprobation and contempt the conduct of the Sixty-eight Apostates,[1] who were so triumphantly held up by the hirelings of Government as the respectable part of the Catholic community. The question was now fairly decided; the aristocracy shrunk back in disgrace and obscurity, leaving the field open to the democracy, and that body neither wanted talents nor spirit to profit of the advantages of their present situation.

The Catholics of Dublin were at this period to the Catholics of Ireland what Paris at the commencement of the French Revolution was to the Departments.[2] Their sentiment was that of the nation, and whatever political measure they adopted was sure to be obeyed. Still, however, there was wanting a personal communication between the General Committee and their constituents in the country, and, as the Catholic question had now grown to considerable magnitude, so much indeed as to absorb all other political discussion, it became the first care of the leaders of the Committee to frame a plan of organisation for that purpose. It is to the sagacity of Myles Keon of Keonbrook in the Co. of Leitrim that his country is indebted for the system on which the General Committee was to be framed anew in a manner that should render it impossible to bring it again in doubt whether that body were or not the organ of the Catholic Will. His plan was to associate to the Committee, as then constituted, two members from each county and great city, actual residents of the place which they represented, who were however only to be summoned upon extraordinary occasions, leaving the common routine of business to the original members, who, I have already related,[3] were all residents of Dublin. The Committee, as thus constituted, would consist of half town,[4] and half country members; and the elections for the latter, he proposed, should be held by means of primary and electoral assemblies, held, the first in each parish, the second in each county and great town. He likewise proposed that the town members should be held to correspond regularly with their country associates, these with their immediate electors, and these again with the primary assemblies. A more simple and at the same time more comprehensive organisation could not be devised; by this means the General Committee became the centre of a circle embracing the whole nation, and pushing its rays instantaneously to the remotest part of the circumference. The plan was laid in writing before the General Committee by Myles Keon, and, after mature discussion, the first part relating to the association and election of the country members was adopted with some slight variation; the latter part, relating to the constant communication with the mass of the people was thought, under the circumstances, to be too hardy and was accordingly dropped *sub silentio*.

About this time it was (viz. [ ])[5] that the leaders of the Committee cast their eyes upon me to fill the station left vacant by Richard Burke. It was accordingly proposed by my friend John Keogh to appoint me their agent, with the title

[1] See above, vol. I, p. 325, n. 1.
[2] i.e. the *départements*, comparable with the counties in Ireland.
[3] See Autobiography (above, p. 298).
[4] i.e. Dublin.
[5] In the MS there is a 5 cm blank. *Life*, i, 62, reads: 'About this time it was that'.

of Assistant Secretary and a salary of £200 a year during my continuance in the service of the Committee. This proposal[1] was adopted unanimously.[2] John Keogh and John Sweetman were ordered to wait on me with the proposal in writing, to which I acceded immediately by a respectful answer, and I was that very day introduced in form to the Sub-Committee, and entered upon the functions of my new office.[3]

I was now placed in a very honorable but a very arduous situation. The Committee, having taken so decided a step as that proposing a general election of members to represent the Catholic body throughout Ireland, was well aware that they would be exposed to attacks of all possible kinds, and they were not disappointed; they were prepared, however, to repel them, and the literary part of the warfare fell of course to my share. On reviewing the conduct of my predecessor, Richard Burke, I saw that the rock on which he split was an overweening opinion of his own talents and judgement, and a desire, which he had not art enough to conceal, of guiding at his pleasure the measures of the Committee. I therefore determined to model my conduct with the greatest caution in that respect; I seldom or never offered my opinion, unless it was called for, in the Sub-Committee, but contented myself with giving my sentiments without reserve in private to the two men I most esteemed, and who had, in their respective capacities, the greatest influence on the body, I mean John Keogh and Richard McCormick, secretary to the General Committee. My discretion in this respect was not unobserved, and I very soon acquired, and I may say without vanity I deserved, the entire confidence and good opinion of the Catholics. The fact is I was devoted most sincerely to their cause, and being now retained in their service I would have sacrificed everything to ensure their success, and they knew it. I am satisfied they looked on me as a faithful and zealous advocate, neither to be intimidated nor corrupted, and in that respect they rendered me but justice. My circumstances were, at the time of my appointment, extremely embarrassed, and of course the salary annexed to my office was a considerable object with me. But tho' I had now an increasing family[4] totally unprovided for, I can safely say that I would not have deserted my duty to the Catholics for the whole patronage of the Government if it were consolidated into one office and offered me as the reward.

In these sentiments, I was encouraged and confirmed by the incomparable spirit of my wife, to whose patient suffering under adversity (for we had often been reduced and were now well accustomed to difficulties) I know not how to render justice. Women in general, I am sorry to say it, are mercenary; and, especially if they have children, they are ready to make all sacrifices to their

[1] In the MS the word 'proposal' is deleted.

[2] On 28 June the General Committee empowered a sub-committee to engage 'a proper person to act as an assistant secretary' until the end of the next session of parliament. On 25 July the General Committee approved the appointment of Tone, who had been engaged by the sub-committee. On 30 July Tone was requested to attend General Committee meetings. (R. Dudley Edwards (ed.), 'The minute book of the Catholic Committee, 1773–92' in *Archivium Hibernicum*, ix (1942), pp 168–70).

[3] In the MS at this point five lines are obliterated.

[4] On 29 Apr. 1791 Tone's third child, William, was born.

establishment. But my dearest Love had bolder and juster views. On every occasion of my life I consulted her; we had no secrets, one from the other, and I unvaryingly found her think and act with energy and courage combined with the greatest prudence and discretion. If ever I succeed in life, or arrive at anything like station or eminence, I shall consider it as due to her counsels and to her example.

But to return. Another rule which I adopted for my conduct was, in all the papers I had occasion to write, to remember I was not speaking for myself but for the Catholic body, and consequently to be never wedded to my own compositions, but to receive the objections of every one with respect, and to change without reluctance whatever the Committee thought fit to alter, even in cases where perhaps my own judgement was otherwise. And trifling as this circumstance may seem, I am sure it recommended me considerably to the Committee, who had been on former occasions more than once embarrassed by the self-love of Richard Burke, and indeed even of some of their own body, men of considerable talents, who had written some excellent papers on their behalf, but who did not stand criticism, as I did, without wincing. The fact is I was so entirely devoted to their cause that the idea of literary reputation as to myself never occurred to me; not that I am at all insensible on that score, but the feeling was totally absorbed in superior considerations; and I think I can safely appeal to the Sub-Committee whether ever[1] on any occasion they found me for a moment set up my vanity or self-love against their interests or even their pleasure. I am sure that, by my discretion on the points I have mentioned (which indeed was no more than my duty), I secured the esteem of the Committee and consequently an influence in their counsels which I should justly have forfeited had I seemed too eager to assure it; and it is to the credit of both parties that from the first moment of our connexion to the last, neither my zeal and anxiety to serve them, nor the kindness and favor with which they received my efforts, were ever for a single moment suspended.

Almost the first business I had to transact was to conduct a correspondance with Richard Burke, who was very desirous to return to Ireland once more and to resume his former station, which the Committee were determined he should not do. It was a matter of some difficulty to refuse without offending him, and I must say he pressed us rather forcibly; however, we parried him with as much address as we could, and, after two or three long letters,[2] to which the answers were very concise and civil,[3] he found the business was desperate and gave it up accordingly.

This was a memorable year in Ireland (1792). The publication of the plan for the new organising of the General Committee[4] gave an instant alarm to all the

[1] In MS 'every', obviously a slip, which is corrected in *Life*, i, 64.

[2] For an excerpt from the letter from Richard Burke to the Catholic Sub-committee of 17 June 1792, see above, vol. I, pp 204–5.

[3] For the text of the letter written by Tone to Richard Burke which was approved of at a meeting of the General Committee on 30 July, see above, vol. I, pp 230–31.

[4] See above, vol. I, pp 198–203. The plan provided that delegates should be elected by each county to serve on the General Committee.

supporters of the British Government, and every effort was made to prevent the election of the country members; for it was sufficiently evident that, if the representatives of three millions of oppressed people were once suffered to meet, it would not afterwards be safe, or indeed possible, to refuse their just demands. Accordingly, at the ensuing assizes, the grand juries universally throughout Ireland published the most furious, I may say frantic, resolutions against the plan and its authors, whom they charged with little short of high treason. Government likewise were but too successful in gaining over the Catholic clergy, particularly the bishops, who gave the measure, at first, very serious opposition. The Committee however was not daunted, and, satisfied of the justice of their cause, and of their own courage, they laboured, and with success, to inspire the same spirit in the breasts of their brethren throughout the nation. For this purpose their first step was an admirable one. By their order I drew up a state of the case, with the plan for the organisation of the Committee annexed, which was laid before Simon Butler and Beresford Burston, two lawyers of great eminence and, what was of consequence here, King's Counsel, to know whether the Committee had in any respect contravened the law of the land, or whether by carrying the proposed plan into execution the parties concerned would subject themselves to pain or penalty.[1] The answers of both the lawyers were completely in our favor, and we instantly printed them in the papers and dispersed them in handbills, letters and all possible shapes. This blow was decisive as to the legality of the measure.

For the bishops, whose opposition gave us great trouble, four or five different missions were undertaken by different members of the Sub-Committee into the provinces, at their own expence, in order to hold conferences with them, in which with much difficulty they succeeded so far as to secure the co-operation of some and the neutrality of the rest of the prelates. On these missions the most active members were John Keogh and Thomas Braughall, neither of whom spared purse or person where the interests of the Catholic body were concerned. I accompanied Mr Braughall in his visit to Connaught,[2] where he went to meet the gentry of that province at the great fair of Ballinasloe. As it was late in the evening when we left town,[3] the postilion who drove us having given warning, I am satisfied, to some footpads, the carriage was stopped by four or five fellows at the gate of the Phoenix Park.[4] We had two case of pistols in the carriage, and we agreed not to be robbed. Braughall, who was at this time about sixty-five years of age and lame from a fall off his horse some years before, was as cool and intrepid as man could be. He took the command, and by his orders I let down all the glasses, and called out to the fellows to come on, if they were so inclined, for that

[1] The case submitted to Butler and Burston and their opinions thereon were published in *H.J.*, 14 Sept. 1792, and are reprinted above, vol. I, pp 275–9.

[2] He relates his visit to Connacht in his Diary for 5–12 Oct. 1792 (above, vol. I, pp 306–11).

[3] Dublin.

[4] Relating the incident in his Diary for 5 Oct. 1792, Tone states 'three footpads near the Park gate' (above, vol. I, p. 307).

we were ready, Braughall desiring me at the same time '*not to fire till I could touch the scoundrels*'.[1] This rather embar[r]assed them and they did not venture to approach the carriage but held a council of war at the horses' heads. I then presented one of my pistols at the postilion swearing horribly that I would put him instantly to death if he did not drive over them, and I made him feel the muzzle of the pistol against the back of his head. The fellows on this took to their heels and ran off, and we proceeded on our journey without further interruption. When we arrived at the inn,[2] Braughall, whose goodness of heart is equal to his courage, and no man is braver, began by abusing the postilion for his treachery, and ended by giving him half a crown. I wanted to break the rascal's bones, but he would not suffer me, and this was the end of our adventure.

All parties were now fully employed, preparing for the ensuing session of Parliament.[3] The Government, thro' the organ of the corporations and grand juries, opened a heavy fire upon us of manifestoes and resolutions. At first we were like young soldiers, a little stunned with the noise, but after a few rounds we began to look about us and, seeing nobody drop with all this furious cannonade, we took courage and determined to return the fire. In consequence wherever there was a meeting of the Protestant Ascendancy (which was the title assumed by that party, and a very impudent one it was) we took care it should be followed by a meeting of the Catholics, who spoke as loud [as], and louder than, their adversaries, and, as we had the right clearly on our side, we found no great difficulty in silencing the enemy on this quarter. The Catholics likewise took care, at the same time that they branded their enemies, to mark their gratitude to their friends, who were daily increasing, and especially to the people of Belfast, between whom and the Catholics the union was now completely established. Among the various attacks made on us this summer the most remarkable for their virulence were those of the grand jury of Louth, headed by the Speaker of the House of Commons;[4] of Limerick, at which the Lord Chancellor assisted;[5] and of the corporation of the city of Dublin, which last published a most furious manifesto threatening us, in so many words, with a resistance by force.[6] In

[1] This appears to be a literary quotation. No source has been found.

[2] Tone states in his diary that they drove on to Kinnegad (see above, vol. I, pp 306–7).

[3] It began on 10 Jan. 1793 (*Commons' jn. Ire.*, xv, 119).

[4] The meeting and resolutions of the grand jury of County Louth are reported in *Faulkner's Dublin Journal*, 11 Sept. 1792. John Foster, speaker of the Irish house of commons and a large landowner in the county, signed the resolutions.

[5] The resolutions passed at a meeting of freeholders of County Limerick on 21 Aug. 1792, said to have been prepared by Lord Fitzgibbon, a landowner in the county as well as lord chancellor, were hostile to the proposal for a catholic convention. Tone found them 'pert and saucy' and wrote 'a flourishing manifesto' in reply. This, however, was 'taken to pieces and at least three fourths struck out' by Grattan, who supplied new passages. Whether it was ever published has not been ascertained. See above, vol. I, pp 255–6, 257.

[6] The members of the corporation, in a long address which referred to the conflict that had been waged in Ireland at the end of the previous century, pledged their lives and fortunes to the maintenance of the protestant ascendancy (*Faulkner's Dublin Journal*, 13 Sept. 1792). In his diary for 13 Sept., Tone dismissed them as 'boobies' and told himself he would 'try and pick a hole or two' in the address. The result was two replies, 'To the corporation of Dublin', dated 15 and 23 Sept. 1792 (above, vol. I, pp 280–83, 287–90).

consequence a meeting was held of the Catholics of Dublin at large, which was attended by several thousands, where the manifesto of the corporation was read, and most ably commented upon by John Keogh, Dr Ryan, Dr McNeven and several others; and a counter-manifesto being proposed, which was written by my friend Emmett and incomparably well done, it was carried unanimously and published in all the papers, together with the speeches above mentioned;[1] and both the speeches and the manifesto had such an infinite superiority over those of the corporation, which were also published and diligently circulated by the Government, that it put an end effectually to this warfare of resolutions.

The people of Belfast were not idle on their part; they spared neither pains nor expence to propagate the new doctrine of the *Union of Irishmen* thro' the whole North of Ireland, and they had the satisfaction to see their proselytes rapidly extending in every direction. In order more effectually to spread their principles, twelve of the most active and intelligent among them subscribed £250 each in order to set on foot a paper whose object should be to give a fair statement of all that passed in France, whither every one turned their eyes, to inculcate the necessity of union among Irishmen of all religious persuasions, to support the emancipation of the Catholics, and finally, as the necessary tho' not avowed consequence of all this, to erect Ireland into a republic, independant of England. This paper, which they called, very appositely, the *Northern Star*, was conducted by my friend Sam. Neilson, who was unanimously chosen editor, and it could not be delivered into abler hands.[2] It is in truth a most incomparable paper and it rose instantly on its appearance with a most rapid and extensive sale. The Catholics everywhere thro' Ireland (I mean the leading Catholics) were of course subscribers, and the *Northern Star* was one great means of effectually accomplishing the union of the two great sects, by the simple process of making their mutual sentiments better known to each other.[3]

It was determined by the citizens of Belfast to commemorate this year the anniversary of the taking of the Bastile with great ceremony. For this purpose they planned a review of the Volunteers of the town and neighbourhood, to be followed by a grand procession with emblematic devices &c. They also determined to avail themselves of this opportunity to bring forward the Catholic question in force, and in consequence they resolved to publish two addresses, one to the people of France, and one to the people of Ireland. They gave instructions to

[1] For a newspaper report of the catholic meeting of 31 Oct. 1792, the counter-manifesto and the speeches, see *Hibernian Journal*, 5 Nov. 1792. Tone stated in his diary for 31 Oct. 1792 that Ryan's speech was 'the best' and that Keogh's was 'rambling and confused but full of matter' (see above, vol. I, pp 320–21).

[2] The twelve subscribers were (in alphabetical order) John Boyle, Robert Caldwell, Henry Haslett, John Haslett, William McCleery, Gilbert McIlveen junr, William Magee, Samuel Neilson, John Rabb, Robert Simms, William Simms and William Tennent. However, they did not all subscribe the same amount. Neilson purchased 13 of the 40 shares; no other proprietor purchased more than three. (R. R. Madden, *The United Irishmen*, 3rd series (3 vols, London, 1846), i, 102.)

[3] There are accounts of the *Northern Star* in Brian Inglis, *The freedom of the press in Ireland, 1784–1841* (London, 1954), pp 92–8, and Nancy J. Curtin, *The United Irishmen: popular politics in Ulster and Dublin, 1791–1798* (Oxford, 1994), pp 202–11.

Dr Drennan to prepare the former, and the latter fell to my lot. Drennan executed his task admirably, and I made my address for my part as good as I knew how.[1] We were invited to assist at the ceremony and a great number of the leading members of the Catholic Committee determined to avail themselves of this opportunity to shew their zeal for the success of the cause of liberty in France, as well as their respect and gratitude to their friends in Belfast. In consequence of all this a grand assembly took place on the 14th of July [1792].[2] After the review, the Volunteers and inhabitants, to the number of about 6,000, assembled in the Linen Hall and voted the address to the French people unanimously. The address to the people of Ireland followed, and, as it was directly and unequivocally in favor of the Catholic claims, we expected some opposition, but we were soon relieved from our anxiety, for the address passed, I may say, unanimously. A few ventured to oppose it indirectly, but their arguments were exposed and overset by the friends to Catholic emancipation, among the foremost of whom we had the satisfaction to see several Dissenting clergymen of great popularity in that country, as Sinclaire Kelburne, William Dixon[3] and Thomas Birch. It was William Sinclaire who moved the two addresses. It is the less necessary for me to detail what passed at this period, as everything material is recorded in my Diary (No. ).[4] Suffice it to say that the hospitality shewn by the people of Belfast to the Catholics on this occasion, and the personal acquaintance which the parties formed, riveted the bonds of their recent union and produced in the sequel the most beneficial and powerful effects.

## Rennes, Sep$^{r}$ 28th, 1796

AS my time is growing shorter, I pass over a very busy interval of my life, all the important events of which are detailed in different diaries among my papers,[5] and I hasten to the period when, in consequence of the conviction of William Jackson for high treason,[6] I was obliged to quit my country and go into exile in America.[7] A short time[8] before my departure my friend Russell being in town, he and I walked out together to Rathfarn[h]am to see Emmett, who has a charming villa there.[9] He shewed us a little study of an elliptical form which he was building at the bottom of the lawn and which he said he would consecrate to our meet-

[1] See Diary entries for 11 and 12 July 1792 (above, vol. I, pp 208–9). It is printed as 'Address of the Volunteers assembled at Belfast to the people of Ireland' (above, vol. I, pp 217–19).

[2] See Diary for 14 July 1792 (above, vol. I, pp 215–17).

[3] i.e. William Steel Dickson.

[4] Blank in MS. Tone is referring to his Diary for 14 July 1792 (T.C.D., MS 2042, ff 7$^{r}$–10$^{v}$, printed above, vol. I, pp 215–17). The original cover of MS 2042 is labelled 'E. 1792'.

[5] The bulk of these have been lost. The interval referred to is from July 1792 to April 1795.

[6] For documents relating to Tone's connexion with Jackson, see above, vol. I, pp 504–18.

[7] In MS at this point three and a half lines are deleted.

[8] Substituted for 'few days', which is deleted.

[9] In 1798 Thomas Addis Emmet sold a piece of ground in Stillorgan, amounting to 3 acres and 30 perches, to the south of the road leading to Kilmacud. His father, Dr Robert Emmet, had a house, Casino, at Milltown. (Registry of Deeds, 513/306; T. A. Emmet, *The Emmet family* (New York, 1898), p. 102).

ings if ever we lived to see our country emancipated. I begged of him, if he intended Russell should be of the party, in addition to the books and maps it would naturally contain, to fit up a small cellaret which should contain a few dozens of his best old claret. He shewed me that he had not omitted that circumstance, which he acknowledged to be essential, and we both rallied Russell with considerable success. I mention this trifling anecdote because I love the men, and because it seems now at least possible that we may meet again in Emmett's study. As we walked together into town, I opened my plan to them both. I told them that I considered my compromise with Government to extend no farther than the banks of the Delaware, and that the moment I landed I was free to follow any plan which might suggest itself to me for the emancipation of my country; that undoubtedly I was guilty of a great offence against the existing government; that in consequence I was going into exile, and that I considered that exile as a full expiation for the offence, and consequently I felt myself at liberty, having made that sacrifice, to begin again on a fresh score. They both agreed with me in these principles, and I then proceeded to tell them that my intention was immediately on my arrival in Philadelphia to wait on the French minister, to detail to him fully the situation of affairs in Ireland, to endeavour to obtain a recommendation to the French Government and, if I succeeded so far, to leave my family in America and to set off instantly for Paris, and to apply in the name of my country for the assistance of France to enable us to assert our independance. It is unnecessary, I believe, to say that this plan met with the warmest approbation and support from both Russell and Emmett; we shook hands and, having repeated our professions of unalterable regard and esteem for each other, we parted, and this was the last interview which I was so happy as to have with those two invaluable friends together. I remember it was in a little triangular field that this conversation took place, and Emmett remarked to us that it was in one exactly like it in Switzerland where William Tell[1] and his two[2] associates planned the downfal[l] of the tyranny of Austria. The next day Russell returned to Belfast.

As I was determined not to appear to leave Ireland clandestinely, whatever might be the hazard to myself,[3] I took care on the day of Jackson's trial to walk up and down in the most public streets in Dublin,[4] and to go, contrary to my usual custom, into several of the most frequented coffee houses and to my bookseller's,[5] which was still more frequented. In this last place I was seen by Lord Mountjoy,[6] who gave himself the pains to call on the Attorney General[7] the next

[1] The legendary Swiss hero. [2] In *Life* 'two' is omitted. [3] In *Life* 'to myself' is omitted.

[4] The trial took place on 23 Apr. 1795. The question of Tone's whereabouts was raised by counsel for the crown in cross-examining Edward Keane, Jackson's legal agent. Keane replied that he did not know where Tone was but he believed that he was not in Dublin. The witness expressed the belief that the crown might have had Tone attend but for 'a compromise with Mr Tone by the government that he was not to be prosecuted'. (*A full report of all the proceedings on the trial of the Rev. William Jackson* . . . (Dublin, 1795), p. 128).

[5] John Archer (d. 1811), bookseller, 80 Dame St. (*Wilson's Dublin Directory*; *D.E.P.*, 16 July 1811).

[6] Luke Gardiner (1745–98), M.P. for Co. Dublin, 1773–89; created Baron Mountjoy, 1789; viscount, 1795; killed at the battle of New Ross (G.E.C., *Peerage*).

[7] Arthur Wolfe.

day and inform him that I was to be found, for that he had seen me in Archer's the day before. The Attorney General gave him however no thanks for his pains, and so the affair ended; my obligation however to his Lordship is not the less for his good intentions. Having made this sacrifice to appearances, I set with all diligence to prepare for my departure. I sold off all my little property of every kind,[1] reserving only my books, of which I had a very good selection of about six hundred volumes, and I determined to take leave of nobody. I also resolved not to call on any of my friends, not even Knox[2] or Emmett, for, as I knew the part I had taken in Jackson's affair had raised a violent outcry against me with a very numerous and powerful party, I resolved not to implicate any of those I regarded in the difficulties of my situation. Satisfied as I was of the rectitude of my own conduct and of the purity of my motives, I believe I should have had fortitude to bear the desertion of my best friends, but, to their honor be it spoken, I was not put to so severe a trial. I did not lose the countenance and support of any one man whom I esteemed; and I believe now[3] that I secured the continuance of their regard by the firmness I had shown all along thro' this most arduous and painful trial, and especially by my repeated declarations that I was ready to sacrifice my life, if necessary, but that I would never degrade myself by giving testimony against a man who had spoken to me in the confidence that I would not betray him. I have said that after Jackson's death[4] I visited nobody; but all my friends made it, I believe, a point to call on me, so that for the short time I remained in Dublin after, we were never an hour alone. My friends McCormick and Keogh, who had both interested themselves extremely all along on my behalf and had been principally instrumental in passing the vote for granting me the sum of £300 in addition to the arrear due me by the Catholics, were of course among the foremost. It was hardly necessary to men of their foresight, and who knew me perfectly, to mention my plans; however, for greater certainty I consulted them both, and I received, as I expected, their most cordial approbation, and they both laid the most positive injunctions upon me to leave nothing unattempted on my part to force my way to France & to lay our situation before the Government there, observing at the same time that if I succeeded there was nothing in the power of my country to bestow to which I might not fairly pretend. It has often astonished me and them also that the Government, knowing there was a French minister in Philadelphia, ever suffered me to go thither, at least without exacting some positive assurance on my part that I should hold no communication with him, direct or indirect. So it was, however, that either despising my efforts, or looking on themselves as too firmly established to dread anything from France, they suffered me to depart without demanding any satisfaction whatsoever on that topic, a circumstance of which I was most sincerely glad, for had I been obliged to give my parole I should have been exceedingly distracted between opposite duties. Luckily, however, I was spared the difficulty, for they suffered me to depart

[1] Tone sold Chateau Boue, his dwelling-house and small strip of land in County Kildare, to Matthew Donnellan (see above, vol. I, p. 533).

[2] George Knox.

[3] *Life* omits 'now'.

[4] On 30 Apr. 1795.

without any stipulation whatsoever. Perhaps it would have been better for them if they had adhered to their first proposal of sending me out to India;[1] but as to that the event will determine.

Having paid all my debts and settled with everybody, I set off from Dublin to Belfast on the 20th of May, 1795, with my wife, sister[2] and three children, leaving, as may be well supposed, my father and mother in very sincere affliction. My whole property consisted in our clothes, my books and about £700 in money and bills on Philadelphia.[3] We kept our spirits admirably. The great attention manifested to us, the conviction that we were suffering in the best of causes, the hurry attending so great a change and perhaps a little vanity in shewing ourselves superior to Fortune supported us under what was certainly a trial of the severest kind. But if our friends in Dublin were kind and affectionate, those in Belfast were if possible still more so. During near a month that we remained there we were every day engaged by one or other; even those who scarcely knew me were eager to entertain us; parties and excursions were planned for our amusements; and certainly the whole of our deportment and reception at Belfast very little resembled those of a man who escaped with his life only by miracle and who was driven into exile to avoid a more disgraceful fate. I remember particularly two days that we passed on the Cave Hill; on the first, Russell, Neilson, Simms,[4] McCracken[5] and one or two more of us, on the summit of MacArt's fort,[6] took a solemn obligation (which I think I may say I have on my part endeavoured to fulfil)[7] never to desist in our efforts until we had subverted the authority of England over our country and asserted her independance; another day we had the tent of the 1st Regiment[8] pitched in the Deer Park,[9] and a company of thirty of us including the family of the Simms's, Neilson's, McCracken's and my own, dined and spent the day together deliciously. But the most agreeable day we passed during our stay, and one of the most agreeable of our lives, was on an excursion we made with the Simms's, Neilson and Russell to Ram's Island, a beautiful and romantic spot in Lough Neagh. Nothing can be imagined more delightful and we agreed, in whatever quarter we might find ourselves respectively, to commemorate the anniversary of that day, the 11th of June. At length the hour of our departure arrived. On the 13th of June we embarked on board the *Cincinnatus* of Wilmington,

[1] An allusion to the proposal made in May 1794 that Tone, in return for a detailed statement by him of conversations between himself, Rowan and the French agent William Jackson, should be permitted by the government to leave Ireland and 'go either to America or the East Indies' (see above, vol. I, pp xxxviii–xxxix and 517).

[2] Mary Tone.

[3] One of the bills is printed above, vol. I, p. 532.

[4] Probably Robert Simms.

[5] Probably Henry Joy McCracken.

[6] MacArt's Fort is on the summit of Cave Hill, 327 metres above sea level. There is a description of the fort and hill in George Benn, *The history of the town of Belfast* (Belfast, 1823), pp 140, 209, 239–40, and a picture of MacArt's Fort facing p. 239.

[7] In MS 'on my part endeavoured to' interlined and 'fulfilled' amended to 'fulfil'.

[8] The 1st Belfast regiment of National Volunteers of which Tone was an honorary member (see above, vol. I, pp 203–4).

[9] The Deer Park was a large plantation of old ash on the east side of Cave Hill (George Benn, *The history of the town of Belfast* (Belfast, 1823), p. 165).

Cap$^{n}$ James Robinson, and I flatter myself we carried with us the regret of all who knew us. Even some of my former friends who had long since deserted me returned on this reverse of my fortune, struck I believe with the steadiness with w[hi]ch we all looked it in the face. Our friends in Belfast loaded us with presents on our departure and filled our little cabin with sea stores, fresh provisions, sweetmeats and everything they could devise for the comfort of my wife and our children. Never while I live will I forget the affectionate kindness of their behaviour. Before my departure I explained to Simms, Neilson and Charles Teeling my intentions with regard to my conduct in America and I had the satisfaction to find it met in all respects with their perfect approbation, and I now looked upon myself as competent to speak fully and with confidence for the Catholics, for the Dissenters and for the Defenders of Ireland.

We were now at sea and at leisure to examine our situation. I had hired a state room, which was about eight feet by six, in which we had fitted up three births [*sic*]. My wife and our youngest little boy occupied one, my sister and my little girl the second, and our eldest boy and myself the third. It was at first grievously inconvenient, but necessity and custom by degrees reconciled us to our situation. Our greatest suffering was want of good water, under which we laboured the whole passage and which we found it impossible to replace by wine, porter or spirits, of which we had abundance. The captain was tolerably civil, the vessel was stout, and we had good weather almost the whole of our voyage. But we were 300 passengers on board of a ship of 230 tons and of course crowded to a degree not to be conceived by those who have not been on board a passenger ship. The slaves who are carried from the coast of Africa have much more room allowed them than the miserable emigrants who pass from Ireland to America, for the avarice of the captains in that trade is such that they think they never can load their vessels sufficiently, and they trouble their heads in general no more about the accom[m]odation and stowage of their passengers than of any other lumber aboard. I laboured and with some success to introduce something like a police and a certain degree, tho' a very imperfect one, of cleanliness among them. Certainly the air of the sea must be wonderfully wholesome, for if the same number of wretches of us had been shut up in the same space ashore, with so much inconvenience of every kind about us, two thirds of us would have died in the time of our voyage. As it was, in spite of everything, we were tolerably healthy. We lost but one passenger (a woman). We had some sick aboard, and the friendship of James McDonnell of Belfast having supplied me with a small medicine chest and written directions, I took on myself the office of physician; I prescribed and administered accordingly and I had the satisfaction to land all my patients safe and sound. As we distributed liberally the surplus of our sea stores, of which we had great abundance, and especially as we gave from time to time wine and porter to the sick and aged, we soon became very popular aboard and I am sure there was no sacrifice to our ease or convenience in the power of our poor fellow passengers to make that we might not have commanded. Thirty days of our voyage had now passed over without any event save the ordinary ones of seeing now a shoal of porpoises, now a shark, now a set of dolphins, the peacocks of the sea, playing about, and once or twice a whale. We had indeed been brought to, when about a week at sea, by the *William Pitt*, Indiaman, which was returning to Europe with about[1] twenty other ships under convoy of four or five men-of-war, but on examining our papers they suffered us to proceed. At length about the 20th of July, some time after we had cleared the Banks of Newfoundland,[2] we were stopped by three British frigates,[3] the *Thetis*, Cap$^n$ Cochran[4], the *Hussar*, Cap$^n$ [Rose],[5] and the *Esperance*, Cap$^n$ Wood,[6] who boarded us and, after treating us with the greatest insolence, both officers and sailors, they pressed every one of our hands save one, and near fifty of my unfortunate fellow passengers, who were most of them flying to America to avoid the tyranny of a bad government at home and who thus most unexpectedly fell under the severest tyranny, one of them at least, which exists. As I was in a jacket and trowsers one of the lieutenants ordered me into the boat as a fit man to serve the King, and it was only the screams of my wife and sister which induced him to desist. It would have been a pretty termination to my adventures if I had been pressed and sent on board a man-of-war. The insolence of those tyrants, as well to myself as to my poor fellow passengers, in whose fate a fellowship in misfortune had interested me, I have not since forgot and I never will.[7] At length, after detaining us two days, during which they rummaged us at least twenty times, they suffered us to proceed. On the 30th of July we made Cape Henlopen, the 31st we ran up the Delaware and the 1st of August we landed safe at Wilmington,[8] not one of us, providentially, having been for an hour indisposed on the passage, nor even seasick. Those only who have had their wives, their children and all, in short, that is dear to them floating for seven or eight weeks at the mercy of the winds and waves can conceive the transport I felt at seeing my wife and our darling babies ashore once again in health and in safety. We set up at the principal tavern, kept by an Irishman, one Captain O'Byrne (I think),[9] for all the taverns in America are kept by majors and captains, either of

[1] MS has 'without', which is obviously a slip.

[2] Another account, in the *Northern Star*, 1 Oct. 1795, gives the date of the incident Tone relates as 25 July and the location as 38° 40' N. by 73° W., which is off New Jersey (see above, p. 1, n. 1).

[3] For another account by Tone of this incident, see above, p. 1.

[4] Alexander Forrester Inglis Cochrane (1758–1832), commanded the *Thetis*, 38 guns, in the north Atlantic for several years; admiral, 1819 (*D.N.B.*). In *Life*, i, 130, William Tone has erroneously inserted 'Lord' between 'Cap$^n$' and 'Cochrane'.

[5] MS blank. 'Rose' is supplied by William Tone (*Life*, i, 130); this must have been Jonas Rose. However, it is stated in David Steel, *Original and correct list of the Royal Navy* (various issues), that the *Hussar*, 28 guns, was commanded by Charles Wemyss (not further identified) and that Jonas Rose commanded the *Esperance*, 22.

[6] Not identified but see preceding note.

[7] In a report made to the French government in Feb. 1796 Tone had stated that 210 of the 220 crew of the frigate which boarded the *Cincinnatus* were Irish (see above, p. 69).

[8] In the state of Delaware, about 45 km from the American capital, Philadelphia.

[9] In the MS a footnote corrects this to 'O'Flyn'. *Life*, i, 130, has 'O'Byrne O'Flynn'. It was in fact Patrick O'Flynn (1749?–1818), capt. in the war of American independence; proprietor since 1789 of the Happy Retreat, at the corner of Third St. and Market St.; an elder in the First Presbyterian church. His inn was frequented by 'the gentry of the town and country round about' and Washington was once a guest. (J. T. Scharf, *History of Delaware, 1609–1888* (2 vols, Philadelphia, 1888), i, 810–11, 844).

Militia or Continentals, and in a few days we had entirely recruited our strength and spirits and totally forgot the fatigues of the voyage.

During our stay in Wilmington we formed an acquaintance which was of some service and a great deal of pleasure to us with a General Humpton,[1] an old Continental officer. He was an Englishman, born in Yorkshire, and had been a major in the 25th Regiment; but on the breaking out of the American War he resigned his commission and offered his services to Congress, who immediately gave him a regiment, from which he rose by degrees to his present rank. He was a beautiful, hale, stout, old man of near seventy, perfectly the soldier and the gentleman, and he took a great liking to us, as we did to him on our part. On our removal to Philadelphia, he found us a lodging with one of his acquaintances and rendered all the little services and attentions that our situation as strangers required, which indeed he continued without remission during the whole of my stay in America, and I doubt not equally since my departure. I have a sincere and grateful sense of the kindness of this worthy veteran.

Immediately on my arrival in Philadelphia, which was about the 7th or 8th of August,[2] I found out my old friend and brother exile, Dr Reynolds, who seemed, to my very great satisfaction, very comfortably settled. From him I learned that Hamilton Rowan had arrived about six weeks before me,[3] from France, and that same evening we all three met. It was a singular rencontre, and our several escapes from an ignominious death seemed little short of a miracle. We communicated respectively our several adventures since our last interview, which took place in the gaol of Newgate in Dublin fourteen months before. In Reynolds's [adventures][4] there was nothing very extraordinary. Rowan had been seized and thrown into prison immediately on his landing near Brest, from whence he was rescued by the interference of a young man named Sullivan,[5] an Irishman in the service of the republic, and sent on to Paris to the Committee of Public Safety by Prieur de la Marne, the deputy on mission. On his arrival he was seized with a most dangerous fever, from which he narrowly escaped with his life; when he recovered, as well as during his illness, he was maintained by the [French[6]] Government; he gave in some memorials on the state of Ireland,[7] and began from the reception he met with to conceive some hopes of success; but immediately after came on the famous 9th Thermidor, the downfal[l] of Robespierre[8] and the dissolution of the Committee of Public Safety. The total change which this

[1] Richard Humpton (d. 1804), capt. in 36th foot, 1761–73; lieut col. in Continental army, 1776; brigadier general, 1783 (*Army list*, passim; F. B. Heitman, *Historical register and dictionary of the United States army* (Washington, 1903), i, 555).

[2] In a letter to Russell dated 'Philadelphia, Aug. 7, 1795', Tone states that he has spent two days there (see above, p. 1).

[3] In fact Rowan arrived at Philadelphia on 16 or 17 July 1795 (Rowan, *Autobiography*, p. 278).

[4] William Tone also inserts 'adventures' (*Life*, i, 131).

[5] See above, p. 143, n. 4. [6] Added in *Life*, i, 131.

[7] For more on Rowan's memorials to the French government, see Marianne Elliott, *Partners in revolution: the United Irishmen and France* (New Haven, 1982), p. 68, citing Archives des Affaires Étrangères, Corresp. Politique Angleterre, cote 588, ff 184–318 passim, and other French archival sources.

[8] Robespierre was arrested on 27 July 1794 (9 thermidor) and was executed on the following day.

produced in the politics of France and the attention of every man being occupied by his own immediate personal safety were the cause that Rowan and his plan were forgotten in the confusion. After remaining therefore several months, and seeing no likelihood of bringing matters to any favorable issue, he yielded to the sollicitude of his family and friends, and embarked at Havre for New York, where he arrived about the middle of June[1] 1795, after a tedious passage of eleven weeks.[2] It is unnecessary to detail again my adventures, which I related to them at full length, as well [as] everything relating to the state of politics in Ireland, about which it may be well supposed their curiosity and anxiety were extreme. I then proceeded to tell them my designs and that I intended waiting the next day on the French minister with such credentials as I had brought with me, which were the two votes of thanks of the Catholics[3] and my certificate of admission into the Belfast Volunteers,[4] engrossed on vellum and signed by the chairmen and secretaries; and I added that I would refer to them both for my credibility in case the minister had any doubts. Rowan offered to come with me and introduce me to the minister, Citizen Adet, whom he had known in Paris, but I observed to him that as there were English agents without number in Philadelphia, he was most probably watched, and consequently his being seen to go with me to Adet might materially prejudice his interests in Ireland. I therefore declined his offer, but I requested of him a letter of introduction, which he gave me accordingly and the next day I waited on the minister, who received me very politely. He spoke English very imperfectly, and I French a great deal worse; however, we made a shift to understand one another; he read my certificates and Rowan's letter, and he begged me to throw on paper in the form of a memorial[5] all I had to communicate on the subject of Ireland. This I accordingly did in the course of two or three days, tho' with great difficulty on account of the burning heat of the climate so different from what I had been used to, the thermometer varying between 90 and 97.[6] At length, however, I finished my memorial, such as it was, and brought it to Adet, and I offered him at the same time, if he thought it would forward the business, to embark in the first vessel which sail'd for France; but the minister, for some reason, seemed not much to desire this, and he eluded my offer by reminding me of the great risque I ran, as the British stopped and carried into their ports indiscriminately all American vessels bound for France; he assured me, however, I might rely on my memorial being transmitted to the French Government and backed with his strongest recommendations; and he also promised to write[7] particularly to procure the enlargement of my brother Mathew who was then in prison at Guise,[8] all which I have since found he faithfully performed.

[1] *Recte* July (see above, p. 336, n. 3).
[2] For an account by Rowan of his adventures after leaving Ireland, see his *Autobiography*, pp 214–48, 264–79.
[3] Above, vol. I, pp 443, 529.
[4] Above, vol. I, pp 203–4.
[5] Above, pp 7–10.
[6] i.e. between 90 and 97 degrees Fahrenheit, or about 32 and 36 degrees Celsius.
[7] He did so on 1 Oct. 1795, adding the memorial to his despatch (see above, pp 23–4).
[8] The memorandum which Tone wrote for Adet on the plight of his brother is printed above, pp 10–11.

I had now discharged my conscience as to my duty to my country, and it was with the sincerest and deepest contristation of mind that I saw this, my last effort, likely to be of so little effect. It was barely possible, but I did not much expect, that the French Government might take notice of my memorial, and if they did not, there was an end of all my hopes. I now began to endeavour to bend my mind to my situation, but to no purpose. I moved my family, first to Westchester, and then to Downingstown, both in the state of Pen[n]sylvania about thirty miles from Philadelphia,[1] and I began to look about for a small plantation such as might suit the shattered state of my finances on which the enormous expence of living in Philadelphia (three times as dear as at Paris or even London) was beginning to make a sensible inroad. While they remained there, in the neighbourhood of our friend General Humpton, whose kindness and attention continued unabated, I made divers excursions, on foot and in the stage waggons, in quest of a farm. The situation of Princeton in New Jersey struck me, for a variety of reasons, and I determined, if possible, to settle in that neighbourhood. I accordingly agreed with a Dutch boor[2] for a plantation of 100 acres with a small wooden house,[3] which would have suited me well enough, for which I was to pay £750 of that currency; but the fellow was too covetous and after all was, I thought, finished he retracted and wanted to screw more out of me, on which I broke off the treaty in a rage, and he began to repent, but I was obstinate. At length I agreed with a Cap[tai]n Leonard[4] for a plantation of 180 acres,[5] beautifully situated within two miles of Princeton and half of it under timber. I was to pay £1,180 currency and I believe it was worth the money. I moved in consequence my family to Princeton, where I hired a small house for the winter, which I furnished frugally and decently. I fitted up my study and I began to think that my lot was cast to be an American farmer.[6]

For myself, I believe, I could have borne it, and for my wife it was sufficient to her that I was with her, her incomparable firmness of mind and never failing chearfulness and equanimity of temper sustaining her, and me also whose happiness depended solely upon hers, under every difficulty; but when we looked on our little children we felt, both of us, our courage fail. Our little boys we could hardly bear to think of rearing in the boorish ignorance of the peasants about us, and to what purpose give them an education which could only tend to discontent them with the state wherein they were thrown and wherein learning and talents

[1] West Chester is in fact about 18 miles, or about 29 km, from Philadelphia.

[2] In *Life*, i, 133, 'farmer' is substituted for 'boor'.

[3] In a letter to his wife dated (incorrectly) 1 Aug. 1795, Hamilton Rowan wrote: 'Mr Tone has bought an hundred acres of ground. The situation is pleasant and within two or three miles of Princeton where there is a college and some good society.' (Rowan, *Autobiography*, p. 282).

[4] Very probably one of the large number of nephews and grand-nephews of Thomas Leonard (d. 1759), a large landowner in the district. The only Capt. Leonard identified is a nephew, Capt. Henry Leonard, who inherited from him 10,000 acres near Squan River. (J. F. Hageman, *History of Princeton* (2 vols, Philadelphia, 1879), i, 42–9).

[5] Almost certainly this is the farm referred to by Tone in his letter to Russell dated 25 Oct. 1795 (see above, pp 29–30, 33).

[6] What follows, up to and including 'But to return', is omitted from *Life*.

were useless? But especially our little girl, now eight or nine years old, was our principal uneasiness; how could we bear to see her the wife of a clown, without delicacy or refinement, incapable to feel or to estimate the value of a mind which even already developed the strongest marks of sensibility and tenderness? For my own part, this idea tormented me beyond enduring; and I am sure no unfortunate lover in the paroxysm of jealousy ever looked forward with greater horror to the union of his mistress with his rival than I did to the probability of seeing my darling child sacrificed to one of the boors by whom we were surrounded. I could better bear to see her dead, for with regard to the delicacy and purity of woman I entertain notions of perhaps extravagant refinement. But to return.[1]

In this gloomy[2] frame of mind I continued for some time, waiting for the lawyer who was employed to draw the deeds and expecting the next spring to remove to my purchase and to begin farming at last, when one day I was roused from my lethargy by the receipt of letters from Keogh, Russell and the two Simms's[3] wherein, after professions of the warmest and sincerest regard, they proceeded to acquaint me that the state of the public mind in Ireland was advancing to Republicanism faster than even I could believe, and they pressed me in the strongest manner to fulfil the engagement I had made with them at my departure and to move heaven and earth to force my way to the French Government in order to supplicate their assistance. William Simms, at the end of a most friendly and affectionate letter, desired me to draw upon him for £200 and that my bill should be punctually paid, an offer at the liberality of which, well as I knew the man, I confess I was surprised. I immediately handed the letters to my wife and sister and desired their opinion, which I foresaw would be that I should immediately, if possible, set out for France. My wife especially, whose courage and whose zeal for my honor and interests were not in the least rebated[4] by all her past sufferings, supplicated me to let no consideration of her or our children stand for a moment in the way of my engagements to my friends and my duty to my country, adding that she would answer for our family during my absence and that the same Providence which had so often, as it were, miraculously preserved us would, she was confident, not desert us now. My sister joined her in these entreaties and it may well be supposed I required no great supplication to induce me to make one more attempt in a cause to which I had been so long devoted. I set off accordingly the next morning (it being this time about the end of November) for Philadelphia and went, immediately on my arrival, to Adet, to whom I shewed the letters I had just received, and I referred him to Rowan, who was then in town, for the character of the writers. I had the satisfaction, contrary to my expectations, to find Adet as willing to forward and assist my design now as he seemed (to me at least) lukewarm when I saw him before in August. He told me immediately that he would give me letters to the French Government recommending me in the strongest manner and also money to bear my expences, if

[1] At this point the text is resumed in *Life*. [2] In *Life*, 'gloomy' is omitted.
[3] Above, pp 17–23. [4] *Life*, i, 134, has 'abated'.

necessary. I thanked him most sincerely for the letters, but I declined acccepting any pecuniary assistance. Having thus far surmounted my difficulties, I wrote for my brother Arthur, who was at Princeton, to come to me immediately and I fitted him out with all expedition for sea. Having entrusted him with my determination of sailing for France in the first vessel, I ordered him to communicate this immediately on his arrival in Ireland to Neilson, Simms and Russell in Belfast and to Keogh and McCormick only in Dublin. To everyone else, including especially my father and mother, I desired him to say I had purchased and was settled upon my farm near Princeton. Having fully instructed him, I put him on board the *Susannah*, Capt[ai]n Baird, bound for Belfast, and on the 10th of December 1795 he sailed from Philadelphia; and I presume he arrived safe, but as yet I have had no opportunity of hearing of him.[1] Having dispatched him I settled all my affairs as speedily as possible. I drew on Simms for £200 agreeably to his letter, £150 of which I devoted to my voyage; my friend Reynolds procured me louis d'ors at the bank for an hundred pounds worth of silver. I converted the remainder of my little property into Bank stock and, having signed a general power of attorney to my wife, I waited finally on Adet, who gave me a letter in cypher,[2] directed to the Comité du Salut Public, the only credential which I intended to bring with me to France.[3] I spent one day in Philadephia with Reynolds, Rowan and my old friend and fellow sufferer James Napper Tandy who, after a long concealment and many adventures, was recently arrived from Hamburgh; and at length, on the 13th of December at night, I arrived at Princeton, whither Rowan accompanied me, bringing with me a few presents for my wife, sister and our dear little babies. That night we supped together in high spirits, and Rowan retiring to the inn immediately after, my wife, sister and I sat together till very late engaged in that kind of animated and enthusiastic conversation which our characters and the nature of the enterprise I was embarked in may be supposed to give rise to. The courage & firmness of the women supported me, and them too, far beyond my expectations; we had neither tears not lamentations, but on the contrary the most ardent hope and the most steady resolution. At length, at four the next morning, I embraced them both for the last time and we parted with a steadiness which astonished me. On the 16th of December I arrived in New York and took my passage on board the ship *Jersey*, Captain George Barons, commander. I remained in New York for ten days, during which time I wrote continually to my family, and a day or two before my departure I received a letter from my wife informing me that she was with child, a circumstance which she had concealed so far, I am sure lest it might have had some influence on my determination. On the first of January 1796 I sailed from Sandy Hook with nine fellow passengers, all French, bound for Havre de Grâce. Our voyage lasted exactly a month,

[1] He arrived safely in Belfast after 28 days' sailing. For this and other information on Arthur Tone, see above, pp 37–8, 265–6.

[2] Above, pp 34–5.

[3] Tone also carried with him to France a ciphered letter of introduction from John Beckley to James Monroe (above, pp 35–6).

during the most part of which we had heavy blowing weather; five times we had such gales of wind as obliged us to lie to under a close-reefed mizen staysail; however, our ship was stout, we had plenty of provisions, wine, brandy and especially what I thought more of, remembering my last voyage, excellent water, so that I had no reason to complain of my passage. We did not meet a single vessel of force, either French or English;[1] we passed three or four Americans bound mostly like ourselves to France. On the 27th we were in soundings at 85 fathoms; on the 28th we made the Lizard and at length on the 1st of February we landed in safety at Havre de Grâce, having met with not the smallest accident during our voyage. My adventures from this date are fully detailed in the diary which I have kept regularly since my arrival in France.[2]

## Diary, 28 September–8 October 1796

T.C.D., Tone papers, MS 2049, ff 133$^{r}$–137$^{v}$; *Life*, ii, 210–14.

No. 10
From September 28th to November the 13th[3]
*Nil desperandum!*
Rennes
1796

### 3 Oct. 1796

The *Journal des Défenseurs de la Patrie*,[4] published under the authority of the Directory, gives the lie, this day, to the arrival &c. of Thomas Grenville, as mentioned in No. 9.[5] I did not much mind the report at the time, but I am much pleased with the spirit of the contradiction, which is by an official note. The Directory seem fully bent on humbling the pride of England, and lay down as a principle that the peace to which they will consent must be one which will 'ravish from her, her maritime preponderance, re-establish the liberty of the ocean, give a spring to the Spanish, Dutch and French marine, and carry to the highest degree of prosperity the industry and the commerce of those nations, whom England has ever regarded as her rivals and her enemies, when they would no longer submit to be her dupes'. If the Directory act up with firmness to these principles and if Spain be not utterly besotted, I think it is impossible but

[1] In his Diary for 17 Feb. 1796, Tone states that they were 'chased by a Bermudian' (see above, p. 57).

[2] Above, pp 40 et seq.

[3] There are no entries for the periods 28 Sept.–2 Oct. and 9–11 Oct. The entries for 12 Oct. and for 14 Oct.–13 Nov. are given as separate documents (below, pp 346–7 and 353–72).

[4] *Journal des Défenseurs de la Patrie* (Paris), 8 Vendémiaire an V (29 Sept. 1796).

[5] See Diary for 27 Sept. 1796 (above, p. 320).

England must be reduced within her proper and natural limits, the first step to which, be it ever kept in mind, is the independance of Ireland.

## 5 Oct. 1796

I find great amusement in chatting with Colonel Shee, who is a very agreeable old man, and has served as a good officer of cavalry now six and thirty years. He told me last night, as I was sitting with him, that Gen[era]l Clarke had written to him that he might have full confidence in me. Nevertheless he does not tell me much, if indeed he knows much himself; that, however, gives me very little concern. I shall learn everything time enough. I collect however that it is resolved, if possible, to turn in a gang of six or seven thousand desperadoes into England who will live at free quarters and commit all manner of devastation. If this takes effect it will embarrass her extremely. She has never yet seen the smoke of an enemy's fire, and I always remember that five thousand ragged, half-starved Highlanders forced their way to one hundred miles distance of London,[1] and might perhaps have atchieved what remained if the Pretender had not been a poltroon. It is, to be sure, a horrible mode of making war; but England shewed the way by disgorging so many hordes of emigrants into France, and the enormities which have been committed in this country in consequence are such as to justify France in adopting any means of revenge; it is, in a word, but strict retaliation. I am curious to see how England will relish a war of *Chouans* in her own bowels. Colonel Shee and I were employed yesterday in digesting and arranging different routes from the several harbours where we might by possibility land to Dublin. I find him very reasonable. We agreed that our first object was to get ashore anywhere, and of course the nearest port to Brest was the best, as we could make any shift when we were once landed, our army being composed of veterans, who have been on service in La Vendée for years, and are steeled against every hardship, having been well used to dispence with clothes, shoes, and even bread at times. Supposing however we had our port to chuse, we both agreed it should be Belfast, or at least as near Belfast as possible; if not, Waterford, or in that neighbourhood. The distance from Dublin is pretty nearly equal. We calculated however for, I believe, a dozen different landing places round the coast. He tells me Hoche has a great magazine of clothing which he took from the British at the time of his famous victory at Quiberon; that is, literally, *tant pris sur l'ennemi*.[2] We talked a good deal of my affairs. I observed that supposing our expedition was, by any unforeseen accident, prevented from taking place, I was a little anxious as to what the Directory might determine with regard to me; that I had almost utterly ruined myself, partly in their service; that since I came to France I had subsisted entirely on my own means, having drawn nothing from the republic but my pay, which he knew was not sufficient to pay my washwoman; that on my journey and during my stay

[1] In 1745 Charles Edward, the Young Pretender, led some five thousand Highlanders south as far as Derby, 200 km from London.

[2] See above, p. 256, n. 3.

in Rennes, I had not drawn even my pay, nor did I intend it, as it was to my own country I looked for indemnification, in case we ever got there; but, I again observed, if our expedition did not take place, I could hardly suppose the Directory would suffer me to be utterly ruined, which must be the case if I were not retained in their service. Shee answered that he had not the shadow of doubt but in that case I would be employed, as he did not think the Directory capable of acting dishonourably by a man who had such strong claims on them, and he added that he was satisfied Gen[era]l Clarke would take effectual measures on my behalf. This was a considerable relief to my mind, on account of my wife and our dear little babies. We then began to build *châteaux en Irlande* as magnificent as any *in Spain*. Shee told me he had some notion in case we succeeded of selling what property he had in France and settling in Ireland. I answered I, for one, should be heartily glad of it, and indeed I spoke but the truth; I added that we should have occasion for his talents, and especially for his long experience as a military man in arranging our army, &c., and in that case I hoped we would find[1] a situation which might recompense him for the services he should have rendered, and the sacrifice he made in quitting his family and exposing his health, which is not very firm, and his person to the fatigues of a voyage, and the perils of a winter campaign. As he seemed very much to relish this discourse, I took the opportunity to throw in a word or two on my own situation and expectations. I reminded him that hitherto I had drawn nothing from either Ireland or France, but on the contrary had sacrificed time, labour, person and property in the common cause of both countries; that I had no doubt, if we succeeded, of being amply recompenced,[2] if I might judge from the generosity which I had experienced from the Catholic Committee, and the noble manner in which they conducted themselves towards me at the time of my quitting Ireland; nevertheless[3] I begged him to remember that the more attention there was shewn to me by the French government, and by the General[4] on our arrival, the greater service it would be in my power to render to France, to Ireland and to our friends embarked in this expedition; that I believed he knew my zeal and affection for the cause of the Republic, as well as my gratitude to the Directory, and I left him to consider whether, in framing our government in Ireland, it might not be desirable for France to have in an efficient station a man on whose principles and attachment she might safely count, a circumstance which might be materially forwarded and most probably secured by the attention on the part of the General to which I alluded; an attention which both Catholics and Dissenters would consider as shewn to themselves much more than to me personally, as I could have no claim upon it, other than as I stood in the capacity of their agent and possessing, as, I would venture to say, I did possess, their confidence. Shee heard me with great attention, and said he saw clearly the advantages resulting from what I proposed; that everything I had said was perfectly reasonable, and he was satisfied the General would see it in the same light and

[1] *Life*, ii, 212, inserts 'for him'. [2] In *Life* what follows up to and including 'Ireland' is omitted.
[3] In *Life* the following five words are omitted. [4] Hoche.

regulate his conduct accordingly. I desired him to think of all I had said and that we would resume the subject once more before our departure.

## 7 Oct. 1796

I like old Colonel Shee more and more; his conversation is my sole resource against the *ennui* which devours me, for as to MacSheehy, he is a sad blockhead. The Colonel was secretary to the late duke of Orleans, for whose memory he cherishes the sincerest regard. He has amused me these two days with an infinity of anecdotes relating to that unfortunate prince, who, I begin to believe, has been most grossly calumniated by all parties in the Revolution.[1] The zeal and affection that Shee manifests for the honor of a man who can no longer serve or prejudice him is with me a strong proof of the goodness of the characters of both.[2] It is to me highly interesting to see the earnestness and warmth with which he labours to impress me with a good opinion of the Duke, and indeed from his report I am satisfied not only of his innocence as to the accusation on which he was guillotined, but as to his general character as a man of honor, courage and probity, and I see that he has been the unfortunate[3] victim of a double cabal of the Court and the Jacobins. '*Mais parlons d'autres choses*.'[4] Gen[era]l Hédouville shewed the Colonel today a letter from Hoche wherein he says he is moving heaven and earth to get things in readiness at Brest, and that he is in hopes that in three weeks we may be getting aboard. The marine agents are scoundrels, and there is a scarcity of seamen; but orders have been this day expedited to the military commanders all along the coast to make diligent search, to secure and send on to Brest all seafaring persons, and there is a reward of six livres a head to the soldiers for all that they can find, which will sharpen them up to the business. It will be November before we arrive, if we are so fortunate as to arrive at all; of course we shall have in that case a winter campaign of it. No matter for that; we are better able to stand it than those who will be opposed to us. The country gentlemen of Ireland, with their warm feather beds, their beef and claret, will make, I think, no great figure before our grenadiers who have been seasoned these four years to all manner of hardships and privations in this execrable war of La Vendée, which Hoche has had the glory of terminating. Damn it, '*We're all Militia captains, and who's afraid of death*?'[5] I have written out about thirty Irish airs for the band of my regiment, if I am to have one, which I doubt a little; whereby I must *insense Hoche* on his return, because '*when both house and lands are spent then learning is most excellent*'.[6] '*Good, good! hold! I meant abominable!*'[7] That is a vile quotation, to tell the God's truth of the matter.

[1] Cf. the Diary for 14 Feb. 1796 where Tone writes unsympathetically of the duke of Orleans, guillotined in 1793 (see above, p. 51).

[2] In *Life*, i, 213, this sentence terminates: '. . . is, at least, a strong proof of the goodness of his own character'.

[3] Omitted from *Life*.

[4] 'But let's change the subject.'

[5] Cf. 'I have had ancestors too! Every man of them colonel or captain in the militia.' (Sheridan, *The rivals* (1775), III, iv).

[6] Samuel Foote, *Taste* (1752), i, 1.

[7] John Dryden, *The Spanish fryar* (1681), II, iii.

### 8 Oct. 1796

I must change my apartment tomorrow to make room for General de Belle,[1] brother-in-law to Hoche, who is just arrived. *À la bonheur!*[2]

*They talk of further alterations*
*Which causes many speculations.*[3]

My quotations latterly are as pert and stupid as you please, but how can I quote when I am in this horrible suspense?

## Matilda Tone to Thomas Russell, 9 October 1796

T.C.D., Sirr papers, MS 868/2, ff 262ʳ–263ᵛ; printed in Bulmer Hobson (ed.), *The letters of Wolfe Tone* (Dublin, [1920]), pp 52–4.

This letter is in Matilda Tone's hand and bears comparison with an earlier letter from her to Russell (above, pp 311–13).

October 9, 1796

My dear Tom,

We set off tomorrow for the back countries,[4] & I cannot begin my journey without bid[d]ing you farewell. We are all in the highest health & spirits, & every precaution is taken to make our journey easy & pleasant. I *fired* at you some time since by Cork, & my heart has smote me for it ever since. 'My dear', says I, 'this is a poor wretch'—'but yet I have a little against thee'.[5] Why did you write as if I was a *fit*? You will judge better than I can express the delight I feel at the prospect of joining my husband. It has no alloy but the sad news we got yesterday of the total defeat of the Austrians in Italy & the deplorable state to which the poor Emperor & the German princes are reduced; there is nothing so sensibly afflicts us as the misfortunes of princes. 'A begging prince, what beggar pities not!',[6] as the sublime Bard hath it. Oh, for Fortunatus' hat[7] that I might look on you all before I set off, [that] I could see Sam. Neilson & his sweet little wife & children.[8] Do you know I dream'd the other night I was gone home & in North Street on my way to R[obert] Simms's, when I awoke myself crying in an extacy, 'I'm in Ireland, I'm in Ireland, I'm in Belfast!', & I cry'd in good earnest to find I was not.

1 Jean François Joseph Debelle (1767–1802) commanded the artillery of the army of the Sambre-et-Meuse, 1796; commanded the artillery of the Irish expedition, 1796; died of fever at Santo Domingo (Six, *Dict. des généraux & amiraux*).

2 Corrected in *Life*, ii, 214, to 'A la bonne heure!', meaning 'Well done!'

3 Jonathan Smedley, *Gulliveriana* (1728).

4 In truth for France.

5 Cf. '"My dear", said Mr Tow-wouse, "this is a poor wretch"' (Henry Fielding, *Joseph Andrews* (1742), i, chap. 11). Matilda Tone's next line does not, however, correspond to Fielding's.

6 *Richard III*, I, iv.

7 James Beattie, 'Epistle to the honourable C.B.' (1776).

8 Samuel Neilson and his wife, Anne, had five children (R. R. Madden, *The United Irishmen*, 2nd ed. (London, 1857–60), iv, 100–40, 150–60).

Oh, this dreadful Buonaparte, there is no knowing what he may not do. I hinted to you in my last that y[ou]r friend '*yes, yes, & no, no*' gave us much pain.[1] I want the Doctor[2] to write to you about him, but he does not like to do it, he says he *hopes* there is no danger of him; to be sure the D[octo]r knows best, but I'm not satisfied.

Never can I find words to express my gratitude to Reynolds for his kind and animated attention to us since we came here; he is one of my first favourites. I never knew a man possess'd [of] better principles or finer feelings. For our third friend,[3] he is, as Dogberry says, '*an old man* & his wits are not as *blunt* as heaven help I cou[l]d desire they were but in faith as honest as the skin between his brows'.[4]

Remember me with sincere aff[ec]tion to all my dear friends, particularly Jane,[5] but don't forget my [*word illegible*]. Never fear, a day will certainly come when every one may do right and be happy; at present, they are incompatible. I will write a few lines to Robert Simms. I hope you will get this safe, but we don't know what to hope, fear or expect from these desperate French.

ever yours

I hear from Arthur that my dear little sister is married.[6] I enclose you a note for her. It contains just nothing. Arthur or his mother will send it for you—it is an amulet. I hope her husband is a sensible man, but I'm afraid he is too handsome.[7]

am yours

What I mention'd to you of your friend is between ourselves, unless you hear from Reynolds.

[Addressed to:]
Thos Russell
Belfast

## Diary, 12 October 1796

T.C.D., Tone papers, MS 2049, ff 137v–138r; *Life*, ii, 214–15.

[1] See above, p. 313. [2] James Reynolds. [3] Probably James Napper Tandy.

[4] *Much ado about nothing*, III, v. This sentence is omitted by Hobson.

[5] Perhaps the 'lovely girl' referred to in Matilda Tone's letter to Russell of 11 Sept. 1796 (see above, p. 312, esp. n. 5).

[6] A few months previously Catherine Witherington (b. 20 Feb. 1775) married John Heavyside who had a post at the Bank of Ireland; he lost this in 1800 and, 'having no remaining support but the interest of his wife's fortune', settled in Wales (Thomas Reynolds, *The life of Thomas Reynolds* (2 vols, London, 1839), i, 120, ii, 238; H. F. Reynolds, 'Witherington of Dublin' in *Notes and Queries*, 12th ser., ix, no. 170 (16 July 1921), p. 44; Margaret Tone to Arthur Tone, 26 or 28 May 1796, T.C.D., Sirr papers, MS 868/2, printed in MacDermot, *Tone*, p. 28).

[7] Margaret Tone wrote that he was 'a young man of no fortune but a most excellent character' (ibid.).

## 12 Oct. 1796

The General[1] returned last night at eight o'clock, having been absent since the 26th of last month. Colonel Shee saw him this morning for a quarter of an hour. He tells me Hoche is bent on going *coûte qui coûte*, and that everything is ready but seamen whom he has given orders to press all along the coast as far as Bourdeaux. Oh, that we were aboard, oh that we were aboard; or rather, indeed, that we were ashore, after being aboard! '*I'gin to be aweary of the sun.*'[2] He told Hoche that we had prepared divers routes during his absence, and he took that opportunity to speak of me, and I suppose he was pleased to say something handsome, but what it was, of course, I did not enquire. I see an article in a French paper[3] that thirty persons have been arrested in Dublin for high treason. Who can they be? Are any of my friends among them, for there are no names mentioned? I hope in God we shall be in Ireland time enough to liberate them, be they who they may; I think General Hoche will be very pretty security for their appearance, and I fancy that even my own bail would not be refused. Colonel Shee and I have been reading over the American Ordonnance,[4] and making our observations on it. If we arrive safe, I will propose adopting it, with a few necessary alterations, as our system. It is excellent, as being clear and concise, for an army that must be made in a hurry.

## *An address to the peasantry of Ireland*, by A Traveller, i.e. Tone, *a.* 14 October 1796

Contemporary print (13 pp) in Archives des Affaires Étrangères, AF III 186, dossier 859; *Life*, ii, 317–24.

The variants between the two versions are too minor to be noted. For Tone's authorship and the dating, see below, pp 353, 357.

### AN ADDRESS
### TO THE
### PEASANTRY OF IRELAND
### BY A TRAVELLER
### 1796

[1] Hoche. [2] *Macbeth*, v, v.

[3] Not identified. The *True Briton* reported that seventeen persons charged with high treason had been arrested in the north of Ireland (*True Briton*, 20, 28 Sept., 5 Oct. 1796).

[4] Perhaps this is a reference to the articles of war approved by Congress in 1786 (*Journal of the Continental Congress* (33 vols, Washington, 1904–36), xxx, 316–22) or to 'An act for regulating the military establishment of the United States', passed by Congress in 1790 and continued in 1795.

## *To the Peasantry of Ireland*

Countrymen,

Great pains have been taken in order to mislead and misinform you on the subject of the French revolution by various descriptions of people whose interest it is, and of course whose policy it ever has been, to keep you in ignorance. They have endeavoured to impress you with horror at the idea of the execution of the king, of the banishment and plunder of the nobility and especially of the clergy; and, in short, have wished to persuade you that the whole French people were a nation of furious cannibals thirsting for blood, eager for plunder, without faith, honour or religion, the enemies and the scandal of the human race. It is time, at last, to shew you the truth, and a residence of some time in France, where I have examined everything carefully with my own eyes, enables me to inform you of the actual state of that country at this hour, particularly as it relates to that numerous and useful body of the community who are, like yourselves, the tillers and cultivators of the earth, by whose labour all the other classes are supported and sustained.

It would be in vain to deny that in the course of the revolution many horrible acts of cruelty and injustice have been committed; the Government was unfortunately for some time in the hands of men utterly devoid of humanity and feeling, who sacrificed without distinction the innocent and the guilty to their own avarice, ambition or revenge; but the French people are not to be confounded with, or made responsible for, the actions of those miscreants, which they regarded with horror and amazement; the public indignation, felt by every man at such atrocious scenes, at length broke out with irresistible fury and those abominable wretches were sent to the same scaffold which had but too long been the instrument of their savage barbarity and wickedness. It has been the policy of your oppressors to dwell upon the crimes which unhappily for a short period disgraced the revolution, which exist no longer and of which no trace remains; it is my business to shew in return the benefits of the same revolution which are at this moment in full effect and which will exist from generation to generation.

Before the revolution, the king, the clergy, the nobility and gentry possessed at least four fifths of all the land in France; the farmers and peasantry there, as with yourselves, were loaded with rents, taxes and tythes. You need not be told that the clergy everywhere know very well how to take care of themselves; their lands paid no tax whatever and they had immense possessions; the gentry, who possessed all the offices of value, civil and military, were likewise exempt from taxes, and of course the whole burthen of the state fell heavy upon the people, who were utterly despised as well as plundered by the other two orders. The inhabitants of the towns, by their trade and manufactures, were enabled in some degree to support the arbitrary impositions of the ancient government; but the condition of a French peasant before the revolution was almost as deplorable as your own.

In the first place, he had his rent to pay to his landlord; that was the least and lightest of his burthens; he had the tythes to pay to the clergy, in which, however, he had one advantage over you in that he paid them to a priest of his own religion; he was tormented with a swarm of begging friars, who at every fresh crop had fresh demands upon his charity for meal, for wood, for meat or for wine; he was obliged, perhaps in the middle of his little harvest, to set off ten, fifteen or twenty miles from his cottage with his horse and cart and work for a fortnight on the public roads, during which time he must support himself and his beast at his own expense and for which he was not to receive one penny; this duty was called in France the *corvée*. He was subject to the capitation tax, which was fixed by the law; he was subject to another tax, called the *taille*, which was settled according to the good will and pleasure of the collector, who judged of his ability to pay according to the appearance he made, so that a peasant was afraid to be seen in a whole coat or to have a good horse in his cart for fear the collector, seeing anything like ease or comfort about him, should make that an excuse for screwing up the tax still higher upon him; for, as I have already said, the only rule for the amount of the *taille* was the pleasure of the tax-gatherer. The peasant was subject to another tax still more odious and unjust, I mean the tax upon industry. The tax-gatherer took upon him to decide how much a man might earn in the year and he rated him accordingly at the price of so many days' labour. Another tax was the heavy excise on tobacco. Another, and a most unjust and iniquitous one as it was managed, was the tax upon salt, the *gabelle*. Every man was obliged to pay for so much salt as the collector supposed he might consume in the year, and this tax, which was a very heavy one, he must pay, even though he did not consume a single grain; it was in vain for the peasant to say he had no occasion for, nor ever used, perhaps, the tenth part of the salt that he was rated at; he was forced to pay equally, and to such a length did they carry this abominable oppression under the old government that if a peasant near the sea coast had two or three sheep and one of them happening to have the scab should follow the natural instinct which would lead it to wash itself in the salt water, the peasant was fined heavily for this indiscretion of his sheep and obliged to pay for having cheated the crown; nay, the very shell-fish which they picked up along the shore they dared not boil in the sea water; the element which God made for the use and convenience of man was forbidden to the French peasant and he must eat his fish raw rather than the king should lose his revenue. If a man used salt which had not paid the duty, he was heavily fined; if he had not money to pay the fine, his little moveables were sold to make it good; if he was caught smuggling this indispensable necessary, he was sent to the gallies, and if with arms in his hands, he was hanged up directly without ceremony. All these heavy taxes and impositions went to the king; and, as the French have a king no longer, I leave you to judge whether the peasants at least have any reason to regret his loss.

I have mentioned the rents which the tenants paid to the gentry, and where the land was let for its value, that was but reasonable; but in most instances, as with you, the farms were let on short leases to the highest bidder and at rack rents, and the tenant was in addition loaded with heavy *corvées*, or duties, of various kinds; he was bound to draw home his landlord's firing, to harvest his corn, to cart his hay and numberless other impositions, one of which, at least, deserves to be mentioned. In some districts the landlord claimed to have the first night of every new married woman and the tenant was of course glad to be permitted to compound this odious demand for the payment of a sum of money. But it was in the execution of the game laws that the tyranny of the French gentry was most remarkable; the crops of the peasants were absolutely laid waste by the immense quantity of hares, rabbits, partridges and pheasants who, seeming to know that they were protected by the law, devoured his property before his eyes; and if the unfortunate peasant, moved either by rage or hunger, killed one of these invaders, he was seized and condemned to the gallies for life, where he was kept chained as a slave to the oar, or, in other cases, compelled to work in prisons or on the fortifications but always in irons and without hope of pardon. To such an extent was this system carried that when his crop of clover or of lucerne was ripe the tenant dared not cut it down without permission of the head gamekeeper, and if one of the under gamekeepers owed him a grudge, he had nothing but to say that there was a partridge's nest in the field; the unfortunate peasant must be content to see his hay rot and waste away before his eyes without daring to put a scythe in the grass; it was of little consequence that his fellow labourer, the horse, or his cow, the support of his children, should starve thro' the winter for want of fodder, provided the game was preserved for the amusement of his landlord. What I have now said is sufficient to give you some notion of the situation of your brother peasants in France before the revolution and I believe you will see that they were, like yourselves, fleeced by the crown, oppressed by the gentry, plundered by the clergy and despised by all. Let me now shew you how they stand since this revolution which the gentry and clergy of Ireland represent in such horrid colours.

The first consequence of the revolution was the abolition of all the unjust and oppressive distinctions which existed in France and a declaration that all men were free and equal in the sight of the law. Another immediate consequence was the removal of all those severe and ruinous burdens which crushed the unfortunate peasant. The *corvée* was abolished, the tax upon salt was repealed, the tax upon tobacco was repealed, the tax upon industry was repealed, the *taille* was repealed, the game laws were repealed, the duties claimed by the landlords, which were called *feudal rights*, were repealed, and lastly tythes were repealed and every one left at liberty to pay the clergy as much or as little as they pleased, or not to pay them at all if they thought proper. You will observe, by what I have now said, that though the gentry and the clergy have suffered by the revolution, the laborious peasantry of France are immense gainers; they are no longer obliged to stand bareheaded like slaves behind their landlords; they are no longer afraid of being sent to the gallies for knocking down a hare or a partridge; their tobacco, for which they used to pay three shillings and six pence a pound, they have now for ten pence; their salt, which used to cost eight pence a pound, is now to be had for one halfpenny or less. If the revolution had done no more than remove the burdens I have just now mentioned, surely it was a blessing to the poor, for whom it seems to have been made; but I will shew that it has done infinitely more and that it has not only removed those unjust and ruinous burdens but it has enabled the peasantry of France, such of them, at least, as were industrious, to acquire a property, which if it had not been for the revolution, they could by no possibility have attained.

All the taxes before mentioned, which were principally paid, as all taxes in the end are principally paid, by the poor, having been repealed, it became necessary to look about for other means to support the government; for this purpose the first step which was taken was to seize upon all the lands of the clergy and set them up to sale. The great body of the gentry, enraged to see the peasantry freed from the yoke and to lose all the immense privileges which they enjoyed under the old government, quit France almost to a man and fled to the different kings of Europe, whom they persuaded to make war on their country in order to restore them to what they called their just rights and to reduce the peasants once more to the condition of slaves and bondmen. In this abominable scheme the king of France was weak or wicked enough to concur and the consequence was that the people cut off his head and changed the form of their government from a monarchy to a republic; they confiscated the property of all those who had deserted their country, as I have mentioned, and who were called emigrants, and they prepared resolutely for that war which they saw ready to break out against them from the four corners of Europe.

What they expected came to pass. All the kings, all the nobility, all the gentry and especially all the clergy joined with all their might to crush the new republic, but in vain, for France alone has defeated the united efforts of all the despots of Europe. It is not necessary for me here to go into a detail on the war further than merely to shew how much the peasantry of France have gained by the very means which were employed by their enemies to reduce them to their former slavery. In order to oppose the attacks of the tyrants, the Republic raised at once no less than fourteen armies, amounting to above one million of men; the expense of arming, clothing and paying those troops amounted to an incredible sum; and as the taxes were almost all repealed in favour of the poor and the sale of the lands of the clergy and emigrants required time, the new government was obliged to issue paper money, which were called *assignats*.[1] This money at first went for its value, that is to say a guinea in paper would bring a guinea in gold or silver; but after some time, as they were obliged daily to issue more and more of this paper, and as gold and silver began to grow scarcer, those that had any hiding it carefully, the *assignats* fell by degrees in their value so that latterly a guinea in gold would bring near a thousand in paper. By this means everything had in fact two prices, one in cash and the other in paper, and the price of all kinds of provisions in *assignats* rose to an astonishing height. This was the harvest of the peasantry of France, for the farmers sold the produce of their lands at this extravagant price, while they paid their rents in *assignats* at their nominal value, that is to say, if the yearly rent amounted to one hundred pounds, for example, the landlord was obliged to take

[1] See above, p. 41, n. 5.

as lawful payment an *assignat* of one hundred pounds, tho' the same *assignat* in the market would not do more than purchase a leg of mutton. By this means the farmers in fact paid, it may be said, no rent, while they sold everything they could raise on the land at tenfold its former price. But this is not all that the revolution has done for the peasantry of France. I have mentioned already that all the lands of the clergy and emigrants, which made perhaps three fourths of the land in the nation, were set up to sale by the government; all the payments for those lands were made in the paper money, which the government was obliged to receive at its nominal value, that is to say, an *assignat* of an hundred pounds was received for an hundred pounds, while at the same time a sack of wheat would bring at market perhaps seven or eight hundred pounds in the same *assignats*. By this means, with the produce of one acre the farmer was enabled to purchase five or six and to secure to himself for ever the land to which he was formerly tenant for infinitely less than he formerly paid as his half year's rent; and in fact at this hour almost all the lands in France are, as they ought to be, the property of those who cultivate them; those who before the revolution were no better than slaves, like yourselves, are now become substantial proprietors and instead of a race of miserable farmers, oppressed by their landlords and fleeced by their clergy, they have obtained for themselves and their children, for ever, every man an estate more or less according to his means and his industry.[1]

I am not afraid of what I have here said being contradicted, either by your landlords or your priests; they know full well that I advance no more than the truth, and now, my countrymen, let me ask you what have you to fear from such a revolution as that of France? The nobleman who loses his title, the bishop who loses his lands, the esquire who loses his feudal rights and the parson who loses his tythes may lawfully cry out against the French revolution, but I cannot see what injury it has done to the peasants, into whose hands it has actually transferred three fourths of the entire landed property of their country.

In all great questions it is but fair to hear both sides, and I believe I have now said sufficient to shew you that those who have hitherto endeavoured to turn your minds against the French republic were actuated by no other motive than their own private interests and the apprehension they felt lest you should shake of[f] the yoke and raise yourselves to the same station of ease and comfort as your brethren, the peasantry of France. I will only add that America, which I have also visited and from whom the French have borrowed many useful hints for their own government, has neither king, nobility nor clergy established by law and it is notwithstanding, I am satisfied, at this hour, the happiest, the most flourishing and the best governed spot on the face of the earth. I leave it to your own good

[1] Tone is not altogether accurate in his description of the agrarian changes in France consequent on the revolution. Certainly tithe (much resented in rural Ireland) was abolished and the *corvée* and feudal dues (neither of which existed in Ireland) were swept away. To what extent land ownership changed presents a problem. Some large noble estates remained and bourgeois purchasers secured much of ecclesiastical and émigré-owned landed property which came on the market. On the whole, it has been stated the transfer of land ownership 'tended to bring small benefits to many and really substantial acquisitions to a small minority' (Norman Hampson, *A social history of the French revolution* (London, 1963), pp 251–4).

sense to draw the conclusion which follows necessarily from the information I have now given you and I remain, with the sincerest wishes for your liberty and prosperity, your friend and countryman.

A Traveller

## Diary, 14 October–13 November 1796

T.C.D., Tone papers, MS 2049, ff 138$^r$–156$^r$; *Life*, ii, 215–34.

### 14 Oct. 1796

The General[1] set off unexpectedly for Paris this day at twelve o'clock. It seems on his visit to Brest he had reason to be discontented with the administration of the Marine; however they promised him fair, and he returned to Rennes, leaving orders with a confidential person to let him know how they were going on. This person has written him word that since his departure all the preparations are slackened, and in consequence he is set off in a rage for Paris, and I trust will return in a few days with full powers to cashier a parcel of those scoundrelly agents of the Marine. I have written, by Col[one]l Shee's desire, a short address to the peasantry of Ireland,[2] explaining to them the great benefits which the revolution has procured to the peasantry of France; this he has translated into French, and gave the copy to the General to read on his way to Paris. I see by two English papers of the 13th and 14th of last month that they are importing daily large quantities of arms, ammunition and artillery into Ireland. I am glad of it for divers reasons; it is also said they are going to restore the fortifications of Derry and to mount 100 pieces of artillery on the walls.[3] This I take to be a rhodomontade, for I cannot see to what end they should fortify Derry. I wish we were once in Ireland and we would make short work with their fortifications. These eternal delays kill me; but then Hoche is a man of the greatest activity and he is embarked body and soul in this business; I am sure he is as earnest to the full as I am myself and that is great comfort to me. I suppose he will be about a fortnight absent.

### 16 Oct. 1796

The General returned unexpectedly this morning at nine o'clock; it seems he met a courier on the road with dispatches, which rendered his trip to Paris unnecessary. Colonel Shee tells me today that it was intended after landing us to dispatch the fleet with three thousand men to the East Indies, but in consequence

[1] Hoche. [2] Above, pp 347–53.

[3] *The Times*, 14 Sept. 1796, reported that ordnance stores were being sent to Ireland and that steps were being taken to repair fortifications of Londonderry.

of a mutiny at the Mauritius[1] that scheme is given up and we are to keep both ships and men. I mentioned to him a report I had heard that we were waiting for cannoniers from the Army of Sambre and Meuse, which I thought very odd, if it was true. He assured me it was no such thing; we have already three companies of cannoniers, and, in short, everything is ready, except the seamen, to procure whom the most positive and pressing orders have been given by the Minister of Marine and by the Directory. He told me also that perhaps about the time of our landing, I would hear of some combustion in England, and that he hoped before we had done we might pay John Bull a visit. According to my laudable custom I did not ask him to explain what this *combustion* was to be. It will probably explain itself time enough.

## 17 Oct. 1796

Our expedition, as well as the life of the General, has had a most providential escape. Last night between nine and ten, as he was returning from the Comédie, with Gen[era]ls Debelle and Hédouville, a ruffian who was posted at a corner fired a pistol at him within five or six yards, which fortunately missed, and the villain instantly ran off, but was stopped by two of the aid du camps [*sic*], who happened to come that way, before he had run an hundred yards; the pistol was likewise found where he dropt it. On his being seized and examined, he confessed that he was hired by a person, whom he described, to assassinate Gen[era]l Hoche, and that he was to have fifty louis for his reward. He threw himself on his knees before Hoche, who behaved incomparably well, and begged for mercy. Hoche desired him to rise,[2] as no man should kneel to him, and to tell the whole truth, assuring him that he had himself not the least resentment against him. The fellow then repeated his story exactly and two of the aid du camps [*sic*] set out with a guard in quest of the other villain, whom they found in bed and brought to head quarters. A magistrate being sent for, the two were confronted, and the latter fellow denying everything the other advanced, they were both, after a long examination, committed to prison. It seems the fellow who fired the shot is a workman employed in the arsenal; the other is lately from Paris and says he is a horse dealer; in order to induce the former to commit the murder, he told him that he was a Royalist, and that it was for the King's service to assassinate Hoche, which, together with the promise of the fifty louis, determined him. The name of the former is Moriau and of the latter Teyssierd. Nothing could be better than the General's behaviour all thro' this affair. For my part, I do not see what the Royalists could promise themselves from his death; at the same time it is beyond

[1] In June 1796 two agents of the Directory who arrived in Mauritius to enforce the decree of 16 Pluviôse An II, abolishing slavery in the French colonies, were hustled back on board ship by indignant colonists while the troops accompanying them were prevented by the colonial national guard from rendering them assistance (C. Northcote Parkinson, *War in the eastern seas, 1793–1815* (London, 1954), pp 96–100).

[2] In *Life*, ii, 216, the preceding two lines read: 'He threw himself on his knees before Hoche, who behaved incomparably well, and desired him to rise'.

all doubt that this villain, Teyssierd, has come down from Paris expressly to have him assassinated. I do not at all suspect the English of assassination, but certainly, at this moment they are much more interested in Hoche's death than that miserable Louis 18th. In short I know not what to think of the motives of this abominable affair. A few days may probably explain it further.[1]

## 18 Oct. 1796

In consequence of the affair of yesterday a search was made in the lodgings of Tessier [*sic*], and a case of pistols, two fusils and three air guns were found, the two last articles buried in the garden; there were also among his papers the directions of several persons in Paris and *in London*! I should be sorry, much as I detest the English nation, to suspect them of such vile and horrible means of effectuating their purpose as that of assassination; yet they have already done several things in this war as bad, at Quiberon and elsewhere.[2] I am very much afraid the English cabinet is implicated in this infernal business, the more so as the General received notice a few days since from the Minister of Justice at Paris to be on his guard, as an attempt was intended to be made on his life by some *English agents!* Hoche is entirely too careless of his person, which, as he is circumstanced, tho' it may be very magnanimous, is not very wise. He was out till past ten o'clock last night. Chatted a good deal today with Col[one]l Shee, who is my only companion here, and whose conversation I find extremely amusing and instructive. He tells me he expects we shall soon set off now; that the General has no confidence in the Marine, but that he is determined if we fall in with the English fleet that fight they shall, for as the military will be at least two to one on board, he will give it out in general orders that the first man, officer or seaman, of whatever rank, that offers to flinch shall be instantly shot on the quarter deck. That is stout of Hoche, or, as P.P. would say, '*manly and decided*'. I had rather however that our valour was tried on *terra firma*, for I am of opinion, with the Turks, that '*God has given the sea to the infidels, and the land to the true believers*'.[3] A seafight is our *pis aller*, nevertheless, if it must be, it must. Those damned Spaniards! Why are they not this moment in Brest Water? They have mortally offended the English by escorting Richéry out of Cadiz, and now they are temporising with half measures, which are always miserable policy, whereas if they joined us instantly, we could strike our blow in security, and the navy of England would be, or I am utterly deceived, no longer formidable to either France or Spain. I wish I was at the head of the Spanish cabinet for one month. Shee told me a good story today.

[1] It seems that royalist agents in Paris decided to assassinate Hoche because of his success in pacifying the Vendée. Charles Jean Martial Teyssière, a horse dealer and *chouan* leader, engaged Jean Marie Moriau, a blacksmith, to shoot Hoche. Teyssière's only link with England was, it seems, a scrap of paper with the address of a person in England on it. Teyssière and Moriau after being captured were tried and found guilty. They both escaped from prison and Teyssière was later killed in a skirmish between *chouans* and government troops. (Lelièvre, 'Jugement contre les assassins de Hoche' in *La Révolution Française*, lxvii (juillet–décembre 1914), pp 165–77).

[2] For Quiberon, see above, p. 19, n. 1.

[3] Source of this quotation not identified.

The English had lodged fifty louis to pay the printer here for a copy of the proclamation which they foresaw Hoche would publish, wheresoever he was bound; he got wind of this and, by Shee's advice, he prepared a proclamation addressed to the Portuguese, and then began to search with great secresy and diligence among the priests for some one who understood Portuguese in order to have it translated. (*It was a pity Mr Fitzsimons, of whose talents for the Portuguese I have already made honorable mention,*[1] *was not here.*) Having thus spread the report among those knaves, he sent off Shee privately to Angers, where there is a printer on whom he has reliance, and caused the proclamation to be printed off there, taking all possible precaution that not a copy should escape. It was very well imagined of Col. Shee, and I have no doubt but those rascally priests will take care the story of the Portuguese proclamation shall find its way to England. All fair! all fair! We talked a little of my affairs, and Col[one]l Shee, after saying some handsome things of my services &c., assured me he would take care, if we arrived safe in Ireland, to state very fully, when and where it might be necessary, of what important consequence my exertions in France had been, &c. He spoke with great friendship and regard, and I have no doubt his representations may be of material use to me. I do not think there is anything wrong or like intrigue in all this. Have I not sacrificed everything to the cause? And have I not rendered some service, and, I may say, essential service to my country? I assured Col[one]l Shee in return that if ever I found myself in a situation which might enable me, he should see the sense I entertained of his kindness for me. There the matter rested, and there I will let it rest.

## 19 Oct. 1796

Since my arrival here, I have not had the least communication with the General;[2] we have scarcely even spoke at meals, when we met, and I began in consequence to grow a little uneasy at it; for as there are two Irishmen here, MacSheehy and Duckett, besides myself, and as the first is a blockhead and the last a scoundrel, I did not exactly know whether the General might not lump us all off together in forming his opinion. I therefore hinted remotely to Col[one]l Shee yesterday my uneasiness at the great reserve on the part of the General towards me, and in consequence of what I said, which was indeed but very little, he spoke to him of it at dinner. The General assured him that he by no means confounded me with the two others, but he observed, which is the fact, that if he was to mark any particular attention for me, it would be immediately observed and set people on making enquiries, which would be very inconvenient, as it was absolutely necessary that I should remain as much *incognito* as possible; he added that in time and place I should see how he wished to treat me. This has satisfied me entirely. Col[one]l Shee also told me that it was a long time a moot point whether our expedition should be undertaken or not, as the Minister of the Marine, Truguet,

[1] See Diary for 3 Apr. 1796 (above, p. 143). [2] i.e. Hoche.

was very much wedded to a scheme he had for India, but that at last with considerable difficulty Gen[era]l Clarke had managed it so that our affair had the preference. If we get once to Ireland, it will be worth fifty of Truguet's scheme.

*At night*. I have mentioned above what the General said yesterday with regard to me. Today after dinner he took Col[one]l Shee aside and repeated his reasons for not being more attentive to me, which he begged of him to explain to me. Col[one]l Shee told him he had done so and that I was perfectly easy on that score. The General then told him he had appointed me to the rank of adjutant general; which will give me, as a military man, very great advantages; and he added that one reason which kept him under restraint as to me was the presence of that rascal Duckett, who had written him an impertinent letter and whom he intended to cashier the next morning; he added many other civilities, to which Col[one]l Shee made the proper acknowledgements on my part. Certainly nothing can be handsomer than this conduct of the General. I am heartily glad, for divers reasons, that he is resolved to send Mr Duckett to wander. Col[one]l Shee then told me that he expects we will set off in four or five days and that he had requested of the General that he and I might travel together, and that the General had given orders to his aid du camp, Poitou,[1] to that effect. The General has likewise read my address to the peasantry of Ireland,[2] which he entirely approves of; so all, as to me at least, is going on as I could desire. Huzza! I am an adjutant general! Well to be sure, but it is droll! Shall I make a good officer? Why not? '*It is a life I have desired; I will thrive*.'[3] We read the King's speech,[4] in which he announces a desire to make peace, but I do not mind that. Shee told me that perhaps at this very hour there was something going on in England which would embar[r]ass them not a little, and that we might perchance hear of it in four or five days; this is at least the third time that he has spoken to me darkly on that subject, but I make it a rule never to press him for explanations. We talked over the plan of an address to the people at large in Ireland inciting them to establish their independance, to be published on our landing, and I sat down beside him and wrote a few pages to begin.[5] I think I will make it a flaming production, but I am tired now, and it is late, and so I will go to bed. I am [a] pretty fellow to be an adjutant general. '*Mr Klinker, Floyd, I wou'd say, hi, hi, hi! I suppose you are too great a man to acknowledge your old acquaintance, ho, ho, ho!*'[6] Well, that is a vile stupid quotation, to tell the God's[7] truth of it; but a soldier is not obliged to quote like a pedant.

[1] Marie Louis Vincent Poitou (b. 1749) joined Legion of Santo Domingo; sous lieut, 1770; lieut, 1772; captain, 1786; returned to France, 1789; aide-de-camp to Hoche, 1795; chef de brigade, 1796 (Archives de la Guerre, dossier).

[2] Very probably *An address to the peasantry of Ireland* by a Traveller (above, pp 347–53).

[3] *Merry wives of Windsor*, I, iii.

[4] At the opening of parliament on 6 Oct. 1796. The speech expressed the hope that 'an immediate and direct negotiation' would lead to 'a just, honourable and solid peace'. (*Journals of the house of lords*, xli, 14).

[5] This was the beginning of another pamphlet, *An address to the people of Ireland on the present important crisis* ([Brest], 1796). It is reprinted below, pp 375–92.

[6] Tobias Smollett, *Humphry Clinker* (1771), letter dated 14 Oct.

[7] *Life* omits 'God's'.

*With their Noveds, and Omurs, and Blueturks, and stuff,*
*By God, they don't signify this pinch of snuff!*[1]

'*Damn Homo, with all my heart! I am sure I have the marks of him sticking in my a— yet.*'[2] Oh Lord, oh Lord, witty quotations for an adjutant general!

## 20 Oct. 1796

This day received my orders to set out for Brest the day after tomorrow, being the 1st Brumaire. Huzza! Huzza! I am to travel in General Debelle's carriage, with Hoche's cousin,[3] and Privat, his aid du camp. Settled all my affairs at Rennes instantly and *hove short*. I am ready at a minute's warning. I have been hard at work today on my pamphlet,[4] w[hi]ch is scurrilous enough. Col. Shee translates it as I go on, for the inspection of the General, and I like it better in his French than in my own English. I think it will do tolerably well, when it is finished.

## 21 Oct. 1796

Last night I met the General in the gallery alone. He immediately came up to me and asked me had I occasion for anything before my departure? I thanked him and replied that I had not. He then continued, 'Because, if you have, I desire you will apply to me as to your friend, without any reserve'. I again thanked him and said that if I was under any necessity, I would avail myself of his permission but that at present I was not. He then said, 'I am not a man to make professions, but I beg you will on all occasions look upon me as your friend and treat me accordingly', or words to that effect. I thanked him for the third time, and so we shook hands and parted. It was very civil of him, and I desired Col[one]l Shee today to let him know again how sensible I was of his kindness.

## 22 Oct. 1796

Set out from Rennes on my way to Brest, with Privat and Marie Hoche. Travelled very agreeably thro' a beautiful country, covered with wood, the very seat of *chouannerie*. The farms beautiful, the towns, for the names whereof I refer to the map, mean, and the villages abominable. England far beyond France in that respect, but very inferior in all the other beauties of a landscape. Halted at Montauban.[5] Our whole caravan amounts to eighteen officers, most of them of the État-Major. Supped very pleasantly. A furious penury of beds. Privat and I,

[1] 'Noveds, and Blutraks, and Omurs and stuff' (Swift, *The grand question debated* (1729), line 160).

[2] Henry Fielding, *Tom Jones* (1749), iii, chap. 12.

[3] Marie-François Hoche (b. 1753), businessman; served from 1789 in the National Guard; captain and aide-de-camp to Hoche; had to retire owing to wounds before he was 38; sought employment from Napoleon (Archives de la Guerre, dossier).

[4] See above, p. 357, n. 5.

[5] A small town in the Ille-et-Vilaine, 34 km west-north-west of Rennes.

to shew a good example, lay rough on a matrass on the floor. Lay awake half the night laughing and making execrable puns. We were not much crowded, there being only nine of us in one small room. I like this life of all things. There is a gaiety and a carelessness about military men, which interests me infinitely. We mess together, &c. I pay nothing, as the General gave orders to that effect to his cousin, and also, as Marie Hoche told me, to treat me with all possible attention and respect, all which is highly agreeable. Once again I like all this mightily.

## 23 Oct. 1796

As yesterday. Halted at Broon,[1] where we slept. Mess pleasant as usual, and good accom[m]odations in the auberge. Two very fine lads of the name of Dalton,[2] nephews of Col[one]l Shee and sons of an Irish officer,[3] are of our party and are particularly civil and attentive to me, for which, if we reach our destination, I will be civil and attentive to them. I like James Dalton, the elder, very much.[4] I wish they could both speak English, which they do but very imperfectly.

## 24 Oct. 1796

Halted at Lamballe.[5] I can see a very great difference in the behaviour of my companions since we set out. While we were at Rennes, nobody was uncivil, but nobody was attentive to me, but now the case is different. I am placed in the seat of honor, lodged single and in the best chamber, while the rest are obliged to fag, &c. I hope I need not say that I give myself no airs on all this. On the contrary I endeavour to recommend myself as much as possible by a very modest and guarded behaviour, and I have the pleasure to see that my discretion in that respect does not pass unnoticed. The alteration in the behaviour of my comrades is so striking that I think it worth mentioning here, and I believe they like me, as well as I like them. It is peculiarly incumbent on a foreigner in the French service to be delicate on all points, and I am at least sensible of what I ought to do, whether I be able or not to execute it. I like the French more and more; their very foibles, of which they have plenty, amuse me, while the singularities of an Englishman are almost always offensive.

[1] *Recte* Broons, 22 km from Montauban.

[2] One was James William Dalton (1766 or 1773–1801), born at Waterford; volunteer in Berwick's regiment, 1791; capt., 1791; aide-de-camp to General Hédouville, Oct. 1795; chef de bataillon, 1796; wounded at Ticino, 1801 (Archives de la Guerre, dossier). The other was his brother, Alexandre Dalton (1776–1859), lieut in Berwick's regiment, 1791; capt., 1795; aide-de-camp to Hoche, 1795; took part in Napoleonic wars; baron of the empire, 1819 (ibid.). See also James Dalton to T. W. Tone, 5 June 1798 (below, vol. III), and *Life*, ii, 640–41.

[3] Not identified.

[4] In *Life*, ii, 221–2, this sentence is amended by William Tone, who served under Alexandre Dalton at Erfurt, 1813–14, to read: 'I like them both, James and Alexander, very much'.

[5] About 27 km beyond Broons.

## 25, 26, 27, 28 Oct. 1796

As usual. Halted at St Brieux, Guingamp (where we remained one day to repose), Belleisle-en-Terre and Morlaix.[1] At Morlaix dined with General Harty,[2] an Irishman in the service of the Republic.

## 29 Oct. 1796

This morning before we set out General Harty sent for me and shewed me an English paper that he had just borrowed, the *Morning Post* of Sept^r^ 24, in which was an article copied from the *Northern Star* of the 16th precedent. By this unfortunate article I see that what I have long expected with the greatest anxiety is come to pass. My dear friends Russell and Sam Neilson were arrested for high treason on that day, together with Rowley Osborne,[3] Haslett, and a person whom I do not know of the name of Shanaghan.[4] The persons who arrested them were the Marquis of Downshire,[5] the Earl of Westmeath[6] and Lord Londonderry,[7] together with that most infamous of all scoundrels John Pollock.[8] It is impossible to conceive the effect this heavy misfortune has upon my mind. If we are not in Ireland time enough to extricate them, they are gone, for the Government will move heaven, earth and hell to ensure their condemnation. Good God! If they fall, where shall I ever find two such men to replace them! My poor friend Russell, with whom I have spent the happiest hours of my life, and whom I love with the affection of a brother; a man who would, I know, sacrifice his life for me or my family, if it were necessary; and Neilson, an honest, a brave, a worthy fellow, a good Irishman, a good republican; both of them men who have rendered such essential service to their country. My heart smites me now for the levity with which I have spoken of my poor Russell in these memorandums under the name of P.P. Well, that levity exists no longer! It is time now to think of other matters. I will not here expend myself in empty menaces which as yet I have not the means to execute. God, I hope, has not so totally deserted me but I may yet arrive in time

[1] A journey of about 105 km from Lamballe. [2] See above, p. 206, n. 2.

[3] Rowley Osborne, chandler and small landowner; presided over the Irish Jacobins in 1792 (Nancy J. Curtin, *The United Irishmen* (Oxford, 1994), pp 139–40, 146; Nat. Arch. (Ire.), Rebellion papers, 620/25/60).

[4] Daniel Shanaghan, attorney's clerk; he was said in July 1796 to have been distributing money among soldiers at Blaris camp (Curtin, *United Irishmen*, p. 171; Rebellion papers, 620/32/35).

[5] See above, vol. I, p. 239, n. 13.

[6] George Frederick Nugent (1760–1814), 7th earl of Westmeath; he was married to a niece of Lord Fitzgibbon (G.E.C., *Peerage*).

[7] In fact it was not Lord Londonderry but his son Robert Stewart (1769–1822), better known as Viscount Castlereagh, who took part in the arrests (*N.S.*, 16 Sept. 1796; *Drennan letters*, p. 24). Londonderry, also named Robert Stewart (1739–1821), was created baron, 1789, viscount, Oct. 1795, earl, 8 Aug. 1796, and marquess, 1816; Castlereagh was chief secretary for Ireland, 1797–1801, and foreign secretary, 1812–22; he succeeded as marquess, 1821 (*D.N.B.*).

[8] John Pollock (d. 1818), attorney; clerk of the crown and peace for Leinster, 1794–1817 (W. J. Fitzpatrick, *The sham squire* (Dublin, 1866), pp 253–8; idem, *Secret service under Pitt* (London, 1892), pp 363–5).

to deliver my friends; if, to my unspeakable loss, I should arrive too late to rescue, at least I shall be able to revenge them, and in that case, *woe to their persecutors*! I see that they have behaved in a manner worthy of themselves and of the cause to which, I fear, they will fall victims. Neilson and Russell surrendered themselves voluntarily. W[illia]m Sampson,[1] too, acted, with the greatest spirit and particularly insulted Lord Westmeath, that contemptible cuckold, two or three times in the grossest manner.[2] This most unfortunate of all events brings to my mind the death of my poor friend Sweetman, which I shall ever regret, and the arrestation of John Keogh, which is mentioned in my memorandums.[3] With regard to Keogh, as I have seen the English papers pretty regularly ever since, and have found no further mention of that affair, I am in great hopes that he was immediately discharged and that nothing disastrous ensued. If ever I return to Ireland God only knows in what state I shall find the invaluable friends I left behind me, or how many of them may be in existence. I am in unspeakable distress at this moment, the more as I can do nothing for their relief. I will go to Hoche the moment I reach Brest and acquaint him with this unfortunate event; but as to him that is unnecessary, for I am sure he is doing his very best to hurry things forward. Good God, if I am so unhappy as to arrive too late, what shall I do? I cannot bear to think of it. If they conduct themselves well, they may postpone their trial for a considerable time, and in that case we may yet save them. It is but forty-five days since they were arrested. But if to my most unspeakable misfortune that should not happen, my only consolation is the hope of revenge. Once again I will not indulge in premature threatenings. If I arrive, and arrive too late, we shall see what is fit to be done.

## 30 Oct. 1796

After halting last night at Landerneau,[4] arrived this day at one o'clock at Brest, having been just ten days on the road. Ran immediately to find the General[5] but he was gone out. Called on Col[one]l Shee and informed him of the situation of our friends; he tells me, if they manage to delay a little, he is in hopes we may arrive time enough to deliver them. God Almighty send! He tells me a relation of

[1] William Sampson (1764–1836), barrister and United Irishman. In 1806 he settled in New York. In 1825 Sampson's daughter Catherine (b. 1796) married Tone's son William. (William Sampson, *Memoirs* (1st ed., New York, 1807), pp 340–43; *D.N.B.*).

[2] The earl of Westmeath at the beginning of 1796 had been the plaintiff in a case of criminal conversation which had attracted widespread attention. Subsequently he had divorced his wife. On the day of the arrests in Belfast, according to the *Northern Star*, he had insisted on searching Mrs Sampson's bedroom though she had 'lain in some days before'. Sampson 'jocularly' assured Lord Westmeath that 'she was not, as some other ladies are, in the habit of privately harbouring gentlemen'. (*The trial on an action for damages brought . . . by the Right Hon. George Fred. earl of Westmeath against the Honourable Augustus Cavendish Bradshaw for adultery with the Right Hon. Mary Anne countess of Westmeath . . .* (Dublin, 1796); *The trial at large on an action for damages brought . . . by the Right Hon. George Fred. earl of Westmeath . . .* (Dublin, 1796); *N.S.*, 16 Sept. 1796).

[3] See Diary entries for 1 Mar. and 9 Apr. 1796 (above, pp 98–9, 148–50).

[4] About 40 km west of Morlaix and 20 km east of Brest.

[5] Hoche.

his,[1] a general officer in the service of the Republic, who was sent by the Executive Directory into Ireland about four months since, is just arrived and will probably be in Brest in about five or six days. He will of course bring us authentic intelligence of the state of the country.

## 2 Nov. 1796

I have been hard at work ever since my arrival on an address to the Irish people,[2] which is to be printed here and distributed on our landing. I have hardly time to eat, but I do not work with pleasure, from the reflection which recurs to me every instant that the men whose approbation I would most covet are perhaps at this moment on trial for their lives. Well, let me, if possible, not think of that longer. I have not yet seen the General. Col[one]l Shee tells me that General Quantin[3] has been dispatched from Flushing with 2,000 of the greatest reprobates in the French army to land in England and do as much mischief as possible; and that we have 3,000 of the same stamp whom we are also to disgorge on the English coast. It is a horrible mode of making war, and such as nothing can possibly justify but the manner in which England has persecuted the Republic. Much as I detest the inhumanity of punishing the inhabitants of a country for the crimes of their rulers, I cannot blame the French when I reflect on the treachery of England at Toulon,[4] on the miseries she has caused in that part of the republic thro' which I have just passed, on her false assignats and counterfeit louis!; but especially on her most atrocious and unheard of system of starving the whole French people, a measure so abominable and which produced such dreadful suffering and misery in France, as justifies any measure of retaliation however terrible. The English ambassador[5] is arrived at Paris. Spain has at length declared war against England and, it is said, begun by taking a man-of-war of 56 guns. Damn them; why are they not today in Brest Water? Corsica is evacuated by the English, so all goes on pretty well.

*Evening*. I have just read in the *Moniteur*[6] the memorial given in by Lord Malmesbury, the English plenipotentiary at Paris, the *mémoire* of Charles De La Croix, and the reply of the Directory, which is admirable. I have not time to

[1] Probably Richard O'Shee (1742–1801), son of Marcus Shee of Sheestown, Co. Kilkenny; col., 87th (formerly Dillon's) regt, 1792; général de brigade, 1796; he seems to have been a fourth-cousin twice removed of Henry Shée (*Burke's landed gentry of Great Britain and Ireland* (London, 1858), p. 896; Richard Hayes, *Biographical dictionary of Irishmen in France* (Dublin, 1949); 'O'Shea of Munster', B.L. Add. MS 45576; see above, p. 163, n. 3).

[2] Probably *An address to the people of Ireland on the present important crisis* ([Brest], 1796). It is reprinted below, pp 375–92.

[3] Pierre Quantin (1759–1824), general of brigade, July 1796; general of division, Aug. 1796 (Six, *Dict. des généraux & amiraux*).

[4] Toulon was delivered to the British on 27 Aug. 1793 by the counter-revolutionary municipal council, but on 17 Dec. was taken by the republic's forces under Bonaparte.

[5] James Harris, 1st earl of Malmesbury (1746–1820), British envoy to France in Oct. 1796 and in July 1797 (*D.N.B.*). His first mission to Paris lasted from mid-Oct. to mid-Dec. 1796.

[6] *Moniteur*, 28 Oct. 1796.

abstract them but the negotiation is at an end for the present. I never thought anything would come of it, for I did not believe Pitt serious, and apparently the Directory is of the same opinion, for it is on that principle they have framed their answer. My Lord Malmesbury may now go back if he pleases. I am curious to know the result of Quantin's expedition, which I presume is the business of which Col[one]l Shee spoke to me indirectly two or three times. I had rather it had followed than preceded ours, for if they commit, as doubtless they will, great enormities, it may alienate people's minds against us, who will make no distinction between one corps of French troops and another. The Spaniards are parading in the Mediterranean to assist us in taking Corsica after the English have evacuated it. Their fashion of making of war puts me in mind of the London alderman's foxhunting. I have worked this day like a horse, and I am as stupid tonight as a horse and in wretched low spirits. Every hour that passes is like an age to my impatience. I do not even sleep.

## 3, 4 Nov. 1796

At work at my pamphlet.[1]

## 4 Nov. 1796

This morning on the parade I met Poitou, the General's first aid du camp, who whispered me that by a vessel from Liverpool which was brought in yesterday intelligence was received that the revolution was effected in Ireland, that the people were all up in arms, and had seized the arsenal in Dublin, and driven 10,000 English troops, being all that were in the country, back to England. I was not a little astonished at this piece of news, and I ran off immediately to Mr Shee, who confirmed it to me; that they had found 30,000 stand of arms in the Arsenal, and that the thing was certain, adding that the General had written off to the Directory last night for positive orders to sail on the return of the courier, with whatever force was ready without waiting for the remainder.[2] He told me further that he expected every moment the captain of the prize in order to examine him, in which he desired my assistance, as the General had written to Joyeuse,[3] the Admiral, to have him sent up. All this I found very circumstantial, yet I felt, I know not what presentiment, that it would turn out at least an exaggeration of

[1] See above, p. 362, n. 2.

[2] Hoche wrote: 'Permettez-moi de partir avec une frégate . . . Je demande une frégate parce que l'escadre n'est pas prête à sortir et que tandis qu'un peuple généreux et confiant dans nos promesses brise ses fers, on nous fait ici les scènes les plus désagréables; quelques rixes de soldats et d'officiers ont déjà eu lieu.' (Hoche to the Directory, 3 Nov. 1796, in Desbrière, *Projets et tentatives*, i, 151). On 7 Nov. 1796, acknowledging Hoche's letter, the Directory stated that it had received with satisfaction his interesting news of a revolution in Ireland and that orders had been given that everything should be done to assist a people struggling to be free (Debidour, *Recueil des actes du Directoire Exécutif*, iv, 228–9).

[3] Louis Thomas Villaret de Joyeuse (1748–1812) commanded French fleet at the battle of the First of June (1 June 1794); he was in command of the Brest fleet destined for Ireland but on 5 Nov. was replaced by Morard de Galles; count of the empire, 1808 (Six, *Dict. des généraux & amiraux*).

the fact. On leaving Mr Shee I met the General himself, who embraced me after the manner of the French, kissing me on both cheeks, and wishing me joy of the event. I returned shortly after to Mr Shee, whom I acquainted with my doubts as to the extent of this report, and I mentioned the anecdote of a Liverpool captain who, seeing the Dublin Volunteers parade on this very day in the year 1779 with their cannon, &c., and their colonel, the Duke of Leinster, at their head, immediately ran down to his ship in a fright, set sail for England and on his landing swore before the Mayor of Liverpool that all Ireland was up in arms, and that he had seen the Duke of Leinster proclaimed King in College Green, which he himself certainly believed. Mr Shee seemed a little taken aback by this anecdote; however, he told me [he] had great hopes that the present news was true, for that to his knowledge 15,000 stand of arms had been lately introduced into Ireland. I asked him was he sure of that, as I did not see where money could be got to purchase them without communicating with so many people as must infallibly lead to a discovery of the affair. He replied they were purchased by one person, who was wealthy, who knew me, and whom I knew, and that in time and place I should learn who it was. I said that satisfied me. In the meantime I cannot form the least conjecture who this person is. 15,000 stand of arms would cost £30,000 and I do not see, among my acquaintance, a man who is at once able and willing to advance such a sum. I think it is hardly W[ ] S[ ].[1] Well, no matter who it is.

At last the author of our intelligence arrived, with two other seamen, taken on their way from Newfoundland about the same time, viz. eight or nine days since. A council was immediately held, consisting of the General,[2] the Admiral,[3] Col[one]l Shee and myself. Our informer said he was an American; that he sailed from Liverpool on a Wednesday; that before his departure news came by the packet that all Ireland was for a republic; that the Liberty boys and the Weavers were up, and the Clear day men;[4] and that he had seen 10,000 English troops embark at Liverpool, three or four days before he left it, in order to quell the insurrection. This was the sum of his information. He added that after they were taken by the French they had fallen in with two fleets; one he judged might be of 20 sail; and in the other he counted 12 sail of line of battle ships, and that he heard there was a third fleet *below again*. I was not disappointed to find the news turn out so different from what it was first reported, supposing even what the fellow said to be true, which it certainly was not; for in the first place he set out with a lie, in saying he was an American, for he was a Scotchman, with a broad accent. He could not tell the day of the month that he sailed, nor the burthen of his vessel. The 10,000 troops he spoke of turned out to be a regiment of Scotch, a regiment of Welsh and *a regiment of Irish*, who were embarked, as he said, on 4 large vessels, and 5 or 6 brigs. Altogether he lied and prevaricated so much that I do not

[1] In the MS the second initial is uncertain but may be S. If so, the person referred to may be William Simms, who had lent Tone £200 to enable him to go from America to France (see above, pp 23, 339). This sentence is omitted from *Life*.

[2] Hoche. [3] Villaret de Joyeuse.

[4] Apparently a confused reference to Defenders and Peep-of-Day Boys.

pay the least attention to his story, so there is an end of the insurrection. I am however heartily glad this event happened, for I hope it will produce positive orders from the Directory to sail immediately.

Dined at head quarters, in state, with the admirals and several captains of the fleet, and the staff of the army—a grand affair. This dinner is to manifest to the public that there is a perfect harmony between the land and sea service, which I am very sorry to see is far from being the case. Sat late at dinner, and after dinner retired to Col[one]l Shee's room with the General, the Admiral, Gen[era]l Debelle and Mr Shee. I did not come in for some time after the others and on my entry I found Hoche pressing Joyeuse extremely to be ready for the expedition, and Joyeuse starting every possible difficulty, particularly on the score of the transports. Hoche then said he would go with the men-of-war only, crowding as many men aboard as they could carry. Joyeuse then came down to 5 sail of the line and 5 frigates, the best sailors who might by dint of seamanship and quick sailing escape from the English who were, he said, in waiting for them off Cape Clear, and who had also *éclaireurs* off Ushant, as every morning the report was two large ships and three frigates being seen there. Col[one]l Shee asked him how many men, for a short passage, could he stow on the fo'c'sle[1] he mentioned? He said 600 on each of the line of battle ships, and 300 on each of the frigates. That makes in all but 4,500 men. The General then said that his word was pledged to the Government and to his friends in Ireland;[2] that the time was even elapsed for which he had engaged himself; that he would go in a single frigate if the Admiral could give him no more, and he pressed him again and again in the strongest manner. Joyeuse still hung back, and I believe he was sorry (to judge by his manner) that he had spoke of even five ships of the line; at length he proposed, merely as I think to gain time, to send out a vessel to reconnoitre and bring positive intelligence of the state of the country, and another to learn the actual position of the English fleet, and upon this proposal, the meeting broke up. I augur the worst possible event from any business in which the marine of France is concerned. Joyeuse wants to prevent our expedition in order to get out to India, where there is more money to be made, and in consequence is throwing every possible difficulty in our way. Attempts are even made to set the soldiers and seamen by the ears; but the Gen[era]l is determined to shoot the very first two who fight, upon the spot; there has been one duel already between Rappatelle,[3] an officer of the État-Major, and a lieutenant of the navy, in which the former was victorious,

[1] In the MS this word is very indistinct and may not be 'fo'c'sle', which does however fit the context. Another possibility is 'force', misspelt 'forced'. *Life*, ii, 228, has 'ships'.

[2] Probably an allusion to promises made to Arthur O'Connor at Angers in Aug. 1796 (see above, p. 215, n. 3, and below, p. 366, n. 5).

[3] Jean Baptiste Rapatel (1776–1814) served in the fleet and was captured, 1 June 1794; released 1795; infantry lieutenant, 1796; captured in Oct. 1798 serving on the *Hoche*; exchanged; served in the army of the Rhine and in Santo Domingo; fell into disgrace along with Moreau and said to have been killed serving with Russian artillery as a colonel (Archives de la Guerre, dossier). William Tone adds the following footnote on him: 'the same who accompanied Moreau in 1813, and in whose arms he died. He was my father's adjoint in this [i.e. the Bantry Bay] expedition.'

having wounded his adversary in two places. From all this I see, first, that if we arrive at all, which is at this moment very doubtful, we shall not arrive in force. No matter. With 5,000 men, the *Artillerie légère*, and Hoche, I have no doubt of success. Would to heaven we were with even that force on the Cave Hill this fine morning. I should soon have my dear and unfortunate friends out of jeopardy! I see likewise that there is no mention whatsoever of the Spanish fleet (damn them) in this affair. They are now parading in the Mediterranean! To be sure the folly of that is beyond all human endurance! The General told me last night that by this there were 5 or 6,000 French he hoped in England playing *le diable à quatre*.[1] I suppose he spoke of Quantin's expedition. This has been an eventful day. I have spent it with celebrated men, and who will hereafter make a figure in history; and yet God knows I am at this moment far from being satisfied. Hoche is behaving incomparably, but for the Admiral.[2] Well, what can't be cured must be endured. Let us see what the Directory will say to us!

## 5 Nov. 1796

At work at my pamphlet.[3] I have no stomach to that business. I dine every day with the General by his orders, which is the greater favour as there are never more than five or six of us, himself, his brother-in-law, Gen[era]l Debelle, Marie Hoche, Col[one]l Shee, Poitou & myself.

## 6 Nov. 1796

Chatting with Col[one]l Shee. I am in great hopes from something he said that we shall turn out Villaret Joyeuse and have an admiral of our own chusing. Perhaps in that case we may get out. I asked him whether, when the General said,[4] in pressing Joyeuse the night before last, that his word was pledged to his friends in Ireland, he spoke really the fact, or said it merely to spur on the Admiral. Mr Shee assured me that Hoche had both seen and spoken with some of the leaders in Ireland.[5] So here are two plots running on at one and the same time, mine and theirs, whoever they are! No matter for that; I am not afraid of our interfering, for our object is, I see, precisely the same, and I am even better pleased to have these invisible co-operators, as it divides the responsibility and does not leave everything resting on my single assertion. I asked Col[one]l Shee, supposing we gave up the transports, how many men could we carry in the men-of-war? He said in 12 sail of the line we could carry 6,000, and in 10 frigates we might have 2,500. So I see our armament is to be of that force. He added however that we must not give

[1] He seems to mean they would be causing mayhem. [2] Villaret de Joyeuse.

[3] Below, pp 375–92. [4] The following seven words are omitted from *Life*.

[5] One was Arthur O'Connor, as noted by William Tone (*Life*, ii, 229). For accounts of the meeting between Hoche and O'Connor, which took place at Angers shortly after 12 Aug., see Arthur O'Connor, *Monopoly, the cause of all evil* (London and Paris, 1848), pp 553–4, and esp. Marianne Elliott, *Partners in revolution: the United Irishmen and France* (New Haven, 1982), pp 100–3.

up the transports, as with them we could land with 20,000, which would settle the business without bloodshed. I answered that, if it were possible, it would undoubtedly be the best way, and I referred him to my memorials[1] for proof that it was my own opinion; nevertheless, if the bringing transports would endanger, perhaps, the success of the entire business, I thought it best to secure the men-of-war, supposing they could carry but 5,000 men, instead of 8,500 which he had calculated, as with that force we should be able to fight it out. He replied, he hoped we would have the transports also, and so it rested. For my part under the circumstances, I would prefer the men-of-war with 6 or 7,000 troops, with which to begin with.[2] I should have no doubt of success; however the business is in better hands.

Mr Shee then told me the General wished to find somebody who would go directly to Ireland, as he had a safe American[3] who would sail at a minute's warning, and also bring back the person who might go, and he was very desirous of intelligence of the state of the country at this moment. I mentioned MacSheehy, and he immediately went for the General, who came accordingly, and we agreed that if MacSheehy had no objections, he should be dispatched tomorrow. I went immediately and found MacSheehy, to whom I opened the business as from myself, and he agreed without difficulty to go if the General desired it. I informed the General of his assent, at dinner, and he desired me to thank him in his name and to desire him to hold himself in readiness for tomorrow, which I did accordingly, and tomorrow we shall see what are his instructions. MacSheehy has behaved very well in this business.[4]

## 7 Nov. 1796

The General has been out on a boating party all day until six o'clock in the evening. On his return he desired me to find MacSheehy, which I did accordingly, and he told him that he must sail that night, as everything was ready, and he gave him verbal instructions which in my mind were very insufficient, and it is the first time I have had reason to find fault with him. He desired him to go to such persons as I should name and learn from them as much as he could on the actual state of the country at this moment, the temper of the people, the number and disposition of the troops, whether the French were expected or desired, and if so, in what part, particularly? I asked him was MacSheehy to tell them nothing in return? He said he must go into no particulars, but tell them in general that the dispositions of France were highly favorable to Ireland and that both

[1] Above, pp 61–70, 88–97.  [2] *Life*, ii, 229, has 'and with that force to begin with'.

[3] Possibly Capt. Reilly, 'an American but of Irish parentage', 'formerly a ship captain employed by the house of Browne and Oakman of Belfast' and in 1796 'a merchant resident in Guernsey'; he seems to have been the master of the *Washington* which left Brest on 7 Nov. 1796 with Hoche's envoy on board (C. J. Woods, 'The secret mission to Ireland of Captain Bernard MacSheehy, an Irishman in French service, 1796' in *Cork Historical and Archaeological Society Journal*, lxxviii (1973), pp 98–100).

[4] For MacSheehy's mission, see Woods, 'Secret mission of Captain Bernard MacSheehy', pp 93–108, and F. W. Van Brock, 'Captain MacSheehy's mission' in *Irish Sword*, x (1971–2), pp 215–28.

Government and people were anxious for their emancipation. He then gave MacSheehy twenty louis, and we took leave. I brought MacSheehy to my lodgings and made him change his dress from head to foot, equipping him with shirts, boots, stockings, waistcoats, coat and cloak, all either Irish or made after the Irish fashion. I then gave him the address of Oliver Bond and Rich[ar]d McCormick. I desired him to call on the former first and to tell him he came from me, at Brest, and to satisfy him[1] I desired him to tell Bond that when Jackson was seized, and Hamilton Rowan and Reynolds escaped, he had advised me to do the same and had offered me money for that purpose, if I wanted it. For McCormick I desired him to tell him that a few days before I left Dublin for America I took him alone into his garden and acquainted him with my plan of pushing on, if possible, for France, and that I had also about the middle of December last written to him, by my brother,[2] from Philadelphia acquainting him with my progress. That I think will satisfy them that he has seen me. I desired him then, in addition to the General's orders, to tell them that he had known me in Paris for some time; that I was now at Brest; that I had the rank of adjudant general in the army of the Republic; and that I was in good repute with the General and the Government; I desired him further to say that an expedition was in great forwardness at Brest; that I had read some months back with great concern an account in a London paper of the arrestation of John Keogh,[3] and within these few days a second account of the arrestation of Sam Neilson, Russell and my other friends at Belfast;[4] that I would on my part move heaven and earth to procure their deliverance; and that I particularly recommended and entreated of them to profit of every possible delay which the forms of the law could give them in order to postpone their trial; and I desired him to press this particularly as I had the strongest hopes that in a short time we should be there to rescue them; finally I desired him to collect as many newspapers as he could for three or four months back, particularly the *Northern Star*, which Bond would furnish him with as being agent for that paper in Dublin. I then walked with him down to the Quay where I saw him join the captain who was in waiting, it being eight o'clock and a fine moonlight night. If they have good weather and a fair wind they may be in Dublin in four days easily; two days will suffice for MacSheehy's business, and four to return makes ten. However, I will allow a fortnight and I attend the expiration of that term with the utmost impatience. In this business, I chose Bond from his honesty and his close connexion with Belfast, and McCormick for a thousand reasons, especially his being secretary of the Catholics and his perfect knowledge of the state of the public mind in Dublin. I hope MacSheehy may acquit himself well.[5] He has not much to do,[6] but then he is blockhead, and I saw also when he came to the push

[1] i.e. Bond, as emended in *Life*, ii, 230.

[2] Arthur Tone.

[3] See Diary for 9 Apr. 1796 (above, p. 148).

[4] See Diary for 29 Oct. 1796 (above, p. 360).

[5] Jane Maryanne MacNeven, a daughter of William James MacNeven, in her account of her father based on information obtained from him during his last illness, states that MacSheehy on arriving in Ireland met not only Bond and McCormick but also MacNeven (Madden, *United Irishmen*, 2nd ed., iii, 203).

[6] In *Life* what follows up to and including 'he could not well go back' is omitted.

that he was not very firm. However, as his word was given and he was before his general, he could not well go back, and I encouraged him for my part as much as I could;[1] so I am in hopes he may do. Here is a fortnight now, dead loss! Damn it, for me!

I had like to forget an odd circumstance. The General desired MacSheehy to learn especially who were the members in the new parliament for the Co. Derry. I observed the new parliament would not be called until next year. The General then said, 'Well, learn who are the candidates; for Derry remember, not Kerry'. I do not for my part understand this.[2] In my mind it is of very little consequence who are either members or candidates for one place or the other. Perhaps Hoche has a mind to set up himself. Seriously, I do not see the drift of this enquiry at all. Well, I will ever leave it, as I always do in similar cases, to explain itself, for '*Quod supra nos, nil ad nos*'.[3]

## 8 Nov. 1796

Grimel, the merchant who procured the American vessel for the General, tells me that MacSheehy was off last night by half after nine o'clock; so that business for so far goes on well.[4]

## 9 Nov. 1796

This day a young man was brought to head quarters who has been taken prisoner[5] on board an American bound from Limerick to Portugal. His name is Barry St Leger.[6] He is an Irishman by birth, but has been bred at Charleston, S.C., where his father is a man of property. He left Limerick the 14th of October and the account he gives is perfectly satisfactory; a great part of it I know myself to be true. He says that everybody in Ireland expects the French; that the gentry are making preparations to receive them; that every magistrate is to raise twenty men who are

[1] In *Life* the rest of this sentence is omitted.

[2] It has been suggested that during the meeting between Arthur O'Connor and Hoche, the possibility of O'Connor becoming a parliamentary candidate for County Londonderry was discussed. In fact towards the end of Oct. 1796 O'Connor announced his candidature for County Antrim. (Frank MacDermot, 'Arthur O'Connor' in *I.H.S.*, xv, no. 57 (Mar. 1966), p. 54).

[3] 'What is above us is nothing to us.'

[4] MacSheehy on his return produced a lively report describing how he accomplished his mission. Landing in England, he travelled to Ireland, spent some days obtaining information about the numbers and distribution of the government forces and the attitude of the people. Then he managed to return to France via England. (Archives des Affaires Étrangères, Mémoires et documents, AE, Angleterre, 1743–1813, cote 53; Woods, 'Secret mission of Captain Bernard MacSheehy', pp 93–108).

[5] *Life* omits 'prisoner'.

[6] Barry St Leger (born *c.*1777). His father owned some land and a distillery near Limerick. At the age of 12 he left Ireland to live with an uncle in the United States. In 1795 he paid a visit to Ireland and was returning to America when the ship he was on board was captured by a French privateer. At Brest he met William Tate, whom he had known in America and who persuaded him to enter the Irish brigade as a sub-lieutenant, under Colonel O'Meara, a relation. He was on board the *Éole* during the Bantry Bay expedition and in 1797 accompanied Tate to Wales, where he was captured. (P.R.O., PC 1/36 A.114).

to preserve the peace, &c.,[1] in place of the militia should these last be ordered to the coast; but he adds also, what I very well believe, that it is universally supposed that the militia would join the French immediately and that a great majority of them are even sworn to do so; that every day persons are arrested, and that just before his departure he heard that John Bagwell,[2] member of parliament for the Co. Tipperary, had been taken up, and a Lord Dosforth,[3] as he pronounced it, in the Co. Armagh. For this last circumstance he must be mistaken.[4] There is Lord Gosford, who is governor of the county, but he I am sure is far from an enemy to the Government. I rather suppose he is head of the Peep o'Day men,[5] and in that case so much the worse for him if we arrive.[6] The result of this young man's account is that Ireland is in a state of the highest fermentation, and that nothing but our presence is wanting to settle the affair at a blow. He spoke very rationally, and in consequence I begged of the General to have him released from prison, so now he has the liberty of the town. There is another circumstance remarkable. The officers of the navy are continually talking of the fleets that England has in the Channel; and that lying Scotch rascal that we examined the other day said he saw three, two with his eyes, and the third I suppose by the second sight. Now St Leger in coming from Limerick to Brest has necessarily made the entire tour of the South of Ireland, the very station where the English fleet must necessarily be, and he saw nothing. The privateer that took him (on the 22d October) sounded the night before under Cape Clear, and he saw nothing; the two English sailors that we examined with the Scotchman, and who came at the same time and nearly in the same track, saw nothing; and almost every day prizes arrive and enter Brest without meeting a single vessel. Now if the English be in force in the Channel, how can all this possibly happen? And if they be not, what precious time are we losing here? And my poor friends in peril of their lives! Well, well! I am half mad with vexation at these eternal delays.

## 10 Nov. 1796

Saw the *Légion noire* reviewed, about 1,800 men; they are the banditti intended for England, and sad blackguards they are; they put me strongly in mind of the Green Boys[7] of Dublin.

[1] This is probably an allusion to the raising of yeomanry corps, the first commissions to which were issued on 31 Oct. 1796 (Allan Blackstock, *An ascendancy army: the Irish yeomanry, 1796–1834* (Dublin, 1998), esp. p. 74).

[2] John Bagwell (1752?–1816), M.P. for Co. Tipperary, 1792–1806; he seconded the address at the opening of the session, Oct. 1796 (*Commons' jn. Ire.*, xvii, 11; *Parl. reg. Ire.*, xvii, 3; R. G. Thorne (ed.), *The history of parliament: the house of commons, 1790–1820*, iii (London, 1986), pp 103–5).

[3] Arthur Acheson (1742?–1807), 2nd Viscount Gosford; created earl of Gosford, 1806 (G.E.C., *Peerage*).

[4] St Leger was wrong in stating that Bagwell and Gosford had been arrested.

[5] *Life*, ii, 232, reads 'Peep-o-Day Boys'.

[6] In fact at the close of 1795 Gosford, presiding as governor of the county at an Armagh county meeting, strongly reprobated the attacks on catholics taking place in the area (*D.E.P.*, 7 Jan. 1796).

[7] According to a pamphleteer, in 1793 the Defenders in Co. Meath 'had conceived that they were to be duped as the *Green Boys* had been some years since' (*A candid and impartial account of the disturbances in the county of Meath*, by a County Meath freeholder (Dublin, 1794), p. 11). In March 1781 a number of recruits

## 11 Nov. 1796

Blank!

## 12 Nov. 1796

Examined (at Mr Shee's apartment) an American captain who is only five or six days from London. He gives us no great encouragement. His account is that Sir John Jervis[1] is off Ushant (as he heard) with eleven or twelve sail of the line; and he himself, coming down Channel, fell in with three different little squadrons, two of four ships each and one of three, which were standing to the westward under easy sail, and were going, as he supposed, to join Admiral Jervis. If that be so they will keep us here as long as they please, for when united they will make 22 sail of the line, and our expedition is but of 12. In that case our only chance is to wait for the first hard gale of wind which may blow them off the coast, and then to make a run for it.

## 13 Nov. 1796

Went, by order of the General,[2] among the prisoners of war at Pontanezen, near Brest, and offered their liberty to as many as were willing to serve aboard the French fleet. Sixty accepted the offer, of whom fifty were Irish. I made them drink heartily before they left the prison, and they were mustered and sent aboard the same evening. I never saw the national character stronger marked than in the careless gaiety of these poor fellows. Half naked and half starved as I found them, the moment they saw the wine before them, all their cares were forgotten; the instant I made the proposal, they accepted it without hesitation. The Englishmen balanced, and several of them asked me, in the true style of their country, 'what would I give them?'; it is but justice to others of them to observe that they said nothing should ever tempt them to fight against their king and country. I told them they were perfectly at liberty to make their choice, as I put no constraint on any man; in the event, of about an hundred English, ten men and boys offered themselves, and of about sixty Irish, fifty, as I have observed; not one Scotchman, tho' there were several in the prison. When I called for the wine, my English recruits begged for something to eat at the same time, which I ordered for them. Poor Pat never thought of eating; but, when his head was a little warm with the wine, he was very urgent to be permitted to go among the Englishmen, and flog those who refused to enter, which of course I prevented, tho' with some little difficulty. '*Arrah, blood and 'ounds, Captain dear, won't you let me have one*

called the Green Linnets were sent in boats from the barracks in Dublin to Poolbeg in order to sail for Jamaica (*H.J.*, 16 Mar. 1781).

[1] John Jervis (1735–1823), created earl of St Vincent, 1797. It was not until towards the end of Dec. 1796 that Jervis, sailing from Gibraltar, reached the mouth of the Tagus. (*D.N.B.*; *Private papers of George, second Earl Spencer, first lord of the admiralty, 1794–1801*, ed. J. S. Corbett (4 vols, n.p., 1913–24), ii, 80–81).

[2] Hoche.

*knock at the blackguards?*[1] I thought myself on Ormond quay[2] once more. Oh, if we once arrive safe on the other side, what soldiers we will make of our poor fellows! They all said they hoped I was going with them, wherever it was. I answered that I did not desire one man to go where I was not ready to shew the way, and they replied with three cheers. It is to be observed that I never mentioned the object of the expedition; they entered the service merely from the adventurous spirit of the nation and without any idea that they had a chance of seeing Ireland again.

## Diary, 18 November 1796

T.C.D., Tone papers, MS 2049, ff 157r–160r; *Life*, ii, 234–7.

No. 11
From November the 18th, 1796, to January 1st, 1797[3]
*Nil desperandum!*
Brest
1796

Vous connoissez l'impétueuse ardeur
De nos Français; ces fous sont pleins d'honneur
Ainsi qu'au bal, ils vont tous aux batailles.

*La Pucelle*,[4] chant 4me[5]

### 18 Nov. 1796

I have made no memorandums these four or five days, for several reasons; one of which was that I had nothing material to insert, and another that I have been indisposed with a slight cold in my head which has made me more stupid than ordinary. Yesterday, as all the world is beginning to embark and arrange themselves, I desired Mr Shee to tell the General[6] that my wish was to serve with the grenadiers on the advanced guard, unless he had occasion for me about his person. Mr Shee replied that the offer did credit to my zeal, but he must see who commanded the grenadiers, that I might not find myself placed, perhaps, under an inferior officer. I answered that they were commanded by my friend Gatine,[7]

[1] Source of quotation not identified. [2] In Dublin.

[3] The Diary entries for 22–30 Nov., 2 Dec., 4–21 Dec., 22–3 Dec. and 24 Dec. 1796–1 Jan. 1797 are given as separate documents (below, pp 396–403, 409, 410–20, 422–5, 427–35).

[4] By Voltaire.

[5] The preceding headings and verse, which were obviously added later than 18 Nov., are omitted from *Life*.

[6] Hoche.

[7] Jean-Baptiste Paul Gastine (b. 1755), private in Garde française, 1771; sergeant, 1782; lieut in National Guard, 1789; adjutant general and chef de brigade, An III (1794–5); served with the armies of the Moselle et Rhin and Sambre et Meuse, rising to rank of adjutant commandant (Archives de la Guerre, dossier).

an adjutant general; that at any rate my wish was to serve in the post of honor where I could most improve myself; and that as to the etiquette of rank we could soon settle that, as I was willing to join as a volunteer. Mr Shee promised to speak to the General, which he did last night when the General told him his intention was to keep me in his family, and that I should embark in the same vessel with himself (*La Fraternité*, a frigate). I am very glad of that, and I should be very glad also to serve with the grenadiers, but I cannot be in two places at once, '*without I was a bird*'. Mr Shee told me the General was very well pleased with my offer. Barry St Leger, the young fellow whom we examined a few days ago, has very spiritedly desired to come with us as a volunteer, and I have, by means of Mr Shee, fixed him in the General's own guards; they are a most noble company of grenadiers, commanded by Captain Bloom,[1] a German, as are almost all the privates, and have distinguished themselves singularly in La Vendée. Bloom has promised me to take care of St Leger, and I hope he will do well. If I had Matt and Arthur here now, I could fix them both; well, if we get safe to the other side, I shall be able to do it there perhaps. We will see.

Today I took occasion to disburthen my mind on the state of our expedition to Col[one]l Shee. I told him the Spanish fleet was, as we know officially, in Toulon, where it was true they might annoy the English commerce in the Mediterranean, which was the only good they could do now that Corsica was restored to the Republic; that instead of mitching[2] in that idle manner at Toulon, they ought to be in Brest Water, which would secure the success of our expedition beyond the possibility of a miscarriage, and by that means cripple the naval power of England for ever; that it was true the French and Spanish navies had never long co-operated successfully, nevertheless that did not apply to our case as our operation was simple, and required only a superiority in the Channel for one week, which would settle the affair as well as a century; that divided as our naval force was now, and watched as we were by the English, it was hardly possible to suppose that we should reach Ireland without falling in with their fleet, and that if they were superior in numbers, or were equal, I gave it as my opinion that they would *infallibly beat us*; that all this risque might be prevented and the matter reduced to an absolute certainty by the co-operation of the Spanish fleet and that consequently their absence proved to me either that the French government had little influence in Spain, or that the Spanish government was infatuated to a degree which I could not conceive and at the reflexion of which I lost all temper; that England would never forgive them the insult of escorting Richéry out of Cadiz; that the consequence of this mode of making war in detail would be that England would beat us first and then send a fleet into the Mediterranean which would beat them soundly, and in this manner destroy us separately; finally I said that as I hoped that, in the worst event, they would not take us all in this expedition, those who escaped would push on for Ireland and make a desperate plunge into the

[1] Not identified.
[2] For this Hiberno-English word, see above, p. 268. The meaning here is 'malingering'.

country. To all this long harangue, which I have detailed here very immethodically, Mr Shee had nothing comfortable or substantial to offer in reply; after heartily damning the Spaniards, in which I was not behind him, he said he had reason to hope we might still get over. I said I hoped it as much as he, but that I hardly expected it. He then said we must not suffer ourselves to see things in too gloomy a light. I replied that my manner of seeing things should not influence my conduct or prevent my doing my duty in the action if we were forced into one, but that at the same time I thought it right to give him my opinion at full length before our departure. The conversation then ended with a second volley of imprecations from both of us on the inconceivable madness of the Spanish government. If they do not pay dear for this system which they have adopted, there is not a drop of water in Brest Harbour. Oh, if we had their 25 sail of the line now idling in Toulon (damn them sempiternally) with Richéry's four or five who have got safe into Rochefort, and our own 12, that would make 40 sail of the line, and then indeed our business would be a party of pleasure, but now see how it is! The English, from the best information that we can collect, are watching us with 25 of the line in three divisions; it is hardly possible but we must fall in with some one of them, and they will delay us, in spite of us, until the others come up, and then they will flog us completely, and give the finishing blow to the French marine, and as for the Spanish after, that will give them no trouble. How terrible to think of all this, and at the same time how simply and easily it might be prevented, and our common adversary humbled for ever! Well, what I cannot remedy it does not signify my grieving at, but if I were King of Spain for six weeks, I think I would settle this affair. Damn them, damn them! I could spend this whole night in cursing them.

One good thing however has happened within these five days. Villaret Joyeuse, the Admiral, is cashiered and we have got another[1] in his place. Joyeuse was a rascal and was underhand giving our expedition all possible expedition.[2] He made the Directory believe we were at a stand for want of seamen, and since his departure we have found out that there is more than enough and, as the chiefs always make the ton,[3] we find already a better spirit rising in the marine; but what can we do with 12 ships?

## To General Louis Nicolas Hyacinthe Chérin, 21 November 1796

Archives de la Guerre, MacSheehy dossier.

Tone informs Chérin that he has just appointed MacSheehy his adjoint and seeks confirmation.

[1] Morard de Galles (see below, p. 401).

[2] The last word is obviously an error. In *Life*, ii, 237, this sentence has been amended to: 'Joyeuse was giving, underhand, all possible impediment to our expedition'.

[3] i.e. create the mood?

Armée
Expédition[n]aire

Brest, le 1[er] frimaire an Cinq
État-major général

L'adjudant général Smith au général Chérin, chef de l'État-Major de l'armée

Mon général,

J'ai l'honneur de vous prévenir que je viens de nommer le citoyen MacSheehy capitaine adjoint aux adjudans pour remplir ces fonctions près de moi. Je vous prie de vouloir bien confirmer ce choix.[1]

Salut et respect
J. Smith

Vû et approuvé par moi
général chef de l'État-Major
général de l'armée Expédition[n]aire
Chérin

## *An address to the people of Ireland on the present important crisis,* *a.* 22 November 1796

The text is taken from the original pamphlet (t.p. + 39 pp), a rare copy of which is in Archives Nationales, AF III 186[b], dossier 859. The pamphlet is reprinted in *Life*, ii, 273–94.

This document is clearly the 'address to the people at large in Ireland inciting them to establish their independance' which Tone began at Rennes on 19 Oct. 1796 (see above, p. 357). He wrote more the next day but progress was interrupted by his departure for Brest. In the first entry in his Diary written at Brest (2 Nov.) he records: 'I have been hard at work ever since my arrival on an address to the Irish people which is to be printed here and distributed on our landing' (p. 362). Three days later he refers to it as 'my pamphlet' (p. 366). In his Diary for 22 Nov. he states: 'I have finished my address to the Irish people' (below, p. 396).

There is a later edition, the title-page of which gives the place and date of publication as 'Belfast, 1796'. But as the 'advertisement' explains that a copy of *An address to the people of Ireland* was found on board the *Hoche* (captured off Lough Swilly in mid October 1798 and brought to shore two weeks later), the pamphlet must have been printed after the beginning of Nov. 1798 and perhaps much later. The publisher's name is not given.

[1] MacSheehy had left for Ireland on 7 Nov. and Tone expected him to return about 21 Nov. (see above, pp 367, 368).

# AN ADDRESS *TO THE PEOPLE* OF IRELAND *ON THE PRESENT IMPORTANT CRISIS*

—Tollas licet omne quod usquam est
Auri & argenti, scutum, galeamque relinques;
Et gladium & thoracem; spoliatis arma supersunt!

Juvenal[1]

[Brest]
1796

## ADDRESS TO THE PEOPLE OF IRELAND

At length the time is arrived when a friend to the liberty and independance of Ireland may venture to speak the truth and examine into the situation and interest of his country without fear of being stopped short by that most unanswerable of all arguments, an information in the court of king's bench at the suit of his Majesty's attorney general.

It is long since every honest Irishman has mourned in secret over the misery and degradation of his native land without daring to murmur a syllable in the way of complaint. Not even our groans were free! Six hundred years of oppression and slavery have passed in melancholy succession over our fathers' heads and our own, during which period we have been visited by every evil which tyranny could devise and cruelty execute; we have been scattered like chaff over the land and our name has been forgotten among the nations; we have been massacred and plundered, insulted and despised; we have been reduced to that lowest state of human degradation, we have almost ceased to respect ourselves; we have doubted whether the opinion of our oppressors was not just and whether we were not in fact framed for that submission to which we have been bent by the pressure of so many centuries of hard, unremitting, unrelenting tyranny.

But if the judgements of Providence be slow, they are certain. The villain must not hope to walk in credit to his grave, nor the tyrant to insult for ever with impunity the misery he has caused. The pride and arrogance of England have at length called down upon her head the tardy and lingering justice which her manifold crimes have so long provoked; the sufferings of Ireland, prostrate and humbled as she has been even to the dust, seem to have awakened the attention of him who rules the destiny of nations; in his goodness and compassion he has at length regarded us and placed in our hands the means, if we have the courage, to be free.

[1] Juvenal, *Satires*, VIII, 123–5. The second line is correctly 'Auri et argenti, scutum, gladiumque relinques' and the third 'Et jaculum et galeam . . .'. Translated into English it could read: 'I mean the poor and the sturdy. You take silver and gold; they still have helmet, sword and shield.'

Without being too much of an enthusiastic visionary, I think I may say I see a new order of things commencing in Europe. The stupendous revolution which has taken place in France; the unparallelled [*sic*] succession of events which have, in defiance of the united efforts of all the despots of Europe, established that mighty republic on the broad and firm basis of equal rights, liberties and laws; the abasement, contrary to all human probability, of her enemies, every one of whom has, in his turn, been forced to yield to her ascendant genius with the exception thus far of Austria and especially of England, whose fall has only been delayed to make her degradation more terrible and the triumph of her victorious rival the more complete. All this, I say, has satisfied my mind that the ancient system of tyranny must fall. In many nations it is already extinct, in others it has received its death wound and, tho' it may for some time train a feeble and lingering existence, its duration is ascertained and its days already numbered. I do not look upon the French revolution as a question subject to the ordinary calculation of politics; *it is a thing which is to be*; and as all human experience has verified that the new doctrine ever finally subverts the old, as the Mosaic law subverted idolatry, as Christianity subverted the Jewish dispensation, as the Reformation subverted popery, so, I am firmly convinced, the doctrine of republicanism will finally subvert that of monarchy and establish a system of just and rational liberty on the ruins of the thrones of the despots of Europe.

But whether this opinion be well or ill founded, the question I mean to examine will not be affected by the result. Fortunately, or unfortunately, for Ireland, her cause is independant of the theory. The object for her immediate consideration is not whether she shall adopt this or that form of government, but whether she shall be independant under any. She has too many solid, substantial, heavy, existing grievances to require much ingenuity or subtle argument to convince her of her interest and her duty; and the question on which we must take an instant determination will, if I mistake not, be decided as soon as it is stated.

The alternative which is now submitted to your choice with regard to England is, in one word, *union* or *separation*! You must determine, and that instantly, between slavery and independance; there is no third way. I will not insult you by doubting what will be your decision. I anticipate your immediate and unanimous declaration which establishes for ever liberty to yourselves and independance to your country.

To a magnanimous people it is unnecessary to prove that it is *base*, to an enlightened people it is unnecessary to prove that it is *ruinous*, to exist in dependance on the will of a foreign power, and that power an ambitious rival. To you this is not a matter of mere speculation. You feel it in your government, in your laws, in your manners, in your principles, in your education; with all the great moral and physical advantages of which you are possessed, you are unnoticed and unknown as a nation in Europe; your bodies and your minds are bent down by the incumbent pressure of your tyrant; she to maintain whose avarice and ambition you are daily forced to spill your best blood, in whose cause you fight without glory and without profit, where victory but rivets your chains the faster, and where defeat adds to slavery, mortification and disgrace. In vain are you placed in the most advantageous position for unlimited commerce, in vain are you blessed with a fruitful soil, with every requisite for trade and manufactures, with inexhaustible mines, with navigable rivers, and with the noblest harbours in Europe. All these advantages are blasted by the contagious presence of your imperious rival, before whose influence your strength is withered, your resources crushed and the rising spirit of emulation strangled in the birth. It is England who debauches and degrades your gentry; it is England who starves your manufacturers to drive them into her fleets and armies; it is England who keeps your wretched peasantry half-fed, half-clothed, miserable and despised, defrauded of their just rights as human beings, and reduced, if the innate spirit of your country did not support them, as it were by miracle, below the level of the beasts of the field; it is England who buys your legislators to betray you and pays them with the money levied on yourselves, it is England who foments and perpetuates, as far as in her lies, the spirit of religious dissension among you and that labours to keep asunder Irishman from Irishman, because that in your cordial union among yourselves she sees clearly the downfall of her usurpation and the establishment of your liberties; it is England who supports and nourishes that rotten, aristocratic faction among you, which tho' not the tenth part of your population has arrogated to itself five sixths of the property and the whole of the patronage and power of your nation; a faction which to maintain itself by the power of England is ready to sacrifice, and does daily sacrifice, your dearest rights to her infallible lust of gold and power.

Look to the origin of your connexion with Britain, that proud and selfish nation, and see what is the foundation of the authority of your oppressors! Six hundred years ago the Pope, *an Englishman*,[1] thought proper to confer the crown of Ireland on Henry the 2d, King of England; and the king of England was pleased in return to guarantee to his countryman, the Pope, the payment of a certain tax, *to be levied on the people of Ireland*.[2] But were the people consulted whose liberties and properties were thus bartered away between these two Englishmen? No such thing. Their independance was sold by one foreigner to the other without their privity or concurrence, and to consummate the injustice of this most infamous and audacious bargain, they were compelled themselves to raise the purchase money of their disgrace *and to pay for being enslaved*. Such was the commencement of the British monarchy in Ireland, and what have been its fruits? Six hundred years of continual intestine wars marked with every circumstance of horror and barbarity, with the desolation of whole provinces, with massacres and confiscation and plunder, with fire, famine and pestilence, with murder to that horrible extent that at length it was decreed, even by your own

[1] Note in original: 'Nicholas Breakspear, Pope, under the name of Adrian the VII[th]'. In fact he was Adrian IV (d. 1159), pope, 1154–9 (*D.N.B.*).

[2] Each household was to pay 'a yearly pension of one penny to St Peter' (Thomas Leland, *The history of Ireland from the invasion of Henry II* (3 vols, Dublin, 1773), i, 9).

legislature, to be no crime in an Englishman to kill *a mere Irishman.*[1] When by these multiplied abominations your strength was exhausted and your spirit broken, when your oppressors made it their boast that you were *brayed as it were in a mortar*, this execrable tyranny of the sword was succeeded by the still more execrable tyranny of the laws, framed with a diabolical sagacity to impoverish and degrade and brutalize you; laws even yet but imperfectly removed and for whose partial repeal, extorted from your reluctant oppressors, you are indebted to the recent union among yourselves, to your consequent spirit, and to the combination of events produced by the French revolution.

But to compensate you for the loss of your independent existence as a nation, for the destruction of your trade and manufactures, the plunder of your property, the interdiction of education to three fourths of your people, and their absolute exclusion from a state of political existence, you have been gravely told that you participated in what is called, in the cant of your enemies, *the inestimable blessings of the British Constitution*!

I will not here enter into a discussion on the merits or demerits of that constitution. You have, all of you, read the productions which have appeared on that subject and it is therefore unnecessary for me to repeat them. On him who is not convinced by the arguments of Payne,[2] the absurdity of hereditary monarchs and hereditary legislators where no man would admit of hereditary cob[b]lers who wished to have his shoes well mended, I despair of making any impression. I will therefore for the sake of argument suppose, tho' I will by no means admit, that this constitution is really as excellent as it is represented to be by its warmest panegyrists, who, by the bye, will ever be found amongst those who exist by its daily destruction, and I answer in the first place that you may, if you chuse, adopt that constitution as your own when your independance is once recognised and you come to organise your government; but to quit this, which I look upon as a wild and idle supposition, I say in the second place that you do not possess this most excellent and happy constitution! that even in England it is disfigured and distorted, but that in Ireland it is so smothered beneath a mass of corruption as to be in effect no more the constitution of England as it exists in theory than it is the constitution of Constantinople or Japan.

In the first place, what is your king? Your king is a foreigner, an Englishman, a native of a country that holds you in utter contempt, whom you never see, nor expect to see, who never condescends to visit Ireland, who, with all the ignorant prejudices and illiberal passions of his nation, distributes from his closet at St James's, by the advice of the British cabinet, the honors and rewards of your country, either amongst English sycophants or more despicable Irish apostates whose strongest recommendation to his royal favor is that they are ready at all times, and without scruple, to sacrifice the interest and independance of their

[1] According to Leland, 'the murder of an Irishman was punishable only by a fine . . ., while the murder of an Englishman was a capital offence in the Irish native' (ibid., i, 279).

[2] Thomas Paine.

native land to the avarice or the ambition of England. Is there a man of you that is not convinced and that has not felt that even the meanest Englishman considers himself as your superior and despises an Irishman in his heart? And have you not had a thousand occasions to know that the king of England holds as rank and vulgar prejudices on that score as the lowest and most ignorant of his vassals, that he regards you not as a nation of valuable subjects but as a rabble of mutinous slaves, and that your whole realm is not of as much importance in his eyes as any one manufacturing town in England? People of Ireland, this is your absentee monarch! This is the idol before whom you are to fall down and to worship, like another Moloch,[1] with the sacrifice of your blood, to pamper whose pride and folly and ambition you are daily called upon to devote your treasures and your lives, your individual liberties and the glory and independance of your native land; and this is the sentiment which is called loyalty by those who wish to deceive and to mislead in order that they may plunder and oppress you.

But perhaps you find in the national spirit, in the patriotism and virtue of the other two estates of your legislature, the Lords and the Commons, a protection from the ruinous effects of an executive power deposited in a foreign country, connected with you by no ties of interest or of glory, actuated solely by selfish motives and illiberal prejudices, and who is represented by a fugacious personage bound by no responsibility and amenable to no tribunal.

See then the redoubtable barrier against oppression which you have in your house of lords! In the very first instance one half of them are Englishmen who never saw Ireland, who have not a foot of property there, who do not think it worth their while even to visit the country from which they derive their titles, but who would of themselves be sufficient to stifle all opposition by their numbers if those noble lords who are in the habit of attending Parliament were to be found, miraculously, in opposition to the mandate of the British Minister. The means by which a peerage is obtained in Ireland and the motives which determine the king of England, *the fountain of honor*, to raise his faithful subjects to that high rank are of sufficient notoriety. It is well known, and has been asserted even in your parliament, that the honors of the peerage are prostituted to the most infamous purposes of corruption, that they are bought and sold, in open market and at a stated price, or made a subject of a more ruinous tho' less disgraceful commerce in debauching the other branch of the legislature; that sometimes a man is made a peer because he can command two votes in the house of commons and sometimes because he can command five thousand pounds in money, sometimes because he has been obedient as a judge in trials when the crown has been concerned, and sometimes because he has been refractory in parliament and it is necessary to appease him. If there were any reason to expect a possibility of patriotism or public virtue from a body thus constituted, there are six and twenty bishops, many of them Englishmen, and all of them expectants of the English government for promotion or translation, ready to strangle it in the birth. Such are the hereditary

[1] Moloch was a Cananean divinity to whom humans were to be sacrificed.

counsellors of the crown in Ireland, the judges in the last resort, the impartial and incorruptible guardians of the Constitution against the incroachments of the people on one side and the king on the other, the people with whom they have no common interest and the king who names the peerage and the episcopacy, who distributes ribbands and stars and mitres, and places and pensions, at his pleasure.

The Crown and the Lords being thus organised against you and having confessedly their own distinct and separate interests to consult, at least it is to be hoped that the third estate, the Commons, your representatives, emanating from yourselves, deriving their existence from the choice of the people of which they make a part, surely they at least will take care of your rights, your liberties and your interest, which are their own; proud of the sacred deposit which you have confided in their hands they will magnanimously resist any attempt of the other two estates, should any such be made, to invade the inalienable privileges of their constituents; amenable to the tribunal of your opinion, they will dread the disgrace which inevitably attaches upon corruption in a legislator, even more than death; should any courtly pandar be found hardy enough to risque the attempt to debauch their stern integrity, they will turn aside from his presence with horror and disgust, if indeed the first emotion of insulted virtue does not rather prompt them instantly to seize the villain, to drag him from his den to public view and denounce him to the Nation as the most atrocious of all parricides, the assassin of his country.

I cannot continue this irony! The subject is too sorrowful to excite any other feeling than indignation. Who are those abominable slaves so impudently miscalled your representatives? How are they chosen? Who are their constituents? Is it not so notorious as no longer to excite surprise, or scarcely resentment, that the most inestimable of your privileges, from which all others depend, the right to chuse your legislators, is made a daily subject of a base and villainous traffic? That a station the most honorable to which a man can aspire, that of representing his fellow citizens in the great council of the nation, is bought and sold, and that seats in parliament are become a subject of dirty, commercial speculation; so that any fellow, even of the most infamous character, provided he can raise three thousand pounds, may in defiance of the public indignation and contempt, place himself triumphantly on the benches of your legislature and make laws to bind millions of men, any one of whom would scarcely trust himself alone in his company, or suffer him to enter his house, without previously locking up his spoons. The temple of your liberties is filled with buyers and sellers, with money changers and thieves, with placemen and pensioners, those unclean and ominous harpies gorged with the public spoil and sucking still, like, like insatiable vampires, the last drainings of the vital blood of their country; with fraudulent bankrupts who take shelter in Parliament from the prosecution of their creditors and purchase with a part of their plunder the privilege to retain the rest in security; with speculating lawyers, who, without principles and without practice, and destitute of talents to rise in their own profession, take up the more gainful trade of making in the legislature those laws which in the courts they are unable to expound, force on their way with inveterate perseverance, a servility that knows no scruple and impudence incapable of a blush, repel their abler and honester brethren who cannot bend to those vile means of advancement and make a short cut thro' parliament to the judgement seat; with those miserable automatons, the humble dependants of great men, who place them as their puppets in the house of commons and whose condition is I know not whether more to be pitied or despised; with young coxcombs of fortune who think *a seat in the house*, like their whores, their horses and their hounds, a necessary appendage to their rank and dignity; even the members for your counties, where, if at all, the public voice might be supposed to have some little influence, even in their election a system of corruption universally prevails, less compendious indeed than that which exists in your boroughs but more scandalous and destructive, I do not fear that any one man in Ireland, even on your treasury bench, will be found with a forehead hard enough to deny one syllable of what I have here advanced, or even to assert that the picture is overcharged. Your parliament has long lost all character, as it has lost all decency; every honest man despises it; the prostitutes who compose it know this and tremble; in vain do they multiply laws for their protection and persecute without remorse the slightest invasion of what they are pleased to vote to be their privileges; the sanction of character is wanting; the public opinion is pronounced against them, and nothing but the pressure of an incumbent force has prevented the indignant spirit of Ireland from bursting forth long since and levelling with the dust the edifice of her oppression.

From a legislature constituted as yours is, no good can flow. Those who compose it have no common interest with the people, they feel that they are but a foreign colony depending entirely for their existence on the connexion with England, whose power alone secures them in possession of their usurpations. If they had the inclination (of which I am far from suspecting them) they have not the courage to be honest. The fact and truth is that the great bulk of the aristocracy of Ireland, conscious that their estates were originally acquired by the most unjustifiable means, either by open robbery, sword in hand, or by the more infamous pillage of the laws, dares not oppose the will of the British minister from the apprehension lest he should withdraw his protection from their party and leave them to the mercy of the majority of their countrymen. It is vain to argue with men under the influence of so extreme a fear. Those of them who are more enlightened and who of course do not dread a resumption of property,[1] which the lapse of time and change of circumstances have rendered impossible, yet affect a terror they do not feel to confirm the delusion of the rest and profit of the panic which in a great degree they have themselves caused and dilgently cultivated, to govern their party and to perpetuate their monopoly in every department of the state. By these means they are enabled to make their bargain with the British

[1] An allusion to the possibility of the property of Irish Jacobites confiscated after their defeat in 1691 being restored to their descendants.

Minister and nothing can be imagined less difficult than the negociation. Their language is simply this.

Maintain us in our places, our pensions and our power; suffer us to support our mistresses, our dependants and ourselves at the public expense; surrender to us, in a word, the entire patronage of the crown. In return we engage to surrender to you the commerce, the manufactures, the liberty and the independance of Ireland; we will support you in every measure which you may devise to impoverish, to divide and to weaken our country; we will abet you in every mad and ruinous war in which you may think proper to embark; we will squander the blood of Ireland without limitation or reserve; *we will stand and fall with England*. Suffer us only in return to appropriate to ourselves such portion of the public treasure as the sacrifices we make to you may appear to deserve.

To a proposition so just and reasonable in itself, it is not to be supposed the English Minister can be so captious as to raise the least objection. He purchases in fact for England every advantage she can possibly derive from the connexion between the countries without putting her to the expence of sixpence, for Ireland, who is sold, is also forced to raise the purchase money; and herein lies the essential difference between the political situation of England and Ireland. In the former undoubtedly the constitution is depraved and degraded, and corruption carried on to an enormous extent; the liberty of the people is, beyond contradiction, sacrificed to the arbitrary will and pleasure of the king; but at the same time their essential interests are in all other respects carefully consulted by the Government. The Minister there studies to advance their trade and manufactures by all possible means, justifiable and unjustifiable, upon the same principle that the farmer manures the soil he means to cultivate and feeds the beasts he destines for labour. Under this point of view I have no hesitation to admit that England is essentially well and wisely governed and a mere merchant or manufacturer who looks no further than his warehouse or his shop has no reason to wish for a change. But do you, my countrymen, lay your hands on your hearts and ask yourselves, 'is all this so with us?'. I do not fear contradiction when I answer for you that the direct contrary is the fact and that your legislators are *hired and paid* by the English Minister (paid with your own money, I beseech you to keep ever in memory) to destroy and smother your arts, manufactures and commerce in the cradle lest they might by possibility interfere with the interest of England who will be ever undoubtedly better pleased to see you a colony of idlers to consume her manufactures and to recruit her fleets and armies than to meet you in the markets of the world, an active, enterprising and industrious rival. No English Minister would have the folly or the impudence to propose to the most corrupt and profligate of his dependants a measure subversive of the interests of the nation, or if he were so utterly infatuated, which is indeed impossible, he would not be Minister for four and twenty hours after. When a member of parliament in England sells himself, it is always with a saving clause; there are things he will not do and which he never will be asked to do; but a member of parliament in Ireland who sells himself (as they all do, or wish to do) is, politically speaking, damned without reserve; the condition of his bargain is to surrender his country for ever to the mercy of England. I do not here speak of your liberties, for in that respect the people of England are nearly as badly off as yourselves, but in the name of God, consider how this connexion affects your interests and see how absolutely and utterly different your condition is from theirs in that respect. The commerce of England is protected and cherished and fostered by the government; on a question of trade all considerations[1] of party vanish; every man, whatever be his political delinquency, is alike eager to forward any measure which promises to be beneficial and even the most abject slaves in the English house of commons are honest upon that score. But how is it with the prostitutes of the Irish house of commons? The indispensable requisite, the fundamental principle of their bargain, I repeat it, is the sacrifice of their country to the avarice and ambition of England. I appeal with confidence to your own unvarying experience to determine whether in Ireland there be any road to preferment other than an implicit deference to the will of the English Minister. Is any man promoted, or will any man ever be promoted, to power or station, at least while the connexion holds, because he is, or is even suspected to be, the friend of his country? Would not such a suspicion operate infallibly to his exclusion? And hence it is that it is impossible under the present system that you ever can have an honest government, because the English Minister, who names your rulers, will be sure to exact from them such conditions and engagements as no honest Irishman can by possibility submit to and consequently none but knaves and sycophants who are ready without scruple to take this abominable covenant can fill place or office; it is not so in England, because there, as I have already said, the essential interests of the nation are equally the object of all parties and a man may accept a situation in the government without sacrificing his integrity or his reputation; but I defy any man to take a share in the measures of the Irish government without a total surrender of all principle and character as an Irishman. Number, I beseech you, your tyrants; consider the most virulent of your oppressors man by man; review the whole of their political career and see what are the means whereby they have become your rulers. Have they any other merit than that of blind submission to the will of England and a profligate eagerness to sacrifice the very existence of Ireland to her arbitrary will and pleasure? Turn then to those who call themselves your patriots and see whether they are not essentially as much your enemies and as ready to prostrate you and themselves at the feet [of] your tyrant as the most impudent and abandoned of her acknowledged hirelings. Do you not go to your legislature, as to a comedy, to be amused by the talents of the actors, well knowing the part which each is to play and what is to be the catastrophe of the piece? Can you not, on every question of importance, determine beforehand with precision how every individual will vote and upon what motives? Do you believe on your honor and conscience that you could find ten men in your entire legislature who act upon conviction or principle? Is not making your laws as much a trade as

[1] Erroneously 'consideration' but the plural is needed.

making your shoes and not the thousandth part so honest or respectable? And if all this be so, what kind of administration is that under which you[1] groan for a brave, a sagacious and an enlightened people with warm hearts, with quick feelings and with strong resentments?

But I waste time in dwelling on grievances and abuses which you all know and feel. The difficulty in enumerating the sufferings of Ireland is not what to chuse but what to reject; so many abominations crowd at once upon my mind and every one more atrocious than the other. Let me turn from a subject so disgusting in all points of view as your actual government and contemplate the brilliant prospect which lies before us, the promised land of liberty and happiness, to secure the possession of which we have but to act with the spirit of men and to profit of the great occasion which providence has at length afforded us. We have now the means, in the first place, to break that execrable slavery by which, under the more plausible name of connexion, we have been chained for six hundred years at the feet of England; we have in our hands independance for our country, the first blessing of nations and liberty for ourselves, without which life is not worth preserving; we shall no longer be dragged perpetually from the line of our obvious interests by the overbearing attraction of our tyrant, nor forced to run and prostrate ourselves at the feet of an English minister, to obtain his permission to regulate concerns of our country. The aristocracy of Ireland, which exists only by our slavery and is maintained in its pomp and splendor by the sale of our lives, liberties and properties, will tumble in the dust; the people will be no longer mocked with a vain appearance of a parliament over which they have neither influence nor control. Instead of a king representing himself, a house of lords representing themselves, we shall have a wise and honest legislature chosen by the people, whom they will indeed represent and whose interest even for their own sakes they will most strenuously support. Our commerce will be free, our arts encouraged, our manufactures protected, for our enemies will be no longer our law-makers. The benches of our legislature will no longer groan under the load of placemen and pensioners, the hirelings of a foreign power and the betrayers of our country; we shall have upright judges to administer the laws, for the road to the judgement seat will no longer be thro' the mire of parliamentary corruption; we shall have honest juries to determine on our liberties, properties and lives, for the Crown will no longer nominate our sheriffs on the recommendation of this or that grandee; the host of useless offices, multiplied without end for the purposes of corruption, will be annihilated, and men will be made hereafter for places and not places for men; the burdens of the people will be lightened, for it will be no longer the custom to buy majorities in Parliament; the taxes which will be hereafter levied will be honestly applied to the exigencies of the state, the regulation of commerce, the support of a constitutional army, the formation of a navy, the making of roads, the cutting of canals, the opening of mines, the deepening [of] our harbours and calling into activity the native energy of the land.

[1] Erroneously 'your'.

Instead of the state of daily suicide wherein Ireland now exists, her resources will at length be actively employed for her interest and her glory. Admission to the legislature will be no longer to be purchased by money and the execrable system of jobbing, so long our disgrace and ruin, will be for ever destroyed. The trade of Parliament will fail, and your boroughmongers become bankrupts. Your peasantry will be no longer seen in rags and misery, their complaints will be examined and their sufferings removed; instead of the barbarous policy which has so long kept them in want and ignorance, it will be the interest as well as the duty of a national government to redress their grievances and to enlighten their minds. The unnatural union between church and state which has degraded religion into an engine of policy will be dissolved. Tythes, the pest of agriculture, will be abolished, the memory of religious dissensions will be lost when no sect shall have an exclusive right to govern their fellow citizens. Each sect will maintain its own clergy, and no citizen will be disfranchised for worshipping God according to his conscience. To say all in one word, *Ireland shall be independant.* We shall be a nation, not a province; citizens, not slaves. Every man shall rank in the state according to his merit and his talents. Our commerce shall extend into the four quarters of the globe, our flag shall be seen on the ocean, our name shall be known among the nations, and we shall at length assume that station for which God and Nature have designed us.

I feel that I am proving an axiom. Can any honest man for a moment doubt that an independant nation will better regulate her own concerns than if she were subjugated to another country, whose interest it is to oppress her? I will therefore assume as a fact that independance is an object of the highest possible advantage to Ireland and I will briefly consider what are the weighty motives, for weighty indeed they must be, which have thus long induced her to forego [*sic*] so great a blessing and to remain in humble subjection to England. The first and most striking and in fact the true reason is the dread of risquing a contest with a power which we are habituated to look upon as our superiour. Every man agrees that independance is a good thing, if it could be had, but dreads to hazard the little he enjoys in surety for the speculation of a greater benefit, the acquisition of which is remote and attended with uncertainty and danger.

Not to dwell upon the pusillanimity of this mode of reasoning, the first answer I have to give is conclusive. It is no longer a matter of choice; we must take our party on the instant and decidedly; we have now all we wanted: allies, arms and ammunition, stores, artillery, disciplined troops, the best and bravest in Europe, besides the countless thousands of our own brave and hardy peasantry who will flock to the standard of the country. The sword is drawn, the Rubicon is passed, and we have no retreat; there remains now no alternative; if we were even inclined, we could not return to the state in which we were three months ago. We must conquer England and her adherents, if any yet she has among ourselves, or they will conquer us, and even then *Vae victis*![1] To the brave and honest majority

[1] Meaning 'Alas, to the vanquished!'.

of my countrymen who are ready to sacrifice their lives for the independance of Ireland, I do not now address myself, but to those timid and cautious speculators who may hang back and wait upon contingencies and fluctuate and balance before they chuse their party, to such men, and I hope at this glorious period few such will be found, I appeal; and I desire them, even for their own sakes, to consider that in a war like that wherein we are now engaged there is no neutrality; we fight for our liberties, dearer far than life, and in such a contest he that is not with the people is against them; him we do not find in the ranks we must hold as an enemy and an enemy in the highest degree, a deserter and a traitor to his country. If any man dreads the issue of the contest, it is notwithstanding the interest, as it is the duty, of even that man to come forward in the defense of the common cause, for it is only in the possibility of disunion among ourselves that England can form the slightest hope of success in the contest.

If she sees all ranks and description of Irishmen united and determined, she will balance, after the experience of America and France, before she will engage in a third crusade against the liberties of an entire nation. The sure way to avert the calamities of war from our country is to shew we are to a man resolved to face them with courage; or if war must be, the infallible means to insure its speedy and glorious termination is to bring to bear on our enemy the consolidated force of the entire nation. In the present crisis it is therefore the interest even of the most cautious man to step forward in the cause of his country, unless he prefers to sacrifice his property, his honor, perhaps his existence, to his fears, for, I again repeat it, *in a war for our liberties we can admit of no neutrality*.

A generous mind is not deterred from a glorious pursuit because it is attended with danger. It is our duty to hazard everything when the object is the independance of our native land were our enemy even more powerful than she has been described or we have been used to conceive her. But let us approach this gigantic figure by which we have been so long kept in awe and see whether our own apprehensions, as well as the artifice of our oppressors, have not magnified the object of our fears. The English fleet is very formidable, but we have little commerce and during the short continuance of the war, we can dispense with it; a shot from a ship will not kill a man a quarter of a mile from the shore and we have no occasion to go upon the seas to meet them. But either I am much deceived or it will be found that so far from England being formidable by her fleet, it is there she will be found most vulnerable. Who are they that man her vessels? *Two thirds of them are Irishmen*;[1] and will those brave and gallant fellows, thousands of whom have been pressed and the rest driven by famine into her service, will they, I say, be ready to turn their arms against their native land, against their fathers, their brothers, their wives, their children and their friends? It is not to be supposed; besides that we have in our hands the means to secure their co-operation in the glorious contest wherein we are engaged, and in due season it will be seen that we want neither the skill nor the spirit to employ them.

[1] See above, p. 4, n. 1.

What I have said of the navy applies, in a great degree, to the army of England; if she is determined to make war upon us, she will not venture to do it with native troops, for there are too many Irish in the ranks; she must therefore do it with forei[g]n mercenaries, if she can find the means to land them; but these mercenaries are not to be had without money and I entreat you to consider what will be the effect of a war with Ireland upon her finances. Four hundred millions of debt is no slight burden and the Minister may not always find lenders. It is no secret that he is at this moment in considerable difficulty, and I take it for granted we shall not be so mad as to part with a shilling of English property until our liberty is established; but supposing he can even find money, money will not do everything, the gold of Carthage did not save her from the iron of Rome, and I doubt whether in the present contest the Bank paper of England will be found more efficacious.

But granting she is formidable, so are we; if she is near us, we are near her; our people are brave, and hardy, and poor; we are not debauched by luxury and sloth; we are used to toil, and fatigue, and scanty living; our miseries, for which we have to thank England, have well prepared us to throw off her yoke. We can dispense with feather beds, with roast beef, and strong beer; war, if it makes any change in the diet of our peasants, must change it for the better; they may in that case taste meat and bread, delicacies to them, and which a great majority of them seldom see; our soil and our climate we can well support; we can sleep in our bogs, w[h]ere our enemies will rot, and subsist on our mountains, where they will starve. We fight upon principle and for our liberties; they fight because they are ordered to do so. We are at home; they are in an enemies' country. Under these circumstances, and especially with a just and righteous cause, he must be timid indeed who could doubt of success.

England with Ireland at her back is undoubtedly formidable; England with Ireland neuter [*sic*] is still respectable; but England with Ireland in arms against her I do not despair of seeing humbled with the dust. Add to what I have said the discontents which exist, even in her own bosom and which every year's continuance of the war will encrease; remember the state of Scotland two years since,[1] and judge whether she may not seize the present great occasion and like ourselves assert her ancient independance; see the mighty French republic, Spain and Holland united against her and friendly to Ireland and then decide which of us has most to dread from the other.

I leave this point, the discussion of which is only necessary for timid souls, and I come to another, addressed to those of a more generous stamp. It may be said that we are indebted to England for protection from our enemies and that we are of course bound in gratitude and honor not to desert her in the hour of difficulty. If this argument were founded in fact I should be ashamed to offer a syllable against it, for with nations, as with individuals, I esteem honor the first of all

[1] Perhaps an allusion to the state trials held in Scotland in 1793 and 1794 and to the convention of British radicals held in Edinburgh in Dec. 1793 (H. W. Meikle, *Scotland and the French revolution* (Glasgow, 1912), chaps 6–7).

objects and no consideration of convenience or interest should be suffered for an instant to stand against it. But, in God's name, who are the enemies against whom we are protected by England? With what one nation on earth have we a shadow of difference? Of what people existing have we reason to complain except England herself? It is true, indeed, that by this baneful connexion, which in a thousand shapes presents itself for the destruction of our interests, we are dragged as reluctant parties into every war wherein her ambition or her avarice induces her to embark; we are forced to forego [*sic*], for the time, the modicum of commerce we possess; we are loaded with taxes, our people are pressed for seamen or listed for soldiers to fight the battles of England in the event of which we have no possible interest, unless indeed it be our interest to be defeated, for the prosperity of England has ever been the depression of Ireland. In this very war which she has in her pride and folly waged against the French Republic we have supplied not less than two hundred thousand of our gallant countrymen to combat against our most essential interests; and this is the protection for which we are to be grateful! If a man sets my house on fire first, even though he should afterwards succeed in extinguishing it, am I to be grateful to such a man? If a man drags me into a quarrel for his interests and wherein I have nothing to do, am I to thank him, even though by our joint exertions I escape with my life after receiving a sound beating and losing a great part of my property? See then whether the protection of England differs in any respect from the cases I have just mentioned, The truth and fact is it is we that protect England; it is our provisions that victual her navy; it is our seamen who man her fleets and our soldiers who fill her armies; this is solid, substantial protection, and now that we are at last about to separate from her for ever, she will soon experimentally feel, to her irrecoverable loss, which of the two nations it is that has thus long protected the other.

Independant of the consideration that this argument is a cowardly one (for what Irishman, what Irishwoman, would in the hour of danger seek shelter under the arm of an Englishman?), it involves a great fallacy, inasmuch as it presumes that without the protection of England we could not exist. It is true that at this hour we have not a navy; neither should we ever have one to the end of time if the connexion with England were so long to continue; but the moment that our independance is established and the resources of our country applied not to debauch and corrupt our rulers to sacrifice our dearest interests but to cherish and bring out the inborn energy of the land, we shall soon see an Irish navy on the ocean, we shall look for protection only to God and our own courage. We have means far beyond those of half of the independant states of Europe, of Denmark, of Sweden, of Portugal, of Naples, of Sardinia. Who at this hour protects America? Who protects Switzerland? The common interest of Europe protects the one, the valour of her people the other. We unite in our case both circumstances. When we have once broken the yoke of England, do not believe that the maritime powers will ever see us return to our bondage; if even our own means were insufficient for our protection (which I will never admit), we should speedily find allies; and I presume there is hardly to be found any Irishman who so little respects his country or himself as to doubt that, with her own resources and the assistance of France, Spain and Holland, Ireland is abundantly competent to her own protection.

There is only one argument more which suggests itself to my mind in support of our dependance upon England and that is that the condition of Ireland is latterly much improved and therefore we should not desire a change.

I admit our condition is improved, and why? In 1779, when England was embar[r]assed by her frantic crusade against America, we extorted from her necessities the extension of our trade;[1] this was a great improvement, but is it the connexion with England we are to thank for that? So far from it that the first improvement in our condition was the step we then made towards independance. In 1782 we broke another and a weighty link of the chain which bound us to England by establishing our exclusive right to legislate for ourselves;[2] this was also a great improvement in our condition inasmuch as it placed us a step farther from England; we had then the means to be honest if our legislators had had the inclination, and if we have not profited of the advantage we then obtained to its full extent, it is because we yet remained too near our enemy and one end of our chain was still in the hands of the despot of England. In 1793, when she was on the point of embarking in her second crusade against France, the union of the dissenters and the catholics took place and three millions of Irishmen were restored in a great degree to their just rights;[3] this was the last great improvement in our condition and of the very highest importance, for by making us at length one people, it has enabled us, if it be not our own faults, to throw off the yoke for ever. Thus it appears that every step that we have made towards independance has in the same degree bettered our condition; that we have become prosperous as we have become free; that while we were bound close to England we were poor and oppressed; that in proportion as we have receded from her baneful influence, we have risen nearer to our proper level. I am ready therefore to allow this argument of the increasing prosperity of Ireland its full force, but I draw therefrom a conclusion very different from those who advance it as a reason for our remaining in subjection to England. For I say that if the imperfect shadow of independance we have enjoyed for the last seventeen years has produced, as all parties will acknowledge it has, such beneficial effects, what may we not expect from a full and complete enjoyment of actual, national independance when the pressure of our ancient tyrant is once removed and we are left at liberty to regulate our own concerns, to study our own interests, to cultivate our means, to augment[4] our

[1] In 1779 there was agitation in Ireland for the removal of legal restraints on her export trade. In Feb. 1780 the British parliament passed an act allowing Ireland to trade with British colonies in America, the West Indies and Africa on equal terms with Great Britain (20 Geo. III, c. 10).

[2] In Apr. 1782 both houses of the Irish parliament agreed to a declaration of rights, in effect an assertion of its exclusive right to legislate for Ireland. Three months later the British parliament passed two acts recognising this right (22 Geo. III, cc 47, 53).

[3] An allusion to Hobart's catholic relief act which extended the parliamentary franchise to catholics, enabled them to hold civil and military offices and removed the bar to their receiving degrees at Dublin university (33 Geo. III, c. 21).

[4] Erroneously 'argument'.

resources, to profit of our natural advantages, in a word to bring into play all the latent energy of our country, '*that noble and neglected island for which God has done so much and man so little!*'[1]

Look, I beseech you, to America! See the improvement in her condition since she so nobly asserted her independance on a provocation which, when set beside your grievances, is not even worthy to be named. Before the struggle, she too was flourishing in a degree far beyond what you have ever experienced; England too was then infinitely more formidable in every point of view than at this hour; but neither the fear of risquing the enjoyments she actually possessed nor the terror of the power of her oppressors prevented America from putting all to the hazard and despising every consideration of convenience or of danger where her liberty was at stake. She humbled her tyrant at her feet, and see how she has been rewarded! Contemplate the situation of America before and since her independance and see whether every motive which actuated her in the contest does not apply to you with tenfold force; compare her laws, compare her government with yours, if I must call that a government which is indeed a subversion of all just principle and a total destruction of the ends for which men submit to be controlled, and see whether it is not worth the struggle to place yourselves in a situation equally happy as hers for yourselves and your friends, and ten times more formidable for your enemies.

I have now done, my countrymen, and I do most earnestly beseech you, as Irishmen, as citizens, as husbands, as fathers, by everything most dear to you, to consider the sacred obligation that you are called upon to discharge, to emancipate your country from a foreign yoke and to restore to liberty yourselves and your children; look to your own resources, look to those of your friends, look to those of your enemies; remember that you must instantly decide; remember that you have no alternative between liberty and independance, or slavery and submission; remember the wrongs you have sustained from England for six hundred years and the implacable hatred or still more insufferable contempt which even at this moment she feels for you; look to the nations of the earth emancipating themselves around you. If all this does not rouse you, then are you indeed what your enemies have long called you—A BESOTTED PEOPLE! You have now arms in your hands, turn them instantly on your tyrants; remember, if this great crisis escapes you, you are lost for ever and Ireland will go down to posterity branded with that infamy of which the history of the world has hitherto, for the honor of human nature, furnished but *one instance*. The Cappadocians had once the offer of liberty; they rejected it and returned to their chains.[2] Irishmen, shall it be said that you furnish the second and more disgraceful instance? No, my countrymen; you will embrace your liberty with transport, and for your chains, you will '*break them on the heads of your oppressors*'; you will shew for the honor of Ireland that

[1] Source of quotation not identified.

[2] About 95 B.C., the Cappadocians were offered their freedom by the Roman senate, but they requested a king and chose a noble, Ariobarzanes.

you have both sensibility to feel and courage to resent and means to revenge your wrongs; one short, one glorious effort and your liberty is established, NOW, OR NEVER; NOW AND FOR EVER!

# To the militia of Ireland, by Sarsfield, i.e. Tone, *a*. 22 November 1796

Contemporary print in Archives Nationales, AF III 186[b], dossier 859; *Life*, ii, 324–6.

A French translation, in the hand of Henry Shee, is with the print in the Archives Nationales.

For Tone's authorship and the dating of this document, see below, p. 396. For a letter from Shee referring to it, see below, p. 402, n. 2.

## To the militia of Ireland

Brave Soldiers,

The occasion so long delayed by every good Irishman to free his country from the tyranny and oppression of England is at length arrived, and you have now an opportunity to employ your valour in defence of your native land. The French republic has supplied us with arms, ammunition and artillery; she has sent us thousands of her best troops, commanded by one of her ablest generals, not to invade our country but to enable us to assert our liberty, and the only return she expects, or desires, is that we shall have the courage to make use of the means which she puts into our hands.

On this great and glorious occasion, shall it be said that the brave militia of Ireland were her only enemies? When thousands and tens of thousands of their countrymen are flocking to the standard of freedom, will they alone hang back? Consider, I beseech you, how the question stands on which you must now decide. You must chuse, and that instantly, between England on the [one] side, and the united nations of France and Ireland on the other, or in other words, between slavery and independence.

Suppose, what I am sure will not happen, that you should be so base as to attach yourselves to the cause of England, and see what you have to expect. In the first place, you will be loaded with the disgrace and infamy of fighting against your country, more terrible, to a true Irishman, than death itself; in the next place, you will have to plunge your bayonets in the bosoms of your parents, your brothers or your friends, or to die yourselves, in return, by their hands; in the next place, if you are defeated, as defeated you infallibly will be, you will have sacrificed your lives without the consolation of suffering in an honorable cause; and, if you were even so unfortunate as to be victorious in the contest, what would be the consequence? After having slaughtered thousands of your countrymen, and after thousands of yourselves had been slaughtered in return, after having brought all the miseries of war upon your native country, you would have the disgrace to see her once more chained like a slave at the feet of England!

What does the enemy offer you, to compensate for this load of infamy and horror? After having forced you into their service by the most outrageous means, by burning your houses, by laying waste your little farms, and hunting you down like wild beast, as you know they have done in half the counties of Ireland, they now call upon you to spill your blood in defence of the very men who have massacred hundreds of your brethren. And if you were weak or wicked enough to obey those tyrants against your country, what would be your reward? After serving the whole of a bloody war, as privates (for I suppose I need not tell you that not a man of you has the smallest chance of ever being made an officer), you will be disbanded, without settlement or provision, and the very best that can happen you is that such of you as have their limbs may return to their spades and drudge once more under their task masters, in the bogs and ditches, for a wretched pittance of sixpence or eightpence a day; the others may go beg.

But suppose, on the other hand, that you act as becomes brave soldiers and good Irishmen who scorn to serve the cause of a tyrant against their native land, and see what a brilliant prospect lies open before you. In the first place, as an Irish national army will be instantly formed, the militia will, of course, have the preference in all promotions, and especially those who are the first to declare for their country. There is not a man of you who has not his chance of being made an officer, for, in framing our army, it will be courage and talents that we shall look for, and not rank or fortune; remember, always, that the most famous of the generals who now command the armies of France have been in the beginning but soldiers like yourselves; you have now in your hands the same opportunity as they had, if you have but the sense and the spirit to seize it, to raise yourselves from the obscurity of your present condition to fame and glory, and at once to establish your own fortune and the liberty of Ireland. At the end of the war, those of you who are not become officers and who wish to retire from the service, instead of being turned loose to shift for yourselves, as will be the case in the service of the enemy, may depend on the justice and gratitude of their country to secure to each a provision in land forever, more or less, according to his rank and merits, where he may retire in ease and comfort, and live with honor and independence.

See now, my brave countrymen, how the matter stands. On the one hand, what does the enemy offer you? Hard service; no advancement; scanty pay; at the end of the war, no provision; infamy, if defeated, when fighting against your native land, or victory, more disgraceful, when its object is to enslave your country. On the other hand, if you follow the call of your interest, your honor, and your duty, you are sure of immediate and rapid promotion; in the service of Ireland you have the chance of arriving at the very highest rank in the army, you have the certainty of a settlement in land at the conclusion of the war, and, above all, what is more interesting to a brave soldier and a good Irishman, you will have the glory of having deserved well of your country and of having contributed, at the hazard of life, to the establishment of her liberties.

Sarsfield[1]

## To the Irishmen now serving aboard the British navy (I), *a.* 22 November 1796

Contemporary print in Archives Nationales, AF III 186[b], dossier 859, and Tone (Dickason) papers; *Life*, ii, 326–8.

A French translation, in the hand of Henry Shee, is with the print in the Archives Nationales.

For Tone's authorship and the dating of this document, see below, p. 396. For a letter from Shee referring to it, see below, p. 402, n. 2.

### To the Irishmen now serving aboard the British navy

Countrymen,

I do most earnestly entreat your attention to the following observations. You will determine yourselves whether I do not speak as well for your own honour and interest as that of your country.

Ireland is now at war with England in defence of her liberties; France is the ally of Ireland and England is the common enemy of both nations. You are aboard the British navy. You will probably be called upon immediately to turn your arms against your native land and the part which you may take on this great occasion is of the very last importance. I hope and rely that you will act as becomes brave seamen and honest Irishmen, and that you will not only refuse to assist in once more enslaving your country but that you will seize the opportunity which is now in your hands to secure her liberty and to make your own fortunes for ever.

Remember that Ireland is now an independent nation. You are no longer subjects of the King of England; you are at the same time a great majority of those who man his fleet in the proportion of at least two to one. What is there to hinder you from immediately seizing on every vessel wherein you sail, man-of-war, Indiaman or merchantman, hoisting the Irish flag and steering into the ports of Ireland? You have the power if you have but the inclination, and it will be your own fault if you are not immediately raised to a situation which in the service of the enemy you durst not even think of.

[1] This is a pseudonym. Patrick Sarsfield (d. 1693), a Jacobite officer, 1689–91, made his reputation by intercepting a Williamite siege train at Ballyneety, Aug. 1690; created earl of Lucan, Jan. 1691; after the treaty of Limerick he encouraged the Irish Jacobite troops to enter the French service; killed at Landen (*D.N.B.*).

Suppose you profit of this favorable moment to do what is but your duty as good Irishmen, that you seize upon the English vessels and bring them into your own harbours. In the first place, every vessel so brought into port shall be sold for its full value, both ship and cargo, and the price faithfully paid you. Those of you who do not chuse to go to sea again shall have an immediate discharge and return to their families with their share of the prize money; and as the vessels will be directly put in commission again under the Irish flag, those brave seamen who wish to serve their country and to make their fortunes at the expense of the common enemy will of course have the first promotion and every man will have his chance of becoming an officer according to his zeal, courage and talents. Instead of being cheated, as you are now, in the division of your prize money where the superior officers swallow up all and leave the brave seamen who have borne the toil and danger almost nothing, where an admiral will get for his share ten thousand pounds while a private mariner gets perhaps twenty shillings, you may depend on a just and reasonable distribution, where every man shall receive his share in a fair proportion to his rank and his merits.

Countrymen, now is your time! Remember that all you seize becomes your own property that moment; remember that you are sure of immediate and speedy promotion in the service of your country; remember that the whole trade of England lies now at your mercy and that it will be your own fault if you do not immediately possess yourselves of her rich East Indiamen, her West Indiamen, her Straights fleet, in a word, of spoil sufficient to enable you to roll in money and to make your own fortunes and that of your families for ever. Remember how you have been pressed in thousands and sent aboard the fleet of the enemy; remember how you have been starved and driven by downright hunger into her service; remember how long she has kept your country in slavery. Now is your time, my brave countrymen, to revenge your own wrongs and those of Ireland!

What is there to hinder you? You are two to one, and if you were but equal in number, I hope there is not a man of you but is as good as an Englishman. How can your officers prevent you, if you are determined to do your duty to your country and yourselves? They are not one to twenty, and it will be your own folly if you allow them for a moment to stand in the way of your advancement on this great occasion. Depend upon it, they dare not stir, if they see you once resolved; you have but to make the attempt and you must succeed.

In one word, what does your country offer you? Immediate promotion in the Irish service and prize money without limits, for the whole trade of England lies at your mercy if you have but the courage to lay hold of it. What does the enemy offer you on the other hand? First, the infamy of fighting against your native land, against your parents, your relations and your friends; next, no chance of plunder, for you know very well that neither France nor Ireland has at this moment any merchantmen at sea; consequently you have nothing to expect but hard blows; and, lastly, your British officers will bestow on you a rope's end, or a cat o' nine tails, in order to keep you to your duty, which, if you let them do, you most richly deserve to suffer both the punishment and the disgrace. Not to speak of your duty to your country as good Irishmen, I leave you to judge which is most for your interest as brave and hardy seamen. Remember once more, now or never! You have the whole navy of England in your power; if you do not avail yourselves of the present opportunity to free your country and to make your own fortunes, you deserve to remain, as you will remain, in poverty and disgrace for ever!

## Diary, 22–30 November 1796

T.C.D., Tone papers, MS 2049, ff 160ʳ–167ᵛ; *Life*, ii, 237–45.

### 22 Nov. 1796

I have been hard at work these three or four days, recruiting and writing. I picked up about twenty very stout hands, which makes eighty in all and cost me five louis, which the republic owes me. I have finished my address to the Irish people,[1] one to the Militia,[2] and one to the Irish seamen;[3] they are all now in the printer's hands, and, to speak honestly, not one of them is any great things. I think I have lost the little facility in writing that I once had. The fact is my mind is so anxious about our business that I cannot write; I do not sleep at nights. The General[4] has been ill with a severe pain in his bowels these three days; we were afraid at first he was poisoned but it proved to be a false alarm; he was at the Comédie last night.[5]

### 23 Nov. 1796

I cannot imagine what delays us now, unless it be waiting for Richéry, who is said to be coming up from Rochefort. Tho' I have the strongest apprehensions that we shall be intercepted by the English, still I wish we were at sea. There is nothing to me so terrible as suspense, and besides the lives of my poor friends in Ireland are in extreme peril. God send we may be in time to save them, but I much fear it. Well, let me not think of that. If we fall in with the English, we must fight them at close quarters, and crowd our tops, the poop and quarter deck with musquetry. It is our only chance; but against superior numbers that will not do. Those infernal Spaniards! They will pay dear for their folly, but what satisfaction is that to us? I was thinking last night of my poor little family till I was as melancholy as a cat. God knows whether ever we shall meet again! If I reach Ireland in safety and anything befals me after, I have not the least doubt but my country will take care of them, and my boys will find a father in every good Irishman; but if I

[1] *An address to the people of Ireland on the present important crisis* ([Brest], 1796), reprinted above (pp 375–92).
[2] 'To the militia of Ireland', reprinted above (pp 392–4).
[3] 'To the Irishmen now serving aboard the British navy', reprinted above (pp 394–6). [4] Hoche.
[5] Tone too attended the theatre at Brest, seeing Voltaire's *Mérope* (1743) (see Diary for 2 May 1797, below, vol. III).

should happen to be killed at sea, and the expedition should not succeed, I dread to think what may become of them. It is terrible! I rely on the goodness of Providence, which has often interposed to preserve us, on the courage and prudence of my wife, and on the friendship of my brother to protect them. My darling babies! I doat on them. I feel the tears gush into my eyes whenever I think on them. I repeat to myself a thousand times the last words I heard from their innocent little mouths. God almighty bless and protect them. I must leave off this subject. I have taken a little boy, whom I found among the prisoners-of-war, as my servant. He is so young that he will not be of much use to me, but he was an orphan and half naked. He is born in Dorsetshire, and his father was an Irish quarter-master of dragoons. He is a natural son. I have rigged him out handsomely, and if he brushes my coat and takes care of my portmanteau with the baggage it is all I require. His name is W[illia]m White.

## 25 Nov. 1796

Col[one]l Shee tells me today that he has it from Bruix,[1] one of our admirals, that in *six days* we shall sail. Would to God it were tonight! There is a fine steady breeze blowing right out of the harbour. In six days it will be the 1st of December; the 1st of January I left Sandy Hook; the 1st of February I arrived at Havre, and if we arrive safe at our destination it is possible that on the 1st of next January I may be once more in Dublin. '*Quanquam, oh!*'[2] General Clark set off nine days ago at a minute's warning for Vienna by way of Italy. That looks like peace with the Emperor, but thank God I see no sign, as yet, of peace with England; on the contrary Lord Malmesbury and my old lover[3] Charles de la Croix are keeping up a very snappish correspondance, which the Directory publishes regularly. I have been hard at work half this day translating orders and instructions for a Col[one]l Tate,[4] an American officer, who offered his services, and to whom the General has given the rank of *chef de brigade* and 1,050 men of the *Légion noire*, in order to go on a buccaneering party into England. Excepting some little errors in the locality (which after all may seem errors to me, from my own ignorance), the instructions are incomparably well drawn; they are done, or at least corrected, by the General himself, and if Tate be a dashing fellow with military talents, he may play the devil in England before he is caught. His object is Liverpool, and I

[1] Eustache Bruix (1759–1805), a naval officer before the revolution. After his return from the Bantry Bay expedition he was minister of the marine, 1798–9 (Six, *Dict. des généraux & amiraux*).

[2] This is a rhetorical particle of transition in objections made by the speaker himself. The meaning here is 'Nevertheless'.

[3] Meaning here 'wellwisher'.

[4] William Tate (b. *c.*1730s?) served as a captain in the American artillery during the war of independence. In 1793 he tried to raise a force in Georgia with the aim of attacking the Spanish possessions in North America. In 1795 he arrived in France and was later appointed by Hoche 'Chef de la 2$^{de}$ Légion des Francs'. In Feb. 1797 he landed at the head of a small expedition at Fishguard in Wales but quickly surrendered. He returned to France on parole in 1798 and left for the United States in 1809. (Archives de la Guerre, dossier; E. H. Stuart Jones, *The last invasion of Britain* (Cardiff, 1950)).

have some reason to think that the scheme has resulted from a conversation that I had a few days since with Col[one]l Shee wherein I told him that if we were once settled in Ireland, I thought we might make a piratical visit in that quarter, and in fact I wish it was we that should have the credit and the profit of it; I should like, for example, to pay a visit to Liverpool myself, with some of the gentlemen from Ormond quay;[1] tho' I must say the citizens of the *Légion noire* are very little behind my countrymen either in appearance or morality, which last has been prodigiously cultivated by three or four campaigns in Bretagne and La Vendée. A thousand of those desperadoes in their black jackets will edify John Bull exceedingly if they get safe into Lancashire. Every day I walk for an hour alone on the ramparts and look down at the fleet which rides below; there are about fifty sail of ships of war of all sizes, of which perhaps twenty are of the line. It is a most magnificent *coup d'œil*, but my satisfaction is always damped by two reflections, first; that my wife and our darling babies, one of whom I have never seen,[2] and perhaps may never see, are most probably at this moment on the ocean exposed to all the perils of a winter passage; the remembrance of the vessel which was wrecked last February at Havre,[3] I may say before my eyes, and of the unfortunate Frenchwoman who was drowned with her two infants shoots across my mind a thousand times a day, and I lie awake, regularly, half the night listening to the wind, every puff of which makes me shudder. Oh my babies, my babies! God almighty will, I hope, preserve you and your mother, whatever becomes of me. I doat upon you, you little things! Well, I am at work for you here, and I am going to fight for you, and if all goes well, there will not be on earth so happy a being as I shall be when I have you all once more in my arms. My other reflection, which also torments me, is the uncertainty of our arrival in Ireland on account of the English fleet. Sometimes I wish for a storm of five or six days to blow them off Brest, but then I think of the danger of[4] my poor little family and I check myself directly; othertimes I wish to wait for those damned infernal blockheads, the Spaniards, if we could get them up from Toulon, but then I think of my friends who are now in prison and whose lives may be sacrificed by our delay. Altogether I scarce know what to wish, and my mind is ten times more troubled and tempestuous than the ocean on which I am gazing. Fortunately the measure does not depend on me. I wait my orders, like every one else, and of course I have no responsibility but for my own personal conduct, and I hope I shall acquit myself at least without discredit. If I could command events, and were sure that Russell and the others could afford the time, what I would wish would be to delay the expedition until the arrival of the Spanish fleet, which I would instantly order up from Toulon; that operation might require at soonest six weeks, and our success

[1] In Dublin. See also Diary for 13 Nov. 1796 (above, p. 372).

[2] Shortly before leaving America nearly a year before, Tone had learnt that his wife Matilda was pregnant (see Autobiography, above, p. 340), and so was now assuming that she had recently given birth to another child. However, there is the possibility that she had had a miscarriage, and this becomes stronger when considered in the light of Tone's letter to her of 13 Jan. 1797 (see below, vol. III, p. 1).

[3] See Diary for 7 Feb. 1796 (above, p. 43).

[4] *Life* omits 'the danger of'.

would then be certain; but what signifies my tormenting myself about what I cannot remedy? The Spaniards won't come, and be damned to them; and we shall be beat first, and they after, and the liberty of Ireland, the lives of my best friends and all my own expectations, will all be sacrificed! Well, I do not care! My mind is getting hardened now, just as it was in Ireland when I expected every day to be seized and hanged.

## 26 Nov. 1796

Today, by the General's orders, I have made a fair copy of Colonel Tate's instructions,[1] with some alterations from the rough draft of yesterday, particularly with regard to his first destination, which is now fixed to be Bristol. If he arrives safe, it will be very possible to carry it by a *coup de main*, in which case he is to burn it to the ground. I cannot but observe here that I transcribed with the greatest *sang froid* the orders to reduce to ashes the third city in the British dominions in which there is perhaps property to the amount of five millions; but such a thing is war! The British burned without mercy in America, they endeavoured to starve 25 millions of souls in France, and, above all, they are keeping at this moment my country in slavery, my friends in prison, myself in exile! It is these considerations which steel me against horrors which I should otherwise shudder to think of; yet I cannot but remark what misery the execution of the orders which I have transcribed and assisted in framing may produce, and how quietly Col[one]l Shee and myself sat by the fire discussing how we might do the greatest possible mischief to the unfortunate wretches on whom our plans are intended to operate. Well, they may thank themselves; they are accomplices with their execrable government, which has shewed us the way in all these direful extremities, and there is not a man of them but would willingly exterminate both the French and the Irish yet once again! The conflagration of such a city as Bristol! It is no slight affair; thousands and thousands of families, if the attempt succeeds, will be reduced to beggary. I cannot help it! If it must be, it must! And I never will blame the French for any degree of misery which they may inflict on the people of England. I do not think my morality, or feeling, is much improved by my promotion to the rank of adjutant general. The truth is *I hate* the very name of England; I hated her before my exile; I hate her since, and I will hate her always!

## 29 Nov. 1796

I have no memorandums to make that are worth a farthing; always waiting and waiting! I declare I am tired of my life, or, as the French say, '*je m'ennuie de ma personne*'. Yesterday at dinner the General[2] was mentioning several deputies who having been in the army before the revolution had profited of the advantages

[1] See Diary for 25 Nov. 1796 (above, p. 397). [2] Hoche.

w[hi]ch their situation in the legislative body gave them to promote themselves to high rank, and he added, 'Well, there is Carnot, of whom they say so much, both good and evil; he was a captain of engineers, before the revolution, and he is a captain of engineers yet'. It is highly honorable to Carnot. Apropos, of the General! there is a charming little aristocrat with whom he is perfectly well, tho' all her relations are *chouans*. In all the hurry of our expedition, he contrived to steal off and spend two days *and nights* with her. Mr Shee and I were in a mortal fright at his absence, for, as we knew where he was gone and on what business, we apprehended some of those *chouans* might waylay and assassinate him; when they attempted it in the middle of Rennes,[1] they might well execute it in a bye road, and if anything happened Hoche, there is an end of our business. It was damned indiscreet in him, but God forbid I should be the man to accuse him, for I have been buffetted myself so often by the foul fiend that it would be rather indecent in me to censure him. (Sings) ''*Tis woman that seduces all mankind!*'.[2] I do not think however (but God knows) that under the circumstances I would have gone catterwauling for two days among the *chouans*. Hoche has all the right in the world (and why not?) to do as he pleases with his own life, but not to knock our expedition in the head. I was very angry with him, which, as I never did a foolish thing myself in my life for the sake of a woman, was but reasonable. It is all nonsense for they do what they please with us, and it is vain talking about it; however I hope he may stop here while he is well. I learn today that the État-Major (myself included) does not embark in the same frigate with the General, and I am very sorry for it, for divers excellent reasons. I should be very glad to have gone with him, but if I cannot I must submit, tho' it vexes me confoundedly. However, I will say nothing of it, but keep my mind to myself, tho' I think the General might have taken me with him. I do not know now on what vessel I am to embark, and I am plaguily angry, if anybody cared. Well, I must take to my old remedy, patience; it is not the first mortification I have met in the business, and it certainly will not be the last. How if I should be taken by the English, for example? Damn it, for me, but I can't help myself, so let the matter lie.

Today the officers of the État-Major gave a grand dinner to four or five of the captains of the fleet; we were about twenty at dinner and very pleasant. '*It cost me eight pence tho', and I had my dinner at home.*'[3] All the captains seemed satisfied that, with the number of soldiers we have embarked, we shall be a match for the English, but what they fear is to meet them on their return after landing us. Would to God we were once landed! What difference does it make to the French? They may as well be blocked up at Cork as at Brest and, if we get safe, that is the worst that can happen them. I cannot express the anxiety of my mind on this subject, but I believe it will be easily conceived that nothing can exceed it. Only think of how deep a stake I have engaged where one of the least[4] considerations is my life. Once for all, I dislike mortally the idea of a sea fight, for in the first place I expect

[1] See Diary for 17 Oct. 1796 (above, p. 355). [2] John Gay, *The beggar's opera* (1728), II, ii.
[3] *Life* omits this quotation. Its source has not been identified.
[4] *Life*, ii, 242, has 'last' instead of 'least'.

we shall be worsted, and perhaps the expedition frustrated; and in the next place I may be killed, and in that case my poor little babies will reap no advantage from my death, whereas, if it was my lot to fall after our landing I should have the consolation of being assured that my country would provide for them, and I can safely say that their future establishment is an object which occupies my mind at this important moment much more than any concern about my own personal safety; not that I wish, at all, to make the idle rhodomontade of saying that I am indifferent about my life; very far from it! I wish to live, and be happy with my dearest love and my friends, and to educate my darling babies; but if it should happen that I should fall in the contest, at least I wish it should be in my own country. If I have my wish, I may say in the words of my poor friend Russell that

*If we meet with a privateer, or a lofty man of war,*
*We will not stay to wrangle, to chatter, nor to jar.*[1]

Poor fellow! His situation at this moment is one of my principal concerns. I trust in God we shall after all be yet in time, in spite of the English fleet, to rescue him and the rest of his fellow sufferers. Well, let me change that subject. Mr Shee shewed me today the proclamation[2] of the General, which is a great favor, as the second in command, Grouchi,[3] has not seen it yet. I need not detail the contents here, as I will take care to have a copy among my papers; it is very incorrectly printed, which is a pity, and I found here and there some expressions which put me in mind of my old friend Captain Poitier.[4]

## 30 Nov. 1796

Today my friend Col[one]l Shee, who has been alarmed with some symptoms of the gout, to which he is a martyr, resolved to go on board *La Fraternité*, while he is yet able to move about; he is near sixty,[5] and with a broken constitution, as may well be supposed after six and thirty years' service, yet he is as bold and as eager in the business as if he were but five and twenty. I went with him aboard, and dined with the Admiral, Morard de Galles,[6] who has succeeded Villaret Joyeuse, and two other admirals, Bouvet[7] and Bruicks.[8] When I was about to leave him, I

[1] Source not identified. In *Life*, ii, 243, the ending of the first line is altered to 'or lofty man of war' and the ending of the second line to 'nor to chatter, nor to jar'.

[2] Probably the proclamation by Lazare Hoche 'To the Irish Nation' and beginning 'Liberty, Equality', a printed version of which is in T.C.D., Tone papers, MS 2050, f. 38. It is in inelegant English and almost certainly not Tone's composition or translation, for which reason it has not been included in this edition.

[3] Emmanuel Grouchy (1766–1847), artillery officer before the revolution; general of division, 1795; chief of staff to Hoche, 1795–6; marshal of France, 1831 (Six, *Dict. des généraux & amiraux*).

[4] See above, vol. I, p. 269, n. 3.

[5] Shée was 57, having been born on 14 Jan. 1739 (Debidour, *Recueil des actes du Directoire Exécutif*, iii, 224). He was to live 24 more years and to have a second career as an administrator.

[6] Justin Bonaventure Morard de Galles (1741–1809) (Six, *Dict. des généraux & amiraux*).

[7] François Joseph Bouvet de Précourt (1753–1832), naval officer before the revolution; admiral, 1793; commanded second squadron in the Irish expedition in 1796; was then not employed for some years; commanded naval force in expedition to Guadeloupe, 1802 (ibid.).

[8] *Recte* Bruix.

took him aside for an instant and told him that, as we embarked on different vessels, I might perhaps not have another occasion to speak to him, and therefore I availed myself of this to observe that, as it was likely we might fall in with the English and of course have an action, I had to entreat of him, in case anything should happen to me and that he got safe to Ireland, to exert himself in behalf of my family by making such a report of my services as he might think just and as they merited. He assured me in case of any accident I might rely upon his zeal and friendship, and he requested at the same time that, if a similar circumstance befel him, I would render his family the same service, which I assured him with great truth and sincerity I would not fail to do, and so we parted.[1] I have a sincere regard for him, and the very best opinion both of his zeal and talents.[2] Well, now that he is aboard, there is a step gained. It seems we (viz. the État-Major) embark aboard *L'Indomptable*,[3] an 80 gun ship, and the finest vessel in the squadron; that is some comfort, however. A young Frenchman, adjoint to Crublier,[4] an adjutant general, applied to me today to be my adjoint, for Crublier, who was a great favorite with the General, has fallen, I apprehend, into some disgrace and does not come with us. This young lad's[5] name is Dorsan,[6] but I do not know him, and he does not speak English, so I told him I left all that to the General and that I would speak to him about it, which I did accordingly, mentioning my own opinion, on which he left me at liberty to do as I pleased, so I will not take him. At night Rapatelle,[7] another young lad, told me he was nominated to be my adjoint, and I like him a great deal better than the other, so I told him I would take tonight to consider of it, and let him know tomorrow the result. I like Rapatelle well enough, but he does not speak English neither [*sic*], so I shall still be in a difficulty. If I had Matt[8] here now I could fix him in a minute *captain and adjoint*. Well,

[1] According to William Tone, some time after Tone's death Shée encouraged Matilda Tone to approach Clarke, Shée's nephew and by then private secretary to Napoleon Bonaparte, the First Consul, for an increase to her pension. Clarke however 'gave no answer and took not the slightest notice'. Shée also urged her to approach Bonaparte through three generals who had known Tone—Grouchy, Hédouville and Lacuée. Though all three applied personally to Bonaparte, she obtained no satisfaction until after the rupture of the treaty of Amiens in 1803. (*Life*, ii, 557–8, 562–4).

[2] Henry Shée in a letter to 'Mon cher Général' dated 'Brest, le 10 Brumaire 5^me^ année' (an error for 'Brest, le 10 Frimaire 5^me^ année', i.e. 30 Nov. 1796) states that he is about to go on board. 'J'ai adressé', he writes, 'il y a 3 semaines au Gén[ér]al Clarke la traduction française de deux adresses, l'une au Peuple d'Irlande, l'autre aux Paysans en particulier. Je vous envois aussi celle de deux adresses, l'une à la Milice, l'autre aux Matelots Irlandais au Service de la Marine Roïale [*sic*] d'Angleterre; quoique l'auteur en soit inconnu j'éspère que ces pamphlets feront un bon effet.' Translations of the last two documents are with Shée's letter and copies of the printed English versions in Archives Nationales, AF III, 186$^b$, dossier 859. The English versions ('To the militia of Ireland' and 'To the Irishmen serving aboard the British navy') are given above (pp 392–6).

[3] Meaning 'untamable' or 'unsubduable'.

[4] Henri Crublier d'Opterre (b. 1772), sous-lieut, 1789; captain, 1792; adjutant general and chef de bataillon, 1795; employed under General Hoche, Sept. 1797; adjutant general at Santo Domingo, 1798–9; retired 1799; recalled in 1809 and served as chief of staff to General Soulier; retired as incapable of fulfilling his functions (Archives de la Guerre, dossier).

[5] *Life*, ii, 244, has 'man's' instead of 'lad's'.

[6] Louis Charles Dorsanne (b. 1768), lieut in 8th regiment, Chasseurs à cheval, and adjutant to General Crublier (Archives de la Guerre, dossier).

[7] See above, p. 365, n. 3.

[8] Mathew Tone.

if I get once to Ireland, I must have *aid du camps* [*sic*] there, and then I will see what can be done. I am now Adjutant General, and of course I will not be put back, if I am not promoted, in my own country. Called in, in the evening, at Grimel's, where all the generals generally go to play cards and trictrac.[1] General Grouchi, who is second in command, got hold of me, and we had a long talk about Ireland; he begged of me to call tomorrow at the printer of the Marine's and see if I could find anything geographical relating to that country, and at all events to call on him tomorrow at eleven, which I promised to do. General Chérin, *chef de l'État-Major*, told me tonight that I shall embark the day after tomorrow, so I came upstairs and packed up my trunk and I am now at single anchor, and this business will at last be brought to a decision. I have been in France exactly ten months tonight! Well, it has not been time misspent. We will see now in a few days what will come of it. At all events I have done my best.

This gap has been occasioned by my being forced to leave my papers in my trunk, for some days, when I could not come at them.[2]

# To Matilda Tone, 30 November–2 December 1796

Tone (Dickason) papers; *Life*, ii, 329–36.
Variants are too minor to be noted.

Head Quarters at Brest, Nov[r] 30th, 1796

My Dearest Love,

I wrote to you on the 26th of May last[3] desiring you to remove, with all our family, to France by the first opportunity, but the ship which carried my letter was taken by the English,[4] so I suppose you never received it. I wrote to you a second time, repeating my orders and giving you very full directions for your conducting yourself in case of my not being in France at the time of your arrival; this letter I gave to the American consul at Paris (who promised to forward it by a safe hand) on the 28th of July last,[5] so I am in hopes it reached you,[6] and by calculating the dates and allowing for your lying in and recovery,[7] I presume you are by this on your passage to Havre and I cannot express the unspeakable anxiety I feel for your safety and that of our dear little babies, exposed to all the inconveniences and perils of a winter passage. I trust in God you will get safe and well, and that by the time you will receive this we shall have finished our business, in

[1] A kind of backgammon.
[2] This sentence is omitted from *Life*. It was evidently written some days after 30 Nov.
[3] See Diary (above, p. 190). [4] See Diary for 5 July 1796 (above, p. 224).
[5] See Diary entries for 28 and 30 July 1796 (above, pp 257, 258). [6] It did (see above, p. 312).
[7] Just before leaving America in Dec. 1795 Tone received a letter from Matilda Tone informing him that she was pregnant (see above, p. 340).

which case you and I will devote the remainder of our lives to each other, for I am truly weary of the perpetual separation that we have lived in, I may almost say, from the day of our marriage.

The Government here has at length seriously taken up the affair of Ireland and in consequence, shortly after my last letter to you, I received orders to join General Hoche (who commands the expedition in chief) at Rennes, where he was quartered. After remaining at Rennes near two months we set off for Brest in order to proceed to our destination, but great bodies move slow; it is only today that our preparations are completed, and the day after tomorrow I expect to embark on board the *Indomptable* of 80 guns. Our force will be of 15 ships of the line and ten frigates, and I suppose, for I do not exactly know, of at least 10,000 of the best troops in France. If we arrive safe with that force I have not the least doubt of success, especially as Ireland is now wound up to the highest pitch of discontent. I have the rank of Adjutant General and I am immediately in General Hoche's family. I offered to serve with the Grenadiers, who will form the advanced guard of the army, as being the post of danger and of honor, but the General refused me, very handsomely, saying that it was necessary for his arrangements that I should be immediately about his person. You see by this that as a military man I am infinitely better off than I had any reason to expect. There is the very best spirit in the troops, both officers and soldiers, and in short nothing can prevent our success, unless it be that we should be totally defeated by the British fleet on our passage. I have no doubt but they are cruising to intercept us and if we fall in with them the engagement will be perhaps the most desperate one that has ever been fought at sea between the two powers, for our orders are to submit (I mean the army on board) to the Captain's orders in everything except to strike to the enemy. Of course, we must fight to the last extremity and I have no doubt but we will do so; if we should even be defeated they will not take us all and in that case those who escape will, I hope, push on for Ireland; in short, once we are at sea, I think we will not turn back without finishing our business.

I would not write thus to terrify you needlessly, but long before you receive my letter the affair will be over one way or the other; I hope happily for us, in which case I once more promise you never to quit you again for any temptation of fame, honor or interest. After all we have suffered, a little tranquillity is now surely due to us.

The circumstances under which I write compel [me] to address you in the most serious style. On the eve of such an expedition as I am about to embark in, and with the prospect of such an action before me as that in which it is likely we may be engaged, I cannot conceal from you nor myself that I have to expect the greatest danger, and it is possible, in short, that I may fall in the contest. Should that event happen I hope you will have the courage to support the loss as may become you, as well for your own sake as that of our dear children. I know by what I feel at this moment how severe will [be] the trial which in that case you will undergo, but the evil will be then inevitable and the duty you owe to our darling babies must incite you to a great exertion of the firmness which I know you possess; and in short whatever the effort may cost you, you must not sink under it. I need not add any cold arguments on the folly of grieving for what is not to be retrieved. I entreat you, as you love me, for your own sake and for that of our little ones, that you may collect all your courage, and should the very worst happen, remember you will be then their only parent. I need not, indeed I cannot, say more.

In case of anything happening to me and that the expedition should succeed, you will of course remove by the first opportunity to Ireland. I do not think so ill of my country or my friends as to doubt that in that case provision will be made for you and my children. In case of my death and the failure of the expedition, I confess I am at a loss to advise you. However, not to be wanting to yourself, you will address yourself by petition to the French Executive Directory and particularly to Carnot, with whom I am acquainted and with whom I have done all my business since my arrival in France, stating the circumstances and praying relief; you will also address yourself to General Clarke, to whom you may write under cover to Carnot, to Colonel Shee, who is my particular friend and embarked with me on this expedition, and, lastly, to General Hoche, who knows my services and will, I am sure, in that case be of use to you. God knows whether all this may produce anything, for the Government here is, I know, in the last distress for money; however, you will at least try. If that fails, as Matt[1] will, I trust in God, be with you, I leave it to your common judgement and prudence to determine what may be most advisable, whether to remain in France or to return to America, in which latter case, as the little you now have will be almost totally gone, you must go to Carolina or Georgia, where alone it will be possible for you to exist and in that case I commit you to the goodness of that Supreme Power who has so often almost miraculously preserved us, entreating only of Matt, as he cherishes the memory of a brother who very sincerely and affectionately loved him, that he may not quit you for a moment while he can be useful to you, but to act as a faithful friend to you and a father to my darling babies.

I have now finished the most painful hour of my life; I have advised and prepared you for the very worst event, and be assured that the prospect of our separation cannot be more terrible to you than it is to me, but I hope we have notwithstanding both of us courage sufficient to contemplate it with steadiness. Let us now turn the picture and see what the bright side of it offers to our view.

If we do not meet the English fleet, or, meeting them, if we force our way and, in short, if I reach Ireland in safety (that is to say with my ten thousand French lovers at my back) there is not a shadow of doubt of our success and when the country is once emancipated there will be, I think, no situation that I will in reason demand which will be refused me and in that case you will see whether or not the principal desire of my life be not to make you happy; indeed, my dearest love, you are the main spring of every action of my life and every thought of my heart. Remember, I am now in the high road to fortune and, I hope, to fame, for if we succeed I think I may say I have earned some reputation, but I can also say that

[1] His brother Mathew.

neither fame nor fortune are an object with me further than as they will enable me to manifest my sense of your goodness and virtues. As I shall arrive there with the rank of Adjutant General and with the favor of the commander-in-chief, and, I hope, the good will of my countrymen, and, as an Irish army will be of course directly formed I shall, I presume, not be offered a lower rank than I now hold, and if I behave, as I hope I shall, in a manner becoming a good officer, I shall have at least as good a chance of promotion as another, so at least I shall be, as Miss Mary,[1] to whom I beg my compliments, used to say, in my *état militaire*. In that case, as I shall have, at least, a regiment, I shall be able to settle Matt to our satisfaction and, I think, as the citizen Arthur[2] has made a voyage also in the cause, I will have a right to demand a place for him also; so Miss Mary will have a chance to see three of her brothers in very gaudy green coats and with long sabres by their sides, and then I hope she will be easy. I wear at present a fine embroidered scarlet cape and cuffs on my uniform and a laced hat, which is only permitted to the general officers, but I shall be happy on the first occasion (would to God it were tomorrow) to change my blue coat for one as green as a leek, which I think will be *more becoming*. If I arrive in safety the other side, the first thing I shall do will be to appoint Matt my aid du camp in his absence, and that will set him going advantageously. In short I have a thousand fine things in my head for you all if Messieurs the English allow me to pass clear, for, as the poet hath it,

> If we meet with a privateer, or a lofty man of war
> We will not stay to wrangle, to chatter, nor to jaw.[3]

It is not our business to fight those gentlemen at sea if we can possibly avoid it and you may be sure we will do everything in our power and I hope yet we may get clear, in which case, as I have already said ten times, you shall see what you shall see.

I have now finished the best and the worst that can happen us, but there remains a third way, which is that it may happen that we should be beaten back in spite of our efforts and that I should, so, return *in safety* to France. In that case, I think, I shall be able to retain my pay as Adjutant General, which, as things go here, will be a vast addition to our little fortune; I will then buy or hire a small farm within a few miles of Paris and devote the remainder of my life to making you happy and educating our children. This last way, tho' not so bad as my first supposition, is yet just now to me a very gloomy prospect, for the reasons I am about to mention.

Since my arrival in France I have had no communication whatsoever with Ireland, but I have seen the English papers pretty regularly by favor of Madgett, who is in the Bureau of the Minister for Foreign Affairs. I had in consequence the mortification to read, in May last,[4] that John Keogh was arrested by order of Government with Sir Edward Bellew (a great aristocrat) and several others.

[1] His sister. [2] His youngest brother.
[3] The last word could also be 'jar', meaning 'wrangle'. Cf. above, p. 401.
[4] *Recte* on 9 April last (see above, p. 148).

However, I watched the papers carefully for some months after and, as I saw no further mention of the business, I am in very great hopes that they were immediately released and that the affair blew over, but I have no certainty. Since that time (indeed within these few days), while we were on our march to Brest, I found an English paper wherein there was an article, copied from the *Northern Star* of Sep[tembe]r 16, by which I saw to my most unspeakable distress and anxiety that Harry Haslet and two persons of the name of Osborne and Shanaghan had been arrested that day at Belfast on a charge of high treason and that Sam Neilson and Russell had surrendered themselves voluntarily.[1] You will judge how I felt this blow! The instant I arrived I ran to Hoche to communicate the news and we agreed immediately to dispatch a proper person to Ireland, on board an American vessel, partly to obtain intelligence but principally to give notice to my friends, thro' a channel which I pointed out, to avail themselves of every chicane and artifice of the law to put off their trials in order to give us time, if possible, to arrive to their relief. This person[2] left Brest the 7th of this month and I trust he arrived safe, but in the meantime I am in the most extreme anxiety and distress of mind. If we reach Ireland, which we may now, as I hope, do in ten days, supposing no unlucky accident, we shall, I trust, be in time to extricate them, but if unfortunately we should be too late for that, at least we shall be in time to revenge them and in that case woe to their persecutors!

While I am on the subject of my friends I am to acquaint you that our poor friend Major Sweetman was unfortunately killed in a duel near London in January last. It was in the English papers I saw this intelligence and I do not think I was ever more shocked in my life; I did not recover my spirits for a month after and even yet I think of his death with the utmost regret, in which I am sure you will join me. Not to speak of my personal regard for him, I need not mention what a loss we have of him at this moment when his courage, talents and patriotism would be of such essential service. I am most sincerely sorry for him on every account, public and private, and I did not think I could have been so affected as I was by his death.[3]

To return to our own affairs. On your arrival at Havre you will of course, agreeably to my former directions, have written to Madgett, who will forward you this, as I send it to him under cover. My first design was that you should go on to Paris, but, on further recollection, living there is so very expensive, as well as travelling also, that you had better fix yourselves, until you hear from me, at some of the villages within a few leagues of Havre, where you will hire lodgings and make your own kitchen &c. There is a village called Yvetot[4] that I think would suit you. If anything should happen to me, you will have no business on to Paris and in that case if your determination be to settle in France, you can fix

[1] See above, p. 360. [2] MacSheehy.

[3] For the circumstances of Edward Sweetman's death, see above, pp 98–9.

[4] Yvetot, 51 km east of Le Havre. Tone passed through it on his journey from Le Havre to Rouen and Paris.

yourself on some little spot in that neighbourhood as well as anywhere else, and Matt must do his best for you all in my place. If you should resolve to return to America you will be near Havre, from whence you will have the most frequent opportunities, *and I confess under the circumstances I would recommend Carolina and especially Georgia, where land is very cheap, before France, where you will labour, I fear, under insurmountable difficulties from your ignorance of the language, customs and manners*. If, as I hope and trust, I arrive safe in Ireland and we succeed, as in that case I think we infallibly shall, still I wish you rather to be at Yvetot, for example, than at Paris for the sake of economy as well as a thousand other reasons. If you do not arrive soon, it is probable you may receive another letter with this, for the very first thing I shall do after our landing will be, you may be sure, to write to you under cover as before to Madgett, and I will also take care to remit you money for your occasions and the very first moment that my duty will permit I will fly with the utmost eagerness to embrace you all. God only knows how I long for that moment.

This letter is dreadfully unconnected, but the fact is I write in a state of the utmost anxiety and incertitude. If I remained in France and you were with my babies on the ocean, it would be full sufficient to keep me in continual uneasiness; or if you were here, safe arrived, and I were embarked, tho' my anxiety would be infinitely lessened, still I should have full sufficient to occupy me; but situated as we are, I have both to encounter; uncertain of your fate and that of our children, uncertain of my own, in which you and they are so deeply interested, I think it is hardly possible to conceive a more painful and anxious situation; add to this that I am obliged to devour my uneasiness from the fear of appearing disheartened at the moment of embarkation. Well, the uncertainty of the affair at least will soon have an end. Ten days, I think, now must settle it and I am sure no extremity scarcely can be so terrible as the state of suspense in which I now find myself. If we succeed in our enterprise, I never will again hazard my happiness and yours for any imaginable temptation of honor or interest; if we fail, at least it is in an honorable cause and on just principles and, in either case, you shall not hear of my behaving in a manner to cause you or my children to blush for me.

I have this moment received orders to embark in half an hour. I have, of course, time to add no more. I recommend you all to the protection of Heaven. God Almighty for ever bless and preserve you. Adieu, my dearest life and soul. Kiss my darling babies for me ten thousand times and love me ever as I love you.

Once more adieu!
T. W. Tone

Brest, Dec$^{r}$ 2$^{d}$, 1796[1]

[1] No address for Matilda Tone is given in the document. Tone states in his Diary for 2 Dec. that before embarking he enclosed it under cover addressed to Madgett.

# Diary, 2 December 1796

T.C.D., Tone papers, MS 2049, f. 168r; *Life*, ii, 245.

1796

2 Dec. 1796

Received my order to embark on board the *Indomptable* of 80 guns, Captain Bedout.[1] Packed up directly, and wrote a long letter of directions to my wife,[2] in which I detailed everything I thought necessary and advised her, in case of anything happening me, to return to America and to settle in Georgia or Carolina; enclosed this under cover to Madgett and at two o'clock arrived on board. We have a most magnificent vessel. Today I command the troops, as the highest in rank, but tomorrow I shall be superseded by the arrival (as I expect) of the whole *État-Major*. I hope in God we are about to set off at last. I see by a proclamation[3] of the Lord Lieutenant's that the North of Ireland is in a flame; if we arrive safe, we will not do much to extinguish it. Well, we shall see.

# From General Louis Nicholas Hyacinthe Chérin, 4 December 1796

Tone (Dickason) papers.

Chérin, through his adjutant general, directs Tone to ensure that a staff officer shall always be on board the *Indomptable*.

| | |
|---|---|
| ARMÉE<br>française | Au Quartier-général de Brest<br>le 14 frimaire an 5e |

LE GENERAL Chef de l'État-Major Général
à l'adjudant général Smith

Il convient, Citoyen, qu'un officier de l'État-major général reste toujours à bord de *L'Indomptable*; ceux qui viendront à terre doivent toujours retourner

[1] Jacques Bedout (1751–1818), born in Quebec; served as officer in navy before the revolution; was captured when in command of *Tigre* in June 1795; commanded the *Indomptable*, 1796 (Six, *Dict. des généraux & amiraux*).

[2] Above, pp 403–8.

[3] The proclamation, which was dated 6 Nov., warned all persons in the disturbed parts of Ulster of the dangers they would incur if they did not desist from treasonable practices (*Dublin Gazette*, 8 Nov. 1796).

coucher à bord. Veuillez bien prévenir de cette disposition & désigner celui de ces officiers qui commencera à rester à bord aujourd'hui.

Salut & Fraternité
Par ordre du Général Chérin
L'adjud$^{t}$ Général
Chasseloup[1]

## Diary, 4–21 December 1796

T.C.D., Tone papers, MS 2049, ff 168$^{r}$–178$^{r}$; *Life*, ii, 245–57.

### 4 Dec. 1796

As it is now pretty certain that the English are in force off Ushant, to the number of sixteen ships of the line and ten frigates, it seems hardly possible that we can make our way to Ireland without falling in with them; and as even the most succes[s]ful action must be attended with damages in our masts and rigging, so that, even if victorious (which I do not expect), we may yet be prevented from proceeding on the expedition, considering the stormy season of the year. I have been devising a scheme which I think, in the present state of things in Ireland, can hardly fail of success. It is this; that three or at most four sail of the fastest going ships should take advantage of the first favorable moment, as a dark night and a strong gale from the North-East, and set off[2] with as many troops as they can carry, including at least a company of the *Artillerie légère*, steering such a course as, tho' somewhat longer, should be most out of the way of the English fleet; that they should proceed round the coast of Ireland keeping a good offing for fear of accidents, and land the men in the North, as near Belfast as possible. If we could land 2,000 men in this manner, with as many stand of arms as we could carry beside, I have no doubt but in a week we would have possession of the entire North of Ireland, and we could certainly maintain ourselves there for a considerable time against all the force which could be sent against us, the consequence of which would be first that the whole South would be disfurnished of troops, which would of course be sent against us, and I also am almost certain that the British fleet would directly quit its station off Brest, where they have been now cruising ten weeks, according to our accounts, as thinking that the mischief was already done and that they were watching the stable when the steed was stolen, in which case the main embarkation might instantly set off, and, landing in the south, put the enemy between two fires, and so settle the business almost without a blow. If this scheme be adopted, it is absolutely necessary that no mortal should

[1] Julien Chasseloup (d. 1800?), adjutant general and chef de brigade. In Thermidor An VI he was directed to go to Brest; he died in Year VIII. (Archives de la Guerre, dossier).

[2] *Life*, ii, 245, has 'slip out' instead of 'set off'.

hear of it but Morard de Galle, Hoche and Col[one]l Shee. The reason of my wishing not to lose an instant, and likewise that we might make the attempt with 2,000 men, contrary to the opinion I have given elsewhere in these memorandums, is that I have seen articles within these few days in the French papers, including among others a proclamation of the Lord Lieutenant dated Nov[embe]r 9th,[1] by which I see that the insurrection is ready every instant to explode in the North, and that they have even gone so far as to break open the Magazine in Belfast and take by force ten barrels of powder. I dread in consequence their committing themselves before they are properly supported. If we were there with almost any number of troops, provided we had arms and artillery, I should have no doubt of success. After deliberating these two days (which I have spent on board) and putting[2] my scheme in all possible lights, I went today at two o'clock on board the *Fraternité* to state it to Col[one]l Shee, who is confined to his hammock with the gout, as he apprehended he should be. I explained it to him at length, and he seemed to relish it a good deal, and as the General[3] dines today on board with the Admiral,[4] he promised he would mention it to him and have his opinion. I should have observed that I begged in case it was adopted to be permitted to go with the first embarkation; we then fixed to meet tomorrow, when he will let me know the result, and so parted. He is a noble old fellow, at his time of life, and with that terrible malady, the gout, to expose himself with so much spirit as he manifests upon this occasion. Apropos, of spirit! My captain, Citizen Bedout, has fought like a lion in this war; he commanded the *Tigre*, which was taken by the English on the 27th of June 1795, and was wounded in four places before he struck to three vessels of three decks, which were on him at once. I mentioned to Col[one]l Shee that if my plan were adopted, I thought he should be named commodore, which is his rank, especially as the *Indomptable* is a remarkably fast-going ship, and he seems heartily bent on our expedition, which is far from being the case with most of the marine. I must wait now 'till tomorrow, and I hope in God my scheme may be adopted, as I am sure it is our best course under the circumstances. I fear it, however, the more as, if it succeeds, it will undoubtedly in some degree lessen the éclat which would attend Hoche if he were the first to land; but I hope he is above such weakness as to sacrifice the success of the measure to his own reputation. We shall see. Today the Admiral has given out in orders that, after tomorrow, no one will be allowed to go on shore, which the French call *lever la planche*. The General sleeps aboard that night, so everything now seems to '*give dreadful note of preparation*'.[5] I wish however that my scheme may be adopted. I am exceedingly well off aboard, and Cap[tai]n Bedout is remarkably civil and attentive; he is a Canadian and speaks very good English.

[1] *Recte* 6 Nov. 1796. It appeared in the *Dublin Gazette*, 8 Nov. 1796.
[2] *Life*, ii, 246, has 'examining' instead of 'putting'.
[3] Hoche.
[4] Morard de Galles.
[5] Line 14 of chorus in *Henry V*, IV.

## 8 Dec. 1796

The uniformity of my life at anchor in the road of Brest does not furnish much matter for observation. I saw Mr Shee yesterday, who is still in bed with the gout. He tells me that he spoke of my plan to the General, who said at once it was impossible, and that he durst not take on himself the responsibility it would induce. His reasons are good; first, if our little squadron fell in with the enemy we must to a moral certainty be taken; next, if we got even clear, and that the remainder of the squadron fell in with the enemy and was beaten, which would most probably be the case, the whole fault would be laid on him, as having weakened the main force by the detachment; and lastly, that from the state of our preparations, being victualled and furnished but for a very short period, we must speedily sail, *coûte qui coûte*, so that the advantage I proposed in drawing off the English fleet would be useless, as we could not afford to wait the time necessary to suffer that circumstance to operate. This last is the best of his reasons, but I remain firmly of opinion that my scheme is under all the circumstances infinitely the best. If we were able to go in force, *à la bonheur*,[1] but as we are not, and as I have no expectation but that we shall be well beaten, and the whole expedition miscarry, I look upon my proposal as a sure means[2] to save so much out of the fire, and perhaps with the force I spoke of, we might succeed, even tho' the main body might miscarry. I say *perhaps*, tho' in fact I have no doubt of it. As to the General's objections on the score of the hazard, undoubtedly there is great hazard, but in the first place I look upon the actual hazard to be much greater on his plan, inasmuch as four ships have an infinitely better chance of escaping the vigilance of Admiral Gardner, who is watching us without, with 18 sail of the line, than fifteen, of which our squadron consists, not including frigates on either side; and as to fighting they will beat us as surely with our fifteen sail as with four, and the consequence will be, of course, the failure of our expedition. In the next place as to the hazard, there is no possibility of executing so great a measure as that which we have in hand without infinite hazard, and as we are undoubtedly the weaker at sea, we are to chuse that party which offers us the least risque, and in that respect I have no doubt of the superiority of my plan. However it is decided otherwise and I must submit. Our force is of fifteen sail of the line, ten frigates, and seven or eight transports; that makes upwards of thirty sail, a force which can never escape the vigilance of the English, unless there should come a furious storm for two or three days without remission, which would blow them up the Channel, and even so, by all I can see of our preparations, we are not ready instantly to avail ourselves of that circumstance, so that in all probability, if a storm were to come to our relief, the enemy would have time to be back again to block us up, or at least to intercept us. Besides the elements seem to conspire against us; in the memory of man there has not been known at Brest so long a succession of fine weather at this season, and we have had now three weeks of

[1] Corrected in *Life*, ii, 248, to '*à la bonne heure*', meaning 'Well done!'.
[2] *Life*, ii, 248, has 'as the best means'.

favorable wind, of which, for obvious reasons, we have not been able to profit; of course, when this weather changes, we must look for the wind in the opposite quarter, which is the prevailing wind in winter, and will block us up as effectually as the English.[1] I am weary of my life, absolutely. If the wind sets in to the westward, and continues there for any time, as is highly probable, the troops will get sickly and impatient, and what is still worse our provisions of all sorts will be exhausted, and so we shall be obliged to give up the expedition from downright poverty. Want of money is the great stumbling block of the French government. These are sad croaking memorandums, but unfortunately they are all too true. Those damned Spaniards! Well, they will lose their American colonies, that is some revenge, and Mr Pitt may profit now of my scheme for the Sandwich Islands.[2] I have now done with my scheme, which is undoubtedly liable to the objections made by the General, but when we have but a choice of difficulties, where is the scheme which is without them?

We had a grand exercise today of great guns and small arms, and both troops and seamen went thro' their business with great activity. I should like to see the same on board an English man-of-war. We did not fire, but two other ships, the *Nestor* and the *Éole*, did. It was a beautiful sight. I saw Mr Shee this evening for half an hour; the gout has got into his left hand and he was dreadfully out of spirits, I think for the first time. He tells me the General thinks that the Marine are trifling with him, on purpose to gain time, until the bad weather sets in, when, if it holds any time as is highly probable, our stores of all sorts will be exhausted and the business must be given up from pure necessity. This I apprehended myself, as I have mentioned on the other side. He says also that Bruicks,[3] a rear admiral, who is charged with the execution of the naval department, and in whose zeal the General had great confidence, has cooled exceedingly within these few days, so much that today, for example, when the General called on him and was pressing him on our affair, instead of answering him, Bruicks was dandling one of his little children. The excuse now is that we are waiting for some charts or plans, which must be washed in water colours and will take up two days! It is a worthy subject for delay in this stage of the business. I begin more and more to think that we shall not get out in force. It is true the General may order us out at his peril, but it is a dreadful responsibility to take on himself, for if any accident happened us, he would have the whole marine on his back, and by what I see of those gentlemen I think they would rather all should fail than their prophecy not be verified; and, by the bye, it is always in their power to make us miscarry, so I think it hardly to be expected of Hoche to go those lengths. A man's own scheme is always lovely in his eyes, but I cannot help wishing that we were out safe, with even four ships, according to my plan, and it seems not impossible but we may come to that at last. Our whole business now (not to speak of the English) turns upon a change

[1] For a well-informed discussion, with sketch maps, of the meteorological conditions prevailing in Dec. 1796, see John Tyrrell, 'The weather and political destiny' in John A. Murphy (ed.), *The French are in the bay: the expedition to Bantry Bay, 1796* (Cork, 1997), pp 25–47.

[2] See above, vol. I, pp 10–16, 68–89.

[3] Corrected in *Life*, ii, 249, to 'Bruix'.

of the wind. In the meantime the troops keep their health and spirits, and are at this moment, as well as every evening, dancing on the quarter deck. Would to God we were all in Ireland, but when will that be? We are 13,500 strong.

## 11 Dec. 1796

Went ashore yesterday to take my leave of Brest. Four of our frigates stood out of the Goulet in the evening, so there are at least symptoms of movement. This morning went on board the *Fraternité* to see Mr Shee, and to my infinite satisfaction saw Richéry in the offing, standing in for the road, where he anchored safely in an hour after. He brings with him five ships of the line and two frigates, of which we shall take three of the line, and the crews of the two others, which are foul; it is a reinforcement of the most infinite consequence to us, and perhaps may enable us to force our way[1] at last. I am astonished how Richéry with his squadron has been able to elude the vigilance of the English; he must be an excellent officer, and I presume we shall have him of course with us. The General comes aboard today, and it is not impossible, if the weather is favorable, but we may sail this night. God send, whatever but is to be the event, for I am tired of this suspense.

## 12 Dec. 1796

The État-Major came aboard last night; we are seven in the great cabin, including a lady in boy's clothes, the wife of a *commissaire*, one Ragoneau.[2] By what I see we have a little army of commissaries, who are going to Ireland to make their fortunes. If we arrive safe I think I will keep my eye a little upon those gentlemen. In consequence of the arrival of Richéry, our squadron will be augmented with two, if not three, ships and with 1,700 men for the army which with 13,400 already on board will make 15,100, a force more than sufficient for our purpose, if, as I always am obliged to add, we have the good fortune to reach our destination in safety.

## 14 Dec. 1796

Today the signal is made to heave short and be ready to put to sea. The report is we shall make sail at 4 o'clock. I am truly rejoiced at it. '*I do agnize, a natural and prompt alacrity*.'[3] Called on my friend Shee, who is better; he is able today to write a little. Recommended my wife and family to his friendship and protection, in case of anything unpleasant[4] happening to me. He promised me heartily to exert himself in their behalf, and I have no doubt he will keep his word, so I have done all that is now in my power to do. Saw Richéry this morning, which I am

[1] *Life*, ii, 250, inserts 'out'.
[2] Perhaps an error for Gatereau, who was a *commissaire de guerre*.
[3] *Othello*, I, iii.
[4] *Life* omits 'unpleasant'.

glad of, as I like to observe the countenances of men who have distinguished themselves.

*Evening*. Having nothing better to employ me, I amuse myself scribbling these foolish memorandums. In the first place, I must remark the infinite power of female society over our minds, which I see every moment exemplified in the effect which the presence of Madame Ragoneau has on our manners; not that she has any claim to respect other than as she is a woman, for she is not very handsome, she has no talents, and (between friends) she was originally a *fille de joie* at Paris; yet we are all attentive and studious to please her, and I am glad, in short, she is aboard, as I am satisfied she humanizes us not a little. General Watrin[1] paid us a visit this evening with the band of his regiment, and I went down into the great cabin, where all the officers mess, and where the music was playing. I was delighted with the effect it seemed to have on them. The cabin was ceiled with the firelocks intended for the expedition; the candlesticks were bayonets, stuck in the tables; the officers were in their jackets and *bonnets de police*, some playing cards, others singing to the music, others conversing, and all in the highest spirits; once again I was delighted with the scene. At length Watrin and his band went off, and, as it was a beautiful moonlight night, the effect of the music on the water, diminishing as they receded from our vessel, was delicious. We are still at anchor, bad, bad!

## 15 Dec. 1796

At eleven o'clock this morning the signal was made to heave short, and I believe we are now going to sail in downright earnest. There is a signal also at the point for four sail of enemies in the offing. It is most delicious weather and the sun is as warm and as bright as in the month of May. '*I hope*', as Lord George Brilliant[2] says, '*he may not shine thro' somebody presently*'. We are all in high spirits, and the troops are as gay as if they were going to a ball.[3] With our 15,000 (more correctly 13,975) I would not have the least doubt of our beating 30,000 of such as will be opposed to us; that is to say, if we reach our destination. The signal is now flying to get under way, so one way or other this affair will at last be brought to a decision. God knows how sincerely I rejoice at it. The wind is right aft. *Huzza!* At one we got under way, and stood out of the Goulet[4] until three, when we cast anchor by signal in the Bay de Camaret, having made about three leagues. Our ship I think would beat the whole fleet. We passed (with easy sail) a frigate, *La Surveillante*, under her top gallant sails, and nothing was able to come near us. We are now riding at single anchor, and I hope we shall set off tomorrow.

[1] François Watrin (1772–1802) joined the army, 1792; sous-lieut, 1793; chef de brigade, June 1795; employed with the army of the Côtes-de-Cherbourg under Hoche, Dec. 1795; general of brigade, 1796 (Six, *Dict. des généraux & amiraux*).

[2] Character in Colley Cibber's *The lady's last stake* (1708).

[3] Cf. the lines from Voltaire's *La Pucelle* which Tone quotes above, p. 372.

[4] The Goulet de Brest is the strait separating the road from the open sea.

## 16 Dec. 1796

At twelve today the *Foug[u]eux*, a 74, ran foul of us, but we parted without any damage on either side. When we were as close as possible, with the muzzles of our guns touching, I saw clearly the impossibility of boarding a ship of the line, from the distance from the gunwale of one to the other. At two, signal to get under way; at half after two made sail; the wind still favorable, but slack. Settled our *rôle de combat*. Chasseloup and Vaudray,[1] with their adjoints, are on the lower deck; Simon[2] and I, with ours, on the main deck; Chérin, I believe, with the captain. I had rather be on the quarter deck, or the poop, where I could see something, however I said nothing. We are all in full regimentals, with our laced hats &c., which is to encourage the troops. I believe our ship will behave well, but it will be still better if we reserve our valour for the shore. At all events two or three days now must, I think, settle the affair.

## 17 Dec. 1796

Last night passed thro' the Raz,[3] a most dangerous and difficult pass, wherein we were within an inch of running on a sunken rock, where we must, every soul, have inevitably perished. I knew nothing about it for my part 'till this morning and I am glad of it. Captain Bedout told me he had rather stand three such engagements as that wherein he was taken than pass again thro' the Raz at night, so it seems the affair was serious; if we had struck, we should have gone to pieces in a quarter of an hour, as the tide runs furiously at the rate of not less than ten knots an hour. Ours is the first squadron that has passed thro' the Raz, which even single ships avoid, unless in case of necessity. This morning, to my infinite mortification and anxiety, we are but 18 sail in company, instead of 43, which is our number. We conjecture however that the remaining 25 have made their way thro' the Yroise[4] and that we shall see them tomorrow morning, at the same time that we much fear that some of our companions have perished in that eternal Raz.[5] We have nothing for it now but to wait till tomorrow.

*At night*. This day has passed without any event; the weather moderate, the wind favorable, and our 18 sail pretty well together. Two of the admirals and the General are with the absent; God send they have escaped the Raz! Rear Admiral Bouvet and General Grouchy, second in command, are with us. I believe there is a rendesvous fixed in case of separation, so tomorrow we shall see. We run on an average 5 and six knots an hour, course W.N.W.

[1] Possibly Georges Michel Leopold Labbé de Waudré who in 1793 was quartier-maître-trésorier in the 7th regiment of artillery (*État militaire de France pour l'année 1793*, ed. Léon Hennet (Paris, 1903)).

[2] Édouard François Simon (1769–1827), chef de brigade, 1795; chief of staff in Hardy's expedition to Ireland, 1798; captured and exchanged; protested against the life consulate; created baron of the empire, 1811 (Six, *Dict. des généraux & amiraux*).

[3] The Raz de Sein, i.e. in a southerly direction.

[4] The Yroise, or Iroise, is the sea lying to the west of Finistère.

[5] In fact the *Séduisant* foundered with the loss of several hundred men (see below, p. 418).

## 18 Dec. 1796

At nine this morning. A fog so thick that we cannot see a ship's length before us. '*Hazy weather, Master Noah!*'[1] Damn it! We may be for aught I know within a quarter of a mile of our missing ships without knowing it. It is true we may also by the same means miss the English, so it may as well be for good as for evil, and I count firmly upon the fortune of the Republic. How, after all, if we were not to join our companions? What will Grouchy and Bouvet determine? We are enough to make the attempt alone, but in that case we must steer for the North of Ireland. If it rested with me I would not hesitate a moment, and as it is I will certainly propose it, if I can find an opening.

> If we are doomed to die, we are enough,
> To do our country loss, and if to live
> The fewer men, the greater share of honor.[2]

This damned fog continues without intermission.

*At night*. Foggy all day, and no appearance of our comerades. I asked Gen[era]l Chérin what we should do in case they did not rejoin us? He said that he supposed Gen[era]l Grouchy would take the command with the troops that we had with us, which on examination we found to amount to about 6,500 men. I need not say that I supported this idea with all my might. The captain has opened a packet containing instructions for his conduct in case of separation which order him to cruise for five days off Mizen Head, and at the end of that time to proceed to the mouth of the Shannon, where he is to remain for three more, at the end of which time, if he does not see the fleet, or receive further orders by a frigate, he is to make the best of his way back to Brest; but we must see, in that case, whether Bouvet and Grouchy may not take on themselves to land the troops. I am glad to see that Chérin is bent on that plan, notwithstanding the interference of his aid du camp, Fairin,[3] who put in his word, I thought, impertinently enough.

## 19 Dec. 1796

This morning, at eight, signal of a fleet in the offing and a *branle-bas général*.[4] Rose directly and made my *toilette*, so now I am ready, *ou pour les Anglais, ou pour les Anglaises*. I see about a dozen sail, but whether they are friends or enemies, God knows. It is a stark calm, so that we do not move an inch, even with our studding sails, but here we lie, rolling like so many logs upon the water; it is most inconceivably provoking! Two frigates that were ordered to reconnoître have not advanced one hundred yards in an hour, with all their canvas out. It is now nine o'clock. Damn it to hell, for a calm! And in the middle of the month of

[1] Source of quotation not identified. [2] *Henry V*, IV, iii.

[3] Antoine Fairin (b. 1750), lieutenant and quarter-master in a regiment of volunteers, 1792; captain, An III; aide-de-camp to General Chérin, Ventôse An IV; chef de bataillon, An VI (Archives de la Guerre, dossier).

[4] *Branle-bas général*, meaning 'pipe to quarters' or 'general alert'.

December! Well, it cannot last long however. If this fleet prove to be our comerades, it will be famous news for us. If it be the English!—well, let them come, and we will do our best, and I think the *Indomptable* will not be the worst fought ship in the squadron! This calm, this calm! it is most terribly vexatious. At half after ten, we floated near enough to one another to recognize the signals, and to my infinite satisfaction the strange fleet proves to be our comerades, so now we are quit for the fright,[1] as the French say; counted 16 sail, including the Admiral's frigate, so the General is safe. The wind, which favored us thus far, has chopped about and is now right in our teeth; that is provoking enough; if we had a fair wind, we should be in Bantry Bay tomorrow morning. At half after one, hailed by a lugger which informed us of the loss of the *Séduisant*, a 74 of our squadron, the first night of our departure, with 550 men of the 94 demi[bri]grade, of whom she saved 33. It happened near the same spot where we were in such imminent danger.[2]

I was mistaken above in saying that the *Fraternité* was with the squadron that joined us; it is Admiral Nielly's[3] frigate, and we know nothing of the other, which has thrown us all into the greatest uneasiness. Admiral Morard de Galles, Gen[era]l Hoche, Gen[era]l Debelle and Col[one]l Shee are aboard the *Fraternité*, and God knows what is become of them. The wind too continues against us, and altogether I am in terrible low spirits. How if those damned English should catch us at last, after having gone on succes[s]fully thus far? Our force leaving Brest Water was as follows: *Indomptable* of 80 guns; *Nestor*, *Cassard*, *Droits de l'Homme*, *Tourville*, *Éole*, *Foug[u]eux*, *Mucius*, *Redoutable*, *Patriote*, *Pluton*, *Constitution*, *Trajan*, *Watigny*,[4] *Pégaze*, *Révolution*, with the unfortunate *Séduisant*, of 74 guns;[5] *La Cocarde*, *Bravoure*, *Immortalité*, *Bellonne*, *Coquille*, *Fraternité*, *Romaine*, *Sirenne*, *Impatiente*, *Surv[e]illante*, *Charente*, *Résolue*, *Tartu*,[6] frigates of 36;[7] *Scévola* and *Fidelle*, armés en flûte; *La Mutine*, *Renard*, *Athalante*, *Voltigeur* and *Affronteur*, corvettes; and *Le Nicodème*, *La Justine*, *Ville d'Orient*, *Suffrein*, *Expérimant* and *Alègre*, transports, making in all 43 sail. Of these there are missing this day at three o'clock the *Nestor* of 74, *La Fraternité, La Cocarde, La Romaine*, frigates, *La Mutine*, *Le Voltigeur* and three others, corvettes or transports.[8]

## 20 Dec. 1796

Last night, in moderate weather, we contrived to separate again, and this morning at eight o'clock we are but 15 sail in company, with a foul wind and hazy. I am in horrible ill humour, and it is no wonder. We shall lie beating about

[1] Rendered in *Life*, ii, 254, as '*nous en sommes quittes pour la peur*'.

[2] i.e. the Raz de Sein (see above, p. 416).

[3] Joseph Marie Nielly (1751–1833), naval officer before the revolution; commanded *La Résolue* in Hoche's expedition to Ireland; baron, 1814 (Six, *Dict. des généraux & amiraux*).

[4] Correctly '*Wattignies*'.

[5] *Life*, ii, 255, inserts in parentheses: '17 sail of the line'.

[6] *Life*, ii, 255, has '*Tatare*'.

[7] *Life*, ii, 255, inserts in parentheses '13 frigates'.

[8] *Life*, ii, 255, is more explicit: 'the *Mutine* and *Voltigeur*, corvettes, and three other transports.

here within 30 leagues of Cape Clear[1] until the English come and catch us, which will be truly agreeable. '*Let me not think!*'[2] I amuse myself at night, when the rest are at cards, walking alone in the gallery, and singing the airs that my poor love used to be fond of

> The wandring tar, that not for years has pressed,
> The widowed partner of his day of rest,
> On the cold deck, far from her arms removed,
> Still hums the ditty which his Susan loved.[3]

I feel now the truth of those beautiful lines. Well, hang sorrow! At ten several sail in sight to windward; I suppose they are our stray sheep. It is scandalous to part company twice in four days in such moderate weather as we have had, but sea affairs, I see, are not our *fort*. Cap[tai]n Bedout is a seaman, which I fancy is more than can be said for nine tenths of his confrères.

## 21 Dec. 1796

Last night, just at sunset, signal for seven sail in the offing; all in high spirits, in hopes that it is our comerades; stark calm all the fore part of the night. At length a breeze sprung up, and this morning at daybreak we were under Cape Clear, distant about 4 leagues,[4] so I have at all events once more seen my country; but the pleasure I should otherwise feel at this event is totally destroyed by the absence of the General,[5] who has not joined us and of whom we know nothing. The sails we saw last night have disappeared, and we are all in uncertainty. It is most delicious weather, with a favorable wind, and everything in short that we can desire, except our absent comerades. At the moment I write this we are under easy sail, within three leagues at most [of] the coast, so that I can discover here and there patches of snow on the mountains. What if the General should not join us? If we cruise here five days, according to our instructions, the English will be upon us, and then all is over. We are 35 sail, at least, in company, and 7 or 8 absent. Is that such a *separation* of our force as, under all the circumstances, will warrant our following the letter of our orders, to the certain failure of the expedition? If Grouchy & Bouvet be men of decision and spirit, they will land immediately, and trust to their success for their justification. If they be not, and if this day passes without our seeing the General, I much fear the game is up. I am in undescribable anxiety; and Chérin, who commands aboard, is a poor creature, to whom it is vain to speak; not but I believe he is brave enough, but he has a little mind. There cannot be imagined a situation more provokingly tantalizing than mine at this moment, within view, almost within reach of my native land, and uncertain whether I shall ever set my foot on it. We are now (9 o'clock) at the rendesvous appointed. Stood in for the coast till 12,

[1] Cape Clear is 20 km east-south-east of Mizen Head. By French reckoning, one marine league ('lieue marine') is 5.56 km. Their distance from Cape Clear was therefore less than 170 km.

[2] 'Let me not think on't' (*Hamlet*, I, ii). [3] R. B. Sheridan, *The rivals* (1775), prologue.

[4] About 22 km. [5] Hoche.

when we were near enough to toss a biscuit ashore. At 12, tacked and stood out again, so now we have begun our cruise of five days in all its forms, and we shall in obedience to the letter of our instructions ruin the expedition and destroy the remnant of the French marine with a precision and punctuality which will be truly edifying. We opened Bantry Bay,[1] and in all my life rage never entered so deeply into my heart as when we turned our backs on the coast. I sounded Chérin as to what Grouchy might do, but he turned the discourse. He is *Taata Enos.*[2] Simon is entirely of my opinion and so is Cap[tai]n Bedout, but what does that signify? At half after one, the *Athalante*, one of our missing corvettes, hove in sight, so now again we are in hopes to see the General. Oh, if he were in Grouchy's place, he would not hesitate a moment. Continue making short boards;[3] the wind foul.

## To the Irishmen now serving aboard the British navy (II), 22 December 1796

T.C.D., Tone papers, MS 2050, f. 15[r].

This and the following two proclamations were written to replace printed material on board the *Fraternité*, which was far out at sea. There was a printing press on board Tone's ship, the *Indomptable*. See below, p. 424, n. 3.

Copy of the Address intended to be published on the landing of the French army in Ireland and which Gen[era]l Chérin and I prepared on board the *Indomptable*, December 22d, 1796.

### To the Irishmen now serving aboard the British Navy

Brave Seamen!

The moment is at length arrived when the Irish nation is about to shake off the yoke of the Tyrant of England and to constitute herself a free and independant state; this splendid enterprise will speedily be accomplished by the aid of a French army now disembarked on her territory, and the people who have received those gallant soldiers as brothers and friends have given a decided proof of their love for liberty.

Imitate your brethren of the Militia, concur in the accomplishment of the National wish, and serve your country by throwing off the yoke of your proud and haughty tyrant, who regards you and every Irishman but as his slaves.

Countrymen, now that the revolution of Ireland is commenced whose great and glorious object is to chase the English from our territory, you have an opportunity at once to serve your country and to make your fortunes. You constitute two thirds of the crews of the British navy. What is there to hinder your seizing the

[1] Meaning they got an open view of Bantry Bay having rounded Cape Clear.

[2] Note by William Tone (*Life*, ii, 256): 'See Cook's *Voyages*'.

[3] i.e. tack frequently.

vessels wherein you serve and bringing them into the Irish harbours? Remember you are two to one! Every vessel so seized shall be sold for your profit; those of you who desire it shall have their discharge instantly; and those who prefer to enter into the service of their country will have the whole trade of England at their mercy.

Independant of your individual profit, think of the service you will render your country, who [*sic*] by your means will recover perfect freedom of commerce and become one of the most powerful maritime states of Europe. I need say no more. Your honor and your interest are equally concerned, and I have no doubt but you will act as becomes brave seamen and good Irishmen.

Bantry Bay

## To the militia of Ireland, 22 December 1796

T.C.D., Tone papers, MS 2050, f. 15[v].

See headnote of preceding document.

Copy of the address to the Militia intended to be published on the landing of the French army in Ireland under the command of the general of division, Emanuel Grouchy, and which General Chérin, chef de l'État-major, and I prepared on board the *Indomptable* of 80 guns, Citizen Bedout, comm[andan]t, in Bantry Bay, December the 22d 1796.

### To the Militia of Ireland

Brave Soldiers!

The army of the French republic has entered your country to assist her in breaking the yoke of England, our natural enemy; the Irish nation declares in favor of the grand enterprise, for the execution of which she has so long sighed. Quit then the colum[n]s of your tyrants and join the warlike and victorious standard of the French; you will not, surely, turn your arms against your country, your fathers, your brothers, your friends! you will not rest confounded in the ranks of the enemy, whom we have so often, with inferior numbers, driven before us on the continent, and who will speedily be chased from the Irish territory.

Come to us with your arms and baggage; reinforce the army which brings to your country liberty and independance; you shall be received as friends and as brothers; you shall obtain promotion such as is due to the patriotism, talents and courage of those brave men who serve with zeal in so glorious a cause, and you may count upon the gratitude of your country that when she is once constituted a free and independent state, which is the only object of our efforts, you shall, every one of you, receive from the property of our common enemies a settlement in land proportionate to your rank and services.

# To the people of Ireland, 22 December 1796

T.C.D., Tone papers, MS 2050, f. 16.

See headnotes of preceding two documents.

Copy of the Proclamation of the General in chief, intended to be published on the landing of the French army in Ireland and which General Chérin and I prepared on board the *Indomptable* in Bantry Bay, December 22d 1797 [*sic*].

## To the People of Ireland

You have long groaned under the intolerable yoke of England, our common enemy; you have long sighed after freedom and independance, and have often made fruitless efforts to attain those blessings, so essential to the happiness and prosperity of a gallant nation. At length the French republic, the natural ally of all who love liberty and have the courage to assert it, offers you the means necessary to enable you to break your chains; she sends you arms, artillery and stores, troops warlike, well disciplined and enured to victory; rise then with an unanimous movement and join your friends; we are your allies and your brothers; united, let us purge the soil of Ireland of your haughty English masters; it is time that their tyranny should cease.

Brave Irishmen, in the name of the French republic, ever faithful to her engagements, I promise you the most inviolable respect for persons and properties, and the free and undisturbed exercise of all religions, without distinction or preference; we come to emancipate, not to conquer your country, and we bring you the succour of which you have need to constitute yourselves an independant nation; persuaded of your true interests, conscious of your own worth, you have but to desire liberty and to obtain it.

The General in Chief

# Diary, 22–3 December 1796

T.C.D., Tone papers, MS 2049, ff 178r–181r; *Life*, ii, 257–60.

## 22 Dec. 1796

This morning at eight, we have neared Bantry Bay considerably, but the fleet is terribly scattered. No news of the *Fraternité*. I believe it is the first instance of an admiral, in a clean frigate, with moderate weather and moonlight nights, parting company with his fleet. Cap[tai]n Gramen,[1] our first lieutenant, told me that his opinion is that she is either taken or lost, and in either event it is a terrible blow to us. All now rests upon Grouchy and I hope he may turn out well; he has a glorious game in his hands, if he has spirit and talents to play it. If he succeeds, it will immortalise him. I do not at all like the countenance of the État-Major in this crisis. When they speak of the expedition, it is in a style of despondence, and when they are not speaking of it, they are playing cards and laughing; they are, every one of them, brave of their persons, but I see nothing of that spirit of enterprise, combined with a steady resolution, which our present situation demands. They stared at me this morning when I said that Grouchy was the man in the whole army who had least reason to regret the absence of the General, and began to talk of responsibility and difficulties, as if any great enterprise was without responsibility and difficulties. I was burning with rage; however I said nothing, and I will say nothing, until I get ashore, if ever I am so happy as to arrive there. We are gaining the Bay by slow degrees, with a head wind at East, where it has hung these five weeks. Tonight we hope, if nothing extraordinary happens, to cast anchor in the mouth of the Bay and to work up tomorrow morning; these delays are dreadful to my impatience! I am now so near the shore that I can see distinctly two old castles, yet I am utterly uncertain whether I shall ever set my foot on it. According to appearances, Bouvet and Grouchy are both resolved to proceed. That is a great point gained, however.

Two o'clock. We have been tacking ever since eight this morning, and I am sure we have not gained one hundred yards; the wind is right ahead and the fleet dispersed, several being far to leeward. I have been looking over the schedule of our arms, artillery and ammunition: we are well provided; we have 41,050 stand of arms; 20 pieces of field artillery and 9 of siege, including mortars and howitzers; 61,200 pounds[2] of powder, 7,000,000 of musquet cartridges and 700,000 flints, besides an infinite variety of other articles belonging to the train; but we have neither sabres nor pistols for cavalry; however we have near three regiments of hussars embarked, so that we can dispense with them. Messieurs of the État-Major continue in the horrors. I find Simon the stoutest of them, and Fairin, Chérin's aid du camp, the worst; he puts me in mind of David in *The Rivals*, but '*I am fighting Bob; and, damn it, I won't be afraid!*'[3] I continue very discreetly to say little or nothing, as my situation just now is rather a delicate one. If we were once ashore, and things turn out to my mind, I shall soon be out of my trammels, and perhaps in that respect I may be better off with Grouchy than with Hoche. If the people act with spirit, as I hope they will, it is no matter who is General, and if they do not, all the talents of Hoche would not save us, so it comes to the same thing at last. At half after six, cast anchor, off Beer Island,[4] being still four leagues[5] from our landing place. At work with Gen[era]l Chérin writing

[1] *Life*, ii, 257, has 'Grammont'. He has not been identified.

[2] *Life*, ii, 257, has 'barrels'. In MS the word, over-written, could be 'pounds' or 'barrels'.

[3] Bob Acres in Sheridan's *The rivals* (1775).

[4] Just inside Bantry Bay.

[5] About 22 km (see above, p. 419, n. 1).

and translating proclamations, &c.,[1] all our printed papers, including my two pamphlets,[2] being on board the *Fraternité*, which is pleasant.[3]

## 23 Dec. 1796

Last night it blew a heavy gale from the eastward with snow, so that the mountains are covered this morning, which will render our *bivouacs* extremely amusing. It is to be observed that of the thirty-two points of the compass, the East is precisely the most unfavourable to us. In consequence we are this morning separated for the fourth time; sixteen sail, including nine or ten of the line, with Bouvet and Grouchy, are at anchor with us, and about twenty are blown out to sea; luckily the gale set off the shore, so I am in hopes no mischief will ensue. The wind is still high, and as usual right ahead, and I dread a visit from the English and altogether I am in great uneasiness. Oh, that we were once ashore, let what might ensue after! I am sick to the very soul of this suspense. It is curious to see how things are managed in this best of all possible worlds. We are here, sixteen sail, great and small, scattered up and down in a noble bay, and so disposed that there are not two together in any spot save one, and they are now so close that if it blows tonight as it did last night, they will inevitably be foul,[4] unless one of them prefers driving on shore. We lie in this disorder, expecting a visit from the English every hour, without taking a single step for our defence, even to the common one of having a frigate in the harbour's mouth to give us notice of their approach; to judge by appearances we have less to dread here than in Brest Water, for when we were there we had four corvettes stationed off the Goulet, besides the signal posts. I confess this degree of security passes my comprehension. This day had passed without the appearance of one vessel, friend or enemy, the wind rather more moderate, but still ahead. Tonight, on examining the returns with Waudrét,[5] *chef de l'état-major d'artillerie*, I find our means so reduced by the absence of the missing, that I think it hardly possible to make an attempt here with any prospect of success. In consequence I took Chérin into the Captain's room and told him frankly my opinion of our actual state, and that I thought it our duty, since we must look upon the main object as now unattainable (unless the whole of our friends returned tomorrow, and the English gave us our own time, which was hardly to be expected), to see what could be best done for the

[1] Three proclamations, 'To the Irishmen now serving aboard the British navy', 'To the militia of Ireland' and 'To the people of Ireland', are given above (pp 420–22).

[2] One pamphlet was *Address to the people of Ireland on the present important crisis* (above, pp 375–92).

[3] There was a printing press on board the *Indomptable*, as is evident in a report made by Grouchy to Hoche on 5 Jan. 1797: 'Chérin, Smilhe [*sic*] [et] le commandant de l'artillerie avaient passé une partie de la journée à organiser avec moi la petite armée forte de six mille quatre cents hommes et quatre pièces de canon. Je leur avais remis une proclamation pour les troupes et une autre pour les Irlandais; elle devait être imprimée pendant la nuit à bord l'*Indomptable*.' (*Mémoires du maréchal de Grouchy par le marquis de Grouchy* (2 vols, Paris, 1873), i, 403).

[4] Amended in *Life*, ii, 258–9, to 'they will inevitably run foul of each other'.

[5] Corrected in *Life*, ii, 259, to 'Waudré'.

honor and interest of the Republic with the force which remained in our hands; and I proposed to him to give me the *Légion des Francs*, a company of the *Artillerie Légère* and as many officers as desired to come volunteers in the expedition, with what arms and stores remained (which are now reduced, by our separation to 4 field pieces, 20,000 firelocks, at most, lb 1,000 of powder, and 3,000,000 cartouches[1]), and to land us in Sligo Bay and let us make the best of our way; if we succeeded, the Republic would gain infinitely in reputation and interest, and if we failed the loss would be trifling, as the expence was already incurred, and as for the *Légion*, he knew of what kind of desperadoes they were composed, and for what purpose, consequently the Republic would be in the worst event well rid of them; finally I added that tho' I asked the command, it was in the supposition that none of the generals would risque their reputation on such a desperate enterprise, and that if another was found I would be content to go as a simple volunteer; this was the outline of my proposal which I pressed on him with such arguments as occurred to me, concluding by observing that as a foreigner in the French service my situation was a delicate one, and if I were simply an officer, I would obey in silence the orders of my superiors, but from my connexions in Ireland having obtained the confidence of the Directory, so far as to induce them to appoint me to the rank of *chef de brigade*, and of Gen[era]l Hoche who had nominated me adjutant general, I thought it my duty both to France and Ireland to speak on this occasion, and that I only offered my plan as a *pis aller* in case that nothing better suggested itself. Chérin answered me that I did very right to give my opinion, and that, as he expected a council of war would be called tomorrow, he would bring me with him, and I should have an opportunity to[2] give my opinion. The discourse rested there, and tomorrow we shall see more, if we are not agreeably surprised early in the morning by a visit from the English, which is highly probable. I am now so near the shore that I can in a manner touch the sides of Bantry Bay with my right and left hand, yet God knows whether I shall ever tread again on Irish ground. There is one thing which I am surprised at, which is the extreme *sang froid* with which I view the coast; I expected I should have been violently affected, yet I look at it as if it were the coast of Japan. I do not however love my country the less for not having romantic feelings with regard to her. Another thing; we are now three days in Bantry Bay; if we do not land immediately, the enemy will collect a superior force, and perhaps repay us our victory of Quiberon.[3] In an enterprise like ours everything depends upon the promptitude and audacity of our first movements, and we are here, I am sincerely sorry to say it, most *pitifully languid*; it is mortifying, but that is too poor a word. I could tear my flesh with rage and vexation, but that advances nothing, so I hold my tongue in general and devour my melancholy as I can. To come so near, and then to fail, if we are to fail! And everyone aboard seems now to have given up all hopes.[4] Well '*'Tis but in vain, &c., &c.*'

[1] Life, ii, 259, has '1,000 lb of powder and 3,000,000 cartridges'.
[2] In *Life*, ii, 260, the following three words are replaced by 'press it'.
[3] See above, p. 19, n. 1.
[4] Remainder of paragraph omitted from *Life*.

# Proclamation by General Emmanuel Grouchy, 24 December 1796

Tone (Dickason) papers.

This proclamation, 'translated into English, was to be distributed on the disembarkation of the army'. It was drafted by General Grouchy, probably with assistance from Tone when the latter was with him on board the *Immortalité* (see Diary for 24 Dec. 1796, below, pp 427–9).

Grouchy addresses himself to the 'peoples of Ireland' and tells them 'it is not war and pestilence that we bring to your homes' but support for your efforts towards 'a free and independent government'. There is a summary of the proclamation in Elliott, *Tone*, pp 326–7.

## Proclamation qui, traduite en anglais, devoit être répandue dès que l'armée eût été débarquée

### Aux Irlandais

Peuples d'Irlande!

Il n'est point la guerre, et ses fléaux, que nous apportons dans vos foyers. Nous venons seconder vos généreux et fréquents efforts vers un gouvernement libre et indépendant. Trop longtems, l'orgueuilleuse Angleterre a apesanti son joug despotique, et sur ses voisins et sur ses propres enfants. Trop longtems elle a regardé l'Irlande comme une province conquise, dont il lui étoit permis d'exporter matelôts et soldats, dont il lui convenoit d'entraver le commerce pour faire fleurir le sien, dont il étoit de sa sagesse d'épuiser les ressources et les trésors pour la mettre dans l'impuissance de réclamer ses droits . . . Combien de fois ne vous êtes-vous pas indignés de l'abusif emploi que fait l'Angleterre des taxes qu'elle vous enlève? Combien de fois n'avez-vous pas réclamé contre les atteintes portées par le parlement britannique aux droits et aux libertés du parlement d'Irlande? Un moment, l'indignation s'est emparée de vous; l'exemple de l'Amérique vous a frappés, et l'Angleterre, glacée d'effroi, à la levée de vos valeureuses milices volontaires, a soulevé pour un instant le sceptre de fer, sous lequel elle ne renoncera jamais à vous courber . . . L'heure sonne où vous pouvez, où vous devez, le briser . . . ce sceptre tirannique. Veuillez une constitution libre et indépendante. Séparez vous à jamais de cette métropole altière. Nous vous offrons nos bras, nous armerons les vôtres. Hâtez-vous, joignez vos phalanges aux phalanges françaises et frappons l'Anglais, notre ennemi commun . . .

Bientôt il aura disparu et avec lui les calamités, inséparables de la guerre et de la présence des armées, telles disciplinées qu'elles puissent être.

Irlandais, la France ne vous envoye point pour vous conquérir. Ne voyez en nous que des alliés fidèl[e]s . . . Nous saurons briser vos fers, mais nous jurons de respecter vos personnes, vos propriétés, vos cultes.

Comptez sur la foy républicaine comme sur la valeur des soldats de la liberté.

Le g[énér]al com[mandan]t l'armée française
Grouchy

Bantry Bay, le 4 nivôse, l'an 5 de la rép[ubliqu]e française

# Diary,
# 24 December 1796–1 January 1797

T.C.D., Tone papers, MS 2049, ff $181^r$–$187^v$; *Life*, ii, 260–69.

## 24 Dec. 1796

This morning the whole État-Major have been miraculously converted, and it was agreed, in full council, that General Chérin, Col[one]l Waudré, chef de l'État-Major d'Artillerie, and myself should go aboard the *Immortalité* and press General Grouchy in the strongest manner to proceed on the expedition with the ruins of our scattered army. Accordingly we made a signal to speak with the Admiral[1] and in about an hour we were aboard. I must do Grouchy the justice to say that the moment we gave our opinion in favour of proceeding, he took his party[2] decidedly and like a man of spirit. We instantly set about preparing the *ordre de bataille*, and we finished it without delay. We are not more than 6,500 strong, but they are tried soldiers who have seen the fire, and I have the strongest hopes that after all we shall bring our enterprise to a glorious termination; it is a bold attempt, and truly original. All the time we were preparing the *ordre de bataille*, we were laughing most immoderately at the poverty of our means, and I believe under the circumstances it was the merriest council of war that ever was held; but, '*des Chevaliers françois, tel est le charactère*'. Grouchy, the commander-in-chief, never since he was adjutant general had so few men under his orders. Waudré, who is a lieutenant colonel, finds himself now at the head of the artillery, which is a furious park, consisting of 1 piece of 8, 1 of 4, and 2 six-inch howitzers; when he was a captain he never commanded less than ten pieces, but now that he is, in effect, general of the artillerie, he prefers taking the field with four. He is a gallant fellow, and offered, on my proposal last night, to remain with me and to command his company, in case Gen[era]l Grouchy had agreed to the proposal I made to Gen[era]l Chérin.[3] It is altogether an enterprise truly *unique*; we have not a guinea, we have not a tent, we have not a horse to draw our four pieces of artillery, the general in chief marches on foot, we leave all our baggage behind us, we have nothing but the arms in our hands, the clothes on our backs, and a good

[1] Bouvet. [2] *Life*, ii, 261, has 'part'.
[3] For this proposal, see Diary for 23 Dec. (above, pp 424–5).

courage; but that is sufficient. With all these original circumstances, such as I believe never were found united in an expedition of such magnitude as that we are about to attempt, we are all as gay as larks. I never saw the French character better exemplified than in this morning's business. Well, at last I believe we are about to disembark. God knows how I long for it! But this infernal easterly wind continues without remorse, and tho' we have been under way three or four hours and made, I believe, three hundred tacks, we do not seem to my eyes to have gained one hundred yards in a right[1] line. An hour and a half's good wind would carry us up, and perhaps we may be yet two days. Damn it, damn it! I learn from a pilot whom I found aboard the Admiral[2] that my friend Hutchins[3] lives within two miles of Bantry and that he is now at home, so perhaps I may see him to-morrow. I wonder what kind of a meeting we shall have. When I saw him last he was a right good fellow, but so many changes happen in twenty months! At all events he will be, I dare say, not a little surprised to see me with a blue coat on my back and a national cockade in my hat.

At six, cast anchor, as usual, having gained not less, I think at least, than fifty yards, to speak within bounds. The rapidity of our progress is the more amazing when it is considered that we have been not much more than eight hours in covering that quantity of ground; and, besides, we have a cool refreshing breeze from the East, which is truly delightful. Well, '*time and tide wait for no man*'.[4] I may say now with the probationary odes,

> *Sometimes it blows, sometimes it freezes,*
> *Just as it pleases.*[5]

Well, let it blow and be hanged! I do not wonder tonight at Xerxes whipping the sea,[6] for I find myself pretty much in the mood to commit some such rational action. To return to our expedition, the more I think of it, the more I find it amusing. As Johnson says, the negative catalogue of our means is extremely copious.[7] In addition to what I have mentioned already, we have no horses for our cavalry,[8] and no cavalry for our horses. Huzza! I apprehend we are tonight six thousand of the most careless fellows in Europe, for everybody is in most extravagant spirits,

[1] *Life*, ii, 261, has 'straight' in place of 'right'.

[2] i.e. aboard Admiral Bouvet's ship, the *Immortalité*.

[3] Emanuel Hutchins (1769–1839), eldest son of Thomas Hutchins of Ballylickey, Co. Cork; graduated B.A., T.C.D., 1790; called to the Irish bar, 1792 (*Burke's landed gentry of Ireland* (1912); *Alumni Dubl.*).

[4] A Scottish proverb?

[5] The 'probationary odes' were part of a collection of satires on Pitt and his followers by various authors first published in book form as *The Rolliad* (London, 1785); they were purported to be the competitive odes of Joseph Warton's rivals for the poet laureateship. The lines Tone quotes are taken from 'Ode on the New Year', purported to be by Lord Mulgrave but in fact by George Ellis. See esp. Lord Braybrooke, 'Authors of *The Rolliad*' in *Notes and Queries*, 1st ser., ii, no. 38 (20 July 1850), p. 114; W. C. Trevelyan, '*The Rolliad*' in ibid., iii, no. 69 (22 Feb. 1851), pp 129–31. The word 'blows' is a misquotation of 'thaws'.

[6] Xerxes (486 B.C.–465 B.C.), king of Persia; invaded Greece in 480 B.C. and was defeated at the battle of Salamis. The story of his whipping the sea is in Herodotus book VII, 34–6.

[7] This saying by Samuel Johnson, except for the words 'of our means', is in his *A journey to the western islands of Scotland* (1775).

[8] Remainder of sentence omitted from *Life*.

on the eve of an enterprise which, considering our means, would make many people serious. I never liked the French half so well as tonight, and I can scarcely persuade myself that the loungers of the boulevards and the soldiers I see about me are of the same hemisphere. To judge of the French rightly, or at least to see the bright side of their character, you must see them not at Paris but in the camp. It is in the armies that the Republic exists. My enemy the wind seems just now (8 o'clock) to relent a little, so perhaps we may reach Bantry tomorrow. The enemy has now had *four days* to recover from his first palpitation and to prepare to receive us; so much the worse, but I do not mind it. We purpose to make a race for Cork, as if the devil were in our bodies, and when we are fairly there, we will stop for a day or two, to take breath and look about us. From Bantry to Cork is about 45 miles,[1] which with all our efforts will take us three days, and I suppose we may have a brush by the way, but I think we are able to deal with any force that can at a week's notice be brought against us. We are not the best dressed body of men in Europe. I think I have seen a captain of the guards in St James's Park that would burn for as much as one of our demi-brigades.

*There's not a rag of feather in our army,*
*Good argument, I hope, we will not fly.*[2]

Apropos! of that quotation. It is inconceivable how well that most inconceivable of all writers, Shakespeare, has hit off the French character, in his play of Henry 5th. I have been struck with it fifty times this evening; yet it is highly probable he never saw a French officer in his life. Well, I have worked hard today; not to speak of my boating party aboard the Admiral, against wind and tide, and in a rough sea, I have written and copied 15 letters, besides these memorandums, which is pretty well for one day. I think I will stop here. I have but one observation to add; there is not, I will venture to say, a grenadier in the *Compagnie Bloom* that will not sleep tonight in his hammock more contentedly than the Archbishop of Dublin in a down bed. I do presume our arrival has put several respectable characters in no small *fuss*; but time will shew more of that!

## 25 Dec. 1796

These memorandums are a strange mixture. Sometimes I am in preposterously high spirits, and other times I am as dejected, according to the posture of our affairs. Last night I had the strongest expectations that today we should debark, but at two this morning I was wakened by the wind. I rose immediately and, wrapping myself in my great coat, I walked for an hour in the gallery, devoured by the most gloomy reflections. The wind continues right ahead, so that [it] is absolutely impossible to work up to the landing place, and God knows when it will change. The same wind is exactly favourable to bring the English

[1] i.e. Irish miles, or 90 km.

[2] *Henry V*, IV, iii. The first line is correctly 'There's not a piece of feather in our host'.

upon us, and these cruel delays give the enemy time to assemble his entire force in this neighbourhood, and perhaps (it is unfortunately more than *perhaps*) by his superiority in cavalry, in artillery, in money, in provisions, in numbers, in short in everything that we want, to crush us, supposing we are even able to effectuate a landing at last, at the same time that the fleet will be caught as it were in a trap. Had we been able to land the first day and to march directly to Cork, we should have infallibly carried it by a *coup de main* and then we should have a footing in the country. But as it is!—if we are taken, my fate will be not a mild one; the best I can expect is to be shot as an *emigré rentré*, unless I have the good fortune to be killed in the action, for most assuredly if the enemy will have us, he must fight for us. Perhaps I may be reserved for a trial, for the sake of striking terror into others, in which case I shall be hanged as a traitor and embowelled &c., &c. As to the embowelling, *je m'en fiche*;[1] if they hang me they are welcome to embowel me, if they please. These are pleasant prospects! Nothing on earth could sustain me now but the consciousness that I am engaged in a just and righteous cause. For my family, I have by a desperate effort surmounted my natural feelings so far that I do not think of them at this moment. This day at twelve the wind blows a gale, still from the East, and our situation is now as critical as possible, for it is morally certain that this day or tomorrow in the morning the English fleet will be in the harbour's mouth and then adieu to everything! In this desperate state of our affairs I proposed to Chérin to sally out with all our forces, to mount to the Shannon and disembark the troops, to make a forced march to Limerick, which is probably unguarded, the garrison being I am pretty certain on its march to oppose us here, to pass the river at Limerick and by forced marches to push for the North. I detailed all this on a paper, which I will keep, and I shewed it to Cap[tai]n Bedout and all the generals on board, Chérin, Simon & Chasseloup. They all agreed as to the advantages of the plan, but after settling it, we find it impossible to communicate with the General and Admiral,[2] who are in the *Immortalité* near two leagues ahead, and the wind is now so high (and foul) and the sea so rough that no boat can live so all communication is impracticable, and tomorrow morning it will most probably be too late, and on this circumstance perhaps the fate of the expedition and the liberty of Ireland depends. I cannot conceive for what the two commanders-in-chief are shut up together in a frigate; surely they should be aboard the flag ship. But that is not the first misfortune resulting from that arrangement. Had Gen[era]l Hoche remained, as he ought, aboard the *Indomptable* with his État-Major, he would not have been separated and taken by the English, as he is most probably at this hour; nor should we be in the difficulties we now find ourselves [in], and which most probably tomorrow will render insurmountable. Well, it does not signify complaining. Our first capital error was in setting sail too late in the day from Camaret bay by which means we were obliged to pass the Raz in the night, which caused the loss of the *Séduisant*, the separation of the fleet, the capture of the General, and above all the

[1] A vulgar expression meaning 'I don't care'.

[2] i.e. Grouchy and Bouvet.

loss of time, resulting from all this and which is never to be recovered; our second error was in losing one entire day in cruising off the bay when we might have entered and effected a landing with at any rate 35 sail, which would have secured everything; and now our third error is having the commanders-in-chief separated from the State Major [*sic*],[1] which renders all communication utterly impossible. My prospects at this hour are as gloomy as possible. I see nothing before me, unless a miracle be wrought in our favor, but the ruin of the expedition, the slavery of my country and my own destruction. Well, if I am to fall, at least I will sell my life as dear as an individual resistance can make it. So now I have made up my mind. I have a merry Christmass of it today!

## 26 Dec. 1796

Last night, at half after six o'clock, in [a] heavy gale of wind, still from the East, we were surprised by the Admiral's[2] frigate running under our quarter and hailing the *Indomptable* with orders to cut our cable and put to sea instantly. The frigate then pursued her course leaving us all in the utmost astonishment. Our first idea was that it might be an English frigate which has been lurking in the bottom of the bay and which took advantage of the storm and the darkness of the night to make her escape, and who wished to separate our squadron by this stratagem; for it seems utterly incredible that an admiral should cut and run in that manner, without any previous signal of any kind whatsoever to warn the fleet, and that the first notice we should have of his intention should be his hailing us in this extraordinary manner, with such unexpected and peremptory orders. After a short consultation with his officers, considering the storm, the darkness of the night, that we have two anchors out, and only one spare one, which is in the hold, Cap[tai]n Bedout resolved to wait at all events till tomorrow morning, in order to be ascertained whether it was really the Admiral or not who hailed us. The morning is now come, the gale continues, and the fog is so thick that we cannot see a ship's length ahead of us, so here we lie, in the utmost uncertainty and anxiety. In all probability we are now left without admiral or general; if so, Chérin will command the troops, and Bedout the fleet, but at all events there is an end of the expedition. Certainly we have been persecuted by a strange fatality from the very night of our departure to this hour. We have lost two commanders-in-chief; of four admirals not one remains; we have lost a ship of the line that we know of, and probably many other vessels of which we know nothing; we have been now six days in Bantry Bay, within five hundred yards of the shore, without being able to effectuate a landing; we have been dispersed four times in four days, and at this moment of 43 sail of which the expedition consisted we can muster, of all sizes, but 14. There only wants our falling in with the English to complete our destruction, and, to judge of the future by the past, there is every probability that that will not be wanting. All our hopes are now reduced to get back in safety to Brest,

[1] *Life*, ii, 265, has 'Etat Major'. [2] Bouvet's.

and I believe we will set sail for that port the instant that the weather will permit. I confess myself, I now look upon the expedition as impracticable. The enemy has had seven days to prepare for us, and three or perhaps four more before we could arrive at Cork, and we are now too much reduced, in all respects, to make the attempt with any prospect of success; so all is over! It is hard, after having forced my way thus far, to be obliged to turn back, but it is my fate, and I must submit. Notwithstanding all our blunders, it is the dreadful stormy weather and the easterly winds which we have had blowing furiously without intermission since we made Bantry Bay that have ruined us. Well, England has not had such an escape since the Spanish Armada,[1] and that expedition, like ours, was defeated by the weather; the elements fight against us, and courage is here of no avail. Well, let me think no more about it; it is lost, and let it go. I am now a Frenchman and I must regulate my future plans accordingly. I hope the Directory will not dismiss me the service for this unhappy failure, in which certainly I have nothing personally to reproach myself [with], and in that case I shall be rich enough to live as a peasant. If God almighty sends me my dearest love and our darling babies in safety I will buy or rent a little spot and have done with the world for ever; I shall neither be great, nor famous, nor powerful but I may be happy. God knows whether I shall ever reach France myself, and in that case, what will become of my family? It is horrible to me to think of. Oh my life and soul, my darling babies, shall I ever see you again! This infernal wind continues without intermission, and now that all is lost, I am as eager to get back to France as I was to come to Ireland.

## 27 Dec. 1796

Yesterday several vessels, including the *Indomptable*, dragged their anchors several times, and it was with great difficulty they rode out the gale. At 2 o'clock the *Révolution* of 74 made the signal that she could hold no longer, and in consequence of the Commodore's[2] permission (who now commands our little squadron) she cut her *only* cable and put to sea. In the night the *Patriote* and the *Pluton* of 74 each were forced to cut and put to sea, with the *Nicodème* flute, so that this morning we are reduced to 7 ships of the line and one frigate. All attempt here is now desperate, but I still think if we were debarked at the mouth of the Shannon we might yet recover all. At 10 o'clock, the Commodore made the signal to get under way, which was delayed by one of the ships which required an hour to get ready. This hour we availed ourselves of to hold a counsel of war at which were present Gen[era]ls Harty and Humbert,[3] who came from their

[1] In 1588. [2] i.e. Bedout's.

[3] Jean Joseph Amable Humbert (1767–1823), private in the National Guard; general of brigade, 1794; served under Hoche at Quiberon, 1795; on board the *Droits-de-l'Homme* on Bantry Bay expedition; shipwrecked, Jan. 1797; commanded Killala expedition, 1798; defeated British force at Castlebar but surrendered at Ballinamuck, Sept. 1798; in Swiss campaign, 1799; in expedition to Santo Domingo, 1801–2; later served with insurgents in South America; died in New York (Six, *Dict. des généraux & amiraux*; *Dict. biog. franç.*).

ships for that purpose, Gen[era]l Chérin, Adjutants Generals Simon, Chasseloup and myself, Lieut. Col. Vaudré,[1] commanding the artillery, and Favory[2] cap[tai]n of engineers, together with Commodore Bedout, who was invited to assist, Gen[era]l Harty as senior officer being president. It was agreed that our force being now reduced to 4,168 men, our artillery to 2 four-pounders, our ammunition to 1,500,000 cartouches[3] and 500 rounds for the artillery, with 500 lbs of powder, this part of the country being utterly wild and savage, furnishing neither provisions nor horses, and especially[4] the enemy having seven days' notice, together with three more which it would require to reach Cork, supposing we even met with no obstacle, had time more than sufficient to assemble his forces in numbers sufficient to crush our little army; considering moreover that this province is the only one of the four which has testified no disposition to revolt, that it is the most remote from the part which is ready for insurrection, and finally Cap[tai]n Bedout having communicated his instructions, which are to mount as high as the Shannon and to cruise there for five days, it was unanimously agreed to quit Bantry Bay directly and to proceed for the mouth of the Shannon without delay, in hopes to rejoin some of our scattered companions, and when we are there we will determine according to the means in our hands what part we shall take. I am the more content with this determination, as it is substantially the same with the paper which I read to Gen[era]l Chérin and the rest the day before yesterday. The wind at last has come round to the Southward and the signal is now flying to get under way. At half after 4, there being every appearance of a stormy night, two or three vessels cut their cables and put to sea. The *Indomptable* having with great difficulty weighed one anchor, we were forced at length to cut the cable of the other, and make the best of our way out of the bay, being followed by the whole of our little squadron, now reduced to 10 sail, of which 7 of the line, 1 frigate, and two luggers or corvettes.

## 28 Dec. 1796

Last night it blew a perfect hurricane. At one this morning a dreadful sea took the ship in the quarter, stove in the quarter gallery and one of the dead lights in the great cabin, which was instantly filled with water to the depth of three feet. Almost the cots of the officers were torn down, and themselves and their trunks floated about the cabin. For my part I had just fallen asleep when I was awakened by the shock, of which I at first did not comprehend the meaning; but hearing the water distinctly rolling in the cabin beneath me, and two or three of the officers mounting in their shirts, as wet as if they had risen from the bottom of the sea, I

[1] Spelling corrected in *Life*, ii, 267, to 'Waudré'.

[2] Julius Favory (b. 1764), a dragoon, 1784; brigadier, 1793; maréchal des logis, An II (1793–4); applied to be sous lieut, An X (1801–2) (Archives de la Guerre, dossier).

[3] *Life*, ii, 267, has 'cartridges'.

[4] *Life*, ii, 267, adds 'as'.

concluded instantly that the ship had struck and was filling with water, and that she would sink directly. As the movements of the mind are as quick as lightning in such perilous moments, it is impossible to describe the infinity of ideas which shot across my mind in an instant. As I knew all notion of saving my life was in vain in such a stormy sea, I took my party[1] instantly and lay down in my hammock, expecting every instant to go to the bottom, but I was soon relieved by the appearance of one of the officers, Baudin,[2] who explained to us the accident. I can safely say that I had perfect command of myself during the few terrible minutes which I passed in this situation, and I was not, I believe, more afraid than any one of those about me. I resigned myself to my fate which I verily thought was inevitable, and I could have died like a man. Immediately after this blow, the wind abated, and at day light, having run nine knots an hour under one gib[3] only during the hurricane, we found ourselves at the rendezvous, having parted company with three ships of the line and the frigate, which makes our *sixth* separation. The frigate *Coquille* joined us in the course of the day, which we spent in standing off and on the shore, without however being joined by any of our missing companions.

## 29 Dec. 1796

At 4 this morning the Commodore made the signal to steer for France, so there is an end of our expedition for the present, perhaps for ever! I spent all yesterday in my hammock, partly thro' sea sickness, and much more thro' vexation. At 10 we made prize of an unfortunate brig, bound from Lisbon to Cork, laden with salt, which we sunk.

## 30 Dec. 1796

On our way to Brest.

## 31 Dec. 1796

Ditto! It will be well supposed I am in no great humour to make memorandums.

This is the last day of the year 1796, which has been a very remarkable one in my history.

# 1797

## 1 Jan. 1797

At light this morning made the Island of Ushant[4] and at 12 opened the Goulet. We arrive seven sail, viz. *L'Indomptable*, 80 guns, *Le Watigny*, 74,

[1] *Life*, ii, 268, has 'part'. [2] Not identified.
[3] *Recte* 'jib'. [4] The île d'Ouessant, about 45 km out from Brest.

*Le Cassard*, 74, *L'Éole*, 74, *La Coquille*, 36, *L'Athalante*, 20, *Le Vautour*, lugger, 14. We left Brest forty-three sail, of which seventeen were of the line. I am utterly astonished that we did not see a single English ship of war going nor coming. They took their measures very ill not to intercept us; but perhaps they have picked up some of our missing ships. Well, this evening will explain all; we shall see now what is become of our four admirals, and our two generals in chief.